Time Out
Budapest

Penguin Books

PENGUIN BOOKS

Published by the Penguin Group
Penguin Books Ltd, 27 Wrights Lane, London W8 5TZ, England
Penguin Books USA Inc., 375 Hudson Street, New York, New York 10014, USA
Penguin Books Australia Ltd, Ringwood, Victoria, Australia
Penguin Books Canada Ltd, 10 Alcorn Avenue, Toronto, Ontario, Canada M4V 3B2
Penguin Books (NZ) Ltd, 182-190 Wairau Road, Auckland 10, New Zealand

Penguin Books Ltd, Registered Offices: Harmondsworth, Middlesex, England

First published 1996
Second edition 1998
10 9 8 7 6 5 4 3 2 1

Copyright © Time Out Group Ltd, 1996, 1998
All rights reserved

Colour reprographics by Precise Litho, 34-35 Great Sutton Street, London EC1
Mono reprographics, printed and bound by William Clowes Ltd, Beccles, Suffolk NR34 9QE

Except in the United States of America, this book is sold subject to the condition that it shall not, by way of trade or
otherwise, be lent, re-sold, hired out, or otherwise circulated without the publisher's prior consent in any form of binding
or cover other than that in which it is published and without a similar condition including this condition being imposed
on the subsequent purchaser.

Edited and designed by

Time Out Magazine Limited
Universal House
251 Tottenham Court Road
London W1P OAB
Tel: 0171 813 3000
Fax: 0171 813 6001
E-mail guides@timeout.co.uk
http://www.timeout.co.uk

Editorial

Managing Editor Peter Fiennes
Editor Dave Rimmer
Deputy Editor Kevin Ebbutt
Consultant Editor Peterjon Cresswell
Researcher Ildikó Lázár
Indexer Dorothy Frame

Design

Art Director John Oakey
Art Editor Paul Tansley
Designer Mandy Martin
Design assistant Wayne Davies
Picture Editor Catherine Hardcastle
Picture Researcher Michaela Freeman

Advertising

Group Advertisement Director Lesley Gill
Sales Director Mark Phillips
Advertisement Sales (Budapest) CoMo Media

Administration

Publisher Tony Elliott
Managing Director Mike Hardwick
Financial Director Kevin Ellis
Marketing Director Gillian Auld
Production Manager Mark Lamond
Accountant Catherine Bowen

Features in this guide were written and researched by:

Introduction Dave Rimmer. **History** Bob Cohen. **Budapest Today** Christopher Condon. **Budapest By Season** Bob Cohen, Peterjon Cresswell. **Language** Bob Cohen. **Folklore** Bob Cohen. **Architecture** Carolyn Smith. **Sightseeing** Bob Cohen, Peterjon Cresswell, Adam Lebor, Dave Rimmer, Carolyn Smith, Helen Teilelbaum. **Museums** Emma Roper-Evans, Helen Teitelbaum. **Art Galleries** Carolyn Smith. **By Area** Dave Rimmer. **Accommodation** Christina Crowder. **Restaurants** Bob Cohen, Peterjon Cresswell, Martin Iain, Adam Lebor, Tim Randall, Dave Rimmer. **Cafés & Coffeehouses** Peterjon Cresswell, Dave Rimmer. **Pubs & Bars** Bob Cohen, Peterjon Cresswell, Tom Popper, Dave Rimmer. **Shopping & Services** Christina Crowder, Simon Evans, Tom Popper. **Baths** Adam Lebor. **Children** Ildikó Lázár. **Film** Simon Evans, John Nadler, Peter Palátsik. **Gay & Lesbian** Douglas Conrad, Christian Heppinstall. **Media** Chris Condon. **Music: Classical & Opera** Steven Loy. **Music: Rock, Roots & Jazz** Peterjon Cresswell, Dave Rimmer. **Nightlife** Simon Evans, Tom Popper, Dave Rimmer. **Sport & Fitness** Christopher Condon, Simon Evans. **Theatre & Dance** Emma Roper-Evans. **Trips Out Of Town** Peterjon Cresswell, Dave Rimmer. **Essential Information** Bob Cohen, Ildikó Lázár, Tom Popper, Dave Rimmer. **Getting Around** Ildikó Lázár, Tom Popper, Dave Rimmer. **Business** Christopher Condon, Tim Smart. **Further Reading** Peterjon Cresswell, Dave Rimmer.

For inspiration, information, moral support and material assistance, the editor must thank:
Steve Carlson, Malcolm Carruthers and everyone at Isys; Bob Cohen, Peterjon Cresswell, Pearl Gluck, Hadley Kincade, Desmond McGrath and Tom Popper in Budapest; Chris Bohn, Matt Brown, Kevin Ebbutt, Julie Emery, Tim Randall and Janet Street-Porter in London; Matthew and Stephanie in an assortment of cities; Annie Lloyd in Berlin; Oran, Hans, Helen, Judit and Judit and all the Young People at Sixtus. *Time Out Budapest Guide* Gold Medal for Horticultural Achievement: Dork Zygotian.

Maps by **JS Graphics**, Hill View Cottage, 17 Beadles Lane, Old Oxted, Surrey RH8 9JG.

Photography by **Hadley Kincade** except for: Page 13, AKG (Archiv Fur Kunst und Geschichte, Berlin); p16, Mary Evans Picture Library; p155, Jules Zalon/Image Bank; p237, Alan Becker/Image Bank; p242, Stuart Dee/Image Bank.

© Copyright Time Out Group Ltd
All rights reserved

Contents

About the Guide

This is the second edition of the *Time Out Budapest Guide*, one of our ever-expanding series on the world's most vital cities. This latest version has been dusted down, smartened up, paraded before a team of experts and sent back out into the world with a whole suitcase full of new tricks. We've reassessed Budapest's attractions, searched out the new and the vital, and mapped the changing shape of this ancient but volatile city.

Though any visit to the Hungarian capital will be enhanced by a copy of this *Guide*, this is not only a book for casual visitors and tourists. While listing the main sights and major monuments, we've also roved far and wide to direct you to Budapest's coolest cafés, darkest dives, most crucial scenes, sharpest shopping opportunities and finest new places to eat. We aim to highlight not only the traditional must-sees, but also the obscure and the eccentric, the most curious backwaters of this most curious capital – places that tourists rarely see.

We've also laboured long and hard to up its user-friendliness. Addresses, phone numbers, transport details, opening times, admission prices and credit card details have all been checked and re-checked. We've added map references to our listings, linked to the maps in the back of this book. We've also tried to note those places where English is spoken, and where you'll get nothing but Magyar.

Checked & correct

All information was thoroughly checked and correct at the time of writing, but please bear in mind that in a city such as Budapest, making a painful transition to a free market economy, things are liable to sudden and unpredictable change. Clubs and bars wink in and out of existence with particular regularity.

Addresses

Budapest is divided into 23 districts, *kerületek*, indicated by a Roman numeral before the street name. District V is the town centre. Postcodes are written in four figures, the middle two indicating the district: 1051 is District V. The postman will recognise both forms but deliver a four digit-coded letter quicker. We've used the Roman numeral form because it's easier for finding your way around town.

Although we've spelled out the words for road (*út*) and street (*utca*), on street signs and in other publications you may see utca abbreviated to *u.*. As some streets in different districts may have the same name, it's always best to pay attention to which one you're heading for on the map. Other terms and abbreviations include: *híd* bridge; *rakpart* embankment; *tér* square; *körút* ring road; *piac* market; *pályaudvar* (abbreviated as *pu.*) station.

Prices

Prices, where listed, should be treated as guideline rather than gospel. Inflation and fluctuating exchange rates mean prices change rapidly, particularly in shops or restaurants. Most are quoted in forints, but some services which cater particularly to foreigners – upmarket hotels for example – give their rates in Deutschmarks. If prices and services vary wildly from those quoted, ask if there's a good reason. If there's not, take your custom elsewhere and then, please let us know. We have endeavoured to give the best and most up-to-date advice, so we always want to hear if someone has been ripped off or given the runaround.

Credit cards

Credit cards are still not widely used in Budapest, although this is slowly changing. The following abbreviations have been used: AmEx: American Express; DC: Diners Club; JCB: Japanese credit cards; MC: Mastercard/Access; V: Visa.

To boldly go

In chapters with no listings, such as History, Architecture or By Area, places **highlighted in bold** are fully listed elsewhere and can be found in the index.

Right to reply

It should be stressed that the information we offer is impartial. No institution or enterprise has been included because it has advertised in our publication. Rigorous impartiality and cosmopolitan critical assessment are the reasons our guides are so successful and well respected. But if you disagree with us, please let us know; your comments on places you have visited are always welcome. You'll find a reader's reply card at the back of this book.

Introduction

This place is ridiculous. That's a compliment, in my book. But what other word can you use for a city where they say 'hello' for 'good-bye', once had Béla Lugosi as Culture Minister, and believe they're all descended from a mythical giant eagle? What else can you call a place where you can't clink beer glasses because of something the Austrians did a century and a half ago? Where they annually parade the streets toting the mummifed right hand of their sainted founding father? Where they use an ass-backwards syntax that was the model for the way Yoda talks in *The Empire Strikes Back*?

Well, you can call it beautiful, because it is. Budapest constantly surprises the visitor, every twist and turn capable of revealing some architectural curiosity or spectacular riverscape. Fans of faded grandeur will feast on its ragged backstreets, curious courtyards and decaying façades. Even jaded expatriates will sometimes be moved to speak of the 'Budapest moment', when the city, caught in an unexpected light, will suddenly reveal itself anew – such as stumbling from some murky club to find classy old neon glowing against a summer dawn. Or looking out from a rattly old tram crossing the Danube to spy a shaft of light breaking through clouds over the Castle. Yes, Budapest is beautiful. Ridiculously beautiful.

History is ever-present, both in the minds of Hungarians, who inhabit a weird psychohistorical landscape in which the Turks invaded yesterday and they're still pissed off about it, and in the very fabric of this pock-marked, bullet-holed city. History has never left Hungary alone and Budapest has been invaded, occupied, burnt down and rebuilt time and time again. But there are gentler reminders of the past, such as lolling beneath a Turkish dome in the healing waters of one of Budapest's baths, or hearing Yiddish spoken in District VII, Central Europe's only surviving Jewish Quarter. At times, sipping an *eszpresszó* in one of the few remaining Habsburg coffeehouses, a peculiar yearning can take hold – a nostalgia for a long-vanished Budapest and its turn-of-the-century Golden Age, a city and a culture almost entirely passed from living memory. Nostalgia for a city one never knew. Ridiculous, really.

But it's no simple proposition, the Hungarian capital. Stunningly divided by the Danube into hilly Buda and flat Pest, the city is likewise culturally tugged in conflicting directions. Is it a passionate southern city, or a hard-working northern

one? Still part of Eastern Europe or attached to the West? The last outpost of Germanic Europe, or the beginning of the Balkans? Both, in every case, and neither. It's Budapest, caught in the middle, alone and unique.

Then factor in a sharp social divide. On one side are the young and the hungry, toting their mobile phones and making the most of new freedoms and opportunities. On the other side are the old and those otherwise unable to adapt, still subsisting within the old state institutions and drowning their economic sorrows in pálinka and cheap wine.

As a visitor, you'll find yourself among the better off. Even on a relatively modest holiday budget you can afford to do pretty much anything you want – check out any cultural or sporting event, ride around everywhere in cabs, dine in the finest restaurants and still have change. Stick to things the Hungarians do and you'll find that this city is so cheap it's, well, ridiculous.

I first visited Budapest on 1 May 1989 – the very cusp of the 'change of systems' – and was so captivated by its idiosyncrasies that I've never stopped coming back for more. Over nearly a decade, I've watched Budapest change, acquiring a glitzy new surface that only partially obscures the doggedly eccentric city underneath. But the Budapest of old is falling down, acquired by property developers, colonised by multinational franchises, and slowly being hammered into the postmodern shapelessness of any late twentieth-century city. For the time being, however, it still offers the best of both worlds – reasonable efficiency with appealingly ragged edges, an affordable level of creature comfort coupled with enough curiosities to keep anyone entertained for a while.

Visit Budapest now, before the whole place turns into one giant Sock Shop – for that will be the most ridiculous thing of all. *Dave Rimmer*

I shop therefore I am

...Get the 'Time Out Shopping & Services Guide', with free shopping discount card – valid at many of London's top stores.

http://www.timeout.co.uk

Amsterdam, Barcelona, Berlin, Boston, Brussels, Budapest, Chicago, Edinburgh, Glasgow, London, Los Angeles, Madrid, Miami, New York, Paris, Philadelphia, Prague, Rome, San Francisco, Sydney, Tokyo & Washington DC.

ATRIUM HYATT BUDAPEST

H - 1051 Budapest

Roosevelt tér 2.

Phone: /361/ 266-1234

Telex: 22-5485

Fax: /361/ 266-9101

MANAGED BY

Location: Located in the heart of Budapest, overlooking the river Danube and Castle Hill, close to the prime shopping area, offices, banks and night-spots.

Accommodation:
- Fully computerized 10-story deluxe hotel
- 355 guest rooms including 27 suites • All rooms have individually controlled air-conditioning, bath, shower, radio, minibar, colour TV with pay-videoprogramme, international dial telephone, facility for connecting lap top pc to the phone on the Regency and Gold Passport floors, personal safes in suites, non-smoking level, two rooms for handicapped guests.

Restaurants and Bars:
- Old Timer Gourmet Restaurant • Atrium Terrace Café Restaurant • Clark Brasserie • Balloon Bar • Cocktail Bar

Conference and Banquet facilities:
- 378 square meter ballroom • 5 function rooms
- All meeting rooms are fully equipped with the latest audio-visual equipment and simultaneous translation system for 6 languages.

Business Center: fully equipped for today's business traveller

Fitness Center: the right place to relax

In Context

Key Events

Early History

c1000 BC Celtic and Illyrian tribes inhabit Danube Basin.
c500 BC Proto-Hungarians begin southwest migration from Siberia.
35 BC Rome Conquers Danube Basin, known as Pannonia.
6 AD Pannonians rebel against Romans.
430-452 Huns make Hungary base for European excursion.

The Hungarians Enter Europe

700-850 Hungarians serve as vassals of the Khazar Empire in southern Russia.
895 King Árpád leads Hungarians across Carpathians into the Danube Basin.
955 King Otto of Bavaria defeats Hungarians at Augsburg, ending period of Hungarian raids on West Europe.
972 King Géza, along with his son Vajk, converts to Western Christianity.
1000 Vajk enthroned as King István (Stephen) with a crown donated by Pope in Rome.
1006 Revolt of pagan Hungarian leaders.
1066 First written example of Hungarian (The Tihány Abbey Codex).
1222 'Golden Bull' signed by nobles at Rakós meadow, defining the Hungarian nation.
1241 Mongol Invasion.
1243 King Béla IV decrees the building of fortified towns. Buda gains in importance.
1301 King Otto dies heirless, ending the House of Árpád.
1310 Robert Charles of Anjou crowned King of Hungary.
1396 Hungarians defeated by Ottoman Turks at Nicopolis.
1456 János Hunyádi defeats Turks at Belgrade.
1458 Hunyádi's son, Matyás, crowned King of Hungary. Budapest's first 'golden age'.
1490 King Matyás dies, leading to chaos between nobles and peasants.
1514 Peasants revolt, unsuccessfully, under György Dózsa. Repressive Tripartum law enacted, reducing peasantry to unarmed serfdom.

The Turkish Era

1526 Turks led by Suliman the Magnificent defeat Hungarians at battle of Mohács. Turning northward, they burn Buda and retreat.
1541 Buda occupied by Turks as provincial capital.
1683 Turks defeated at Siege of Vienna.
1686 Habsburgs defeat Turks at Siege of Buda. Buda burned. Again.
1699 Turks relinquish claims to Hungary at Peace of Karlowitz.

The Habsburg Era

1703 Hungarians led by Ferenc Rákóczi rebel unsuccessfully against Austrians.
1723 Habsburgs claim right to rule under the Hungarian crown.
1740-1780 Empress Maria Teresia institutes social reforms. Immigration encouraged.
1808 The Embellishment Act sets guidelines for the urban development of Buda and Pest.
1839-1849 Construction of the Chain Bridge across the Danube.
1848 Hungarians rebel unsuccessfully against the Austrians. Again.

1867 Ausgleich signed, uniting Austria and Hungary as equals.
1870 Imperial railway system established with Pest as hub.
1873 Pest, Buda, and Óbuda united as a single city, Budapest.
1896 Budapest hosts Hungarian Millennial Exhibition.
1901 Hungarian Parliament Building, the world's largest, opened.
1914 Austria-Hungary enters World War I.
1918 Austria-Hungary loses World War I.
1918 Hungary declares independence from Austria.
1919 Hungary declares shortlived Soviet Republic under Béla Kun. Romanian Army occupies Budapest. Admiral Horthy returns. 'White Terror' against leftists.
1920 Treaty of Trianon signed. Hungary loses two thirds of its territory to neighbouring states of the 'Little Entente'.
1938 Hungary, now allied with Nazi Germany, receives a part of Slovakia under the Second Vienna Awards.
1940 Hungary awarded most of Transylvania by Germany. Hungarian troops assist in Nazi invasion of Yugoslavia.
1943 Hungarian Army defeated by Russians at Battle of Stalingrad.
1944 Admiral Horthy kidnapped by Nazis, fascist Arrow Cross Party begins murders and mass deportations of Jews to concentration camps.
1945 Red Army captures Budapest.

Communist Hungary

1945 Communist Party given control of occupied Hungary.
1946 Hungarian monarchy abolished and a Hungarian People's Republic declared.
1948 Land ownership collectivised.
1949 Mátyas Rákosi, Communist Party chief, institutes a show trial against traditional Hungarian Communist Party leaders. All are executed.
1953 Stalin dies. Rákosi temporarily replaced with Imre Nagy, and then by Ernö Gerö. Hungary beats England 6-3 at Wembley.
1956 Hungarians revolt against Russian occupation. An independent Hungarian Socialist State is proclaimed under Imre Nagy, but falls to Russian tanks after two weeks. Budapest in ruins again. Janos Kádár placed in power by Russians.

The Kádár Era

1963 Kádár declares a partial amnesty for those jailed for their role in the 1956 revolt.
1968 Hungary aids Russia in crushing the Prague Spring in Czechoslovakia. Kádár institutes his 'New Economic Mechanism' allowing restricted private enterprise.
1978 The Crown of Saint Stephen is returned to Hungary by the United States.

The Change of Systems

1989 János Kádár dies. Mass demonstrations in streets of Budapest. 'Reform Communists' declare intention to allow democratic elections. East Germans flee to west via Hungary. The Communist Party declares itself defunct.
1990 Hungarian elections elect conservative government headed by the Hungarian Democratic Forum. With József Antáll as Prime Minister and Árpád Göncz as President Hungary is declared a Republic.
1994 Socialist Party trounces Hungarian Democratic Forum in second democratic election. Gyula Horn named Prime Minister.
1997 Hungary provisionally invited to join Nato.

History

Marauding Mongols, Ottomans, Habsburgs, Nazis and the Red Army have all fought over the strategic importance of Budapest.

Digging deep for Magyar roots.

Early History

Budapest's strategic and majestic geographical location has long made it the key to the major events and trends in the history of the Danube basin. Perched on limestone hills which rise abruptly above the Danube, some 20 kilometres below the dramatic bend which sends the river flowing southward to the Black Sea, Buda's location offers a virtually impregnable defensive position and potential control of Central Europe's main waterway to all those who occupy it.

The earliest history of the region, like that of so much of Europe at the time, was a decidedly lowbrow affair. Archaeologists have turned up evidence of human habitation as early as 500,000 BC. Agricultural communities sprang up around the River Tisza, where large neolithic sites have been discovered. During the first millennium BC,

Illyrian populations shared the plains with groups of Celtic peoples, known as the Eravi. The recent excavation of a large Celtic site on Gellért Hill is the first Eravi settlement found in Budapest itself.

It isn't until the expansion of the Roman Empire under Julius Caesar that the Danube basin enters written history. The region was conquered without resistance in 35 BC, officially incorporated into the Roman Empire in 14 BC under the name Pannonia, then promptly revolted against Rome in 6 AD. This encouraged the Romans to build up their defences through military settlements. Several Hungarian towns begin their modern existence at this point, including Pécs, Szombathely and Buda.

Known to the Romans as Aquincum for the copious mineral waters that flow from the limestone rocks of the Buda hills, Roman Buda was a modest trading town on the very edge of the Roman Empire. Today, one can visit the ruins of classical Aquincum in the Óbuda district (*see chapters* **Sightseeing** *and* **Musuems**), which boasts the remains of an ancient amphitheatre. More Roman ruins (the aptly named 'Minor Aquincum') can be seen along the Danube in Pest, at Március 15 tér just north of the Erzsébet bridge.

THE ASIANS ARE COMING!

As the Roman Empire withered, political and cyclical climatic changes in Central Asia forced the first of a series of migrations of various Altaic peoples westward in what becomes known, depending on to whom you are speaking, as either the 'Age of Barbarians' or the 'Age of Migrations'. The Romans, no longer able to maintain their overextended Empire against repeated waves of Goths, Gepids, Alans and Vandals, began to withdraw from Pannonia.

In 430, the Huns, a central Asian confederacy of Turkic-speaking nomads, burst into Europe. Under the leadership of Attila they defeated the armies of Romans and vassals alike until finally, in 453, the Pope came in person to beg mercy. Attila returned to Pannonia without sacking Rome, but died mysteriously on the very night of his wedding to the princess Ildikó.

With the death of their leader, the Huns returned to their central Asian homelands. Next out of Asia were the Avars in the seventh century. They,

Tribes and tribulations

Ever since the Hungarians arrived in Europe, conjecture as to their origins has been rife. The Byzantines mislabelled them 'Turks' or 'Ungeri' after the 'Ten Arrows' confederation of Central Asian tribes. Medieval Hungarian chroniclers recorded that the Hungarians came from 'Magna Hungaria' somewhere in the east, and ever since King Béla IV sent the monk Julianus to the Volga to search for those lost Magyars, Hungarians have been diligently researching their origins.

For a long time, Hungarians were fascinated by the myth of Hun origins. Poet János Arany's epic poem about the Huns, written in the nineteenth century, influenced several generations of Hungarians into believing a literary device to be the explanation of their national origins. (Attila is still a common first name here).

In the 1840s, explorer Sándor Körösi Csoma travelled to Tibet and China in search of lost Hungarians. He didn't find any, but he did remain convinced that the Uighur Turks were the ancient progenitors of modern Hungarians. This idea

found eager adherents during the pre-World War II epoch among right-wing 'Turanian' parties, who envisioned a Turko-Uralic master race including both the Hungarians and the Japanese. Strangely enough, the idea has recently been revived, and Hungarian archaeologists are again digging around in Uighur cemeteries.

Political prejudice has led some Hungarians to the idea that descent from the Uralic Voguls and Ostyaks, who live in what used to be the Soviet Union, was a commie plot to tie the Magyars to Mother Russia. A favourite alternative theory is that Hungarians are descendants of the Sumerians, and thus, by extension, are the founders of modern civilisation. This is supported by the fact that half a dozen Sumerian vocabulary items sound vaguely Hungarian.

Given the way the political wind blows, there is always room for another theory. Assorted Hungarian 'linguists' have published studies 'proving' that the Hungarians are related to the Incas, the Australian Aboriginals, the California Miwok Indians and the Tibetans.

in turn, came under pressure from the Bulgar Empire, another Turkic-speaking confederacy from the Volga steppes. Meanwhile, Transdanubia in the west was being populated by more sedentary, agricultural Slavs, most closely related to today's Slovenians. Many place names bear witness to early Slav settlement, such as Pécs, Debrecen, Balaton and Visegrád.

The Hungarians Enter Europe

The origins of the Hungarian people is a topic debated to this day, most loudly by Hungarians themselves (*see* **Tribes and tribulations**). The Magyars are a branch of the Finno-Ugric language grouping, a subgroup of the Altaic language family which includes the Finns, Turks, Mongolians and a host of Siberian peoples. (*See also chapter* **Language**.) The earliest Hungarian homeland was in the dense forests between the Volga river and the Ural mountains. Hungarian's closest linguistic relatives today are Vogul (Mansi) and Ostyak (Hanti) spoken by 35,000 fur trappers and fishermen on the left bank of the Ob river in the northern Ural region of Siberia. You can still buy 'three fish' using Hungarian if you ever find yourself on the Ob in need of lunch.

These proto-Hungarians broke off from their northern relatives around 500 BC and moved south into the central Volga region. In the first centuries

AD, the Hungarians came into contact with Turkic cultures pushing west; one group became known as the Huns. It is possible that some Magyars rode with Attila, but historically speaking, the Magyars first became known in the seventh and eighth centuries as vassals of the Turkic-speaking Khazar Empire between the Black and Caspian seas. The Khazars engaged nomadic tribes, such as the early Hungarians, to act as border guards.

In the ninth century, the Hungarians left their base in 'Levedia' (today's Ukraine) and settled in the land of 'Etelköz', meaning 'between the rivers', in today's Moldavia. From here they raided deep into Frankish Europe. St Cyril described the horde of Magyars he met in 860 as *luporum more ululantes*, 'howling in the manner of wolves'. Faced with a howling gang from Asia pillaging the Holy Roman Empire, western Christendom reacted by amending the Catholic mass with the words 'Lord save us from sin and the Hungarians'.

While the main Magyar armies spent the spring of 895 raiding Europe, their villages in Etelköz were devastated by Bulgars and Petchenegs. The surviving tribes of Magyars, led by their king, Árpád, fled across the Verecke pass in the northern Carpathians and on to the Hungarian plain in 895. Meeting little resistance from the local Slavs, Goths and Avars, the Hungarians pushed their competitors, the Bulgars, south of the Danube, and began raiding as far west as France, Germany and northern Spain. The Hungarians were defeated by King Otto I at the Battle of Augsburg in 955. Retiring to Pannonia, the Hungarians realised that alliance with a major power might be a good idea. This meant dealing with the Christian Church.

Hungary was sandwiched between the Holy Roman and Byzantine empires and King Géza, Árpád's grandson, requested missionaries be sent from Rome to convert the Magyars to the western Church, a fact still trumpeted by Hungarians as a decision to be 'linked with the west'. King Géza was baptised along with his son, Vajk, who took the name István (Stephen) upon his accession to the Hungarian throne on Christmas Day 1000.

King István didn't have an easy time convincing his countrymen. Tribes loyal to the older, shamanic religion led a revolt against István in 1006. One consequence was the death of Venetian missionary Saint Gellért (Gerard), who was put into a spiked barrel and rolled down Gellért Hill into the Danube by miffed Magyar traditionalists. King István crushed the revolt and set about destroying the power of the chieftains by appropriating their land and setting up a new class of nobles. He also began minting coins, forging alliances, building castles and all the other things that early medieval rulers did on the road to feudalism.

Medieval Hungary

With St Stephen's conversion to Christianity, Hungary had made a religious and political commitment to the Holy Roman Empire. But the country was still in a state of cultural flux between east and west, as symbolised by the mixed Byzantine/Roman manufacture of St Stephen's crown (*see page 22* **Two bent half-crowns**). Budapest itself was, at this time, of little importance. The main centres of power were the King's palace in Székesfehérvár, the Queen's residence in Veszprém and the seat of ecclesiastical power in Esztergom.

Stephen's son, Imre, died young, and the next 200 years saw a succession of weak kings and struggles for the throne of the House of Árpád. Turning mounted central Asian nomads into medieval European serfs did not prove an easy task and revolts among the tribal Magyar nobility were common until the late twelfth century.

The tensions between the landowning nobility and the office of the King were eventually settled by the signing of the 'Golden Bull' under King András in 1222. This document granted the landed nobility exemption from taxation (among other privileges), it recognised the 'Nation' as such and it laid the framework for an annual assembly of nobles, the Diet. This was to be held in Rákos meadow in Pest; the annual gathering of the nation's high and mighty provided a push that helped Pest grow into a central market town.

All was going well, in a medieval kind of way, when the next big gang from central Asia gate-crashed central Europe. The Mongol invasion of 1241 devastated Hungary as towns were sacked, crops were burned, and entire regions depopulated. The Mongols retreated a year after the death of Genghis Khan, but the experience was sobering for King Béla IV, who ordered a series of defensive castles to be built. Buda became the site of one such castle, and once built, it soon came to dominate the Hungarian realm.

In order to repopulate the devasted countryside, Béla IV invited foreign craftsmen, traders, clergy and peasants from the west, especially Germans, Czechs and Italians. Central Asian Cumans and Jász who had fled the Mongol onslaught were granted land east of Pest as border guards.

Béla's son, King András III, died without leaving an heir, thus ending the House of Árpád. Robert Charles of Anjou was crowned King of Hungary in 1310. Under his son, Louis the Great, Hungary's frontiers were extended by alliance to include Dalmatia, the Banat of Serbia and part of Poland.

In 1396, Hungary's King Sigismund led an ill-fated attack on the Turks at Nicopolis, ending in a defeat that marked the beginning of the Turkish advance into Europe. Things went from bad to worse until a Transylvanian prince, János Hunyadi, stemmed the Turkish advance in Serbia and finally regained control of Belgrade in 1456. Church bells rang all over Europe. Hunyadi's death soon after led to the usual bloody struggle for the throne, and in 1458 one of Hunyadi's sons, Mátyás Corvinus, found himself king by default at the age of 16.

With Mátyás, Buda became the true focus of Hungarian life, a position it has never surrendered since. Revered as Hungary's 'Renaissance King', Mátyás undertook extensive building within **Buda Castle**. Among his achievements was the Royal library, one of the world's largest, intended to attract wandering scholars to Buda.

Mátyás also created one of the first standing armies in European history. Comprising professional soldiers, foreign and domestic, the 'Black Army' was able to keep both Turks and rebellious nobles at bay. Meanwhile, his second wife, Queen Beatrice, introduced courtly customs and fashions from her native Italy to the relatively backwoods court of Hungary.

Hungarian historians refer to these years as the 'Hungarian Renaissance' a term which should be taken with a few grains of salt. Still, as medieval courts go, Mátyás' showed a distinctly humanistic streak. Mátyás spent a lot of his time galloping around the countryside, disguised as a lowly peasant and seeking out injustices in the feudal system, which, given the nature of medieval society, must have been quite an easy job. Even to this day, his

Dome sweet dome – Turkish influence still evident at the Király baths.

name still symbolises justice and good governance. 'Mátyás is dead' goes the oft-spoken Hungarian saying, 'and justice died with him.'

Certainly, when Mátyás died heirless in 1490, the legacy of culture and order he had built more or less collapsed. It soon became business as usual for the unruly nobility, who chose a Bohemian, Ulászló, as king. Under Ulászló the nobles began appropriating common land and taxes, they sold off the Buda library and dismissed the standing army. In 1496 a pogrom against the Jews broke out in Buda, and the survivors then fled en masse to Bulgaria.

In 1514 the Pope ordered a new crusade against the Turks. Hungary's peasantry, under the leadership of György Dózsa, a Transylvanian Captain, rallied near Pest and turned against the nobles. As is usual with peasant revolts, the peasants were quickly and soundly defeated. Dózsa was executed in particularly artful fashion: he was enthroned as 'king of the peasants' on a red-hot iron dais.

With Dózsa's defeat the nobility voted in a new law which superseded the Golden Bull of 1222. The Tripartum law, which was effectively in force right up to 1848, reduced the peasantry to serfdom and forbade them to bear arms. The timing could not have been worse.

Turkish Rule

When the young Hungarian King Lajos II, with 10,000 armoured knights, met the Turkish cavalry on the swampy plains of Mohács on 29 August 1526, 80,000 Ottoman spahis routed the Hungarians in under two hours. King Lajos, thrown from his horse, drowned in a muddy stream, trapped in heavy armour. After Mohács, the Turks turned north, sacking and burning Buda. They retreated briefly, but returned in 1541 to occupy the castle. Thus Buda became the seat of power in Ottoman Hungary, rebuilt as a Turkish provincial capital.

Hungary was divided in three. A rump Hungary ruled by the Habsburgs existed in the west and north. The Turks controlled the heartland with Transylvania nominally independent as a principality under Turkish control. While the countryside became a theatre of border warfare on the marches of Ottoman Europe, Buda developed into a provincial Ottoman town. The **Mátyás templom** (Matthias Church) was converted into a mosque, and the thermal springs inspired the construction of Turkish baths (*see chapter* **Baths**). An Ottoman chronicler recorded that Buda boasted four major mosques, 34 smaller mosques, three dervish monasteries, and ten schools.

Sephardic Jews, refugees from the Spanish Inquisition, settled along today's Táncsics Mihály utca. Muslim Gypsies, known as 'Copts' (that is Egyptians) settled around the Vienna Gate working as armourers. The bulk of Buda's Turkish residents lived below the Castle in today's Víziváros, behind Batthyány tér and around today's Bem tér. Bosnians and Serbs worked in the Ottoman gunpowder factories and conducted trade along the Danube. This neighbourhood, between the Castle and Gellért Hill became known as Tabán (from the Turkish *tabahane*, or armoury). The neighbourhood continued to be a centre for southern Slavs, and it was here that the modern Serbo-Croatian literary language was created during the nineteenth century (Tabán became a night-life centre for artists and peasants until the quarter was torn down on the orders of Admiral Horthy in the 1930s: he felt it spoiled his view from the palace.)

Pest was a city mostly populated by Magyars. Few Hungarians resided in Buda, since there were no churches there. The upheaval of the Protestant Reformation made itself felt throughout the Hungarian region during the Turkish occupation. The rulers didn't care about the theological squabbles of their Christian subjects. Still, anti-clericalism and wariness of the Catholic Habsburgs among the petty nobles made an attractive recruiting ground for Protestant reform in Hungary, while the austere tenets of Calvinism found eager adherents in the Great Plain.

The Turkish defeat at the siege of Vienna in 1683 signalled the end of the Turkish threat to Christian Europe. In 1686 the Habsburgs turned the tables on the Ottomans, attacking their stronghold at **Buda Castle** and defeating the Turks after a six-week siege. The victors looted and pillaged Buda and Pest, so that Buda was again reduced to a pile of post-war rubble, while Pest was virtually depopulated. After a further decade of war the Turks lost the rest of their Hungarian realm and relinquished their claims at the Peace of Karlowitz in 1699.

Habsburg Budapest

At the beginning of the eighteenth century, both Buda and Pest were ruins. As an Austrian principality, Hungary was ruled by Vienna, but governed as a province from Pozsony (today's Bratislava). The Habsburgs suspended the constitution and placed the country under military occupation. Counter-Reformation measures were then undertaken to ensure nobles' loyalty to their Catholic Habsburg rulers, including the sale of 42 Protestant pastors as galley slaves in Naples. In the meantime, claims for land redistribution after 150 years of Turkish rule was proving fertile ground for corruption.

In 1703 the Hungarians rebelled, led by the Transylvanian magnate Ferenc Rákóczi. Once again Hungary was shattered by a War of Independence. This one lasted eight years and ended with the signing of the Treaty of Szatmár. Rákóczi died in Turkish exile. To prevent further rebellion by the feisty Hungarians, the Austrians blew up every castle in the country and ordered that the walls be dismantled from each fortified town or church. Today, the visitor to Hungary can view the ruins of many such castles, but if you want to see the intact versions you will have to go north to Slovakia.

Buda's strategic and economic value was not lost on the industrious Austrians. Rebuilding would take some time, but it is during this period that Buda and Pest began to acquire the central European character that makes this city at times seem even more *mitteleuropäisch* than its sister, Vienna.

The reign of the Empress Maria Theresa (1740-80) marks the beginnings of the real integration of Austria and Hungary. Hungary's nobility began to look more and more towards Vienna as the centre of power. While the upper crust built baroque palaces and commissioned ornate churches, the majority of the peasantry lived as impoverished serfs using medieval agricultural technology.

One of the Austrians' ambitious programmes was to repopulate Hungary with immigrants from throughout the Habsburg realms. Lands left fallow by centuries of war and rebellion were laid open for settlement. In the west and south, German settlers from Swabia, known as Svábs, were given land, while Slovaks, fleeing overpopulation in the Carpathian highlands, settled on the great plains. Buda was reborn as the German town of Ofen, while Pest developed into a commercial centre for the grain and livestock produced on the Hungarian plains and shipped along the Danube.

Evidence of this immigration policy is still very much present to this day in the makeup of Budapest's suburban villages. In the Buda hills, villages such as Budakeszi and Zsámbék can boast bilingual Sváb communities. In the Pilis Hill villages to the north of Budapest you can find Svábs mixed with Slovaks, Gypsies, and Serbian communities, all refugees who fled here during Turkish times.

Meanwhile, Jews began moving back to the city from Bohemia and Galicia, settling in Pest, just beyond the the now dismantled city walls in what is today District VII. This neighbourhood became the centre of Hungarian Jewry, and is still the most complete Jewish quarter remaining in eastern Europe, known, since World War II, as the Ghetto. (*See chapters* **Budapest By Area** *and* **Sightseeing**.)

'Arise Hungarians!' – Lajos Kossuth, voice of nationalist sentiment, points the way.

Apart from a few revolts (such as the Transylvanian Székely Rebellion in 1764), the eighteenth was a relatively quiet century, in which Hungary was seen as an agricultural backwater feeding an ever more industrialised Austria. Maria Theresa's successor, Joseph II (1780-90) began a reform programme of taxing noble estates, granting rights to serfs and constructing hospitals and schools. Ever the pragmatist, Joseph retracted these reforms on his deathbed, allowing his more conservative-minded successor, Leopold II (1790-92) to reinstate the wonderful world of feudalism.

Repercussions of the French Revolution were felt all across Europe; Hungary was no exception. A conspiracy of Hungarian Jacobins was nipped in the bud, although their ideas gained an audience through the Hungarian-language writings of Ferenc Kazinczy. As the nineteenth century dawned, Hungarians eagerly embraced the Magyar tongue as a revolutionary and literary language. After centuries of war, immigration, and official neglect, the Hungarian language was now spoken only by peasants, and only in the Calvinist east of the country did any of the nobles continue to speak Magyar.

Loath to use German, the language of the occupying Austrians, many continued to use Latin between themselves, using Hungarian, or any of the other local languages, only when speaking to peasants. Hungarian now began to revive as a literary language, uniting people as 'Hungarian' instead of 'Habsburg'.

REFORM

The period of national revival in the early nineteenth century is known in Hungary as the Reform. Buda and Pest perked up under the Embellishment Act, an 1808 law which began to plan the city on more modern development ideas. After a particularly nasty year of Danube floods in 1838, first Vienna and then Pest were redesigned along a pattern of concentric ringed boulevards.

The personality who embodies the Hungarian national emergence in the early nineteenth century was Count István Széchenyi (1791-1860). A figure of amazing energy, Széchenyi – as a writer, entrepreneur, ardent capitalist and patron of the arts – set the trend among the nascent urban nobility by being an ardent Anglophile. Having visited England several times, he introduced such British inventions as flush toilets, steam shipping on the Danube and horse racing, as well as founding the Hungarian Academy of Sciences.

Among Széchenyi's English inspirations was the first bridge across the Danube. Hitherto traffic between Buda and Pest had been conducted by ferry or by a rather clumsy removeable pontoon bridge. Széchenyi imported the English designer William Tierney Clark and Scotsman Adam Clark as supervising engineer and the Széchenyi

Rebel leader and magnate Ferenc Rákóczi ended his life in Turkish exile.

Lajos Batthyany's place of execution marked with the Eternal Flame.

Lanchíd (Chain Bridge) was constructed between 1839-49 (*see chapter* **Sightseeing**).

While Széchenyi championed the ideal of economic development within the Habsburg Empire, other members of the Hungarian Diet were less accommodating to the Austrians. Lajos Kossuth, one of the now landless gentry who were flocking to Pest, became an eloquent voice of nationalist and liberal sentiment against Austrian rule.

Pressure on Habsburg internal affairs elsewhere led to a lessening of repression in 1839, and a reform-orientated liberal Diet was convened, led by Ferenc Deák. Lajos Kossuth became the editor of the leading Hungarian newspaper, the *Pesti Hírlap*, and his editorials lambasted the Austrian administration. Kossuth stressed increased political independence from Vienna, and his uncompromising stand led to his becoming the bitter opponent of Count Széchenyi.

Against this background the Parisians rose and overthrew the French monarchy for the second time. Civil nationalist uprisings spread across Europe like wildfire, threatening the old monarchical order. On 3 March 1848, Kossuth delivered a parliamentary speech demanding an end to the feudal sysytem – tax privileges, serfdom, the whole lot. On 13 March, the revolutionary spirit reached the streets of Vienna.

THE REVOLT OF 1848

Two days later, on 15 March 1848, Kossuth met with the cream of Hungarian dissident liberals in the Pilvax coffeehouse in Pest to develop a revolutionary strategy. Among them was the poet Sándor Petőfi who, later that day, famously read his newly penned poem *Nemzeti dal* ('National

Where Petőfi said his piece – the steps of the National Museum.

Sándor Petőfi – poet killed in action.

Song') on the steps of the **National Museum** – an event still commemorated annually. A proposal for a liberalised constitution with Hungary given far-reaching autonomy was dispatched to Vienna that day and consented to by the Hungarian Diet and the frightened Imperial government. On 7 April the Emperor sanctioned a Hungarian Ministry headed by Lajos Batthyány, and including Kossuth, Széchenyi and Deák. Hungarian was made the language of state; freedom of the press, assembly and religion were granted; noble privileges were curtailed; and peasants were emancipated from serfdom.

This might have satisfied less demanding nationalist sentiments, but Kossuth, as Finance Minister, wanted a financial and military structure separate from the Imperial Austrians. The new Hungarian Diet went against the Emperor and voted in funding for the creation of a 200,000-man army. Kossuth's intentions were noble, but his tactic was shortsighted. Hungary's minorities comprised over 50 per cent of the population, and they essentially lost all rights under the new constitution. Vienna, occupied with its own security problems, organised a Croatian invasion of Hungary to induce a compromise and soon the entire region was at war. The Hungarians could not expect much aid from the ethnic minorities within the scope of Kossuth's rather narrow nationalism.

During the early, heady days of the rebellion, Pest was the scene of fervent pro-independence sentiment. But Buda and Pest fell early to the Austrian Army and the Hungarian government moved to Debrecen while fighting continued. By the spring of 1849, the Hungarian troops had the upper hand.

A newly enthroned Habsburg Emperor, Franz Joseph, appealed to the Tsar of Russia for help in defending the endangered European institution of absolute, incompetent and unresponsive monarchy. The Tsar, of course, agreed. With the help of Russian troops the rebellion was quickly, and brutally, crushed, and Kossuth, like his predecessor Rákóczi, fled to Turkey.

Petőfi was killed on a battlefield in Transylvania and Count Széchenyi suffered a nervous breakdown and spent the rest of his days in a sanatorium. The Hungarian generals who surrendered to the Russians at Arad were shamefully executed, and the anniversary of that day is still a national day of mourning.

TURNING DEFEAT INTO GOLDEN AGE

With the crushing of the 1849 rebellion, Hungary fell into one of its periodic post-defeat depressions. Thousands went into exile. Hungarian prisoners were made to construct a huge Austrian military blockhouse, the **Citadella**, atop Gellért Hill. Its guns were intended as a deterrent to any future Hungarian attempts to dislodge Habsburg power.

The Austrians' military defeat in Italy in 1859, however, made accommodation with the Magyars a political necessity. In Pest, the remnants of the Liberal Party coalesced around Ferenc Deák, who published a basis for reconciliation with the Austrians in 1865.

The *Ausgleich*, or Compromise, of 1867 made Hungary more of an equal partner in the Habsburg Empire. Austria-Hungary was to be a single nation with two governments and two parliaments, although ruled by Habsburg Royalty who would recognise the legitimacy of the unclaimed crown of St István. New tariff agreements made Hungarian products more competitive than before, and the agreement allowed for the establishment of a Hungarian army. In 1868, Transylvania, in violation of previous agreements, was incorporated into Hungary proper, while Croatia was unhappily subordinated to the Hungarian Crown.

THE RISE OF PEST

The 50 years between the signing of the Compromise and World War I are rightly remembered as the Golden Years of Budapest. The city boomed with new industry and building, and the population exploded from 280,000 in 1867 to almost a million on the eve of war. In 1867 Buda and Pest together were the seventeenth largest city in Europe; by 1900 Budapest was the sixth.

Part of the prosperity was due to the better trade position won by Hungary in the 1867 agreement. With trade tariffs reduced, Hungarian products quickly flooded the rest of the Austrian Empire and came into demand abroad. The Danube provided the main route for grain sold north to Germany and for manufactured goods shipped south towards the Balkans. An extensive rail system was introduced with Pest as its hub. In 1870 Pest appointed a Council of Public Works, modelled on the London Metropolitan Board of Works, to supervise the reconstruction of the city.

Buda, Óbuda and Pest were officially united as a single city, Budapest, in 1873. There were monumental urban development projects, including the construction of boulevards such as Andrássy út and the Nagykörút (*see chapter* **Budapest By Area**). Gentry and noble families competed to have palaces constructed in the garden suburbs that sprung up around the old city centre.

Hungarian culture was focused on the Pest side. Buda was primarily a German-speaking town of dour burghers and irrelevant nobility, but arts and politics were increasingly being conducted in Hungarian on the Pest side. The booming growth of the Hungarian language went hand in hand with the Magyarisation policies of Prime Minister

Kálmán Tisza (1875-90). Tisza suspected that the Austrians could endanger Hungary's newly strengthened position by leverage among the non-Hungarian minorities of the Empire just as it had in 1848. His response was a programme designed to assimiliate the assorted Croats, Slovaks and Romanians of the Hungarian realm.

Tisza declared that all schools would have to teach in Magyar, and attempts were made to have Magyar become the language of churches. The assimilation policy laid the groundwork for the minority unrest and resentment that festers to this day among Hungary's neighbours.

The corollary to the minority issue, however, was that adoption of Hungarian became the linguistic ticket to success in Budapest. A lively literary life began to grow in Hungarian, as artists, students, politicians and other society figures met to congregate, socialise and exchange ideas in Pest's many coffeehouses.

THE 1896 EXHIBITION

By the 1890s, Budapest was the fastest-growing metropolis in Europe. The Emperor Franz Joseph, on the twenty-fifth anniversary of the 1867 agreement, issued a decree that Budapest was to be a capital equal to that of Austria. Budapest became the focus of a new sense of Hungarian national confidence. In anticipation of the millennial anniversary of the Honfoglalás, the Hungarian invasion of the Danube Basin, a huge exposition was planned for 1895. The untimely death of the exhibition's designer caused a minor delay, but with typical Hungarian aplomb this was duly taken care of by an official declaration that the invasion had occurred in 896, and since then the history books have been amended to include the new date.

The Millennium celebration in the **Városliget** (City Park) became an overt expression of this new national confidence. Continental Europe's first underground railway whisked visitors beneath Andrássy út to the fairground at today's **Hősök tere** (Heroes' Square), where they were met by the gargantuan memorial to King Árpád and his tribal Magyar chieftains. A miniature of Transylvania's Vajdahunyad Castle was constructed to house exhibits and today still houses the **Agriculture Museum**. Across the way, the Wampetics Gardens, the home to celebrity chef Károly Gundel (now the **Gundel** restaurant), served up traditional Hungarian cuisine prepared with a touch of French flair making Hungarian food the culinary fad of the new century.

Bordering on the obsessive

The Hungarian obsession with the Trianon Treaty reminds even the most casual visitor that in this part of the world the wounds of history have still to heal.

When the Treaty Conference in Versailles dealt with Hungarian territorial claims after World War I, Hungary sent its best diplomats but was in a terrible bargaining position – on the losing side and surrounded by states which had gained military control of Hungarian regions inhabited by disgruntled minorities. The Serbs, Czechoslovaks and Romanians who, aligned with France, were known as the Little Entente, all pressed claims for regions previously part of Hungary.

The treaty did contain some glaring injustices. Romania was granted not only Transylvania, but also the mostly Hungarian towns of Szatmár, Nagyvárad (Oradea), Arad and Temesvár (Timișoara) simply because the rail line which linked them seemed a strategic prize. Southern Slovakia ended up containing large regions with a dense Hungarian minority simply because the Danube formed a neat frontier.

Throughout the 1920s and 1930s it seemed that there was no other political goal besides the regaining of lands lost in the treaty. The slogan of 'Nem! Nem! Soha!' ('No! No! Never!') was chanted as speech after speech was made condemning the treaty. Ire about Trianon and an attempt to reclaim former territories was a direct factor in Hungary's decision to align with Nazi Germany.

In most cases, the treatment of the newly created Hungarian minorities in the lost Trianon regions was remarkably bad. Language rights were lost, schools were closed, and most of the talented Hungarians left for 'Small Hungary'.

Today, Hungarians remain outraged over Trianon and politicians regularly invoke the treaty. In 1990, when Hungary's then Prime Minister József Antall claimed that he was the 'Prime Minister of 15 million Hungarians', neighbouring countries rounded on him to accuse him of 'Trianon Revisionism'.

Today, Hungarian minorities in former Yugoslavia, Romania and Slovakia feel that their rights to self-determination in simple things such as schooling and choice of names are under attack. The thousands of Transylvanian Hungarians who live and work illegally in Budapest are a reminder that flawed treaties never die – they just age gracelessly.

TOWARDS THE TWILIGHT

In the wake of the Millennium celebration, Hungarian confidence in the bright future was at an all-time high. The turn of the century was the golden age of Hungarian literature and arts. Mór Jókai was one of the most widely translated novelists in the world. Endre Ady's volume of new poetry, *Új versek*, sparked a veritable literary explosion. Béla Bartók and Zoltán Kodály were creating the study of ethnomusicology and composing masterpieces of modern music based on Hungarian folk traditions. Budapest became the in-spot for the vacationing upper crust of Europe.

Amid the heady confidence in culture, politics began to take an ominous turn. The city had largely been developed on credit, and the apparent opulence of Pest façades to this day contrasts with the poverty of the courtyards within. Working class unrest had first asserted itself on the first great May Day demonstration in 1890 and its influence grew over the next decade.

The new Hungarian **Parliament** building, opened in 1902, was the largest in the world, naively anticipating a long and prosperous rule. It was never a site for decorous politics, however, as representatives were not allowed to read speeches, leading to a tendency for rambling outbursts, nationalist *braggadacio* and occasional riots among the representatives, as in 1904. The ageing Deák wing Liberals were challenged by newer right-wing elements who introduced Austrian-influenced anti-Semitism, previously alien to Hungarian political and social life, into political dialogue.

THE LIGHTS GO OUT

National tensions within the Habsburg Empire came to a head in the years just before World War I. Hungary's Magyarcentric and high-handed administration of the majority of peoples within the realm had helped fuel resentment and nationalism.

When Gavrilo Princip, the leader of a minor Serb radical student group in Habsburg-occupied Sarajevo shot dead the Archduke Franz Ferdinand, war was declared against Serbia. What should have been a minor provincial police action rapidly turned into World War I.

Although Hungary could count itself lucky that the war was not fought on Hungarian land, by 1918 the Habsburgs, with Hungary beside them, faced defeat along with their German allies.

The Horthy Era

With the signing of the Armistice on 11 November 1918, World War I came to an end, and with it the Austro-Hungarian Empire. Hungary declared its independence as a republic on 16 November, with Mihály Károlyi as president. The country was faced by serious shortages, unresolved minority

Béla Lugosi – Culture Minister as vampire.

problems, and a ring of unsympathetic neighbours aligned with France. No clear demarcation line existed in the border regions, and Serbian troops occupied Pécs while the French camped in Szeged.

Hungarian diplomatic efforts at the Peace Conferences in Versailles went badly, and when the allies showed their determination to hand over two-thirds of Hungary's territory to the neighbouring states of the Little Entente, the Károlyi government resigned and handed power to the Social Democrats. They in turn made a coalition with the new Hungarian Communist Party.

On 21 March the Hungarian Soviet Republic was declared by Béla Kun, who went about forming a Red Army, nationalising banks and sending emissaries to the new Soviet Union. Kun hoped, as much as any Hungarian nationalist, to regain the territories lost in the war, but the Soviets did not heed his calls for aid. In response to the threat of expanding Bolshevism, Czech and Romanian armed forces entered Hungary. The Hungarians fought doggedly, but nevertheless the Romanian Army reached Budapest on 3 August 1919. Kun and his ministers fled to Vienna, most never to return (among them László Moholy-Nagy, the Bauhaus genius, and Béla Lugosi (*see above*), under-Minister of Culture and future Dracula). The Romanian Army did little to endear themselves to the citizens of Budapest. They bivouacked in the middle of the posh Oktogon intersection and plundered the city at will, finally leaving Budapest in November 1919.

Hungary entered a new phase of history when Admiral Miklós Horthy, hero of the Battle of Rijeka, entered Budapest from Szeged mounted on a white horse at the head of 25,000 Hungarian troops. The weeks that followed were known as the 'White Terror', as Communists, Social Democrats and Jews were hunted down and killed for collaboration with the Kun regime. On 25 January

1920, elections brought in a Christian-right coalition Parliament, with Admiral Horthy acting as regent in place of a claimant to the crown. Hungary was now a political incongruity – a monarchy without a king, led by an admiral without a navy.

On 4 June 1920, the Treaty of Trianon was signed in France (*see page 15* **Bordering on the obsessive**). Traffic in Budapest came to a halt, shops closed, black flags flew from buildings. Overnight, Hungary lost two thirds of its territory and a third of its Hungarian population. Budapest was now the only major city in Hungary, a city of one million in a country of seven million. Refugees clogged the city, unemployment raged and the economy virtually came to a standstill.

THE 'SILVER AGE'

A new political coalition, led by the Christian National Party and the peasant-orientated Smallholders' Party, came to power under the leadership of Count Gábor Bethlen, a hard-nosed conservative. He kept left and right in check and worked abroad to gain international credit and sympathy.

In October 1921, Habsburg pretender Charles IV flew in from Switzerland to head a monarchist coup with the help of loyalist troops. Horthy crushed the coup at the airfield in Budaörs, assisted by a paramilitary militia led by radical right-wing leader Gyula Gömbös. Their relationship would have serious consequences, as Gömbös's increasingly anti-Semitic appeals to nationalism became more and more the accepted political tone.

The Horthy governments advocated economic growth of rural areas and referred to Budapest as a somehow 'un-Hungarian' den of iniquity. Yet Budapest continued to be the economic and social focus of the nation's growth. Financial stability returned in the late 1920s, but when world stock prices collapsed in 1929, labour discontent rose sharply. Count Bethlen resigned and Horthy appointed Gyula Gömbös as Prime Minister.

Budapest in the 1920s and 1930s was not quite as dark as politics would suggest. Whereas the turn of the century was referred to as Budapest's Golden Age the inter-war period is remembered as the Silver Age, at least in art and society.

During the 1920s, Hungary's spas and casinos were the playgrounds of European high society. The Prince of Wales, the King of Italy, Evelyn Waugh and countless millionaires flocked to Budapest for the good life it promised, including the legalised brothels that offered both discretion and the *filles hongroises* who were well known for their beauty. When HL Mencken visited in 1930 he wrote to his wife: 'This town is really astounding. It is far the most beautiful that I have ever seen. I came expecting to find a dingy copy of Vienna but it makes Vienna look like a village.'

Culturally, Budapest was experiencing a renaissance. The coffeehouses still provided a home for an active literary output that was gobbled up by an adoring public. Avant-gardists grouped around Lajos Kassák and his Bauhaus-influenced journal *Ma* (*Today*), while liberal nationalists such as Gyula Illyés created a distinctly Hungarian genre of literature known as the *népi írók* ('folky writers'), focusing on peasant themes and village histories.

THINGS GO ASTRAY

Nevertheless, the organic make-up of Budapest society was coming apart. The Jews of Hungary were the first to feel the changing winds when access to higher education and certain professions were curtailed under the Numerus Clausus law in 1928. Prime Minister Gömbös was attracted by dreams of a Fascist Hungarian-Italian-German 'axis' (Gömbös coined the term), and worked to bring Hungary closer to Nazi Germany. German investment gained the Fascists influential friends and Oktogon was even renamed Mussolini tér.

When Germany annexed Austria and invaded the Sudetenland in 1938, Hungarian hopes for regaining the lands lost in the Trianon treaty soared. The second Vienna Award in November 1938 returned a part of Slovakia to Hungary, and in 1940 Hungary was awarded most of Transylvania. When Germany declared war on the United States after Pearl Harbor in 1941, Hungary immediately followed suit.

Still, all was not entirely fine between the Hungarians and the Germans. Gömbös had died and the new Prime Minister, Count Pál Teleki, who mistrusted the Nazis, worked to keep Hungary out of combat and resisted German demands for increased deportations of Jews. Teleki, an anglophile noble of the old school, would not stand for Germany infringing on Hungarian sovereignty *vis-à-vis* its own citizens, even Jews. Hungary, however, invaded Yugoslavia alongside the Germans in 1941, and when Vojvodina was returned, Hungarian troops took part in massacres of Jews and Serbs. When Hungary joined Germany in the invasion of Russia, Count Teleki did the noble thing and committed suicide.

Hungary's participation in the Russian invasion was disastrous. At Stalingrad in January 1943 the Russians captured the entire Hungarian second army. As the Soviets closed in on Budapest, American and British bombing sorties against Hungarian arms factories began to level parts of Angyalföld and Zugló in Pest. The Nazis tightened their internal control of Hungary with the arrival of German troops in March 1944. Hungarian officials continued to resist German demands for more Jewish deportations, but it became harder when Adolf Eichmann moved his SS headquarters to the Buda Hills. Jews were herded into the Ghetto in District VII, while the **Astoria Hotel** across the street served as Wehrmacht Headquarters.

In October 1944, Admiral Horthy saw that there was no hope in continuing the war and made a speech calling for an armistice. The SS responded by kidnapping Horthy and on the morning of 15 October 1944 German troops occupied the **Buda Castle Palace**. The Nazi puppet Ferenc Szálasi and his Fascist Arrow Cross Party took control of Hungary. Extra trains were put on to take Budapest's Jews to the gas chambers at Auschwitz. Arrow Cross thugs raided the ghettos, marched Jews to the Danube bank and shot them. With Russian tanks at the outskirts of Pest, Jews were marched to concentration camps in Austria.

Many of the Jews who survived owed their lives to Raoul Wallenberg, a Swedish diplomat posted in Budapest. Wallenberg had safe houses set up for Jews around Budapest, and issued many with fake Swedish passports. One moment Wallenberg would be charming in negotiations with German officers, and the next he would be personally pulling Jews off trains bound for Auschwitz. When the Russians surrounded Pest, Wallenberg drove off to meet them. He was never seen again. Soviet authorities claimed he died in 1947, but survivors of the Siberian prison camps reported that he may have been alive as recently as the 1970s. A memorial stands to him in Buda.

Just as Marshal Malinovski's tanks were about to enter Budapest in November 1944, Stalin gave a personal order for the Red Army to split and pursue German divisions in south Hungary. The Germans made a last-ditch stand in Budapest. The result was that Budapest and its citizens were caught in the crossfire of an artillery battle that lasted months, killing many more civilians than combatants. The Russians advanced west through Pest's neighbourhoods in bloody door-to-door fighting. By the time the Red Army took control of Pest, the Germans had entrenched themselves in Buda around Castle Hill. While Russian tanks could easily control Pest's boulevards, the fighting in Buda's twisting, medieval streets was hellish. By the time the Germans finally surrendered on 4 April 1945, the castle was in complete ruins, and not one bridge was left standing over the Danube

Communism

When Budapest residents finally climbed out of their basements and shelters, it was as if they had been transported to some desolate planet. One of Europe's most beautiful cities had been reduced to a heap of smoking rubble. Rebuilding Budapest would occupy its citizens for the next 30 years.

The task of restoring order fell to the Soviet military government, who placed loyal Hungarian Communists in all positions of power. Nevertheless, an election held in November 1945 was won by the Smallholders' Party, the only legiti-mate pre-war party still in existence. Even with vote rigging, the Communists only garnered 17 per cent, but Soviet authorities insisted they remain in power, and nobody was in a position to argue.

In February 1946, the Monarchy was abolished and a Hungarian Republic proclaimed. Two weeks later the Paris Peace treaty was signed, compounding the loss of land under Trianon by granting a slice of east Hungary to the USSR. Communist authorities controlling the Interior Ministry set up a secret police force, known as the ÁVO and run by László Rajk, to root out dissent. Thousands were picked up off the streets and sent to the Soviet Union for *malenkaya robota* ('a little work'). Many were never heard from again.

Changes in the social fabric of Budapest were also part of post-war city planning. Budapest neighbourhoods lost some of their unique social identity as the Communists attempted to homogenise areas in support of a classless society. Apartments went to whomever the local *tanács* (council – a new term translated from the Russian 'soviet') decided. The empty flats left by the annihilation of the Jews in Budapest's Districts VII and VIII were given to migrant workers, many of them Gypsies. Other neighbourhoods, now anonymous block jungles such as Lágymányos or Angyalföld were envisaged as 'Workers' Utopias'.

The Communists went forward with the nationalisation of industry and education. In 1948 a plan was introduced to collectivise landholdings, effectively neutralising the Smallholders' Party. The Communist hold on Hungary was complete.

Tensions arose between those Hungarian Communists who had spent the war in the Soviet Union and those who had lived underground in Budapest. In 1949, the scales of power tipped in favour of the Moscow loyalists, led by Mátyás Rákosi. Using the spectre of pro-Yugoslav 'Titoism' as a weapon, old-time party members – among them secret police chief László Rajk – were tried as foreign spies and executed.

By the early 1950s, Hungary was one of the dimmest lights trimming the Iron Curtain. Informers were everywhere, classic Hungarian books were banned, church leaders imprisoned and middle class families persecuted as class enemies.

During his years in power Mátyás Rákosi pursued a cult of personality that even Stalin found embarrassing. Rákosi's face was on huge street murals, his picture hung in every office. Children wrote poems about him while peasant women embroidered his ugly mug on pillows of red silk.

A brief respite came with Stalin's death in 1953. Rákosi was removed from office and replaced with Imre Nagy, a more humanistic Communist with a sense of sympathy for Hungarian national ideals. It didn't last long. Rákosi, backed by Moscow, accused Nagy of 'deviationism' and came back into power in 1955.

The statue of General Bem – rallying-point for the 1956 revolution.

HUNGARIAN REVOLUTION OF 1956

By June 1956, well known Hungarian intellectuals and writers began openly to criticise the Rákosi regime, using the forum of the Petőfi Writers' Circle for unprecedented free debate. The Kremlin, now led by Krushchev, poured oil on the flames of discontent by replacing Rákosi with the equally despicable Stalinist, Ernő Gerő.

On 23 October 1956, Budapest students marched to the statue of the 1848 Polish hero General Bem (*see above*) to express solidarity with reform policies taking place in Poland. The demonstration continued across the river to Parliament, its ranks swelled by thousands of workers, then moved to the Hungarian Radio Headquarters on Bródy Sándor utca behind the National Museum. During the demonstration, sharpshooters from the ÁVH (as the ÁVO were now known) on the roof of the Radio building shot into the crowd. Police and members of the Hungarian Army who were in the area responded by attacking the ÁVH men, and street fighting broke out. When Russian tanks showed up, they were met by determined fire from partisan freedom fighters who had been armed by rebel workers from the arms factories in 'Red Csepel', one of the staunchest Communist districts in Budapest.

By 23 October, all of Hungary was in revolt. The statue of Stalin which stood near Heroes' Square was sawn off at the ankles, pulled down and spat on by angry crowds. ÁVH men were pulled out of the Interior Ministry and executed on the street. Imre Nagy was reinstated as Prime Minister and

General Pál Maléter pledged the loyalty of the Hungarian Army to the new government. Many political prisoners were freed.

After the first few days of fighting, Russian troops began a hasty retreat from Hungary on 29 October. For the next few days a dazed euphoria swept the nation. Hungarians believed that the West would come to their aid, as promised daily by Radio Free Europe. It was an unfortunate miscalculation, compounded by the Suez Canal Crisis, which distracted Western attention.

On 1 November, claiming Hungary had illegally seceded from the Warsaw Pact, Russian tanks re-invaded and on 4 November once again entered Budapest. As tanks rolled down the boulevards, Hungarians put up a dogged defence. Battles took place at the Kilián Army Barracks (corner of Üllői út and József körút) and the fortress-like **Corvin cinema** nearby. In Buda, armed workers fought to prevent the approaching tanks from entering Pest through Széna tér. At Móricz Zsigmond körtér students stopped tanks by spreading oil on the cobbled streets and pulling grenades on strings underneath the stalled vehicles.

Soon, however, Hungarian resistance was brutally crushed. Imre Nagy took refuge in the Yugoslav embassy, but was captured when he accepted an armistice agreement. He and most of the other members of the Hungarian revolutionary council were executed in secret. Thousands of Hungarians were sent to prison and 200,000 fled the country.

Unknown freedom fighter of the 1956 uprising – commemorated at the Corvin cinema.

THE KÁDÁR YEARS

The stranglehold lasted until the 1960s, when amnesties were granted and János Kádár began a policy of reconciliation. His was a balancing act between hard-line Communism and appeasing the population. While Hungary maintained a strong Cold War stance and toed the Moscow line, Hungarians enjoyed a higher standard of living than most of Soviet eastern Europe. Hungary was known as 'the happiest barracks in the bloc'.

Life under Kádár meant more food in the shops, but it also meant banned books and 'psychological hospital' prisons for dissenters. Unlike his predecessors, Kádár allowed limited celebration of certain national traditions. Petőfi and Kossuth were extolled as precursors of the proletarian revolution. During the 1960s, Hungary finally began to resemble its old self. The rubble from World War II and the 1956 revolution was cleared away, historic buildings were restored. Tourism began to grow, although Western visitors were still followed around by government spies after dinner.

Kádár's balancing act was well proven in 1968. When Czechoslovakia irked the Soviets with the reform atmosphere of the Prague Spring, Hungarian troops loyally participated in the invasion. At the same time Kádár introduced his 'New Economic Mechanism', an economic reform that broke with hard-line Communist theory and laid the ground for entrepreneurship. Kádár came to represent 'Communism with a human face'.

During the 1980s, however, it became obvious that the 'New Economic Mechanism' was flawed.

Hungary became ever more dependent on foreign trade, and inflation rose. The black market in Western goods belied the ability of a command economy to provide basic goods and services, and Hungary's relations with its Warsaw Pact neighbours began to show signs of strain.

A growing number of writers and other public figures started to test the limits of open criticism, and by the 1980s Hungary was the centre of eastern Europe's boom in underground *samizdat* literature. Typically, the Hungarian government was not pleased, but instead of jailing dissidents outright, authorities played a cat-and-mouse game with *samizdat* publishers, prosecuting them not for what they had written but for distributing their literature without using the national postal service, an economic crime. Western support for open debate came in odd ways. Billionaire Hungarian financier George Soros made deals to supply basic materials for hospitals and educational institutions. Soros also provided scholarships for Hungary's dissidents to study democratic practice at Universities in the West, and made the production of *samizdat* literature commonplace by flooding the country with free photocopy machines.

As it became obvious that the aged Kádár was no longer fit to rule, younger party members began to take positions of power. Known as the 'Miskolc Mafia', after the city where they had begun their political careers, many, such as Prime Minister Károly Grósz and his successor Miklós Németh, openly tolerated debate, while opening more doors for 'market socialism' and freer expression.

GOODBYE, IRON CURTAIN

In 1989 the bubble burst. In June, people took to the streets to rebury the remains of Imre Nagy. It was a hero's funeral attended by thousands. Soon after, a huge demonstration was held at Heroes' Square to protest against Romania's treatment of its Hungarian minority. Allowing public protest was a major shift in government policy.

Two events in the early summer of 1989 signalled the end of Communism. One was the government declaration that political parties could form to discuss the future possibility of free elections. The second was the mass exodus of East Germans to the West through Hungarian territory. When Hungary ceremonially cut the barbed wire fence on its Austrian border, thousands of East Germans poured into Hungary on 'vacation'. Those wishing to go to the West were housed and fed by the Hungarian government. East Germany's faltering Communist government was incensed when trainloads of refugees were taken by the Hungarian government on 'tours' that dropped them conveniently by the Austrian border.

Hardline Communists in Hungary were alarmed and some factions called out the old Communist Workers' guard in August 1989. An armed militia of geriatric hardliners, the Workers' Guard, shot several East Germans before the more moderate Hungarian Army protested and put an end to the vigilantism. The failure of the Workers' Guard marked the end of Communist hegemony.

Soon the 'reform Communists' led by Imre Pozsgay announced that free elections would take place in 1990. The Communist party threw in the hat, changed its name to the Hungarian Socialist Party and declared that it was running in the elections.

Hungary had tipped over the first domino. The collapse of Communism followed throughout eastern Europe. Hungarians breathed a sigh of collective relief, and then got down to the very Hungarian business of politics.

Post-Communist Hungary

Early 1990 was a period of intoxicating possibilites for Hungarians. All talk was focussed on newfound freedoms, democracy and market capitalism. A new era had dawned and many Hungarians were quick to position thermselves in the emerging social and economic picture. Just as many, however, found themselves bystanders, watching the changes from afar, confused and frustrated by yet another upheaval in history. With elections set for March 1990, Hungarians set about forming political parties – loads of them. Eventually, of 150 or so parties, about six became contenders. The old dissidents coalesced around the Free Democrats (SZDSZ) while a national student activist group formed the

Young Democrats (FIDESZ, which has now added NPP – 'National Middle Class Party' – to the name). The communists split into the socialist party (MSZP) and the hardcore Workers' Party (Munkáspárt). Christian Democrats and the reformed Smallholders' Party held broad appeal. The Hungarian Democratic Forum (MDF) represented a mixed bag of nationalist and conservative views.

The SZDSZ and the MDF ran neck and neck during the first democratic elections since World War II, with the MDF winning the first round of elections. During the run-offs, however, the MDF began to use nationalist, sometimes anti-Semitic rhetoric, which many interpreted as an attempt by the MDF to present themselves as *népi-nemzeti* ('folkish-national') conservatives. It was rhetoric that would pigeonhole the MDF for the next five years, eventually weakening their voter base and causing splits within the party.

With a conservative, MDF-led coalition in Parliament, medical historian József Antall became Prime Minister, while dissident playwright Árpád Göncz assumed the largely ceremonial position of President. The 'change of systems' (*rendszerváltás*) brought more than just democratic government. The face of Budapest swiftly changed as new businesses started to open and the bright windows of western fast-food restaurants and brand-name

Soviet memorial on Szabadság tér.

clothing shops began replacing the city's classy old neon. Business centres sprouted all over the city. Street names were changed, so that Lenin Boulevard and Marx Square were no longer, and their respective statues and monuments were sent to the **Statue Park**. The ubiquitous red stars were taken down, and a law was signed that made any public use of 'symbols of tyranny' (such as red stars, hammers and sickles, as well as swastikas) a criminal offence.

DISTURBING SIGNS

As the economic changes took place, a new class arose in Budapest,. the entrepreneur or *menedzser*. Many young Hungarians found opportunities working in Western businesses. Many others, especially from the older generation who were used to being looked after from the cradle to the grave, found the changes confusing, and Hungarians have been overwhelmed by new regulations. Unemployment rose sharply as state industries were privatised or shut down. The standard of living for many dropped below Communist-era levels, when prices were fixed and services subsidised by the state. Hungarians began to learn the joys of income tax. The difference between the quality of life in Budapest and the rest of Hungary, particularly in the new 'rust belt' of the previously industrial north-east, swift-

ly increased. Crime rose as the divide between rich and poor grew sharper, although rates remain laughably low compared to virtually any other world capital, and violent crime is rare.

Prime Minister Antall, whose illness had been an increasingly public secret, died in December 1993. Stiff and paternalistic, he had appealed to those Hungarians who found his aristocratic bearing attractively old-fashioned, a welcome return to pre-Communist times. Others were surprised by Antall's inability or unwillingness to condemn right-wing radicals within his governing coalition. The MDF likewise became embroiled in a long and protracted war between the government and the media over the control of state TV.

Hungary's severe economic problems, including foreign debt, an unwieldy privatisation process, and a small internal market, have made the expected post-communist boom appear to fizzle, and the ruling MDF coalition paid the price by losing the 1994 election to the Socialist Party, led by Gyula Horn, the man who, as Communist Foreign Minister, had given the order to open the borders in 1989. But whatever nostalgia voters may have had for the 'good old 1980s' was dashed when the Socialists, along with their coalition partners the SZDSZ, prescribed a no-nonsense policy of austerity and belt tightening.

Two bent half-crowns

The greatest treasure of the Hungarian nation is, indisputably, the crown of St Stephen. Much more than a mere relic of a bygone king, to Hungarians it symbolises their independence and alone confers legitimacy on the governments of the nation.

Born Vajk, son of Grand Duke Géza who converted to Catholicism and great-great grandson of Árpád, St Stephen (Szent István in Hungarian) assumed the throne in 1000 AD. The upper part of the crown was a gift from Pope Sylvester II in Rome, and is decorated with gems and small images of eight of the apostles, while the lower part of the crown is of Byzantine manufacture and was added later by King Géza I. It is thought the two crowns were probably joined together during the reign of King Béla III (1172-96).

Stephen's acceptance of the crown acknowledged fealty to the Holy Roman Empire. It is just the sort of bauble a medieval Pope might give to a recently converted pagan chieftain he wasn't too sure about, but the crown is nevertheless an impressive bit of Byzantine-Gothic

finery and, under constant armed guard, is exhibited in the **National Museum** along with St Stephen's golden orb and embroidered coronation cape.

The crown has had some interesting adventures. During the Mongol invasion in 1242 it was smuggled to safety in the back of a hay cart. Somewhere along the way it got dropped and the crown acquired a sportingly bent look.

As the symbol of the legitimacy of Hungarian governments, the Habsburgs carried the thing off to Vienna for a while. Under the Dual Monarchy it was understood that the Habsburg emperors would rule Hungary in the name of St Stephen's crown, and would travel to Budapest for a special coronation ceremony.

At the end of World War II, the crown was again smuggled out of Hungary, this time by forces wishing to deny legitimacy to the Communists. It languished in Fort Knox until 1978 when President Jimmy Carter decided to return it to Hungary. Emigrant Hungarians in the US were outraged that Carter would thus legitimise a Communist government.

This has meant constant and sweeping devaluations of the forint, slashes in social funding, rocketing energy prices and shock-therapy privatisation measures to get Hungary on track for eventual membership of the European Union. Meanwhile, Hungary has been invited to join NATO, and Hungarian engineers have served in the UN Peacekeeping force in Bosnia. An influx of American peacekeeping troops brought back memories of other, less friendly occupying armies, but all they seemed to occupy in Hungary were a few discothèques around Lake Balaton and Pizza Huts.

With elections slated for 1998, the ruling Socialist coalition has more than its share of woes. Several cabinet-level scandals and an atmosphere of influence peddling mark a 'business as usual' style of government that draws sharp criticism from the man in the street. Meanwhile, several parties have split (including the MDF), changed their policies completely (FIDESZ) or simply disappeared. While the tenor of political debate is tense, politics remains in the realm of the abstract. Hungarians view politics the way they view football – passionately partisan, and from a safe seat in the stadium.

Yet regardless of the changes that sweep through Hungary every few decades, Budapest remains one of the world's most wondrous cities, managing to maintain its beauty and dignity without hiding the wrinkles and warts that provide it with such a sense of character. Budapest wears its age and scars of its history for all to see.

Home for heroes of labour – socialist realism in dignified retirement at the Statue Park.

Budapest Today

The Hungarian capital might have a glitzy new confidence, but there is also a Budapest that's been left behind.

Budapest is an exception to Hungary. Big and burly, rapid – or at least trying – and young. And it's got something new, something alien to the country for most of a century: confidence.

Pessimism is the Hungarian disease. Ask a Budapester about the outlook for the country's economy or the national football team's chances of qualifying for the World Cup finals and you can bet on a deflated reply. But ask them about Budapest, their darling city, and a flicker may appear. You'll still get complaints about traffic and dog shit, but you won't hear the voice of defeat. For Budapest, when sliced from the rump, is no longer trapped by the nostalgia and malaise that still grip many a Hungarian mind.

This city is not simply thinking about what was, about the turn-of-the-century magnificence that history conspired to destroy. Nor is it dwelling on the experience of four debilitating, decades caught on the wrong side of the Iron Curtain. Budapest is somehow slipping those bonds, transforming itself from a decaying Habsburg time capsule with recent Cold War scars to a bubbling hub of business and finance, construction, crime and pop culture — just another piece of the postmodern megalopolis.

All of that is changing the face of Budapest. South of the city centre, just before the river reaches the industrial area of Csepel, an impressive new bridge spans the Danube. Along the Nagykörút, the semi-circular Grand Boulevard that arches through Pest, a massive, three-year effort has replaced several kilometres of tram lines, water mains and roadway. Theatres and historic buildings are being renovated. A fourth subway line is planned. City Hall is preparing to give itself a huge facelift that will completely remake Deák tér. And everywhere, private money is pouring into the construction of new and the refurbishment of old buildings. And it remains to whether the spoils will go to only a few, but for now, after two years of Thatcherite economic policies that have slashed debts and deficits, the economy is roaring back, providing jobs and lowering inflation. There is even talk of Budapest becoming the financial capital of eastern-central Europe.

Modern Magyar malls and surviving communist cars – a Trabi at the Duna Plaza.

The changing face of Budapest – confident, glitzy, reflective.

Confidence seeps from it all. None of what first swept into town in the early 1990s is a novelty anymore. Budapest is used to it now. No one notices the glass towers. Glitzy shops and fast food don't intrigue. Kids no longer stare at foreigners. The towers and the fast food and the foreigners aren't, well, aren't foreign any more. They're just Budapest and the wonder has been replaced by nonchalance.

Budapest today has little to do with the categories into which we often try to stuff it. Oh yes, it's a city in transition nearly a decade after the fall of the Berlin Wall, still struggling to shake off the chill of Communism. Yes, yes, a population learning to cope with the insecurity and harshness of a capitalist free market. But what does that say about the skateboarders flinging themselves around the plaza at Hősök tere, who, at 12 or even 15 years old, don't really remember anything about one-party rule? And what of those just a little older still, the children of 'Goulash Communism', toting around their mobile phones? These are the people who grab your initial attention in Budapest and there were no 'good-old-bad-old-days' for them. They exist only in today's Budapest, yet they could be from anywhere.

The confidence has another face, too. It's short-haired and it's been lifting weights. At night you'll see the enforcers of the capital's biggest growth industry: organised crime. They man the doors to nightclubs and bars, looking nasty and providing 'security'. Somehow you get the feeling Budapest would be a lot safer if it weren't for all the security. The goons are the muscle for Hungarian, Russian, Ukrainian and even Chinese gangs that use extortion to skim millions from the earnings of small businesspeople. The gangs control prostitution and smuggling operations and also make good theatre – theatre that can unfortunately turn very dangerous, very quickly if the wrong word is given to the wrong bouncer. (*See also page 206* **The Doormen of Doom**.) With the help of these lads, the hand grenade recently made its biggest splash in Budapest since the Red Army was chasing the Wehrmacht when an apparent turf war resulted in lots of late-night attacks designed to destroy property and intimidate. Crime, danger, large thugs with little brains – reasons to make any big city dweller feel at home in Budapest.

Each year it seems Budapest is further drawn inexorably into the brash, faceless everywhere and nowhere of the modern city. In 1997, Hungary was formally invited to join the grand political-military alliance that is NATO. If completely impractical and woefully expensive, that move is still enormously important to a people who feel they have been excluded for half a century from their rightful place in the West, a word that carries more weight as a psychological definition than a geographical delineation. As important as NATO, and certainly more practical, is Hungary's application for entry into the European Union. With some luck, Hungary will be a full member by 2002. So the steady melding of Budapest's inhabitants with every other big city citizen will continue, probably even accelerate. But it's far from complete.

Budapest hasn't completely transformed into the familiar, and it's definitely not all shiny and new. You can still find with ease the softer, unchanged pockets of Budapest. Silent courtyards rimmed with window flowers, mysterious passageways smelling of lilacs and dust. Crumbling backstreet houses pockmarked by the bullets of 1945 or 1956. Coffee bars and corner pubs suspicious of strange tongues spoken by funny-looking visitors. You can also find the Budapest that has for these few years of full-fledged capitalism been spiralling downward at an appalling pace. There is nothing quaint about this other, barely hidden face. Dingy, decaying blocks of concrete flats with hallways stinking of urine. A Gypsy mother begging from the grimy floor of an underpass. Proud pensioners picking through the trash in the dead of night, looking for empty bottles to return for change. This is the Budapest left behind. The Budapest that isn't being thrown a life line by new jobs and rising wages.

Poverty, of course, doesn't set Budapest apart from the western megacity. Beggars are easy to find in Paris and Amsterdam, too. So also for the oases of stillness and dated charm that lie beneath the bustle and glitz of any modern capital. Truly to discover in Budapest a place that you have never been, a different kind of wandering is needed – a wander into the Magyar mind. Hidden like the courtyards and passageways of Pest, some things lie deep in the Hungarian imagination that truly set it apart.

Perhaps it is their origins deep in central Asia or maybe the 1,000 years at the edge of the Balkans. One famous son, the physicist Edward Teller, once remarked that Hungarians were descended from Martians. Whatever the reason, if you listen and watch closely enough, Budapest can still feel a million miles from western Europe.

In February of 1997, for instance, sudden rumours abounded that one of the country's largest banks, Postabank, one still owned by the state, was about to collapse. Within 24 hours, despite assurances from the government that the bank was in no crisis, every Postabank branch in the land was flooded with depositors seeking to withdraw their funds. The panic was not limited to fearful widows in the countryside. It was led by the handsome young professionals of Budapest. They lined up in droves to grab their money, continuing the business of the day via cell phone from the queues. Depositor insurance? Not good enough. Pleas from the finance minister? He's lying. Common sense as to whether the government would allow one of the country's most important financial institutions to sink? Shrug.

The bank called the public 'stupid' and, in typically cryptic fashion, government officials mused publicly that political mischief was behind the scare, though no one ever validated this. Eventually it was revealed that Postabank, though never near collapse, had indeed been operated shoddily and had piled up an inordinate amount of bad debts – enough to force the government to bail it out with a $66 million loan. The press, in typical lapdog fashion, responded with weak criticism and no investigation of the state-owned bank, which coincidentally just happens to have extensive holdings in the media.

And finally came the icing on this decidedly Balkan cake. Postabank bought four huge advertorials in *Világgazdaság*, the country's leading economic daily (and part-owned by Postabank) to defend itself with reams of pseudo-intellectual drivel. This included gems such as, 'It is not our task to decide what the single truth is, if only because in many cases it doesn't exist at all', and 'Are we able to assess the events of the recent past without fear of falling into the mistake of subjectivity? Who knows?'

(To cap it all, the advertorials came out simultaneously with a survey showing that only 13 per cent of Hungarians understood that copy concluded with an '[x]' designated editorial that had been paid for, and presumably concluded it was the newspaper that was spouting this rubbish. *See also chapter* **Media**.)

So Budapesters are, after all, Hungarians. And Hungarians are, after all, not quite dissolved into the modern Euro-mash. They thrive on conspiracy theorising and absolutely refuse to hold public officials accountable for almost anything, deferring feudally to anyone in charge. They go to pig killings in November and December, rural rituals of slaughter and consumption (*see page 30* **Porky gets the chop**). They watch the skies on June 8 – *medárd* – a day that will tell, they say, whether the summer will be wet or dry. They put their family name before their given name, as do the Koreans and Chinese. They are a lonesome people whose Asian language mixes with no other. They are also the same people who wallow in the disasters of their history – so many of them self-inflicted – with a national anthem that dolefully intones: 'We have suffered all the sum, for sins of past and those to come.'

Even in Budapest. The confident capital.

Another protest about Budapest's banks.

Budapest by Season

From fireworks for a founding father through pagan perfume and pálinka days to celebrating the withdrawal of Soviet troops.

Hungarian traditions have lasted generations of bitter winters and boiling summers, let alone two World Wars and 40 years of Communism. Although economic influences from the West try and push new traditions like Valentine's Day, they tend to attract more adverse publicity than business. Whitsun has only recently come back into the calendar. Christmas is a sedate family occasion, New Year a party affair, and every day at a workplace is an excuse for celebrating some colleague's Name Day (*see also page 265* **What's in a name?**).

(*see also page 265* **What's in a name?**)

Information & Tickets

For regular information on events, read *Budapest Week* or the *Budapest Sun*, English-language weeklies available at most newsstands. Or try:

Tourinform
V. Sütő utca 2 (117 9800). M1, M2, M3 Deák tér. **Open** 8am-8pm daily.

Interart Festivalcenter
V. Vörösmarty tér 1 (117 6222). M3 Vörösmarty tér. **Open** 10am-6pm Mon-Fri; 10am-2pm Sat.

Central Theatre Booking Office
VI. Andrássy út 18 (312 0000). M1 Operaház. **Open** 9am-1pm, 2pm-6pm, Mon-Thur; 9am-5pm Fri. **Branch**: II. Moszkva tér 3 (135 9136). M2 Moszkva tér. **Open** 10am-1pm, 2pm-6pm, Mon-Thur; 10am-5pm Fri.

Public Holidays

New Year's Day (1 Jan); **Revolution Day** (15 Mar); **Easter Monday; International Labour Day** (1 May); **Whit Monday; Saint Stephen's Day** (20 Aug); **Remembrance Day** (23 Oct); **Christmas Day, Boxing Day** (25, 26 Dec).

Spring

The joys of a Hungarian spring are announced by scuffles in Post Office queues as everyone desperately tries to hand in their tax returns by the March 20 deadline. Metro station entrances are full of grandmothers from the villages jostling to sell lucky snowflowers. Bunches are laid at Sándor

All kinds of people celebrate **March 15**.

Petőfi's statue on March 15, the first national holiday of the new season.

March 15 Public Holiday
Revolution Day commemorates poet Sándor Petőfi reciting his *Nemzeti Dal* (national song) on the steps of the National Museum in 1848, the event commonly held to have launched the national revolution. Budapest gets decked out in red, white and green and there are gatherings at Petőfi's statue in Március 15 tér and outside the National Museum.

Budapest Spring Festival
Tickets and information: *Budapesti Fesztivalkozpont, VIII. Rakoczi ut 65, VI/66 (133 2337). M2 Blaha Lujza ter/tram 4, 6.* **Box office** *Feb-Mar* 10am-6pm Mon-Fri.
Problems with funding have reduced the biggest event in the arts calendar to a two-week festival of mainly local talent in the classical music field. Some dance and folk acts are also featured at several venues in the city. *See chapters* **Theatre & Dance** *and* **Music: Classical and Opera**.

Easter Monday
Public holiday
The most drunken occasion in a calendar chock-full of them, Easter Monday is when men go door-to-door indulging in the pagan rite of *locsolkodas*, the splashing of womenfolk with cheap perfume, and are presented with large doses of pálinka in return. The fun traditionally starts as early as 6am, and by 9am every male is past caring. By 10am the streets get ugly. Don't leave the house after 1pm if you can possibly help it.

Labour Day
1 May (public holiday).
No longer a forced wave at medal-festooned leaders along Dósza György út, May Day still brings a few old Communists out of the woodwork and into the main parks to indulge in beer, sausages and a moan about today's prices.

IFABO

Hungexpo, Budapest International Fair Centre, X. Albertirsai út 10 (263 6000). M2 Örs vezér tere then bus 100. **Date** May.

Hungary's largest computer fair, with more than a thousand companies showing off the latest communications and data processing technology.

Summer

Summer is the season of no shame. Budapesters strip to the bare essentials as the temperature climbs into the forties. At weekends and for most of August, they leave the heat and traffic fumes for the tourists, and there are open-air festivals at Szeged, Diósgyőr Castle in Miskolc, Győr and Pécs. Don't even think about getting any business done in town after 10am on a Friday.

Book Week

Information *Mariann Csizmadi, Hungarian Publishers' Association, 10th floor, V. Vörösmarty tér 1 (118 4651). M1 Vörösmarty tér.* **Date** first weekend in June.

For more than 60 years Hungarian writers have gathered together, a chance for those living in Transylvania, Slovakia and Vojvodina to catch up on the latest news from the centre of Hungarian-language publishing. Expect a large open-air fair and short theatrical performances in Vörösmarty tér (M1 Vörösmarty tér) and readings at the **Petőfi Museum**, *V. Károlyi Mihály utca 16 (117 3611). M3 Ferenciek tere.*

World Music Day

Information Malacka BT, VIII. Mikszath Kalman ter 2 (118 0684). **Date** nearest weekend to June 21.

Introduced by then French Minister of Culture Jacques Lang, brought to Budapest thanks to the funding and enthusiasm of the French Institute, Hungary takes World Music Day seriously. In 1997, 50 towns hosted some 300 rock, folk and jazz bands over mid-summer's weekend, with a dozen major venues in Budapest alone. All entertainment is free, and generally open-air. Look out for the more eclectic acts in Klauzal ter.

WOMUFE

XI. Budai Parkszínpad. Tram 6/bus 1, 7, red 7, 27, 40, 127, 153 to Móricz körtér. **Information** Mandel Produkcios, I. Attila ut 13 (06 23 417 938). Bus 5. **Date** June.

Budapest's annual World Music Festival is staged near the supposedly bottomless lake in the park between Kosztolányi Dezső tér and Móricz Zsigmond körtér. Organiser Robert Mandel, one of the world's leading exponents of the cranklute, doesn't have much funding so the three-day programme tends to be a hot-potch of whoever's on tour at the time.

Kriminalexpo

Budapest Kongresszusi Központ, XII. Jagelló út 1-3 (161 2869). Bus 8, 8A. **Information** Compexpo, V. Kálvin tér 5 (117 6760). **Date** June.

Budapest, although much safer than most European cities of its size, is a crossroads for international crime. Since 1992, the Kriminalexpo has brought traders together to ply the wares for businesses and individuals to protect themselves against both domestic and international versions.

Budapesti Bucsú

Information *Budapesti Fesztivalkozpont, VIII. Rakoczi ut 65 VI/66 (133 2337). M2 Blaha Lujza ter/trams 4, 6.* **Date** last weekend in June.

The city celebrates the 1991 withdrawal of Soviet troops from Hungary. A weekend of music, dance and theatre in assorted parks and public spaces around town.

Book Week – *all the Magyar lit fit to print.*

Bastille Day

Institut Francais, I. Fő utca 18 (202 1133). M2 Batthyany ter/bus 86. **Date** nearest Sunday to July 14, from 8pm.

Free open-air ball between the Danube and the French Institute, who celebrate Bastille Day by inviting leading accordion players from France, laying out a decent spread of French wines and snacks, and then setting off loads of fireworks. Expect a big crowd.

Open-air Theatre Summer Festival

Information *Szabad tér Színház, XII. Városmajor (175 5922).* **Date** June-Aug.

Outdoor music, dance and theatre at three main venues: Margaret Island Open-air Theatre (111 2496); Hilton Hotel Dominican Yard, I. Hess András tér 1-3 (175 1000); and the Buda Park Stage, XI. Kosztolányi Dezső tér (166 9849). Performances are mostly Hungarian only, but this need not matter for the children's puppet theatre in the afternoons.

Budafest

Information *VIP-Arts Management, VI. Hajós utca 13/15 (332 4816/302 4290). M1 Opera.* **Date** mid-Aug.

A week of top-flight performances at the Opera House, VI. Andrássy út 22 (153 0170). Budafest is the major arts festival in town over the summer, bringing foreign ballet and opera stars to entertain bewildered rich Americans.

Hungaroring

Information *MAMSZ, XIV. Dózsa György út 1-3 (117 2811).* **Date** second weekend of Aug.

Talks between the government and the Grand Prix organisation in 1997 have extended the contract of this traditional loss-maker into the next century. The most prestigious sporting event in the Hungarian calendar, the Hungaroring weekend means that the city's hotels are full, restaurants packed and bars overflowing. The course itself is at Mogyorod, 24km east of Budapest on the M3 motorway. (*See chapter* **Sport & Fitness**).

Sziget Fesztival

Information *Sziget Csoport Kulturalis Egyesulet, XI. Lonyai utca 18b (218 8693).*

Grown considerably in stature since its introduction in 1993, the Sziget Fesztival attracts hundreds of acts and over 100,000 music fans to a normally deserted island in the Danube for a week's cut-price entertainment. Expect half-a-dozen name acts from the West and anyone who's anyone in Magyar music. (*See chapter* **Music: Rock, Roots & Jazz**).

St Stephen's Day

Public Holiday. **Date** 20 Aug.

The day when Hungarians celebrate their founding father, Szent István. At 9pm there is a fireworks display from Gellért Hill, best viewed from a boat on the Danube. The day also marks the festival of the new bread and every town, village and hamlet stages minor events, the most notable being the Flower Carnival in Debrecen.

Autumn

The Indian Summer of early autumn sees the city at its best, slowly emptying of tourists, and with its cultural life starting up again. Bars, clubs and concert halls re-open their doors to local audiences still bronzed from summer weekends at the Balaton.

Budapest International Wine Festival

Information *Bacchus Arts Studio Kft., V. Vorosmarty ter 1 (117 7031). M1 Vörösmarty tér.* **Date** Sept.
Grape harvesting (*szüret*) involves wine tasting, folk dancing and general merriment. In Budapest, under-funded wine companies woo international buyers with chamber concerts in the Castle District and wine tasting and folk dancing in Vörösmarty tér. For a better feel of a real *szüret*, head out of town to Székszard or Eger.

Budapest Autumn Festival

Information *Budapesti Fesztival Kozpont, VIII. Rakoczi ut 65 VI/66 (133 2337). M2 Blaha Lujza ter/tram 4, 6.*
Date late Sept-mid-Oct.
A contemporary arts festival with the accent on film, fine arts, dance and theatre.
Venues: *Nemzeti Szinház, VII. Hevesi Sándor tér 4 (341 3845). Trolleybus 73, 76.*
Petöfi Csarnok, Városliget, XIV. Zichy M. utca 14 (343 4327). M1 Széchenyi fürdö.
Várszinház, I. Szinház utca 5-9 (175 8011). Bus 16 or castle minibus.
Ernst Museum, VI. Nagymezö utca 8 (341 4355). M1 Operaház.

Budapest Music Weeks

Information *Nemzeti Filharmónia, V. Vörösmarty tér 1 (*118 0314*). M1 Vörösmarty tér.* **Date** 25 Sept-end Oct.
For the last 30 years this festival, which begins on the anniversary of Bartók's death, has opened the concert sea-son. Classical concerts take place at either the Vigadó, V. Vigadó tér 5 (117 222), M1 Vörösmarty tér; or at the Zene-akadémia, VI. Liszt Ferenc tér 8 (341 4788), M1 Oktogon/tram 4 or 6.

Music Of Our Time

Information *Nemzeti Filharmónia, V. Vörösmarty tér 1 (118 0314). M1 Vörösmarty tér.* **Date** late Sept.
A ten-day contemporary music festival featuring a select group of composers. The event has rather lost its impetus since the organisers, Nemzeti Filharmónia, formerly the state concert ticket agency, has lost most of its funding.

Remembrance Day

Date 23 Oct (public holiday).
The anniversary of the 1956 Uprising is a national day of mourning. When Soviet tanks put down the rebellion, 30,000 people died and 200,000 fled the country. Former leader Imre Nagy was executed. He was secretly buried at Plot 301 in Ujköz Cemetery, where wreath-laying ceremonies take place on this day every year. There is also a flag-raising ceremony in Kossuth tér, an event which right-wing nationalist groups have tried to take over in recent years. The date of 23 October also marked the of the new republic in 1989.

Winter

Temperatures fall below zero as stores fill for the Christmas rush in December. Outside Budapest, villagers gather for the *disznóvágás*, pig-killing (*see page 30* **Porky gets the chop**). The winter gloom does not begin to lift until March.

Mikulás

St Nicholas' Day. **Date** 6 Dec.
On the eve of 6 December, children put out their shoes on Budapest's window sills for Santa to fill with chocolates, fruit and little pressies. He is assisted by *krampusz*, the bogey-

Sziget Festival – *hundreds of acts, thousands of fans, and a great deal of dancing 'til dawn.*

man, who threatens to steal naughty children from their beds. In most cases the bogey-man's appearance is token: small *krampusz* puppets, hung on a gilded tree-branch, *virgács*, are also left by Santa.

Christmas

Date 25, 26 Dec (public holiday).
Trees and tacky presents line the Nagykörút from mid-December. The traditional Christmas meal is carp, happy to be out of the Danube mud and in the clear water of the Hungarian family's bathtub – until the evening of 24 December, when the festive meal and present-giving take place. Christmas is a family affair and apart from special events in major hotels, the city shuts up shop for two days from lunchtime on 24 December. Those staying in Budapest would be advised to accept any invitation going or curl up at home with a hefty novel. Life doesn't get back to normal until after New Year.

Szilveszter

New Year's Eve. **Date** 31 Dec.
Szilveszter is when everyone takes to the streets in style, down the Nagykörút and around Blaha Lujza tér in particular. Most major places of entertainment will put on some kind of special event. Buses and trams in Budapest run all night long. The national anthem solemnly booms out of everyone's radios at midnight. Afterwards, it's Champers, kisses, handshakes and fireworks. Merriment continues into the next day, a public holiday, when *kocsonya*, a dish made from pork fat, is liable to wobble its way into your hungover consciousness.

The Farsang Season

Date Feb.
Masked balls, *farsang*, test Hungarians' ingenuity to make the wildest fancy dress. The wildest ball of all is at Mohács, site of the Turkish victory over the Hungarians in 1526. The *busójárás*, the masked procession the last weekend before Lent on Carnival Sunday, is a re-enactment both of spring rites and of the battle. For more information, contact the Bartók Béla Művelődési Központ, Vörösmarty utca 3, Mohács 7700 (69 311 828).

Hungarian Film Festival

Date Feb.
Tickets and information: *Filmunio Hungary, VI. Városligeti fasor 38 (351 7760). Bus 33/trolleybus 33.* **Open** 8am-4.30pm Mon-Thur; 8am-2pm Fri.
Since 1969 the Magyar Filmszemle has been struggling to attract the film world to the cinemas of Budapest during a long weekend in early February. Translations are provided for the main features. *See chapter* **Film**.

Porky gets the chop

Hungarians keep their rural roots greasily alive by participating in the annual ritual of the *disznovagas*, or pig-killing. A combination of gore, feast and ritual, pig-killing usually takes place outdoors in the winter or late fall, when cold weather keeps the fresh pork from decay. As a statement of rural self-sufficiency, pig-killing is so self-defining in the culture that the Communists sought to ban it in one of those moves guaranteed to make everyone hate their guts. People simply continued killing their pigs in secret, until the government gave up and lifted the ban.

Even urban Hungarians continue the ritual, travelling out to Uncle Laszlo's farm to reassert their peasant roots and play their role in the Hungarian family version of *Friday the Thirteenth Part XXI: Porky's Demise*. And although one can get any and all imaginable pig parts from your neighbourhood butcher's, it's just not the same as doing the little fellow in yourself. The family pig-killing is cathartic, and its traditions are an alchemical mystery that turns happy little porkers into gold.

The ritual begins at dawn, when a local professional pig-killer/butcher known as the *boller* arrives. Today, with fewer people living off the land, he often provides the pig as well. The family serves rounds of over-proof pálinka starting at dawn, followed by more at ten minute intervals. Rich families used to hire musicians to be present, but today they merely slip in a cassette of special 'pig-killing music' played by any of Hungary's cheesy saxophone and Casio organ wedding bands. The innocent porker is often simply shot, but part of the merriment involves ingenious folk devices to whisk the little guy to pig heaven: home-made zip guns, explosive spears, even gas chambers.

After being dispatched, the porcine carcass is charred with butane torches to remove the hair, and his blood is drained into vats for use in blood sausage (*veres hurka*). By this time everybody is in high appetite, of course, and extremely well dosed with plum brandy. The whole family helps prepare the meat for salamis, sausages, bacons, hams and dozens of other essential Hungarian pork products. The fat is rendered into lard, and the cracklings are served (along with more pálinka) as a pre-lunch snack. The best cuts are reserved for whoever is still standing by lunchtime. Fresh roast pork, fried blood sausage and innard soup are laid on for the hungry butchers.

If invited to visit a Hungarian home at Easter, there is a good chance that the patriarch of the house will fetch from the back pantry some ancient dessicated brownish object and encourage you to eat it, claiming it is his finest ham. Maybe it was. Eat it anyway. If you are a vegan, or the thought of all this blood makes you squeamish, you could always try going out to the western suburb of Vecses to watch how they turn cabbages into sauerkraut. But somehow this just isn't the same.

Language

Hungarian may be maddeningly difficult, but a little of the local lingo goes a long, long way.

Easy, simple, clear Hungarian.

Perhaps nowhere else in Europe will the traveller be confronted by as great a linguistic barrier as in Hungary. The Hungarian language is renowned the world over for its difficulty, which for most foreigners boils down to the fact that Hungarian bears absolutely no resemblance to any language they may have previously encountered. In other countries, picking up a bit of the local lingo can be an enjoyable pastime. A few words of Portuguese? *Não problema.* A bit of Plattdeutsch? *Kein Problem.* A smattering of any Slavic tongue? *Nema problema.* Hungarian? *Nincs semmi gond!*

Hungarian is a Finno-Ugric language, part of the greater family of Altaic-Uralic languages that includes Turkish, Finnish and Mongolian. Much is made of Hungarian's relationship to Finnish, but that kinship is distant indeed. As the main language of the Ugric stock, Hungarian is related most closely to two small languages in the Ural mountains of north-west Siberia, Vogul and Ostyak. When the Hungarians moved southward and adopted the equestrian and agricultural cultures of the southern steppes they adopted many terms from Turkic and

Iranian languages, such as names for livestock and farm implements (the words for 'customs official' (*vám*) and 'bridge' (*híd*) are borrowed from the Alan language, spoken today in Ossetia).

After the Magyars established themselves in Europe their language became infused with many Slavic, Latin and, later, German terms. The first written document containing any Hungarian – a few score place names in a mostly Latin document – was the 1055 deed of foundation for Tihany Abbey, these days preserved at Pannonhalma Abbey near Győr. Hungarian has shown itself to be an extremely conservative language, and medieval Hungarian is easily understood by a modern Magyar. There are various regional accents but relatively few dialects, although Budapest boasts a slangy style of rapid-fire speech peppered with foreign vocabulary, especially borrowings from Yiddish, Gypsy and German.

There are so few terms in Hungarian that are cognate with words from the Indo-European language family that every new word requires prodigious feats of learning. Then comes gram-

Teach Yourself Magyar

Maddeningly difficult though Hungarian may be, learning a few words and phrases will make life easier – both for you, and for any Hungarians you may encounter. *Igen* (yes), *nem* (no) and *jó reggelt* (good morning), *jó napot* (good day) and *jó estét* (good evening) are all fairly easy, but you'll probably find *viszontlátásra* (goodbye) a mouthful. In shops and among friends you can use the informal short version, *viszlát*.

Meanwhile, *szervusz* is an all-purpose, informal greeting meaning either hello or goodbye, as is the even more informal *szia*. Older women still like to be greeted with *kezét csókolom* (literally, 'I kiss your hand'). Confusingly, but inevitably, Hungarians usually use the English 'hello' to mean 'goodbye'.

The word *kérem* serves a lot of purposes. Its first meaning is 'please', but it also means 'excuse me' when trying to attract the waiter's attention; it can be the answer to *köszönöm* (thank you), and if you pronounce it as a question, it means 'pardon?'. If you don't understand what you are being told, you can also say *Bocsánat, nem értem* (Sorry, I don't understand). And then *Nem beszélek magyarul* (I don't speak Hungarian), although that will probably have become obvious by this point.

Hol van? (where is it?) is useful. The answer will probably include a lot of *itt* (here), *ott* (there), *innen* (from here), *onnan* (from there), *jobbra* (to the right), *balra* (to the left) and *egyenesen* (straight ahead).

Hungarian makes a noun plural by adding '-k' and sometimes a link vowel to a noun. *Busz* (bus) becomes *buszok*, *csirke* (chicken) becomes *csirkék*. You don't form the plural, though, when stating the number of things, such as *négy alma* (four apples) or *száz forint* (one hundred forints).

Shop assistants rarely speak anything other than Hungarian. *Mennyibe kerül?* (how much is it?), *ez* (this), *az* (that) and some adjectives such as *kicsi* (small), *nagy* (large), *régi* (old), *új* (new), *piros* (red), *fehér* (white) and *fekete* (black) should help.

When asking for something say *Kérek egy/kettő/három jegyet/kávét* (I want a/two/three tickets/coffees). Finally, if you are completely lost, try *Beszél itt valaki angolul?* (does anyone speak English here?).

Pronunciation

Accents denote a longer vowel, except for é (ay) and á (as in father). The stress is always on the first syllable. Double consonants are pronounced longer (*kettő, szebb*).

Add 't' to nouns when they are the object of the sentence: 'I would like a beer' is *Kérek egy sört* (*sör* + t).

a – like 'o' in hot
á – like 'a' in father
é – like 'a' in day
í – like 'ee' in feet
ö – like 'ur' in pleasure
ü – like 'u' in French tu
ő, ű – similar to ö and ü but longer
sz – like 's' in sat
cs – like 'ch' in such
zs – like the 's' in casual
gy – like the 'd' in dew
ly – like the 'y' in yellow
ny – like the 'n' in new
ty – like the 't' in tube
c – like 'ts' in roots
s – like 'sh' in wash

Useful Phrases

Yes *Igen*
No *Nem*
Maybe *Talán*
(I wish you) good day *Jó napot (kívánok)* (formal)
Hello *Szervusz* (informal); *Szia* (familiar)
Goodbye *Viszontlátásra* (formal)
'Bye *Viszlát*

---

mar. Beginners memorise a whole series of conjugations simply to begin mangling the idea of 'I have' (*nekem van* 'it is for/of/to me'). Prepositions come after the noun as suffixes, and their use is usually quite different from English, so that you have to know that 'to go to' may be different if you're going to a place that is enclosed, geographical, or personal (*házba*, to the house; *Pestre*, to Pest; *hozzánk*, to our house). Furthermore, each Hungarian town has its own post-preposition to indicate that you are in that town. You can be 'in London' (*Londonban*) but you are in *Budapesten, Pécsett, Debrecenben*. Easy, simple, clear Hungarian.

Luckily, Hungarian has a few features that make things easier. There is no gender, not even a different pronoun for 'he' and 'she'. Past and future tenses are relatively easy and regular. And Hungarians are delighted to hear foreigners attempt their language. If you intend to stay for more than a few weeks, the best book to learn Hungarian is probably *Colloquial Hungarian* by Jerry Payne (Routledge Publishers, London). *See also chapter* **Further Reading**.

A good rule of thumb is that the younger the Hungarian, the more likely they will be to speak English. Today Hungarians are becoming more aware of the need to learn foreign languages.

How are you? *Hogy van?* (formal) *Hogy vagy?* (familiar)
I'm fine *Jól vagyok*
Please *Kérem*
Thank you *Köszönöm*
Excuse me *Bocsánat*
I would like *Kérek...* (an object)
I would like (to do something) *Szeretnék...* (add infinitive)
Where is...? *Hol van...?*
Where is the toilet? *Hol van a wc?* (**wc** *vay tzay*)
Where is a good/cheap/not too expensive restaurant? *Hol van egy jó/olcsó/nem túl drága étterem?*
When? *Mikor?* **Who?** *Ki?* **Why?** *Miért?* **How?** *Hogyan?*
Is there...? *Van...?*
There is none *Nincs*
How much is it? *Mennyibe kerül?*
Open *Nyitva*
Closed *Zárva*
Entrance *Bejárat*
Exit *Kijárat*
Push *Tolni*
Pull *Húzni*
Men's *Férfi;* **women's** *Női*
Good *Jó;* **bad** *Rossz*
I like it *Ez tetszik*
I don't like it *Ez nem tetszik*
I don't speak *Nem beszélek*
Hungarian *Magyarul*
Do you speak English? *Beszél angolul?*
What is your name? *Mi a neve?*
My name is... *A nevem...*
I am (English/American) *(angol/amerikai) vagyok*
Railway station *Pályaudvar*
Airport *Repülőtér*
Ticket office or **cash desk** *Pénztár*
I would like to go to Pécs *Pécsre szeretnék menni*
I would like two tickets *Két jegyet kérek*
When is the train to Vienna? *Mikor indul a bécsi vonat?*
(At) three o' clock *Három óra (kor)*
I feel ill *Rosszul vagyok*
Doctor *Orvos*
Pharmacy *Patika/Gyógyszertár*
Hospital *Kórház*
Ambulance *Mentőautó*
Police *Rendőrség*

Days of the week
Monday *Hétfő*
Tuesday *Kedd*
Wednesday *Szerda*

Thursday *Csütörtök*
Friday *Péntek*
Saturday *Szombat*
Sunday *Vasárnap*

Numbers
zero *nulla*
one *egy*
two *kettő* (note the form 'két', used with an object: **két kávé** *two coffees*)
three *három*
four *négy*
five *öt*
six *hat*
seven *hét*
eight *nyolc*
nine *kilenc*
ten *tíz*
eleven *tízenegy*
twelve *tízenkettő*
thirteen *tízenhárom*
twenty *húsz;* **twenty-five** *húszonöt*
thirty *harminc*
thirty-four *harmincnégy*
forty *negyven*
forty-one *negyvenegy*
fifty *ötven*
sixty *hatvan*
seventy *hetven*
eighty *nyolcvan*
ninety *kilencven*
one hundred *száz*
one hundred and fifty *százötven*
two hundred *kettőszáz*
three hundred *háromszáz*
one thousand *ezer*
ten thousand *tízezer*
one million *millió*
one billion *milliárd*

Crucial Phrases
Where is a good bar? *Hol van egy jó kocsma?*
What are you having? *Mit tetszik inni?*
Cheers! *Egészségedre* (Egg-aysh-ayg-ed-reh!)
God! You drink like a brushmaker! *Istenem! Úgy iszol, mint egy kefekötő!*
Which football team do you support? *Melyik foci csapatnak drukkolsz?*
I love you *Szeretlek*
It is hopeless *Reménytelen*
Could you call a cab for me? *Tudna nekem egy taxit hívni?*
It's all the same to me! *Nekem nyolc!*

Private language schools these days do a booming business teaching English and German, but under Communism, Hungarians were forced to study Russian in school, and it became a badge of pride to fail the eight-year course – not the best experience of foreign language acquisition. Standards for foreign language ability have stayed rather low as the 'Welcome In Hungary' sign on the way into town from Ferihegy airport, or a glance at any English-language menu will confirm (*see page 132* **'Good Hungarian Grubs'**). Common errors include such appetising terms as 'paste covered with greaves' for noodles with bacon bits, and 'fried innard glands' for sweetbreads.

Much of the blame for such merry mistranslations must lie with one László Országh, who edited the standard post-war Hungarian-English dictionary. Országh was a less than spectacular linguist who was known to confiscate his students' copies of other English dictionaries and tear them up in front of his classes.

Országh's main experience with native English-speakers came during his term as a prisoner of war in 1945. The only available native Anglophone was an errant bachelor from Nottingham who was paid for his assistance in beer. Not surprisingly, some of the entries in Országh's dictionary are quite bizarre.

(Cynanchium vincetoxicum)
vadpástétom *n,* game-pie
vadpecsenye *n,* game, *[őz, szarvas]* (a course of) veni
vádpont *n,* count (of indictment); ~ok counts of
indictment, heads of the charge, gist; *a követk*
~okkal vádolják he is charged on the following cou
vadréce *n, (állt)* wild-duck, mallard *(Anas platyrhynch*
vadregényes *a,* romantic
vadregényesség *n,* wildly romantic character/aspe
nature (of sg)
vadrepce *n, (növ)* wild rape/charlock *(Sinapis arvens*
vadrózsa *n, (növ)* hedge/wild rose, dog/briar/bramb
-rose *(Rosa canina)*
vadrózsabokor *n,* wild rose, dog-rose (bush)
vadság *n,* **1.** *[tulajdonság]* wildness, fierceness,
rocity, ferity, savageness, savagery, *[modorbe*
lack of civility, ruffianism rowdyism, barbarit
[brutalitás] brutality, *[tartózkodás]* unsociabilit
shyness **2.** *[állapot]* wildness, (state of) savege
vadspenót *n, (növ)* English/false mercury, good Kin
Henry *(Chenopodium bonus Henricus)*
vadsugárzás *n, (műsz)* spurious radiation
vadszag *n,* game smell, smell of game
vadszamár *n,* **1.** *(állt)* wild ass *(Equus asinus africanus*
[dzsiai] onager *(E. onager),* **2.** *[emberről; iron*
egregious ass, dolt
vadszőlő *n, (növ)* wild vine, woodbine, Virginia creepe
ampelopsis *(Ampelopsis sp.)*
vadsztrájk *n,* wildcat strike
vádtanács *n,* grand jury
vadul¹ *[-t, -jon] vi,* **1.** become wild/savage, *[futballisto*
stb.] lose one's temper, run amok, get rough/dirty
see red **2.** *[élénkké válik]* become shy, become averse
to company
vadul² *adv,* wildly, savagely, fiercely, *[durván]* coarsely,
furiously, madly; ~ *csahol [kutyafalt...*

Merry mistranslations – see 'vadspenót'.

Many of these Országhisms are stubbornly defended by Hungarians, including translating *vadspenót* (wild spinach) as 'English/false mercury, good King Henry', and *fesztelnít* (to unscrew) as 'to uncock the cock'. The dictionary also includes strange idiomatic explanations, such as 'to sit down under an insult' and 'in consequence of the lucky concurrence of circumstance' (we'll meet again).

Another infuriating feature of Hungarian English is that translations attempt to use the most convoluted English constructions possible – a hangover from the dense Hungarian literary style and a mistrust of colloquialism in print. Hungarian uses the article before each noun, so translations abound in 'the' constructions, such as 'The Students of the School of the Agriculture study the biology and the animals'.

All these linguistic difficulties are well worth the effort, however, since every Hungarian knows that Hungarian is the perfect language. This is a qualitative judgement that any Hungarian will be happy to explain to you. Shakespeare, you will be informed, sounds much better in Hungarian than in the original English. The same holds true for Woody Allen films, Winnie-the-Pooh and Flintstones cartoons (which are dubbed in squeaky voices, in rhyme). The verb for 'to explain' is *magyarázni*, which is to say, to 'Hungarianise'. This may sound absurd, but Hungarians are very proud of their unique ability to understand Hungarian.

'Az Anyád!'

Writer George Konrad once observed that a foreigner watching two Magyars screaming at each other in a café might imagine them to be involved in some great verbal fight – while in fact they are actually just chatting amicably, if colourfully.

Hungarians swear with a vengeance. In fact, some linguists claim that Hungarians swear more frequently, and with a broader vocabulary, than almost any other people in the world. The frequency of profanity can make learning Hungarian tricky – many beginners simply don't realise that *kurva jó* ('whore good') actually means 'fucking good', and that although your grocer may use it when describing a tomato, you may not reply in kind.

We don't recommend that you actually use any of the expressions listed below, but knowing a few of them will make listening in to bar conversations a more edifying and engaging touristic experience.

● **Most common general profanity**: *Kurva*. Literally, it means 'whore', but is used in a peculiarly adverb-like way to mean 'fucking'. Most commonly encountered as a simple amplifier, such as *kurva jó* ('very good') or *kurvára tetszik* ('I really like it').

● **Runner up**: *Bassza meg!* (colloquial for 'Fuck it!') Be careful not to confuse it with the related, but more provocative *baszd meg* ('fuck you!'), which will get your butt kicked (*seggbe rúgás*) very quickly.

● **Quickest way to get your nose flattened in a pub**: Using *az anyád!* ('your mother!') or any of its creatively appended variations, the most common being *Menj az anyád picsájába* ('climb back into your mother's cunt').

● **English profanity least used in Hungarian**: 'Arsehole'. The closest Hungarian correlate is *seggfej* ('arse-head'), but the term is much more coarse and provocative than in English. Try the jolly-sounding *fasz kalap* ('dick-hat') or the less provocative *kocka fej* ('block-head'). Note that Hungarian lacks an equivalent of the English 'geek', 'twerp', 'anorak' or 'trainspotter'.

● **Least biologically sound profanity**: *Lófasz a seggedbe!* ('A horse dick up your arse!')

● **The poetry of love**: Lovemaking (*szeretkezés*) seems to bring out the worst in any language. Hungarians generally use *baszni* ('to fuck'), but also *dugni* ('to stuff') and *kefélni* ('to screw').

● **Most delectable term of derision**: *Szarházi senki!* ('Shithouse nobody'.)

● **Most commonly used term of material derision**: *Lószar!* ('Horseshit!') which can be used to describe shoddy goods, bad pay, or less than perfect fish soup.

Folklore

Avoid the kitsch, drink a pálinka, and get into a bit of boot-slapping.

When Béla Bartók and Zoltán Kodály roamed the countryside collecting folk songs at the turn of the century, they were not just creating the science of modern ethnomusicology. They were also helping to cement the identity of the modern Hungarian nation to its rural folk traditions. Twentieth-century Hungarian culture still flexes between classical and folk traditions in art, literature and music. Many urban Hungarians are not far removed from their rural past, and often all it takes is a fiddler and a shot of home brew to make an modern office worker jump into an ancient boot-slapping dance.

Hungarians know their folk culture is a tourist draw, and can turn on the kitsch with a vengeance. Avoid commercial 'folklore tours' – tourists are bussed out to the Puszta for 'genuine folkloric shows' that include a bit of costumed dancing, a Gypsy orchestra, a horse show with costumed *csikós* cowboys, and dinner at a country *csárda*.

If you really want to see a village full of peasants in embroidered vests and odd hats dancing to discordant fiddles amid thatched homes, you will have to do what Hungarians do – go to Transylvania, the multi-ethnic region of Romania that has avoided much of the twentieth century. Modern Magyar villages are much of a muchness since Kádár provided cheap loans to replace traditional thatched houses with boring box-like homes. Traditions do still survive, but tend only to be passed on when there is nothing good on cable TV. Nevertheless, within an hour of Budapest there are several villages that come close to being living museums.

VILLAGES & REGIONS

Hollókő, in Nógrád hill country, is a well-preserved Palóc village with old-style wooden houses, a ruined castle and a magnificent wooden church to which older women still wear folk costumes on Sunday. Peasants sell embroideries and beadwork in front of their houses, and visitors can stay in peasant homes renovated in traditional style. Hollókő is on the UNESCO list of world treasures and there are bus tours to the region. Check with local travel agents or call **Nógrád Tourinform**. Other villages in the Galga valley and Nógrád region are less spectacular, but just as authentic.

Other village regions worth seeing include the Őrség, near Szentgotthárd along the Austrian border, or the Szatmár and Nyírség region near the Soviet border. Closer to home, villages to the north of Buda in the Pilis hills, particularly Csobánka

The Dance House scene – a whirl of activity.

and Pomáz (on the HÉV commuter train near Szentendre) are pleasant for an afternoon walk. Both are home to multi-ethnic populations of Serbian, Slovak, Sváb German, Gypsy and Hungarian backgrounds.

West of Budapest is a series of pleasant villages easy to reach by local buses from Moszkva tér. Budakeszi (bus 22) was originally a Sváb German village known as Wudigeiss, but today is more or less a village suburb of Buda, with pleasant restaurants and beer gardens for the yuppies who are snatching up peasant homes here. You can see ornately carved wooden gates at the entrances to homes built by the Székelys who were settled here from Romanian Bukovina in the 1940s.

But the easiest way to see real live old ladies wearing strange embroidered things on their heads is to go to any of the vegetable markets that ring the downtown. At Bosnyák tér (bus 7) market, the peasant women who sell in the rear of the market continue to wear folk costumes, as do the women who sell on the terrace of the Skála Open Market in Buda (end of the number 4 tram line).

GYPSIES

One group preserving a visible folkloric identity are the Gypsies, or Roma. Stereotypes of Hungary always include the romanticised Gypsy musician, serenading noblewomen beneath moonlit castle windows. Truth is, there are half a million Magyar Gypsies and their life is anything but romantic.

The Roma are a European nationality without a nation. Their language, Romanes, is related to northern Indian tongues such as Hindi and Punjabi, and it is conjectured that they left India due to war or famine around the eighth century. The majority of Roma in Hungary are Oláh, or Vlach Gypsies (*vlashiko roma* in their own language), who arrived after the abolition of slavery in Romania in 1855. They guard their traditions closely, and the women continue to wear the traditional voluminous skirts. Many came to Budapest in the postwar period to find work in construction sites.

The Hungarian 'musician Gypsies' form a separate group among Roma, with their own dialect of Romanes and a hereditary tradition of professional musicianship. Few still speak Romanes, and most work in agriculture and industry since the market for violin bands has shrunk.

As all over Europe, in Hungary Gypsies face massive discrimination. Most live at or below the poverty level, with only menial or unskilled employment. Most Hungarians see Gypsies as nothing but a bunch of thieves and beggars, while police tend to treat them all as potential criminals. But although the most visible Gypsies may be the women begging coins downtown, the vast majority is working in regular, if low-paid, jobs.

Today Gypsies are organising to demand basic rights. There are Roma political parties and schools for Gypsy children, taught in Romanes. A Gypsy cultural revival has blossomed and bands such as Kalyi Jag, Ando Drom, and Romanyi Rota have produced recordings of traditional Roma music, predominantly vocal backed with guitars, mandolins and milk-churn percussion.

That's All Folk!

Shopping for Hungarian folk CDs is like walking into the Louvre and asking for 'paintings'. There is so much you can get lost, and some of the stuff in the bins truly deserves to stay there, but there is a lot of wonderful music you will never find outside of Hungary.

The state label, Hungaroton, issued some amazing folk recordings in the days of vinyl, and is slowly re-releasing some of it on CD. Smaller labels have also entered the fray, but distribution is poor and some of the best music remains hard to track down. Try the **Kodály Zoltán Music Store**, the shop at **Fonó** or the **Rózsavölgyi Zenemübolt** (*see chapter* **Shopping & Services**).

If you want the romantic restaurant Gypsy music, ask for *cigany zene* or *magyar nota*. If it's hardcore village recordings you're after, ask for *eredeti nepzene* (authentic folk music) or *tanchaz zene* (Dance House music). If seeking some traditional Gypsy music ask for *eredeti cigany nep zene*. Otherwise, here are a few more specific suggestions:

Márta Sebestyén

Vocalist Márta Sebestyén brought Hungarian folk wide exposure through her adventuresome work with French techno artists Black Forest and as the voice on the *English Patient* soundtrack. She remains active in the trad scene, and her first solo album *Dudoltam En*, recorded with Muzsikás, remains a classic.

Muzsikás

One of the first revivalist bands, Muzsikás did their homework in the villages when the old masters were still alive and kicking. Now they are the old masters. *Arrol Nem Hajnalik* is their best album, along with the more recent *Osz Az Ido*.

Kali Yag

In 1978 Gusztav Varga, a Gypsy from east Hungary, started this traditional band in a worker's hostel. Their first album, *Gypsy Folk Songs from Hungary*, is still one of their best: relentless guitar, mandolin, water jug and vibrant, melodic vocals.

Vujicsics

In the 1600s, thousands of Serbs and Croats fled the Turks and moved north to Budapest. Their identity in Hungary is strongly linked to family dances, and Vujicsics plays the mandolin-manic tamburica style in the best of the tradition. Their new CD, *Samo Sviraj*, is tops.

Compilations

Tancház Talalkozo is a monster Easter weekend folk festival that brings together the best of the Dance House movement. Any of the annual compilation CDs they've been producing since 1985 will provide Transylvanian music, minority bands, and young singers galore. *Uj Elő Népzene*, if you can find it, is another broad-based compilation of old and new dance house stuff.

Traditionalists

Recordings of the village masters, like The Palatka Band or Sándor 'Netti Fodor', contain traditional music that is still being played off the beaten track in Transylvania and east Hungary. Some of the best, if your ears don't mind the scratchy recording quality. Look also for the CD *Folk Music From Szatmar*.

Nógrád Tourinform
3170 Szécsény, Kulturcentrum, Ady Endre utca 12 (06 32 370 777/fax 06 32 370 170). **Open** 9am-5pm Mon-Fri. Some English spoken. **Map A1**

Folk Arts
Collections

Museum of Ethnography
Néprajzi Múzeum
V. Kossuth Lajos tér 12 (332 6340). M2 Kossuth tér/tram 2. **Open** 10am-6pm Tue-Sun. **Admission** Ft220; Ft100 concs; free Tue. EB Ft180; ET Ft3,000. Some English spoken. **Map C2**
In a beautiful nineteenth-century palace that was once the Finance Ministry, the Néprajzi has the most complete collection of ethnographic material in Hungary. The recently opened permanent exhibition of folklore includes costumes, household objects and tools from all of Hungary's historical regions, but most of the accompanying descriptive information is only in Hungarian. *See also chapter* **Museums**.

The Open Air Village Museum
Szabadságforrás út, Szentendre (26 312 304). Bus 8 from HÉV terminal. **Open** *1 Apr-31 Oct* 9am-5pm Tue-Sun. **Admission** Ft200; Ft100 children. Some English spoken.
Designed in the 1950s to ease 'ethnographic' research by transporting village homes to Szentendre, this Skansen-like village exhibits peasant homes with original furnishings, wooden churches and farm implements.

Purchasing Folk Arts

The state-owned folklore shops (*népművészeti bolt*) are full of kitsch. You can find cute little folk dolls, factory-produced weaving and machine-carved woodwork, although some stuff is worthwhile. Ceramic plates with floral patterns, or the matt black ceramics of the Great Plains are a good buy, although a visit to a flea market will produce finer quality pieces, even antiques, for half the price.

Folk textiles may be the perfect gift: easy to pack, light, and impossible to break in transit. Since most of these items are intended for local use, the prices can be shockingly affordable. The revival of interest in folklore among young Hungarians has provided a ready market for authentic village costumes and weavings from Transylvania, and peasants now come to Budapest to sell their wares. Find the women who sell textiles and other folk arts on the streets around Parliament and at Moszkva tér.

You'll recognise these women by their costumes. White kerchiefs and red skirts signal the women of the Transylvanian village of Szék, while yellow kerchiefed women in green wool vests and skirts are usually from the Kalotaszeg region (*see also chapter* **Shopping & Services**).

Folk Music & Dance

Budapest is one of the few capitals in Europe with an active traditional music and folk dance scene. Young Hungarians are wildly enthusiastic about their folk music. A visit to a Dance House

Váci vendor – who are you trying to kitsch?

(*Táncház*) is one of the best ways to meet Hungarians and learn directly what it is that makes them so, well, Hungarian.

The Dance House Movement, as it is now called, began in the early 1970s among young Hungarians tired of the centrally-dictated versions of folklore and syrupy 'restaurant music' favoured by state programmers. Fiddler Béla Halmos and singer Ferenc Sebő pioneered the revival by going to the elder village musicians to encourage a direct link to music traditions still strong in the countryside. The search for 'pure sources' of folk music led to Transylvania, where isolation had preserved the context of ancient music.

By the 1970s, folk music was becoming rare in Bartók's homeland. Old women still sang, but their grandchildren preferred the Beatles to ancient ballads. Communalisation put the shepherds out of business, along with their music, and recorded music was putting the village Gypsy bands to pasture. The younger musicians revitalised traditional music at just the right time, and soon it was a mark of rebellion to have a fiddle band at your wedding or to know a few old dances.

Back in Budapest, urban bands opened up Dance Houses based on the Transylvanian model – rented rooms where young people made their own entertainment with fiddles, dancing and lots of illicit plum brandy. The most famous of the Dance House bands, Muzsikás, used the raw, traditional sounds of the Transylvanian string bands, the shepherds' goatskin bagpipes, and the directness of folk song texts sung by Márta Sebestyén to protest the government's strongarm cultural policies, providing a musical voice to the dissident movement in a way that local rock never did.

Today the Dance Houses are still going strong. Bands that play Budapest weekly include Téka, the Ökrös Band, Kalamajka and Méta. Basic instrumentation includes lead violin, gut strung bas, and the kontra, a three-string viola with a flat bridge that enables it to play full, rich chords in the skewed rhythms of Transylvania. Extra fiddles, cimbalom (hammered dulcimer), duda (double chanter bagpipes), hurdy gurdy or reeds may round out the ensemble. Traditional Gypsy string bands from Transylvanian villages also make regular appearances in Budapest's Dance Houses.

Bands such as Kali Jag, Ando Drom, and Romanyi Rota perform the music of Hungary's contemporary Gypsy communities. Keep an eye on **Almássy tér Recreation Centre** for these events. Dance Houses tend to be open from October through May. There is usually a weekly summer Dance House somewhere in town but venues change. Check *Budapest Week* listings for information. Admission is around Ft100-Ft250.

Csángó Dance House

Marczibányi tér Művelődési Ház, XII Marczibányi tér 5/a, (212 5789). M2 Moszkva tér. **Open** 8pm-midnight Wed. Closed July-August. **Admission** Ft200. No English spoken. **Map A2**
Csángó music is the latest folk craze. The Csángós are two pockets of Hungarians, one in the Gyimes region of Transylvania, one in the Szeret valley of Moldavia, who play a rough, energetic music reflecting the oldest Magyar traditions. Using the gardon (a cello-shaped string instrument hit with a stick), the koboz (similar to the Arabic oud but smaller and louder), fiddles and Moldavian flutes, Csángó music as played by the house band Tatros has injected the Budapest folk scene with a loud and rocking rhythm.

Fonó Budai Zeneház

XI. Sztregova utca 3 (206 5300). Tram 47. **Open** 4pm-midnight daily. Concerts at 8pm. **Admission** Ft300. Some English spoken.
A new club dedicated to acoustic music, mostly folk and jazz, with special Dance House nights Tuesday and Thursday. Acoustically perfect, and in summer action moves outside to their breezy garden. There's also an excellent café and CD shop, and the Fonó runs its own label and recording studio.

Gyöker Dance House

Gyöker Restaurant, VI. Corner of Eötvös utca and Szobi utca (153 4329). M3 Nyugati. **Open** 9pm-1am Fri. **Admission** Ft200. Some English spoken. **Map D2**
The Gyöker was opened by a folk musician to provide a home to Budapest's active folk scene. Some kind of concert goes on almost every day, but Fridays are a treat with the real hard core of the Transylvanian folk scene. Good food. Usually the only Dance House open in summer.

Kalamajka Dance House

Belvárosi Ifjusági Művelődési Ház, V. Molnár utca 9, (117 5928). M3 Ferenciek tere. **Open** 8pm-1am Sat. Closed mid-June to mid-Sept. **Admission** Ft200. Some English spoken. **Map C5**
The biggest weekend dance. Dancing and instruction on the second floor and jam sessions and serious pálinka abuse on

the fourth. The Kalamajka band is led by Béla Halmos, a pioneer of the Dance House movement, and usually there are guest performances by traditional village bands.

Méta Dance House

Józsefvárosi Club, VIII. Somogyi Béla utca 13 (118 7930). M3 Blaha Lujza tér/tram 4, 6. **Open** 7pm-midnight Sun. Closed mid-June to mid-Sept. **Admission** Ft150. Some English spoken. **Map E4**
Small weekend get-together for serious dance fanatics in the basement of a local school. Excellent band featuring a woman lead fiddler and music from the Hungarian plains.

Muzsikás Club

Marczibányi tér Művelődési Ház, XII. Marczibányi tér 5/a (212 5789). M2 Moszkva tér. **Open** 8pm-midnight Thur. Closed mid-June to mid-Sept. **Admission** Ft200. Some English spoken. **Map A2**
Renowned folk band Muzsikás host a 'club' every Thursday. Not as much dancing, but a chance to hear Muzsikás and friends jam and relax in an informal atmosphere.

Téka Dance House

District Culture House, I. Bem Rakpart 6 (201 0324). Tram 19. **Open** 7pm-midnight Fri. Closed mid-June to mid-Sept. **Admission** Ft200. No English spoken. **Map B3**
The Téka band have for years been standard bearers of the traditional music craze. This is a dancer's paradise, and beginners should make an effort to go early to learn the basic steps from Csidu, one of Hungary's best, and funniest, dance masters. Village guests and concerts all for the same entrance price.

Festivals

The best festivals are during the summer, especially the Kaláka festivals in Miskolc and Sopron, which also showcase foreign acts. The National Folk Festival (Országos Táncházatalálkozó) is held at the Budapest Sportcsarnok at the end of March. (Information from the Professional Association of Folk Dancers – Szakmai Ház: 201 3766.)

Performances by professional folk dance troupes, such as the State Folk Ensemble (*see chapter* **Theatre & Dance**), the Duna Folk Dance Ensemble and the Bartók Dance Ensemble most often take place at the Budai Vigadó, I. Corvin tér 8 (along Fő utca near Batthyány tér in Buda, 201 5928, M2 Batthyány tér) or the FSZMH Fővárosi Culture Center, XI Fehérvári út 47 (181 1360, tram 47). Almássy tér Recreation Centre also hosts special folk music events.

Almássy tér Recreation Centre

Almássy téri Szabadidőközpont
VII. Almássy tér 6 (267 8709). M2 Blaha Lujza tér. **Open** 8am-8pm or later depending on events. Closed in summer. English spoken. **Map E3**

Kodály Zoltán Music Store

V. Múzeum körút 21 (117 3347). M2 Astoria. **Open** 10am-6pm Mon-Fri; 9.30am-1.30pm Sat. **Credit** AmEx, EC, V. Some English spoken. **Map D4**
Budapest's widest selection of Hungarian folk and traditional music, as well as world music from elsewhere. There's also classical music and lots of old vinyl.

Architecture

The use of architecture as propaganda, to reinvent history and even 'speak Hungarian' means Budapest's buildings are not always quite what they seem.

In 1904, leading Budapest modern architect Béla Lajta complained about the international styles that dominated the city: 'The visitor from abroad should find houses here that speak Hungarian, and those houses should teach him to speak Hungarian himself.'

Attempts to create a distinctive sense of place have preoccupied Budapest's architects since the early nineteenth century. Successive waves of occupation have left the city's architecture polarised: between that of its occupiers and that of supporters of the national cause. Hungary's own imperial position during the Dual Monarchy has also left its mark. Class antagonisms, state ideology and commercial colonisation have put Budapest's buildings into the frontline.

Things are not always what they seem. Architectural style and form have been consciously used as propaganda and history has been reinvented time and time again.

Pre-World War I

Repeated sieges of Castle Hill destroyed the pre-Turkish city, yet Habsburg rebuilding after the seventeenth-century reconquest of Buda often incorporated medieval ruins. Reconstruction after World War II uncovered many more Gothic remains, which were then combined with the restoration. Baroque façades, particularly on I. Úri utca, often include Gothic windows and door frames. Reconstructed merchants' houses can be found on I. Tárnok utca 14 and 16 and distinctive sedilias, seats for servants in the gateways of mansions, can be seen at I. Országház utca 9, I. Szentháromság tér 5 and 7.

DOMES & ROSES

A century and a half of Turkish occupation has also left surprisingly little trace. Many churches were turned into mosques. The **Belváros Parish Church** still contains a *mihrab* (prayer niche) and the Alsó Viziváros Parish Church on I. Fő utca 32 has the distinctive ogee-shaped Turkish windows on its south wall. Minarets were destroyed once the Habsburgs recaptured the city in 1686 and mosques were turned back into churches. Even the tiny domed **tomb of Gül Baba** was consecrated as a chapel by the Jesuits.

The greatest Turkish contribution to Buda was the bathhouses. The **Rudas**, **Rác**, **Király** and Császár (part of the **Lukács** complex) baths are still in use under their original copper domes.

BAROQUE AROUND THE CLOCK

The Habsburg reconquest found Budapest with a largely Protestant population. The Baroque style was critical to the Counter-Reformation, its curving sensuality and rich iconography a deliberately seductive contrast to Protestant austerity. The **Church of St Anne** on Batthyány tér is one of Hungary's most striking Baroque monuments.

Hungarian Catholic authorities revived the medieval cult of the holy kings. Frescoes and altar statues of István, László and Imre can be seen in the Krisztinaváros and Erzsébetváros Parish

*The **Church of St Anne** – strikingly baroque.*

József Finta – Postmodern Paranoia

High-tech, eclectic, monumental – the work of József Finta dominates new building in Budapest. Hallmarked by the depthlessness and pastiche of much 'postmodern' architecture, his approach is most prominently paraded in the **Kempinski Hotel**, and the Budapest Police Headquarters near Árpad híd. His earlier, less flamboyant hotels have meanwhile blighted the Pest side of the Danube since the late 1960s.

Beginning his career in one of the design 'factories' of the 1960s – a period of anonymity, kitsch and a tendency to humourless and unintentional parody – Finta progressed from prefab concrete housing estates, such as Kelenfoldi (XI. Étele út), to his first major commission, the Intercontinental (now the **Marriott**) Hotel, completed in 1969. Amazingly, this blot on the Danube Corso was a wild success. More commissions for hotels followed, including the **Novotel**. The amenability of his style with the culture of 'the emerging markets' smoothed Finta's passage through the political transition of the late 1980s and has ensured his dominance today. The **Hotel Taverna** and the International Trade Center on V. Váci utca, the Dom International Trade Center on Bajcsy-Zsilinsky út and the **Hotel Liget** all reflect the glossy taste of the Hungarian nouveau riche.

Finta's architectural nihilism becomes more pronounced after the end of Communism. Each façade of the Kempinski Hotel (completed 1992) relates to the street it faces, not to the hotel itself. The building has such an identity crisis that there's not even a clearly defined main entrance. Inside the lobby, the mix of art-deco pomposity and high-tech glamour is jarring and disorientating. There's also a distinct paranoia in Finta's later works. The reflective glass and polished marble shells of the Police Headquarters, the Bank Center on the Sas utca corner of Szabadság tér (*above*) or the **Duna Plaza** shopping mall repel the city like casino mirrors – not so much reflecting as deflecting, granting these buildings a sinister 'invisible' quality. Despite the proliferation of surveillance cameras, users and passers-by are able to imagine themselves unseen. Real life is indeed elsewhere.

Finta's futuristic and alien façades are ultimately a mere distraction from the failures of the present. Never mind the shrinking of the economy. Forget the escalating crime rate. Instead, just marvel at the way in which the Budapest Police Headquarters (XIII. Teve utca), with the red lights gleaming on its metallic tower, looks like nothing so much as a giant, menacing cockroach.

Churches (I. Krisztina tér and VII. Rózsák tere). Szent István's Holy Right Hand resides to this day in the **Basilica**.

The largest secular Baroque buildings are military. The Városház (City Hall) at V. Városház utca 9-11 was built as a hospital for veterans of the war against the Turks. The **Citadella** fortress on Gellérthegy was built to assert Habsburg control after the Hungarian defeat in 1849.

The aristocratic mansions and artisans' houses of the Castle District have been faithfully restored. The rich terracotta pinks and ochres, greens and blues of the façades are complemented by the elegant patterns of doors and window grilles. The former Erdődy Mansion (Táncsics Mihály utca 4), now the **Music History Museum**, and the tiny mid-eighteenth-century Baroque courtyard blocks all over the Castle District are particularly inviting. Houses in the *copfstil*, a Hungarian late Baroque style, can be found at Fő utca 20 and Batthyány tér 3. Their characteristic undulating tiled roofs have little eye-like windows peeking out.

PANNONIAN MODERN CLASSICS

The Embellishment Committee, set up in 1808 to develop Pest, chose the neo-classical style for areas such as the Lipótváros, challenging the feudalism of aristocratic Buda. The cultivation of national identity and the aspiration to a modern industrial economy is clear in the surviving neo-classical monuments. Pannonia, with the Hungarian coat of arms on her shield, sits in the tympanum of the **National Museum**. Mihály Pollack's Grecian design followed the idiom set by the British Museum and the Altes Museum in Berlin, and was the fourth museum of its kind in the world. The 1830s also saw the construction of the Lánchíd, the first permanent crossing over the Danube.

DUAL MONARCHYLAND

In the decades of the Dual Monarchy after 1867, Budapest expanded with astonishing speed. Preparation for the 1896 Millennial celebrations spurred the building of the capital's most important monuments. The **Opera House, Parliament,** the rebuilding of the **Mátyás templom**, expansion of the **Castle**, and the current layout of the **Városliget** all date from this time.

Monumental planning was designed to legitimise the city's new status as an imperial capital. Boulevards such as Andrássy út, Bajcsy-Zsilinszky út and the Nagykörút were carved through the poorer areas of the city and facilitated the policing of growing unrest.

A selective reinvention of Hungarian history pervades these new monuments. Both the neo-Gothic style of the Mátyás Templom and the neo-Romanesque **Fisherman's Bastion** romanticised medieval Christian values. The **Turul statue** by the Palace and the intricate ironwork of the Parliament gates allude to the mythical pagan-divine ancestry of Árpád, legendary founder of the Hungarian nation.

The 1896 exhibition had a profound impact on design in the years that followed. But all that remains of the structures that filled the park is Vajdahunyad Castle, a Disney-like fantasy that now houses the **Agriculture Museum**.

OCCULT & ORNAMENTATION

The extravagantly vulgar decoration that characterises the eclectic and neo-Renaissance styles reflected the ambition of the growing bourgeoisie. Buildings were designed from pattern books. Neo-Gothic and neo-Renaissance entrance halls clash with neo-Baroque ornamentation, but the eclectic extravagance of the now crumbling courtyard blocks of Districts V, VI, VII and VIII is superficial. Façades decked with cherubs, devils, and voluptuous caryatids hide courtyards with the sparsest of detail, and where entire families often lived in only one room.

Allusions to alchemy and freemasonry abound. The neo-Gothic entrance hall of V. Báthori utca 24, where sphinxes sit on Hermes' winged helmet, is particularly intriguing. The blatant masonic symbolism of leading nineteenth-century architect Miklós Ybl's Opera House is echoed in his Várkert Bazár (now the Várkert Casino at I. Ybl Miklós tér) and the Basilica.

Colossal debts incurred in the city's expansion are reflected in the opulence of financial institutions. The proportions of the former Stock and Commodity Exchange (now the headquarters of Magyar TV) on **Szabadság tér** were deliberately distorted to overawe with the power of money. The former headquarters of the Domestic Savings Bank, now the **British Embassy**, at V. Harmincad utca 6, is one of the few accessible to the visitor. The magnificent undulating glass ceiling of the former cashier's hall has survived virtually intact.

MODERN TIMES

The new construction techniques of the late nineteenth century were used to the full. The recently renovated **Nagy Vásárcsarnok,** and **Nyugati station,** built between 1874-77 by the Eiffel company, revel in palatial use of iron and glass.

Experimentation with new materials was one of the driving forces behind Art Nouveau. The villas and apartment blocks of Districts VI and VII beyond Oktogon are the best examples, particularly along VI. Városligeti fasor and VII. Munkácsy Mihály utca, although the rich marble and tiled interior of the **Zeneakadémia** is also worth seeing.

Characteristically curvaceous iron doorways with flower and bird motifs can be spotted all over the centre, notably at **Gresham Palace**. The Metro Klub at VII. Dohány utca 22 is a rare Hungarian example of the more geometric Viennese secessionist style.

The decorative arts and fine craftsmanship were integral to Art Nouveau. The Hungária mosaic rising above V. Szervita tér on the former Turkish Banking House (now Dr Jeans at ground level) is particularly striking.

MAGYAR MOTIFS

Questions of national identity preoccupied intellectuals throughout the nineteenth century and were paralleled by attempts to develop a national style of architecture. Disillusionment after defeat in the Second War of Independence led to the belief that Hungary's salvation lay in its eastern origins and folk culture. Frigyes Feszl's ornamentation for the **Vigadó** included frog fastenings from Hussar's uniforms, the faces of moustachioed Hungarian peasants and Tibetan heads.

The **Central Synagogue** is also in the Moorish and Turkish-inspired Romantic style. Orientalism resonated later in the designs of the **Párizsi udvar** and the **Museum of Applied Arts.** Zsolnay tiles, manufactured in Pécs, were important in creating a distinctive sense of place and frost-resistant glazes ensured that their rich colours survived. The deep blue wallpaper-like façade of Lechner's Thonet House (V. Váci utca 11a) is particularly beautiful. Ancient middle eastern symbolism is evident in Béla Lajta's mausoleums in the Jewish part of **Újköztemető cemetery** and in his motifs on the Parisiana nightclub, now the **Új Színház.**

Ödön Lechner made it his life's cause to develop a distinctive Hungarian architecture. He believed that the new idiom should emerge with the use of modern materials and structural applications, yet also made a serious study of Hungarian folk art which he brought to life in three dimensions. The gracious curves in the Museum of Applied Arts, the Geological Institute on XIV. Stefánia út 14 and the magnificent former **Royal Post Office Savings Bank** are enhanced by soft colours and light that give his buildings a magical aura. The playful surreality of his decoration is comparable to that of Antoni Gaudí.

A group of architects called A Fiatal Csoport ('The Young Ones'), originally students of Lechner's, looked to medieval folk architecture as the 'true' basis for an authentic national style and conducted detail-collecting expeditions much like the musical odysseys of Bartók and Kodály. Their style has become known as 'National Romantic' and can be seen in the **Wekerle Estate** in Kispest built between 1909-14.

Béla Lajta, on the other hand, another student of Lechner's, pursued an urban version of the Hungarian idiom. His 1911 Rózsavölgyi House on V. Szervita tér (now the **Rózsavölgy** music shop) is a forerunner of internationalist avant-garde architecture. Here the use of folk art is purely decorative, confined to patterns on the copper skirting.

The tension between these two trends – urban modernist versus rural romantic – continued to dominate the architecture of the interwar period.

Between the Wars

The Hungarian utopian avant garde was centred around the journal *Ma* (*Today*), edited by the poet and painter Lajos Kassák. The Horthy dictatorship forced Kassák (whose futurist poems and constructivist paintings reside at the **Kassák Museum**) and several other leading avant gardists into exile. László Moholy-Nagy and Marcel Breuer found fame at the Bauhaus, as did Ernst Kállai in the Der Stijl group. But many important figures, such as Lajos Kozma and the Bauhaus-trained Farkas Molnár, remained.

Kozma's **Átrium cinema** and apartment block can be found at II. Margit körút 55. The former Manfred Weiss Pension Office apartment block at II. Margit körút 17 is notable for the lifts in glass tubes centred in the eliptical staircase. Molnár's houses can be found in District II, particularly along Pasaréti út. Both architects were among those who designed the 1931 **Napraforgó utca experimental housing estate**.

Not all modern architects were leftists, however. An enormous Nietzschean superman looks down with disdain from the apartment block at VI. Bajcsy-Zsilinszky út 19, built in 1940.

HOMELANDS & GARDENS

Garden suburb developments were common under the Horthy regime, constructed mainly for refugees fleeing territories lost after Trianon. The residents of Szent Imre Kertváros in Pestszentlőrinc (District XVIII) paid for the construction of the garden suburb themselves, and it was planned to reflect the traditional communities they had left behind. Though now in a sad state of disrepair, many of the tiny houses mimic the neo-Baroque mansions of the aristocracy.

Public buildings of the Horthy era, such as the enormous Szent Imre Church on XI. Villányi út 23-25, as well as many of the larger mansions on

Nietzschean disdain on Bajcsy-Zsilinsky út.

The **Geological Institute** *designed by Ödön Lechner – Hungary's answer to Antoni Gaudi.*

Gellérthegy, were also designed in a neo-Baroque style, a reaction to the liberalism and supposed immorality of the city.

Post-World War II

Shock at war devastation was intensified by subsequent social upheaval. Rebuilding Budapest became a national priority of psychological and political importance. The policy of reconstruction, which took decades, was to restore historic buildings to their prewar state. Restoration of the Mátyás templom, for instance, faithfully executed Schulek's original design.

The need for a sense of historical continuity followed through during the Rákosi regime. The radical replanning of Budapest didn't get very far, but the regime did attack the 'the visual landscape of everyday life'.

Streets were renamed rather than obliterated and the names of Communist leaders were used alongside those of Hungarian national heroes. The occasional corner still displays the old street signs, crossed through since being renamed again after the demise of Communism. Shopfronts were another battleground. The campaign to end competition between individual shops led to the destruction of many Art Nouveau interiors. Király utca still sports several painted glass shop signs of the Rákosi era, all in the same gold typeface and dark backgrounds.

Rákosi-era architecture was a relatively restrained version of totalitarian classicism. The elegant porticos of the Hungarian Optical Factory (MOM) on XII. Csörsz utca 35-47 are reminiscent of 1930s Italian modernism. The College of Fine Arts at II. Zugligeti út 9-25 and the Dubbing Film Studio at II. Hűvösvölgyi út 68 have been recommended for national protection.

Architecture was actively used as propaganda. Housing estate and factory design were promoted as monuments of working class achievement. The workshops of the Csepel Car Factory (Autógyár tér, Szigethalom) have an almost organic form, their skylights curved like shark fins. Fifty thousand people laboured 'voluntarily' to build the **Népstadion** with its Stalinist statues, the major monument of the Rákosi regime.

Tenement blocks sprang up to cope with the postwar housing crisis. They were comfortable but small, the absence of privacy compounded by thin walls. Social activity was meant to take place in the workplace and in the specially built culture houses, which are still important in city life.

Soviet war memorials turned Budapest into a necropolis. Tombs were built in public places such as the park on XII. Csörsz utca and Ludovika Gardens in Csepel (District XXI). Separate areas for Soviet solders were also laid out in **Kerepesi cemetery**.

The **Liberation Memorial** on Gellérthegy and the memorial to Soviet soldiers in **Szabadság tér** symbolised Hungarian military defeat. Statues of Stalin and Lenin once standing in the Városliget were infused with an almost religious significance. Stalin was pulled down in 1956, but other statues,

Népstadion – *major Stalinist monument.*

including the Soviet soldier from the Liberation monument, can now be found in the **Statue Park.**

1956 AND ALL THAT

The Kádár government was quick to eradicate most signs of the uprising, although bullet holes can be seen down many side streets and the **New York Kávéház**, its façade smashed into by a tank, is still unrepaired today.

The thaw after Stalin's death in 1953 gradually worked its way into the architecture of the city. Eszpresszó interiors celebrated with rock 'n' roll décor. The Origo Eszpresszó in the bus terminus at II. Pasaréti tér still has groovy 1960s light fittings, and is kitted out in the ubiquitous brown and orange. Neon signs from this period still grace the Ferenc körút and the waterfront near Boráros tér (look out for the 'Traktoroexport Moscow USSR' sign, though its days are probably numbered). Others around town say simply 'shoeshop' or 'food', but notice the figure with flames rising from an out-stretched neon finger advertising the national gas company above Deák tér, or the daring typography of the Sztár Fodrász on VI. Király utca 72 – the politically correct place to get your hair done.

Kádárism was a disaster for architecture, which was relegated to a subsection of the building industry. Prefabricated concrete housing estates such as József Attila Housing Estate on IX. Üllői

út were the result, though the Óbuda Experimental Housing Estate on III. Bécsi út is still acclaimed for its varied housing and attention to detail.

Ironically it is the work of Imre Makovecz, then excommunicated from the profession, that has brought modern Hungarian architecture international renown. He claims to invoke the magic latent in peasant folk culture. His yurt houses on Sashegy in District XII and on II. Törökvész lejtő draw on the symbolic form of Siberian nomad shelters. His approach is best suited to meta-physical exploration, as in his interior for the Mortuary Chapel in **Farkasréti cemetery**.

RETAIL NIGHTMARES

These days the spotlight has returned to Buda-pest's shopfronts and interiors. Western retail logos and brash fast-food chains now dominate the Nagykörút, though some of the classy old neon still survives.

Old-style shop fronts and signs are again sym-bolising resistance, this time to rampant commer-cialism. Erma's at VII. Erzsébet körút 62 suggests a 1930s elegance, the genteel place to buy your underwear. Ancient dingy eszpresszó bars such as the **Majakovszkij** at VII. Király utca 103 or the **Mignon** at V. Károly körút 30 hold out against the tide of change, while the brass-and-mirror tack in newer bars feigns membership of the affluent West. **Café Mozart**, the ultimate in postmodern indelicacy, reduces a vibrant coffeehouse culture to a mythologised 'central European experience'. But a local sense of irony prevails in the pastiche. **Marxim** pizzeria serves up Stalinist kitsch with tomato ketchup. The Statue Park attempts to con-struct a critique of Stalinism while treating the statues with dignity in their obsolescence.

The city has been reduced to theatrical back-drop. Juxtaposed with crass western commercial-isation, crumbling nineteenth-century architecture achieves a dignity it would have lacked in its prime. The 1994 collapse of an apartment building on Ó utca in the centre of Budapest highlighted the poor state of the city's infrastructure. Historic landmarks of the poorer areas, such as the **Gozsdu Udvar**, are literally rotting away. Little maintenance has been done since World War II although several of the most important buildings have been renovated in the past few years.

While George Morriose's French Institute at I. Fő utca 17 enhances the Buda waterfront, post-modern Hungarian architecture has little to rec-ommend it. High-tech hotels catering to a foreign élite, such as József Finta's **Kempinski Hotel**, are complemented by his sinister **Duna Plaza** shop-ping mall. More successful as a tourist destination for provincial Hungarians than as a commercial venture, this giant mall looks and feels like a sci-ence fiction set. Budapest residents have become strangers in their own city.

Sightseeing

IGUANA
bar & grill

Kick Ass Mexican food

1054 Budapest • Zoltán u. 16.
Reservation: 131-4352

Sightseeing

Budapest can seem like one big sight with each phase in its history, from the Ottoman period until the Communist days and from renaissance to revolution, leaving its mark on the city.

Catch a tram 47 one sunny afternoon across Szabadság híd and take in the view upriver. Gellért Hill and the Liberty Memorial loom in shadow to the left; Castle Hill and the Royal Palace rise above the river beyond it, catching the light. The cityscape is set off against distant villa-speckled hills, bissected by the Danube which sparkles in the sun. Sometimes Budapest just seems to be one big sight.

The area covered by the city has been settled since pre-Roman times. Wars, invasions, revolutions and occupations, from the Mongol horde who gatecrashed in 1241 through to the aerial bombardments and street battles of 1945, have wiped out much of what was here before the latter half of the nineteenth century. Even the Castle District is largely a reconstruction of a reconstruction.

Nevertheless, from the Ottoman period until the Communist days, each phase in Budapest's history has left its mark, and there are even some extant Roman ruins, though these are poorly cared for. In particular, the expansion of Pest and the invention

of Hungarian national identity that took place in the late nineteenth century, when the country finally attained a measure of autonomy within the Austro-Hungarian Dual Monarchy, have left both a series of grandiose monuments and some extraordinary architecture. Much of this costs nothing to see. Such admission prices as there are will usually be negligible, although guided tours can be costly. Even the farthest flung sights – such as the ruins and museums of Óbuda, assorted cemetries and architectural experiments on the outskirts of town – are easily accessible by public transport. Apart from in the most-visited places, however, English documentation will be thin on the ground.

In this chapter we've singled out the most important sights and rounded up an assortment of others. Areas where sights are clustered together include the Castle District, Gellért Hill, the Városliget/Hősök tere, District VII and Lipótváros, the northern part of District V. (*See also chapters* **Budapest By Area**, **Museums** *and* **Architecture**.)

Budapest by night – the **Royal Palace** *and* **Chain Bridge**.

AIRPORT PROGRAM OFFICE
• organization of foreign and domestic programs

TERMINAL 1 GALLERY Tel.: 296-6556 Fax: 296-8547
Opening hours: from 8 a.m. to 6 p.m. on weekdays

LRI-VIP SERVICE BUSINESS CENTER
• meeting rooms for 6-300 persons • office services
• hostess and interpreter • message service
Opening hours: 7 a.m. to 10 p.m.
Terminal 1 Tel.: 296-7357 Fax: 296-6854, Terminal 2 Tel.: 296-8706 Fax: 296-8791

GENERAL AVIATION SERVICES
• full handling of small planes • catering service

LRI AIR CARGO
Postal address: 1675 Budapest-Ferihegy P.O.Box: 53.
Opening hours: from 7 a.m. to 7 p.m. Tel.: 296-7028, 296-7882

MINIBUS SERVICE
Transfer of passengers from the airport to the city and vice versa
Tariff is 1200 Ft per person Tel.: 296-8555

AIRPORT MINIBUS SERVICE
BUDAPEST FERIHEGY - AIRPORT

AIRPORT RENT A CAR
Rentals available: VW, Polo, Golf, Passat, Vento and Seat Ibiza
passenger cars and minibusses
Opening hours: from 8 a.m. to 10 p.m. every day Phone/Fax: 296-7170

*Budapest's **Central Synagogue** – second-largest in the world. See page 61.*

Calling Card Number
836 000 6780
M K SHEERAN

Without it, you're nowhere.

The AT&T Global Calling Card. It'll save you.

If you want to get somewhere fast, it pays to travel with the AT&T Global Calling Card. It costs nothing to get, and has all the calling conveniences of the AT&T Calling Card. Plus, it offers competitive prices and a 10% discount on calls you make to and from any one country you choose—all on one simple bill to your credit card. You can save on every card call you make around the world. But you need the AT&T Global Calling Card to enjoy the savings. To get an application or information about our services call our local office at 267-1980 Ext. 2156.
And if you wish to access **AT&T Direct**[SM] Service to place a call with your AT&T Calling Card or to call collect, from Hungary dial 00-800-01111*.
You just won't find benefits like these with any other card.

*Public phones require coin or card deposit.

©1997 AT&T

Buda

The Castle District

We've picked out the most obvious items, but the whole Castle District, both beautiful seen from across the Danube and fascinating to explore close up, is one great big attraction – UNESCO has designated it a World Heritage Sight. Built, destroyed and rebuilt throughout the centuries, when the Red Army took Castle Hill in 1945 only four out of 200 buildings were still habitable. Post-war reconstruction has recreated much of the Buda of the Habsburgs. The street pattern of the medieval city has been retained, together with much of the architectural detail – some restored, some unearthed by wartime bombing for the first time in centuries.

Heading for the hills

Not all Budapest sights are glued to the spot. The city has an assortment of enjoyably eccentric conveyances apart from the **Sikló** (funicular) which runs from Clark Ádám tér up to Castle Hill.

The cog-wheel railway, for example, built by a Swiss company in 1872, takes you right up Széchenyi-hegy for the price of one BKV ticket. It runs from opposite the Budapest Hotel, two stops from Moszkva tér on tram 56 or 18. Last train down is at 11.30pm.

Across the park from the cog-wheel railway is the terminal of the narrow-gauge Children's Railway (*gyermekvasút*) which wends through the wooded Buda hills to Hűvösvölgy. Formerly the Pioneer Railway run by the Communist youth organisation, many of the jobs are still done by children. Trains leave hourly 9am-5pm and tickets cost Ft60 adults, Ft30 children.

Another way up into the hills is the chair-lift (*libegő*) up to Jánoshegy – at 520 metres the highest point of Budapest, the air thankfully free of Trabant fumes. Take the 158 bus from Moszkva tér to the terminus at Zugligeti út. It costs Ft100 (Ft60 children) and runs between 9am-5pm from May-September, 9.30am-4pm October-April. There are cafés and bars at the top, and you can walk up ten minutes to Erszébet lookout tower or the Jánoshegy stop on the children's railway.

The ordinary tram 2, meanwhile, which runs up the Pest bank of the Danube from Vágóhíd to Margaret Bridge, passing Gellért Hill, Castle Hill, Parliament and all the bridges, has to be the second most beautiful public transport ride in Europe. (First prize must surely go to a *vaporetto* down Venice's Grand Canal.)

*The **Libegő** – a journey off the beaten track.*

All aboard!

First and last experience of Hungary for many travellers, Budapest's main railway stations are its real frontiers.

Keleti announces the East. Armies of students hustling for youth hostels assault your train; tannoy voices are incomprehensible to foreign ears; departure boards announce destinations both exotic and dangerous; money-changers hustle for hard currency; Chinese and Gypsy families decant to sell their wares.

This Beaux Arts palace, originally finished in 1884, has been undergoing renovations that will last until at least summer 1998. Paintings in the international ticket hall are by Mór Than and Károly Lotz, decorators of the Opera House and Parliament. Oeil-de-boeuf windows line the curving roof and the lacy ironwork on the main gates contrasts with the heaviness of stone.

Outside stands a statue of Gábor Baross, pioneer of the phenomenal Hungarian rail expansion that began in 1867 and was used by the Hungarians to keep its empire's minorities dependent: all railway lines had to go through Pest. To this day there is still no direct line from Vienna to Zagreb.

With St Stephen's crown perched on its apex, Nyugati is Budapest's oldest station. Constructed by the Eiffel Company (1877), the symmetry of its main shed and the weightlessness of the thin cast iron supports calm the pressure of departure. The ironworked arching is more reminiscent of Parisian greenhouses than a hectic railway terminus and the outside world seems remote as yellow trams blur through the glass façade. Postmodernity has cheapened its refinement. With boilers of occasional 'nostalgia' trains snorting steam, it's still possible to imagine Nyugati's heyday. But the Beaux Arts restaurant is now a McDonald's with synthetic plants and bulbous white lights.

Déli, ruining the view from Castle Hill, is the newest of Budapest's stations. While its prewar terminus was the haunt of newlyweds off to honeymoon in Venice, modern Déli brings you back down to earth. The stench of urine hits as you leave the metro. Fly-posters peel and people sleep rough. This really is the last resort. Finished in 1977, György Kővári's design exemplifies Communist shoddiness and superficiality. Its metal cladding is buckling and the marble facing falling off in dirty great lumps.

Carvings and figureheads still sprout from painted walls. Fountains and statues litter the streets and squares. The best time to look around is early in the morning before the tourists all decant from their coaches. Go for a stroll and, if you imagine away the parked cars, Buda castle looks much as it did hundreds of years ago. (*See also chapters* **Budapest By Area** *and* **Museums**.)

Fisherman's Bastion

Halászbásztya
I. Várhegy. Várbusz/bus 16. **Admission** Ft150. **Open** 24 hours daily. **No credit cards.** Some English spoken. **Map A3**
There are several explainations why this vantage point has a piscine name. Some claim the Fisherman's Guild defended this part of the Castle; others that there was a medieval fisherman's quarter down below. Certainly no one ever cast a line into the river from up here. Built between 1890-1905 by Frigyes Schulek and intended to harmonise with his romanticised reconstruction of the nearby **Mátyás templom**, there are seven turrets, one for each of the original Hungarian tribes. It's worth Ft100 for the view.

Mátyás templom

I. Szentháromság tér 2. Várbusz/bus 16. **Open** 7am-7pm daily. **Admission** free. Some English spoken. **Map A3**
This neo-Gothic extravaganza takes its name from the great Hungarian King Mátyás the Just (aka Good King Mátyás) who twice got married here. Parts date from the thirteenth century, but much was reconstructed in the nineteenth century and like most of the Castle District the church is a historical mish-mash. When Istanbul, rather than Vienna, ruled Buda, the church was converted into a mosque. The building suffered terribly during the 1686 siege of Buda and was mostly restored in the nineteenth century by Frigyes Schulek, who returned to the original thirteenth-century plan

The **Royal Palace***, see page 53.*

*The **Turul** has landed – feathered friend and mythical Magyar forefather.*

but also added his own decorative details, such as the gargoyle-bedecked stone spire. The interior is almost cloyingly detailed and includes the entrance to the Museum of Ecclesiastical Art in the crypt (*see chapter* **Museums**).

Royal Palace

I. Budavári palota. Várbusz/bus 16. **Open** times vary depending on museum. Some English spoken. **Map B4**
The former Royal Palace has been destroyed and rebuilt many times. What you see today is a postwar reconstruction of an architectural hotch-potch from the eighteenth, nineteenth and twentieth centuries. The first royal residence here was constructed by King Béla IV after the 1241 Mongol invasion. It was probably under the reign of King Mátyás (1458-90) that the Royal Palace reached its apogee. Mátyás' Renaissance-style palace had hot and cold running water and fountains and gargoyles that sometimes spouted wine. This palace was badly damaged during the Turkish siege of 1541 and the area was completely laid waste when recaptured from the Turks in 1686. Empress Maria Theresa caused a new 203-room palace to be built towards the end of the eighteenth century. This was even further badly damaged in the 1848-49 War of Independence, then reconstructed and expanded once more, only to be trashed yet again at the end of World War II. That battering revealed Gothic and Renaissance foundations, which have been included in the painstaking postwar reconstruction. Visitors are thus greeted by a mélange of architectural styles including Baroque and Gothic elements. The Palace now houses a complex of museums, including the **Budapest History Museum**, the **Hungarian National Gallery** and the **National Széchényi Library**.

Turul Statue

I. Szent György tér. Várbusz/bus 16/Sikló. **Map B4**
Wings outstretched and with a sword grasped in fierce talons, Gyula Donáth's giant bronze eagle (1905), visible from across the Danube, shrieks at tourists getting off the nearby Sikló. The best view is from the steps leading down to the

Palace where his pained expression smacks more of constipation than ferocity. This mythical protector of the Hungarian nation raped the grandmother of Árpád, legendary conqueror of the Carpathian Basin, and sired the first dynasty of Hungarian kings. Later he flew with the invading tribes, carrying the sword of Attila the Hun. In Siberian mythology the eagle is the creator of world, lord of the sun. By claiming ancestry from this creature, ancient Magyars believed they were descended from gods. In the nineteenth century romanticised eastern origins stressed a cultural and ethnic difference from the hated Austrians. Yet by 1896 Habsburg Emperor Franz Joseph was portrayed as the second Árpád, founder of the thousand-year Dual Monarchy. The Turul myth, co-opted to serve this new master, was positioned here by the Palace. The turul-eagle is a common motif on turn-of-the-century Budapest buildings. The main gates of the Parliament building have a row of fierce wrought-iron specimens and golden turuls guard the Szabadság hid.

Gellért Hill

Cave Church

Sziklatemplom
XI. Gellérthegy (185 1529). Just up from Szent Gellért tér, opposite the side of the Gellért Hotel. Tram 19, 47, 49/bus 7. **Open** 8am-9pm daily; mass at 11am and 5pm.
Admission free. No English spoken. **Map C5**
Although the caves were inhabited 4,000 years ago, the Cave Church was only dedicated in 1926. It feels much older. The church was popular enough to be expanded in 1931 by Count Gyula Zichy, archbishop of Kalocsa, who had helped re-establish the Hungarian Paulite order of monks. The monastery next door opened in 1934, and the white-robed monks resumed their work after an interval of 150 years – their order had been dissolved by Emperor Joseph II and sent into exile. The Communists jailed the monks in the 1950s and the cave was boarded up for decades, re-opening in August 1989. Visiting is a spooky experience, a gloomy organ booming against a backdrop of the Hungarian flag being devoured by two bleeding hearts.

FAMILIES' FAVORITE!

BUDAPEST ZOO

The WILDEST PLACE in town since 1866

**In Városliget (City Park), near Hősök tere (Heroes's Square)
(Metro line No. 1 - station: Széchenyi fürdő)
(Trolley bus No. 72 - station: Állatkert (Zoo)**

One of the most interesting monument zoos in the world

**2500 animals of 400 species, 2500 plant species,
the best park and resort area of the city.**

**OPENING TIME: FROM 9.00 AM TO SUNSET
BUDAPEST ZOO AND BOTANICAL GARDEN
BUDAPEST, XIV., VÁROSLIGETI KRT. 6-12.
TEL.: 343-6883, 343-6075**

Citadella

XI. Gellérthegy. Bus 27. **Map B5**
After the failed Hungarian revolution of 1848, the
Habsburgs built the Citadella in 1851 as an artillery
redoubt. Its commanding view put the city within easy
range should the Magyars choose to get uppity again. The
Ausgleich of 1867 that gave Hungary a measure of autonomy under the Dual Monarchy meant that its guns were
never fired in anger against the city. In fact the new administration planned to destroy it as a symbol of reconciliation,
but that proved too costly. The site now houses a youth
hostel, restaurant and disco as well as an exhibition of the
area's history since its earliest settlement by the Celts. It's
quiet up here and the views north and south along the
Danube are splendid.

Gellért Statue

XI. Gellérthegy. Tram 18, 19/bus 7. **Map B5**
A short walk down the hill from the Citadella is the enormous statue of St Gellért. Built in 1904, this 11-metre sculpture of the bishop raising his cross dominates the Buda
side of the Elizabeth Bridge. Below it is an artificial water-
fall, which dates from the same time. Like so many
Hungarian heroes Bishop Gellért (Gerard) met a tragic end
– originally an Italian missionary, he was the country's
first Christian martyr and legend has it that in 1046 he was
nailed into a barrel by pagans and rolled down Gellért Hill
into the Danube.

Liberation Monument

Felszabadulási emlékmű
XI. Gellérthegy. Bus 27. **Map C5**
Perched above the Citadella and visible from all over the city
is the 14-metre Liberation Monument. It was originally commissioned as a memorial to the son of Admiral Horthy,
Hungary's pre-war and wartime dictator. But his son was
killed while test-piloting a plane during World War II and
then in 1945 the Soviets arrived. A rapid switch of ideologi-
cal allegiance proved simple for sculptor Zsigmond
Kisfaludy-Stróbl. A palm branch was substituted for the pro-
peller blade the statue was originally supposed to be
holding, and – hey presto! – the same design was transformed to commemorate the liberation of Budapest from the
Horthyites by the Red Army. Local wits dubbed Stróbl

'Strébel' – which means to 'climb' or 'shift from side to side'.
Political zig-zags aside, the sculpture is impressive, and the
view from it even better. The statues of Soviet soldiers which
once stood below have been moved to the **Statue Park** (*see
chapter* **Museums**).

Elsewhere in Buda

Church of St Anne

Szent Anna templom
I. Batthyány tér 8 (201 6364). M2 Batthyány tér. **Open**
for services at following times: 6.45am-9am, 4pm-7pm
Mon-Sat; 7am-1pm Sun and public holidays. **Admission**
free. No English spoken. **Map B3**
Visited at dusk, as weary shoppers pop in to say their
prayers, St Anne's captivates the senses. The whispering of
catechisms echoes around its emptiness and there's a
faint smell of incense. Earthquakes, floods, metro construction and Stalinism couldn't destroy one of Hungary's finest
Baroque monuments. If you only visit one church in
Budapest, this should be it. Construction began in 1740, to
the plans of the Jesuit Ignatius Pretelli. Máté Nepauer, a
prominent architect of the Hungarian Baroque, oversaw its
final completion in 1805. The façade is crowned by the eye-
in-the-triangle symbol of the Trinity, while Faith, Hope and
Charity loiter around the front door. Larger-than-life statues
are frozen in performance on the High Altar, framed by marble columns representing the Temple of Jerusalem. The
Trinity above is held aloft by angels, cherubim strike poses
around the supporting altars, and a heavenly orchestra
perches atop the undulating line of the organ pipes. Despite
the melodrama St Anne's feels remarkably suburban. The
flowers and framed oval paintings of saints and notables
make it easy to imagine you're admiring the chintz in God's
front room. Speckled turquoise-green walls and potted trees
framing the altar of St Francis Xavier add to the cosy effect.

Clark Ádám tér

I. Clark Ádám tér. Tram 19/bus 16, 86, 105. **Map B4**
Adam Clark was responsible for building one of Budapest's
most famous landmarks, the Lánchíd (Chain Bridge), the
first permanent crossing of the Danube. William Tierney
Clark (no relation) actually designed the thing but it is the
Scottish engineer who has been honoured with a small

The Buda of the Ottomans

There are only a few traces left of the century
and a half when Buda was a distant outpost of
the Ottoman Empire.

The Pasha's residence, the 'serai', was on
today's Színház utca in the Castle District, while
the 'Red Hedgehog House' on I. Hess András tér
housed members of the Janissary corps. Most
buildings left by the Ottomans either fell into
disuse in the eighteenth century, or were
destroyed in 1945. A few Turkish gravestones,
topped by turban-like carvings, can still be
found in the bushes beneath the southern wall
of Buda castle, above Attila út.

There are still the **Rudas** and **Király** baths,
however (*see chapter* **Baths**), and the **Tomb of
Gül Baba** on II. Mecset utca. This last resting
place of the Bektashi dervish is the world's

northernmost Islamic place of pilgrimage. The
Buda hills were also home to Sufi dervish sects.

On the Anjou Bastion in Castle Hill, just west
of the **Museum of Military History**, stands
the grave of the last Pasha of Budapest, Vizir
Abdurrahman Abdi Arnaut Pasha, with an
inscription in Turkish and Hungarian advising
future generations that the Pasha wasn't such a
bad fellow, as Turkish pashas go. He was killed
at the age of 70 near this spot in 1686, as
Habsburg-led forces took the Castle. The
National Museum in Pest also displays an
Ottoman Pasha's tent, captured during the wars
of the seventeenth century.

Perhaps the gentlest reminder of the Ottoman
years are the fig trees, the northernmost in the
world, that still grow on Gellért Hill.

square at the foot of the bridge. Adam Clark, is remembered for preventing the Austrians blowing up the nearly completed bridge in 1849. He also had to talk the Hungarian General Dembinszky out of setting fire to it, and later constructed the tunnel that cuts under Castle Hill. The elongated dough-nut-shaped thing nestling in the bushes by the Sikló is Budapest's kilometre zero – the point from which distances from the capital are measured – making Clark Ádám tér the official centre of town.

Funicular

Sikló

I. Clark Ádám tér. Tram 19/bus 16, 86, 105. **Open** 7.30am-10pm daily. 2.30pm-10pm every second Monday. **Tickets** Ft180; Ft100 children. Some English spoken **Map B4**.

The fastest way to get to the Castle District from the bottom of the Chain Bridge; the mini-funicular railway crawls slowly up the side of Castle Hill in a minute or two. The panorama of Pest unfolds as you ascend. Until it was hit by a shell in the Soviet bombardment of 1945, the sikló had functioned continually since it first climbed up the hill in 1870. It was restored and electrified (it was originally hauled by a steam engine) in 1986.

Tomb of Gül Baba

Gül Baba Türbéje

II. Mecset utca 14 (no phone). Tram 4, 6. **Open** 10am-4pm Tue-Sun. **Admission** Ft30; Ft10 concs. **No credit cards.** Some English spoken. **Map D1**

Perched at the top of Buda's last surviving Turkish street is the northernmost Islamic place of pilgrimage in Europe. Gül Baba was a Turkish Dervish, whose name means 'father of roses'. According to local folklore, he introduced the flower to Budapest, thus giving the area Rózsadomb (Rose Hill) to the area. (Actually he died just after the capture of Budapest in 1541 and never had time to plant any roses.) Inside the mausoleum are verses inscribed by Turkish traveller Evliya Tselebi in 1663 as well as antiquities and furnishings donated by Hungarian Muslims. It's a peaceful spot, recently renovated and suffused with the air of tranquillity that always shrouds Islamic holy sites.

Pest

Basilica of St Stephen

Szent István Bazilika

V. Szent István tér 33 (117 2859). M3 Arany János utca. **Open** at mass times 7am-9am, 5.30pm-8pm, daily. *Treasury* 10am-5pm Mon-Sat, 1pm-5pm Sun. **Admission** Ft80, Ft40 concs. *Tower* 9am-5pm daily. **Admission** Ft200; Ft100 concs. Some English spoken. **Map C3**

For evening concerts, tickets from VII. Erzsébet körút 29. Designed in 1845 by József Hild, but only consecrated in 1905, the Basilica is Budapest's largest church. Construction was so disrupted by wars and the deaths of its two major architects that one wonders if God actually wanted it built at all. The original dome collapsed in an 1868 storm. An exasperated Miklós Ybl, its new architect, had the entire building demolished and rebuilt the original neo-classical edifice in the heavy neo-Renaissance style favoured by the Viennese court. In World War II the Basilica was devastated by Allied bombing. Restoration only began in 1980 and has yet to be finished. The interior is best appreciated during the evening choral and organ concerts. Gyula Benczúr's painting of Szent István offering the Hungarian crown to the Virgin Mary and Miksa Róth's stained glass windows depicting the Holy Kings decorate the Chapel of the Sacred Right. Here lies the main reason to visit. The mummified fist of Szent István lives in a Mátyás templom-shaped trinket box – a bit like Thing from the Addams Family. Ft20 in the slot lights up this gruesome relic.

Danube bridges

Budapest is the most Danubian of all the settlements on central Europe's main waterway. The river defines the city, separating the mentalities of Buda and Pest. On a national level the bridges join rural Hungary with cosmopolitan Europe – an economic necessity recognised by Count István Széchenyi, who organised the construction of the Lánchíd (Chain Bridge), Budapest's first modern bridge. It replaced the iced-over pontoon bridge he had been unable to cross to visit his dying father.

But the Danube has been a psychological as well as a political frontier since it formed the *limes* of the Roman Empire, separating urban imperialism from the nomadic cultures of the unconquered plains beyond. The Romans built the first permanent crossing: a wooden construction which stood not far from today's Árpádhíd.

Projections of national and civic self-image characterise the design of today's bridges. The Lánchíd, guarded by stone lions and lit up at night, has a strength and grandeur despite its postcard picturesqueness. It opened in 1849 after the defeat of the Independence movement, yet crystallises the optimism of metropolitan expansion and national ambition. Conversely, the mythical turuls and the shields of 'Greater' Hungary on Szabadság híd (Freedom Bridge, 1896 – originally named Franz Joseph I Bridge and perhaps Budapest's most beautiful) betray an ambivalence towards the future.

The views from the Elisabeth (Erzsébet) and Margaret (Margit) Bridges are more memorable than the structures themselves. But Margaret Bridge has a Parisian sophistication, mirroring the self-perception of Pest's emerging bourgeoisie.

While the bridges opened up new areas of Budapest for development, the older city suffered. Construction of Erzsébet híd (1903) destroyed Pest's medieval centre and the Tabán near Castle Hill. Hungary's first heritage campaign was formed to save the Inner City Parish Church and the road off the bridge obligingly swerves round it.

The Danube bridges have a strategic vulnerability, their destruction a blow to civic and national pride. The Austrians attempted to blow up the Lánchíd in 1849. The Nazis demolished them all in 1945. Memorials to a temporary bridge which carried public transport until 1956 can be found near the Parliament and on the opposite quay at Batthyány tér.

Trusted .
by the world
to send money
in minutes.

(01) 267 4282 **WESTERN UNION | MONEY TRANSFER®**
The World's No 1 Money Transfer Service.

International
Agenda

**The best weekly entertainment
listings from around the world**

Every Wednesday in *Time Out, Time Out New York & El Pais*

http://www.timeout.co.uk

Amsterdam, Barcelona, Berlin, Boston, Brussels, Budapest, Chicago,
Edinburgh, Glasgow, London, Los Angeles, Madrid, Miami, New York, Paris,
Philadelphia, Prague, Rome, San Francisco, Sydney, Tokyo & Washington DC.

*The **Inner City Parish Church** – Pest's oldest building.*

Inner City Parish Church

Belvárosi Plébiánatemplom
V. Március 15 tér (no phone). M3 Ferenciek tere. **Open**
9am-12.30pm, 6pm-7pm, Mon-Sat; 6.30am-7.30am, 6pm-
7pm, Sun; *Latin Mass* 10am Sun. Some English spoken.
Map C4
Founded in 1046 as the burial site of the martyred St
Gellért, this is Pest's oldest building, although little of its
original structure remains. It's an extraordinary mixture
of styles – Gothic, Islamic, Baroque and neo-classical – testifying to the city's turbulent history. The beauty of its
interior is in the light and shadow of the Gothic vaulting.
Side chapels contain their own altars. Most of the older detail
is in the sanctuary, around the altar, but dodge the 'Stop
tourists!' signs or visit on Sunday after Latin mass to see
them. Behind the High Altar you'll find Gothic sedilias and
a Turkish prayer alcove, surprisingly intact from when the
church was used as a mosque. Outside, it's still possible to
make out the Gothic stones. The remains of the Roman outpost Contra Aquincum lie north of the church.

City Park

Városliget
VI. Dózsa György út. M1 Hősök tere. **Map F1**
The Városliget, laid out by the French designer Nebbion, is
where Budapest comes to stroll. Towering over the greenery and the small artificial lake, used for boating in summer
and ice-skating in winter, both activities strangely embellished by booming disco hits from the late 1970s, is
Vajdahunyad Castle. This is a Disneyfied version of the
Hunyad clan's castle that still stands near Hunedora in
Romania. Together with neighbouring buildings the castle
embodies every architectural style in Hungary up to the nineteenth century. The Baroque part houses the **Agriculture
Museum**. In the courtyard stands Miklós Ligeti's sculpture
of the hooded Anonymus, chronicler to the court of Béla III.
People take snaps of each other sitting his lap, as if to avoid
the constant gaze of the postcard and balloon vendors. There
is also a statue of George Washington in the park, erected in

1906 in gratitude to America for providing a home for Hungarian immigrant communities, whose contributions paid
for the statue. Apart from the **Transport Museum**, the
Széchenyi Baths complex, the **State Circus**, the restaurants **Robinson** and **Gundel**, and the **Petőfi Csarnok** concert hall (*see chapter* Music: Rock, Roots & Jazz) outside of
which is a weekend flea market (*see chapter* **Shopping**), the
Városliget is also home to the city's **Zoo** and **Vidám Park**.
Hősök tere (Heroes' Square) is essentially the park's
main entrance.

Former Royal Post Office Savings Bank

Magyar Királyi Takarék Pénztar
V. Hold utca 4 (311 4432). M3 Arany János utca. **Open**
9am-2pm Thur, or call to arrange a tour. Some English
spoken. **Map C3**
Ödön Lechner's recently restored 1901 masterpiece (as pic-
tured on the front cover of this *Guide*) is Budapest's most
innovative building, worthy of a Gaudi or Jujol. The buildings all around allow only tantalising glimpses of its flash-
ing white ceramic or writhing gold serpents crowning
green tiles. Lechner's finesse lies in the restraint of his folk-
motif detailing combined with a meticulous attention to
form. The exuberant colours and sinuous shapes put eclectic Budapest to shame. The bank was founded for peasants and other working people. The folk-art sources and
playfulness of the decoration are part of the bank's acces-
sibility. The lights flanking its entrance writhe like sea
horses and Zsolnay bees march up to hives perched on top
of the verticals. Floral motifs pattern its upper reaches, like
the embroidery on those white lace tablecloths sold around
Váci utca. The cashier's hall is the only part accessible to
the visitor. Lechner's irreverent style was abhorred by the
establishment of the day and banned from public buildings in 1902. Now part of the National Bank, this, alas, was
his last major commission. Other Lechner buildings worth
seeing include the **Museum of Applied Arts** and the
Institute of Geology at XIV. Stefánia út 14. (*See also chapter* **Architecture**.)

Gozsdu udvar

VII. Dob utca 16/Király utca 15. M2 Astoria, M1, M2, M3 Deák tér/tram 47, 49. **Map D4**

Built at the turn of the century, Gozsdu udvar was once the heart of Budapest's working-class Jewish quarter, crammed with dozens of tiny shops and tradesmen. The seven courtyards, which stretch for 200 metres between Király utca and Dob utca, echoed to the sounds of German and Yiddish, Hungarian and Romanian as newcomers poured into Budapest to try to make new lives for themselves as restrictions on Jewish life were eased. Many of those families vanished in the Holocaust. The authorities recently emptied most of the complex out yet again, but still haven't got around to much-needed renovations. You can smell the damp as you walk through. But Gozsdu udvar retains its atmospheric feel, especially at night. Visit now before they end up knocking it all down.

Great Market Hall

Nagy Vásárcsarnok

IX. Fővám tér (218 5322). Trams 2, 47, 49. **Open** 6am-5pm Mon; 6am-6pm Tue-Fri; 6am-2pm Sat. **Credit** (at main cash register) AmEx, DC, EC, JCB, MC, V. **Map D5**

The grand three-storey Great Market Hall was opened in 1897. It was a spectacular shopping mall in its day, featuring barges gliding down an indoor canal, used to deliver the stallholders' goods, with a railway line that went up to the market's gates. Under the Communists the building gradually began to crumble and fall apart, but Budapest city council decided to restore the site and the market reopened in 1994 with a gleaming new Zsolnay tile roof. Even without the indoor canal, it is still pretty grand. About 30,000 shoppers a day pass through the hall, trawling the 180 stalls.

Gresham Palace

V. Roosevelt tér 6. Tram 2. **Map C3**

Beautifully situated, its iron peacock gates in line with the Lánchíd, the Gresham Palace is crumbling away. Designed by Zsigmond Quittner and built in 1906 for the Gresham Insurance Society (a gold-haloed relief of Charles Gresham, the company's founder, still surveys the Danube) it had all the latest gadgets in its prime, including the central vacuum system, a Hungarian invention. The glass-roofed arcade is a public right of way and it's possible to sneak up the stairs and find stained glass windows by Miksa Róth. The Gresham was in the frontline at the end of World War II and

---

Jewish Budapest

Beyond the **Central Synagogue** lies Budapest's historic Jewish quarter, established in District VII in the eighteenth century and peaking in the second half of the nineteenth century, as the Jewish population of the city grew from 16 per cent in 1872 to 21.5 percent in 1900.

The block behind the Central Synagogue has the **Jewish Museum**; the Heroes' Synagogue (1931), named for Jewish soldiers killed in World War I; and the Károly Goldmark cultural hall. The headquarters of many Jewish organisations are located just around the corner at VII. Síp utca 12 (M2 Astoria).

Imre Varga, who sculpted the Holocaust memorial in the Central Synagogue's courtyard, also created a statue of Raoul Wallenberg, the Swedish diplomat who saved more than 20,000 Budapest Jews. Communist authorities insisted it be placed far from the city centre – so today it stands out in Buda on II. Szilágyi Erzsébet fasor (tram 56).

The Orthodox community complex is at the corner of Dob utca and Kazinczy utca – dominated by a 1910 synagogue whose façade gracefully negotiates the curve of Kazinczy utca. It is in use but needs restoration. Nearby is the Fröhlich Cukraszda at VII. Dob utca 22, still serving up kosher pastries for the observant. The Rumbach Sebestyén utca Synagogue – a Moorish structure designed by Viennese architect Otto Wagner – can only be seen from the outside. Restoration has bogged down amid ownership disputes, and its future is unclear.

Nearby, the **Gozsdu udvar**, a series of interlocking courtyards which was once packed full of tradesmen's workshops, runs from Dob utca through to Király utca.

Though Király utca was 70 per cent Jewish a century ago, the only remaining religious building is a small 'hidden' synagogue just off it at VI. Vasvári utca 5, currently used by Hasidic Jews. There are several such in Budapest; to get around the prohibition against Jewish land ownership, the community would rent all the flats in a building, enabling them legally to build a house of worship in the courtyard.

As some Jewish families grew wealthier, they left District VII and built the upper-class, elegant Bauhaus buildings in District XIII around Pozsonyi út and Szt István Park. Many would later serve as Wallenberg's safe houses, protecting Jewish families during the war.

The past ten years have seen some revitalisation within Budapest's Jewish community, estimated at over 80,000. Eastern Europe's only rabbinical centre is at VIII. József körút 27. There are four Jewish day schools and a newly opened community centre (VI. Révay utca 16). District VII, although it is no longer majority Jewish, remains the heart of the Jewish community.

Budapest's oldest synagogue, dating back to medieval times, is in the Castle District at I. Táncsis utca 26. András Landherr's 1821 Óbuda Synagogue, one of Budapest's earliest neo-classical buildings and now a TV studio closed to the public, is at III. Lajos utca 163 (HÉV Árpád híd/tram 1).

further damaged in 1956. Home to a raucous cabaret in the 1930s, the arcade now boasts a casino, hairdresser and Chinese restaurant. Residents have blocked the sale of the building to a hotel chain which would have restored the façade but left them homeless. The Gresham Palace will thus continue to crumble for some time to come.

Heroes' Square

Hősök tere
VI. Hősök tere. M3 Hősök tere. **Map E1**
As a symbol of confident nineteenth-century nationalism, Heroes' Square is unbeatable. Completed for the 1896 Magyar Millennium that celebrated the anniversary of Hungarian tribes arriving in the Carpathian basin, the grandiose use of space encapsulates the conviction that Hungary then was a nation going places. It's flanked by the **Műcsarnok** and the **Museum of Fine Arts** and centred on the Archangel Gabriel, perched on top of a 36-metre column and staring boldly down Andrássy út, Budapest's answer to the Champs-Elysées. Gabriel gets pole position because, according to Hungarian legend, Pope Sylvester II sent a crown to King Stephen after his personal intervention. Perched in the two colonnades are statues of assorted Hungarian kings and national heroes, from St Stephen to Lajos Kossuth. Now often crowded with skateboarders in reversed baseball caps, Heroes' Square has witnessed many key events of modern Hungarian history – most recently the ceremony to mark the reburial of Imre Nagy, leader of the 1956 revolution, the event that in June 1989 marked the the re-birth of democracy in Hungary. Nagy's remains are at **Újköztemető Cemetery.**

Central Synagogue

Nagy Zsinagóga
VII. Dohány utca 2 (342 8949). M2 Astoria. **Open** *synagogue* 10am-3pm Mon-Fri; 10am-1pm Sun. **Entrance** Ft400. *Museum* 10am-3pm Mon-Fri; 10am-1pm Sun. **Admission** Ft200. *Heroes' Temple prayer* 6pm Fri; 9am Sat. **Credit** AmEx, DC, EC, JCB, MC, V. English spoken. **Map D4**

St Stephen looms at **Heroes' Square.**

Designed by Lajos Förster and completed in 1859, this is the second-largest synagogue in the world after New York's Temple Emmanuel. Seating 3,000 and too big to heat, it has never been used in winter. The synagogue is a monument to the patriotism of the Hungarian Jewish bourgeoisie. Newly cleaned brickwork glows in blue, yellow and red, the heraldic colours of Budapest. Fresh gold leaf gleams on Moorish domes, their orientalism a reaction against Austrian rule. Interlaced eight-pointed stars in the brick detailing, continued in the stained glass and mosaic flooring inside, are a symbol of regeneration – appropriate once again after the recently completed $10 million, ten-year facelift financed by the Hungarian government and Tony Curtis' Emmanuel Foundation. The divisions of its central space are based on the cabbalistic Tree of Life, giving it a similar floor plan to a Gothic cathedral. The dark wooden pews are numbered, some poignantly tagged with names of those long dead, and its freshly painted ceiling entwines Stars of David outlined in gold leaf. An inscription of Jaweh surrounded by a blaze of glory radiates above the Arc of the Covenant, lit from overhead by an opening in its cover-

Parizsi Udvar – *neon signs glow enticingly from the cavernous interior. See page 63.*

RESTAURANT
Művészinas

Budapest, VI. Bajcsy-Zsilinszky út 9.
Telefon: 268-1439. Fax: 269-6889
Nyitva/Open: 12 - 24.

Irish Pub
& RESTAURANT

On the Renault boat, in front of the Hotel Forum, the best panoramic view of the city

Charcoal Grilled Dishes - Home-made Recipes

Columbus

AUTHENTIC IRISH PUB
OPEN YEAR ROUND FROM NOON TILL SUNRISE
Phone-266-9013, 266-7514

fausto's
Ristorante

*Fausto di Vora warmly invites you to come
in and sample his authentic Italian cuisine.*
Hours: Mon-Sat. 12-3, 6:30-11
Closed Sunday

VII. Dohány u. 5. • Budapest
Tel./Fax: 269-6806

restaurant.cafe

Open noon – 12 pm

Szarvas Gábor út
Buda
Pest
Moszkva tér

H-1125 Budapest, Szarvas Gábor út 8/D
Tel: (36-1) 275-2115
Reservation: 275-1039

ing dome. The synagogue's annex, the Heroes' Temple, designed by Ferenc Faragó and László Vágó in 1929-31, is a memorial to Hungarian Jews who died fighting in World War I. The simple concrete arching colonnade encloses the Garden of Remembrance, now a mass grave for Jews massacred by fellow Hungarians in 1945. Imre Varga's weeping willow memorial to those killed in concentration camps is visible from Wesselényi utca. Family names of the dead are inscribed on its leaves. Towards the end of World War II, 20,000 Jews were herded inside here, 7,000 of whom perished within.

New York Kávéház

VII. Erzsébet körút 9/11 (322 3849). M2 Astoria. Tram 4, 6. **Open** *café* 9am-midnight; *restaurant* 6.30pm-11pm. **Credit** AmEx, DC, EC, JCB, MC, V. English spoken. **Map E4**

Don't visit for the mediocre restaurant or the overpriced cappuccino (*see also chapter* **Cafés & Coffeehouses**) but do go look at the architecture. Built in 1894 by Alajos Hauszmann (the architect also then responsible for renovations to the Royal Palace) the spectacular neo-Baroque interior with twisting columns, cheeky cherubs, lush velvets, marble and gold leaf caused a sensation at its opening and still draws crowds of tourists to what was once the main hangout of literary and artistic Budapest. Nymphs and satyrs cavort around the ceilings, and 'New Yorkia' brandishes a miniature Statue of Liberty near the expresso bar. Peering through the plastic plants you can also spot caricatures of the journalists of the 1950s and '60s who made it their haunt, a refuge from the newspaper offices that used to occupy the upper floors. Rammed by a tank in 1956, its façade still hasn't been renovated. Visit before it all falls down.

Opera House

Operaház

VI. Andrássy út 22 (153 0170). M1 Opera. **Open** *box office* 10am-7pm Tue-Sat; 10am-1pm, 4pm-7pm, Sun. Guided tours available in English 3pm, 4pm daily Ft700 (further info 131 2550 ext 156). Doors for performances open 6pm. **No credit cards**. English spoken. **Map D3**

Miklós Ybl's neo-Renaissance Opera House was the most culturally significant of the monuments built to commemorate the Millennium celebrations. Completed in 1884, it was also one of the few actually finished in time. Although financial constraints forced Ybl to scale down his original proposals, the interior is still lavish. Seven kilograms of gold were used to gild the intimate auditorium and 260 bulbs light up the enormous chandelier. Its cultural importance has always been linked to Hungarian national identity. Ybl, who personally supervised every detail, subverted the implied colonialism of the Viennese-favoured neo-Renaissance style by incorporating masonic allusions, such as the smiling sphinxes and the alchemical iconography on the wrought-iron lampposts. Ferenc Erkel, the Opera's first director, was responsible for composing the doleful Hungarian national anthem. Operas by Erkel, Liszt, Kodály and Bartók are still prominent on the programme. (*See also chapter* **Music: Classical & Opera.**)

Párizsi udvar

V. Ferenciek tere 10-11/Petőfi Sándor utca 2-8. M3 Ferenciek tere/bus 7. **Map C4**

Henrik Schmahl's Párizsi udvar was completed in 1913 and still functions as a bustling shopping arcade today. Gold leaf mosaics announce its presence to the street, neon signs glow enticingly from the cavernous oriental interior, and 50 nude ceramic figures solicit from portholes above the third storey. Outraged critics charged the arcade with 'lacking good taste and discretion' – not bad going considering the moral and aesthetic standards prevalent at the time. It began life as the Inner City Savings Bank, a function made perfectly clear in its ornamentation. Bees, the symbols of thrift, can be found throughout the building, while heavenly banking is presided

Parliament *– like a pointy Prussian helmet.*

over by the archangel Gabriel on the white pyrogranite reliefs below the gable. Classical-style mosaics with gorgons' heads and theatrical masks smother the porch, juxtaposed with Islamic geometric motifs. This curious eclecticism continues once you're inside the arcade, which is best viewed from the Piccoló Bar. Alcohol can only heighten the effect of the intricate detailing although you wouldn't want to be sitting there if any more panels fall out of Miksa Róth's arched glass ceiling. The mock grandeur of the arcade tails off sadly into Kigyó udvar, 1970s strip lighting starkly filtered through metal lattice. Gone are the days when they made tack with flair.

Parliament

Országház

V. Kossuth Lajos tér (268 4437). M2 Kossuth Lajos tér/tram 2. Tours in English. When Parliament is sitting: 10am Wed-Sun. In recess: 10am, 2pm Mon-Fri; 10am, 12.30pm Sat; 10am Sun. **Tickets** Ft700; Ft300 concs from Door 10 to right of main entrance. EB Ft250. **No credit cards**. English spoken. **Map B2**

Centrepiece of the extraordinary invention of national history that transformed Budapest at the turn of the century, Imre Steindl's Országház was completed in 1902, six years too late for the Millennium celebrations it was intended to crown. The building is an exercise in establishment kitsch and the freshness of its 1980s restoration denies it the authority that age and decay might have lent. Bright lights and 88lbs of gold leaf bestow a glittering vulgarity. The spiky profile dominates the Pest embankment of the Danube. The incongruous neo-Renaissance dome is crowned by a neo-Gothic spire, making it look much like one of those pointy Prussian helmets. Ferocious turul birds guard the main entrance and shields of Hungarian nobilty line the façades – an equation of national citizenship with the aristocracy (at the time of its construction, only five per cent of Budapest's adult population had the vote).

Angels support the coat of arms of pre-Trianon Hungary, the empire a gift from God. The dome is 96m high, an allusion to the Carpathian conquest of 896. Underneath, 16 Zsolnay Hungarian rulers perch on supporting columns. The guided tour will take you to the chamber of the former Upper House. Note the numbered cigar holders outside the door, where members left their havanas burning during debates, and the shield of Transylvanian prince János Hunyadi, vanquisher of the Turks, where a wolf bays at a crescent moon beside a gold star.

Serbian Orthodox Church
Szerb templom
V. Szerb utca 2-4 (137 4230). M3 Kálvin tér. **Open** *for High Mass only* 10.30am Sun. Service 60-90 minutes. ET by appointment. Some English spoken. **Map C5**
Announced at the corner of Veres Pálné utca by painted tiles of St George spiking the dragon, this secluded church was begun in 1698 after the Turkish defeat, and modified in the mid-eighteenth century. Built to serve the Serbian craftsmen and merchants who lived in this waterside district, it still has a congregation of their descendants, plus refugees from the recent war. The church is only open for Mass on Sundays. It's an overpowering experience. With clouds of incense and votive candles flickering, the service is sung throughout by priests. Acoustics are superb. As the litany reverberates around the glowing ochre interior, the light picks out the gold leaf of the neo-Renaissance iconostasis which hides the gleaming altar. The congregation stands during mass. Carved wooden pews with high arms provide something to lean on as your head goes dizzy and the ethereal blue of the ceiling frescoes starts to spin. Visitors leave spellbound.

Szabadság tér
V. Szabadság tér. M2 Kossuth Lajos, M3 Arany János utca. **Map C3**
Constructed during Hungary's brief flirtation with imperialism and conceived as the hub of the fin-de-siècle economy, Liberty Square was intended to be an image of imperial prosperity, its air of permanence masking the volatility of economic expansion. It's still dominated by the Dual Monarchy's central bank (now the National Bank number 9) and the Hungarian Stock Exchange (now headquarters of Magyar Televízió at number 17). Symbolism was paramount for the builders of Szabadság tér. Built on the site of the Habsburg barracks where leaders of the nascent Hungarian nation had been imprisoned and executed in 1849, they attempted to defeat their former oppressors through the weight of architecture. Nationalism triumphed at the expense of good design. The former Stock and Commodity Exchange was completed in 1899. With distorted perspective and exaggerated scale, the huge proportions of its entrance and central vaulted hall are terrifying. In the 1920s Szabadság tér became the site of the 'sacred flagstaff', a Hungarian flag flown at half mast over a mound of soil from territory lost at Trianon. Following World War II, the Soviet army erected an obelisk commemorating its dead on top of the flagstaff, destroying the sacred mound. The obelisk still stands, with a star on top and reliefs of Soviet soldiers besieging Budapest on the base. One nationalist memorial remains. The 'eternal flame', a block away up Auflich utca on the corner of Báthory utca, commemorates Count Lajos Batthyány, prime minister of the 1848 provisional government, imprisoned in the Új Épület and executed by firing squad in 1849. The American Embassy is housed at number 12.

Új Színház
VI. Paulay Ede utca 35 (269 6021). M1 Opera. **Open** for performances. **Tickets** from box office or Andrássy út 18. **Closed** mid-June-Sept. **No credit cards.** No English spoken. **Map D3**
Originally built as the Parisiana nightclub (1910), Béla Lajta's striking symmetrical geometric design peeps out

Margaret Island

Neither Pest nor Buda, the Margaret Island (Margitsziget), which stretches from Margit híd to Árpád híd, a walk of about 20 minutes, is named after the thirteenth-century King Béla IV's ultra-pious daughter, St Margaret. The ruins of her Dominican nunnery still stand on the island's east side not far from the remains of a Franciscan church. Margaret Island is also known as 'Rabbit Island', a reference to ancient times when this island was wooded, difficult for humans to get to, and filled (presumably) with rabbits.

In summer the island is jammed with people heading to either the Hajós Alfréd swimming pool or the Palatinus strand to swim and splash about. The Hajós pool complex includes a diving pool, an open-air pool and a children's pool. At the Palatinus, as well as at the Thermal Hotel Margitsziget, there are thermal baths fed from springs on the island. (*See also chapters* **Sport & Fitness** *and* **Baths**.)

Several relics survive from the island's time as a religious centre. On the east side are the ruins of the Dominican church and convent, where there is a shrine to St Margit herself. Further north is the Premonstratensian Chapel, orginally built in the twelfth century on an older site and reconstructed in 1930-31. North of the Dominican ruins is an array of busts and sculptures of Hungarian artists and writers, near the Open-Air Theatre and the UNESCO-protected water tower.

In the summer it's possible to hire bicycles (bring ID to leave as a deposit) or strange pedal-powered and canopied two-seater contraptions. Lazier visitors can ride in a horse-drawn buggy.

For all its central location Margaret Island feels pleasantly distant from the city. Private cars are banned and the island is the ideal place for an afternoon spent lazing about or strolling among the 10,000 trees.

"a true bit of SoHo"

OPEN: 11 AM-4PM
FRI-SAT: GARAGE PARTY
(MUSIC NIGHTS)

GIANT SCREEN:
SPORTS CHANNEL
SEPARATE BAR FOR
THE MOST SPECIAL COCKTAILS
IN THE TOWN

This place drives me crazy!

V. DISTRICT ARANY J. U. 9.
TEL.: 302-6473

MUSIC CLUB

fat 1927 mo's

SPEAKEASY

open for lunch too!

Great food, including
mouth-watering steaks,
lively atmosphere and
live music mon. – wed.
open: noon – 2 AM (and later)

Budapest V. Nyári Pál u. 11.
Tel: 267-3199

Miyako

Japanese Bar & Restaurant

Tempura! Yakitori!
Maki sushi! Ramen!
Happy Hours: 16.00 - 19.00
Drink two, Pay one!
1137 Bp., Visegrádi u. 1.
Tel: 111-3023,
Open: 9 am - 1 am

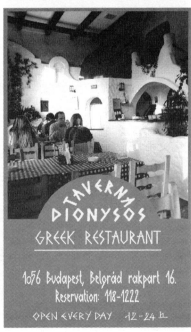

TAVERNA
DIONYSOS
GREEK RESTAURANT

1056 Budapest, Belgrád rakpart 16.
Reservation: 118-1222
OPEN EVERY DAY 12-24 h

Of cabbages and courtyards

The city's inner life – a District VI courtyard.

While Budapest's eclectic facades present a paradoxical unity to the streets, the courtyards beyond tell their own individual stories. Here, in the *udvar*, is the city's inner life.

Most of Budapest's nineteenth-century apartment houses were built, according to the common central European pattern, around these inner courtyards. Some are locked to the street, but if the door's open there's no reason not to wander inside and look. Some contain statuary or secret gardens – perhaps venerable and ivy-clad, or else charmingly makeshift with tin cans for plant pots. Some have tattered balconies with wrought-iron railings supported only with the aid of wooden scaffolding; others rise in triumphant neo-Renaissance archways, cascading towards the sky.

Drinking troughs are a common feature, dating back to the days when horses were tethered where now cars are parked. At one time each courtyard would have an old lady in one of the ground-floor flats, who'd provide coffee or simple food at one or two tables. People would go courtyard crawling: 'I hear Káti néni at number 23 cooks a fine stuffed cabbage...'

Some courtyards cut through whole city blocks, providing secret routes for those in the know. Most famous of these is the Gozsdu udvar, seven linked courtyards connecting VII. Dob utca 16 and VII. Király utca 13, but there are many smaller ones. A beautiful yard with shady chestnut trees runs between V. Sas utca 6 and V. Oktober 6 utca 5. A yard containing several small shops cuts off the corner between VII. Dohany utca and Rákoczi út.

On such busy commercial streets, most courtyards contain a business or two. You can take a coffee at the Auguszt cukrászda as you admire the neo-Renaissance courtyard at V. Kossuth Lajos utca 14-16. Similar courtyards can be found all the way along Rákoczi út (number 7 is especially stunning; 25 and 26 are also worth a peek). In parts of District VII, some courtyards seem to lead you out of the city altogether. Walk through the arched doorway of VII. Király utca 25 and it's as if you've stepped hundreds of miles to the south and into the outskirts of some blasted Balkan town.

In District VIII, in those shabby streets beyond the Nagykörút, courtyards possess an almost medieval life. Here glimpse from the streets by all means – dusty, overgrown spaces where ragged children play and old wives thrash the life out of dusty carpets – yet think twice about wandering into their world. This is Fort Apache – The Udvar.

They came, they saw, they left ruins

Although the Roman camp at Aquincum in what is today Óbuda was one of the most developed in Europe, there is little left of it today. Apart from **Aquincum Museum**, the carcasses of two amphitheatres are all that will really interest the lay visitor.

The Romans arrived here at the time of Christ. The province of Pannonia was a buffer zone protecting central Europe from unwashed heathens such as the Hungarians. Aquincum was its capital and they first set up a garrison around what is now III. Flórián tér. The military amphitheatre on the corner of III. Nagyszombat utca and III. Pacsirtamező is in need of serious weeding. The gates are open should you wish to do some. In its heyday it seated some 14,000 spectators.

Further up Pacsirtamező utca, at number 63, are the ruins of the soldiers' baths, encased in glass but closed to visitors, and at Flórián tér a few columns stand defiantly under the Szentendrei út flyover. All these ruins are in serious need of care and attention.

The civilian town developed in 2 AD further north by the HÉV stop Aquincum. This is also the site of Budapest's Hell's Angels chapter, who zoom past the bits of aqueduct still standing by the main road to Szentendre. This road now divides **Aquincum Museum** from the civilian amphitheatre opposite. This amphitheatre is more intimate and accessible, hence the litter and graffiti.

To protect the crossing point over the river in Pest, the Romans built Contra Aquincum. Its stubby remains are now part of the small park in Március 15 tér where owners let their dogs loose around the smelly stones.

By the fourth century, the Romans had left Aquincum to the Huns, the Hell's Angels, the Hungarians and their dogs.

---

from behind the far grander Ballet School on Andrássy út. It's well worth the short detour. Nine ceramic angels with gold inlaid wings carry turquoise mosaiced plaques with the letters of its name. The polished granite of its façade is punctuated by grey monkeys. Ziggurat motifs on the door, continued inside, hint at the possible Babylonian origins of his inspiration. Meticulously restored inside, it now functions as a children's theatre. Most productions are in Hungarian, but it's worth the price of a ticket simply for the interior.

Vidám Park
XIV. Állatkerti körút 14/16 (343 0996). M1 Széchenyi fürdő. **Open** *summer* 9.45am-8pm Tue-Sun; *winter* 9.45am-sunset Tue-Sun. **Admission** Free; rides Ft200-Ft500. **No credit cards.** No English spoken. **Map F1**
The old-style rides in this vintage amusement park – a beautiful Victorian merry-go-round, an assortment of ancient test-your-strength machines, 'dodzsem' cars, laughably tame ghost trains, the world's slowest big wheel and a wooden roller coaster that appears to be held together by chewing-gum and string – are gradually being replaced by more modern western rides. Though it's recently been acquired by a western company, and further modernisations are clearly imminent, the Vidám ('Fun') Park still retains an appealingly ramshackle charm. The Barlangvasút a János Vitéz – a 'cave railway' featuring cutesy dioramas from Sándor Petőfi's children's poem Kukorica Jancsi, recited over speakers as you ride through – is one defiantly Hungarian attraction. There's also an amusement park for toddlers next door. (*See also chapter* **Children**.)

Zoo
Állatkert
XIV. Állatkerti út 6-12 (343 6075). M1 Széchenyi fürdő. **Open** *summer* 9am-7pm Tue-Sun; *winter* 9am-4pm Tue-Sun. **Admission** Ft500 (donation); Ft300 adults; Ft250 students; Ft200 children. EB Ft200. **No credit cards.** No English spoken. **Map E1**
Budapest's Zoo, completed in 1911, once had buildings which placed every animal in an architectural surrounding supposedly characteristic of its place of origin. All that remains of these are Neuschloss-Knüsli's extraordinary Elephant House and Main Gate. There's also a Palm House built by the Eiffel company. The Zoo is badly in need of renovation and many of its cages and pens with their morose-looking inhabitants would not pass muster in the west. New management is beginning to tackle these urgent problems, however, and Ft110 million was recently set aside to improve the Africa House complex, giving lions, panthers, leopards and elephants a bit more room to breathe and prowl. Children can pet tame animals in the Állatsimogató (stroking zoo), only open in the summer. (*See also chapter* **Children**.)

Farther Flung

Caves

Budapest's caves are unique because they were formed by hot thermal waters underground, rather than by cold rainwater from above. This created unusual rock formations rather than gigantic dripstone columns or cave chambers. Szemlő-hegy and Pálvölgy were only discovered this century. Both provide a cheap, refreshing afternoon's entertainment. For the Catacombs of Buda Castle, *see chapter* **Museums**.

Szemlő-hegy
II. Pusztaszeri út 35 (325 6001). Bus 29. **Open** 10am-3pm Wed-Fri; 10am-4pm Sat-Sun; tours every hour. **Admission** Ft160; Ft80 concs; EB Ft50. **No credit cards.** Some English spoken.
Szemlőhegyi Cave is one of rare beauty, formed by thermal waters. Its entrance was only discovered in 1930 and it was

---

*Budapest's **Zoo** – extraordinary architecture, same old animals.*

Potholing made easy – **Pálvölgy**.

opened to the public 56 years later. Although the tour is short, some 2km covered in 25 minutes, the weird and bulbous mineral formations spark the imagination. The air is clear and clean; Szemlő-hegy is an underground therapy centre for those suffering from respiratory illnesses. The hourly guided tours are in Hungarian or German, but an English tour can be booked in advance. At the entrance you'll find a café and a modest exhibition room.

Pálvölgy

II. Szépvölgyi út 162 (325 9505). Bus 65, 65A. **Open** 10am-4pm Wed-Sun; tours every hour. **Admission** Ft160; Ft80 concs; EB Ft50. **No credit cards.** Some English spoken.
Just a ten-minute walk from Szemlő-hegy, Pálvölgy is the only Buda cave that evokes the sense of awe and curiosity that drove explorers underground in the early part of the twentieth century, when these caverns were discovered. A sign warns three groups against entering: children under four and the physically and alcoholically challenged, so don't visit the bar by the entrance until after you've negotiated the 600-odd steps, steep climbs and low-hanging rock formations. This is the longest, most impressive cave in the Buda hills and potholers uncover new sections every year. Hourly guided tours last 30 minutes; English-speaking tours by appointment.

Cemeteries

Farkasréti Cemetery

Farkasréti temető
XI. Némedvölgyi 99 (166 5833). Tram 59 from Moszkva tér/bus 8, 8A, 53. **Open** 7am-9pm Mon-Fri; 9am-5pm Sat, Sun. **Admittance** free. No English spoken.
Tucked away in the hills of District XI, it's here you'll find

one of the most outstanding works of Imre Makovecz – the mortuary chapel (1975). Giant wings of the souls of the dead open to lead you inside the wooden-ribbed oesophagus of a mythical beast. Be discreet on entering as the chapel is in pretty much constant use. In the cemetery itself you'll find the grave of Béla Bartók and lots of intriguing winged wooden grave markers. Look out for inscriptions in an ancient runic Székely alphabet. Detailed maps of the cemetery's 'residents' can be picked up from the information building to the left of the main gate.

Kerepesi Cemetery

Kerepesi temető
VIII. Fiumei út 14 (333 9125). M2 Keleti/tram 23, 24, 28. **Open** 7am-8pm daily. **Admission** free. No English spoken. **Map F4**
Declared a 'decorative' cemetery in 1885, Kerepesi is where you'll find the names behind the streets. Politicians, poets, novelists, singers and industrialists, chosen by governments to represent the way they wanted their eras remembered. Street names might change, but corpses are not disinterred, giving you a comprehensive overview of the Hungarian establishment of the last 100 years. Monumentally planned, it's a popular place for a stroll. Wide leafy avenues direct you towards strategic mausoleums – romantic novelist Mór Jókai and arch-compromiser Ferenc Deák, bourgeois revolutionary Lajos Kossuth and that other nationalist favourite, Count Lajos Batthyány. Nearby, music hall chanteuse Lujza Blaha is tucked up in a four-poster bed, serenaded by adoring cherubs. Toeing the party line in death as in life, the regimented black granite gravestones of communist cadres carry identical gold stars, while the totalitarian proportioned Worker's Pantheon has its own special gate on to Fiumei út. Anarchist poet Attila József, thrown out of the 1930s Communist party but rehabilitated during the 1950s, was buried here more than 20 years after his suicide. Styles of burial have changed over the years. Thousands mourned the first prime minister of post-Communist democracy, József Antall, in a candle-lit vigil, yet his grave is marked by a simple cross.

Újköztemető Cemetery

X. Kozma utca 8-10 (260 5549). Tram 28, 37. **Open** dawn-dusk, hours vary depending on season; always open *Aug-Apr* 7.30am-5pm, *May-July* 7am-8pm, daily. **Admission** fee only for cars. No English spoken.
It's surprisingly lively for a place of the dead. The main entrance bustles with old women selling flowers and the gravestones are packed in close. People visit to see the final resting place of Imre Nagy, the prime minister who defied the Soviets in 1956. You'll find him in Plot 301, with 260 others executed for their part in the Uprising, in the farthest corner of the big map to the right of the entrance. Empty coach parks, a traffic barrier and police guard let you know you've arrived. Transylvanian markers outline the mass grave behind a Székely gate proclaiming a 'National Pantheon'.

Housing Estates

Napraforgó utca experimental housing estate

Napraforgó utcai Mintatelep
II. Napraforgó utca 1-22. Tram 56/bus 5.
Built in 1931, the 22 houses on this fascinating street exemplify different styles of the modern movement. Modelled on the Deutsche Werkbund's Weißenhofsiedlung in Stuttgart and sponsored by Budapest's Municipal Council, it was intended to demonstrate the possibilities of combining industrial production methods with traditional craftsmanship. Key movers of the estate were Lajos Kozma and KR Kertész. Kozma, who had worked with Béla Lajta on the Rózsavölgyi House (*see chapter* **Architecture**), designed

numbers 5, 6 and 8, complete with portholes and rounded balconies. Kertész's villas are the most didactic. While the brick detailing and ceramic icons of number 9 exude a folksy traditionalism, the smooth white planes of number 11 celebrate the machine aesthetic of the avant garde. But Napraforgó's charm is that this is not presented as 'great' architecture. These are people's homes.

Wekerle Housing Estate

Wekerle lakótelep
XIX. Kispest. M3 Határ út/bus 48, 99.
Like a rustic Transylvanian version of an English garden suburb, the Wekerle (1910-14) started life as the Kispest Worker and Clerk Settlement and is still mainly working class. The architects, Fiatal Csoport (the 'Young Ones'), strove to improve the national standard of proletarian and peasant housing. A sense of unreality pervades the estate. Bicycling old ladies career down ash-lined lanes. Snack bars are run from garages, but there are few shops. The estate has its own kindergartens, schools and police station. Kós Károly tér, surrounded by apartment blocks, is the centrepiece. Pitched roofs tower over long thin windows and wooden balconies. The wooden arch over the junction of Hungária út and the square have recently been restored. There's a cinema and a bar, but the Catholic church takes central place. The residents' association at number 10 has a noticeboard displaying the millions of forints you now need to buy a Wekerle flat. Architectural romanticism is fashionable again.

Farkasréti Cemetery, *see page 70.*

Bullet holes and battle scars

Budapest has seen more than its share of violent conflict. Over the centuries marauding foreign armies have seen fit to practise a severe form of urban planning in Budapest. They would flatten it. Buda Castle, for instance, has been burned 86 times since it was erected in the 13th century.

The events which have most marked the face of the modern city are World War II and the uprising of 1956. Although today it is often hard to match which war fits which mortar shell damage or bullethole, it pays to keep one's eyes open to the historical witness of certain neighbourhoods and squares.

The World War II battle between the Soviet Red Army and the Wehrmacht involved months of house-to-house fighting that pulverized the city. The fighting in Pest was particularly heavy near Keleti train station and the nearby race track, which the Nazis had converted into an air field. Bullet- and shell-scarred buildings are still typical in the poverty belt of District VIII.

The Soviet assault on the Nazi strongholds in Buda was among the most horrific battles. The shell of the one time War Ministry in Disz tér still stands unreconstructed to give an idea of the extent of damage. The urban spaces around Deli station and Moszkva tér owe their wide-open vistas to the devastating damage of 1945.

A decade after the war, Hungarians again saw their city afire in the 1956 rebellion against the Russians. In the opening days of the conflict, Kossuth tér and the gardens around the Hungarian Radio building by Kálvin tér were the scenes of bloody fighting. A giant bronze statue of Stalin was torn down at Heroes' Square – the hand is now in the National Museum, preserved by someone in a flower garden until 1989. Some of the stiffest resistance occurred at the corner of Üllői út and the Nagykörút in Pest, where the rebel Hungarian Army's Killian barracks were pounded by Soviet artillery. Nearby rebels made forays from the fortress-like Korvin köz, now the site of a multiplex cinema. There's a modest commemorative plaque on the front of the building that is still regularly draped with fresh wreaths and flowers.

After the rebellion had been crushed, the city set itself to rebuild again. While walking the city, look at the outlines of the roofs of buildings. One can often see where the bomb damage was repaired, and a single concrete modern building set amid older homes is a dead giveaway that the former house was bombed. Today many of the scars, particularly along main streets, have been repaired while commemorative wreaths bear witness to the past. But bullet scars remain in profusion, a mute scream of twentieth century history.

Museums

Major institutions are catching on to the post-communist tourist boom, slowly overcoming money problems, and enlivening exhibitions to make them less musty and more must-see.

National Museum – *following the Grecian idiom of the British prototype. See page 74.*

Money is still the problem with Budapest's museums. The city has now managed to get itself on the international circuit and places like the **National Gallery** have pulled off shows like Picasso Sculpture or Baroque Art from Colombia. Yet so often paintings are badly lit and in bad condition. The **Fine Arts Museum**, for example, which houses a magnificent Spanish collection, is dingily lit and in some wings even electricity is scarce. Many museums have vast amounts of space they're unwilling to utilise, preferring to keep things in the basement. Or they use spaces without publicising them, so you wander through a museum and miss half of its treasures. Many exhibits are crammed into dim, musty rooms while historical displays tend to ignore most of the twentieth century and Jewish and Gypsy participation in Hungarian society.

However, the idea of interactive shows has finally got to Hungary with the **Palace of Wonders** and the **Natural History Museum** trying to provide interesting hands-on displays. Things are also looking up for the major institutions. The **National Museum** and **Budapest History Museum** have recently been restored, reorganised and expanded. Others, such as the **Ethnographic**, **Applied Arts**, **György Ráth**, **Kiscelli** and **Music History** museums offer excellent permanent displays despite other shortcomings. Even the blandest have important or amusing highlights. The socialist-era desire to promote working-class occupations and culture has resulted in some exhibits you'd probably never find outside the former Eastern bloc (though maybe you would not want to).

Take a look at the buildings the museums are housed in before you enter: the National Gallery is in the old Royal Palace; the Applied Arts Museum was designed by the Art Nouveau master Ödön Lechner; the Ethnographic Museum is in a magnificent pile originally intended for the Supreme Court while the Kiscelli Museum is housed in a Baroque monastery.

English-language booklets and captions have come on a lot in recent years so that if you visit the bigger institutions you should be able to find your way round without much trouble. Temporary exhibitions and small museums, however, rarely provide adequate English translations, if any at all. Where indicated below, there's an English booklet (EB) available – an Ft80 booklet, for example, is noted as EB Ft80. Most are an inexpensive investment, given how low museum admission prices usually are in Budapest. For the exceedingly penurious, the large institutions often have one free day a week.

Opening times are typically 10am-6pm from Tuesday to Sunday, with last tickets given out 30-45 minutes before closing. Almost all (notable exceptions being the Budapest History Museum, the Jewish Museum and Statue Park) are closed Mondays. Between November and March, most close an hour or two earlier than indicated below, and some small museums shut entirely for the winter, as well as in July or August. Art and music are frequently combined, with concerts held in the grander buildings or, of course, other music-related museums – especially during the spring and autumn festivals and in the summer.

The *Budapest Week* and *Budapest Sun* list concerts and temporary exhibitions. Where listed, credit cards can be used for entry and purchasing books and souvenirs.

National Institutions

Museum of Applied Arts

Iparművészeti Múzeum

IX. Üllői út 33-37 (217 5222). M3 Ferenc körút/tram 4, 6. **Open** 10am-6pm Tue-Sun. **Admission** Ft120; Ft30 concs; free Tue. No English spoken. **Map D5**

Established in 1872 to showcase Hungarian art objects and furnishings which had won acclaim at international expositions, it found its permanent home in this magnificent Ödön Lechner-designed building opened at the 1896 Millennium. The permanent exhibition of furniture and objets d'art, 'Style Periods of the Applied Arts in Europe', is clearly explained in English with much historical context. A far-sighted purchasing policy at the Paris Exhibition in 1900 meant the Applied Arts Museum was well furbished with Secession, Jugendstil and Art Nouveau pieces right from the outset of the style. An exhibition entitled 'Secession, the Dawn of the twentieth century' which runs until the end of the century includes Viennese furniture, Tiffany glass and Morris wall hangings as well as Hungarian *objets d'art* such as glass by the famous Miksa Róth and tiles by the great Zsolnay factory in Pécs which cover the building inside and out. Other important items are collecting dust in the back – few visitors find out about the Fabergé eggs, Tiffany glass and Lalique crystal in a back room near the staircase.

Museum of Ethnography

Néprajzi Múzeum

V. Kossuth Lajos tér 12 (332 6340). M2 Kossuth tér/tram 2. **Open** 10am-6pm Tue-Sun. **Admission** Ft220; Ft100 concs; free Tue. Call to arrange guided tour in English, Ft3,000 for parties up to five. EB Ft180. No English spoken. **Map C4**

Despite its poor planning and unwillingness to rotate an enormous collection (too much of which languishes in the basement), this extremely worthwhile museum offers a comprehensive illustration of Hungarian village and farm life, folk customs and gorgeous folk art. Each display is accompanied by a good English text, rendering the rented cassette from the front desk unnecessary. The exhibition starts one flight up on the left with regional folk costumes. A 1909 map gives a colour-coded breakdown of the many ethnic minorities in the region. The museum also usually has two or three temporary photo exhibitions on at a time – recent topics included contemporary Israeli photography, Norwegian folk art and Nomads and city dwellers. It also usually hosts the World Press Photo exhibition every March, and holds fairs at Christmas and Easter inviting folk groups from all over the region to sell their wares, do dance displays and perform mystery plays – so, very much a place that looks at the folk tradition as a living one. The building is anything but folky, though – a monumental, gilt-columned edifice with ceiling frescoes by Károly Lotz, constructed in 1893-96 to serve as the Supreme Court, though it never did. The management appears to do as much catering as curating – on many days you'll find the centre hall set up for banquets.

Museum of Fine Arts

Szépművészeti Múzeum

XIV. Hősök tere (343 9759). M1 Hősök tere. **Open** 10am-5.30pm Tue-Sun. **Admission** Ft200; Ft100 concs. English tours (Ft1,500 for up to five people) can be arranged on the spot in summer, otherwise contact Zoltán Bartos on ext 137. Some English spoken. **Map E1**

While the National Gallery is Hungary's chief venue for Hungarian art, the country's major display of European art is here. Unfortunately, lack of funds means galleries are poorly lit and some wings are in dire need of repair. However, it has recently reorganised its magnificent Spanish collection, putting all El Greco and his school into one place along with the Madrid School and Southern Spanish Art, thus doing justice to the best Spanish collection outside Spain. The basics of this were acquired by the Esterházy family in 1818, who later added Goyas and Riberas. Other highlights include an excellent Venetian collection (particularly Titian and Giorgione), a beautiful Durer, several Breughels, and a doubtful but beautiful Raphael and some Leonardos. The vast collection of drawings and graphics from the Renaissance to the present is generally rotated in small, temporary exhibits. The museum also stages major temporary exhibitions in the grand, eclectic halls leading from the entrance.

Hungarian National Gallery

Magyar Nemzeti Galéria

I. Buda Palace, Wings B, C, E (175 7533 ext 423). Várbusz from M2 Moszkva tér/bus 16. **Open** Apr-Oct 10am-6pm Tue-Sun; Nov-Mar 10am-4pm. **Admission** Ft150; Ft40 concs; guided tour Ft2,000 up to five people. Some English spoken. **Map B4**

This vast museum's purpose is to chronicle art by Hungarians since the founding of the state, and requires more than one visit to take in all of the permanent exhibits of paintings, sculptures, ecclesiastical art, medallions and graphics. The two collections considered most important are its fifteenth/sixteenth-century winged altarpieces (so-called because of their ornately carved pinnacles which create a light, soaring effect); and its mid-nineteenth- to early twentieth-century art. Most of the work here is derivative of major European art movements such as Classicism, Impressionism, Fauvism and Art Nouveau. There are depictions of Hungarian history by Viktor Madarász and lively sculptures of Hungarian peasants by Miklós Izsó. Also worth seeing are the works of impressionist József Rippl-Rónai, Hungary's answer to Whistler (he even painted his mother), and if you go to the upper galleries there are some great early twentieth-century painters such as the symbolists Lajos Gulácsy and János Vaszary, the mad, self-taught genius Tivadar Kosza Csontváry and the tragic figure of István Farkas who as a Jew was murdered at the end of the war. The Gallery, along with the Museum of Fine Arts (devoted to non-

Hungarian works) also hosts important temporary exhibitions. For a separate, Ft50 entrance fee, one can enter (with a guide only) the Palatine Crypt beneath the museum, built in 1715 as part of the Habsburg reconstruction of the palace.

National Museum

Nemzeti Múzeum

VIII. Múzeum körút 14-16 (138 2122). M3 Kálvin tér/tram 47, 49. **Open** 10am-6pm, *winter* 10am-5pm, Tues-Sun. **Admission** Ft250; Ft100 concs; guided tour in English, Ft2,000 for parties up to five. Some English spoken. **Map D4**

The oldest museum in Budapest (and the fourth such to be built anywhere at all – Mihály Pollack's design followed the Grecian idiom of the British Museum) was also the site of the reading of Petőfi's 'National Song' on 15 March 1848, which heralded the start of the revolt against Habsburg rule. The two permanent exhibitions are the History of Hungary from the establishment of the state up to the nineteenth century, and the History of Hungary in the twentieth century. The former takes in the sainted King Stephen, crowned the first king of Hungary in 1000, (his crown and coronation robes are on display – *see also page 22* **Two bent half-crowns**). It continues through the Ottoman occupation in the sixteenth century, the revolution of 1848 and the Magyar millennium in 1896, with jewels, armour, flags, documents, old photographs and paintings. The twentieth-century part begins with the collapse of the Monarchy, and continues through World War I, the 1919 revolution and the restoration of dictatorship in 1920, with contemporary propaganda, suites of furniture and shop window displays. Watch out for the wonderful posters of happy workers waving to a fat bald Rákosi (Hungary's Stalin) as he leads them forward to Socialism.

National Széchényi Library

Országos Széchényi Könyvtár

I. Buda Palace, Wing F (175 7533). Várbusz from M2 Moszkva tér/bus 16. **Admission** Ft40, Ft20 concs, for exhibits; passport required to enter library. **Open** 10am-4.30pm Mon, Tue; 10am-6pm Wed-Fri. Some English spoken. **Map B4**

The seven-storey national library houses over two million books plus even more manuscripts (as well as collections on music, theatre history, graphics, newspapers and journals), with the aim of gathering anything related to Hungary or in Hungarian published anywhere in the world. If you wish to conduct research there or just look round, bring your passport and ask for English-speaking staff who will help you with the interesting (if a bit noisy) retrieval system by which books are sent down on automated carts. The library is named after Count Ferenc Széchényi (father of the nineteenth-century reformer, István) who donated his library to the state in 1802. The institution possesses volumes (codices, or *corvina* in Hungarian) which belonged to King Mátyás – owner of one of the largest libraries in Renaissance Europe. These are rarely displayed, however. The exhibits on the first floor usually concern Hungarian and German writers, but there are occasional displays of book illustrations. The library also offers an interesting way to reach the Castle if you're coming from the west side of Castle Hill; there's an elevator (Ft10) that takes you from the bottom of the hill (near buses 78 and 5 or tram 18 in the Tabán) into the library wing of the palace.

History

Agriculture Museum

Mezőgazdasági Múzeum

XIV. Vajdahunyad Castle in Városliget (343 8573). M1 Hősök tere. **Open** 10am-5pm Tue-Sat; 10am-6pm Sun. **Admission** Ft100; Ft50 concs. EB Ft100. No English spoken. **Map F1**

Antique ploughs and the history of cattle breeding sit oddly inside the mock-Baroque wing of a fake Transylvanian

castle – built for the 1896 Magyar Millennium exhibition and the only structure to have survived. The dozen exhibits range from snoozers such as the History of Grain Production to one on the Hungarian ritual pig-killing (*see page 30* **Porky gets the chop**), but the building is definitely worth a look and the hunting hall has rows of stuffed stags and shelved antlers beneath a magnificently vaulted and painted ceiling. There are also occasionally interesting temporary exhibits on such subjects as Jews in the Hungarian countryside, or life in a medieval village. The castle is surrounded by a moat which transforms into a beautiful winter ice rink.

Aquincum Museum

Aquincumi Múzeum

III. Szentendrei út 139 (250 1650). HÉV Aquincum. **Open** *ruins (Apr-Oct)* 9am-6pm Tue-Sun; *museum* 9am-5pm Tue-Sun. **Admission** Ft100; Ft50 concs. EB Ft400. No English spoken.

Workers' housing estates and a highway dwarf the numerous Roman ruins scattered throughout Óbuda. The largest concentration is at this site, where most of Aquincum's 4,000 or so residents lived. This was the capital of Pannonia Inferior, the Roman province that covered most of what is now western Hungary. The exhibit tells of a comfortable town doing well from the garrison stationed at what is now the Árpád Bridge. Famed for its spas and good waters, unfortunately very little remains except a remarkable water organ found at the site in 1931 – the only one ever found that was complete enough to be replicated. Within the vast Flórián tér underpass, the so-called Baths Museum – ruins of Roman baths – are closed indefinitely but you can pretty much view these unexciting remnants from outside the glass enclosure. There's a small amphitheatre across the road by the HÉV station, usually open the same hours, or by request at the museum. Likewise, the Hercules Villa is out of the way on a suburban street and merely comprises what little is left of a Roman official's villa, with a few faded pieces of mosaic depicting the legendary strongman.

Hercules Villa, III. Meggyfa utca 19-21 (250 1650).

Budapest History Museum

Budapesti Történeti Múzeum

I. Buda Palace, Wing E (155 8849). Várbus from M2 Moszkva tér/bus 16. 10am-6pm Mon, Wed-Sun. **Admission** Ft100; Ft50 concs; free Wed. Some English spoken. **Map B4**

The main exhibit on Budapest starts from the earliest tribal settlements, with lots of interesting artifacts, photos of excavations and good descriptions in English. Recently renovated, the museum has made great efforts to present the city in an interesting historical light. Budapest in Modern Times, for example, tracks over its identity as a big urban centre, a metropolis that prompted even the lethargic Habsburgs into making it their royal seat. The display focuses on certain key symbols of the city: Charles of Lothringen's triumphal Arch to celebrate the defeat of the Ottomans; the Danube as the element that both divides and unites Budapest; the 1 May 1919 red drapes which represent the socialist idea; and contemporary urban sites including the hotels and bank centres of József Finta contrasted with Imre Makovecz's organic villas and yurt houses (*see chapter* **Architecture**). A dark room is full of ghoulish Gothic statues pre-dating King Mátyás' unearthed at the castle. The lower levels are partially reconstructed remains of his palace, including a vaulted chapel and music room. The upper floor houses temporary exhibits, usually on other historical topics. A museum to see if you are interested in the city and urban life.

Catacombs & Wax Museum

Panoptikum

I. Úri utca 9 (212 0207). Várbusz from M2 Moszkva tér/bus 16. **Open** 9.30am-8pm Tue-Sun; closed Dec-Jan. **Admission** Ft600; Ft400 concs. EB free. **Credit** AmEx, DC, JCB, MC, V. English spoken. **Map B3**.

The worst – and most expensive – exhibit in Budapest unfortunately offers the only way into Castle Hill's 10km network of underground caves and man-made passageways (*see also* *chapter* **Sightseeing**). This poor excuse for a museum, for which there are mandatory tours in bad English every 15 minutes, offers mouldy, sloppy wax figures of medieval Hungarian historical figures and a few torture instruments.

Museum of Military History

Hadtörténeti Múzeum
I. Tóth Árpád sétány 40 (156 9522). Várbusz from M2 Moszkva tér. **Open** 10am-5pm Tue-Sat; 10am-6pm Sun. **Admission** Ft100; Ft50 concs; free Sat; Ft500 guided tour. Some English spoken. **Map A3**
Permanent displays in this former eighteenth-century Castle District barracks include the 'History of Hand Weapons' from the stone axe to the pistol and 'Thirteen Days' – a look at the street-fighting of the 1956 revolution. Recent exhibitions have looked at Hussars, toy soldiers, fighting techniques of the eighteenth century, and other martial excitements.

Óbuda Local History Exhibit

Óbudai Helytörténeti Gyűjtemény
Zichy Mansion, III. Fő tér 1 (250 1020). HÉV Árpád híd. **Open** 2-6pm Tue-Fri; 10am-6pm Sat, Sun. **Admission** Ft50; Ft25 concs. No English spoken.
A single corridor of the mansion displays old photos and artifacts on Óbuda, plus rooms set up in Secession and Sváb (ethnic German) styles, and a delightful room full of toys, including a Herend tea service for dolls.

Semmelweis Museum of Medical History

Semmelweis Orvostörténeti Múzeum
I. Apród utca 1-3 (175 3533). Tram 18. **Open** 10.30am-5.30pm Tue-Sun. **Admission** Ft80; Ft40 concs; EB Ft600; Ft500 guided tour in English. Some English spoken. **Map B4**
Known as the 'saviour of mothers', Dr Ignác Semmelweis (1818-63) discovered the cure for puerperal fever, blood poisoning contracted during childbirth. He was born in this building and it displays his possessions, but more interesting is the exhibit on the history of medicine. The items, from all over the world, include a medieval chastity belt, eighteenth-century beeswax anatomical models and a portrait of Hungary's first female doctor, Vilma Hugonai. Another room contains the 1786 Holy Ghost Pharmacy transported whole from Király utca.

Statue Park

Szobor Park
XXII. Balatoni út (227 7446). Yellow bus for Érd from Kosztolányi Dezső tér/tram 49. **Open** *May-Sept* 8am-8pm, *Oct-Feb* 10am-dusk, daily. **Admission** Ft100; Ft80 concs; EB Ft400. Some English spoken.
One of Europe's most unique museums is a dumping ground on the south-west edge of the city for the politically undesirable monuments of the Communist era. The outdoor museum was opened in 1993 after the 42 works were removed from prominent positions in the city. The latest acquisition is the statue of Vladimir Illich Lenin that used to stand outside the gates of the Ironworks on Csepel Island (*see chapter* **By Area**) and now joins comrades Marx, Engels and Béla Kun. Lenin raises his right hand, which once pointed towards the factory as if to usher the workforce in; legend has it he was once offered bread and dripping by grateful proletarians on their way through the gates. Most of the statues are in blocky socialist-realist form, and some are quite massive – such as a terrifying sailor modelled on a call-to-arms poster by the 1919 Communist government, or the Soviet soldier that used to guard the Liberation Monument. With your ticket you'll get a sheet outlining the statues' layout, date, artist and former location, but for further information you'll need to purchase the Ft400 catalogue. The ticket booth also sells commie kitsch and drinks such as the 'Molotov cocktail'.

Arts

Ferenc Hopp Museum of Eastern Asiatic Arts

Kelet-Ázsia Művészeti Múzeuma
VI. Andrássy út 103 (322 8476). M1 Bajza utca. **Open** 10am-6pm Tue-Sun. **Admission** Ft80; Ft20 concs; free Tue. EB Ft850. No English spoken. **Map E2**
One of two major Asian art collections in Budapest (the other is at the **György Ráth Museum** nearby), this features ancient works, including Buddhist art from China dating as far back as the tenth century; Lamaist scroll paintings; and Gandhara sculpture, third- to sixth-century Indian art influenced by ancient Greece. By the end of his life and after five trips round the world, Hopp (1833-1919), a successful businessman turned collector, had amassed over 4,000 pieces.

György Ráth Museum

VI. Városligeti fasor 12 (342 3916). Trolleybus 70, 78. 10am-5.45pm Tue-Sun. **Admission** Ft 80; Ft20 concs; free Tue. No English spoken. **Map E2**
Chinese and Japanese works make up this excellent collection in the former home of the artist and art historian who collected them. The displays are accompanied by English texts more detailed than most in Hungarian museums. Note the wonderful snuff bottles, scroll paintings and tools in the Chinese collection, and the miniature shrines, Samurai armour and finely carved lobster on a lacquer comb in the Japanese rooms upstairs. There are also temporary exhibitions from other Far Eastern countries.

Kiscelli Museum

III. Kiscelli utca 108 (188 7817). Tram 17 then bus 165. **Open** 10am-6pm Tue-Sun. **Admission** Ft150; Ft50 concs; free Wed; EB Ft100. Some English spoken.
This Baroque Trinitarian monastery (built 1745) atop a wooded hill in Óbuda houses an important collection of

Still life at the **Kiscelli Museum.**

Where do you find out what's happening in London ?

http://www.timeout.co.uk

Time Out

Your weekly guide to the most exciting city in the world

Hungarian art from about 1880-1990. The works, displayed upstairs, include late nineteenth- to early twentieth-century masters and paintings influenced by the Impressionists, pre-Raphaelites, Cubists and Surrealists. Among them are Rippl-Rónai's *My Parents After 40 Years of Marriage*, János Kmetty's cubist *City Park*, and works by Alajos Stróbl, Károly Ferenczy, Margit Anna and many others. There are also engravings of eighteenth- to nineteenth-century Budapest – you'll recognise the vantage point from what is now Petőfi bridgehead in Pest in a 1866 engraving by Antal Ligeti, showing the newly built Chain Bridge, the church at Kálvin tér, the Castle Hill and Citadella, and the twin domes of the Central Synagogue. Downstairs are the Golden Lion Pharmacy (formerly at Kálvin tér), old printing presses (you can print out Petőfi's 'National Song' and take it home with you), and classical statuary from early nineteenth-century Pest façades. The most atmospheric part of the complex, however, is the ruined church, its bare brick walls left intact after bombing in World War II and now transformed into a dim, ghostly gallery. These days it's often used to stage operas, fashion shows and other performances.

Zsigmond Kun Folk Art Collection

Kun Zsigmond Népművészeti Gyűjtemény
III. Fő tér 4 (no phone). HÉV Árpád híd. **Open** 2-6pm
Tue-Fri; 10am-6pm Sat, Sun. **Admission** Ft60; Ft20
concs. EB Ft30. Some English spoken.
'Zsigi bácsi' (Uncle Sigi), as the attendants affectionately refer to him, is a centenarian ethnographer who formerly lived in this eighteenth-century apartment. It now serves as a showcase for his charming collection of folk art: about 1,000 pieces from all over nineteenth- and early twentieth-century Hungary, including handpainted furniture, textiles, pottery and carvings. Particularly notable are ceramics from his hometown Mezőtúr in northern Hungary and the replica of a peasant stucco oven.

Literature

Petőfi Museum of Literature

Petőfi Irodalmi Múzeum
V. Károlyi Mihály utca 16 (117 3611). M3 Ferenciek tere.
Open *Apr-Oct* 10am-6pm Tue-Sun; *Nov-Mar* 10am-4pm
Tue-Sun. **Admission** Ft60; Ft20 concs. No English
spoken. **Map C4**
Budapest's main museum on Hungarian literature does a half-hearted job. Much of it is in any case lost on the rest of the world because of the obscure language and a hard-to-translate idiom. There's also almost nothing in English at this museum about the romanticised portraits and personal effects of Sándor Petőfi and other writers on display. Recent exhibits included the snoozeworthy 'A Hundred Years of the Hungarian Pedagogical Institute'. The building warrants some historical explanation but this too is neglected. It was the Budapest mansion of the aristocratic Károlyi family, whose most famous scion, Mihály, was born here and headed Hungary's first, but short-lived, democratic government in 1918. There used to be a memorial to him here, but this was removed (possibly because the conservative government elected in 1990 didn't like him). There are also a number of preserved apartments of other late, great and largely untranslated Hungarian writers. These, which have little English documentation, include:
Endre Ady Memorial Room (Ady Endre Emlékszoba)
V. Veres Pálné utca 4-6 (137 8563). M3 Ferenciek tere.
Open 10am-6pm Wed-Sun. **Admission** Ft60; Ft20 concs.
Mór Jókai Memorial Room (Jókai Mór
Emlékszoba) *XII. Költő utca 21 (156 2133). Bus 21.*
Open 10am-2pm Wed-Fri; 10am-4pm Sat, Sun.
Admission Ft60; Ft20 concs.
Attila József Memorial Room (József Attila
Emlékszoba) *IX. Gát utca 3 (117 3143). Tram 24.* **Open**
10am-4pm Tue-Sat; Sun 10am-3pm. **Admission** Ft60;
Ft20 concs.

Music

Béla Bartók Memorial House

Bartók Béla Emlékház
II. Csalán utca 29 (176 2100). Bus 5. **Open** 10am-5pm
Tue-Sun. **Admission** Ft100; Ft50 concs. No English
spoken.
The composer lived here with his wife and two sons from 1932 until he left an increasingly fascist Hungary in 1940. The house has some of his original furnishings and an exhibit of Bartók memorabilia, such as the folk art collection that he amassed while travelling the region to collect folk tunes. This includes photos, letters and notes and there are also paintings, graphics, sculptures and commemorative of the composer. Chamber concerts are often held here on Fridays (*see chapter* **Music: Classical & Opera**). In good weather they take place outside, by Imre Varga's Bartók statue.

Kodály Memorial Museum & Archive

Kodály Emlékmúzeum és Archivum
*VI. Andrássy út 87-89, in courtyard (322 9647). M1
Kodály körönd.* **Open** 10am-4pm Wed; 10am-6pm Thur-
Sat; 10am-2pm Sun. **Admission** Ft50; Ft30 concs. Some
English spoken. **Map E2**
This was where Zoltán Kodály lived from 1924 until his death in 1967. His library, salon and dining room were left in their original state, with an eclectic range of furnishings as well as folk art objects the composer bought while collecting songs. His bedroom displays manuscripts including parts of the *Psalmus Hungaricus* and *Buda Castle Te Deum*.

Franz Liszt Museum

Liszt Ferenc Múzeum
*VI. Vörösmarty utca 35 (322 9804 ext 16). M1
Vörösmarty utca.* **Open** 10am-6pm Mon-Fri; 9am-5pm
Sat. **Admission** Ft80; Ft30 concs; free Mon. Some
English spoken. **Map D3**
Free concerts most Saturday mornings. Liszt lived here from 1881 until his death in 1886. The three-room apartment is preserved with his furniture and other possessions, including a composing desk-cum-keyboard. Text in English.

Museum of Music History

Zenetörténeti Múzeum
*I. Táncsics Mihály utca 7 (214 6770). Várbusz from M2
Moszkva tér.* **Open** 4-8pm Mon; 10am-6pm Wed-Sun.
Admission Ft80; Ft50 concs. EB Ft20. No English
spoken. **Map A3**
Beethoven was a guest here in 1800, when it was the palace of the Erdődy family. Within are many gorgeous, seventeenth- to nineteenth-century classical and folk instruments. These vary from delicately ornamented lyres and a unique, tongue-shaped violin in the classical section, to the gardon (a crude cello), bagpipes and cowhorns in the folk section. The minimalist, orderly arrangement of the exhibit puts the beauty of the instruments in full focus. As well as temporary exhibits of musically themed contemporary art, there is also a collection of Bartók manuscripts. Summer concerts are sometimes held in the garden at the back.

Theatre

Gizi Bajor Theatre Museum

Bajor Gizi Színészmúzeum
XII. Stromfeld Aurél út 16 (156 4294). Bus 112. **Open**
2-6pm Tue-Thur; 10am-6pm Sat, Sun; closed in July and
August. **Admission** Ft50; Ft25 concs. No English spoken.
This lovely, turn-of-the-century villa was once home to theatre and film actress Gizi Bajor (1893-1951). The exhibit is devoted to actors of the Hungarian National Theatre and early cinema, with lots of old photographs and Bajor's original furnishings.

Religion

Bible Museum

Biblia Múzeum
IX. Ráday utca 28 (no phone). M3 Kálvin tér. **Open**
10am-5pm Tue-Sun. **Admission** free. EB Ft160. No
English spoken. **Map D5**
'3,000 years of the Holy Bible', mainly facsimiles, pictures
and texts in a dusty room at a Calvinist seminary, is mostly
the sort of exhibit to which reluctant Sunday school students
are dragged. There are some interesting items, though,
such as a 1534 Hebrew Bible from Basle and a 1599
12-language New Testament from Nuremberg. In the corridor are missionary Bibles in languages such as Tamil,
Khmer and Cherokee.

Ecclesiastical Art

Egyházművészeti Gyűjtemény
I. Mátyás Templom, Szentháromság tér (no phone).
M2 Moszkva tér then Várbusz/bus 16. **Open** 9am-7pm
daily. **Admission** Ft80; Ft30 concs. Some English
spoken. **Map A3**
The exhibit begins in the partially reconstructed medieval
crypt (take the stairs down from the south-east aisle of the
church), in which there's a red marble sarcophagus containing bones from the Royal Tomb of Székesfehérvár and
mediocre photos of the church taken after a 1994 terrorist
bomb. A passageway leads back up to the St Stephen chapel,
with walls showing scenes from the life of the first
Hungarian king. The chapel and gallery above contain ecclesiastical treasures, nothing remarkable since the country's
best are at Esztergom.

Jewish Museum

Zsidó Múzeum
VII. Dohány utca 2 (342 8949). M2 Astoria/tram
47, 49. **Admission** Ft400. Ft 200 concs. free for children.
Credit AmEx, DC, JCB, MC, V. **Admission Apr-Oct** 10am-3pm Mon-Fri; 10am-1pm
Sun. **Map D4**
This small museum displaying mainly eighteenth- to nineteenth-century ritual objects from central and eastern Europe, is located in a wing of the Central Synagogue complex
and on the site where Zionist leader Theodor Herzl was born.
Everything is well-documented in English, and there are
English-speaking staff and tours. The collection is arranged
in three rooms according to function: Sabbath, holidays, and
life-cycle ceremonies. The fourth room covers the Hungarian
Holocaust – one photo shows corpses piled up in front of this
same building after a massacre by Hungarian Arrow Cross
fascists. What is missing from the museum – actually, from
virtually all Hungarian museums – is any historical exhibit
on pre-war Hungarian Jewry, though there are plans to open
an archives section and create exhibits on the topic. Though
the museum was founded in 1931 when Hungarian Jews
were feeling fairly secure, many more objects were given to
the collection after their owners were murdered in the
Holocaust. In 1993, over 80 per cent of the collection was
stolen but then recovered eight months later in Bucharest.

The Lutheran Museum

Evangélikus Múzeum
V. Deák tér 4 (117 4173). M1, M2, M3 Deák tér/tram
47, 49. **Open** 10am-6pm Tue-Sun. **Admission** Ft200;
Ft50 concs. EB Ft80. Some English spoken. **Map C4**
Adjoining Budapest's main Lutheran Church, this museum
traces the history of the Reformation in Hungary. On display is a facsimile of Martin Luther's last will and testament (the church archive has the original); the first book
printed in Hungarian, a New Testament from 1541; and a
pulpit cover from 1650 with an embroidered tableau of the
12 apostles (who for some reason all have red noses) – in
Lutheran churches usually one item with graven images
was permitted. A small display commemorates Gábor
Sztehló, a pastor who rescued over 2,000 Jewish children

Jewish Museum *– where Zionism was born.*

during World War II. There's some English text but also
usually an English-speaking attendant who can better
explain the exhibits.

Trades

Museum of Commerce & Catering

Kereskedelmi és Vendéglátói Múzeum
I. Fortuna utca 4 (175 6249). Várbusz from M2
Moszkva tér. **Open** Mar 15-Sept 30 10am-6pm Tue-Sun;
Oct 1-Mar 14 10am-4pm. **Admission** Ft80; Ft30 concs.
No English spoken. **Map A3**
A fascinating small museum. The Commerce section features
a mock-up of an old grocer's shop and advertisements from
1900 through to the middle of this century, including
Hungary's first electric billboard – a low-tech affair that the
attendant will turn on for you. It advertises Buck's Beer, with
a goat leaping toward a frothy mug. A bizarre highlight is a
stuffed dog atop a His Master's Voice phonograph – which
raps its paws against the glass case. The recently added permanent exhibition 'Hospitable Budapest: Tourism and
Hospitality in the City 1873-1930' includes objects, photos
and furniture from some of Budapest's magnificent old
hotels and coffee houses plus documentation about how the
city was transforming itself from a an imperial seat to a
bustling twentieth-century metropolis throughout this period. There are only a few captions in English, but the exhibits
are colourful, visual and intriguing.

Golden Eagle Pharmaceutical Museum

Arany Sas Patikamúzeum
I. Tárnok utca 18 (175 9772). Várbusz from M2
Moszkva tér/bus 16. **Open** 10.30am-5.30pm Tue-Sun.
Admission Ft60; Ft20 concs. EB Ft600. Some English
spoken. **Map A3**

The Golden Eagle was the first pharmacy in Buda established after the expulsion of the Turks, though it was originally in nearby Disz tér and didn't move here till the mid-eighteenth century. The house, however, dates from the fifteenth century (one of the oldest in the Castle District). The museum is an eye-catching hodgepodge of Hungarian and pharmaceutical history in the Castle District – jugs and bottles from every era and part of the world, and old, handpainted Hungarian pharmacy furnishings. Highlights are an excellent reconstruction of an alchemist's laboratory; mummy powder from Transylvania (believed to cure epilepsy); and a large painting of a sweet-faced nun performing, as monks and nuns did in the Middle Ages, the duties of a chemist. The staff speak English, German or French and can show you around.

Industry

Foundry Museum

Öntödei Múzeum
II. Bem József utca 20 (201 4370). Tram 4, 6. **Open** 10am-5pm daily. **Admission** Ft90; Ft40 concs. EB Ft50. No English spoken. **Map B2**
The original building of the Ganz Foundry (1845-1964), one of the big players in Hungary's industrial revolution, displays historical exhibits on metalwork, and cast-iron products from giant tram wheels and turn-of-the-century street lamps to decorative architectural elements and a woman-shaped stove.

Milling Industry Museum

Malomipari Múzeum
IX. Soroksári út 24 (215 4118). Tram 2, 4, 6. **Open** 9am-2pm Mon-Thur (or by appointment). **Admission** free. EB free. No English spoken. **Map D6**
The museum's environs – the working class District IX – are a freeze-frame from Hungary's Communist years. There's even a quote from Karl Marx right as you enter: 'The history of machinery can be followed through the development of the flour-milling industry'. Inside are lots of nineteenth- to early

twentieth-century cylinder mills (*hengerszék*) and charming models (including a wind-operated ship mill). Be warned, though: the old *bácsi* doesn't always turn up to open the place.

Capital Sewerage Works Museum

Fővárosi Csatornázási Művek Múzeuma
II. Zsigmond tér 1-4 (188 6572). Tram 17. **Open** 10am-3pm Mon-Fri. **Admission** free. EB free. Ring bell at gate. No English spoken.
Yes, this place is for real, and even whiffs just a little bit (it's still in operation). The museum is located in a modest, rather pretty brick and stucco building (1912) full of curvy, shiny, black pumps which look like giant snails. There's also a Secession-style Siemens switchboard.

Hungarian Museum of Electrotechnics

Magyar Elektrotechnikai Múzeum
VII. Kazinczy utca 21 (322 0472). M2 Astoria/tram 47, 49. **Open** 11am-5pm Tue-Sat. **Admission** free. Some English spoken. **Map D4**
Housed in a 1930s transformer station, the outside of which looks like a set from Terry Gilliam's *Brazil*. Men in white coats demonstrate things that crackle and spark and proudly present the world's first electric motor, designed by a Hungarian Benedictine monk. There are also old household appliances and an exhibit on the electrification of the Iron Curtain. The collection of consumption meters is amusingly tedious, as are the switches throughout the ages.

Leisure

Sport & Training Museum

Testnevelési és Sportmúzeum
XIV. Dózsa György út 3 (252 1696, ask for Sport Museum). M2 Népstadion. **Open** 10am-4.30pm Sat-Thur. **Admission** 50Ft; 30Ft concs. No English spoken.
Part of the huge 'People's Stadium' sports complex. Temporary exhibits on current and past sports themes, in Hungarian only.

Still in working order and even whiffing a bit – the **Capital Sewerage Works Museum***.*

Stamp Museum

Bélyeg Múzeum
VII. Hársfa utca 47 (342 3757). M1 Vörösmarty utca.
Open 10am-6pm Tue-Sun. **Admission** Ft50; Ft30 concs.
Some English spoken. **Map D3**
Thousands of stamps from every corner of the world. Kept
in a large room above a post office, the collection resembles
a well-organised card catalogue, with 3,000 pull-out boards
of stamps organised by continent and country.

Natural History

Natural History Museum

Természettudományi Múzeum
*VII. Ludovika tér 2 (313 0842). M3 Klinikák or
Nagyvárad tér/tram 24.* **Open** 10am-6pm Mon, Wed-Sun.
Admission Ft200. Ft90 concs; free for under-8s. EB
Ft300. Some English spoken. **Map F6**
The permanent show 'Human Beings and Nature in
Hungary' looks at the geological changes in the region and
the way humans have made use of the natural resources
available. The exhibition uses graphics, photos and interactive devices as well as displays to take you over the millen-
nia. There are also temporary exhibitions; recent ones have
included: 'Mummies', expedition photos from Malaysia, min-
erals and fossils. Outside the museum is a park full of old
fossils and stones.

Public Services

Museum of Firefighting

Tűzoltó Múzeum
*X. Martinovics tér 12 (261 3586), inside fire station.
Tram 28.* **Open** 9am-4pm Tue-Sat, 9am-1pm Sun.
Admission free. EB Ft150. No English spoken.
History of firefighting in Hungary, with items and repro-
ductions from Aquincum, statues of St Florian (the patron
saint of firemen), old photos and engravings, a horse-
drawn engine from 1899, and the first motorised water-
pump, brought to Hungary from England by Széchényi's
son Ödön in 1870. There's also the original motorised dry
extinguisher invented by Hungarian Kornél Szilvay in
1928. In a still-functioning fire station, next door to an Art
Nouveau church.

Géza Kresz Emergency & Ambulance Service Museum

Kresz Géza Mentőmúzeum
V. Markó utca 22 (312 3430, ext 4179). M3 Nyugati.
Open 9am-2pm daily. **Admission** Ft50, concs free. No
English spoken. **Map C2**
Dr Kresz (1846-1901) founded Hungary's first volunteer
ambulance service in 1887. Medical rescue history here is
covered in excruciating Hungarian-only detail. Listed open-
ing hours may prove unreliable.

Postal Museum

Posta Múzeum
*VI. Andrássy út 3 (269 6838). M1, M2, M3 Deák
tér/tram 47, 49.* **Open** 10am-5.30pm Tue-Sun.
Admission Ft50; Ft30 concs. No English spoken.
Map C3
The richly frescoed and wainscoted former apartment of the
wealthy Saxlehaner family now displays all things relating
to the Hungarian postal service. The frescoes in the entrance
and stairway are by Károly Lotz, whose work also adorns
the Opera House. The second room somehow manages both
to preserve the appearance of a bourgeois home and to look
like a workaday post office. Further on are old delivery vehicles and wartime radio transmitters. The good English text
at the front desk will guide you through.

Telephone Museum

Telefónia Múzeum
*I. Uri utca 49 (212 2243). Várbusz from M2
Moszkva tér.* **Open** 10am-6pm Tue-Sun. **Admission**
Ft30; Ft10 concs. No English spoken. **Map A3**
Though touted as great for kids, you'd have to have a doc-
torate in engineering to understand the long, dry, techie text
in Hunglish (though there's an interesting page of references
to phones in Hungarian literature). It might have once been
exciting for Magyar kids, not whom didn't have phones
at home until recently (an irony since the switchboard was
invented by a Hungarian, Tivadar Puskás – many dealing
with the Budapest phone system may suspect that they're
still using his model). In any case, kids can call old-fashioned
exchanges, or dial up a bad Hungarian pop song on a c1970
phone, and there are lots of old equipment and photos.

Science

Palace of Wonders

Csodák Palotája
XIII. Váci út 19 (201 9483). M3 Lehel tér. **Open** 9am-
5pm Tue-Fri; 10am-6pm Sat-Sun. **Admission** Ft350;
Ft200 concs. Some English spoken. **Map D2**
Central Europe's first interactive science museum. Although
on nothing like the scale of London's National Science
Museum – it's on the top floor of an old warehouse building
– it does boast such wonders as a whispering mirror, a flying carpet and an independent-minded shadow. Kids can
push, pull and press to their hearts' delight as there are a host
of devices that light up, make noises and react to commands.
You can also try out a video telephone, have an adventure on
the internet, and take a short rest on a Fakir's bed.

Transport

Transport Museum

Közlekedési Múzeum
XIV. Városligeti körút 11 (343 0565). Trolleybus 72, 74.
Open 10am-5pm Tue-Fri; 10am-6pm Sat, Sun, holidays.
Admission Ft100; Ft50 students; Ft30 children; free for
under-6s. EB Ft170. No English spoken. **Map F2**
Remains of the pre-war Budapest bridges are displayed in
front of this large museum, which covers every aspect of transport in Hungary in exhaustive but Magyar-only detail.
However, guided tours in English can be arranged in advance.
Kids should enjoy the antique cars, trams, steam train and
model boats, and can try out some of the engines in the big
hall on the ground floor, but that's it for hands-on stuff. The
railroad models include a realistic miniature Hungarian countryside, with Stalinist high-rises on the town outskirts and A-
frame weekend cottages, demonstrated on the hour. The other
part of the museum, Air & Space Travel, is a five-minute walk
away, on the second floor of the Petőfi Csarnok concert hall
(open 10am-6pm Tue-Sun, closed Nov-Mar, same admission
fees). Small planes, gliders and helicopters fill two halls – the
oldest a 1921 Junkers F13 and a replica of a 1909 monoplane.
The aerospace section is dead boring.

Underground Railway Museum

Földalatti Múzeum
*Inside Deák tér metro station, near Károly körút exit. M1,
M2, M3 Deák tér/tram 47, 49.* **Open** 10am-6pm Tue-Sun.
Admission Ft60 or one transport ticket; free children.
Some English spoken. **Map C4**
If you're passing through Budapest's main metro intersection, pop in to have a look at several original carriages from
continental Europe's first underground, built in 1896. There
are plans, as yet vague, for the museum to start running 'nostalgia tours', with the original train running from Hősök tere
to Deák tér.

Art Galleries

Hungarian masters might be dead, but political repression and cultural isolation have prompted innovative, subversive work.

Despite a cultural bias against the visual, Hungary has produced some of the most innovative artists of the twentieth century. Many, such as Victor Vasarely, László Moholy-Nagy and István Kantor (Monty Cantsin) had to leave the country to gain international recognition. Others, such as Miklós Erdély and György Galántai, remained knowing that they were fated for relative obscurity and worse: ignored by the West while undermined by the Socialist regime. State repression against awkward characters continued right up until the late 1980s and several 'deviant' artists only avoided starvation through the charity of friends.

Political and cultural isolation has had a profound effect on the Hungarian art scene. Far from defeating artistic expression, the degree of repression and censorship before 1989 helped produce its own subversion. The need to get around strict regulations prohibiting the reproduction of samizdat manuscripts led many otherwise 'secular' publications to be declared artworks, encouraging the spread of mail art. Self-conscious obscurantism, for example in videos produced by Group K3/the Indigo group, enabled artists to undermine the socialist-realist documentary genre by playing games with the production of meaning. Art using communication media, particularly video and mail art, is where Hungary is now most internationally renowned. Look out for the **Artpool**-organised part of the Budapest Autumn Festival and for lectures and performances at **c3** and those organised by the **Media Research Foundation**. (*See pages 70-71* **Pushing The Envelope**.)

Hungary rarely honours its own. You'll need to visit the smaller collections and galleries to discover the vitality and humour of contemporary Hungarian art. Surrealism and constructivism are still strong. Watch out for exhibitions by El Kazovszkij (like a macabre De Chirico) and contemporary constructivist painters, such as Ákos Matzon, István Haáz and Tamás Szikora, based in Szentendre. Communist educational policies denied many artists the opportunity to study their chosen subject, but they also enabled several to develop industrial skills such as welding. Look out for Galántai's sound sculptures and János Sugár's furniture/alchemy-related works.

Antique hunters and those seeking cheaper early twentieth-century artworks should scout around the many galleries on V. Falk Miksa utca,

although the stack 'em high, price 'em low atmosphere that prevails in several is off-putting for the serious art connoisseur.

Many galleries close during July-mid August. Do ring first. Current information on temporary exhibits and performances can be found in *Pesti Est* or either of the English-language papers.

Public Galleries & Spaces

Budapest Galéria Kiállítóterem

Budapest Gallery Exhibition Space
V. Szabadsajtó út 5 (118 8097). M3 Ferenciek tere. **Open** 10am-6pm Tue-Sun. **Admission** Ft50; Ft25 children. **No credit cards**. Some English spoken. **Map C4**
Twentieth-century documentary photography, architecture and commercial graphic design as well as contemporary art are exhibited here. The Budapest galéria also runs the **Kiállítóháza** (*see below*), the **Imre Varga Collection** (*see below* **Collections**) and is responsible for the caretaking and installation of public monuments in the city.

Műcsarnok – *pillar of the establishment.*

Koller Galéria – *with the ambience of an art-lover's drawing-room. See page 67.*

Budapest Galéria Kiállítóháza

Budapest Gallery Exhibition House
III. Lajos utca 158 (188 6771).Tram 1. **Open** 10am-6pm
Tue-Sun. **Admission** Ft50; Ft25 children. **No credit
cards.** Some English spoken.
Exhibition space also housing a collection of classicist sculptures by Imre Varga's tutor Pál Pataszay.

Dorottya Galéria

V. Dorottya utca 8 (266 0223). M1 Vörösmarty tér.
Open 10am-6pm Mon-Fri, 10am-2pm Sat. **Admission**
free. **No credit cards.** Some English spoken. **Map C4**
An airy gallery linked to the **Műcsarnok** and devoted to
work that pushes the boundaries of 'art' such as set design,
installation, media art.

Ernst Múzeum

VI. Nagymező utca 8 (341 4355). M1 Opera. **Open**
10am-6pm Tue-Sun. **Admission** Ft50; Ft25 children; Tue
free. **No credit cards.** No English spoken. **Map D3**
Recognisable by its beautiful brass art nouveau doors, this
was designed as an exhibition space in a block of artists' studios commissioned by the private collector Lajos Ernst in
1912. These days it is run by the Műcsarnok and shows contemporary Hungarian avant-garde as well as smaller international exhibits of quality. Always worth a visit.

Ludwig Museum Budapest/Museum of Contemporary Art

*Wing A, Buda Palace, I. Dísz tér 17 (212 2534). Várbusz
from M2 Moszkva tér/bus 16.* **Open** 10am-6pm Tue-Sun.
Closed July, Aug. **Admission** Ft100; Ft50 children. **No
credit cards.** Some English spoken. **Map B4**
Interesting collection of eastern European painting and
sculpture, much of it dealing ironically with totalitarianism
and Communism's last days. Upstairs are pieces donated by
German businessman Peter Ludwig including a 1950s
Picasso and American pop artists Warhol, Lichtenstein and
Oldenburg. Central space often hosts travelling exhibits.

Műcsarnok

Palace of Exhibitions
XIV. Dózsa György út 37 (343 7401). M1 Hősök tere.
Open 10am-6pm Tue-Sun. **Admission** Ft200; Ft100
children. **Credit** (shop only) AmEx, DC, MC, JCB, V.
Some English spoken. **Map E2**
Budapest's largest and most prestigious contemporary exhibition and installation space also has a lively lecture and film
programme as well as occasional performances by internationally renowned artists. It also hosts art workshops for
kids on Sundays. Tours are offered and there is a library and
archive (open 10am-6pm Mon-Fri). There are no permanent
exhibits. Check current programme for details.

Vigadó Galéria

V. Vigadó tér 2 (117 6722). M1 Vörösmarty tér/tram 2.
Open 10am-6pm Tue-Sun. **Admission** free. **No credit
cards.** No English spoken. **Map C4**
Next to the concert hall of the same name, a prominent and
roomy exhibition space for members of the Hungarian
Creative Artists Assembly. The link with a state organisation lends an establishment feel to the place. Nevertheless it
has one of the most extensive programmes of exhibitions in
Budapest.

Commercial Galleries

Bolt Foto Galéria

*VIII. Leonardo da Vinci utca 40 (324 7769/fax 312
1603). M3 Klinikák.* **Open** 2pm-6pm Tue-Sat.
Admission free. **No credit cards.** English spoken.
Map E5
A contemporary photo gallery jointly owned by twenty
artists. Exhibitions change monthly. Much of the work is
experimental and in mixed media, blurring the boundaries
between painting and traditional photography. Definitely
worth the trek.

Dovin Galéria

V. Galamb utca 6 (118 3524). M1 Vörösmarty tér. **Open** noon-6pm Mon-Fri; 11am-2pm Sat. **Admission** free. **Credit** AmEx, MC, V. English spoken. **Map C4**
Established in 1993 and dealing in younger contemporary artists, including Márton Barabás, contemporary surrealist El Kazovszkij and László Révész.

Galéria 56

V. Falk Miksa utca 7 (269 2529). M3 Nyugati. **Open** noon-6pm Tue-Sat. **Admission** free . **No credit cards.** Some English spoken. **Map C2**
Leading commercial space for household-name American artists. Pop art and derivatives figure strongly – Lichtenstein, Mappelthorpe, Rauschenberg and the like. Owner Samuel Havadtöy (Yoko Ono's husband) also promotes up-and-coming Hungarian artists that catch his eye.

Gulácsy Galéria

V. Semmelweiss utca 4 (117 8245). M2 Astoria/tram 47, 49. **Open** 8.30am-4pm Tues-Fri. **Admission** free. **No credit cards.** Some English spoken. **Map D4**
Owned by a collective of 15 painters and sculptors. Representative slice of contemporary Hungarian scene.

Koller Galéria

I. Táncsics Mihály utca 5 (156 9208). Várbusz from M2 Moszkva tér/bus 16. **Open** 10am-1pm, 2pm-5pm Tue-Fri; 10am-1pm, 2pm-6pm Sat-Sun. **Admission** free. **Credit** AmEx, DC, MC, V. Some English spoken. **Map A3**
With the ambience of an art lover's drawing room, this secluded gallery (go through the courtyard and up the stairs at the end) is crowded with early twentieth-century etchings, watercolours and small sculptures of many different genres. A treat if you can get past the dragon that guards the hoard.

Mai Manó Fotógaléria

VI. Nagymező utca 20 (302 4398). M1 Opera. **Open** 2pm-6pm Mon-Fri. **No credit cards.** Some English spoken. **Map D3**
The camera-toting cherubs on the gaudy façade is a giveaway that this 1894 building originally housed a photographer's studio. The cosy exhibition space upstairs displays contemporary as well as retrospective photography; art as well as commercial work. Well-stocked general art bookshop.

Qualitás Galéria

V. Haris köz 1. 4th floor (118 4438/fax 266 3508). M3 Ferenciek tere. **Open** 11am-6pm Mon-Fri; 11am-1pm Sat; closed in July. **Admission** free. **Credit** AmEx, DC, JCB, MC, V. English spoken. **Map C4**
Loaded with cash and want to buy dead Hungarian painters? Qualitás deals in the names that fill the National Gallery – such as impressionist József Rippl-Ronai, symbolist László Mednyánszky and *plein air* painter Béla Czóbel. Do Hungary a favour: take these paintings out of the country.

Roczkov Galéria

VI. Andrássy út 1 (213 5155). M1, 2, 3 Deák tér, M1 Bajcsy-Zsilinszky ut. **Open** 2pm-6pm Mon-Fri, 11am-2pm Sat. Closed in July. **Admission** free. **No credit cards.** Some English spoken. **Map C3**
Tiny gallery in a courtyard, run by award-winning Serbian graphic artist Milorad Krstic, notorious for his hilarious 'Freudian' interpretations of current news events and his obsession with the erotic potential of the former-Yugoslavian train network. Also the occasional show by the Balkan art-anarchists Bada Dada and Dr Máriás.

Stúdió Galéria

V. Képíró utca 6 (267 2033/fax 266 6502). M3 Kálvin tér. **Open** 2pm-6pm Mon-Sat when there's a show. **Admission** free. **No credit cards.** Some English spoken. **Map D5**

Hosts some of the city's most entertaining exhibitions and performances, including the Gallery by Night events at the **Budapest Spring Festival** (*see chapter* **Budapest By Season**). Check local listings press for details.
e-mail: studio@visio.c3.hu

Vantage Galéria

V. Magyar utca 26 (137 0584). M2 Astoria/tram 47, 49. **Open** 2pm-7pm Tues-Fri. **Admission** free. **No credit cards.** English spoken. **Map D4**
Airy space devoted to the best of contemporary Hungarian photography, with art, experimental and occasionally documentary exhibitions. Originally set up in 1995 on a ship moored on the Danube near Győr, this Budapest base opened in November 1996. Works in storage also for sale.

Várfok 14 Galéria

I. Várfok utca 14 (213 5155). M2 Moszkva tér. **Open** 10am-6pm Tue-Sun. Closed in July. **Admission** free. **Credit** AmEx, MC, JCB, V. Some English spoken. **Map A3**
One of the first commercial galleries in the city, displays well-known modern artists such as El Kazovszkij, Imre Bukta and András Böröcz among others of the contemporary Hungarian avant-garde. A newer, more spacious gallery upstairs hosts individual shows.

Institutions

British Council

VI. Benczúr utca 26 (351 2037). M1 Bajza utca. **Open** Library 11am-6pm Mon-Thur; 11am-5pm Fri. Closed in August. **Admission** free. **Map E2**
The British Council has a far lower profile than other foreign cultural institutes and no exhibition space, although it is a frequent sponsor of events in the city, as well as the organiser of occasional arts festivals. Grappling with the problems associated with promoting a non-existent 'British' identity, it tends to highlight self-consciously regional culture (Scottish, Northumbrian etc). Underfunded library is a godsend for longer-term residents and English teachers.
http://www.britcoun.org

c3

Centre for Culture and Communication
I. Országház utca 9 (214 6856/fax 214 6872). Várbusz from M2 Moszkva tér/bus 16. **Open** 10am-6pm Mon-Fri; *Labs* (by appointment) 9am-9pm Mon-Thur; 9am-6pm Fri; 10am-6pm Sat-Sun. **Admission** free. English spoken. **Map A3**
Bristling with bright young things and flash computer gadgetry, this Soros-funded centre was surrounded by controversy at its foundation in 1996. Critics accused it of undermining the grassroots net access campaign while leav-

Várfok 14 – *a pillar of the avant garde.*

Top of the Ops – illusory perspectives at the **Vasarely Múzeum**. *See page 69.*

ing more traditional art media high and dry. A year on it seems to have found its feet predominantly due to the presence of video artist Kathy Rae Huffman on its board. Catch the screening of experimental videos and occasional lectures by passing media glitterati such as Victor Burgin or Stelarc.
e-mail: info@c3.hu
http://www.c3.hu

Institut Français
I. Fő utca 17 (202 1133/fax 202 1323). M2 Batthyány tér/tram 19. **Open** 9am-7pm Mon-Fri; 9am-1pm Sat. **Admission** to exhibitions free. Some English spoken. **Map B3**
George Morriose's pastel pink and green cube on the Buda embankment (*see chapter* **Architecture**) is the liveliest of the foreign cultural centres. A vibrant film and performance programme is complemented by exhibitions of modern art and photography (French and Hungarian). It also has a café and bookshop. Check listings papers for details.

Goethe Institut
VI. Andrássy út 24. (153 2233/fax 251 8755). M1 Opera. **Open** 10am-6pm Mon-Fri. **Admission** to exhibitions free. **No credit cards**. English spoken. **Map D3**
Increasingly active with a regular programme of exhibits and performances by both German and Hungarian artists. They also sponsor film retrospectives of German filmmakers at the **Örökmozgó** cinema (*see chapter* **Film**), writers' readings and the occasional concert on Margaret Island.
e-mail: goethebp@mail.matav.hu.
http://www.goethe.de

Media Research Foundation
V. Váci utca 44 (117 4462/fax 342 7918). English spoken. **Map C4**
Film, video and new media artists headed by internationally renowned sculptor and filmmaker János Sugár, once a student of Miklós Erdély. The MRF specialises in bringing theoreticians and artists together in a sometimes uncom-

fortable but always catalytic alliance. Despite lack of funds and personnel they remain at the sharper edge of European media art and hacking culture. Look out for the occasional exhibition, film festival or performance.
e-mail: sj@dial.isys.hu
http://www.isys.hu/metaforum

Instytut Polski
Polish Institute
VI. Nagymező utca 15 (131 1168). M1 Opera. **Open** 10am-4pm Mon-Fri. **Admission** to exhibitions free. Some English spoken. **Map D3**
Brings the lively Polish alternative arts scene to Budapest, as in, for example, their 1997 festival of groundbreaking experimental theatre, film and video, and legendary Polish graphic/poster art. The gallery, on the corner of Andrássy út, hosts more unconventional and adventurous exhibitions than the other state-funded institutions.

Collections

Imre Varga Exhibit
Varga Imre Állandó Kiállítás
III. Laktanya utca 7 (250 0274). HÉV Árpád híd. **Open** 10am-6pm Tue-Sun **Admission** Ft100; Ft50 children. **No credit cards**. No English spoken.
Varga was the favoured sculptor of the Kádár regime, but his talent is unquestionable. Political themes dominate the official works: nuclear apocalypse, Jewish resistance, a crop of emaciated poets and national heroes. Yet his figures are distinguished by their evident humanity and emotion. The garden houses some of his most touching portaits, those of martyred poet Miklós Radnóti and sculptor Alajos Stróbl.

Kassák Múzeum
Zichy mansion, III. Fő tér 1 (168 7021). HÉV Árpád híd. **Open** 10am-6pm Tue-Sun. **Admission** Ft50; Ft20 children. **No credit cards**. No English spoken.
Lajos Kassák (1887-1967), a poet and constructivist painter,

Anna Margit–Amos Imre Múzeum – *where lyricism partners Surrealism. See page 70.*

was the leading advocate in Hungary of all strands of the early European and Russian avant-garde through his journals *A Tett* (*Action*) and *Ma* (*Today*), on display in this tiny exhibit of his book design, publishing, poetry, painting and sculpture. The Kassák circle (including surrealist poet Tibor Déry and László Moholy-Nagy) was held together not by a style but by a belief that 'art transforms us and we become capable of transforming the world'. This disdain of propaganda brought him into sharp conflict with left governments as well as the Horthy régime who forced him briefly into exile. The gallery also hosts contemporary exhibits.

Molnár C. Pál Magángyüjtemény

XI. Ménesi út 65 (185 3637). Tram 61. **Open** *May-June* 3pm-6pm Tue-Thur; *Oct-Apr* 3pm-6pm Tue-Thur; 10am-1pm Sun. **Admission** Ft90; Ft50 children. **No credit cards.** English spoken. **Map B5**
In the former studio of graphic artist, painter and illustrator Pál C. Molnár (1894-1981) you can meet his daughter, Éva Csillag, who entertains visitors with stories about Hungary's most famous surrealist painter and graphic artist. M-C P, as he signed his paintings, was preoccupied with Christian themes and created many altar pieces. This private collection also contains many of his best-known graphic works.

Vasarely Múzeum

III. Szentélek tér 6 (188 7551/250 1523). HÉV Árpád híd. **Open** 10am-6pm Tue-Sun. **Admission** Ft50 children free. **No credit cards.** Some English spoken.
A vast exhibit that takes you through Victor Vasarely's development as an artist – from commercial graphic design as a student of Sándor Bortnyik to eventual fame in Paris as one of the founders of the Op Art movement in the late 1960s. Described by André Breton as 'the true surrealist painter', Vasarely's play with spatial disorientation and illusory perspective brims over from the many monumental canvasses. The Pécs-born artist's smaller kinetic sculptures deploy the distortion of geometry through parallel glass and the shifting forms of the moiré effect.

Szentendre

Don't be fooled by the Baroque churches and the Mediterranean ambience. There is a quiet tension, in this picturesque artists' colony town 20km north of Budapest, between the iconoclastic artistic community, the 'official' aesthetics of the state-funded galleries and the hordes which descend to coo over the naive ceramics of Margit Kovács. While you might still catch the spontaneity and spirit of the 1970s experimental scene with a performance by István ef Zámbó's Happy Dead Band, it's easy enough simply to beat the crowds by visiting the galleries, which include two run by the artists.

The original artists' colony was founded in the early 1920s as a temporary summer retreat. It became more established in the 1930s and 1940s, when surrealist and constructivist painters took up base here – trends which are still strong. After World War II, the town became the centre of the 'European School' – artists who saw links with major European art trends as the key to a healthy local artistic culture, controversial in the Rákosi era. The permanent colony was established in 1968, providing residence for 12 artists. These days about 150 artists make up the colony.

Anna Margit – Ámos Imre Múzeum

2000 Szentendre, Bogdányi utca 10 (no phone). HÉV Szentendre. **Open** 10am-4pm Tue-Sun. **Admission** Ft90; Ft50 children. **No credit cards.** Some English spoken.
Two very different personalities, lyric painter Imre Ámos and his partner surrealist Anna Margit lived together at this address before the Holocaust swallowed up Ámos in 1944.

Premonitions of death and apocalypse overshadow Ámos'-work upstairs mingling with Chagallesque symbolism of rural Jewish life. This incredibly moving exhibit also has documents from Ámos' forced labour in the Ukraine. Downstairs, Anna's naive surrealist portraits combine peasant characters with allusions to totalitarian insanity as she dealt with her grief at the loss of her husband. Anna Margit died in 1991 and is buried in the courtyard. The paintings in the museum were selected by herself before her death.

Art.éria

2000 Szentendre, Városház tér 1 (26 310 111). HÉV Szentendre. **Open** 10am-6pm Tue-Sat. **Admission** free. **Credit** AmEx, DC, MC, JCB, V. Some English spoken.
The first private gallery in Szentendre and owned by 20 artists, jointly run with the **Műhely** on Fő tér. This tiny space crammed with paintings tends to exhibit wilder art than its sister gallery, such as work by autodidacts István ef Zámbó and László fe Lugossy as well as more established artists Imre Bak, Imre Bukta, Pál Deim and András Wahorn.

Barcsay Múzeum

2000 Szentendre, Dumtsa Jenő utca 10 (no phone). HÉV Szentendre. **Open** 10am-4pm Tue-Sun. **Admission** Ft90; Ft50 children. **No credit cards.** No English spoken.
One of the larger Szentendre museums containing the constructivist works of Jenő Barcsay. Much of his inspiration was evidently drawn from the town and its buildings, such as the Klee-derivative works from around 1945 and the minimalist geometry of pieces from the late 1960s, 1970s and 1980s which have the precision of architectural plans. His use of colour is particularly striking – sombre rather than vivid, some with the richness of orthodox icons. The gallery also contains his mosaics and tapestries.

Czóbel Béla Múzeum

2000 Szentendre, Templom tér 1 (26 312 721). HÉV Szentendre. **Open** 10am-4pm Tue-Sun. **Admission** Ft90; Ft50 children. **No credit cards.** No English spoken.
One of Hungary's most prominent twentieth-century painters, Béla Czóbel (1883-1976) joined the Fauvist movement in Paris and hung out with Matisse before retreating to the artists' colony in Szentendre. Here he created his best work, such as the bikini-clad Venus of Szentendre (1968), displayed here amid romanticised scenes of markets and the rather passionless portraits of his prewar years.

Ferenczy Múzeum

2000 Szentendre, Fő tér 6 (26 310 790). HÉV Szentendre. **Open** 10am-4pm Tue-Sun. **Admission** Ft90; Ft50 children. **No credit cards.** No English spoken.
The works of the family Ferenczy are spread over four floors of one of the first museums to be opened in Szentendre. Károly Ferenczy was a founder of the Nagybánya colony of Impressionists. His wife Olga Fialka was an established Wiener Biedermeier painter. His eldest son Valér was only a mediocre talent, but the twins Béni (a sculptor) and Noémi Ferenczy (who created symbolist gobelin works) both earned a reputation as exalted as their father's. Noémi's dabbling in theosophy is revealed in her use of allegory.

Pushing the Envelope

Mail art, video, performance, installation, fax and xerox: their popularity with artists rests on their potential to break the boundaries of establishment art. In Budapest, the iconoclasm of this tradition was tied to the struggle for an autonomous culture, and thus acquired an edge it lacked elsewhere. Regarded with paranoia during the Kádár era and historically shunned by mainstream gallery culture, these days intermedia events and exhibitions continue to flourish at the **Műcsarnok** and smaller institutions such as the **Liget**, **Bartók 32** and **c3**.

Miklós Erdély (1928-1986), probably the most influential fine artist of the Hungarian post-war generation, was the key pioneer. From his retrospectively titled 'Unguarded Money' – a 1956 action collecting money for families of those killed in the uprising – he began reusing accidentally found celluloid in cinematic montage. His filmmaking and photography won him the most renown, but he was also a poet, performance artist, playwright and painter. His work is preoccupied with repetition and similarity, and with a symbolic use of unusual materials (bitumen, goose fat, snow, carbon paper) which has been compared to that of Joseph Beuys. The archive of his videos, writing and recordings of performances and lectures is at Artpool.

A Neoist – milking it in Budapest.

Kmetty János Múzeum

*2000 Szentendre, Fő tér 21 (26 310 790). HÉV
Szentendre.* **Open** 10am-4pm Tue-Sun. **Admission**
Ft90; Ft50 children. **No credit cards.** No English
spoken.

Cubist János Kmetty (1889-1975), a member of the Kassák
circle, studied in Paris and worked in Szentendre from 1930
onwards. Among the many Cezanne-inspired still lifes are
frequent self-portraits revealing a suspicious weasel-like
man glaring out of the canvases. Experimentation with
stained glass led to self-conscious angularity in his painting,
enhancing this aggressiveness towards the viewer. A rather
disturbing collection.

Kovács Margit Múzeum

*2000 Szentendre, Vastagh György utca 1 (26 310 790).
HÉV Szentendre.* **Open** *summer* 10am-4pm Mon; 10am-
6pm Tue-Sun. **Admission** Ft250; Ft150 children. Shop.
No credit cards. English spoken.

Margit Kovács (1902-77) was probably the most popular
Hungarian 'sculptor' (really, a ceramicist) ever. In the low-
est-common-denominator aesthetics that dominated Kadár-
era officially approved art, Kovács was queen. To be fair, her
work is not entirely kitsch. There are certain votive aspects
to her ceramics, more reminiscent of Etruscan or Persian religious mythology than Hungarian folktales. Her later work
reveals her fear of death as she battled with cancer. In an
eighteenth-century house behind Fő tér – overpriced, overcrowded and almost certainly not worth the effort if you're
pushed for time.

Műhely Galéria

*2000 Szentendre, Fő tér 20 (26 310 139). HÉV
Szentendre.* **Open** 10am-6pm Mon-Sat. **Admission** free.
Credit AmEx, DC, MC, JCB, V. English spoken.

Twenty-five contemporary artists based in Szentendre own
this friendly gallery, run in conjunction with the Art.éria up
the road. Many different styles are represented although constructivist and surrealist painters are the strongest. Look out
for work by Ákos Matzon, István Haaz, Tamás Szikora. If
you want to pick up a painting by Margit Anna or Béla
Czóbel this is also the place to do it.

Vajda Lajos Múzeum

*2000 Szentendre Hunyadi utca 1 (no phone). HÉV
Szentendre.* **Open** 10am-4pm Tue-Sun. **Admission** Ft90;
Ft50 children. **No credit cards.** Some English spoken.

The montages and surrealist paintings of Lajos Vajda, a
member of the Kassák circle, while not as apocalyptic as that
of Imre Ámos, are a powerful commentary on looming disaster as World War II approached. Like Ámos, Vajda died
in the Holocaust. While his montages comment on current
political events in much the same way as did those of John
Heartfield, his paintings are the most disturbing: vegetation
twisted with violent energy into a war dynamic. Gentler are
his city scenes with their disorientating multiple perspectives. Downstairs is another gallery with other Szentendre-
based surrealist painters. Look out for Endre Bálint's ghostly
village scenes such as 'The shop window of an undertak-
er'(1970) and geometric dancing insects of 'The wedding of
the cricket' by Dezső Korniss (1948).

Sculptor and mail artist György Galántai was
another pivotal figure in the Kádár-era opposition and often worked with Erdély. With his
partner Júlia Klaniczay, Galántai published the
samizdat *Artpool Letter*. The Artpool archive,
founded in 1979, and illegal though largely tolerated until 1989, holds extensive archives of
underground art, music and literature from the
1960s to 1989 and probably the most extensive
mail-art collection in the world.

Other Hungarian mail-art 'groups' include
Xertox headed by Robert Swiekievicz, one of the
most significant Fluxus artists in Hungary,
Szolnok-based Inconnu and the mysterious
International Parallel Union of Telecommunications ('Neo-Socialist Realist Catabasis-diagnos-
tic around the clock by appointment only').

The Árnyékkötők group have been working
with fax and xerox since 1989. You can find their
magazine at the Írók Boltja bookshop (*see*
chapter **Shopping & Services**) and their
Black-Black Galéria in a semi-derelict
District IX basement. Gyula Máté uses wire-
brushed toner to create works with a textured
formalism of fine art quality. Photocopiers turn
out to be a surprisingly versatile medium –
Zsusza Dárdai uses them to unveil hidden connections between human aura and electricity.

These days the subversion has turned on the
avant-garde itself. Ottó Mészáros recently created artworks out of smashed eggs at the Black-
Black Galéria, while the flaming steam irons and
coat hanger cult parties of István Kántor (Monty
Cantsin) and his Neoist shock troops bamboo-
zled Budapest in the summer of 1997. Confusion
and cacophony also reign at performances of
István ef Zámbó's Happy Dead Band and
Serbian art-anarchists BadaDada and Dr Mariás.

Artpool Art Research Center

*VI. Liszt Ferenc tér 10 (268 0114/fax321 0833). M1
Oktogon/tram 4, 6.* **Open** 2pm-6pm Wed, Fri. Closed
July-August. **Admission** free. Shop. **Map D3**
e-mail: artpool@artpool.hu

Bartók 32 Galéria

*XI. Bartók Béla út 32 (186 9038). Tram 18, 19, 47,
49/bus 7.* **Open** 2pm-6pm Tue-Sun. **Admission** free.
Map C6

Liget Galéria

XIV. Ajtósi Dürer sor 5 (253 3373). Bus 30, 74, 75.
Open 2pm-6pm Tue-Sun. **Admission** free. **Map F2**

Black-Black Galéria

IX. Balázs Béla utca 20 (280 1113). M3 Klinikák.
Open for specific performances and exhibitions.
Admission fee depends on events. Check listings
papers for details. **Map E6**
e-mail: zservin@figyelo.hu

GRAND CASINO

BUDAPEST

1052 Deák Ferenc u. 13.
Open: 14:00 - 05:00

Slots

Stud Poker

American Roulette

Punto Banco

Black Jack

Craps

RESTAURANT
Open:
19:00 - 01:30
Tel/Fax: 118-9929
Next to Hotel Kempinski

By Area

By Area

Pest is flat, Buda is hilly, and the Danube is never blue.

In **Clark Ádám tér**, near the funicular that leads up to the **Castle District**, stands a thing like a giant, elongated doughnut. This is the Zero Kilometre Stone, the point from which all distances to Budapest are measured and thus the official centre of town. And centre it is, between the Danube, central Europe's main waterway, and the Castle District, the rocky promontory that throughout history offered a controlling vantage over the river – together the main reason why there was ever a settlement here in the first place. From this square the Chain Bridge stretches over the Danube into Pest. Completed in 1849, it was the first permanent crossing over the river (before that were only rickety pontoon bridges in summer, occasional ferries or perilous treks across thin ice in winter). It was this bridge that allowed the subsequent incorporation of Buda, Pest and Óbuda into one single city in 1872. Other routes from here prod north and south along the Danube, while the tunnel conveys traffic beneath Castle Hill and into Buda beyond.

The Danube sweeps by strong and wide, though here it is at its narrowest and currents are relatively weak. The river, too, is one area of Budapest – the only city on the river's long course between Black Forest and Black Sea where the Danube flows straight through the middle. There are quiet parks on its Margaret and Óbuda islands. Spectacular views from its bridges – upstream from Szabadság híd or downstream from Margaret híd – form part of the urban landscape, even though the waterfront is sadly underused once away from the stretch with all the major hotels.

Always present in the panorama from the Buda Hills, the Danube asserts itself even when out of sight. Come down one of the Pest streets leading to the embankment and the light changes as you approach the river, a result of reflection off the water and the sudden open space. The Danube is never blue, however. More usually it's a dull and muddy brown.

For a map showing Budapest district by district *see page* **287**.

Buda

Older than Pest, more conservative and residential, and notably devoid of decent bars, Buda is sort of disjointed. The Castle and Gellért Hills carve up the central area into a patchwork of separate parts.

Throughout history, the Castle District has offered a controlling vantage over the Danube.

The most surprising thing about the **Castle District** – *people actually still live there.*

The continuation of the Nagykörút runs round the back of these two urban hummocks, losing definition between Moszkva tér and Móricz Zsigmond körtér, the north and south hubs of public transport on this side of the river. To the north and west of the central area, smart residential districts amble up into still higher hills – green and spotted with villas in a way that, from a distance, is reminiscent of Los Angeles.

Castle District

Wandering around the streets at the north end of the Vár – the Castle District – you'll see surnames against the doorbells of small Baroque houses. This is perhaps the most surprising thing about this whole historic area: people still live here.

Without that reminder, the Vár appears to be nothing but one big tourist attraction – and certainly no visit to Budapest is complete without at least one afternoon up here. Apart from the obvious major landmarks – the former **Royal Palace** complex, the **Mátyás templom** and the **Fisherman's Bastion** – the narrow streets and open squares that top this 60-metre hill also contain no fewer than nine museums, from the dreary waxworks in the **Panoptikum** through appealing oddities such as the **Museum of Commerce & Catering** to national institutions such as the **Széchenyi Library** and the **National Gallery**, as well as assorted other churches, mansions and statues. Practically every building, as the ubiquitous stone plaques with their Hungarian-only

inscriptions indicate, seems to have been declared a Műemlék – an historic monument.

The air of unreality is abetted by the quiet. You have to have a permit, or else be staying at the **Hilton Hotel** to bring a car into the Castle District, and though there are plenty of parked vehicles, there is no through traffic. A few souped-up horses and carts with traditionally costumed coachmen (you can rent them at Szentháromság tér) clatter along backstreets bearing parties of sightseers. The small Várbusz comes up from Moszkva tér to circle the district every few minutes. But otherwise the only street noises are the prattle of tour groups and the whirr of Japanese video cameras. Most of the shops are tourist-orientated, selling lacy folk items, overpriced antiques, 35mm film, postcards and strings of dried paprika. Locals have to dive downhill to Moszkva tér or **Déli station** to buy their bread and túró.

But the feeling that all here is not really real is an accurate one. Buda Castle has been destroyed and rebuilt so many times that virtually nothing historically authentic remains. Though it was inhabited in celtic times, the first major settlement on this hill was in the thirteenth century. That was promptly trashed by the Mongols.

King Mátyás built a Renaissance palace, then the Turks showed up in 1541 and wrecked the place again. Everything they built was in turn destroyed when Habsburg-led armies chased them back out in 1686. Rebuilt once more, it was damaged during the 1848-49 War of Independence, rebuilt again in the latter half of the nineteenth

Gellért Hill rises above the Tabán.

century, somehow managed to get through World War I unscathed, and was pounded back into rubble in 1945.

Postwar reconstruction, which took decades, has both followed the way things were before the war, and incorporated earlier bits and pieces unearthed in wartime ruins. Many Baroque houses were built on medieval foundations, and all this has been faithfully reproduced.

A lot of it was only simulated history anyway. Bits of the Mátyás templom date back to the thirteenth century, but the nineteenth-century reconstruction by Frigyes Schulek, who also designed the phony ramparts of the Fisherman's Bastion, romanticised the thing according to then current notions about Hungarian national identity. Add touches such as the **Sikló** – funicular – and the **Turul Statue**, and what you get is a sort of historical theme park: Dual Monarchyland.

The Royal Palace, which looks splendid from over the river, is pretty boring up close. Nothing here now but the museums. Even the Habsburgs, for whom it was originally built, never stayed here much. The crenellated Fisherman's Bastion, guarded by a statue of St Stephen, offers fantastic views across the Danube and Pest, but isn't quite the same now one can't wander at will, and instead must pay an entrance fee to help save 'this internationally recognised value of Hungarian architecture'. Here one can sit and drink the worst and most overpriced beer in Budapest – we'd swear it must be watered down – and listen to competing music from the violinist in one of the turrets, and cocktail piano drifting up from the terrace behind the mirror glass Hilton which has somehow managed to worm its way into this UNESCO-protected area.

Tóth Árpád sétány, the promenade on the other side, overlooks ugly Déli station, the houses of Krisztinaváros, and a telecommunications centre that looks like something out of *Thunderbirds*. It's pleasant under the chestnut trees, especially at sunset. Relatively tourist-free, this is where the old folk of the Castle District come to stroll.

If you walk up to the north end of the hill, along the Anjou Bastion past the artillery pieces behind the **Museum of Military History**, you'll find the Memorial to the last Pasha of Buda. Vizir Abdurrahman Abdi Arnaut Pasha was killed and buried here in 1686. 'A valiant foe', reads the inscription, 'may he rest in peace'. People still sometimes leave fresh flowers at his grave. The nearby Vienna Gate, which looks much older, was built in 1936 to commemorate the 250th anniversary of the victory over the Turks.

In a way the only real piece of history in the whole Castle District is the wrecked stump of the former Ministry of Defence, down at the south end of Disz tér, unrestored and bullet-pocked from the last desperate battles between Nazis and Soviets.

Little happens up here at night, although it can all be very atmospheric in the dark. The **Király** is the only restaurant we'd recommend. If you want to pause for a coffee or beer in the middle of all this relentless sightseeing, both the **Café Miró** and **Café Pierrot** are refreshingly unhistorical.

The Tabán, Gellért Hill & Surrounds

Krisztinaváros sits below the Castle District to the west. Apart from the enormous, and enormously ugly, Déli pályaudvar – the station for trains to the Balaton, Croatia and other points south-west – there isn't much noteworthy about the area.

South of here, between Castle Hill and **Gellért Hill**, is the Tabán. Now a public park, this was

Cave Church – *worship on the spooky side.*

*The girders of **Szabadság híd** loom over heavy traffic on Szent Gellért tér.*

once an ancient and disreputable quarter inhabited by Serbs, Greeks and Gypsies, most of whom made their living on the river. The Horthy government levelled it in the 1930s and only a few bits and pieces remain. Appropriately enough for an area once renowned for its gambling dens, one of these is the **Várkert Casino**, housed in a Miklós Ybl-designed neo-Renaissance-style pump house (it used to furnish water for the Royal Palace) near the **Semmelweis Museum of Medical History**. Ybl also designed the nineteenth-century exterior of the **Rác baths**, over on the other side of the park below Gellért Hill. The original domed Turkish pool survives within.

On the other side of the roads which feed traffic on and off Erzsébet híd (Elizabeth Bridge), the only building between Gellért Hill and the Danube, stands the **Rudas**, most beautiful, atmospheric and (though men-only) least gay of all the Turkish bathhouses. It doesn't look much from outside, though. On the cliff behind it, over the road from the number 7 bus stop, plaques note several springs that emerge from the hill at this point, variously christened Rákóczi, Gül Baba, Beatrix, Kinizsi and Musztafa. This last is named for Sokoli Mustapha, pasha from 1566-78, who caused the Rudas to be constructed.

Gellért Hill rises steep at this point. Looking up you'll sometimes see rock climbers scaling the limestone cliffs with ropes. An easier route is the path that leads up to the **statue of martyred Archbishop Gellért**, enclosed by a colonnade and brandishing a crucifix at motorists crossing Erzsébet híd. Paths meander up and around the

hill and it's easy to find your way to the top. Villas dot the south and west slopes but here there are only trees, through which one catches steadily more spectacular views of the Danube and Pest rooftops beyond. Once this hill was covered in vines, but a nineteenth-century epidemic of phylloxera destroyed them all. Some fig trees still flourish, though, brought here by the Turks in the sixteenth century.

The grim **Citadella** on the 230-metre summit was built by the Austrians to assert their authority after the 1848-49 War of Independence. Its artillery were never used against the city and portions of it were symbolically dynamited when Budapest and Vienna kissed and made up with the Ausgleich of 1867. It's now a quiet spot with extraordinary views and contains a variety of tourist amenities, although the Hungarian army still sets up camp here every August to supervise the **St Stephen's Day** fireworks. The **Liberation Monument**, a figure apparently doing some form of aerobics with a palm frond, towers above the ramparts, flanked below by sprightly statues of Progress and Destruction.

From here any number of paths lead down the other side of the hill. On the way you might pass the **Cave Church**, an odd and somewhat spooky place of worship run by monks of the Hungarian Paulite order. The white-robed brothers live in the pseudo-historical monastery just around the hill facing the river. At the Buda foot of Szabadság híd (Freedom Bridge) stands the four-star **Gellért Hotel**, an imposing Art Nouveau edifice with a complex of thermal baths and swimming pools behind. This is Budapest's most famous hotel, built 1912-18. The first-class **Gellért Eszpresszó** is a good spot for coffee and cakes, although the terrace is rather noisy. Even if you don't want to swim or soak, it's worth poking your head round the **Gellért baths'** entrance in Kelenhegyi út just to clock the impressively ornate secessionist foyer. Refreshment in less ornate surroundings can be found at the nearby **Libella** on Budafoki út 7.

The **Technical University** stands to the south of the Gellért on what was once a marsh, and Bartók Béla út runs round the south side of the hill. From about 200 metres down, the view of Szabadság híd's green metal girders sweeping across the line of the road is a unique piece of cityscape. This busy shopping street and some of the roads off it (Mészöly utca, Lágymányosi utca) also have an assortment of interesting turn-of-the-century buildings, notably Ödön Lechner's number 40, and József Fischer's numbers 15B and 49.

Roads off to the right lead up to the residential district of Gellért Hill, where the former School of State Management, academy for the Communist elite, stands tall and still somehow a little proud. A statue of **Géza Gárdonyi**, famous for authoring an adventure novel about the 1552 Siege of **Eger**, one of Hungary's few famous victories, occupies the triangle where Bercsényi utca meets the main road. The **Café Ponyvaregény** at Bercsényi utca 5 is a handy stop for refreshment.

Just beyond Móricz Zsigmond körtér, terminus for assorted trams and buses and very much the border between the city centre and the outlying industrial suburbs to the south, is a small park, whose theatre, the Budai Parkszinpad, is the venue for the annual **World Music Festival** each June. The park also contains the **Park Café Restaurant**, Budapest's home-grown answer to the Hard Rock chain, an austere statue of Bartók and a supposedly bottomless lake (actually four metres deep). The Baroque façade of Szent Imre's church over the way on Villányi út lends some historical atmosphere, but like so much else in Budapest, it's a bit of a fake, built in 1938.

The Víziváros (Water Town)

From the north-east side of the Castle District, ancient streets cascade down towards the Danube. The Víziváros (Water Town) is one of Budapest's oldest districts. It's a quiet and conservative area where nothing very much happens, stretching about a mile north from Clark Ádám tér to the foot of Margaret Bridge, gradually widening west away from the river and towards Moszkva tér.

Main street is Fő utca (it means just that: 'main street') a thoroughfare of Roman origin that runs parallel to the Danube-hugging Bem rakpart. Down here are medieval houses, Baroque churches, small squares and narrow roads leading up to the Castle. George Mauroius's French Institute at

Fő utca – a thoroughly Roman thoroughfare.

number 17 is one of the city's few decent postmodern buildings, with an impressive and prominent waterfront location.

The space in front of it somehow invites you to stroll across and wonder whether the French are trying to make amends for 1920, when their support for the Little Entente was instrumental in Trianon's dismemberment of Hungary, or just ostentatiously asserting Gallic culture. The flashy fireworks they let off here every 14 July, Bastille Day, suggests the latter. A nineteenth-century water meter a little further down towards the Chain Bridge, by the stop for tram 19, often contains miniature art installations.

Batthyány tér is the centrepiece of the Víziváros, opening from Fő utca out on to the Danube where Parliament looms rather largely on the opposite bank. It's a busy and interesting square, with a desultory flea market in the middle and an assortment of notable, mostly eighteenth-century architecture round the edges. The **Church of St Anne** on the southern side is one of Hungary's finest Baroque buildings, with a decidedly camp interior. The middle-class ladies of Buda gather for coffee and cakes in St Anne's former presbytery, now the **Angelika** café, where light seeps in through atmospheric stained glass windows. Number 4 was built in 1770 as the White Cross Inn and is these days called the Casanova House – he supposedly once stayed here – while number 3 next door is a rare example of a late Baroque style called **copfstil**. The 1902 market hall now houses a modern supermarket with depressing piped Muzak. The floating **Hotel Dunapart**, complete with Korean gift shop, is moored nearby, as is the Titanic nightclub.

Batthyány tér is also a public transport hub: various buses leave from here, and underground there is both a station on the M2 line and the southern terminal of the HÉV line that runs north to **Szentendre**. The station boasts Budapest's first privately owned public convenience, which has clean towels and plastic flowers.

Further north along Fő utca at 70-72 is the forbidding Military Court of Justice, used as a prison and headquarters by both the Gestapo in the Nazi times, and the secret police in the Stalinist 1950s. Here Imre Nagy and associates were tried in secret and condemned to death after the 1956 revolution. A block away are the **Király baths**, another leftover from the Turkish days and, unlike the others, interesting to view from outside as well as in.

The street ends at Bem tér, where there's a statue of General Joseph Bem. A Pole, Bem led the Hungarian army in the War of Independence. On 23 October 1956, this small square was the site of a huge demonstration – partly because people wished to express their approval of political changes in Poland. It was the beginning of the revolution that was to end so starkly just three blocks back down the road.

Moszkva tér & the Rózsadomb

Coming up the escalator from Moszkva tér metro, you see concrete supports which fan beautifully across the ceiling above the mouth of the tunnel. Outside, though, the station building looks tired and tatty. On the terrace above, where you can sit, drink a beer and watch the action in the square from the rooftop eszpresszó, grass grows up from cracks in the concrete.

Ugly and dilapidated, Moszkva tér, a major public transport hub connecting the Buda Hills to the rest of town, bustles with lowlife. From 5am it's an unofficial labour market: Romanians and Gypsies gather outside the station, waiting for someone to come along and hire them for a day's work. All day long, as trams going in several directions pull in and out and small buses nip up to the Castle District, police check the papers of anyone sitting around who looks like they might be an illegal immigrant. Hungarians from rural areas also cluster here, selling flowers, fruit and lace tablecloths to rush-hour crowds.

In nearby Retek utca, the **Szent Jupát** restaurant serves cheap and hearty platefuls deep into the night. The **Auguszt Cukrászda** on Fény utca serves some of the city's finest cakes and pastries. A short walk on to Kis Rókus utca, up one side of the enormous Ganz tram factory, leads to the **Marxim**, where pizzas are served up with Stalinist kitsch. But despite all the bustle there's not really much life around here. Moszkva tér is

On the opposite bank from Parliament, **Batthyány tér** *is the main square of Víziváros.*

Ugly, dilapidated and bustling with lowlife – **Moszkva tér.**

principally a tawdry transition zone where people pass through but rarely stop.

And very different from the Rózsadomb, which it serves. Down near the Buda foot of Margaret Bridge, you can walk up the narrow, cobbled Gül Baba utca and come to the **tomb of Gül Baba**. The northernmost Islamic holy place in Europe and a peaceful spot, this is the resting-place of a Turkish dervish credited with introducing roses to Budapest. It's also the foot of the Rózsadomb – Rose Hill – Budapest's most fashionable residential district.

This villa-speckled hill has long been known as the 'millionaires' district'. Whereas in cities such as London, Paris and Berlin the rich settled in western areas while prevailing winds blew industrial effluent towards working-class east ends, in Budapest avoiding the smoke has always been a matter of altitude. It was said in Communist times that inhabitants of the airy Rózsadomb had the same life expectancy as in Austria, while the citizens of polluted Pest below had the life expectancy of Syria: two continents in one city.

Unless you're either staying here or visiting one of the area's many restaurants – places such as the **Vadrózsa**, **Remiz** or **Kikelet**, all with beautiful gardens for summer dining – there aren't many reasons to go to the Rózsadomb. The yurt houses designed by Imre Makovecz on Törökvész utca are one architectural attraction. The fascinating **Napraforgó utca experimental housing estate**, where each house has been built in a different style of the modern movement, is another. Near the pic-

turesquely decayed concrete bus terminal at Pasaréti tér (the Origo eszpresszó here is worth a look for its tatty 1960s fittings) stands the **Bartók Memorial House**, the composer's former residence, now a concert venue as well as a museum. The **Szépvölgy** and **Pálvölgy caves** burrow beneath the outskirts of this area. But otherwise you'll see a lot of embassies, flash cars, tasteless new villas and a huge variety of Hungarian 'Beware of the Dog' signs.

The Buda Hills

From opposite the cylindrically ugly Budapest Hotel on Szilágyi Erzsébet fasor, you can catch the cog railway up to the summit of Széchenyi Hill, a ride of about 20 minutes. There's no view to speak of, unless you count the large building festooned with radar dishes, but you immediately feel as if you're out of the city. It's quiet and in summer there's a cool breeze.

There are wooded hills all around the western fringes of Buda, most of them criss-crossed with hiking trails. At weekends these can get quite crowded. You can ramble all you like, but take a good map, a strong pair of hiking boots and keep a sharp eye out for rampaging wild boar.

Otherwise, you can walk across the park from the cog railway terminal and hop on the narrow-gauge **Children's Railway**. This was formerly the Pioneers' Railway, named for the Communist youth organisation whose membership supplied the conductors and ticket collectors. Its charming

*The **Rózsadomb** rises above Margaret Bridge.*

trains, open to the breeze and still manned by children, snake hourly through the Buda Hills. The line meanders through woodland and retains a vaguely socialist flavour: the kids wear uniform hats and neckerchiefs, salute guards at stations, punch all tickets conscientiously and insist you remain seated when the trains are in motion. Many of the stations still sport murals of idealised socialist youth diligently enjoying their leisure time.

Near the end station of Hűvösvölgy you'll find a small amusement park and the popular **Náncsi Néni** restaurant. Or you can get off earlier at János-hegy, from where it's a brisk 15-minute walk up to the 527-metre summit of Budapest's highest hill. Here the view from the Erzsébet lookout tower puts the city in context: the Buda Hills roll around and behind; Castle Hill looks small and barely significant down below; the Danube bisects the entire landscape; way over on the other side, the outskirts of Pest shade into a patchwork of fields that in turn disappear into a flat, dusty horizon – the beginning of the Great Hungarian Plain.

From a terminal by the buffet below, the **libegő** – chair-lift – will convey you back down into urban Buda, the city spread grandly before you as you ride. Be warned, though: if you get the last Children's Railway train, you won't make it over the hill in time to catch the final chair-lift.

Pest

Though the south part of District V, the Belváros (Inner City), dates back to medieval times, the current shape of Pest – as resolutely flat as Buda is jaggedly hilly – is essentially nineteenth century. Its great boulevards were laid out in 1872, the same year that the three towns of Buda, Pest and Óbuda were merged to form one single city.

The main lines can be quickly drawn: a concentric series of semi-circular boulevards is cut through by several avenues that radiate from the centre. The spaces outlined by these major roads contain the various different districts. The two big circular roads – Kiskörút and Nagykörút (Small and Great Boulevards) – both have their own atmosphere and take on some of the character of the districts they traverse. A journey along them is thus an introduction to the whole of central Pest.

Kiskörút

The southern half of the Kiskörút follows the line of the old city walls – extant portions of which can be seen in Bástya utca behind Vámház körút and also a few yards down Ferenczy István utca off Múzeum körút. The Kiskörút begins at Fővám tér at the Pest foot of Szabadság Bridge, Gellért Hill standing craggily opposite. Marxist philosopher and literary critic George Lukács used to live just by here, in a fifth-floor flat at Belgrád rakpart 2. On the south side of the small square are two buildings: the **Budapest University of Economic Science**, facing the Technical University over the river; and the recently restored **Nagy Vásárcsarnok** (Great Market Hall), an indoor emporium of stalls selling every kind of meat, fish, vegetable and fruit. The former, designed by Miklós Ybl in neo-Renaissance style, was originally the Main Customs Office (hence Fővám – 'main customs'). The latter was in those days the city's main wholesale market. At one time an underground canal ran from the Danube, taking barges through the customs house and into the market.

Vámház körút leads up to Kálvin tér, named after the ugly Calvinist church on the square's south side. This was once the city's eastern gate and, with the ugly pink, postmodern Korona Hotel bridging Kecskeméti utca (its saving grace is the **Korona Passage** pancake place on the ground floor), still feels somewhat gate-like. From here two roads stab out eastwards into the city: Baross utca, which runs through the heart of District VIII, and Üllői út, which forms the border of Districts VIII and IX and leads eventually to Ferihegy airport. Ráday utca, a narrow commercial street leading off to the south-west, has some interesting shops and bars, including the **Shiraz Persian Sandwich Club** and **Paris, Texas**.

The next stretch is Múzeum körút, named for the **National Museum** on the east side. The

Madach utca – *built in the thirties as the start of a never-completed new avenue.*

fourth institution of its kind in the world when it was built between 1837-47, it was then so far out of town that cattle are said to have once wandered in. St Stephen's rather bent Crown is the main treasure here. Every 15 March the neo-Classical building gets decked out in red, white and green and crowds fill the forecourt to hear speeches from the steps. This is to commemorate the moment in 1848 when Sándor Petőfi launched the revolt against the Habsburgs by standing here and reading out his evidently inflammatory National Song. On the next corner is the century-old **Múzeum restaurant**, while over the road are some of Budapest's biggest antiquarian booksellers.

Múzeum körút ends at **Astoria**, where the grand but faded 1912 hotel dominates the intersection it has christened. Westwards, Kossuth Lajos utca leads towards the Danube and Elizabeth Bridge. East of here it continues as Rákóczi út towards **Keleti station** which, on a clear day, you can spy in the distance. The **Népstadion**, Hungary's biggest sports arena, lies beyond it.

Károly körút continues on up to Deák tér, passing on the right the enormous **Central Synagogue** which guards the entrance to District VII, and a huge apartment block, bridging Madach út, that looks like 1950s Soviet architecture but was actually built in the late 1930s. It was intended as the start of a new avenue, but never got further than a couple of blocks.

The 47 and 49 trams run this far up the Kiskörút and Deák tér is the central hub of Budapest's transport network: all three metro lines intersect in the station below, where there's also the cute little **Underground Railway Museum**. Sütő utca, off Deák tér to the south-west by the austerely neo-Classical Lutheran Church, has the main office of **Tourinform** – best place in town to pick up free maps, find details of cultural events and answer such niggling little queries as this book may not already cover.

The old city walls here curved west to meet the river at Vigadó tér. The Kiskörút, however, flattens out and continues on up north past the **Basilica of St Stephen** and down Bajcsy-Zsilinszky út, a drab boulevard named after a right-wing politician who turned anti-fascist. His half-sitting, half-standing statue in Deák tér supposedly depicts the moment he was arrested in Parliament. With his hand outstretched, he looks like a man outraged because his pint of beer has just been stolen.

Bajcsy-Zsilinszky út is boring and undistinguished, save for the enormous figure who languishes on top of a building at the corner of Ó utca, and the startling glimpse of the **former Royal Post Office Savings Bank** afforded by looking left down Nagysándor utca, a street which also contains the excellent **Via Luna** restaurant. On the corner of Alkotmány utca, just before the Kiskörút joins the Nagykörút at Nyugati tér, stands **Beckett's** – the huge Irish pub and restaurant that provides expensive beer, bad music and Sky Sports for Budapest's expatriate business community.

Nagykörút

At exactly 4,114 metres, the Nagykörút is the longest thoroughfare in the city, running from Petőfi Bridge in the south to Margaret Bridge in the north and passing through Districts IX, VIII, VII, VI and XIII en route. Trams 4 and 6 run the whole distance, starting at Móricz Zsigmond körtér in Buda, and ending up back on that side of the river in Moszkva tér.

A busy commercial boulevard built, like much of nineteenth-century Pest, entirely in eclectic style, it is curiously lacking in two things: decent bars or restaurants, and any kind of shop where you might actually want to buy something. Nevertheless it's here, rather than on upmarket Váci utca, that the real day-to-day business of downtown takes place. American fast food franchises thrive on every other corner, but new western logos haven't quite driven out all the beautifully dated neon signs.

On the Ferenc körút stretch you'll see people dressed in green and white – supporters of **Ferencváros FTC**, the local football club, Hungary's most popular and known for its right-wing following. The ugly concrete building on the south-west corner of the Üllői út intersection is known as the Lottóház – its apartments were given away as prizes in the 1950s. The contrast with Ödön Lechner's extraordinary and colourful **Museum of Applied Arts** round the corner couldn't be more complete. The building on the south-east side is a former army barracks. This and the **Corvin multiplex** tucked away in Corvin köz behind the intersection were the scenes of fierce fighting during the 1956 revolution.

Continuing north as József körút, the boulevard acquires a disreputable air as it passes through District VIII. Sleazy bars advertise 'leszbi sex shows', a bingo hall does a brisk trade and prostitutes ply their wares day and night around Rákóczi tér. One shop on this stretch (it's on the west side, near the Baross utca tram stop) sells absolutely nothing but soda syphon chargers.

At Blaha Lujza tér, Népszínház utca runs away south-east towards **Kerepesi cemetery** and the vast and seedy **Józsefvárosi piac**, the place to buy Chinese tat. Rákóczi út runs back towards Astoria and on up to Keleti station, its façade quite distinct from this vantage. Frank Zappa fans will appreciate **Z Hangelemez** in the courtyard of Rákóczi út 47, one of Budapest's more curious record shops. 'Blaha', as it's universally known, has the **Centrum Corvin** department store (now unfortunately updated from the intriguing Communist cornucopia of old) and an M2 metro station.

As it passes into District VII and its name changes to Erzsébet, the körút gets noticeably glitzier. Cinemas and theatres begin to appear.

Váci utca – *brash, tacky, full of life.*

This is the best stretch for elegantly quaint neon. A block up from Blaha the venerable **New York Coffeehouse**, rammed by a tank in 1956, stands in dire need of renovation. A few blocks further on the other side, its postmodern grandchild, the dreadful **Café Mozart**, stands in equally dire need of demolition. You almost wish Soviet tanks would come back just to ram this place, too. The **Fészek restaurant** and artists' club, a block away down Dob utca, has managed to survive the twentieth century intact, and offers peaceful summer dining in a picturesquely tatty inner courtyard, formerly a monk's cloister.

Crossing Király utca, a lively street worth delving into, Erzsébet changes into Teréz körút as it stumbles into District VI. The **Zeneakadémia**, Budapest's principal concert hall, is a block west down Király on the corner of Liszt Ferenc tér.

Oktogon, where the Nagykörút intersects broad Andrássy út, is the grandest intersection, once lined with coffeehouses but now sadly dominated by burger joints. In the Communist days this was November 7 Square; under Horthy it was named after Mussolini. The M1 metro stops here, on its way underneath Andrássy út to **Heroes' Square** and the **Városliget** (City Park) beyond.

Teréz körút is the flashiest segment of boulevard and brightest at night. Here there are more cinemas and the respectable **Béke Radisson**

*The **Nagykörút** crosses Rakoczi út at Blaha Ljuza tér.*

Hotel in the run-up to the Nagykörút's most magnificent landmark: **Nyugati station**. Built by the Eiffel company in 1874-77 (in the low-rent shopping complex underneath, everything seems to be named after Eiffel: tacky shops, amusement arcades, dowdy coffee bars) it's a pale-blue palace of iron and glass. The panes in front allow you to see inside the station, making arriving and departing trains part of the city's street life. In the early 1970s this became literally so, when one engine crashed through the façade and came to rest at the tram stop. Over the road, the mirror glass frontage of the Skála is by contrast oddly forbidding for a department store, despite attempts to enliven the square with summer lunchtime concerts. Two of Budapest's most happening nightclubs are in the vicinity. **E-Play** occupies two floors of Nyugati's eastern tower. Behind the station on Váci út, **Bahnhof** is housed in an old train shed and employs the city's most evil bouncers.

Views of Nyugati from Szent István körút are spoilt by the unsightly road bridge carrying traffic over Nyugati tér between Bajcsy-Zsilinszky út and Váci út, which leads on up to the busy Lehel tér produce market. The only stretch that isn't named after a Habsburg, Szent István körút is also the only part where there's very much of interest at night. **Okay Italia** and **Pinocchio** do a roaring trade, while **Sziesta** purveys pizzas until 4am. The **Franklin Trocadero** is a decent Latin dance club on a good night, and the **Süss Fel Nap** cellar disco on Honvéd utca was in summer 1997 certainly the hottest spot in town. The streets beyond

in Újlipótváros have a number of busy bars, including the **Zöldség-Gyümölcs** and **Yes**, making this an admirable locality for late-night pub-crawling.

Built in the 1930s and originally a middle-class Jewish district, Újlipótváros and its main thoroughfare, Pozsonyi út, is also lively by day, with lots of small shops, a busy street life and the Szent István Park opening out on to the Danube. There's nothing in particular to go to see, but these are amiable streets for an afternoon stroll.

Centrepiece of this last stretch of körút is the stubbily Baroque **Vígszínház** (Comedy Theatre). Built in 1896 and renovated in 1995, this has pretensions of grandeur, but in a certain light looks like nothing so much as a tawdry end-of-the-pier attraction. Szent István körút ends at Jászai Mari tér, terminus of the number 2 tram. Here traffic sweeps on to Margit híd (Margaret Bridge), a Y-shaped construction that leads not only to Buda and the Rózsadomb, but also to the traffic-free and wooded park of **Margaret Island**.

Belváros

Trace the line of the Kiskörút on a map as far as Deák tér. Now move your finger west along Harmincad utca, past the Erzsébet tér bus station and the **Kempinski Hotel**, past the British Embassy and the neighbouring **Sushi** bar. Dogleg into Vörösmarty tér, sweep by the **Gerbeaud** patisserie and the terminus of the Millennial Metro, and go down to the Danube at Vigadó tér. The area you have outlined, bounded by the river to the west, is the Belváros, or Inner City.

The area south of Kossuth Lajos utca is one of Pest's most appealing quarters. Though the Danube is mostly invisible (one or two streets that run out on to it offer sudden, startling views of Gellért Hill) its narrow, quiet streets feel like a waterfront district. Apart from the old Customs House (now the Economic University) on the Kiskörút – the dock for international Danube traffic (notably **jetfoils to Bratislava and Vienna**), complete with customs area, is on this stretch of riverfront. The still-functioning gear-repair shop at Belgrád rakpart 18 (next door to the **Govinda** Hare Krishna restaurant) with its beautiful old sign and window display of cogs, cogs and more cogs, is a relic from an earlier era of river travel.

The south stretch of Váci utca, between Kossuth Lajos utca and Fővám tér, has recently been pedestrianised and a new life is slowly seeping into the area as fashion shops and terrace cafés begin to open up next to older antique and collectors' shops. Though it's never too busy, either by day or night, this area offers a host of decent restaurants and bars: **Taverna Dionysios** (one of the few establishments actually to use the waterfront), the **Amstel Bar**, **Capella**, **Latin Kocsma**, **Fregatt**, **Fatál** and the **Adria** are all within a block or two of each other. The **Janis Pub**, **Old Amsterdam** and the **Irish Cat** are all also nearby, making this perhaps Budapest's premier district for pub-crawling – particularly as the streets are so atmospheric at night.

The **Serbian Orthodox Church** nestles in a garden up Szerb utca, near the **Rhythm 'n' Books** shop which offers world music and English-language reading materials. The former home of chanteuse and actress Katalin Karády – Hungary's answer to Marlene Dietrich – is around the corner at Nyári Pál utca 9, complete with plaque where flowers are still left to her memory. But this is a quarter for quiet strolling rather than serious sightseeing.

All this changes at Ferenciek tere (named for the Franciscan Church which stands near the University Library). The extraordinary 1913 **Párizsi udvar** on the other side of Kossuth Lajos utca heralds the beginning of Budapest's prestige shopping district, though around here there are also more notably ancient monuments, including the **Inner City Parish Church**, Pest's oldest building, down towards the bridge. From here on up to Vörösmarty tér, Váci and its environs are pedestrianised and bustle with street hustlers and expensive shops, both aiming their pitch at the equally numerous tourists.

Although the westerner will not find it very impressive (it's mostly souvenir shops and drab western retail chains) Hungarians are proud of Váci utca. It's what they think the tourists want.

Budapesters will invariably bring visitors to Váci, although they rarely shop here (too expensive) and more or less visit as tourists themselves. Brash, tacky, full of life and, nearly a decade after communism, still remarkably bare of decent clothes shops, it remains interesting principally for anthropological reasons: grab a table outside **Gerbeaud** or the **Anna Café**, prepare yourself for a heftier bill than you'd receive elsewhere in town, and settle back to study the holidaying habits of the lesser spotted Austrian package tourist.

At night, it's a different story. A few restaurants and bars stay open, but after about 11pm the area is mostly deserted save for sex bar touts handing leaflets to such foreigners as remain on the streets. Vörösmarty tér, which on summer days is full of café tables or hosting some seasonal event such as **Book Week** or the **Budapest International Wine Festival**, at night is patrolled by prostitutes, who'll cheerfully approach any passing male. There's nothing threatening about the atmosphere, though. In Budapest even the sex industry seems vaguely conservative and respectable.

The area west of Váci, between Petőfi Sándor utca and the Károly körút, is mostly pretty dead, dominated by two huge bureaucratic complexes: the Budapest City Hall and the Pest County Hall. Narrow streets and small squares lead through to Deák tér. Szervita tér has the Hungaria mosaic top-

*The garden of the **Serbian Orthodox Church**.*

*The Hungarian **Parliament** (left) apes the British Parliament's style and riverside location.*

ping number 5 and Béla Lajta's **Rózsavölgyi House** next door, still occupied by a communist-era **music shop** offering, among a stock of modern CDs and an excellent classical section, an assortment of bizarre vinyl bargains.

The Danube Korzó (or Corso), Budapest's premier promenade, is almost as busy as Váci. It begins at the convergence of Március 15 tér, with its stubby Roman ruins, and Petőfi tér, with its statue of the national poet. From here up until Vigadó tér is the city's main **gay cruise**, though you'd not notice if you weren't looking for it. At Vigadó tér are buskers, stalls selling handicrafts and folkloric souvenirs and the **Vigadó** itself, Budapest's second-best concert hall. The Korzó continues from here on up to Roosevelt tér, where statues of Deák and Széchenyi stand among the trees and the **Gresham Palace** faces off against the Chain Bridge.

Between the Korzó and the Danube run the tracks for the number 2 tram; on the river itself, various odd attractions – an Irish restaurant called, for some reason, Columbus, on one moored boat; a Renault car showroom on another. Above tower many of Budapest's most prestigious hotels, including the **Marriott** and **Atrium Hyatt**, all of them architecturally quite uninspiring. But these need not spoil the view of the Chain Bridge ahead and Castle District opposite. Particularly when lit up at night and reflecting in the river, whether under a clear, starry sky or softened by trails of autumn mist, these form one of the most magical urban landscapes in the world.

Lipótváros

The northern part of District V – the Lipótváros – is Budapest's quarter for business and bureaucracy. There are few shops in this area, though **Bestsellers** bookstore on Oktober 6 utca is an obvious rallying-point for Anglophones. Once almost totally devoid of decent bars and restaurants, these broad, blocky late-nineteenth century streets, almost Prussian in feel, have now begun to acquire a little life at night and in places positively buzz at lunchtime. **Lou Lou, Gandhi, Café Kör** and **Iguana** all offer more than acceptable eats, while the stretch on Nador utca between Vértanuk tér and Zoltéan utca, with its various 24-hour presszós, seems to be becoming a local hub for nightlife.

In the backstreets round here you might also be approached by Transylvanian village women selling illicitly imported lace. On Vértanuk tér, standing at the crest of a small bridge and looking both wistfully towards Parliament and determinedly away from the Soviet obelisk, is Tamás Varga's 1996 statue of Imre Nagy, tragic hero of the 1956 uprising.

The remarkably ugly Basilica of St Stephen points its façade down Zrinyi utca towards Gresham Palace and the river. There's nothing much to see inside, save for the mummified right hand of St Stephen, contained in a box and lit up for Ft20 like something in a fairground sideshow. József Finta's glossy new postmodern building for the national bank, cousin to his Kempinski Hotel

The statue of 1956 Prime Minister Imre Nagy looks back towards **Parliament**.

a few blocks south, adds a forbidding blue glass and polished granite sheen to the south-east corner of **Szadadság tér**, Budapest's late nineteenth-century financial centre. It's dominated by the National Bank, the American Embassy, the huge and authoritarian Magyar Televizió headquarters (formerly the Stock and Commodity Exchange) and the Soviet obelisk which stands on the site of the former Sacred Mound of soil from territories lost at Trianon. It's an unappealing space which, for all its size, is easily missed as no major roads pass through.

Note, though, on the east side, the small statue of US General Harry Hill Bandholtz. An officer of the peace-keeping force in 1919, he saved the treasures of the National Museum from rampaging Romanian soldiers by 'sealing' the doors with the only official-looking seals he had to hand: censorship seals. The Romanians saw the American eagle, and backed off down the steps.

Apart from General Bandholtz, every notable landmark in this part of town seems to have some kind of nationalist function. A diagonal block away from the institutions of Szabadság tér, the Eternal Flame burns on the corner of Hold utca and Báthory utca to commemorate Count Lajos Batthyány, prime minister in the revolutionary government, and executed by Habsburgs at this spot on 6 October 1849. Even the brightest spot of this sombre, officious quarter – Ödön Lechner's startlingly ornate and colourful former Royal Post Office Savings Bank – was built around forms Lechner considered to

be 'original' pre-Christian Hungarian patterns and thus the basis for a new nationalist architecture. Behind the US Embassy and a block south of the Eternal Flame, it's one of the city's most extraordinary buildings. The only pity is that there's nowhere to step back and take a good look at it.

The same can't be said of the **Parliament**, one of Budapest's most conspicuous structures. Built, like the rest of Lipótváros, at a time when Hungary, getting its first and only taste of empire, was in a position to boss around a few Slovaks, Romanians and Croats, this was the largest parliament in the world when it opened in 1902 – larger even than the British Parliament (whose neo-Gothic style and riverside location it aped), then still administering the biggest empire the world has ever seen. The Hungarian Parliament's 691 rooms have never been fully utilised, even in the 16 years before Trianon dismembered Magyar imperial pretensions. The business of governing Hungary today takes up only 12 per cent of the space. (Offices for the various parties are down the road in the Fehérház – 'White House' – at Széchenyi rakpart 19, formerly the Communist Party headquarters.)

The **Museum of Ethnography**'s positioning, opposite Parliament on Kossuth Lajos tér and looking pretty governmental itself, says much about how seriously Hungarians take their folk traditions. Along Balassi Bálint utca to the north, the venerable **Szalai Cukrászda** serves coffee and pastries to a city-wide clientèle.

Andrássy út, District VI & the Városliget

Andrássy út, built between 1872-85 with the continent's first electric underground railway running underneath, is the spine of District VI. Intended as Budapest's answer to the Champs-Elysées, it stretches for 2.5 kilometres and has had a variety of names: Sugárút (Radial Avenue), Andrássy út (after the nineteenth-century statesman), Sztalin út and the tongue-twisting Népköztársaság útja (Avenue of the People's Republic) before being renamed Andrássy once more in 1989.

Like much of Dual Monarchy Budapest, Andrássy út today seems a little too grand for its own good: there isn't enough wealth and power in contemporary Budapest to flesh this avenue out with the kind of shops and businesses that might do its proportions justice. Even on the liveliest stretch – between Bajcsy-Zsilinszky út and Oktogon – there isn't much save banks and supermarkets, stationery chains and electrical stores, plus one or two car showrooms. The **Művész** coffeehouse and **Irók Boltja** (Writers' Bookshop) are down here, though, as are the **Belcanto** and **Bombay Palace** restaurants.

Few individual buildings stand out from the uniform eclectic style, with two notable excep-

tions: Miklós Ybl's **Opera House**, where the appeal of the architecture is perhaps greater than the quality of the productions, and Béla Lajta's extraordinary 1910 Parisiana nightclub (now **Új Színház**), a worthwhile 50-metre detour down Dalszinház utca.

Nagymező utca, with the main **MÁV office** on the corner (best place to get advance train tickets), was once known as Budapest's Broadway – a name still echoed on a couple of shop signs. Here there are some West End-style theatres (including the **Operetta**) and a couple of nightspots, notably the **Piaf**, after-hours hangout for the older arty set. This area to the north and west of Andrássy – a triangle also bounded by Teréz körút and Bajcsy-Zsilinszky út – is by day a dull commercial district (although it does include **Wave** and **Trance**, two of the city's better specialist record shops) but by night offers a cluster of eccentric bars and restaurants. **Mirtusz, Kétballábas, Pizza Bella, Picasso Point, Marquis de Salade, Cactus Juice** and **Crazy Café** are all around here.

More nightlife can be found on Liszt Ferenc tér, which leads from Andrássy up to the Zeneakadémia, and the square bustles on a summer evening with tables outside **Incognito, Pompeii, Palacsinta Porta** and **Café Mediterran**.

One curiosity on this stretch. In the courtyard of Andrássy út 27 there's the Esperanto centre. Hungary is the only country in the world with state exams in Esperanto, and where the 'universal tongue' (modelled on Romanian and invented by a Pole) is accepted as a second language for university entrance requirements. It's taught in about 30 schools and an estimated 50,000 Hungarians speak it – meaning, ironically, they have not one language nobody else in the world understands, but two. At the shop you can buy 'Saluton el Hungario' postcards and Bulgarian 7-inch Esperanto singles.

The middle stretch of Andrássy út – between Oktogon and the Kodály körönd – is the most boring part, mainly institutional and bureaucratic buildings. The unprepossessing number 60, though, was once feared enough to make people cross the road to avoid it. These days sporting a Chemokomplex sign, it was secret police headquarters for both the Horthy and Communist regimes. The **Lukács** at number 70 is one of Budapest's more venerable coffeehouses. Closed to the public for a while in the 1950s, when it became the secret police cafeteria, it reopened for a few decades, closed again in 1995, and as this book went to press was apparently about to reopen as a combination coffeehouse and bank headquarters. Over the road at number 69 there's the neo-Renaissance Képzőművészeti Főiskola (Old Exhibition Hall), now the College of Fine Arts, which also contains the **Budapest Puppet Theatre**.

The 'Little Metro' runs below **Andrássy út**.

Gozsdu udvar – *deserted and decaying, but a taste of the old Jewish Quarter.*

Kodály körönd is the Rond-Point of Andrássy út, and was clearly once very splendid. The four palatial town houses that enclose it are dilapidated but still fascinating. The composer Zoltán Kodály used to live in the turreted number 87-89, and his old apartment now serves as the **Kodály Memorial Museum**.

The final stretch of Andrássy út is wider than the rest of it, mostly occupied by villas set back from the road. This is Budapest's main diplomatic quarter and many embassies are here and on the surrounding streets (Benczúr utca is shady and quiet and full of Art Nouveau mansions). The Yugoslav embassy where Imre Nagy holed up for a while in 1956 is the last building on the southern corner by Hősök tere. This stretch also features the **Made Inn Music Club**, a combination disco and terrace restaurant that also occasionally features live acts.

Hősök tere (Heroes' Square), flanked by the **Museum of Fine Arts** and the **Műcsarnok** (Exhibition Hall) and offering the Archangel Gabriel amid a pantheon of Hungarian heroes, is a monumental celebration of mythic Magyardom, these days mostly inhabited by skateboarders. The **Városliget (City Park)** beyond is Pest's most interesting park, with a boating lake, the **Széchenyi baths**, the **Zoo**, **Vidám** (Amusement) **Park** and **Petőfi Csarnok** concert hall among its amenities. Once the site of the 1896 Magyar Millennium exhibition, the theme-park feel of the place survives in the Disneyfied mock-Transylvanian design of Vadjahunyad castle, now home

for the **Agriculture Museum**. This and Hősök tere form the heart of Dual Monarchyland, while the **Gundel** restaurant nearby offers an expensively recreated taste of the old days.

District VII

Like so much else in Budapest that dates from the latter half of the last century, the Central Synagogue on Dohány utca is grandiose and simply enormous – so big it's impossible to heat and has never been used in winter. Though tucked discreetly behind the junction with Károly körút – you don't see the thing until you're almost upon it – the building stands like some twin-domed Moorish fortress, guarding the district behind.

District VII, or Erzsébetváros, between the Kiskörút and the Nagykörút, Andrássy út and Rákóczi út, is Budapest's Jewish quarter, established here in the eighteenth century when Jews were still forbidden to live within the city walls. These days people call it 'the Ghetto', although it never was one until 1944-45, when Arrow Cross fascists walled off this whole area and herded the Jewish community inside. The junction by the Central Synagogue was one of two entrances.

It's not as picturesque or as ancient as Prague's Jewish quarter, but although 700,000 Hungarian Jews were murdered in the Holocaust, enough survived to mean that District VII is still the heart of a living community. You can hear Yiddish spoken on Kazinczy utca, or eat a kosher pastry at the **Fröhlich Cukrászda** on Dob utca. Several syn-

Hidden Hasidic prayer house on Vasvári utca.

District VII market hall on the east side. In summer, old men play cards and chess under the trees. The best taste of how it once was is afforded by the **Gozsdu udvar** – a linked series of courtyards running between Dob utca and Király utca, still inhabited by workshops, labs and hairdressers, even though most of the apartments are currently empty.

Király utca was 70 per cent Jewish at the turn of the century. It's still full of character and commotion, with old communist-style shop signs, curious courtyards and an informal market for dodgy goods on the corner of Kis Diófa utca. The backstreets round here are dark, narrow, tatty and full of odd detail. Sip utca has some fascinating buildings, including the secessionist Metro Klub on the corner of Dohány utca sporting one of Budapest's best old neon signs, and a number 11 with neo-Gothic doorways, gargoyles and the statue of a seventeenth-century halberdier. Kazinczy utca is intriguing too, with the stretch between Wesselényi utca and Király utca containing the 1930s **Hungarian Museum of Electrotechnics** in a sort of junior totalitarian style, the Orthodox synagogue, angled to the bend of the street, and a final stroll up to the **Wichmann** bar, a lonely but welcoming tavern that by night casts an almost medieval glow.

A fine mini-pub crawl can be had around here, taking in the Wichmann, **Sixtus** and Incognito and Café Mediterran up on Liszt Ferenc tér, and then maybe moving over Andrássy to Piaf and beyond. If walking alone, though, be just a little bit wary at night.

District VIII

Although its tabloid nickname, Csikagó (Chicago), originated with the fast construction rate round here late last century, District VIII is indeed what the name also suggests: a crime-ridden, run-down area that is Budapest's red light district and heartland of the mafia, both Ukrainian and Chinese. (If Pest ever acquires a Chinatown, this is where it will be.)

Bounded by Üllői út and Rákóczi út, the pie-slice shape of Józsefváros, as it's also known, has its point at the National Museum. In Pollack Mihály tér behind, former mansions rub shoulders with the ugly socialist-realist Magyar Rádió headquarters, scene of much bloodletting in 1956. The bars **Nothing But The Blues** and **Darshan** are on a lively stretch of Krudy Gyula utca and jazz venue **Big Mambo** is a short walk away down Mária utca near the corner of Pál utca. This short, unprepossessing street was the scene of Ferenc Molnár's well-known novel *The Paul Street Boys*.

On Rákóczi út and in the streets beyond the Nagykörút, District VIII is at its seediest. Grass grows up through cracks in the pavement. Prosti-

agogues in the area are still active – the small Heroes' Temple behind the newly renovated Central Synagogue, the Orthodox synagogue on Kazinczy utca and a hidden Hasidic prayer house in the courtyard of Vasvári utca 5 – and a number of Jewish organisations have their headquarters at Sip utca 12.

This community has survived both an exodus of younger, wealthier Jews into less noisy and congested districts, and postwar attempts by the Communist government to homogenise the area. If you'd survived the Holocaust, you got to keep your flat. Workers brought into Budapest to work on the reconstruction of the city were housed in the empty properties.

Many of these were Gypsies and District VII is now also the Gypsy quarter – although the heart of Gypsy territory is beyond the Nagykörút, an area of broken phone boxes, repair shops and dingy borozós where people have wine for breakfast. In that area there's the hideous **Nemzeti Színház**, which looks more like a National Car Park than a National Theatre, as well as the **Stamp Museum**, but otherwise it's pretty devoid of particular things to see. Ármin Hegedűs's 1906 Primary School at Dob utca 85 is definitely worth a detour, though.

The heart of the Jewish quarter is Klauzál tér, featuring assorted Jewish businesses and the tutes work the squares and street corners. Many of the shops are Chinese discount stores or sad old repair shops. Eclectic façades are shabby, bullet-pocked and crumbling while overgrown inner courtyards, many still with their racks for beating carpets, buzz with a ragged, almost medieval life. It's a fascinating area, and not as dangerous as it sounds, as long as you look as if you know what you're doing. Venture into a bar or two and you'll find a warm, though starkly impoverished, neighbourhood atmosphere. Just don't knock over any drinks or wave your wallet around, and remain a little watchful on the streets.

Other Hoods

Óbuda

The oldest part of the city (in archeological terms, at least), Óbuda was a separate village until 1873 and still feels very different from the rest of Budapest. The Romans established the town of **Aquincum** here, although no one knew it had been there until late in the nineteenth century. The Magyars set up shop here when they arrived in the ninth century, christening it Buda, which got changed to Óbuda (Old Buda) when the first Royal Palace went up on Castle Hill.

Apart from the Communists erecting clusters of tower blocks and a flyover right over Flórián tér and its Roman baths, the area has been pretty much forgotten about ever since. Locals consider themselves independent of Budapest – the chant of Óbuda's second division football club (III. kerület TVE) is 'Come on you district!' In the last century there was some industry – mainly shipbuilding and viticulture – but all you'll see now are rows of rickety old peasant houses and run-down bars, with some new shops going up in plastic neo-Baroque style.

Apart from Aquincum's Roman ruins and a couple of art museums (the **Kiscelli**, the **Vasarely** and the **Budapest Galéria**) the only reasons to come up here are for the stretch of bars and stalls selling cheap fish on the Danube by Római Fürdő. For a week or so every August, the area buzzes as Hungary's rocking youth crams out Óbuda island for the **Sziget** festival.

Csepel

Budapest's industrial District XXI perches at the very tip of Csepel Island, in the middle of the Danube to the south of the city centre. Militant, proud, and independent-minded, it was known as 'Red Csepel' in the interwar years, and in 1944 held one of the few successful acts of mass resistance against the Nazis as locals refused to be evicted en masse. In 1956 its local workers' council was, in turn, one of the longest to hold out against the Soviets.

Óbuda – *long ago a Roman outpost.*

It's easily reached by the HÉV from Boráros tér, an interesting ride running down by the Danube and then over the area of waste ground that might have housed Expo '96, had Hungary not fessed up to the fact that it couldn't afford it.

Szent Imre tér is the centre. Down the end of Tanácsház utca is the main gate for the enormous Csepel Iron and Metal Works. Founded as the Manfred Weiss Works and for a while in the 1950s named after Mátyás Rákosi (the huge Lenin statue which once stood outside the gates is now a feature of the Statue Park), it's no longer one monolithic state enterprise but still employs thousands of people in the area.

Although it is not strictly speaking allowed, it's easy to get inside: tell them you're visiting the Gyártörténi Múzeum (which exists on Központi út inside, but is invariably closed) and they'll issue you with a pass resembling a raffle ticket. After that, feel free to poke around among this cornucopia of ducts and chimneys, back lanes with corrugated tin roofing and ivy-covered brick, desolate workshops full of interesting debris, and odd old Communist displays of nuts and bolts. There's even some street life in the complex, including a few cafés and a bicycle shop.

Around Béke tér, near the terminus of the HÉV, various run-down but friendly bars provide a dilapidated dose of the local pride.

DANUBIUS
THERMAL HOTEL
HELIA

Enjoy romantic Budapest
with services of a luxurious hotel!

* A centrally located superior first class hotel in modern ambience
* Comfortable guest rooms with a charming view onto the river Danube,
Margaret Island and Buda Hills
* Gastronomical pleasures in our Jupiter restaurant
* Conference and banquet facilities in 8 fully equipped rooms
for 900 delegates
* Extensive Business Center for heavy scheduled businessmen
* Fashionable Fitness Complex with swimming-pool, Jacuzzi, sauna, gym,
thermal and steam baths, the use of which is free for hotel guests.
* Modern Therapy Section with wide range of treatments
and highly qualified multilingual staff
* Newest beauty-treatments for ladies: oxygen therapy, fragrant bath
and body-shaping massage.

Helia for you

H-1133 Budapest, Kárpát u. 62-64. HUNGARY
Tel.: (36-1) 270-3277 Fax: (36-1) 270-2262
E-mail: hhelia@mail.matav.hu

Consumer Budapest

CORINTHIA
AQVINCVM HOTEL
★ ★ ★ ★ ★
BUDAPEST

Half a dozen reasons why to visit Aquincum Corinthia Hotel

Ideal location. Fresh air & ample parking.
Hospitality – personalized service.
Good value for money.
Comfort. Both for business and leisure.
Wide range of facilities.
Reliability.

Why not?...Comfort, service & style
Of course Aquincum Corinthia!

H-1036 Budapest, Árpád fejedelem útja 94.
Phone: (36-1) 250-3360
Fax: (36-1) 250-4672

Accommodation

Booking ahead is the key to finding the right place – be it a luxurious spa hotel, a Buda hill panzió or a cheap room in downtown Pest.

In Budapest accommodation boils down to two basic questions. Pest or Buda? And, is the place you'd like to stay already booked? The first is mere preference. Accommodation in Pest puts you in the heart of the downtown within minutes of the major sights, shopping, museums and nightlife. The ideal *panzió* (pension) in Buda places you a little farther from the centre, but will reward with a pleasant, cool garden and a view out over the city.

Answering the second question is more of a challenge. It isn't to say that there aren't plenty of rooms – the number of hotels in Budapest has steadily increased since 1990. Rather, finding a room in the right location, and in the right price range can be difficult; especially in the Moderate and Budget categories. Thus, booking in advance is advised whenever possible; a fax in English at least two weeks before you plan to arrive with a follow-up call should suffice. Receptionists in nearly all of the hotels and *panziók* listed here speak enough English to handle a basic telephone conversation. One helpful innovation is the Hungary Info Web Site (*http: //www.hotelinfo.hu*) which allows you to look up information on almost all of the hotels in Budapest and Hungary.

If you have arrived without booking ahead, IBUSZ (open 24 hours daily) is reliable for local accommodation in a hotel, *panzió* or private room and will book free of charge. Though they do have their favourites (not always the best), don't be afraid to ask them for help in contacting a specific place. American Express books hotels for a $20 service fee. If booking yourself, Tourinform can provide a free brochure with current listings for most of the hotels and *panziók* in Hungary.

High season runs from late spring through early autumn with prices increased accordingly. During the spring festival (late April-early May) and the Hungarian Grand Prix (second week of August) it is best to book at least a month in advance to be sure to get something in your price range.

With the exception of the **Hilton** in the Castle District and the **Kempinski** on Erzsébet tér, the major hotels line the Pest bank of the Danube, just south of the Chain Bridge. All of them were either built after 1990 or have been renovated since then. While they claim to be five-star hotels, and services are extensive, there's little feeling of luxury,

except perhaps at the Kempinski. Digital phone extensions for laptops are a recent innovation in all but the Hilton. Less expensive hotels are scattered around the city offering either the convenience of central location, or the quiet of the Buda hills. Among these hotels, those built after 1990 or under private ownership tend to have better rooms, more facilities and friendlier staff.

Most of the communist-era hotels – despite, in some cases, renovations that have traded 1970s kitsch for the 1990s model – still impose average restaurants and a cavalier attitude towards service. On the bright side, alternatives in the moderate price ranges are increasing every year. *Panziók* offer many of the same services found in hotels, but with a more personal touch. A number of small, medium-range hotels (usually west-European owned), such as the **City Panzió Pilvax** and **City Panzió Mátyás**, have recently opened in the central districts. Not pretending to cater to the business élite, and providing only the most essential services, they make their best impression with competent, friendly staff and tastefully furnished rooms. Both these and *panziók* will often give generous rate reductions for stays longer than a few days.

Spa hotels are another interesting alternative. Budapest is the only European capital with hot springs and the city has long been the destination for travellers seeking the benefits of the warm mineral-laden water. The **Thermal Hotel Helia**, **Gellért**, **Hotel Aquincum**, **Thermal Hotel Margitsziget**, and the adjacent **Ramada** all have spa facilities on the premises and are recommended in that order. Stay for a few nights, or book in for a one- or two-week 'cure' at a special price. Find not only swimming, sauna, and thermal pools of varying temperatures, but medical and beauty services that include massage, mud baths and hydrotherapy. *See also chapter* **Baths**.

Private rooms (*fizetővendég szolgálat*) are the least expensive option in the city outside of the youth hostel scene (between Ft3,000-Ft5,000 for a double per night). IBUSZ books private rooms and Keleti station is the hunting ground for Hungarians with rooms to let. Ask to see where you'll be staying before accepting a room or agreeing to a price – breakfast of some kind should be included. Though many are very comfortable indeed, rooms and their owners receive only cursory inspection by the tourism board. Beware of ending up stranded in a cramped District XVI apartment with a landlady from hell looking through your dirty socks and expecting you to be home before ten.

Finding a more permanent residence in Budapest is, if anything, even harder than finding a hotel. Word of mouth is best for inexpensive digs, followed by the *Expressz* daily classified ad paper (*see chapter* **Media**). Watch out, though; most apartments are listed by agencies that will charge Ft2,500 to give you a list of addresses which may or may not be out of date. If you have a bit more money to spend, try one of the real estate agents advertised in *Budapest Week* or *Budapest Sun*. Though they offer more expensive properties, they are more likely to give you an honest deal. Housing is still subsidised and most of the people you might sublet from are paying ridiculously low rents. Foreigners are expected to fork out, though. Expect to pay up to Ft45,000-Ft55,000 per month plus utilities for a two-room flat in the centre.

Prices in the Hungarian tourist industry are pegged to the Deutschmark and hotels list their prices in this currency, although payments can be made in forints. We have, therefore, listed hotel prices in this guide in Deutschmarks. At the time of going to press, DM1 was buying around Ft105 though this will doubtless change. Also 15 per cent VAT will often be added.

Unless otherwise noted, breakfast is included in the price. In most cases, this consists of a cold buffet of bread, cheeses and cold-cuts. Hotels in the expensive range and some *panziók* offer an 'American' breakfast which includes hot and cold buffet. Price categories are as follows: a double room in a De Luxe hotel costs DM330 or more; an Expensive hotel DM230 or more; a Moderate hotel DM120 or more; the rest are Budget.

Top Tips

A somewhat less-than-definitive selection:

Best place to pretend to have conquered Europe over a cappuccino and scones:
Hotel Astoria

Best communist-era light fittings:
Hotel Agro

Most ferocious old lady on reception (and most unpronounceable name):
Vasutas Egyesületek Vendégszobaháza

Best place to imagine you're a superstar or plot your next leveraged buy-out:
Hotel Korvinus Kempinski

Most luxurious accommodation for backpackers:
Hostel Marco Polo

Finest view from breakfast terrace:
Molnár Panzió

Best deal for well-located, nondescript room in the city centre:
City Panzió Mátyás

Most affordable faded downtown grandeur:
Hotel Metropol

Best place to pacify your gout in an old-fashioned spa atmosphere:
Hotel Gellért

Most genteel atmosphere for the seasoned traveller:
Ábel Panzió

Grandest foyer for budget accommodation (just don't show anyone your room):
Hotel Kulturinov

Only five-star hotel with riverside location whose view isn't spoilt by the Budapest Hilton:
Budapest Hilton

Booking

American Express
V. Deák Ferenc utca 10 (266 8680/fax 267 2028). M1, M2, M3 Deák tér. **Open** *Sept-May* 9am-5.30pm Mon-Fri; 9am-2pm Sat. *June-Aug* 9am-6.30pm Mon-Fri; 9am-2pm Sat. **Credit** AmEx. **Map C4**
Information, exchange and hotel reservations for a $20 fee.

IBUSZ
V. Apáczai Csere János utca 1 (118 3925/118 5776/fax 117 9099). M1 Vörösmarty tér. **Open** 24 hours daily. **Map C4**
Perhaps the only useful remnant of socialist tourism in Hungary, the now privatised IBUSZ books for approximately 80 per cent of Budapest's hotels and *panziók* free of charge, and will often be able to give a better rate than you would get by going directly to the hotel. Courteous though often harried staff will also help you find a private room, or a short-stay apartment (up to 2-3 weeks), as well as booking flight tickets, arranging private sightseeing tours and changing money.

Tourinform
V. Sütő utca 2 (117 9800/fax 117 9587). M1, M2, M3 Deák tér. **Open** 9am-7pm Mon-Fri; 9am-4pm Sat-Sun. **No credit cards. Map C4**
A branch of the Hungarian tourist board, Tourinform will cheerfully provide accurate answers to the most obscure questions about anything having to do with tourists in Hungary. No room booking, but stop by to get useful brochures and a comprehensive Hungarian hotel booklet.
e-mail: tourinfo@tourinform.hu
http://www.hungary.com/tourinform/

De Luxe

Buda

Hotel Aquincum

III. Árpád fejdelem útja 94 (250 3360/250 4114/fax 250 4672). HÉV Árpád híd. **Rates** *single* DM290; *double* DM 340; *suite* DM480. **Credit** AmEx, DC, EC, JCB, MC, V.
Actually one of the more pleasant hotels in Budapest, the Aquincum ranks near to the five-star downtown hotels in overall services, but misses the mark for style of both décor (cheesy and brash) and service (obsequious and smug). Though bit of a haul from the centre, the Aquincum is still good value and the extensive spa facilities make up for a few more minutes in a taxi. Skip the restaurant, though. *See chapters* **Baths** *and* **Sport & Fitness**.
Hotel services *Air-conditioning. Babysitting. Bars (3). Beauty salon. Car park (DM18). Conference facilities. Currency exchange. Disabled: access. Fax. Laundry. Lift. Non-smoking rooms (16). Restaurants (2). Safe. Sauna. Solarium. Swimming pool.*
Room services *Hair-dryer. Mini-bar. Radio. Room service. Telephone. TV.*

Hilton Hotel

I. Hess András tér 1-3 (214 3000/fax 156 0285). M2 Moszkva tér, then Várbusz. **Rates** *single* DM280-DM330; *double* DM365-DM415; *suite* DM530-DM820; *extra bed* DM85; *breakfast* DM29. **Credit** AmEx, DC, EC, JCB, MC, V. **Map A3**
Spectacular views over the Danube are the trade-off for a location away from central Pest (and rooms without views make up for the lack with extra space). It's designed around a seventeenth-century façade (once part of a Jesuit cloister) and the remains of a thirteenth-century Gothic church, with a small, open-air concert hall between the two main wings, used for summer opera performances. Also interesting is a walk through the remains of the cloister to the Faustus wine cellar where Hungarian vintages can be sampled or purchased. The Hilton is among the few Budapest hotels to create a sense of luxury and service is among the best in town. Booking several weeks in advance is advised.
e-mail: hiltonhu@hungary.net
Hotel services *Air-conditioning. Babysitting. Bars (2). Beauty salon. Business centre. Car park (DM29). Casino. Coffee shop. Conference facilities. Currency exchange. Disabled: access. Fax. Laundry. Lift. Non-smoking rooms (50). Restaurants (2). Safe. Sauna. Solarium. Swimming pool.*
Room services *Hair-dryer. Mini-bar. Radio. Room service. Safe. Telephone. TV.*

Pest

Atrium Hyatt Budapest

V. Roosevelt tér 2 (266 1234/fax 266 9101). M1 Vörösmarty tér. **Rates** *single* DM310-DM430; *double* DM410-DM490 *suite* DM500-DM1000; *extra bed* DM60-86; *breakfast* DM26. **Credit** AmEx, DC, EC, JCB, MC, V. **Map C4**
Standard but pleasant rooms open off the central atrium from which the hotel takes its name. Centrally located with Danube views and catering mainly to business travellers, the Atrium is rather cavernous, designed in faintly cheesy 1970s American style (fountains, potted palms, indoor terrace bar with cane furniture). Otherwise, the service is polite and the Balloon Bar remains an excellent spot with an unequalled view of the river, Chain Bridge and Castle Hill beyond. For those wanting to entertain on a grand scale, the Hyatt will rent and cater the nearby Ethnographic museum.
e-mail: atriumhyatt@pannoniahotels.hu
Hotel services *Air-conditioning. Babysitting. Bar. Beauty salon. Business centre. Car park (Ft3,000).*

Atrium Hyatt – *cavernous but courteous.*

Casino. Coffee shop. Conference facilities. Currency exchange. Fitness centre. Laundry. Lift. Massage. Non-smoking rooms (43). Restaurants (3). Safe. Sauna. Solarium. Swimming Pool.
Room Services *Hair-dryer. Mini-bar. Radio. Room service. Safe. Telephone. TV.*

Hotel Inter-Continental

V. Apáczai Csere János utca 12-14 (117 9111/fax 117 9808). M1 Vörösmarty tér. **Rates** *single* DM300-DM360; *double* DM360-DM400; *triple* DM380-DM420; *suite* DM500-DM700; *breakfast* DM19-DM29. **Credit** AmEx, DC, EC, JCB, MC, V. **Map C4**
The takeover of the old Forum hotel by Inter-Continental in May 1997 encouraged high hopes for what is potentially a top-notch hotel. As this book went to press, however, it remained to be seen whether Inter-continental's management would make much needed renovations to what were formally rather drab rooms, and whether it would work to create a more friendly atmosphere among staff who in the past could only rarely capture the refined, professional style essential to anything calling itself a five-star hotel. Nonetheless, every room in the Inter-Continental has a Danube view and the lobby continues to hum with business deals in the making. With luck, the Bécsi Kávéház on the first floor will keep up its tradition of fine pastries (*see chapter* **Cafés & Coffeehouses**).
e-mail: budapest@interconti.com
Hotel services *Air-conditioning. Babysitting. Bar. Beauty salon. Business centre. Car park (DM25). Casino. Coffee shop. Conference facilities. Currency exchange. Disabled: access. Fax. Laundry. Lift. Massage. Non-smoking rooms (50). Restaurants (2). Sauna. Solarium. Swimming pool.*
Room services *Hair-dryer. Mini-bar. Radio. Room service. Safe. Telephone. TV.*

TAVERNA
Hotel & Restaurant Co.

WELCOME TO HUNGARY AND TO OUR ELEGANT HOTELS AND PENSIONS WITH EXCELLENT SERVICES!

Hotel Taverna****

H-1052 Budapest, Váci utca. 20.
Tel.: (361) 138-4999
Fax: (361) 118-7188
E-mail: hotel@hoteltaverna.hu
Internet:
http://www.hoteltaverna.hu

The only hotel in the elegant pedestrian and shopping zone, in Váci utca. Restaurant, brasserie, Zsolnay Café, Grill bar, air-conditioned rooms and garage available.

Hotel Liget***

H-1068 Budapest, Dózsa Gy. 106.
Tel.: (361) 269-5300
Fax: (361) 269-5329
E-mail: hotel@liget.hu
Internet: http://www.liget.hu

The Hotel Liget close to the famous Heroes's Square with air-conditioned rooms, bar, sauna, solarium and garage available. Museums and entertainment facilities nearby.

City Panzió*** Chain in Budapest
Pensions in the inner city of Budapest, three-star hotel comfort at the most reasonable rates.

City Panzió Mátyás***

H-1056 Budapest,
Március 15. tér 8.
T. (361) 138-4711
Fax: (361) 117-9086
E-mail: matyas@taverna.hu

City Panzió Pilvax***

H-1052 Budapest,
Pilvax köz 1-3.
T. (361) 266-7660
Fax: (361) 117-6396
E-mail: pilvax@taverna.hu

City Panzió Ring***

H-1037 Budapest,
Szt. István krt. 22.
T. (361) 340-5450
Fax: (361) 340-4884
E-mail: ring@taverna.hu

Ground services:

Taverna Tourist Sevice: transfer services, guaranteed programmes, ticket and restaurant booking, tailor-made programmes and packages

Information:

Taverna Hotel & Restaurant Co., Sales Department, H-1056 Budapest, Molnár u. 28.
Phone: 361-118-0436, Fax: 361-138-4622,
Internet: http://www.taverna.hu, E-mail: sales@taverna.hu

The **Hilton** – *among the few Budapest hotels to reflect a sense of luxury. See page 113.*

Hotel Korvinus Kempinski

V. Erzsébet tér 7-8 (266 1000/fax 266 2000). M1, M2, M3 Deák tér. **Rates** *single* DM410-DM450; *double* DM490-DM530; *suite* DM710-DM3,500; *extra bed* DM80; *breakfast* DM29. **Credit** AmEx, DC, EC, JCB, MC, V. **Map C4**

Built in 1992, the Kempinski is perhaps the only hotel in Budapest which offers true luxury in both service and facilities. Designed specifically for the hotel, Art Deco furnishings are unusual in rooms and bathrooms bigger than average, with extras such as down duvets and slippers. Suites are bigger than most Budapest apartments and there are extensive fitness and leisure facilities. Staff are attentive to detail and courteous without being stifling, though the Kempinski Grill isn't spectacular. Madonna called the Kempinski home when she was here to shoot *Evita*. *e-mail: hotel@kempinski.hungary.net*

Hotel services *Air-conditioning. Babysitting. Bars (2). Beauty salon. Business centre. Car park (Ft2,500). Coffee shop. Conference facilities. Currency exchange. Disabled: access. Fitness centre. Laundry. Lift. Non-smoking rooms (60). Restaurants (2). Sauna. Solarium. Swimming pool.* **Room services** *Hair-dryer. Mini-bar. Radio. Room service. Safe. Telephone. TV.*

Marriott Hotel

Apáczai Csere János utca 4 (266 7000/fax 266 5000). M1 Vörösmarty tér. **Rates** *single* DM310-DM400; *double* DM360-DM420; *suite* 700-DM2,050; *breakfast* DM29. **Credit** AmEx, DC, EC, JCB, MC, V. **Map C4**

Every room has a Danube view and the staff get top marks for excellent service. One of the favourites with the local business community for conferences, the Marriott has a reputation for looking after its guests. Rooms are well furnished and the Marriott offers extras like theme brunches and a well appointed fitness room also looking over the river. The business lounge on the top floor has one of the best views in the city, though it's restricted to guests in the 'Concierge'-level rooms. Madonna may have stayed at the Kempinski while filming *Evita*, but all of her staff stayed at the Marriott.

Hotel services *Air-conditioning. Babysitting. Bar. Business centre. Car park (Ft2,800). Coffee shop. Conference facilities. Currency exchange. Disabled: access. Laundry. Lift. Non-smoking rooms (180). Restaurants (3). Sauna. Solarium. Swimming pool.* **Room services** *Hair-dryer. Mini-bar. Radio. Room service. Safe. Telephone. TV.*

Radisson SAS Béke Hotel

VI. Teréz körút 43 (301 1600/fax 301 1615). M3 Nyugati. **Rates** *single* DM230-DM290; *double* DM290-DM350; *suite* DM600; *extra bed* DM60. **Credit** AmEx, DC, EC, JCB, MC, V. **Map D2**

Cordial service, from well-turned-out doormen to helpful desk staff, and an excellent location near Nyugati station on the glitziest stretch of the körút. Rooms are comfortable with handsome, tasteful furnishings. Full buffet breakfast in the skylit Shakespeare room is pleasant and the pastries in the excessively pink Zsolnay Coffee Shop are recommended (*see chapter* **Cafés & Coffeehouses**).

Hotel services *Air-conditioning. Babysitting. Bars (2). Beauty salon. Business centre. Car park (Ft2,500). Casino. Coffee shop. Conference facilities. Currency exchange. Disabled: access. Fax. Laundry. Lift. Massage. Non-smoking rooms (30). Restaurants (2). Safe. Sauna. solarium. Swimming Pool.* **Room services** *Hair-dryer. Mini-bar. Radio. Room service. Safe. Telephone. TV.*

Thermal Hotel Helia

XIII. Kárpát utca 62-64 (270 3277/fax 270 2262). Trolleybus 79 Dráva utca. **Rates** *single* DM200-DM280; *double* DM240-DM320; *suite* DM460-DM660. **Credit** AmEx, DC, EC, JCB, MC, V.

Budapest's most modern spa hotel is Finnish-owned and decked out in Scandinavian style – warm, pleasant pastel shades and a great deal of pine furniture. Tall glass windows bring light into the spacious two-storey lobby, and link it to the conference rooms on the second level. The white-tiled pool areas also benefit from lots of natural light and the

Most of Budapest's five-star hotels stand to attention along the Pest bank of the Danube.

Helia's spa facilities are by far the cleanest in town (*see chapters* **Baths** and **Sport & Fitness**). Rooms are comfortable and light and all suites have their own sauna. Above-average breakfast and lunch buffet. Five rooms with exceptional facilities for wheelchairs.

e-mail: hhelia@mail.matav.hu

Hotel services *Air-conditioning. Babysitting. Bar. Beauty salon. Business centre. Car park (free). Conference facilities. Currency exchange. Disabled: access. Fitness centre. Hair-dryers. Laundry. Lift. Massage. Restaurants (2). Safe. Sauna. Solarium. Swimming Pool.*

Room services *Mini-bar. Radio. Room service. Telephone. TV.*

Millennium Court Executive Residences

V. Pesti Barnabás utca 4-6 (266 7000/fax 266 5000). M3 Ferenciek tere. **Rates** (pending) DM4,200-DM5,000 per month. **Credit** AmEx, DC, EC, JCB, MC, V. **Map C4**

Due to open shortly after this book went to press (and thus we can't speak for its quality) the Millennium Court is intended to give five-star hotel services to travellers spending more than a few weeks in Budapest by converting the historic Vasudvar into short-term residential apartments and a high-end shopping arcade. Bi-weekly housekeeping and a shopping service are planned as well as facilities to assist residents with visas, residence permits and finding longer-term housing. It looks good in the brochure but the details remain to be seen. The Millennium Court is owned by Marriott, who can provide information – that's their number listed above.

Hotel services *Air-conditioning. Babysitting. Bar. Beauty salon. Business centre. Car park. Casino.*

Expensive

Thermal Hotel Margitsziget

XIII. Margitsziget (311 1000/fax 269 4589). Bus 26 from Nyugati. **Rates** *single* DM 220-260; *double* DM270-DM310; *suite* DM370-DM420; *extra bed* DM50. **Credit** AmEx, DC, EC, MC, V.

A bustling place in the summer, the rooms are small with outdated furnishings reflecting the somewhat 1970s feel of the entire hotel (service included). Air-conditioning is often inadequate and in summer open windows invite copious mosquito bites. However, the spa facilities are extensive, the terrace restaurant next door at the Ramada is pleasant, and the park spreading over the rest of the island is a nice retreat. Order your taxi from the concierge, though; taxis waiting outside the hotel are known to overcharge. *See chapters* **Baths** and **Sport & Fitness.**

Hotel services *Air-conditioning. Babysitting. Bars (2). Beauty salon. Business centre. Car park (DM17, free outside). Conference facilities. Currency exchange. Disabled: access. Hair-dryers. Laundry. Lift. Non-smoking rooms (46). Restaurant. Safe. Sauna. Solarium. Swimming Pool.*

Room services *Mini-bar. Radio. Room service. Telephone. TV.*

Ramada Grand Hotel

XIII. Margitsziget (311 1000/fax 269 4589). Bus 26 from Nyugati. **Rates** *single* DM180-DM270; *double* DM230-DM310; *apartment* DM350-DM520, *extra bed* DM50. **Credit** AmEx, DC, JCB, MC, V.

Sharing the same spa facilities as the Thermal Hotel Margitsziget (they are reached through an underground tunnel so you can scurry through in your dressing gown), the Ramada has a much more pleasant atmosphere and bigger, cleaner rooms. Though not air-conditioned, most rooms have a balcony and all contain period furnishings that reflect the hotel's 100-year history. The charming lobby and outside terraces serving the restaurant, ice-cream shop and pizzeria foster a turn-of-the-century feel.

Hotel services *Babysitting. Bars (2). Beauty salon. Business centre. Car park (Ft1,800, free outside). Coffee Shop. Conference facilities. Currency exchange. Disabled: access. Fax. Fitness centre. Laundry. Lift. Non-smoking rooms (20). Restaurant. Safe. Sauna. Solarium. Swimming Pool.*

Room services *Hair-dryer. Mini-bar. Radio. Room service. Telephone. TV.*

Buda

Hotel Gellért

XI. Szt. Gellért tér 1 (166 6867/fax 166 6631). Tram 18, 19, 47, 49 Gellért tér. **Rates** *single DM180-DM220; double DM280-DM320; suite DM430-DM500; extra bed DM100.* **Credit** *AmEx, DC, EC, JCB, MC, V.* **Map C5**

Once one of Budapest's most spectacular spa hotels, the art nouveau Gellért (built 1912-18) earned its reputation in the interwar period – Budapest's 'silver age'. Restaurateur Károly Gundel, who also then ran the Városliget restaurant which still bears his name, entertained visiting dignitaries with Hungarian delicacies. In 1927, when he took over the restaurant here, the swimming pool and terraces were created out back. Built on the site of an old Turkish Bath house, the spa facilities also date from the interwar period and radiate period charm (also worth visiting in their own right: *see chapters* **Baths** *and* **Sport & Fitness**). Since World War II the hotel has been somewhat neglected, and the staff can still sometimes be less than attentive to details. But things are looking up, as owner Danubius began major renovations in the autumn of 1997. Most rooms should be completed by the late spring of 1998. In any case, all of the rooms are different, so its worth taking the time to look at several. The coffee shop is excellent, though the terrace bar is somewhat spoiled by over-abundant midges and heavy traffic outside.
Hotel services *Babysitting. Bar. Beauty salon. Business centre. Car park (free). Casino. Coffee shop. Conference facilities. Currency exchange. Laundry. Lift. Massage. Restaurant. Safe. Sauna. Solarium. Swimming pool.* **Room services** *Hair-dryer. Mini-bar. Radio. Room service. Telephone. TV.*

Hotel Flamenco Budapest

XI. Tas vezér utca 7 (372 2000/fax 165 8007). Tram 61 Tas vezér utca. **Rates** *single DM150-DM200; double DM180-250; suite DM250-350; extra bed DM50-DM60.* **Credit** *AmEx, DC, EC, JCB, MC, V.* **Map B6**

A truly repulsive socialist-era concrete and glass exterior makes the Flamenco's tasteful and elegant interior all that much more surprising. Staff is friendly and professional too – another pleasant surprise. The atrium coffee shop is especially nice, as is the outside terrace restaurant with its view of the adjacent park and supposedly bottomless lake. The cave-like nightclub is to be joined by additional conference facilities and the swimming pool in the basement. Enormous suites and not too far from the central business district.
Hotel services *Air-conditioning. Babysitting. Bar2 (2). Beauty salon. Business centre. Car park (DM15 underground, DM5 on the roof). Casino. Coffee shop. Conference facilities. Currency exchange. Disabled: access. Fax. Laundry. Lift. Non-smoking rooms (30). Restaurants (2). Safe. Sauna. Solarium. Swimming pool.* **Room services** *Hair-dryer. Mini-bar. Radio. Room service. Safe. Telephone. TV.*

Novotel Budapest Centrum

XII. Alkotás utca 63-67 (209 1990/fax 166 5636). Tram 61 from Moszkva tér. **Rates** *single DM164; double DM164-DM230; suite DM299; extra bed DM33-DM43.* **Credit** *AmEx, DC, EC, JCB, MC, V.* **Map A5**

The Budapest Conference Centre next door and a convenient location for motorists are the only outstanding features. Catering almost solely to businessmen, average rooms go with the 1982 tower construction. Extensive facilities include shops, various choices for eating and drinking and Budapest's very first bowling alley. Just as well, really, as there's little else going on in this drab part of town.
Hotel services *Air-conditioning. Babysitting. Bars (2). Beauty salon. Business centre. Car park (DM15). Conference facilities. Currency exchange. Hair-dryers. Laundry. Lift. Massage. Non-smoking rooms (40). Restaurants (3).* **Room services** *Mini-bar. Radio. Room service. Safe. Telephone. TV.*

Pest

Hotel Astoria

V. Kossuth Lajos utca 19-21 (117 3411/fax 118 6798). M2 Astoria. **Rates** *single DM141-DM184; double DM184-DM242; suite DM250-DM320.* **Credit** *AmEx, DC, EC, JCB, MC, V.* **Map D4**

Built between 1912-14 and lending its name to the busy intersection on which it stands, the Astoria is reasonable, central and reeks of old Mitteleuropa. At different points in history, this was the where the National Council met and formed an independent government during the upheavals of October 1918, the favourite hangout of Nazi officials during World War II, and the headquarters for Soviet forces during the 1956 revolution. The elegant panelled and chandeliered Art Nouveau coffee lounge on the ground floor recalls the atmosphere of pre-war Budapest. These days still managed by the state-owned HungarHotel chain, the service is somewhat offhand. The spacious rooms on the street side are noisy, the smaller rooms in back more peaceful. The once popular bar has been converted into a McDonald's, but the baroque dining room has to be one of the most spectacular places to breakfast in Budapest. *See chapter* **Cafés & Coffeehouses**.
Hotel services *Babysitting. Cafe. Car park (DM25). Casino. Conference facilities. Currency exchange. Disabled: access. Fax. Hair-dryers. Laundry. Lift. Restaurant. Safe.* **Room services** *Mini-bar. Radio. Telephone. TV.*

Hotel Erzsébet

V. Károlyi Mihály utca 11-15 (138 2111/fax 118 9237). M3 Ferenciek tere. **Rates** *single DM135-DM210; double DM150-DM250; triple DM280-DM340.* **Credit** *AmEx, DC, JCB.* **Map C4**

Stark but spacious – **Hotel Liget**, *page 121.*

Pannonia Hotel Nemzeti – the blue venue for watching busy Blaha bustle by, page 121.

The dark wood and beige interior betrays communist-era origins, but staff are friendly enough and rooms air-conditioned. The restaurant/bar downstairs is rather naff with rustic illustration of the epic adventures of Hungarian folk-tale hero János Vitéz and the upstairs restaurant looks and feels like a cafeteria. But the central location, conference facilities and good discounts for groups make it popular with business travellers who want a downtown location without downtown prices.
Hotel services *Air-conditioning. Bar. Car park (free). Casino. Conference facilities. Currency exchange. Fax. Gift shop. Laundry. Lift. Hair-dryers. Restaurants(2). Safe.*
Room services *Minibar. Radio. Telephone. TV.*

K+K Hotel Opera
VI. Révay utca 24 (269 0222/fax 269 0230). M1 Opera. **Rates** *single* DM180-DM220; *double* DM240-DM260; *suite* DM350-DM540; *extra bed* DM55-DM70. **Credit** AmEx, DC, EC, MC, V. **Map C3**
The ultra-modern interior radiates Austrian efficiency and the location on a quiet street right around the corner from the Opera and Andrássy út can't be beat. Quiet, immaculate rooms, service with attention to detail, and a big buffet breakfast make a pleasant stay almost inevitable. No restaurant, but there are plenty of eateries in the vicinity.
Hotel services *Air-conditioning. Babysitting. Bar. Car Park (DM15). Conference facilities. Currency exchange. Fax. Laundry. Lift. Snack bar.*
Room services *Hair-dryer. Mini-bar. Radio. Room service. Safe. Telephone. TV.*

Hotel Mercure Korona
V. Kecskeméti utca 14 (117 4111/117 9117/fax 118 3867). M3 Kálvin tér. **Rates** *single* DM196-DM227; *double* DM227-DM268; *extra bed* DM52. **Credit** AmEx, DC, JCB, MC, V. **Map D5**
Built in 1990 and pinkly dominating one side of Kálvin tér. Black columns and an abundance of green marble make the reception area feel somewhat like the inside of a fish tank. Service has been known to verge on the surly, but rooms are

nice enough, fitness facilities extensive, breakfast buffet ample, and the coffee bar in the connecting bridge between the two buildings is a great place to sip a cappuccino while watching traffic whizz around the busy intersection below.
Hotel services *Air-conditioning. Babysitting. Bars (2). Beauty salon. Business centre. Car park (DM18). Coffee Shop. Conference facilities. Currency exchange. Disabled: access. Fax. Laundry. Lift. Massage. Restaurants (2). Safe. Sauna. Solarium. Swimming Pool.*
Room Services *Mini-bar. Radio. Room service. Safe. Telephone. TV.*

Hotel Taverna
V. Váci utca 20 (138 4999/fax 118 7188). M3 Ferenciek tere. **Rates** *single* DM170-DM191; *double* DM218-DM247; *triple* DM267-DM306. **Credit** AmEx, DC, EC, JCB, MC, V. **Map C4**
A standard business hotel right in the middle of the Váci pedestrianised zone with one of the most informative tourist information centres in the city. Some of the rooms are rather cramped, but the management will give significant discounts for longer stays.
e-mail: 100324.235@compuserve.com
Hotel services *Air-conditioning (96 rooms). Babysitting. Bar. Beauty salon. Car park (DM25). Conference facilities. Currency exchange. Fax. Gift shop. Laundry. Lift. Non-smoking rooms (45). Restaurant.*
Room services *Hair-dryer. Mini-bar. Radio. Room service. Safe. Telephone. TV.*

Moderate
Buda

Alba Hotel Budapest
I. Apor Péter utca 3 (175 9244/fax 175 9899). Bus 16 Clark Ádám tér. **Rates** *single* DM165-DM200; *double* DM180-DM200; *triple* DM230-DM250 **Credit** AmEx, DC, JCB, MC, V. **Map B3**

Owned by a Swiss chain and positioned at the foot of Castle Hill. The top three floors are air-conditioned and give a pigeon's eye view of the Víziváros. Rooms are spartan but spacious enough with large, well-lit bathrooms, and the three-bedded room is almost big enough to be a suite. The lobby is also rather stark, with only a small bar, but there's a large breakfast buffet and a Greek restaurant next door.
Hotel services *Babysitting. Bar. Car park (DM25). Conference facilities. Currency exchange. Fax. Hair-dryer. Laundry. Lift. Safe.*
Room services *Mini-bar. Room service. Telephone. TV.*

Orion Hotel

I. Döbrentei utca 13 (156 8583/fax 175 5418). Tram 18, 19/bus 78 Krisztina körút. **Rates** *single* DM95-145; *double* DM130-DM185; *extra bed* DM37. **Credit** AmEx, DC, EC, MC, V. **Map B4**
Frequented by academic guests of local universities, the Orion is small but convenient for the centre. Rooms are clean but plain, the Tabán and Castle Hill are just outside the door, and the restaurant serves inexpensive Hungarian food.
Hotel services *Air-conditioning. Bar. Currency exchange. Fax. Lift. Restaurant. Safe.*
Room services *Hair-dryer. Mini-bar. Radio. Room service (drinks). Telephone. TV.*

Petneházy Country Club Hotel

II. Feketefej utca 2-4 (176 5992/176 5992/fax 175 5738). Bus 56 (red) Adyliget. **Rates** *small bungalow (2-4 people)* DM165-DM195; *large bungalow (4-6 people)* DM210-DM245; *extra bed* DM30. **Credit** AmEx, DC, EC, JCB, MC, V.
Doubling as a country club for the local bourgeoisie, this hotel is actually 45 private bungalows – four of which have disabled access – with a central building housing the reception, pool, restaurant and other services. A location far from the centre is made up for by a peaceful setting and loads of facilities for sport lovers – horseback riding next door, organised bus and boat excursions, and traditional pig-killing parties during winter months (*see chapter* **By Season** *and* **Sports**).
Hotel services *Babysitting. Bar. Bicycles. Car park (free). Conference facilities. Currency exchange. Disabled: access. Fax. Laundry. Restaurant. Safe. Sauna. Solarium. Swimming pool.*
Room services *Kitchen. Mini-bar. Radio. Room service. Safe. Sauna. Telephone. TV.*

Hotel Victoria

I. Bem rakpart 11 (201 8644/fax 201 5816). Bus 16 Clark Ádám tér. **Rates** *single* DM185; *double* DM150-DM195; *extra bed* DM60-DM80. **Credit** AmEx, DC, EC, JCB, MC, V. **Map B3**
One of Budapest's first private *panziók* occupies a townhouse site below the castle, facing the Danube and within easy reach of the main sights. Rooms are big, commanding a view of the river and it's far less expensive than the hotels on the Pest side. No restaurant, but the friendly staff can recommend good choices in the neighbourhood. American breakfast.
Hotel services *Air-conditioning. Babysitting. Bar. Car park (free). Casino. Coffee shop. Conference facilities. Currency exchange. Fax. Laundry. Lift. Sauna.*
Room services *Hair-dryer. Mini-bar. Radio. Room service (drinks). Safe. Telephone. TV.*

Pest

Hotel Art

V. Királyi Pál utca 12 (266 2166/fax 266 2170). M3 Kálvin tér. **Rates** *single* DM130; *double* DM170; *suite* DM250; *extra bed* DM45. **Credit** AmEx, DC, EC, JCB, MC, V. **Map D5**

Dunapart *– a floating option, see page 123.*

Near the quiet end of Váci utca, this newish small hotel is convenient for the centre and there are several good bars in the neighbourhood. The attempt at Art Deco – marble accents, frosty light fittings and an abundance of angular columns – leaves the common areas rather cold, but the rooms are very good for the price. American breakfast.
Hotel services *Air-conditioning. Bar. Car park (Ft1,800). Currency exchange. Disabled access. Fax. Fitness centre. Hair-dryer. Laundry. Lift. Safe. Sauna.*
Room services *Minibar. Room service. Telephone. TV.*

Hotel Central

VI. Munkácsy Mihály utca 5-7 (321 2000/fax 322 9445). M1 Bajza utca. **Rates** *single* DM180; *double* DM190; *suite* DM200-DM220. **Credit** AmEx, EC, V. **Map E2**
Once owned by the Hungarian Communist Party, though the present owners don't like to talk much about the past. In its current incarnation, the Central is a pleasant place in its own sort of way. The dark furnishings complement the 1930s building and the quiet setting of the embassy district, resulting in an intriguing time-warped feel. Staff and services are fine (ask the bell boy about the Central's most famous visitors), but take your meals elsewhere.
Hotel services *Bar. Car park (free). Currency exchange. Fax. Laundry. Lift. Restaurant. Safe.*
Room services *Hair-dryer. Mini-bar. Radio. Telephone. TV.*

City Hotel

XIII. Szent István körút 22 (111 4450/fax 111 0884). M2 Nyugati. **Rates** *single* DM54-DM123; *double* DM75-DM156; *suite* DM103-DM223; *extra bed* DM17-DM36. **Credit** AmEx, DC, EC, MC, V. **Map C2**
A brand new hotel, the City comes highly recommended for a comfortable stay in the heart of the city. Opened in May 1996, the hotel is immaculate and tastefully decorated in blue and cream with light pine accents. The breakfast room is bright and airy, and the prices are some of the best in town with generous discounts for long-term stays. Services are minimal, but there are numerous restaurants in the imme-

BUDAPEST

HILTON

"There's no place like...
HILTON MINI...home"

Do not bother searching through the whole city for the right place to stay.
We have everything you will need for your temporary residence in Budapest.

**Stay in a duplex suite, located in the baroque wing of the hotel,
furnished in contemporary style:**

Downstairs: living room, toilette
Mezzanine
Upstairs: bedroom, bathroom
Total: 68m²
Electricity: 110/220 V, converter available
Color TV set on both levels
Direct telephone line, telephone socket is suitable
for computer hook up

The Mini Home is available for a minimum stay of one month at a super rate of:

★ DM 4500 + 12% VAT / MONTH ★

Discounts and benefits:

25% on Food & Beverage consumption, garage and laundry
telephone costs at PTT charge
free newspaper daily

Make yourself at home in Hilton's MINI HOME!

H-1014 BUDAPEST, HESS ANDRÁS TÉR 1-3.
TEL.: (36-1) 214-3000 FAX: (36-1) 156-0285
e-mail: hiltonhu@hungary.net

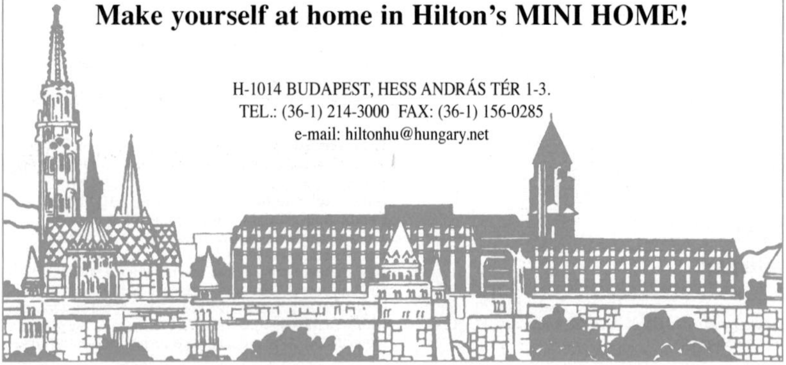

diate vicinity, and easy public transportation links to just about anywhere in town.
e-mail: 100324.235@compuserve.com
Hotel services *Currency exchange. Car park (Ft1,500). Laundry. Safe.* **Room services** *Mini-bar. Radio. Telephone. TV.*

City Panzió Pilvax
V. Pilvax köz 1-3. (266 7648/fax 117 6396). M3 Ferenciek tere. **Rates** *single DM67-DM123; double DM94-DM156; suite DM201-DM223; extra bed DM30-DM36.*
Credit AmEx, V. **Map C4**
The breakfast room and outside terrace of the Pilvax were one of the favorite haunts of Hungarian heroes Sándor Petőfi and Mór Jókai, and in later days, dissidents of the communist era. Inside is a brand new modern hotel in the heart of the city. Uninspiring but clean and efficient. Long-term guests should negotiate a discount.
e-mail: 100324.235@compuserve.com
Hotel services *Bar. Car park (free). Conference facilities. Currency exchange. Fax. Laundry. Restaurant. Safe.* **Room services** *Mini-bar. Radio. Telephone. TV.*

City Panzió Mátyás
V. Március 15 tér 8 (138 4711/fax 117 9086). M3 Ferenciek tere. **Rates** *single DM54-DM123; double DM74-DM156; apartment DM129-DM223; extra bed DM17-DM36.* **Credit** AmEx, DC,EC, JCB, MC, V. **Map C4**
Part of the Taverna group, the Mátyás offers excellent value at a great location. Like its newer sister the City Hotel, the two-year-old *panzió* offers friendly staff and well appointed rooms with no frills. No bar, but most of Pest's great attractions are just steps away by foot or public transport. A bonus is the adjoining Mátyás Pince Restaurant, well-known for classic Hungarian food and Gypsy music.
e-mail: 100324.235@compuserve.com
Hotel services *Currency exchange. Laundry. Safe.* **Room services** *Mini-bar. Radio. Telephone. TV.*

Grand Hotel Hungaria
VII. Rákóczi út 90 (322 9050/fax 351 0675). M2 Keleti. **Rates** *single DM150-DM220; double DM180-DM270; suite DM210-DM370; extra bed DM100.* **Credit** AmEx, DC, EC, JCB, MC, V. **Map E4**
A jovial atmosphere pervades a lobby buzzing with tour groups. Budapest's largest hotel has 511 rooms and extensive, though not exceptional, restaurant and conference facilities. Rooms are generally comfortable but vary greatly in size, so look first to make sure you don't get one of the broom cupboards. The tennis court is an open-air, roof-top affair.
e-mail: grandhun@hungary.net
Hotel services *Air-conditioning. Babysitting. Bars (2). Beauty salon. Business centre. Car park (Ft2,250). Conference facilities. Currency exchange. Fax. Fitness centre. Laundry. Lift. Restaurants (2). Safe. Sauna. Solarium. Tennis court..* **Room services** *Mini-bar. Radio. Room service. Telephone. TV.*

Hotel Liget
VI. Dózsa György út 106 (269 5300/342 7586/fax 342 5185). M1 Hősök tér. **Rates** *single DM134-DM209; double DM148-DM224; extra bed DM43-62.* **Credit** AmEx, DC, JCB, MC, V. **Map E1**
Though pleasantly situated next to the Városliget, the Liget has a rather stark modern feel. Recently built by an Austrian-Hungarian firm, and part of the Taverna group, the place targets people on the move. Common areas are minimal and the entrance and outside terrace are dominated by the ramp to the car park. However, the 139 rooms are clean, spacious and 55 of them have air-conditioning.
e-mail: 100324.235@compuserve.com
Hotel services *Air-conditioning. Bar. Business centre. Car park (DM15). Coffee shop. Conference facilities.*

Present tents – **Romai-Parti Diák Camping**.

Currency exchange. Laundry. Lift. Massage. Non-smoking rooms (24). Safe. Sauna. Solarium.
Room services *Mini-bar. Radio. Room service. Safe. Telephone. TV.*

Pannonia Hotel Nemzeti
VIII. József körút 4 (269 9310/fax 314 0019). M2 Blaha Lujza. **Rates** *single DM100-DM150; double DM110-DM190; extra bed DM40-DM45.* **Credit** AmEx, DC, EC, JCB, MC, V. **Map E4**
Watching Budapest walk by from the red velvet chairs in the time-worn lobby that looks out over busy Blaha Lujza tér is one of the best ways to see the city. This plus the grand stairway and dining room and the friendly staff are this 100 year-old hotel's best features. Renovations continue, and all of the street-facing windows are sound-proofed, but ask to see one of the new rooms as the old ones are rather dark.
e-mail: nemzeti@pannoniahotels.hu
Hotel services *Air-conditioning. Bar. Currency exchange. Fax. Hair-dryers. Laundry. Non-smoking rooms (5). Restaurant. Safe.* **Room Services** *Mini-bar. Radio. Telephone. TV.*

Budget

Buda

Ábel Panzio
XI. Ábel Jenő utca 9 (185 6426/209 2537/209 2538). Tram 61. **Rates** *double DM90.* **No credit cards.** **Map A6**
The most beautiful *panzió* in Budapest. An ivy-covered turn-of-the-century house set on a quiet sidestreet and fitted with period furniture in common areas. The neighbourhood is quiet and safe, a couple of tram stops from Móricz Zsigmond

Comfort Health & Recreation:
DANUBIUS HOTELS GROUP

Have you decided to take a break - to relax and enjoy life by concentrating on the essentials? Are you seeking regeneration, fitness and a few quiet days? Do you wish to be spoiled and to recover from your daily stress? Get the values you really need - now!
Special offers for weekends, city-breaks and spa treatments and as well as sport and beauty packages are at our guests' disposal. Trips and tours tailored to meet individual requirements and guide services are also available.

HOTELS IN BUDAPEST
Budapest Hilton*****de luxe • Danubius Hotel Gellért****
Danubius Thermal Hotel Margitsziget**** • Danubius Grand Hotel Margitsziget****
Danubius Thermal Hotel Helia**** • Radisson SAS Béke Hotel****
Park Hotel Flamenco**** • Grand Hotel Hungaria**** • Hotel Budapest****
Hotel Astoria*** • Hotel Erzsébet*** • Hotel Stadion*** • Hotel Expo***
and
First class spa & city hotels throughout the country and resort hotels at Lake Balaton.

Information & Reservation:

DANUBIUS HOTELS GROUP	DANUBE TRAVEL LTD.	DANUBIUS HOTELS
H-1051 Budapest,	6 Conduit Street	D-70182 Stuttgart
Szent István tér 11.	London W1R 9TG	Gaisburgstr. 29
Tel.: 361 374 7229	Tel.: 44 171 493 0263	Tel.: 49 711 247082
Fax: 361 269 2669	Fax: 44 171 493 6963	Fax: 49 711 232924

Internet: www.hungary.net/danubius • www.hungary.net/hungarhotels
E-mail: danubius@hungary.net • hhmktg@hungary.net
or at any UTELL, SRS, and Hilton Int. reservation office

DANUBIUS HOTELS GROUP

körtér. Rooms are sunny and clean with simple modern furniture. Breakfast around a common dining table overlooking a terrace and well-kept garden recalls a mode of travelling long since past. Book in advance.
Hotel services *Bar. Car park (free). Casino. Coffee shop. Conference facilities. Fax. Hair-dryer. TV.*
Room services *Safe. Telephone.*

Hotel Agro

XII. Normafa út 54 (175 4011/fax 175 6764). Bus 21 Normafa. **Rates** *single* DM85-DM115; *double* DM100-DM145; *suite* DM150-DM175; *extra bed* DM25. **Credit** AmEx, DC, EC, MC, V.
Perched high up in the Buda hills, the Agro isn't a rest home for skinheads, as the name might suggest. Rather, the former guest house for Hungary's agricultural élites has gone public but continues to radiate its best socialist-era charm. Rooms aren't anything exceptional, but the views from the rooms and the restaurant are great. A drink or two in the boozer (and a quick round on the bowling alley) are a must for anyone seeking to catch a taste of Hungary's not-so-distant past.
Hotel services *Bars (2). Car park. Coffee shop. Conference facilities. Currency exchange. Fax. Laundry. Lift. Restaurant. Sauna. Swimming pool.*
Room Services *Hair-dryer. Minibar. Radio. Safe. Telephone. TV.*

Beatrix Panzió

II Széher út 3 (275 0550/fax 176 3730). Tram 59 Farkasréti tér. **Rates** *single* DM70-DM90; *double* DM80-DM100; *triple* DM90-DM120; *apartment* DM130; *extra bed* DM10.* **No credit cards.**
The twelve rooms here are comfortable, though nothing special. The location is a couple of tram stops from Moszkva tér, but on a quiet residential street. Guided tours available of the city and other destinations in Hungary and there are weekly summer barbeques in the pretty garden at the rear. American breakfast.
Hotel services *Bar. Car park. Currency exchange. Disabled access. Fax. Safe. Sauna.*
Room services *Telephone. TV.*

Buda Center Hotel

II. Csalogány utca 23 (201 6333/fax 201 7843). Bus 39 Fazekas utca. **Rates** *single* DM65-DM100; *double* DM80-DM120; *triple* DM90-140; *extra bed* DM20. **Credit** AmEx, EC, MC, V. **Map A2**
Conference facilities are in the office space which takes up the other half of the building; services are minimal. Nevertheless, rooms are small but clean with new furniture. The downstairs bar has an impressive selection of beers (including Guinness) and there's a sleepy (but decent) Chinese restauraunt in the foyer.
Hotel services *Air-conditioning. Babysitting. Bar. Car park (DM10). Conference facilities. Currency exchange. Fax. Hair-dryers. Laundry. Lift. Game room. Non-smoking rooms (10). Restaurant. Safe.*
Room services *Mini-bar. Telephone. TV.*

Budai Sport Centrum

XII. Jánoshegyi út (395 6492/395 6493/fax 395 6192). Bus 21 (red) Jánoshegy. **Rates** *single* Ft5,600; *double* Ft6,700; *apartment* Ft6,700. **No credit cards.**
High above the city on János Hill with a lovely view down over Pest, it's about 20 minutes from Moszkva tér by bus and is the place for Budapest's most inexpensive rooms with a view. Lots of sport and relaxation possibilities in the acres and acres of parkland nearby.
Hotel services *Bar. Car park (free). Fax. Laundry. Lift. Massage. Restaurant. Safe. Sauna. solarium. Swimming pool.*
Room services *Hair-dryer. Mini-bar. Radio. Room service. Safe. Telephone. TV.*

Kulturinov – *grand, vaulted foyer. Page 124.*

Charles Apartment House

I. Hegyalja út 23 (201 1796/212 2584/fax 202 2984). Bus 8 or 112 Mészáros utca. **Rates** *single* DM59-DM72; *double* DM63-DM76; *triple* DM75-DM90. **Credit** MC, V. **Map B5**
Spacious studio flats in a converted apartment block are fully self-catering, though the young and enthusiastic staff remain on hand at the reception 24 hours. The flats consist of kitchen, generous bathroom and very large bedroom/sitting-room, all with magnificent views over Buda – possibly the best value for long-term accommodation in the city.
Hotel services *Air-conditioning (some rooms). Photocopying . Car park (Ft900). Currency exchange. Disabled access. Fax. Hair-dryer. Laundry. Lift. Safe.*
Room services *Mini-bar. Telephone. TV.*

Hotel Dunapart

I. Szilágyi Dezső tér, Alsó rakpart (155 9244/fax 155 3770). M2 Batthyány tér. **Rates** *single* DM80-DM110; *double* DM100-130; *triple* DM120-DM160; *extra bed* DM15. **Credit** AmEx, DC, EC, JCB, MC, V. **Map B3**
Tiny air-conditioned cabin rooms look out towards an unusual water-level view of Parliament from this floating hotel, moored near Batthyány tér on the Buda side of the river. The restaurant is rather expensive, but the fine view toward the chain bridge from the terrace on the back deck is well worth it on summer evenings. The inexplicable Korean gift shop is a recent addition.
Hotel services *Air-conditioning. Bar. Car park (free). Currency exchange. Fax. Laundry. Restaurant. Safe.*
Room services *Radio. Room service. Telephone. TV.*

Hotel Express

XII. Beethoven utca 7-9 (tel/fax 175 3082). Tram 59 Királyhágó tér. **Rates** *single* DM30; *double* DM55; *dormitory* DM23. **No credit cards.**
One of the few remaining cheap hotels in Buda is frequented by people with backpacks. Rooms are clean, if a bit worn,

and bathroom and showers are in the hall. Friendly communal breakfast room and quiet secluded location not far from Moszkva tér.
Hotel services *Car park (free). Conference facilities. Currency exchange. Fax. Safe.*

Kulturinov Hotel

I. Szentháromság tér 6 (155 0122/fax 175 1886). M2 Moszkva tér then Várbusz. **Rates** *single* DM95; *double* DM120; *triple* DM150; *extra bed* DM45. **Credit** AmEx, DC, JCB, MC, V. **Map A3**
Location and price are the attractions in a building that also houses the Hungarian Cultural Foundation and some of the National Archives. Upstairs and to the right from the huge vaulted entry, the cell-like rooms have few luxuries, but the Mátyás templóm and Castle District are just outside the door.
Hotel services *Bar. Babysitting. Car park. Conference facilities. Currency exchange. Fax. Gift Shop. Safe. Telephone. TV.*

Molnár Panzió

XII. Fodor utca 143 (tel/fax 395 1872). Bus 53 Rácz Aladár utca. **Rates** *single* DM70-DM90; *double* DM90-DM110; *triple* DM100-DM130. **Credit** AmEx, DC, EC, MC, V.
High on a Buda hill and now boasting three-star services, the Molnár recently completed a new building, adding 23 new rooms and a small conference space. All rooms have unique features and are tastefully decorated. Some nestle under wood panelled eaves; others have sunken bathtubs and windows looking out over Pest. There's even a little A-frame cabin in the beautiful back garden. Opt to share a bathroom and shave a little off the price. Service is meticulous and the terrace restaurant downstairs is an excellent spot for summertime meals.
Hotel services *Bar. Beauty salon. Car park. Conference facilities. Currency exchange. Fax. Fitness room. Laundry. Restaurant. Safe. Sauna.*
Room services *Mini-bar. Telephone. TV.*

Queen Mary Hotel

XII. Béla Király út 47 (274 4000/274 4001/274 4002/fax 156 8377). Bus 28 Béla Király út. **Rates** *single* DM72-DM115; *double* DM80-DM130; *triple* DM85-DM150; *apartment* DM95-DM180. **Credit** AmEx, DC, JCB, MC, V.
Popular with families bringing their children to the nearby Pető Institute (for children suffering from cerebral palsy), this quiet *panzió* high in the Buda Hills will gladly arrange discounts for extended stays.
Hotel services *Bar. Car park (free). Currency exchange. Fax. Laundry. Restaurant. Safe. Sauna. Solarium.*
Room services *Mini-bar. Telephone. TV.*

UhU Villa

II. Keselyű utca 1 (275 1002/fax 176 3876). Tram 56 Vadaskerti utca. **Rates** *single* DM90; *double* DM100; *apartment* DM140; *extra bed* DM30. **No credit cards.**
An excellent *panzio* nestled among tall fir trees in a quiet valley ten minutes from Moszkva tér. The turn-of-the-century villa has small but cosy rooms and a quaint charm pervades the common areas. American breakfast in the solarium overlooking the lovely flower garden is the perfect prelude to a short walk down the hill to the tram and the heart of Budapest.
Hotel services *Bar. Car park (free). Fax. Safe. Solarium.*
Room services *Mini-bar. Telephone. TV.*

Walzer Hotel

XII. Németvölgyi út 110 (319 1212/fax 319 2964). Tram 59 Liptó utca. **Rates** *single* DM138; *double* DM188; *triple* DM240; *suite* DM330. **Credit** AmEx, DC, EC, JCB, MC, V.
In a quiet hillside garden neighborhood, the Walzer is a recently built mansion in which rooms with reproduction Biedermeier furniture look into Farkasréti cemetery (*see*

chapter **Sightseeing**) across the street. Immaculate, spacious bathrooms, pleasant common areas and a well-appointed dining room with adjoining lawn.
Hotel services *Babysitting. Car park (free). Currency exchange. Fax. Laundry. Lift. Restaurant. Safe.*
Room services *Mini-bar. Radio. Telephone. TV.*

Pest

Hotel Benczúr

VI. Benczúr utca 35 (342 7970/342 7975/fax 342 1558). M1 Hősök tere. **Rates** *single* DM90-DM130; *double* DM110-DM150; *triple* DM150-DM180. **Credit** EC, MC, V. **Map E2**
The main attractions of this rather stuffy hotel are reasonable prices for a central location and adequate services. Tacky décor has survived an early 1990s renovation, as did rather dark, cramped rooms. The desk staff have difficulties with anything other than basic English, but you can get your teeth fixed by the in-house dentist.
Hotel services *Bars (2). Car park (DM5). Casino. Conference facilities. Currency exchange. Dentist. Fax. Laundry. Lift. Restaurant. Souvenir shop. Thai massage.*
Room services *Mini-bar. Telephone. TV.*

Hotel EMKE

VII. Akácfa utca 1-3 (342 0197/322 9230/fax 322 9233). M2 Blaha Lujza tér/tram 4, 6. **Rates** *single* DM75-DM120; *double* DM95-DM150; *apartment* DM125-DM180; *extra bed* DM30. **Credit** AmEx, DC, EC, MC, V. **Map E4**
What looks from the outside to be an unrelieved socialist monstrosity rewards inside with newly remodelled rooms (common rooms are set to be overhauled in the winter of 1999). Not a lot of services and no restaurant, but the location is excellent next to Blaha Lujza tér. Friendly, relaxed staff are helpful without imposing. Special group rates. Named after the famous coffeehouse which once stood on the

Mansion worth mentioning – **Walzer Hotel.**

Invasion of the hostel hustlers – if you have a backpack, they'll find you. See page 127.

same block (now the Chicago restaurant) which was in turn named after the Hungarian acronym for the Transylvanian Public Education Association.
e-mail: emke@pannoniahotels.hu
Hotel services *Car park (DM15). Currency exchange. Fax. Laundry. Lift. Non-smoking rooms (30). Safe.*
Room services *Mini-bar. Radio. Telephone. TV.*

King's Hotel
VII. Nagy Diófa utca 25-27 (352 7621). M2 Blaha Lujza.
Rates *single DM105; double DM120-DM140; triple DM155.* **Credit** AmEx, DC, MC, V. **Map D4**
A welcoming family-run hotel in the heart of the Jewish quarter with a variety of room-types to suit particular needs. It has the prize attraction of a Mehadrin kosher restaurant (about half of the guests are Orthodox Jews) where your visit may coincide with one of the many Hasidic weddings the hotel hosts.
Hotel services *Air-conditioning. Currency exchange. Fax. Laundry. Lift.Restaurant. Safe.*
Room services *Safe. Telephone. TV.*

Hostel Marco Polo
VII. Nyár utca 6. (342 9586/342 9587/342 9588/fax 342 9589). M2 Blaha Lujza tér. **Rates** *dormitory Ft2,900; double Ft9,200; quad Ft14,800; breakfast Ft300.*
No credit cards. Map D4
Opened in July 1997, and equipped with a cyber café and in-house Guinness pub, the Marco Polo is the youth hostel of the twenty-first century. A bed will set you back a bit more than at most hostels, but in exchange you get ultra-cleanliness, security and privacy. Twelve-bed dormitory rooms have two showers *en suite* and are divided into bunked cubby holes. Lockers are big and secure while double and quad rooms are up to hotel standards. Quiet enclosed terrace, laundry and e-mail lifeline (address not fixed at time of going to press) an added bonus.
Hotel services *Air-conditioning. Bar. Currency exchange. Fax. Laundry. Restaurant. Safe.*
Room services *Telephone.*

Medosz Hotel
VI. Jókai tér (374 3000/fax 132 4316). M1 Oktogon.
Rates *single DM55-DM69; double DM60-DM72.* **No credit cards. Map D3**

Not the most luxurious hotel in the city centre, but certainly one of the least expensive and with a surprising range of services. Rooms are simple though perhaps a bit stuffy, the beds kind of lumpy and service is haphazard tending toward surly. But it's steps away from Oktogon and the Opera House and an alternative if you'd prefer rubbing shoulders with a Czech tour group instead of a bunch of backpackers.
Hotel services *Bar. Car park (free). Conference facilities. Currency exchange. Fax. Lift. Restaurant. Safe. Solarium.* **Room services** *Radio. Telephone. TV.*

Metropol Hotel
VII. Rákóczi út 58 (342 1175/fax 342 6940). M2 Blaha Lujza. **Rates** *single DM35-DM70; double DM57-DM95 triple DM75-DM120.* **No credit cards. Map E4**
Old and tatty but with a certain charm. Rooms looking out over busy Rakoczi út will be noisy in the morning; and in summer lack of air-conditioning may pose a dilemma between quiet and cool. However, the Metropol offers clean, if spartan, rooms and some have interesting (if rather rickety) old furnishings. Choose to have shower *en suite* (but no toilet), or opt for one down the hall for a cheaper rate. Mind the dodgy restaurant.
Hotel services *Bar. Currency exchange. Fax. Laundry. Restaurant. Safe.*
Room services *Radio. TV.*

Richter Panzió
XIV. Thököly út 111 (363 3956, 363 5761/fax 363 3956). Bus 7 Amerikai út. **Rates** *single DM80-DM120; double DM90-DM140; quad DM140-DM220; extra bed DM20.* **No credit cards. Map F3**
On the inner edge of a Pest garden suburb, the Richter stands in a pleasant neighbourhood less than ten minutes from the city centre by bus. Staff are helpful, though rooms are no better than basic and services are minimal. They do have a Jacuzzi, though.
Hotel services *Bar. Car park. Currency exchange. Fax. Jacuzzi. Laundry. Safe. Sauna.*
Room services *Telephone. TV.*

Vasutas Egyesületek Vendégszobaháza
VI.Szinyei Merse utca 4 (269 4942/fax 131 9148). M1 Kodály körönd. **Rates** *single Ft2,700; double Ft4,700; triple Ft7,100.* **No credit cards. Map D2**

i-D

ALL THE STYLE THAT'S FIT TO PRINT!

Don't miss out on your monthly fix of i-Deas, fashion, clubs, music, people...

FROM ALL GOOD NEWSAGENTS/BOOK STORES PRICED £2.50

Special US Subscription offer only £60. Call + 44 171 813 6170 or e-mail: David.Pepper@i-Dmagazine.co.uk

YOU'RE IN BUDAPEST NOW BUT WHEN IN NEW YORK CITY

CHECK OUT HOTEL 31 MOVING COOL INTO MID-TOWN

CALL FOR OUR BROCHURE:
120 E 31ST STREET
NYC 10016
TEL: 212-685-3060
FAX: 212-532-1232

15% discount for Time Out readers

http://www.timeout.co.uk

Amsterdam, Barcelona, Berlin, Boston, Brussels, Budapest, Chicago, Edinburgh, Glasgow, London, Los Angeles, Madrid, Miami, New York, Paris, Philadelphia, Prague, Rome, San Francisco, Sydney, Tokyo & Washington DC.

The unpronounceable Hungarian Railway Association Guest House happens to be conveniently located in the heart of the embassy district between Oktogon and Hősök tere, and a stay here will definitely put you a few steps back into Hungary's recent past. This communist-era relic offers simple, inexpensive accommodation that is an alternative to the backpacking scene. Rooms are spartan and clean, with communal showers, toilets, TV lounge and breakfast room. Your biggest challenge may be the ferocious matron at the desk. **Hotel services** *Fax. Lift. Massage. Safe. TV.*

Youth Hostels

Between the beginning of July and the end of August, if you haven't already reserved a room, Keleti Station is the most reliable place to find a hostel – and don't worry, if you have a backpack, they'll find you. Usually paid on commission, packs of t-shirted hostel-hustlers rove the station, often boarding trains on the final approach to get a jump on the competition. If you somehow miss the barrage (and it can make for a pretty off-putting arrival in the city), go to the Travellers Youth Hostel information desk (open daily 7am-10pm; tel 06 60 332 236) where you can choose from among ten different student halls of residence in varying price ranges. Expect to pay between Ft1,000-Ft2,000 for dormitories and Ft2,000-Ft4,500 for singles and doubles. You don't have to have an ISIC or Youth Hostel card, but production of one will get you a discount. Services are minimal, though most hostels don't have a curfew. Breakfast is extra, but sheets and hot showers are usually provided. The hostels listed below are open all year round.

Backpack Guest House

XIII. Takács Menyhért utca 33 (185 5089). Bus 7 Tétényi út. **Rates** *dorm* (5-7 bed) Ft1,000. **No credit cards. Map A6**
The party hostel in Budapest is always packed with international youth looking to spend their travellers' cheques in a place where beer is affordable. Kitchen walls covered with pictures and postcards lend a homey atmosphere to late-night drinking sessions assisted by the recently added bar and TV lounge. World traveller/owner Attila is rarely at home, but make friends with Alex the Irish Setter. Caving, water skiing and bridge-jumping excursions for the brave. *Bar. Laundry (Ft600). TV.*

Caterina Youth Hostel

VI. Andrássy út 47 (291 9538/342 0804/fax 352 6147). M1 Oktogon. **Rates** *dorm* DM10; *5-bed apartment* DM14 per person. **No credit cards. Map D3**
In a magnificent nineteenth-century apartment block near Oktogon, the columned balconies and marble statues on the stairs give a glimpse of the city's grander side. The Caterina provides a more genteel atmosphere for the budget traveller than most hostels; but in exchange for quiet, extra cleanliness and comfort, you'll find that the converted apartment's owner expects you to look after her house and not trail your muddy shoes on the carpet – not a bad trade-off, really. *Front-door keys. Full kitchen. Laundry. Fax. Lift. Telephone. TV.*

Citadella Hotel

XI. Citadella sétány (166 5794/fax 186 0505). Bus 27 from Móricz Zsigmond körtér. **Rates** Ft1,129. **No credit cards. Map B5**

Sleep in ten-to-14-bed dormitories inside the Fortress overlooking the Danube on the top of Gellért hill. Standard hotel rooms are also available. One of the most popular cheap lodgings in town if only for the spectacular views while clambering back up the hill after a night on the town. *Bar. Currency exchange. Fax. Safe (Ft150).*

Lotus Youth Hostel

VI. Teréz körút 56, 3rd floor (302 2984/fax 223 5856). M3 Nyugati pályaudvar. **Rates** *dorm* 990Ft; *double* Ft4,000. **No credit cards. Map D2**
The Lotus has a Far Eastern theme but is essentially a friendly, basic hostel with informal and easy-going staff for whom nothing is too much trouble. The only hurdle is finding the entrance – through a courtyard shopping arcade with no visible signs – but the staff will meet new arrivals on the street if they phone in advance. Sightseeing tours arranged. *No curfew. No lock-out. Full kitchen. Breakfast available. Towel and sheet hire. Laundry. Currency exchange. Fax. Lift. Safe. Individual lockers.*

Diák Sport – Travellers Youth Hostels

XIII. Dózsa György út 152 (140 8585/129 8644/fax 120 8425). M3 Dózsa György út. **Rates** *single* Ft1,800; *double* Ft2,800-Ft3,600; *dorm* Ft1,500. **No credit cards. Map F3**
A converted dormitory, this hostel is open all year. The same people run ten other similar places in summer, plus an information booth and a horde of unemployed students foisting leaflets at Keleti to book them. *Bar. Kitchen. Laundry. Lockers. Safe.*

Camping

Numerous camping grounds surround Budapest, though services and prices vary. Pick up a handy brochure and map covering all of Hungary free at **Tourinform**. For group camping, contact individual sites. Prices vary depending on size of sites and facilities availble. Several are by the Danube and offer open-water swimming, though considering the polluted state of the river, this is not advised (nor is eating anything you fish out of it). In general, expect to pay Ft300-Ft600 for a tent site, Ft800-Ft1,500 for a caravan site and Ft350-Ft550 per person plus a small tourism tax.

Csillebérci Autóscamping

XII. Konkoly Thege utca 21 (156 5772/fax 175 9327). Bus 21 (red) Normafa.
Bungalows for rent. Showers. Restaurant. Post office. Swimming pool. Tennis.

Hárs-Hegyi Camping

II. Hárshegyi út 5-7 (115 1482/fax 176 1921). Bus 22 from Moszkva tér.
Bungalows for rent. Showers. Restaurant. Post office.

Római-Parti Diák Camping

III. Királyok útja 191 (06 62 321 103). Bus 34.
Auto repair. Bungalows for rent. Car wash. Fishing. Food shop. Petrol station. Swimming.

Tündérhegyi 'Feeberg' Camping

XII. Szilassy út 8 (06 60 336 256). Bus 28 from Moszkva tér.
Bungalows for rent. Showers. Swimming pool.

Zugligeti 'Niche' Camping

XII. Zugligeti út 101 (200 8346). Bus 158 from Moszkva tér.
Bungalows for rent. Disabled: access. Showers. Restaurant.

Restaurants

From cheap and hearty Hungarian food, to ethnic cuisine from all over the world – dining in Budapest is on the up.

Dining out in Budapest has improved markedly in the last couple of years. There have always been fine restaurants, if one was prepared to pay top dollar. There have also always been cheap places to dine simply but heartily. What's new is a welcome increase in the number of mid-range eateries offering decent cuisine and an enjoyable ambience at prices that won't wallop the wallet – such as **Café Kör**, a central European-style bistro, or **Iguana**, a Tex-Mex expat joint with Budapest prices for American service. Italian food is now particularly well represented, with a host of new places opening in the wake of **Okay Italia**'s success – places like **Via Luna**, **Pinocchio**, **Pizza Bella** or the Iberian-accented **Ristorante Italiano y Español**.

Somewhat further upmarket, places like **Lou Lou**, **Due Lampioni** and **Chez Daniel** are beginning to demonstrate that fine dining doesn't have to be stuffily formal, and that fine ingredients can be an excuse for culinary invention, rather than an end in themselves, as still seems to be the case in older establishments such as **Vadrózsa**.

Asian cuisine is also on the march. The Chinese **Xi-Hu**, the Indian **Shalimar**, the Korean **Naphaz**, and the Japanese **Shiki** and **Miyako** are among the best of new ethnic restaurants in Budapest, taking advantage of the increasing availability of exotic ingredients and offering food and service to a genuine standard.

What hasn't changed much is Hungarian food. Hungary does have a distinct and developed, if somewhat second-rank, cuisine, but decades of communism have taken their toll on its development – nobody has tried to spruce up Magyar fare since Károly Gundel in the early part of this century. Most Hungarian food is old-fashioned – heavy, bland, rich and, contrary to legend, under-spiced. Especially in cheaper places, it's sort of central European school dinners. Aficionados of game and goose liver will enjoy themselves, though, and the fogas, a pike-perch indigenous to Lake Balaton and featured on many menus, is one of the world's most delicate freshwater fish.

We've recommended the best of Hungarian dining at both ends of the price spectrum. For most Hungarians, lunch is the main meal. Dinner in the evening is still often accompanied by Gypsy musicians and Hungarian wines that get better by the year (although in restaurants they're often disgracefully overpriced). Service varies from slow to very slow and, where good, is usually quite formal.

Although you can always find something to eat in the small hours (*see chapter* **Nightlife**), most places tend to wind down before midnight. Vegetarians must work hard to find anything interesting. Hungarian restaurants provide little other than trappist cheese or mushroom caps, boringly breaded and fried (often in goose fat) and served up with tartar sauce. The few dedicated vegetarian restaurants tend to be either dour (**Vegetárium**, **Mirtusz**, **Govinda**) or blissed out (**Gandhi**) and there's an annoying tendency to serve up meatless dishes with live acoustic guitar. But decent salad bars are on the increase, ethnic

Top tips

A selection of Budapest's best restaurants for:

Elegant dining at bargain prices:
Fészek

Nouvelle cuisine in Magyar portion sizes:
Lou Lou

A safe haven in the mean streets around Váci utca:
Cyrano

No-frills pasta and pizza:
Pizza Bella

Expats at play:
Iguana

Authentically rustic ambience:
Nancsi Néni

Off-the-scale cholesterol count:
Hax 'n' Király

Mixing with the Mob:
Rus' Étterem

Weird English menu items:
Barokk

High-quality Hungarian cuisine with all the trimmings:
Gundel

cuisine offers some herbivorous diversity, and contemporary Budapest is more veghead-friendly than ever before.

Averages listed below are for a starter and main course. We've organised restaurants according to price: **Inexpensive** means an average of less than Ft1,200, **Moderate** is between Ft1,200-Ft2,500, and **Top Range** anything upwards of that. Note, though, that prices on any Hungarian menu vary wildly. Even in some of the more expensive places, it's still possible to dine on the relative cheap.

We've also included some of the better étkezdék – cheap and cheerful diners where Hungarians take lunch – and a selection of fast food that you won't already know from back home.

Top Range

Adria Grill
II. Zilah utca 9 (175 7363). Bus 49. **Open** noon-midnight daily. **Average** Ft3,000. **Credit** AmEx, EC, V. English spoken.
A modern villa in a smart residential area whose main attraction is a nicely maintained garden. All the stranger that the inside bit is decorated with plastic flowers. Vast lumps of grilled meat are the specialities and the leg of veal, recommended for two, would be enough for four normal people. The potato soup is a meal in itself.

Barokk
VI. Mozsár utca 12 (131 8942). M1 Oktogon. **Open** noon-midnight daily. **Average** Ft3,000. **Credit** AmEx. English spoken. **Map D3**
A theme restaurant complete with staff in period costume, taped Baroque music and metal platters on the table. Gilt-framed paintings and Louis-XV style chairs lend a luxuri-

ous feel. The menu is in extraordinary language: 'Grilled lifer from Kosmarok', 'The eatable of Grudinovich in salsa and ginger' and 'roste of cu'. Fortunately there are elaborations in modern English. In spite of the weird dishes the menu is broad and user-friendly, and despite the gimmicks this is a really good restaurant.

Belcanto
VI. Dalszínház utca 8 (269 3101/269 2786). M1 Opera. **Open** 6pm-midnight daily. **Average** Ft3,500. **Credit** AmEx, DC, MC, V. English spoken. **Map D3**
In a splendid Baroque room, with unique entertainment: stars from the Opera next door wander around delivering hits of the 1890s and standards of the 1980s. Just when you think the coast is clear, the entire waiting staff appears as a chorus line. The menu is upmarket, in keeping with the furs and jewels which appear as the Opera finishes, but not really first-class. Their various steak options are the best bet. Service is pretty good, considering the waiters have to remain aware their cue might be coming up at any moment. Best time is just before the Opera tips out. A special place, and a wonderful spot for a party. Booking essential.

Chan-Chan
V. Sö utca 3 (118 4266). Tram 47, 49. **Open** noon-4pm, 6pm-11pm daily. **Average** Ft2,800. **Credit** AmEx, MC, V. English spoken. **Map D5**
Run by Laotians, Budapest's only Thai restaurant occupies a generous cellar space decked with fish tanks, Buddhist tat and signed photos of celebrity diners. The menu is long and meat-heavy, but includes a big assortment of prawn, squid and fish dishes and a small vegetarian selection. Soups are particularly good and their spring rolls are the finest in Hungary. Immaculate service. The only drawback is the rotten syrupy muzak, though sometimes they switch this off.

Chez Daniel
VI. Sziv utca 32 (302 4039). M1 Kodály körönd. **Open** noon-3pm, 7pm-midnight daily. **Average** Ft2,800. **Credit** AmEx, DC, JCB, MC, V. English spoken. **Map D2**

Fish tanks, Buddhist tat and Hungary's finest spring rolls – Thai one on at **Chan-Chan**.

THE JOHN BULL® PUB™

John Bull is a timeless, quality franchise system.
Its style blends the feel of an original British pub with
the golden age elegance of the Victorian era. Business
people and tourists are drawn to its friendly atmosphere
and excellent, famous English beers.

Budapest:

John Bull Pub Kft. Head Office
1136 Budapest, Tátra u.31.
Tel /fax: 270-3475
1386 Budapest, Pf 906/103
270-3476

John Bull Pub "Angol Söröző"
1052 Budapest, Apáczai Csere J. u. 17.
Tel: 138-2168

John Bull Pub "Víghajós"
1118 Budapest. Budaörsi út 7.
Tel./Fax: 319-8751
8752

John Bull Pub "Vadász"
1054 Budapest, Podmaniczky tér 4.
Tel: 269-3116

John Bull Pub "Automobile"
1122 Budapest, Maros u. 28.
Tel./Fax: 156-3565

John Bull Pub "Palota"
1157 Budapest, Erdőkerülő u. 3-5.
Tel: 271-8205

John Bull Pub "Little Horse"
2092 Budakeszi, Fő tér 5.
Tel: 06 23 452 313
Fax: 06 23 451 949

Vidék:

John Bull Pub "Perkovátz ház"
9400 Sopron, Széchenyi tér 12.
Tel./Fax: 06 99 316 839

John Bull Pub "Korona"
4400 Nyiregyháza, Dózsa György u. l.
Tel: 06 42 409 300
Fax: 06 42 409 339

John Bull Pub Pécs
7621 Pécs, Széchenyi tér 1.
Tel: 06-72 325 439
Fax: 06-72 325 490

John Bull Pub Szeged
6720 Szeged, Oroszlán u. 6.
Tel: 06-62 484217

John Bull Pub "Crown"
Tel: 06-22 316 505
8000 Székesfehérvár, Szent István tér 14.

Erdei John Bull Pub
4026 Debrecen, Piac u. 28.
Tel./Fax: 06-52 424 026

John Bull Pub "Britannia",
"Chelsea Rock Bar"
3525 Miskolc Hunyadi u. 3.
Tel: 06-46 350 524
Fax: 06-46 354 110

Currently Budapest's best French restaurant, though local gourmets have begun to mutter about falling standards. The restaurant is in a six-table cellar space, complemented in summer by a peaceful back courtyard (separate entrance to the left) that manages a remarkably Mediterranean atmosphere despite an assortment of *Brazil*-like ducts. The food – Gallic standards with nouvelle cuisine leanings – is mostly seasonal stuff, so ignore the menu and go for the specials. Service is knowledgeable if a little disorganised.

Due Lampioni

II. Frankel Leó utca 30-34 (326 4818). Tram 4, 6. **Open** noon-11pm Tue-Sat; noon-10pm Sun. **Average** Ft2,600. **Credit** AmEx, DC, MC, V. English spoken. **Map B1**
Cool, clean shiny joint near the Buda foot of Margaret Bridge serving Sicilian food in understated surrounds – a long room with a tiled floor, brick archways and a traditional pizza oven at the back. Prices are heftier than average, with huge portions as one compensation, and a better than usual vegetarian selection as another. Seafood and properly *al dente* pasta are stars of the show (the farfalle with shrimps and porcini wins special applause) and in general this is much more inventive than most Budapest Italian restaurants.

Fausto's

VII. Dohány utca 5 (269 6806). M2 Astoria/tram 47, 49. **Open** noon-3pm, 7pm-11pm Mon-Sat. **Average** Ft3,000. **Credit** AmEx, MC, V. English spoken. **Map D4**
Possibly the best restaurant in Budapest just now, though getting glib and in danger of resting on its laurels. Fausto's is small, slick, elegant, unpretentious and offers inventive Italian dishes that make good use of local ingredients. Excellent wine list, too. Booking recommended, as is sitting with your back to the disconcerting perspectives of the Venetian canal mural.

Gundel

XIV. Állatkerti út 2 (321 3550/fax 342 2917). M1 Hősök tere/trolleybus 72, 75, 79. **Open** noon-3pm, 7pm-midnight daily. **Average** Ft6,000. **Credit** AmEx, DC, MC, V. English spoken. **Map E1**
Still the city's most famous restaurant, in the interwar years this was the focal point for elegant, aristocratic Budapest and the international wealthy who came here to play. Originally opened in 1894 as the Wampetics, it was taken over in 1910 by chef Károly Gundel. He proceeded to Frenchify Hungarian cuisine, inventing many now standard dishes, such as the ubiquitous Gundel pancakes. A tourist trap under communism, in 1991 it was acquired by Hungarian-American restaurateur George Lang and given a multi-million-dollar makeover with the aim of recreating the glory days. It's a huge place, in an Art Nouveau mansion by the Zoo, with a ballroom, garden and terrace, and several private dining rooms as well as the large main room hung with paintings by nineteenth-century Hungarian masters. Tables are laid with Zsolnay porcelain and sterling silver and the Gypsy band is slick. The menu is, not surprisingly, a little old-fashioned, and starters and desserts tend to outshine the main courses, but award-winning chef Kálmán Kalla has created both fine versions of Hungarian standards, and Hungarianised versions of international dishes. A long and authoritative list of Hungarian wines is rounded off with excellent sweet Tokaj from the restaurant's own vineyard. Service is smooth and formal, if at times a little glib, and dining at Gundel is always a memorable experience. If you're only going to splash out once in Budapest, this is the place to do it, but don't expect to escape for less than Ft10,000 a head.

Hong Kong Pearl Garden

II. Margit körút 2 (212 3131). Tram 4, 6. **Open** noon-11.30pm Mon-Sat; noon-11pm Sun. **Average** Ft2,500. **Credit** AmEx, DC, V. Some English spoken. **Map B2**
The huge Hong Kong skyline is a mite tacky and the one big room lacks atmosphere, but this place on the Buda foot of

Király – *bring on the kilted dancing girls.*

Margaret Bridge offers probably the best Chinese food in town. The extensive menu spans many regional styles, with a big selection of seafood, excellent duck, lobster fresh from the tank by the door and a couple of interesting vegetarian items. Service occasionally scatterbrained.

Király

I. Táncsics Mihály utca 25 (212 9821). Várbusz. **Open** noon-midnight daily. **Average** Ft4,500. **Credit** AmEx, DC, JCB, MC, V. Some English spoken. **Map A3**
Every place in the Castle District tends to be tourist-oriented and overpriced, but here at least the service and food (mostly well-presented Hungarian standards) are to a genuine standard. Tread carefully with the outrageous wine list, though. The main room is a pleasant semi-circular space with stone walls and heavy furnishings. Strange floor show with Gypsy band and dancing girls in kilts.

Kisbuda Gyöngye

III. Kenyeres utca 34 (168 6402). Tram 17. **Open** noon-midnight Mon-Sat. **Average** Ft2,600. **Credit** AmEx, MC, V. Some English spoken.
Sidestreet favourite with Óbuda locals. Walls are panelled with parts of old wardrobes and the seating is an assortment of old and not always terribly comfortable kitchen chairs. A pretty general Hungarian menu with some interesting daily specials. The venison fillet with wild mushrooms and a brandy sauce is a real plateful and demonstrates the best of the kitchen.

Légrádi Testvérek

V. Magyar utca 23 (118 6804). M3 Kálvin tér/tram 47, 49. **Open** 6pm-midnight Mon-Sat. **Average** Ft3,500. **Credit** AmEx. English spoken. **Map D5**
One of the oldest upscale restaurants in Budapest. The basement is a comfortable drawing room which sells very simi-

'Good Hungarian grubs'

Budapest restaurateurs are renowned for many things, but the quality of their written English is not one of them. Hungarian menus, when scrutinised closely, can offer a lot more than mere food.

Choose from among the 'Good Hungarian Grubs'. Start with a 'Soup of Grandmother', perhaps. Then maybe a 'Risotto from the Woods' or some 'Ham from Parma with Milky Bits'.

You want fish? Why not go for a 'Grilled little Octopussy' or a 'Long Noodle with Fish in the Carman's Way'? Maybe some 'Scallops drunk by Metaxa' or a plateful of 'Grandad spicy fishes fried in plenty of oil'. And there's nothing to beat a pizza festooned with 'Clambs, Scrabs & Polip'.

Steel yourself for 'Spaghetti rolled up in Alfol' or a 'Steak Metallurgic Style' with a healthful 'Germ Salad' on the side. Perhaps you might sample the 'Grilled Lifer from Kosmarok' or the 'Soul stuffed with Cheese'. Few can resist a 'Crips Roasted Sucking Pig'. And after a fine 'Cock's Testicle in a Cheese Sauce', what better dessert than 'Curd Square Pasta with Pig's Cracklings', or, for those with a sweeter tooth, 'The Layering of the Tarts'?

---

lar contemporary Hungarian food to its sister restaurant, Légrádi Antique. Friendlier than the Antique although the kitchen isn't quite as good.

Le Légrádi Antique

V. Bárczy István utca 3-5 (266 4993). M1, M2, M3 Deák tér/tram 47, 49. **Open** noon-3pm, 7pm-midnight Mon-Fri. 7pm-midnight Sat. **Average** Ft3,500. **Credit** AmEx, DC, MC, V. English spoken. **Map C4**
Difficult to find (it's hiding in an antique shop – take the staircase opposite the door), this special restaurant is elegant and comfortable, with heavy antique furniture and waiters wearing tails. The hors d'oeuvres trolley selection is limited but represents a true taster session of the best of Hungarian cooking, including fish terrine, foie gras, miniature portions of steak tartare and quails' eggs. The main courses include pork stuffed with goose liver, excellent steaks and a wide selection of game and local fish. Gypsy music in the evenings.

Lou Lou

V. Vigyázó Ferenc utca 4 (312 4505). Tram 2. **Open** noon-3pm, 7pm-midnight Mon-Fri; 7pm-midnight Sat. **Average** Ft2,600. **Credit** AmEx. English spoken. **Map C3**
Dark green woodwork and pale ochre walls hung with old prints and photographs complement nouvelle cuisine-style food served in Hungarian-sized portions. Typical dishes are salmon steak with a lemongrass sauce or rack of lamb in a parmesan jacket with tomato vinaigrette. Excellent food, charming place, agreeable service, just seven tables. Limited vegetarian options the only drawback. Booking advised.

Naphaz

III. Dereglye utca 5 (388 2530). Bus 60, 86. **Open** noon-3pm, 6pm-midnight daily. **Average** Ft3,000. **Credit** AmEx, MC, V. English spoken.
The finest of the city's Korean restaurants, with pleasant surroundings and real downtown Seoul atmosphere. All the most popular Korean specialities – bulgogi, pulgobi, bibimpap and different kinds of kimchi – can be found, served authentically with metal dishes and chopsticks, and with hot pepper sauce aplenty for aficionados. Soju (Korean sake) is available and service is quietly efficient and polite.

Robinson

XIV. Városliget, tósziget (343 0955). M1 Hősök tere. **Open** noon-4pm, 6pm-midnight daily. **Average** Ft5,300 daily menu; Ft2,500 regular menu. **Credit** AmEx, DC, JCB, MC, V. English spoken. **Map E1**
So-called because of its location on an 'island' (about a yard from the shore) in the Városliget duckpond, Robinson has a wonderful waterside terrace but otherwise just doesn't get there. The menu veers wildly from cheap and plain (stuffed peppers at Ft720, beef stew at Ft850) to expensive and incomprehensible ('The favourite of Molnár Anikó' at Ft2,500). Service is bumbling, the wines are exorbitant, and there's an outrageous ten per cent slapped on the bill for the 'music' – three guys with guitars and bongos doing crap versions of old Santana numbers.

Shiki

II. Zsigmond tér 8 (335 4249). Bus 6, 86/tram 17. **Open** noon-3pm, 6pm-11pm daily. **Average** Ft3,000. **Credit** AmEx, MC, V. Some English spoken.
On any given evening, a good percentage of the Japanese business community can be found here. The menu is large and confusing and contains some items best left to the initiated, like natto, but the real reason people eat here is the fresh sushi and sashimi, skillfully prepared to order by a Japanese chef. For those with a low threshold for cold pressed rice, there are good grilled dishes, comforting stews and delicious steaks. Sake and Japanese beer is available at a price, and the Hungarian dining room staff are polite, friendly and helpful in choosing your Japanese meal.

Szindbád

V. Markó utca 33 (332 2966/332 2749). M3 Nyugati tér. **Open** noon-3pm, 6pm-midnight Mon-Fri; 5pm-midnight Sat-Sun. **Average** Ft3,500. **Credit** AmEx, DC, JCB, MC, V. English spoken. **Map C2**
Very much a business venue. The bar area is full of heavy chesterfields and the dining room is comfortable in a formal sort of way. The menu contains a few surprises, but the main emphasis is on Hungarian international cuisine and this they do well. Not a spot to relax 'à deux' but good for a more formal dinner. Attentive and clever service.

Vadrózsa

II. Pentelei Molnár utca 15 (326 5807). Bus 91. **Open** noon-3pm, 7pm-midnight, daily. **Average** Ft3,800. **Credit** AmEx, DC, JCB, MC, V. English spoken.
In a beautiful small villa halfway up the Rózsadomb, this was once one of Budapest's few top-flight restaurants, but is these days past its best. Their custom of eschewing a written menu, and inviting guests to choose from a plateful of raw ingredients such as goose liver, fogas, wild boar, venison, filet mignon and Russian caviare, harks back to black market days when so much fine meat was something pretty special. The resulting meals are well-prepared but a little

plain. In the main wood-panelled room a mournful pianist plays with the air of one who has seen regimes come and go. Elegant garden for summer dining.

Xi-Hu

V. Nádor utca 5 (137 5679). Tram 2. **Open** noon-midnight daily. **Average** Ft2,600. **Credit** AmEx, MC, V. Some English spoken. **Map C3**

One of Budapest's finer Chinese restaurants. Dishes are well prepared and presented, utilising specially imported ingredients where necessary. The fish dishes are spectacular, and enormous, though the locally sourced fish can sometimes taste rather muddy. Live lobster – a rarity in this land-locked country – is available at a price, as are some Cantonese dishes including cha shiu and dim sum (towards the back of the menu, names given in Mandarin). One charmingly surreal touch is the downstairs karaoke bar, where homesick Chinese can be heard crooning off-key Cantopop favourites. Efficient service; good wine cellar.

Moderate

Bagolyvár

XIV. Állatkerti út 2 (next door to the Gundel) (321 3550 ask for Bagolyvár). M1 Hősök tere. **Open** noon-11pm daily. **Average** Ft1,800. **Credit** AmEx, DC, V. English spoken. **Map E1**

In a mock Transylvanian castle attached to Gundel and owned by the same people, the 'owl castle' is run by women because proprietor George Lang reckons that they are the best home cooks and this place is all about home cooking. The menu varies daily and features some very good soups and other basic offerings. A roulade of fresh breads, served with various spreads, is part of the starter.

Bagolyvár – *home of home cooking.*

Biarritz

V. Kossuth Lajos tér 18 (111 4413). M2 Kossuth tér/tram 2. **Open** 11am-11pm daily. **Average** Ft2,000. **Credit** AmEx, MC, V. English spoken. **Map C2**

Centrally located yuppie haunt, with a modern and often innovative Hungarian menu. Good cream of cranberry soup, nicely moist lamp chops that retain their natural juices. Other favourites such as mozzarella and tomato salad and steaks with grilled potatoes also score high marks for artistic but unpretentious presentation. Biarritz's location near the White House, the modern riverside office building that houses MPs, ensures a steady stream of custom, attracted as much by the pleasant terrace as the high-quality food.

Bombay Palace

VI. Andrássy út 44 (132 8363/131 3787). M1 Oktogon/tram 4, 6. **Open** noon-2.45pm, 6pm-11.15pm daily. **Average** Ft2,500. **Credit** AmEx, DC, JCB, MC, V. English spoken. **Map D3**

A local branch of the international chain in suitably palatial premises with marble floors, chandeliers and so many service staff they often sort of mill around aimlessly. The fare is excellent, displaying no particular regional bias: a good tandoori selection, many vegetarian options and a fine basket of assorted nan breads to clean your plate afterwards.

Café Kör

V. Sas utca 17 (111 0053). M3 Arany János utca. **Open** 10am-10pm Mon-Sat. **Average** Ft1,700. **No credit cards.** English spoken. **Map C3**

With a comfortable, bistro-like atmosphere more reminiscent of Vienna or Berlin than Budapest, Café Kör has both a great bar and some small café tables as well as more a formal dining space. Furnishings have been chosen with care and a simple Hungarian-international menu is complemented by daily specials. Service is slow and the salads are a tad tired, but steak tartare, fogas or the best fried cheese in town will not disappoint. Good spot for breakfast, served until 11.30am. Business crowd at lunchtimes.

Carmel Pince

VII. Dob utca 31 (entrance from Kazinczy utca) (322 1834/342 4585). M2 Astoria. **Open** noon-11pm daily. **Average** Ft1,800. **Credit** AmEx, DC, JCB, MC, V. English spoken. **Map D4**

Not a Kosher restaurant but, right next door to the Orthodox synagogue, it is defiantly Jewish – and maybe plays up the fact just a little too much. The vaulted cellar is comfortable and shows the maturity of age, with an easy ambience afforded by stained glass and interesting nick-nacks. The food is traditional Hungarian Jewish with goose as the speciality. The cooking is all right and the service normally helpful.

Cyrano

V. Kristóf tér 7-8 (266 3096). M1 Vörösmarty tér. **Open** 11am-5pm, 6.30pm-midnight, daily. **Average** Ft2,500. **Credit** MC. English spoken. **Map C4**

Just off the brash end of Váci and really the only place to dine in that neighbourhood. The menu is long – mostly French-accented Hungarian and international dishes with some vegetarian options – but inconsistent. The pasta is particularly poor, but chicken and game dishes, salads and some imaginative starters should not disappoint. The main room is beautiful, crowned with the chandelier used in Depardieu's movie of the same name. In summer the terrace is great for people-watching as passers-by pause to splash in the small fountain outside. Booking essential for terrace tables.

Fatál

V. Váci utca 67 (entrance in Pintér utca) (266 2607). Tram 2, 47, 49. **Open** 11.30am-2am daily. **Average** Ft1,500. **No credit cards.** Some English spoken. **Map C5**

No, you won't get food poisoning – the name means 'wooden platter' and Fatál is a country-style restaurant with mock

TAVERNA
Hotel & Restaurant Co.

COMPLEX SERVICES AND
HIGH QUALITY HOSPITALITY
You get all you need in Hungary from us!

The only Hungarian chain in Budapest!

Mátyás Pince restaurant
H-1056 Budapest,
Március 15. tér 7.
Tel: (361) 118-1693

Ménes csárda
H-1051 Budapest,
Harmincad u. 4.
Tel: (361) 117-2703

Századéves restaurant
H-1052 Budapest,
Pesti B. u. 2.
Tel: (361) 118-3608

Ádám-Éva restaurant
H-1061 Budapest,
Andrássy út 41.
Tel. (361) 352-1338

Gambrinus restaurant
H-1066 Budapest,
Teréz krt. 46.
Tel: (361) 312-7631

Fesztivál restaurant
H-1061 Budapest,
Andrássy út 11.
Tel. (361) 268-1440

Pilvax restaurant
H-1052 Budapest,
Pilvax köz 1-3,
Tel: (361) 266-7660

Napoletana restaurant
H-1052 Budapest,
Petőfi S. tér 3.
Tel. (361) 118-5714

Aranybárány csárda
H-1051 Budapest,
Harmincad u. 4.
Tel: (361) 117-2703

Corso restaurant
H-1052 Budapest,
Petőfi S. u. 3.
Tel. (361) 118-5628

Information:
Taverna Hotel & Restaurant Co., Sales Department
H-1056 Budapest, Molnár u. 28.
Phone: 361-118-0436, Fax: 361-138-4622
Internet: http://www.taverna.hu, E-mail: sales@taverna.hu

It's no goal for gourmets, but you can feast on football kitsch at **Kétballábas.**

stained-glass windows serving hearty portions of well-cooked traditional food that even includes a few vegetarian choices. Service is indifferent, though. Booking essential.

Hax'n Király
VII. Király utca 100 (351 6793). Trolleybus 70, 78. **Open** noon-midnight daily. **Average** Ft1,800. **Credit** MC. English spoken. **Map E3**
Entertaining Bavarian restaurant serving delicious pig hocks spit-roasted in full view of the assembled carnivores. Both the limited starter selection and the main courses are all about meat and lots of it. The hocks are the speciality and one between two is a massive portion of high-fat food. At least nobody around you will be muttering about cholesterol, they will just be tucking in and enjoying themselves.

Iguana
V. Zoltán utca 16 (131 4352). M3 Arany János utca/tram 2. **Open** 11.30am-midnight. **Average** Ft1,600. **Credit** AmEx, V. English spoken. **Map C3**
American-owned Tex-Mex joint that, opening in summer 1997, immediately became expat central. Excellent bar, American-style service and flexible menu of margaritas and Mexican standards. It's a big place in a good location: a quiet street just off Szabadság tér and next to the MTV building, which means the occasional Hungarian TV personality rubbing shoulders with all the foreigners. The food is merely average, though not overpriced, and service isn't quite as good as it thinks it is. Disappointing choice of tequilas, too. But this is a fun place which seems to do its best.

Jorgosz Tavernája
VII. Csengery utca 24 (351 1289). Tram 4, 6. **Open** noon-midnight daily. **Average** Ft1,300. **Credit** AmEx, MC, V. English spoken. **Map D3**
Cellar restaurant decked in Aegean blue and white, with Greek music in the background and an enormous menu of Hellenic specialities: 40 starters, 32 meaty mains, 13 vegetarian selections and a dozen seafood dishes. The decidedly dizzy service is little help in negotiating all this, but it's hard not to find at least one dish tempting.

Kéhli
III. Mókus utca 22 (250 4241). HÉV Árpád híd/tram 1. **Open** 5pm-midnight Mon-Fri; noon-midnight Sat-Sun. **Average** Ft2,300. **Credit** AmEx, MC, V. Some English spoken.
Rated by many as Budapest's best Hungarian restaurant. The main area with its Gypsy band is difficult to get into without booking first, but there are several other rooms in which to perch and which also fill up every night. One of the best specialities is a rich bone marrow soup: first drink the soup, then scrape out the marrow and spread it on toast with garlic. Portions are mountainous. There are normally a few tourists looking for the real Hungarian experience, but the great atmosphere is provided by the largely Hungarian clientèle – so maybe this is the real Hungarian experience.

Kétballábas
VI. Teréz körút 36 (entrance in Dessewffy utca) (269 5563). M1 Oktogon/tram 4, 6. **Open** noon-midnight daily. **Average** Ft1,500. **Credit** AmEx, EC, JCB, MC. Some English spoken. **Map D2**
No gourmet paradise, but not bad considering it's owned by a footballer – György Bognár, capped 50 times for Hungary. The name means 'two left feet' and the décor is soccer kitsch with mementoes from Bognár's career, and a large goal apparently dragged in from the local park. It's an interesting place to catch major matches on television, when György often invites along old football stars and sports journalists for a meal of two halves. The menu is Hungarian and international, leaning a little heavily on the microwave, but the broccoli cream soup is not a bad warm-up before kick-off.

La Fontaine
V. Mérleg utca 10 (117 3715). Tram 2. **Open** noon-midnight daily. **Average** Ft1,800. **Credit** JCB, MC, V. Some English spoken. **Map C3**
Beautiful roomy bistro space with mirrors and long windows, but a small and somewhat dreary French menu. Vegetarians can forget it. The bar, shipped specially from Paris along with most of the furniture, is the best feature.

Hungarian wine (1): Fine vintage quality

Hungary is a major wine producer. The two best-known wines are Tokaji, a dessert-style wine that's inspired hundreds of poetic eulogies, and Bulls Blood, a heavy red blend that has received thousands of curses the morning after. But there are wine regions all over the country, and, apart from the large regional wine companies, also many boutique wine producers as well as thousands of private vintners growing anything from a few litres for private use to a few thousand for public sale.

There are thus some very fine, and very expensive, Hungarian wines on offer. Most are named after their grape variety and area of production. The main white wine areas are Balaton, Etyek and Szekszárd. The best grape varieties are Chardonnay, Riesling (Olaszrizling) and Pinots Gris and Blanc. All should provide dry, reasonably fruity wine. Etyek Chardonnay can be particularly good, and Balaton rizling is on most menus.

The main red grapes are Cabernet Sauvignon, Merlot and Kékfrankos – though check this last is *száraz* (dry) rather than *félédes* (half-sweet). The region with the best reputation for reds is Villány; those of Szekszárd and Eger are also worthwhile.

Some of the best Villányi comes from Bock or Gere. Bátapáti and Morcseny wines dominate Szekszárd. Some very pleasant Balaton wines are produced under the label 'Volcanic Hills', and the Dörgicse vineyard has a growing reputation.

Bulls Blood is called Egri Bikavér in Hungarian. It is a strong, dry and reasonably consistent red blended from Cabernet Sauvignon, Cabernet Franc, Merlot and Kékfrankos.

The origins of Tokaji go back to an inconvenient Turkish invasion which delayed the vendage until the 'noble rot' had reduced the grapes to raisins. A vintage Tokaji Aszú with five or six *puttonyos* (a measure of sweetness), drunk as a dessert wine, is an experience both for the palate and, if you're not wary, the wallet as well.

Lancelot
VI. Podmaniczky utca 14 (302 4456). M3 Nyugati/tram 4, 6. **Open** noon-1am daily. **Average** Ft1,500. **Credit** AmEx, MC, V. English spoken. **Map C2**
Bizarre medieval theme restaurant where vast portions of meat are served at long wooden benches by a platoon of attractive waitresses in skimpy 'medieval' costumes. The food is based on the sort of stuff Hungarians ate several hundred years ago, mostly meat and lots of it, so don't expect much subtlety. A fun venue for a group night out.

Leroy's Country Pub
XIII. Visegrádi utca 50 (140 3316). M3 Lehel tér. **Open** noon-1am Mon-Thur, Sun; noon-2am Fri-Sat. **Average** Ft1,800. **Credit** AmEx, MC, V. Some English spoken. **Map C2**
American theme bar decked out with old enamel signs, wire netting and a load of ramshackle furniture. The clientèle tend to be local 'entrepreneurs' who spend most of their time on the mobile phone. The accompanying molls spend fortunes on blond rinses and very little on cloth. Despite all this, the food is wholesome, the steaks are among the best in Budapest and there is normally a good buzz in the air.

Les Amis
II. Römer Flóris utca 12 (212 3173). Tram 4, 6. **Open** 10am-midnight Mon-Sat. **Average** Ft1,800. **No credit cards.** Some English spoken. **Map A1**
Tiny, popular neighbourhood place on a quiet street. The menu reflects the limited cooking facilities behind the small bar. The only hot starter options are soups, followed by a section of 'frying pan foods', 'grill foods' and a small range of fogas dishes. A friendly spot. Tables outside in summer.

Mare-Monti
VII. Damjanich utca 40 (342 9948). Trolleybus 70, 78. **Open** noon-midnight daily. **Average** Ft1,300. **No credit cards.** Some English spoken. **Map F2**
Out in the Városliget end of District VII, this is like a local Italian joint transplanted from, say, Brooklyn: rotund Sicilian proprietor, scatty but entertaining service, no-frills menu of basic but tasty pasta and pizza, steak and chicken, served at big wooden tables. The sea and mountains are on a lurid mural covering one wall. Handy in a locality otherwise poorly served for decent eateries.

Marquis de Salade
VI. Hajós utca 43 (302 4086). M3 Nyugati. **Open** noon-midnight daily. **Average** Ft1,400. **No credit cards.** Some English spoken. **Map C3**
Big selection of salads, augmented by steaks plus dishes from Italy, China, North Africa, Bangladesh and the Russias. The self-service salad bar is badly lit and the contents often past their best by the evening, making this a better spot for a light lunch than a sit-down dinner, though vegetarians will sigh with relief at any time of day. The steaks push up the average price; it's possible to eat here very cheaply.

Miyako
XIII. Visegrádi utca 1 (111 3023). M3 Nyugati/tram 4, 6. **Open** noon-1am daily. **Average** Ft1,500. **Credit** AmEx, MC, V. English spoken. **Map C2**
A big, airy room with tables and a smaller traditional Japanese room above, available for hire with a special menu. The decor (kites, fans) is understated, the service is friendly and efficient, and a wide-ranging Japanese menu covers all bases, though not always successfully. The tempura is poor

and sushi merely average, but tofu and noodle dishes are well-prepared and there are loads of intriguing starters. Weekday lunch menu for Ft580; plenty for vegetarians.

Múzeum
VIII. Múzeum körút 12 (138 4221). M3 Kálvin tér. **Open** noon-midnight daily. **Average** Ft2,500. **Credit** AmEx. English spoken. **Map D5**
High ceilings, tiled walls, tall windows providing plenty of light and well-spaced tables add to the fin-de-siècle ambience at the ever-popular Múzeum, founded in 1885. The menu is impressive with an enormous difference in price from one dish to another – you can spend a fortune here or you can dine very cheaply. The Hungarian-international food is good, if unexceptional. Vast, well-presented portions, smooth service and the pleasant surrounds keep this old place buzzing.

Náncsi Néni
II. Ördögárok út 80 (176 5809). Tram 56 then bus 157. **Open** noon-11pm daily. **Average** Ft1,500. **Credit** AmEx, MC, V. English spoken.
City-dwellers flock here at weekends, pretending it is in the country, although actually it is now well into suburbia. Both location and food retain a rustic charm, with a leafy garden, extravagant portions and reasonable prices. The food is Hungarian home cooking with excellent soups and the Túrós Gombóc dessert – a cannonball-sized dumpling stuffed with cottage cheese – as specialities. Notably child-friendly.

Okay Italia
XIII. Szent István körút 20 (131 6990). M3 Nyugati/tram 4, 6. **Open** noon-midnight daily. **Average** Ft1,300. **No credit cards.** English spoken. **Map C2**
These days there's plenty of competition, but this place was a revelation for Budapest when it opened in late 1993: simple, good, reasonably priced Italian food in an unpretentious atmosphere. Staffing the place with good-looking women in very short skirts was part of a strategy which proved so popular they opened up a second branch round the corner, universally known as 'Okay 2'. The branches have slightly different menus, each offering a good general selection of familiar if unadventurous dishes.
Branch: V. Nyugati tér 6 (332 6960).

Pinocchio
XIII. Szent István körút 10 (132 0587). Tram 4, 6. **Open** noon-midnight daily. **Average** Ft1,500. **No credit cards.** Some English spoken.
If Okay Italia is full, try this nearby place – one of the many Italian joints that have sprung up in Okay's wake. The entrance is on Tatra utca, where summer tables outside complement a cellar space within. Standard Italian menu.

Remiz
II. Budakeszi út 5 (275 1396). Bus 22. **Open** 9am-1am daily. **Average** Ft2,000. **Credit** AmEx, MC, V. English spoken.
Perhaps too well aware of its enviable reputation for the wonderful sheltered garden and separate grill kitchen that churns out summer barbie-type food. There are a few vegetarian dishes and the Russian caviare is the cheapest in town. The grills, proudly borne around on wooden platters, tend to be murdered rather than cooked. Patchy service but the staff normally speak good English.

Ristorante Italiano y Español
I. Attila út 125 (212 3759). M2 Moszkva tér/tram 4, 6, 18. **Open** noon-midnight Mon-Fri; 2pm-midnight Sat. **Average** Ft1,300. **No credit cards.** Some English spoken. **Map A3**
A relaxed, unpretentious joint – white walls, simple furniture – with a Spanish chef and a Uruguayan owner who will serve you himself. The pasta's cheap but tuck into the Iberian side of the menu – the Spanish roast vegetable starter, gazpacho and tortilla won't disappoint. Nor will the paella, nicely moist and served on a cast iron skillet. The only drawback is a limited and overpriced wine list (Ft2,000 for an indifferent Chianti). Otherwise, a fun and worthwhile place.

Rus' Étterem
XIII. Béke út 37 (270 0384). Bus 4/tram 14 to Fáy utca. **Open** noon-midnight daily. **Average** Ft2,300 **Credit** AmEx, MC. Some English spoken.
The Rus' specialises in Russian peasant food: thick soups, pickles, black bread, Chicken Kiev and incomparable

Hungarian wine (2): Recycled Fanta bottle quality

While it is hard to stop praising the noble Tokaji or Egri Bikavér, a couple of litres of Csopaki Rizling drunk from recycled pop bottles will get you there faster, cheaper and more authentically.

Hungarians drink vast amounts of less than noble wine every day, whether in the neighbourhood borozó or at home, bought from the 'Termelői Bor' (Grower's Wine Shops) down the street. Although a booze licence is neither cheap nor easy to come by, a quirk of Hungarian law makes it legal to sell wine with only a membership in a wine grower's association. Thus home-made wine shops and borozós can number two a street in working class neighbourhoods. You walk in with your jerry can or empty cola bottles and choose your brew from the array of wines – usually from whatever region the store is affiliated with.

Since almost every region of Hungary produces wines, however, there are bound to be a few klinkers. The flat and sandy southern plains around Csongrad produce a weak and sour 'sand wine', famed for its hangover-producing qualities. The Jasz region east of Pest also grows wine – if that is what you can call something which produces hallucinations that alligators are growing out of your head. These are usually called 'fröccs wines' – fit only for mixing with soda water.

The best cheap wine in Budapest is found on Saturdays behind the Bosnyák tér market, where growers from Tokaj truck in their finest and sell it in cola bottles for about a fifth of the commercial bottled price.

Taverna Dionysos – *by the Danube, not the Aegean, but almost more Greek than Greece.*

'Sibirskiye pel'meni' – garlicky, dill-scented ravioli served with butter, sour cream or vinegar. For the wealthy there are gourmet treats like real Russian caviare, but you hardly ever see the regulars order it. The zakuski (hors d'oeuvres) menu is authentic, broad, and just the thing to eat your way through with a bottle of ice cold vodka (the vodka is often Belgian, but very good). Dodgy Russian 'businessmen' love this place, perhaps because of the live Russian music: cabaret singers and musicians are imported regularly from Moscow. On weekend nights the patrons can be a startling bunch – complete with Ukrainian 'escorts' and armed guards.

Seoul House

I. Fő utca 8 (201 7452). Tram 19/bus 2, 86, 105. **Open** noon-11pm Tue-Sun. **Average** Ft1,900. **Credit** AmEx, DC, JCB, MC, V. Some English spoken. **Map B3**
Budapest's second-best Korean restaurant. Décor is a mite bleak, but it's usually full. Table-top barbecues allow those in the know to order strange and wonderful dishes they can cook themselves. A favourite is bulgogi, marinated beef. Modumjeon, Korean stuffed vegetables, fried tempura-style, is a recommended starter and arrives at the table cooked.

Shalimar

VII. Dob utca 50 (267 0662). Tram 4, 6. **Open** noon-4pm, 6pm-midnight daily. **Average** Ft2,000. **Credit** AmEx, MC, V. English spoken. **Map D3**
Before this place opened there were two choices for decent Indian food in central Budapest: a) go to the Bombay Palace or b) forget it. In a cellar made Indian-like with assorted statues and trinkets, here the cooks are Indian and the wait staff Hungarian – thus service is erratic while the food is excellent, including tandoori dishes, eight types of bread and a host of excellent vegetarian options (try the Spicy Tomato Shahi Paneer). Ten per cent discount in the afternoons.

Taverna Dionysos

V. Belgrád rakpart 16 (118 1222). Tram 2, 47, 49. **Open** noon-midnight daily. **Average** Ft1,500. **Credit** AmEx, MC, V. English spoken. **Map C5**

The hyperreal whitewashed and blue interior looks more Greek than Greece; the terrace, on the Danube overlooking Gellért Hill, can be noisy but boasts a unique view. The service is a bit offhand, but it's a well-run place offering acceptable versions of all the Aegean standards. Non-carnivores will enjoy picking among the starters. Excellent tiropita.

Tian Tan Chinese Restaurant

V. Duna utca 1 (118 6444). M3 Ferenciek tere. **Open** 11.30am-midnight daily. **Average** Ft2,500. **Credit** AmEx, MC. English spoken. **Map C4**
With its labyrinthine interior of dark lacquer and back-lit multicoloured panels, dotted with fountains, fish tanks and jade sculptures, entering this place is like stepping into some kind of Chinese computer game. The menu is huge, with 14 categories of main course including good duck and shrimp and some tasty tofu variations, but by international standards the food is competent rather than outstanding. Possible to eat cheaply if you lay off the seafood.

Sushi

V. Harmincad utca 4 (117 4239). M1 Vörösmarty tér. **Open** noon-3.30pm, 5pm-10pm daily. **Average** Ft1,500. **Credit** AmEx, MC, V. English spoken. **Map C4**
Surprisingly good sushi and sashimi (Ft350-Ft600 per piece) in this simple, clean, traditionally styled sushi bar next to the British embassy. Vegetarian seaweed rolls are also on the short menu, along with one excellent tofu dish. Attracts a cosmopolitan crowd, including many Japanese. Food is good value but the alcohol overpriced: Kirin beer at Ft750, jars of hot sake at Ft800.
Branch: Hilton Hotel (214 3000 ext 236).

Via Luna

V. Nagysándor József utca 1 (312 8058). M3 Arany János utca. **Open** 11am-11.30pm Mon-Fri; noon-11.30pm Sat-Sun. **Average** F1,500. **Credit** AmEx, MC, V. English spoken. **Map C3**
Attractive, spacious and efficient with a long though somewhat old-fashioned menu of traditional Italian fare, includ-

ing 25 pasta dishes and appetisers so generous you could make a meal from them alone. Roomy, well-spaced tables encourage relaxed conversation while the food arrives almost too quickly. The short wine list is a mite overpriced but good value otherwise and possibly the best profiterole in town.

Inexpensive

Falafel

VI. Paulay Ede utca 53 (no phone). M1 Oktogon/tram 4, 6. **Open** 10am-8pm Mon-Fri; 10am-6pm Sat. **Average** Ft500. **No credit cards.** Some English spoken. **Map D3**
Budapest's best salad bar: build your own falafel or fill your own salad bowl. Tables upstairs or, if you feel like dining on a bench in nearby Liszt tér, takeaway cartons available.

Fészek

VII. Kertész utca 36 (corner of Dob utca) (322 6043). Tram 4, 6. **Open** noon-1am daily. **Average** Ft1,100. **Credit** AmEx, MC, V. Some English spoken. **Map D3**
An artist's club since the turn of the century but in practice open to anyone (with a Ft100 entrance fee in the evening), Fészek offers elegant dining at bargain prices. The ornate high-ceilinged main room is attractive enough, but the real bonus is the appealingly dilapidated Venetian-style courtyard, formerly a monk's cloister and one of the most beautiful places in central Pest to spend a long summer lunchtime. Service can be slow, sullen and inaccurate, but the food is all right and the atmosphere relaxing.

Gandhi

V. Vigyázó Ferenc utca 4 (269 4944). Tram 2. **Open** noon-10.30pm daily. **Average** Ft750. **Credit** AmEx, MC, V. English spoken. **Map C3**
Cellar vegetarian place decked in warm colours where a small fountain and a gallery of gurus (Gandhi, the Dalai Lama and the like) set the somewhat blissed-out tone. Two daily set menus (one 'lunar', one 'solar'), plus soups and an interesting salad bar. Lots of juices and teas. No smoking.

Govinda

V. Belgrád rakpart 18 (118 1144). Tram 47, 49. **Open** noon-9pm Tue-Sun. **Average** Ft800. **No credit cards.** Some English spoken. **Map C5**
Budapest's Hare Krishna restaurant, offering an edible but drab Indian vegetarian set meal and little else of note except a decent home-made gingery lemonade. Nice location by the Danube, but unfortunately no tables outside.

Gyökér

VI. Eötvös utca 46 (153 4329). M3 Nyugati. **Open** 4pm-2am Mon-Thur; 4pm-4am Fri; 6pm-4am Sat; 6pm-2am Sun. **Average** Ft1,000. **No credit cards.** Some English spoken. **Map D2**
The name means 'roots', which explains tree stumps dangling from the ceiling and refers to the fact that, owned by a musician, this is the folk scene's favourite restaurant. Late evenings there is often some sort of jam session as musicians drop by for a bite of the inexpensive and unusually grease-free Hungarian food. There are often also more formal concerts in a separate room, including a Friday night *táncház* (dance house) led by Transylvanian group Újstilus. Cover charge for concerts about Ft200. (*See also chapter* **Folklore**.)

Horváth

I. Krisztina tér 3 (175 7573). Bus 4, 78/tram 18. **Open** noon-11pm daily. **Average** Ft1,100. **Credit** MC, V. Some English spoken. **Map A4**
Good choice for a genuine Hungarian local restaurant that has happily taken on board western standards of cuisine and presentation. Décor somewhat hotel-like, but service is snappy. Fine draught Gosser beer nicely washes down Hungarian classics, all executed with style and flair. Excellent steak

tartare, pungent beef stroganoff. Also try chicken with pistachio accompanied by apple salad. Large portions, low prices, speedy service, a reasonable wine list, as well as an excellent selection of spirits and digestifs.

Kikelet

II. Fillér utca 85 (212 5444). Bus 49. **Open** noon-11pm daily. **Average** Ft1,000. **No credit cards.** Some English spoken.
In a strangely out of place log cabin, but it's the rustic, shady garden that attracts. The furniture has seen better days and the food is basic: a few typical Hungarian dishes, mostly prepared to order with that essential local cooking utility, the frying pan. The grills are good and come served with a decent salad. Main attractions are affordable prices and the ambience, which is wonderful on a balmy summer's evening. Cheap, cheerful and unpretentious.

Kulacs Étterem

VII. Osvát utca 11 (352 1734). M2 Blaha Lujza tér. **Open** 10am-midnight daily. **Average** Ft1,000. **Credit** AmEx, DC, JCB, MC, V. Some English spoken. **Map E4**
This is where, in 1927, László Jávor wrote the song *Szomorú Vasárnap*. Translated as 'Cloudy Sunday', it became a huge hit for Billie Holiday. For a while it was the fashion for young men to dress in black, pin the lyrics to their clothes as a suicide note, and throw themselves off the nearest Danube bridge. Less melodramatic these days, Kulacs offers a straightforward Hungarian menu, a pianist in one room, and some of Budapest's most authentic Gypsy music in the other.

Marxim

II. Kisrókus utca 23 (115 5036). Tram 4, 6. **Open** 11am-1am Mon-Fri; 11am-2am Sat; 6pm-1am Sun. **Average** Ft400. **Credit** AmEx, DC, JCB, V. Some English spoken. **Map A2**
In an appropriately industrial setting behind the old Ganz tram factory, the theme of this pizzeria is Communist kitsch. There's a showcase of Stalinist trinkets by the door, red flags and trade union banners festoon the interior, chicken-wire separates the tables and the pizzas have names such as Anarchismo and Gulag. Alas, it isn't only the décor which harks back to Communist days: the pizzas are so tough they can bend the cheap cutlery.

Mérleg Vendéglő

V. Mérleg utca 6 (117 5910). Tram 2. **Open** 11am-11pm Mon-Sat. **Average** Ft800. **Credit** AmEx, MC, V. Some English spoken. **Map C3**
Slick, economical and deservedly popular restaurant in the heart of the Belváros. More of a lunch spot than a site for a leisurely dinner, the Merleg is always crowded with civil servants and politicians and you may have to share a table, otherwise book. The best bargains are the set daily menus, usually including a soup, main dish and dessert, although portions are smaller than the same dishes à la carte from the standard Hungarian menu. Excellent palacsintas.

Mirtusz

VI. Zichy-Jenő utca 47 (131 5920). Tram 4, 6. **Average** Ft900. **Open** noon-midnight daily. **Credit** MC, V. Some English spoken. **Map D3**
Cheap but not terribly cheerful cellar restaurant, decorated with earth tones and pressed leaves and following the inexplicable local practice of accompanying vegetarian food with live acoustic guitar. Decent value and dishes that demonstrate some imagination, such as seitan Provençal or Transylvanian soya ragout, though the kitchen should be cautioned on the use of salt and service is slow and dizzy. Avoid the gazpacho, more like a drowned salad than a soup.

Művész

XIII. Vigszínház utca 5 (339 8008). M3 Nyugati/tram 4, 6. **Open** 9am-midnight daily. **Average** Ft1,000. **No credit cards.** Some English spoken. **Map C2**

香 港 明 珠 酒

HONG KONG PEARL GARDEN

1027 Budapest, Margit krt. 2 • Tel: 212-3131, 212-3948 • Fax: 212-5524

Budapest's finest Cantonese
cuisine served in an elegant,
comfortable setting

CLASSIC CANTONESE

The million-forint meal

In early summer 1997, the story flashed around the globe. A party of four Danes had wandered into the Halászcsárda on Ferenciek tere, eaten a modest meal, and wound up with a bill for Ft1,300,000 – around £4,300. 'As far as I'm concerned,' the restaurant's owner told *Népszabadság*, 'we can charge tourists anything we like.'

A host of similar horror stories soon also came to light: people charged outrageous prices in tourist parts of town – the £200 pork chop, the £500 bottle of sparkling wine – and then intimidated into forking out. Individuals were beaten up or held hostage while others were escorted in search of cash by a bevy of crop-haired bruisers.

Galvanised by the unwelcome publicity, the city government boldly leapt into action. Despite receiving mafia death threats, Judit Xantus, local government official in charge of issuing licences to places of entertainment, closed the Halászcsárda on a technicality, but also swooped on an assortment of essentially innocent venues. The Amstel River Café was closed for failing to list the amount of decilitres in a glass of wine. Amadeus had only posted menus in English and German. Even **Cyrano**, the one restaurant in the Váci area that we'd actually recommend, was

closed for neglecting to have their complaints book notarised by the responsible authority.

The situation has settled down now, and the worst offenders are out of business, but it's still wise to be cautious in restaurants and bars around the Váci utca area. Don't eat anywhere that doesn't have prices clearly listed on the menu. Examine the small print for surcharges. Be wary of any place with lots of short-haired thugs hanging about. And don't go anywhere if invited by a beautiful woman who approaches you on the street. She's probably a *konzum lány* – 'consume girl' – and likely to have both very expensive tastes, and a very brutal collection of male colleagues.

If you stick to places listed in this *Guide*, you're unlikely to have any problems – although please let us know if you do. Meanwhile, avoid the following establishments, all of which have been the subject of complaints to the US Embassy, to American Express, or to the Budapest Consumer Protection Office: Black and White, Fortuna Cabaret, Labirintus, La Luna Bar, Mizrah Café, Muskátli Eszpresszó, Piccoló Eszpresszó, Pigalle Bar, Secret Club, Tropical Bar, and Waikiki Restaurant.

Romantic venue, behind the Vigszinház, with a Hungarian chef who clearly takes time and trouble to produce quality meals. Hearty meat soup, one portion easily enough for two, and fine poultry dishes such as rooster in wine sauce or stuffed hen. Reasonably priced. Straightforward breakfast menu from 9am-11am, lunches and dinners thereafter.

Palacsinta Porta

VI. Liszt Ferenc tér 3 (no phone). M1 Oktogon/tram 4, 6. **Open** 11.30am-11pm Mon-Sat. **Average** Ft700. **No credit cards**. Some English spoken. **Map D3**
Big selection of savoury or sweet crepes, plus a small selection of salads and soups, served up at summer tables in between Pompei and Incognito on Liszt tér's outdoor nightlife strip. Average food, nice prices, excellent location.

Pizza Bella

VI. Teréz körút 32 (332 4462). M1 Oktogon/tram 4, 6. **Open** noon-11.30pm Mon-Sat. **Average** Ft1,100. **No credit cards**. Some English spoken. **Map D3**
Small, beautiful, and Pizza Bella is a tiny, no-frills Italian joint serving some of the best pasta and pizza in town, though very little else. Simple, unfussy touches (even the wall-to-ceiling murals somehow manage to be unobtrusive), friendly service and a fine house grappa.

Pompei

VI. Liszt Ferenc tér 3 (351 8738). M1 Oktogon/tram 4, 6. **Open** noon-1am daily. **Average** Ft700. **Credit** AmEx, MC, V. Some English spoken. **Map D3**
Classical kitsch, wobbly tables and uninspiring pizzas. Cheap, though, and an excellent location with summer tables outside on one of Pest's premier people-watching spots.

Rosenstein Vendeglő

VIII. Festetics György utca 7 (entrance on Mosonyi utca) (113 4196). M2 Keleti. **Open** noon-11pm Mon-Sat. **Average** Ft1,100. **No credit cards**. No English spoken. **Map F4**
District VIII is not best known for its cuisine, but Rosenstein is a welcome addition to Budapest's small range of fine quality but moderately priced Hungarian eateries. Its name is Jewish, and despite Israeli wines on the wine list, most of the food is high-quality Magyar home-cooking with a modern twist. Excellent goose liver, while the veal ragout soup is a meal in itself. Extraordinarily long menu, with numerous variations on the theme of fish, beef, poultry and game. Booking essential in the evenings at this pleasant place.

Semiramis

V. Alkotmány utca 20 (111 7627). M3 Nyugati/tram 4, 6. **Open** noon-9pm Mon-Sat. **Average** Ft650. **No credit cards**. Some English spoken. **Map C2**
Small, friendly Syrian joint offering usual spread of middle eastern stuff: lentil soup, lamb and chicken dishes, salads, kebabs. The chicken and spinach especially recommended. Cheap and cheerful without frills or pretensions.

Taverna Ressaikos

I. Apor Péter utca 1 (212 1612). Tram 19/bus 2, 86, 105. **Open** noon-midnight daily. **Average** Ft1,250 **Credit** AmEx, MC. English spoken. **Map B3**
Greek place that's a useful spot if you're stuck down the Lánchíd end of Fő utca. Five per cent added to your bill when the 'orchestra' (a small and not terribly good Greek folk group) is playing. Greek fare of average character but the salads are worth investigating. Summer tables outside.

Vegetárium

V. Cukor utca 3 (267 0322). M3 Ferenciek tér. **Open** noon-10pm daily. **Average** Ft1,000. **Credit** AmEx, JCB, MC, V. English spoken. **Map C4**

Once Budapest's only vegetarian restaurant, but now poultry and fish have arrived on a menu 'prepared in accordance with dietary principles carefully worked out with the help of foreign consultants'. There is beer and wine, a few vegan and macrobiotic dishes among more standard vegetarian fare, and strictly no smoking. The atmosphere is austere, the food plain and solid. Usually a queue in the evenings when a classical guitarist entertains diners at booth tables.

Étkezdék

The étkezde is the Hungarian equivalent of the English caff: small, cheap and often family-run places which provide simple home cooking. They have few vegetarian options but offer a hearty lunch for between Ft450-Ft700 for two courses.

Házias Étkezde

I. Várfok utca 8 (115 2931). Várbusz from M2 Moszkva tér. **Open** noon-5pm Mon-Fri; noon-4pm Sat. **Average** Ft500. **No credit cards**. Some English spoken. **Map A3**

Five minutes' walk from the Castle District, the Házias is a tiny eatery with a limited menu and no alcohol. The food is standard, but you will welcome the lack of tourist kitsch.

Kisharang Étkezde

VI. Október 6 utca 17 (332 9348). M3 Arany János utca. **Open** 11am-8pm Mon-Fri; 11.30am-3.30pm Sat-Sun. **Average** Ft500. **No credit cards**. Some English spoken. **Map C3**

*The **Kádár** – reflecting former glories.*

The Little Bell bustles near Budapest's business quarter: quick, clean and efficient. You're as likely to sit next to a chap in a pinstriped shirt as a granny gulping goulash. Main dishes are not for the meek and are served with rice, parsley potatoes and salad. They can be ordered in half-portions or the staff will lovingly wrap leftovers for Ft15. Vegetable porridge, *főzelék*, is the ideal winter warmer.

Lukrécia Snackbar

V. Váci utca 65 (118 1098). Tram 2, 47, 49. **Open** 10am-6pm Mon-Fri. **Average** Ft450. **No credit cards**. Some English spoken. **Map C5**

In the unfashionable end of Váci utca and run by a batty woman who would be perfectly at home running a Torquay boarding house. Go early because some of the main dishes disappear before mid-afternoon. Draught light and dark beer.

Karcsi Ételbár

VI. Jókai utca 20 (312 0557). M1 Oktogon/M3 Nyugati/tram 4, 6. **Open** 11am-10pm Mon-Fri. **Average** Ft500. **No credit cards**. Some English spoken. **Map D3**

Two menus, one changed weekly, the other the chef's regular specialities. Two set menus – a soup, a main course and a pudding – also change weekly. Service a little slow but the customers seem to have time to spare.

Kádár Étkezde

VII. Klauzál tér 10 (no phone). Trolleybus 74. **Open** 11.30am-3.30pm Tue-Fri. **Average** Ft450. **No credit cards**. Some English spoken. **Map D3**

Signed celebrity photos on the walls testify to former glory. Menu changed daily to keep the regulars' interest, with a fair selection of puddings. Pay at the cash desk by the door.

Tüköry Söröző

V. Hold utca 15 (269 5027). M3 Arany János utca. **Open** 10am-11pm Mon-Fri. **Average** Ft500. **No credit cards**. Some English spoken. **Map C3**

A cheap restaurant rather than the beer hall its name suggests. Tables fill from around noon. Grab one by the window and watch shoppers come and go at the indoor market next door. Menu changes weekly.

Fast Food

Eating on the hoof is a daily necessity for many Hungarians, a fact not lost on proliferating American fast-food chains. Small bakery kiosks sell cheap snacks at main metro stations. Look out also for falafel stalls, such as the one at Mignon presszó by Deák tér metro. Indigenous street eats are ever harder to find; for a round-up of possibilities, *see page 143* **Steamed pig's head to go**.

Duran Szendvics

V. Bajcsy-Zsilinszky út 7 (342 7124). M3 Arany János utca. **Open** 8am-6pm Mon-Fri; 9am-1pm Sat. **No credit cards**. Some English spoken. **Map C3**

Viennese Imbiß chain offering more than 20 kinds of small, delicately made open sandwiches at around Ft60. Excellent cappuccinos as well. Takeaway boxes for up to 25 items. **Branch**: V. Október 6 utca 15 (332 9348).

Házi Rétes

VII. Király utca 70 (no phone). Tram 4, 6 Király utca. **Open** 9am-7pm Mon-Fri; 9am-3pm Sat. **No credit cards**. Some English spoken. **Map D3**

As the sign says, 'Ahogy Nagymama Sütött' – just how Grandma used to make. The best takeaway strudel in town: apple, cherry, plum and cabbage at around Ft70 a throw.

Steamed pig heads to go

Budapest bristles with brand-name burgers, but there are alternatives to the styrofoam lunch.

In butchers' look for the steaming vats of hot *kolbász* sausage, the rotisseries crammed with *grill csirke* (grilled chicken) and the hot boxes filled with liver and blood sausages (*májas* and *véres húrka*) and fatty pork ribs (*oldalas*). You can also get a steamed pig head (*féj hús*) served and eaten with ears, snout and all. Don't let the bristles put you off! Order your portion by size (*tíz deka* is a 100-gram snack, *husz deka* a hefty lunch) and ask for bread (*kenyer*), pickles (*savanyuság*), mustard (*mustár*) or horseradish (*torma*). Pay at the cashier, return your receipt to the server, and wolf it down at the stand-up counter along the wall.

Vegetarian fast food is anything bought in a bakery and munched at a bus stop. Here the *kifli*, a cheap croissant, is king. Strudels and *pita* (crumbly shortcake filled with apple or cherry) run a close second. *Pogácsa*, available at bakers or most bars, are scones baked with salt and lard, and sometimes with cheese or pork cracklings. Bar food otherwise means either a *meleg szendvics* ('warm sandwich'), a thick slice of stale bread with mystery meat or mushrooms and cheese grilled on to it, or *zsíros kenyer* – 'lard bread'. A slice is smeared with pig fat, salted, dusted with paprika, and topped with sliced onions.

Hungarians find the concept of salad puzzling. A traditional Hungarian salad consists of either pickled vegetables, or half a lettuce doused with vinegar. There are plenty of 'salad bars' serving some downright disgusting concoctions. Canned vegetables or economy meats are mixed with sour cream and mayonnaise and given exotic foreign names: 'French salad' (peas and spuds), 'Swedish Salad' (mushrooms and tomato paste), 'German Salad' (hot dogs sliced with onions) or 'Mexican Salad' (anything with corn in it). Approach such salads with caution – they can go a bit off by the early afternoon.

Pizza is ubiquitous and unexceptional. Hungarians dress theirs with ketchup and add odd toppings such as pineapple ('Hawaiian pizza') and corn (yes, 'Mexican Pizza'). Closely related, yet starkly Magyar, is *lángos*, a deep-fried dough on sale at marketplaces, stations and strands. Of all Magyar delicacies, *lángos* is the one most missed by emigré Hungarians. Slathered with sour cream, cheese and garlic paste there is nothing better. Or greasier. Or worse for your cholesterol count. But hey, you're on holiday!

Hét Torony

VI. Nagymező utca 21 (111 5654). M1 Oktogon/tram 4, 6. **Open** 10am-midnight daily. **No credit cards.** Some English spoken. **Map D3**
Slightly upmarket Turkish eatery, hence the higher prices, but worth it for the comfort of the upstairs section despite the hippie trappings of the decor.

Korona Passage

V. Kecskeméti utca 14 (117 4111). M3 Kálvin tér/tram 47, 49. **Open** 10am-10pm daily. **No credit cards.** English spoken. **Map D5**
Upmarket cafeteria with the best takeaway pancakes in town. Impressive salad bar to boot.

Marie Kristensen Sandwich Bar

IX. Ráday utca 7 (218 1673). M3 Kálvin tér/tram 47, 49. **Open** 10am-9pm Mon-Fri. **No credit cards.** English spoken. **Map D5**
Budapest's first sandwich bar, and a little pricey, but worth the indulgence given Budapest's lack of breakfast options. The salmon salad baguette is especially recommended.

New York Bagel

VI. Bajcsy-Zsilinszky út 21 (111 8441). M3 Arany János utca. **Open** 7am-10pm Mon-Fri; 9am-10pm Sat-Sun. **No credit cards.** English spoken. **Map C3**
Several kinds of bagels and toppings, from modest cream cheese spreads to the Atlantis sandwich, smoked salmon, cream cheese and tomato for Ft597. Summer terrace.
Branch: East-West Business Centre, VIII. Rákóczi út 1-3 (266 7770).

Pizza Kuckó

VII. Károly körút 1 (no phone). M2 Astoria/tram 47, 49,/bus 7, 9. **Open** 9am-9pm Mon-Fri; 9am-2pm Sat. **No credit cards.** Some English spoken. **Map D4**
Popular Hungarian kiosk standing proudly before its American counterpart. A handful of varieties of pizza slices, often served painfully slowly.

Pizza Mix

V. Mérleg utca 10 (117 3579). Tram 2. **Open** 11am-10pm Mon-Sat. **No credit cards.** Some English spoken. **Map C3**
Order by filling in a form at the counter specifying the toppings of your choice, perhaps giving yourself a ridiculous name for when they call out your order. A large pizza is Ft420 plus Ft30 per topping.

Shiraz Persian Sandwich Club

IX. Ráday utca 21 (217 4547). M3 Kálvin tér/tram 47, 49. **Open** 10am-10pm Mon-Sat; noon-10pm Sun. **No credit cards.** Some English spoken. **Map D5**
Small place offering a selection of cheap middle eastern specialities – kebabs, falafel, gyros – all served with salad and pita bread. Restful seating area upstairs.

Szultán Büfé

VII. Király utca 80 (351 8987). Tram 4, 6 Király utca. **Open** 10am-10pm Mon-Sat. **No credit cards.** Some English spoken. **Map D3**
Cheap Turkish standard fast-food fare, with an excellent çorba soup well worth Ft200, bread and tea thrown in free.

The Magyar menu

If you're coming to Hungary for its spicy food, prepare for disappointment. The typical menu (*étlap*) relies on heavy, bland portions of pork (*sertés*) or chicken (*csirke*), garnished with over-cooked vegetables. Meats are mainly stewed (*pörkölt*) or breaded (*rántott*). Salads (*saláták*) are often sour, pickled affairs. Even the goulash (*gulyás*) is a thin disappointment, soup rather than stew. Bean soup (*bableves*) is a better bet.

Starters (*előételek*) feature breaded cheese (*sajt*) or mushrooms (*gomba*); *Hortobágyi palacsinta*, a pancake in meat sauce, and goose liver, *hideg libamáj*, are hardy perennials. Soups (*levesek*) are based on rich meat stock. Only cold fruit soup, *gyümölcsleves*, passes the veggie test. Spicy fish soup, *halászlé*, is worth investigating.

Main courses (*főételek*) may feature *töltött káposzta* (stuffed cabbage rolls in meat sauce); *paprikás csirke* (chicken in sour cream and paprika sauce); *sertésborda* (pork chops with different fillings); *vaddisznó pörkölt* (wild boar stew) and *fogas* (pike-perch from Balaton). Tournedos Rossini and Beefsteak (*marhabélszín*) Budapest Style (with stewed paprika) are common. These will be served with a side dish (*köretek*) of potatoes (*burgonya* or *krumpli*), rice (*rizs*) or noodles (*galuska*). Hungarians love desserts (*desszertek*). *Somlói galuska*, sponge cake soaked in cream, rum and chocolate sauce, and Gundel pancakes (*palacsinta*), fruit-filled, covered in chocolate sauce and flamed in rum, are ubiquitous. Some menus have strudel (*rétes*) and most offer *fagylalt*, ice cream.

Useful Phrases

I'd like a table for two. *Két fő részére kérek egy asztalt.*
Are these seats taken? *Ezek a helyek foglaltak?*
I'd like the menu, please. *Kérem az étlapot.*
I didn't order this. *Én nem ezt rendeltem.*
I am a vegetarian. *Vegetáriánus vagyok.*
I am diabetic. *Diabetikus vagyok.*
Do you have...? *Van...?*
Bon appétit! *Jó étvágyat!*

Basics

Ashtray *Hamutartó*
Bill *Számla*
Bread *Kenyér*
Cup *Csésze*
Fork *Villa*
Glass *Pohár*
Knife *Kés*
Milk *Tej*
Oil *Olaj*
Pepper *Bors*
Salt *Só*
Spoon *Kanál*
Sugar *Cukor*
Water *Víz*

Meats (*Húsok*)

Bárány Lamb
Bográcsgulyás Thick goulash soup
Borjú Veal
Comb Leg
Jókai bableves Bean soup with pork
Kacsa Duck
Kijevi pulykamell Cheese-filled turkey in breadcrumbs
Liba Goose
Marha Beef
Máj Liver
Mell Breast
Nyúl Rabbit
Pulyka Turkey
Sonka Ham
Szarvas Deer

Fish/Seafood (*Hal/tengeri gyülmölcs*)

Halfilé roston Grilled fillet of fish
Homár Lobster
Kagyló Shellfish, mussels
Lazac Salmon
Pisztráng Trout
Ponty Carp
Rák Crab, prawn
Tonhal Tuna

Salads (*saláták*)

Cékla Beetroot
Fejes saláta Lettuce salad
Paradicsom Tomato
Uborka Cucumber
Vitamin saláta Mixed salad with mayonnaise

Vegetables (*Zöldség*)

Karfiol Cauliflower
Kukorica Sweetcorn
Lencse Lentils
Paprika Pepper
Sárgarépa Carrot
Zöldbab Green beans
Zöldborsó Green peas

Fruit (*Gyümölcs*)

Alma Apple
Dinnye Melon
Dió Nut, walnut
Eper Strawberry
Gesztenye Chestnut
Meggy Sour cherry
Narancs Orange
Őszibarack Peach
Szilva Plum

Drinks (*Italok*)

Ásványvíz Mineral Water
Bor Wine
Édes bor Sweet wine
Fehér bor White wine
Kávé Coffee
Narancslé Orange juice
Pálinka Fruit brandy
Pezsgő Sparkling wine
Sör Beer
Száraz bor Dry wine
Vörös bor Red wine

Cafés & Coffeehouses

Step back in time to sip cappuccino and sample a slice of literary life amid the grand remnants of Habsburg coffeehouse culture, or travel back to 1965 in one of the city's many eszpresszós.

Budapest caters well for the coffee drinker. The post-communist acceleration in the pace of daily life hasn't quite eradicated the luxury of sitting down for a quiet cappuccino and watching the world hurry by. Indeed, the fact that many Hungarians now need at least two jobs to survive has sharpened the necessity for the caffeine fix. From the humble eszpresszó or the classy cukrászda to the grand remnants of Habsburg coffeehouse culture and modern cafés in a variety of idioms, the city teems with opportunities to satisfy that caffeine craving and binge on a dangerously affordable variety of accompanying confections.

Coffee arrived in Hungary with the Turks, and coffeehouses were a feature of Budapest long before they appeared in Paris or Vienna. But it was along Viennese lines that the Budapest coffeehouse (kávéház) developed and the institution reached its heyday in the final decades of the Habsburg Empire. At the turn of the century there were nearly 600 coffeehouses in Budapest. Only a handful have survived.

In the nineteenth century, coffeehouses both embodied a Habsburg ideal – that people of all classes, races and nations could mingle amicably under one roof – and were a breeding ground for burgeoning Magyar culture. A list of regulars at the Café Japan (now the Írók Boltya bookshop on Andrássy út; *see chapter* **Shopping**) reads like a who's who of Hungarian painting. Writers gathered in droves at the New York Kávéház. Even the 1848 national revolution against Budapest rule started in a coffeehouse – the Café Pilvax, now a shoddy branch of a Hungarian fast-food chain.

Combining the neighbourliness of a local pub, the facilities of a gentleman's club and the intellectual activity of a free university, coffeehouses were places to feel at ease. You could wolf down a full meal or linger for hours over one cup of coffee. Writers were provided with free pens and paper. Regular groups of playwrights and sculptors, painters and musicians, would congregate at particular tables. A journalist didn't even need to leave his regular spot to catch the latest stories and scandals, compose an article or even dispatch it to the paper – coffeehouse regulars could send and receive messages.

The cream of the crop was the **New York Kávéház** (also known as the Café New-York) which opened in 1894. Its century-long demise epitomises the fate of kávéház culture. On opening, the marble and bronze interior was decorated with frescoes from leading painters and every literary figure used to hob-nob at its tables. It thrived on between the wars, when visiting Hollywood moguls were as vital to the atmosphere as the literary set. Then fascism, war and the Communists came along, between them destroying not just the actual coffeehouses, but also the social classes and independent artistic scene which had brought them life. The New York was turned into a sports shop, only later to reopen as the Café Hungaria. Now re-named New York, it just about still functions – a shoddy state-run trap for tourists who come to gawp at an Art Nouveau interior defaced with appalling communist-era light-fittings.

There are other survivors. **Gerbeaud** has lorded it over Vörösmarty tér since the 1870s. The **Lukács** on Andrássy út was reopening as this book went to press. The **Művész** is probably the best surviving coffeehouse, and still retains a semblance of some literary life. But most coffeehouses are these days too expensive for Hungarians. Meanwhile, something of the old literary café tradition survives in the various Budapest bookshops which also serve coffee, such as the **Litea** in the Castle District, or the Írók Boltya on Andrássy út.

Eszpresszós – smaller, seedier and markedly less inspiring – had grown in popularity during the 1930s Depression. These were encouraged in the coffeehouse's place and flourished in the 1960s. The city is full of them, and we've listed some of the more intriguing examples of the genre. *See page 149* **Eszpressz Yourself.**

The cukrászda is a confectioner's or pastry shop which also serves coffee. You can buy cakes to take away or consume on the premises. Some are self-service, stand-up joints best suited to the urgent caffeine fix. Others are essentially sit-down cafés. The smaller cukrászdak are often family businesses, and some have been flourishing for generations.

While the cukrászda upholds tradition, an assortment of modern cafés struggle to reinvent the coffeehouse for the 1990s. We've listed the best of these, such as **Café Ponyvaregény**, **Café Miro**, **Talk Talk** and **Café Gusto**, and they're usually more cosmopolitan in style and a better bet for breakfast (not a great Magyar tradition) than the older places.

Hungarian coffee protocols are a hybrid of Italian and Austrian. Ask for a *kávé*, and you'll get a simple espresso with sugar and milk on the side. A *dupla* is a double measure. Be careful when ordering a cappuccino, as you sometimes get it German-style with a huge gloop of whipped cream. For a large, milky coffee resembling a French *café au lait*, order a *tejeskávé*. Certain more cosmopolitan cafés offer a Viennese *mélange* (like a cappuccino without chocolate or cinnamon) or the Italian *macchiato*, an espresso 'stained' with a dash of steamed milk. Decaffeinated is *koffeinmentes*.

Buda

Castle District

Café Miró
I. Úri utca 30 (175 5458). Várbusz from M2 Moszkva tér/bus 16. **Open** 9am-midnight daily. **No credit cards.** Some English spoken. **Map A3**
Although, like everywhere in the Castle District, frequented mostly by tourists, this newish place has managed to resist the temptation towards the phonily historical. Décor and furniture has been designed in the shapes and colours of Joan Miró. The green metal chairs look crazy but are surprisingly comfortable; extraordinary sofas and hatstands impel you to pause and admire. The service ranges from cute to barely competent but there's a fine selection of salads, sandwiches and cakes.

Litea
I. Hess András tér 4 (175 6987). Várbusz from M2 Moszkva tér/bus 16. **Open** 10am-6pm daily. **Credit** AmEx, DC, EC, JCB, MC, V. English spoken. **Map A3**
Inside the Fortuna Passage, an attractively glass-roofed bookshop/café with tables scattered among the shelves. Teas are the speciality here, but they also serve coffees, cakes and ices, and their stock of English-language books – mostly stuff about Budapest or translations of Hungarian lit – is as good as you'll find in any non-specialist shop. Courtyard tables, too.

Pierrot
I. Fortuna utca 14 (175 6971). Várbusz from M2 Moszkva tér/bus 16. **Open** 11am-1am daily. **Credit** AmEx, DC, EC, JCB, MC, V. English spoken. **Map A3**
Essentially a café but with a long Hungarian-international menu if you feel like a meal (and eating it off rather low café-style tables). Otherwise, crepes are the speciality, served in a quiet, comfortable room with a piano, cane chairs, discreet lighting and paintings of Pierrots. It's far from cheap, even for this area, but service is fine, the wares are nicely presented and it does offer some respite from the tourist hordes. Long menu of cocktails and coffee specialities.

Ruszwurm Cukrászda
I. Szentháromság utca 7 (175 5284). Várbusz from M2 Moszkva tér/bus 16. **Open** 10am-7pm daily. **No credit cards.** English spoken. **Map A3**
Budapest's oldest cukrászda has been going since 1827 and still retains some 1840s Empire-style cherrywood fittings. These days it's tourist hell, though, and you're unlikely to be able to sit down for coffee, cakes or ices without a long wait. In the inner salon you must 'omit smoking'.

Tabán, Gellért Hill & Surrounds

Café Déryné
I. Krisztina tér 3 (212 3804). Tram 18/bus 78, 105. **Open** 9am-11pm Mon-Sat; 9am-9pm Sun. **No credit cards.** Some English spoken. **Map A4**
A modern café where down-at-heel locals pop in to read the daily papers while entrepreneurs do deals over mobile phones. It's a largish place in fake 'old' style, dominated by a grand piano. The cake counter is impressive and there's a decent variety of pastries, salads, sandwiches and ices. Service is brisk and flexible. Summer tables outside.

Erzsébet Híd Eszpresszó
I. Döbrentei tér 2 (212 2127). Bus 5, 7/tram 18. **Open** 9am-11pm daily. **No credit cards.** English spoken. **Map B5**
Refurbished but cramped inside, the attraction here is the terrace, looking out over the Danube and the busy flyover above. The clientèle is mixed, the décor in the narrow bar area kitsch, cake selection minimal, but the Buda bank of the river so as underused as a drinking venue that even the most modest of presszós will do on a baking hot afternoon.

Gellért Eszpresszó
Hotel Gellért, XI. Szent Gellért tér 1 (185 2200). Tram 18, 19, 47, 49. **Open** 8am-9pm daily. **Credit** AmEx, DC, EC, JCB, MC, V. English spoken. **Map C5**
Elegant but conservative café of the Gellért Hotel (its slightly chintzy décor is essentially a Communist idea of what German tourists find congenial) offers coffees, teas, cakes and strudels and a terrace marred by traffic noise. Stiff but efficient service and an assortment of daily papers, including some in English. Excellent spot for a coffee after a soporific stint in the Gellért baths.

Café Ponyvaregény
XI. Bercsényi utca 5 (06 30 606 609). Tram 18, 19, 47, 49/bus 7. **Open** 10am-2am Mon-Sat; 3pm-2am Sun. **No credit cards.** English spoken. **Map C6**
Coffeehouses never occupied basements, yet something of the old tradition does persist in this modern cellar space – the name means 'pulp fiction' and there are both bookshelves on the walls and daily papers in those Cuban bamboo holders. Mainly frequented by young Hungarians chatting over coffees (the classic range), cocktails (seven pages on the menu) or snacks (a basic assortment of cheap pastries). Furniture and crockery have been chosen with care and this is a relaxing spot to talk, read or indulge in an hour or two's battery-charging indolence.

Víziváros

Angelika
I. Batthyány tér 7 (212 3784). M2 Batthyány tér. **Open** 10am-10pm daily. **No credit cards.** Some English spoken. **Map B3**
In the former crypt of St Anne's Church on Batthyány tér, the Angelika is a refined café where the middle-class ladies of Buda come to gossip. When the sun streams through the stained-glass windows on a September afternoon, it's a most atmospheric venue for coffee and cakes. Terrace open in summer.

Moszkva tér & Rózsadomb

Café Gusto

II. Frankel Leó utca 12 (316 3970). Tram 4, 6. **Open** 10am-10pm Mon-Sat. **No credit cards**. Some English spoken. **Map B2**
Classy joint a short walk from Margaret Bridge, with a terrace overlooking a quiet sidestreet. Inside, the kind of place you wouldn't be embarrassed taking an Italian friend to, with coffee to match, possibly the best in town. Excellent selection on the menu, including fish and other seafood, fresh orange juice and decent salads.

Rózsadomb

II. Margit körút 7 (212 5145). Tram 4, 6. **Open** 9am-10pm daily. **No credit cards**. Some English spoken. **Map B2**
An inaccurate reflection of its namesake, the posh and barless residential area in the hills beyond, this humble eszpresszó is an oasis of low-priced entertainment. This is presszó life at its best, a celebration of the tacky and the tasteless. As cheap a draught Borsodi as anywhere in town.

Pest

Belváros

Anna Café

V. Váci utca 7 (266 9080). M1 Vörösmarty utca/tram 2. **Open** *winter* 8am-midnight daily. **Credit** AmEx. English spoken. **Map C4**
Pricey, touristy and somewhat characterless but offering an

excellent spot to watch the ceaseless flow of shoppers and tourists. The pastries and coffee are pretty good too. At night the crowd in here, like those roaming the street outside, begins to get a little dodgy.

Astoria Café

V. Kossuth Lajos utca 19-21 (117 3411). M2 Astoria. **Open** 7am-11pm daily. **Credit** AmEx, DC, JCB, MC, V. Some English spoken. **Map D4**
Elegant without being either overbearing or overpriced, the high-ceilinged café of the Astoria Hotel has big windows, large and comfortable leather chairs, and offers basic coffee, cakes and snacks. Once the haunt of both Nazi (1944-45) and Soviet (1956) officialdom, and despite being part of a state hotel chain for decades, the Astoria has managed to retain its turn-of-the-century feel. Cafés don't come more grandly *mitteleuropäisch* than this.

Auguszt Cukrászda

V. Kossuth Lajos utca 14-16 (137 6379). M2 Astoria. **Open** 10am-6pm Tue-Fri; 10am-2pm Sat. **No credit cards**. English spoken. **Map C4**
A venerable institution, run by the Auguszt family since 1870. Strictly speaking, this one is the branch, but their flagship Buda premises and bakery (near Moszkva tér) offer only a stand-up shelf for consuming their excellent coffees, pastries and cakes (and some memorabilia to peruse while munching). Here there are tables both within the cosy shop, and out in the expansive Neo-Renaissance courtyard. A speciality is the E-80 cake (chocolate with a marzipan filling, coffee icing and almonds), created for the 80th birthday of Elemér Auguszt, father of current owner József.
Branch: II. Fény utca 8 (135 8931).

Eszpressz Yourself

Somewhere in Budapest it is forever 1965. This is achieved without wax figures of pop stars, fickle flashbacks of fashion or vinyl reissues. It is the real McCoy – preserved, pickled and presented as it would have been 30 years ago: the presszó.

The smaller, seedier and cheaper offspring of the more cultured kávéház, presszós (or more correctly, eszpresszós) sprang up during the Great Depression of the 1930s. After communism frowned upon coffeehouse culture as a decadent bourgeois throwback, presszós ruled. Their heyday was the 1960s, when they became the domain of bored youngsters seeking solace in their neon lights, chrome coffee machines, jukeboxes and lurid décor.

Well, what would you have done? Studied your Lenin and Marx for homework, run a few more laps around the track or caught another dreary Soviet film at the pictures? Would you hell. You would have been straight down the presszó: catching the latest beat tune to drift over from the West, two forints a song, scaring up the opposite sex and somewhere along the line establishing your identity with all the other spotty weirdos who would later marry and get rehoused in some distant tower block.

Presszos grew old with the remaining clientèle, Casio tunes lulling divorced housewives into a false sense of security and belonging. The jukeboxes fell into disrepair, any western tune you wanted was right there in Vienna, and all that remained was the neon and the décor, right out of an East German airport waiting room.

Gorgeously tatty examples of the genre, such as the **Majakovskij**, **Rozsadomb** or **No. 1** (*below*) can still be found, as charming as a newsreel of the Beatles, as irrelevant as a reunion concert of their many Hungarian imitators.

All stacked up at the **Művész.** *Page 149*

Bécsi Kávéház

Inter-Continental Hotel, V. Apáczai Csere János utca 12-14 (117 9111). M1 Vörösmarty tér/tram 2/bus 15. **Open** 9am-9pm daily. **Credit** AmEx, DC, JCB, MC, V. English spoken. **Map C4**
Probably the best cakes in town. Three long rows of them laugh at you from the display counter – a Viennese ('Bécsi') selection at Budapest prices. The place itself is pleasant enough, with tables sectioned off by glass dividers, allowing privacy as you scoff down your daily fix of gateau. Also on the menu are a dozen types of coffee and ice creams.

Gerbeaud

V. Vörösmarty tér 7 (118 1311). M1 Vörösmarty tér. **Open** 9am-9pm daily. **Credit** AmEx, DC, JCB, MC, V. Some English spoken. **Map C4**
On this imposing site since 1870, and with turn-of-the-century fittings, these days Gerbeaud's elegance is mostly reserved for tourists, who stop off after a stroll up Váci. It was here that Emil Gerbeaud invented the cognac cherry and there is still a huge choice of patisserie items, both Hungarian and Viennese. Service runs from rude to efficient, and the outside tables are a fine spot for people-watching.

Gourmand

V. Semmelweis utca 2 (118 0892). M2 Astoria/tram 47, 49/bus 7. **Open** 8.30am-midnight Mon-Sat; 11am-10pm Sun. **No credit cards**. English spoken. **Map D4**
At first glance, a typical Pest cukrászda, a cake shop perched on the corner of Kossuth Lajos utca with a few tables outside in summer. The real treat is the extraordinary upstairs room, with seating arranged as if it was an auditorium, the hemispherical bar its stage. At times it feels as though the place ought to be revolving. Chasing your coffee with one of their lethal 'Puszta cocktails' will assist in achieving this effect. Excellent venue for an intimate rendezvous.

Ibolya

V. Ferenciek tere 5 (267 0239). M3 Ferenciek tere/bus 7. **Open** *summer* 8am-11pm Mon-Sat; noon-8pm Sun; *winter* 7am-10pm Mon-Sat; noon-8pm Sun. **No credit cards**. Some English spoken. **Map C4**
Opposite the ELTE University Library, Ibolya is among the best and most central of the surviving communist-era eszpresszós: staff are slow, but you can have fine salads, sandwiches and drinks. Avoid the microwaved meat. Take a seat on the terrace if you prefer traffic fumes to cigarette smoke.

Mignon

V. Károly körút 28 (117 5702). M1, M2, M3 Deák tér/tram 47, 49. **Open** 8am-9pm Mon-Sat; 9am-8pm Sun. **No credit cards**. English spoken. **Map C4**
What other major European capital could have such tack, neon and cheap booze at its epicentre? Right by the Károly körút exit of Deák tér metro station, the Mignon is a classic presszó right where a bank or hotel should be. In fact, it's where a bank or hotel will be once they knock down this communist-era row of shops before the end of the century. For the time being, enjoy the Mignon's small-time mafia clientèle, painfully slow service and summer terrace out back.

Múzeum Cukrászda

VIII. Múzeum körút 10 (266 4526). M2 Astoria/tram 47, 49/bus 7. **Open** 24 hours daily. **No credit cards**. Some English spoken. **Map D4**
By night a haunt for boozehounds and ne'erdowells, by day an innocent cukrászda, with a decent selection of cakes, sandwiches and salads. The modest terrace is as good a place as any to sink a beer or coffee after a hard morning's trekking around the nearby National Museum, and what the place lacks in décor it makes up for in intimacy and reasonable service. Check out the marzipan cartoon animals on the counter. *See also chapter* **Nightlife**.

Talk Talk

V. Magyar utca 12-14 (266 2145). M2 Astoria/tram 47, 49/bus 7. **Open** 9am-1.30am daily. **No credit cards**. English spoken. **Map D4**
Newish, and still one of the few cafés in Budapest with a decent breakfast selection (mostly German-style plus eggs and omelettes) also serves up a big selection of coffee specialities, light meals, imported beers and cocktails. The concrete-based tables are wobbly and the music (mostly mainstream rock) varies from loud to way too loud. Mainly frequented by young Hungarians in Italian fashions.

Lipotváros

István Cukrászda

V. Október 6 utca 17 (131 3274). M3 Arany János utca. **Open** 10am-6pm daily. **No credit cards**. No English spoken. **Map C3**
Nicest feature of this small cake shop is the dumb-waiter that ushers your purchase upstairs. Order at the counter, then proceed to the small upper room. The arrival of your coffee and cake will be heralded by an emphatic buzz. Can be a bit airless in summer but a handy spot to read whatever you just bought at nearby Bestsellers bookshop.

No. 1 Presszó

V. Sas utca 9 (267 0235). M3 Arany János utca. **Open** 9am-midnight Mon-Fri; 4pm-midnight Sat. **No credit cards**. No English spoken. **Map C3**
Finest presszó in the downtown area, with an atmosphere straight out of the 1960s slap in Budapest's business quarter. The prominent bar counter is offset by a spacious room of brown furniture, incongruous paintings and a small statue, the occasional bleep of mobile phone quickly dealt with while patrons conduct the more serious business of draught Zipfer and Unicum chasers. Cocktails of questionable parentage share the menu with toasted sandwiches and cappuccinos served like ice-cream cornets. As far away from the city beat as it is possible to get in the same postal district.

Szalai Cukrászda

V. Balassi Bálint utca 7 (269 3210). Tram 2. **Open** 9am-7pm Mon, Wed-Sun. **No credit cards**. Some English spoken. **Map B2**
Just north of Parliament, an excellent old family-run cukrászda with a city-wide reputation for its cakes and pastries. These can be consumed sitting on stools at one of half a dozen low tables, or carried away in handsome boxes. A few large, gilt-framed mirrors challenge the tawdriness of the modern brand-names festooned on walls also hung with ancient and modern certificates testifying to the quality of the wares. Beautiful old weighing machine on the counter.

Andrássy út & District VI

Lukács

VI. Andrássy út 70. M1 Vörösmarty utca. **Map D3**
At the time of going to press, this historic *kávéház* – designated a national monument – was about to reopen as the head offices of the CIB Hungária Bank, with the original coffeehouse area restored and functioning amid all the financial activity. Bizarre notion, but maybe worth a look.

Művész

VI. Andrássy út 29 (352 1337). M1 Opera. **Open** 9am-midnight daily. **No credit cards.** Some English spoken.
Map D3
Perhaps the last real turn-of-the-century coffeehouse in Budapest, with excellent coffee, unpretentious period décor, a good, though limited, selection of cakes, savouries and ice creams, and some genuine life apart from the tourist trade. The name means 'artist' and you still see people annotating manuscripts at corner tables, next to gaggles of gossiping old ladies. It's also a favoured haunt of the less business-orientated expat crowd. On Pest's grand boulevard, not quite opposite the Opera, the outside tables are a grand spot in summer.

Perity Mestercukrászdá

VI. Andrássy út 37 (352 8031). M1 Oktogon/tram 4, 6.
Open 8am-10pm daily. **No credit cards.** Some English spoken. **Map D3**
Marked by multi-coloured barber-pole things that contrast oddly with the marble façade, here cakes are dispensed either through a hatch on to the street, or within for consumption at a handful of tables. Despite the grand location, it's cheap enough for Hungarians to frequent. Worth looking in just to note the splendid communist-era chandelierthing, or observe the 'Barby' cakes (made to order complete with voluminous iced dresses for a mere Ft5,500) in the glass case by the door.

Zsolnay Kávéház

Béke Radisson Hotel, VI. Teréz körút 43 (301 1600). M3 Nyugati/tram 4, 6. **Open** 10am-10pm daily. **Credit** AmEx, DC, JCB, MC, V. Some English spoken. **Map D2**
Café on the first floor of the Beke Radisson Hotel, as bright and elegant as the ceramics produced by the man after whom it is named. Vilmos Zsolnay's bust sits proudly on the fireplace at the end of a long, sunlit room embellished with chandeliers and a pianist knocking out a few Cole Porter numbers. Decent range of cakes, ice creams and breakfast options, but the Zsolnay is seen in its best light in the late afternoon.

District VII

Fröhlich Cukrászda

VII. Dob utca 22 (121 6741). M2 Astoria/tram 47, 49.
Open *summer* 10am-6pm Mon-Thur; 7.30am-4pm Fri;
8am-8pm Sun. *winter* 10am-5pm Mon-Thur; 7am-2pm Fri;
8am-8pm Sun. **No credit cards.** English spoken. **Map D4**
Recently renovated baker's serving kosher pastries in the heart of Budapest's Jewish quarter, and very much part of the local community. Old Mr Fröhlich still stumbles out of the bakery covered in flour, only to be shooed back out of sight by his wife at the counter. The traditional *flodni* – with layers of apple, poppy seeds and hazelnuts – is the star of the pastry counter. Various teas complement the coffee dispensed from a beautiful old Casino espresso machine.

Majakovskij

VII. Király utca 103 (342 5732). Trolleybus 70, 78.
Open 6am-10pm Mon-Fri; 7am-8pm Sat, Sun. **No credit cards.** No English spoken. **Map D3**
Classic *eszpresszo* that would fit well with the Stalinist edifices in Statue Park. Today the Majakovszkij still stands

Kosher coffee at the **Fröhlich Cukrászda**

proudly among the dust, filth and neon of Király utca, a street once also named after the Russian poet and revolutionary. (*See also chapter* **Architecture**.)

Café Mozart

VII. Erzsébet körút 36 (352 0664). Tram 4, 6.
Open 9am-11pm Mon-Fri, Sun; 9am-noon Sat. **No credit cards.** English spoken. **Map D3**
Laughable simulation of coffeehouse culture: waitresses in Baroque costume, phony period furniture, crap *mitteleuropäisch* murals, inept portraits of Mozart and 62 different kinds of coffee, all with straight-faced descriptions so absurd it's almost worth going in just to deride the menu. ('Espresso: strong, black coffee made out of carefully selected coffee beans, served in a small cup'). Overlit, sterile and naff as ninepence, this is the unacceptable face of capitalist Budapest. Avoid also its sister establishment, the equally asinine Café Verdi at Astoria.

New York Kávéház

VII. Erzsébet körút 9-11 (322 3849). M2 Blaha Lujza tér/tram 4, 6. **Open** 9am-midnight daily. **Credit** AmEx, DC, MC, V. Some English spoken. **Map D4**
Budapest's most famous coffeehouse is a sad ruin of its former magnificent self. Opened in 1894 to a design by Alajos Hauszmann and once the main haunt of Pest's artistic life, it's been run down by decades of communism and is now too expensive for the locals. Tourists who can afford what is more of a museum than a living coffeehouse (and can find their way in through the wooden scaffolding that's been holding up the façade since 1956 when a Soviet tank slammed into it) are greeted with some of the most indifferent service in town. The sumptuous interior is still worth a look. But unless someone buys up the state-run hotel chain of which this is a part, it's likely to deteriorate even further. A tragedy. (*See also chapter* **Sightseeing**.)

Pubs & Bars

Bright bars, dingy dives, tacky theme pubs, worm-eaten wine cellars.

Hungarians drink like brushmakers, as the saying goes here. Budapest's savage drinking culture has traditionally been fuelled by cheap wine, but Hungary's position at the crossroads between spirit-swilling Slav countries and the beery expanses of Germanic Europe has also affected local customs. Add nearly a decade of cosmopolitan western influences and you get a mixed bag of drinking habits and places to indulge them.

Most of them aren't too sophisticated, with dreary décor, terrible toilets and the radio tuned to some top 40 station. Hungarians aren't that bothered as long as they've got a drink in front of them. Standing at counters is rare and table service, though the norm, varies from slow to practically stationary. Bar snacks are starchy and simple: either the *pogácsa*, a salty scone, or bread and dripping with raw onions.

There are two traditional mainstays: the borozó, a cheap and unpretentious wine cellar; and the söröző, a beer bar inferior to those of Germany or the Czech Republic. The latter are beginning to decline in importance, overwhelmed by 'drink bars' (*see page 152* **Inside the 'Drink Bar'**) and wave of tacky theme pubs that represent a misguided attempt at 'western' sophistication. Borozós are dank, dark and start filling before dawn. Here wine is priced by the decilitre and ladled from tureens, often mixed with soda water to create *fröccs* – spritzers – or, if it's red wine, cola. Specify the mix you prefer.

Hungarian beer is acceptable if cold. Borsodi is your best option on draught, otherwise Austrian and German brews are widely available. Beers are either light (*világos*) or, more rarely, dark (*barna*). The younger generation have taken to drinking pints (*korsó*; a smaller glass is a *pohár*) instead of the wine their dads drank. No one clinks their beer glasses, though. Doing so yourself will either cop some nasty looks, or else induce an intoxicated historical lecture. The Austrians were clinking beer glasses, you will be informed, while executing Hungarian generals after the failed 1848 uprising against Habsburg rule.

Hungarians drown their historical memory with shots of Unicum, the national drink, or rounds of pálinka, fruit brandy. The latter comes in several fiery varieties. Stick to either *szilva* (plum) or *vilmos* (pear) pálinka, and tread carefully if anyone offers you lethal, home-brewed *házi pálinka*. Unicum, a herb liqueur made to a secret recipe that was smuggled out of the country during Communist times

Drink a pálinka, awake with a stinker.

and has now been brought back, is an acquired taste. Bittersweet and minty, some call it The Accelerator. Drink five beers and feel bloated. Drink five beers and whack back one Unicum and feel like five more beers – and several more Unicums. After that, cancel tomorrow's sightseeing plans.

Prices vary wildly. The borozó clientèle can get shitfaced for a handful of coins. Beer drinkers will be paying around Ft200-Ft250 for their pint. Pubs appealing to Budapest's expatriate community will happily charge double that.

The area around the south end of Váci utca is decent for pub crawling, with an assortment of bars lurking in its waterfront backstreets. The patch around Oktogon and the Opera offers a more refined crawl, with Liszt tér as summer drinking central. District VII features many of the city's more intriguing bars, more spread out but still within strolling distances, with lots of places sprouting around Almássy tér. Borozós mostly close around 8pm. Most pubs and bars stay open until midnight-2am, though there are plenty still going if you want to continue until dawn. *See also chapters* **Nightlife** *and* **Cafés & Coffeehouses**.

Buda

Tabán, Gellért Hill & Surrounds

Libella
XI. Budafoki út 7 (209 4761). Tram 18, 47, 49. **Open** 8am-1.30am Mon-Sat. **No credit cards.** Some English spoken. **Map C6**
Café/bar attracting an underground clientèle, with arty photos and paintings, and a good place to collect flyers for gallery openings or alternative theatre performances. Dark and light beers on draught, chess games in the corner. Two minutes from the Gellért Hotel.

Park Café
XI. Kosztolányi Dezső tér 2 (166 9475). Tram 49/bus 7.
Open 10am-2am Mon-Thur; 10am-4am Fri-Sat. **No credit cards.** Some English spoken. **Map B6**
In the small park area between Kosztolányi Dezső tér and Moricz Zsigmond körtér, this is a restaurant, really, valiantly if misguidedly attempting to become Budapest's Hard Rock Café. But the bar is the real attraction, running right along one wall of the rock memorabilia-bedecked main room, curving out into the attractive terrace area beside the small park lake and fountain, and staffed by people who actually know how to mix a drink. The cheerful, neon-accented exterior looks like something from the Flintstones kind of way. Menu of burgers and 'international' items, average Ft1,700.

Café Zacc
XI. Bocskai utca 12 (209 1593). Tram 18, 47/bus 7.
Open noon-2am Mon-Fri; 10am-2am Sat; 3pm-midnight Sun. **No credit cards.** Some English spoken. **Map B6**
Modest but fun-loving bar a short hop from Moricz Zsigmond körtér, named after the bits left at the bottom of your coffee. Its décor wavers between pop-art and a local youth club, with customers to match. Decent sounds, much football talk, and a grimly imaginative range of cheap and lethal cocktails. Tables outside in summer.

Víziváros

Belgian Brasserie
I. Bem rakpart 12 (201 5082). M2 Batthyány tér/tram 19. **Open** noon-midnight daily. **No credit cards.** Some English spoken. **Map B3**
Just round the corner from the French Institute, with a summer terrace looking out on to the Danube, and offering a dozen or so Belgian beers – Leffe, Chimay, Hoegarden, Duvel – at prices varying from Ft350-Ft420. The menu has mussels at Ft950 and herring starters at Ft500. The décor is a little contrived, with a miniature Mannekin Pis by the toilets, a portrait of King Léopold overseeing a back room, and a model of a fat, bald Belgian monk greeting visitors at the entrance. But the bar counter is perfect for serious drinking.

Moszkva tér & Rózsadomb

Calgary
II. Frankel Leó utca 24 (115 9087). Tram 4, 6, 17.
Open 11am-4am Mon-Fri; 3pm-4am Sat-Sun. **Credit** AmEx, DC, JCB, MC. Some English spoken. **Map B2**
From the outside the Calgary, in the shadow of Margaret Bridge, looks like any corner bar. Step inside and it's like Steptoe and Son's front room. Run by a radio star from the 1950s, the Calgary attracts a variety of faded actresses, antiques collectors and misplaced alcoholics. Downstairs among the ornaments you'll can admire a record player and Hungarian pop hits from the 1960s. There's no menu, but ask if the fish soup is on.

Móri Borozó
I. Fiáth János utca 16 (no phone). M2 Moszkva tér. **Open** 2pm-11pm Mon-Fri; 2pm-9pm Sat, Sun. **No credit cards.** No English spoken. **Map A2**
Comfortable wine bar singled out by its younger clientèle. In the 1970s Moszkva tér was a major meeting place for young rockers with nowhere else to go. It still attracts the leather waistcoat brigade, one generation down from the messy mac merchants who usually frequent these joints. Friendly atmosphere, Innstadt beer on draught, and the wine is cheap and plentiful.

Oscar Café
II. Ostrom utca 14 (212 8017). Tram 4, 6. **Open** 3pm-4am daily. **No credit cards.** No English spoken. **Map A3**

Getting discreetly zonked at **Café Zacc.**

Large and efficient pub with a Hollywood theme, a long bar, and lots of young Hungarians debating whether to go back to his place or hers. A menu containing both snacks and full meals, and a short but sensible cocktail selection plus staff skilled enough to mix them properly, make this is a useful spot in the Moszkva tér area. Music is mostly the out-of-date chart disco stuff you seem to hear everywhere in this town.

Vox
II. Marczibányi tér 5A (315 0592). M2 Moszkva tér/tram 4, 6, 18. **Open** 1pm-3am daily. **No credit cards.** Some English spoken. **Map A2**
Handy if you're visiting the concrete and brick Művelődécsi Központ culture centre, scene of many dance houses (*see chapter* **Folklore**), but otherwise rather out of the way. Vox occupies the culture centre's basement and has its own separate entrance. The bar is pleasant if unremarkable, occasionally hosting bands and DJs. The airy terracing outside, its concrete surfaces daubed with primitive fish pictures, is the best feature – a fine spot to relax on a hot summer night. Amstel at Ft180 a korsó.

Pest
Belváros

Amstel Bar
V. Váci utca 61 (267 0296). M3 Ferenciek tere/tram 47, 49. **Open** 8am-6am Mon-Sat; 10am-6am Sun. **No credit cards.** Some English spoken. **Map C4**
It's been here for ever, this small corner place, and despite a better selection of alcohol brands and new tables outside on the recently pedestrianised end of Váci utca, it remains largely unchanged in atmosphere since Communist times. The circular bar is beautiful, the staff usually know what they're doing, the atmosphere is relaxed and it's open until the crack of dawn.

Fregatt

V. Molnár utca 26 (118 9997). Tram 2, 47, 49.
Open 3pm-1am Mon-Fri; 5pm-1am Sat-Sun. **Credit**
AmEx. Some English spoken. **Map C5**
For years this was the main hangout for Anglophone
expats and those who wished to meet them. On a Friday
night you'd have trouble getting in the door. But life has
moved on from Budapest's first English-style pub and
though the barmen still ring a bell when one of them gets
a tip, the thing doesn't chime so often. Quiet, air-conditioned, some rudimentary food and a depressing tendency
to play the Gypsy Kings.

Galéria

V. Vitkovics Mihály utca 6 (266 4566). **Open** 10am-11pm
Mon-Sat; 11am-11pm Sun. **No credit cards**. No English
spoken. **Map C4**
This serene and pretty bar has been here forever, tucked
away in a quiet Belváros backwater. The Gallery has paintings up for sale displayed around a cosy bar area and back
room, embellished by vases of dried flowers and dinky stools
that look like hat boxes. In summer there are a couple of
small tables outside, though actually finding a seat free at
one of these is a rare event indeed.

Irish Cat

V. Múzeum körút 41 (266 4085). M3 Kálvin tér. **Open**
11am-2am daily. **No credit cards**. Some English
spoken. **Map D5**
Every major European city seems to have an Irish pub that
functions as a meat market. This is Budapest's. Crowded bar
area with intimate wooden booths and back section for overspill and smooching. Packed after midnight.

Janis Pub

V. Királyi Pál utca 8 (266 2619). M3 Kálvin tér. **Open**
4pm-2am Mon-Thur; 4pm-3am Fri-Sat; 6pm-2am Sun. **No
credit cards**. Some English spoken. **Map D5**
Quiet pub tucked away in the narrow backstreets between
Kálvin tér and Ferenciek tere. Ms Joplin would have been
pretty disappointed if someone had dragged her here,
although Southern Comfort can be had to chase the Guinness. Attracts an expatriate and native crowd.

Latin Kocsma

V. Havas utca 2 (267 0260). Tram 2, 47, 49. **Open**
noon-2am Mon-Sat. **No credit cards**. Some English
spoken. **Map C5**
Curious but cosy bar just off the Belgrád rakpart. Walls are
covered with logs, the seating is a forest of carved tree
stumps and there's a beautiful neon 'coctail' sign above the
bar. Here Latin music is the order of the evening – either genuine Mexican muzak on the tape player, or live between 9pm
and midnight on Mon, Wed and Fri, when Chilean guitarist
friends of the management gather here to jam.

Sport Planet Café

*V. Kecskeméti út 1 (267 0226). M3 Kálvin tér/tram 47,
49.* **Open** 10am-2am daily. **No credit cards**. Some
English spoken. **Map D5**
Budapest's only sports bar, with a few Hungarian touches
among the Americana, such as a framed front page from the
Népsport which carried the news of Hungary's victory over
England in 1953, plus Warhol-style portraits of disgraced
swimming manager Gyorgy Zemplenyi. Full American
menu, but a disappointingly small range of beers. Bundles
of television sets but alas no Sky Sports.

Inside the 'Drink Bar'

There are hundreds of charming places to drink
in Budapest, but often the nearest joint turns out
to be a 'drink bar'. Beware: the convenient
answer is not always the right one.

You can't always tell these small, soul-free
establishments by their labels, but you'll know
you've stumbled upon a drink bar when you sit
down, place your order, clock the lack of atmosphere and the tacky decor – usually something
metallic and mirrored. Music will be provided
by a Hungarian top 40 station.

The classic drink bar only has room for four or
five stools. You will probably be served by a
young barmaid with a short skirt and a matching
attention span, serving up overpriced bottled beer
and shots of Johnnie Walker. If there's anyone else
around, they're likely to be either clones of the barmaid or else clones of her mafia boyfriend.

Most drink bars sprang up around the time
Communism fell. When everyone was suddenly allowed to open their own business, well-
meaning Hungarians with a little savings
sought to realise their dreams. Sadly, you can't
build a bar on dreams, and many of these mini-
enterprises have already closed. The rest of
them probably should.

But drink bars do have a sort of minimalist
appeal. Imagine the least you would need to be
served a drink in public: a bar and someone
standing behind it with alcohol. A Zen drinker,
or a drinker with an interesting companion to
speak to, needs nothing more.

If you forgot to bring someone with you, you
can expect any conversational ploy to fail mis-
erably. The barmaid may be willing to go
through her English vocabulary: 'Bruce Willis...
Pretty woman... Laugh, laugh me do!' She'll
think it's just charming that you don't speak any
Hungarian. You'll smile at each other, useless-
ly, for a second before she turns her back on you,
starts cleaning some glasses that weren't dirty,
and pretends that the two of you aren't the only
people sharing a space the size of a closet.

Maybe another patron will wander in. He'll
have a shaved head and a body the size of a
small mountain. Just for fun, ask for a fancy
cocktail. If the barmaid knows it, she'll be proud
to demonstrate. If, as is more likely, she is
stumped, she'll shrug her shoulders and look at
her huge boyfriend. Then both of them will stare
at you like you're a trouble maker. At least they
will have noticed you.

Lipotváros

Beckett's
V. Bajcsy-Zsilinszky út 72 (111 1033). M3 Nyugati.
Open *bar* noon-2am daily. **Credit** over Ft3,000: AmEx, DC, JCB, MC, V. Some English spoken. **Map C2**
Enormous Irish pub and principal watering hole for Budapest's Anglophone expat business community. Although pricey for Budapest, some Hungarians do wander in too. Friday night is the liveliest, as consultants and chancers quaff away the cares of the week, and the place can also heave for major sports events on Sky. The live music, which usually starts around 11pm, is loud and mostly dreadful – trad jazz or Beatles impersonators.

Andrássy út & District VI

Cactus Juice
VI. Jókai tér 5 (302 2116). M1 Oktogon/tram 4, 6. **Open** noon-2am Mon-Thur; noon-4am Fri-Sat; 4pm-2am Sun. **No credit cards**. Some English spoken. **Map D3**
Wild West theme pub with wooden panels, rifle cases, iron stoves and other suitable fittings placed with some attention to detail. A joint to meet friends and sit at tables, rather than somewhere to get to know strangers at the bar, it's mostly patronised by young Hungarians. Big menu of burgers and rudimentary Tex-mex items and HB at Ft220 la korsó. It could be a great place if they played some country & western, but the music is mostly old disco with a bit of the ubiquitous Gypsy Kings thrown in.

Crazy Café
VI. Jókai utca 30 (302 4003). M3 Nyugati. **Open** 11am-1am daily. **No credit cards**. Some English spoken. **Map C2**
Its name and the long row of beer signs outside refer to the ridiculous choice of drinks: up to 18 types of draught beer, nearly 100 types of bottled beers, and some 50 cocktails. Two restaurant areas serving pizzas and Hungarian standards, two bars and an area for live music and karaoké.

Incognito
VI. Liszt Ferenc tér 3 (267 9428). M1 Oktogon. **Open** 10am-midnight Mon-Fri; noon-midnight Sat-Sun. **No credit cards**. Some English spoken. **Map D3**
Large bar area with walls covered in classic jazz LP sleeves. Although it has an adventurous drinks menu – 20 types of coffee, ten teas, two dozen cocktails – the Incognito isn't as cool as it thinks it is. It could be the loud jazz, it could be the dim lighting, it could be the extortionate prices. At its best in summer, when the outside tables fill up night and day.

Jet Station
VI. Teréz körút 51-53 (311 1538). M3 Nyugati/tram 4, 6. **Open** noon-2am daily. **Credit** EC, MC, V. Some English spoken. **Map D2**
Run by members of the Jet Stream Flying Club, so unsurprisingly and not unsympathetically themed around flight, from wall designs of hot air balloons to airmen's artefacts under the glass bar counter. Unfortunately the scores of multinational beer and cigarette logos spread around this large, cool, cellar bar give more of an impression of a Grand Prix driver's overalls. Summer terrace, and a full menu of pub grub and lunchtime specials.

Café Mediterran
VI. Liszt Ferenc tér 10 (342 1959). M1 Oktogon/tram 4, 6. **Open** 10am-2am daily. **No credit cards**. No English spoken. **Map D3**
Thanks to the popularity of this place and Incognito (*see above*) across the way, pedestrianised Liszt tér bustles until the early hours. Of the two, the Mediterran is preferable.

Smaller, less pretentious and certainly redder than its rival, this is a smart, friendly bar for an Amstel or three. The terrace gets very popular in summer. The Undergrass disco (*see chapter* **Nightlife**) is down in the cellar.

Picasso Point
VI. Hajós utca 31 (269 5544). M2 Opera. **Open** 9am-2.30am Mon-Thur, Sun; 9am-4am Fri-Sat. **No credit cards**. Some English spoken. **Map C3**
Picasso once attracted a pseudo-arty expat crowd. What's left of them tend to sit in the comfortable large upstairs bar, while Hungarians gyrate in the darker downstairs disco. Decent bar food; occasional live acts and arts events.

Underground
VI. Teréz körút 30 (111 1481). M3 Nyugati/tram 4, 6. **Open** 3pm-3am daily. **No credit cards**. Some English spoken. **Map C2**
Popular subterranean space with curious décor intended to evoke Kustirica's film of the same name. There's a good, long bar, a young and fashionable crowd, decent and reasonably priced food (average Ft800) and DJs playing trip hop and acid jazz. What more could you want, apart from a little less pushing and shoving? *See also chapter* **Nightlife**.

District VII

Dam Coffee
VII. Almássy tér 7 (06 30 341 416). **Open** 6pm-3am daily. **No credit cards**. Some English spoken. **Map E3**
Themed like an Amsterdam coffee bar – right down to the king-size papers on sale, though something to roll up in them is less reliably available, especially if no one knows your face. Drinks are complemented by a selection of munchies.

Galéria
VII. Akácfa utca 30 (06 60 332 079). Tram 4, 6 Wesselényi utca. **Open** noon-midnight daily. **No credit cards**. Some English spoken. **Map D3**
Intimate gallery bar area up a winding staircase, with a full pub menu, occasional live jazz in the corner, and lively young clientèle. Service is glacially slow.

Óbester borozó
VII. Huszár utca 5 (351 3890). M2 Keleti/bus 7. **Open** 9am-midnight daily. **No credit cards**. No English spoken. **Map E3**
Smoky wine bar with convenient opening hours and comfortable seating, attracting both classic wine-nosed users and a younger crowd eager for a game of darts. It even does a modest range of bar snacks, as well as the usual spritzers and pálinka chasers. As dirt cheap as any other wine bar in Pest.

Portside
VII. Dohány utca 7 (351 8405). M2 Astoria/tram 47, 49/bus 7. **Open** noon-2am Mon-Thur; 11am-4am Fri-Sat; noon-2am Sun. **Credit** AmEx, V. English spoken. **Map D4**
A huge and nautically-themed English-run cellar pub. Early evenings it's patronised by a smart, youngish and largely Anglophone crowd – guys in suits and ties, and women who like guys in suits and ties. Later on it's even younger and even more of a meat market free-for-all. Efficient staff, a big menu (average Ft1,800), pool at Ft300 an hour, and the same old disco standards, played rather too loud for comfort. Packed at weekends.

Sixtus
VII. Nagy Diófa utca 26-28 (352 1479). M2 Blaha Lujza tér/tram 4, 6/bus 7. **Open** 5.30pm-1am Mon-Sat. **No credit cards**. English spoken. **Map D4**
Tiny Irish-run establishment that is the principal haunt of Budapest's artier and more academic Anglophone expats –

Every dog has his day at the incomparable **Wichmann**.

basically a sort of bohemian Beckett's. With a small bar in front and a few tables in the back – both rooms decorated with theatre posters – it can get uncomfortably crowded, especially at weekends. The insider atmosphere – everyone knows everyone else – may also prove off-putting. But the staff are sweethearts, a korsó of Kaiser is Ft180, and there's usually some decent vegetarian food for Ft300 a plateful of whatever they happen to have on that night. Music veers from the Pogues to Coltrane.

Wichmann

VII. Kazinczy utca 55 (342 6074). M1, M2, M3 Deák tér/tram 47, 49. **Open** 6pm-2am daily. **No credit cards.** Some English spoken. **Map D4**
Owned by former world champion canoeist Tamás Wichmann, this rough and smoky bar with no sign outside (it's just south of the corner with Király utca) seems largely un-touched by recent history. Wine is appallingly cheap, young customers cluster around big and sociable wooden tables, and the staff have a daft sense of humour. This is the place to toast Oscar Wilde with Transylvanian English Lit students, or hear the staff singing the Hungarian equivalent of rugby songs. A fine establishment.

Districts VIII & IX

Darshan

VIII. Krúdy Gyula utca 8 (266 7797). M3 Kálvin tér/tram 47, 49. **Open** 8pm-1am daily. **No credit cards.** Some English spoken. **Map D5**
Imaginatively designed bar with a laid-back feel and a reasonable taste in music – mainly ambient and acid jazz – the Darshan could do with a more varied selection of drinks – only one beer and a desultory selection of spirits. The grand and Gaudi-ish mosaic entrance and gallery space make it worth a visit all the same. Sluggish counter service only is another drawback. At press time they were planning to start opening for breakfast.

Paris, Texas

IX. Ráday utca 22 (218 0570). M3 Kálvin tér. **Open** 10am-3am Mon-Sat; 4pm-3am Sun. **No credit cards.** Some English spoken. **Map D5**
Pleasant bar on a lively street, decorated with dozens of peri-od portrait photos. The atmosphere is reminiscent of an Amsterdam 'brown café'. Upstairs is a relaxed bar area ideal for afternoon drinking and a roomy saloon in back to catch the evening overspill, downstairs there's a pool table and the occasional jazz or blues gig. Cheap beer on Sundays and Mondays; tables outside in summer. Pizza can be ordered from the restaurant next door.

District XIII

Akali Borozó

XIII. Szent István körút 2 (112 2861). Tram 2, 4, 6. **Open** 5.30am-11.30pm Mon-Fri; 8am-10.30pm Sat; 7am-9.30pm Sun. **No credit cards.** No English spoken. **Map C2**
Friendly borozó on the Pest side of Margaret Bridge. Wine tureens, bread and dripping, and a clientèle with faces like let-down balloons. Ground-level wine bar, so good for late-afternoon views of Nagykörút action from the doorway.

Zöldség-Gyümölcs De Luxe

XIII. Kresz Géza utca 17 (06 60 314 698). M3 Nyugati/tram 4, 6. **Open** noon-3am Mon-Thur; 5pm-5am Fri-Sun. **No credit cards.** Some English spoken. **Map C2**
This out-of-the-way establishment has an appealing warren of cellar spaces, assorted games machines, a small, sealed-off dancefloor (enter via the airlock contraption near the toi-lets) and seems to subsist mainly on a young, pre-Bahnhof crowd (*see chapter* **Nightlife**). Fine big bar for perching, cheap drinks, indomitable staff, an acceptable selection of snacks, well-meaning but inconsistent music and rarely a crowd big enough to do all this justice.

Shopping & Services

Choice is increasing and there are still great buys to be had, although standards of service can leave something to be desired.

Váci utca seen from Vörösmarty tér – Budapest's main shopping street.

To stroll down Váci utca or one of the other major shopping avenues in Budapest is to see a city trying very hard to be hip, trendy, and above all, 'Euro'. Sidewalk cafés and expensive boutiques are continually sprouting up, radiating out from the pedestrianised upmarket Váci utca. Long gone are the days when polyester reigned supreme and peanut butter and Marmite were worth their weight in gold as trade items between expats. The advent of shopping malls on Budapest's outskirts combined with an influx of brand-name shops in the centre has led to Europeanised standardisation of the clothing, appliances, services and food available and is gradually leading to a decline in the neighbourhood businesses and speciality shops that were the hallmark of Hungary's late Communist period.

The greater availability of goods hasn't fazed Hungarians who gleefully sally forth to stock up on bigger TVs and the latest bathroom fixtures, and the dedicated shopping visitor shouldn't be afraid to dive into the fray as there are still a lot of great buys in the city. The main shopping areas are in Pest with the pedestrian street Váci utca (both the north and the south sides) at its heart. Other major shopping streets are along the two ring roads and Rákóczi út. While most Socialist-era souvenirs have found their way into expensive shops, shopping in Budapest has its own unique rewards. Antiques and old books are interesting and decently priced, while handmade porcelain, folk art and Hungarian wines are unique and relatively cheap purchases. Hand-tailored clothing, handmade shoes and fashion by local designers are where the

inter CHANGE

Regional Agents of

WESTERN UNION | MONEY TRANSFER™

The fastest way to receive money worldwide. ™

Hungary – Czech Republic – United Kingdom – Italy – Netherlands

Hotline: (36 1) 266-4995

INTERNATIONAL BUREAU DE CHANGE FOREIGN EXCHANGE SPECIALISTS

To serve all your currency exchange needs.

Telephone (36 1) 266-6411

CITY CENTRE

- Budapest V, Váci utca 25.
- Budapest V, Váci utca 30.
- Budapest V, Deák F. u. 17.
- Budapest V, Kristóf tér 2.
  (Open 24 hours)
- Budapest V, Vörösmarty tér 1.

STATIONS

- Keleti (Eastern) Railway Station
  Budapest VII, Baross tér
  (Open 24 hours)
- Nyugati (Western) Railway Station
  Budapest VI, Teréz krt.
- International Bus Station
  Budapest V, Erzsébet tér

city's true bargains are to be found, and a trip to the market – for fresh produce, antiques or just junk – is a must on any itinerary. For children's clothing and toys *see chapter* **Children**.

Compared to western Europe, services in Budapest are relatively inexpensive and of surprisingly good quality. This is the place to treat yourself to little luxuries like a facial or a massage, have a suit made or get your watch repaired, all for a fraction of what it would cost back home. That said, actually being served can be a different matter. Once positioned behind a counter, Hungarians are notorious for being at best indifferent, and at worst downright rude. Patience, persistence and politeness pay off when you've spoiled someone's day by walking into their shop, but for every surly waitress there's also a charming old néni to send you off with a smile.

The PhoneBook, now in its fourth edition, is an invaluable aid to navigating the vagaries of the service sector. It can be purchased at most English-language bookshops, or pic ked up free from CoMo Media (V. Kossuth Lajos utca 17/266 4916/fax 117 9695/*comoc@ind.eunet.hu*/open 9am-5pm Mon-Fri).

Központi Antikvárium – *see page 163.*

Váci utca, and in the traditional antiques district around Falk Miksa utca. For bargains, spend a morning at **Ecseri** or the **Bolhapiac** for one-off treasures. *See below* **Markets**.

BÁV

V. Bécsi utca 1-3 (117 2548). M3 Ferenciek tere. **Open** 10am-6pm Mon-Fri; 10am-1pm Sat. **Credit** AmEx, MC, V. **Map C4**

A Venus de Milo sign hangs outside each of the many branches of BÁV – the state-owned chain of pawn shops. Each store has a different focus and the central warehouse has several auctions every year. While you're unlikely to find a genuine collector's item, prices here are generally lower than other antique shops. For information about auctions (*árverés*) contact Burján Imréné on 217 6072 extension 287 or go in person to the auction house at IX. Lónyay utca 30-32 (M3 Kálvin tér).

Branch: VI. Andrássy út 27 (342 5525).

Judaica Gallery

VII. Wesselényi utca 13 (267 8502). M2 Astoria/tram 47, 49. **Open** 10am-6pm Mon-Thur; 10am-2pm Fri. **Credit** AmEx, EC, M, V. English spoken. **Map D4**

A comprehensive selection of new and antique merchandise related to Hungarian Jewish culture. Expect frayed prayer books, Korond-style pottery with Hebrew sayings, paintings and drawings by local artists, embroidered Challah covers and a good selection of books in English on Jewish themes.

Moró Antik

V. Szent István körút 1 (312 7877). Tram 4, 6 Jászai Mari tér. **Open** 11am-6pm Mon-Fri. **No credit cards.** English spoken. **Map C2**

Ancient swords and guns and odd oriental curios line the walls, shelves and even ceiling of this tiny shop. Specialising in the weapons of the eighteenth century, for 25 years owner Lajos has collected interesting relics relating to the evolution of warfare. If you can actually catch him in the shop, the conversation alone is well worth the time.

Nagyházi Galéria

V. Balaton utca 8 (131 9908/312 5631/fax 131 7133). Tram 4, 6 Jászai Mari tér. **Open** 10am-6pm Mon-Fri; 10am-1pm Sat. **Credit** AmEx, DC, EC, JCB, MC, V. English spoken. **Map C2**

Budapest's largest antiques house. The shop is full of furniture, paintings, porcelain and jewellery among all kinds of odds and ends. Three catalogue auctions per year plus smaller auctions in the shop every month.

Standard opening hours are 10am-6pm Monday-Friday and 10am-1pm on Saturdays. Basic supplies – simple groceries, tobacco and booze – can be procured at an ABC or 'non-stop' at any hour and there's at least one in every neighbourhood (*see page 163* **Shop around the clock**). Late opening on Thursday evenings (until 7pm) is mostly confined to Váci utca. On Saturday afternoons and Sundays, head to the Castle District, Váci utca or one of the malls to shop; almost everything else will be closed.

The *rögtön jövök* (back in ten) sign you might find hanging on a locked door during business hours means 'I may be back at some distant and unspecified time in the future, if ever'. If no one shows up in a few minutes, try the next day (or the day after that). Similar signs appear in late July and August when many small shops close for summer vacations. The sign will usually indicate the date when they'll re-open. Almost everything is closed around major holidays, including 15 March, 20 August, and 23 October. Everything closes at Christmas – even non-stops – on 24-25 December.

The antiques market is dominated by eighteenth- and nineteenth-century, Habsburg-style furniture, with bits and pieces of Art Nouveau and Art Deco thrown in. While the wares are competitively priced compared to Vienna, dealers here generally know the value of their collections. Antiques shops are concentrated in the Castle District, on

Relikvia
*I. Fortuna utca 14 (175 6971/fax 156 9973). Várbusz from
M2 Moszkva tér/bus 16.* **Open** 10am-6pm. **Credit** AmEx,
DC, EC, JCB, MC, V. Some English spoken. **Map A3**
Three sister shops hold some of Budapest's finest furniture,
paintings, porcelain, lace and knick-knacks. Not a lot of bar-
gains to be found here in the prime tourist territory of the
Castle District, but a visit is sure to yield interesting finds.
The third shop is in the Hilton Hotel.
Branch I. Fortuna utca 21 (155 9973).

Auctions and Appraisals

See also **BAV** and **Nagyházi Galéria**.

Blitz Gallery
V. Falk Miksa utca 30 (332 0401). Tram 2, 4, 6. **Open**
10am-6pm Mon-Fri; 10am-1pm Sat. **No credit cards.**
Some English spoken. **Map C2**
Though smaller in size, Blitz has a larger turnover than
Nagyházi. Specialising in twentieth-century paintings and

A taste of communism

Despite the influx of capitalist goodies, the determined shopper can still find a taste of communism in Budapest. The big western sweet
manufacturers who gobbled up the old state
concerns quickly realised that there were many
consumers with strong loyalty to the brands of
the old regime. So chocolate bars such as
Kapuciner, Sport Szelet and Balaton survived.
The problem for most Hungarians is that multi-
nationals only wanted to keep the name for
brand recognition. That all-important taste has
been cynically adjusted to fit western notions of
how a chocolate bar should be.

The coffee-flavoured Kapuciner once had all
the subtlety of a cheap espresso from the local
bufé but is now a weak *café au lait*. Sport Szelet

Magyar munchies – still on the shelves.

used to contain some suspiciously strange
crunchy bits which have now disappeared along
with half the flavour. The wafer bar Balaton no
longer has the rough cooking chocolate coating
but comes in two versions Classic (dark) and
Milk . Even the Boci bars, given out by grandparents on Sunday afternoons, now come in
three versions with the old ladies complaining
that the 'original' is nothing of the sort.

But for Hungarians robbed of childhood tastes
there was worse to come. Scores of products simply disappeared as the market was flooded with
German chocolate and American cola. Never
again, they thought, would a picnic basket include
a bottle of Traubisoda (a fizzy grape drink) and a
packet of ZiZi (sweetened and coloured rice).

But if capitalism is capable of destroying
decades of tradition it also has the ability to
recreate them if there is a market. In recent years
small factories have begun re-producing some
of the old favourites. The most visible comeback
has been that of Traubisoda. The manufacturers have even made two versions – one in a giant
plastic two-litre bottle and one in the old green
bottle. Wherever it is found it is snaffled up.

Another fizzy drink, Marka, in its smaller 'three
swigs' bottle has also made a welcome return. The
older generation are now waiting for the reap-
pearance of Bambi, the disgustingly tart syrup-
based drink, and Limo – a packaged powder
which becomes a fizzy drink when water is added
(most kids never bothered, though; they just
dipped their fingers in and ate it like sherbert).

But you have to be a smoker to enjoy the most
obviously Communist product in the store.
Munkás (Worker) is a filterless blast from the
past. Clearly designed to reduce the numbers of
workers reaching pensionable age, the only western brand it comes anywhere near resembling is
Capstan Full Strength and probably only
Cabinet from the German Democratic Republic
has ever come close to it in the lung destruction
department. Kossuth is a slighter milder version.
Designed for intellectuals, it nevertheless does
an excellent job of browning the wallpaper.

sculpture, a single auction can see up to Ft30 million spent. Annual auctions are held in April and November in the Kempinski Hotel.

RFR Kft./Profila

VII. Szentkirályi utca 6 (267 2494/267 2495). M2 Blaha Lujza/tram 4, 6. **Open** 9am-5pm Mon-Fri. **Credit** AmEx, EC, MC, V. Some English spoken. **Map D4**
Stocks stamps, postcards, old phone cards, coins and other valuable paper things. The main office on Szentkirályi utca displays the valuables, but pick up catalogues for bi-annual auctions from Kazinczy utca.
Branch: VII. Kazinczy utca 3A (268 0198).

Art Supplies & Stationery

Ápisz

VI. Andrássy út 3 (122 6347/268 0534). M1 Bajcsy-Zsilinszky. **Open** 8am-8pm Mon-Fri; 9am-1pm Sat. **Credit** EC, M, V. No English spoken. **Map C3**
The main Hungarian chain of stationery stores. Stocks paper, pens, office supplies, string, tape, band-aids, aluminium cooking tins and floppy disks – almost all Hungarian-made and inexpensive.
Branch: VII. Rákóczi út 64 (342 1228).

Interieur Studio

V. Vitkovics Mihály utca 6 (137 7005). M2 Astoria/tram 47, 49/bus 7. **Open** 10am-6pm Mon-Fri; 10am-2pm Sat. **No credit cards**. Some English spoken. **Map C4**
Two little shops next to each other, Interieur supports local crafts-people making paper, boxes, and household knick-knacks. Also stocks stationery, dried flowers, essential oils and bath supplies, and offers a gift-wrapping service.

Leonart

VI. Bajcsy köz 3 (153 3750). M3 Arany János utca. **Open** 9am-5pm Mon-Fri. **No credit cards**. Some English spoken. **Map C3**

Pick up larger office supplies like Canson white boards and flip charts as well as international brand names for painting, graphic arts, silk screening, watercolour and drawing. Frames and mats also available.

Pirex

VI. Paulay Ede utca 17 (322 7067). M1 Opera. **Open** 8.30am-5pm Mon-Fri. **Credit** AmEx, EC, MC, V. Some English spoken. **Map D3**
Big and sophisticated selection of office stationery and supplies. Basic graphic art materials and computer stuff, too.

Books

See also **Judaica Gallery** under **Antiques**.

Bestsellers

V. Október 6 utca 11 (312 1295). M3 Arany János utca. **Open** 9am-6.30pm Mon-Fri; 10am-6pm Sat. **Credit** AmEx, DC, MC, V. English spoken. **Map C3**
The largest selection of contemporary literature and popular fiction in English in Budapest. Also newspapers and periodicals in English. Prices are steep. Efficient ordering service.

CEU Academic Bookshop

V. Nádor utca 9 (327 3096). M1, M2, M3 Deák tér. **Open** 9am-6pm Mon-Fri; 9am-6.30pm Wed; 10am-4pm Sat. *Summer* 10am-4pm Mon-Fri. **Credit** AmEx, DC, MC, V. English spoken. **Map C3**
Attached to the Central European University, stocking books with an academic focus. During 'happy hour' on Wed, 4.30pm-6.30pm, there's a ten per cent discount.

Helikon

VI. Bajcsy Zsilinszky út 37 (302 4406). M3 Arany János. **Open** 10am-7pm Mon-Fri; 10am-1pm Sat. **Credit** AmEx, EC, MC, V. English spoken. **Map C3**
Extensive collection of books in English including art/coffee table books, local history, guide books, general English lit-

Bestsellers – *browsing through Budapest's biggest selection of English-language books.*

American Express
is your answer to
efficient and high
quality travel services

• Airline Tickets • Cardmember Services •
• Travelers Cheques • Foreign Exchange •
• Sightseeing Tours • Clients' Mail •
• Hotel Reservations • MoneyGram • Money Order •
• Worldwide Customer Care •
• Meetings • Special Group Arrangements •
• Conferences • Incentives •
• Business Travel Service •

TRAVEL
RELATED
SERVICES
An American Express company

AMERICAN EXPRESS
1052 Budapest, Deák Ferenc utca 10.
Telephone: Travel Service (36-1) 266-8680, Card Service (36-1) 267-2024
Opening hours: October - May: Monday-Friday 9.00 a.m.-5.30 p.m.,
Saturday 9.00 a.m.-2.00 p.m. Travel and Foreign Exchange Services
2.00 a.m.-5.30 p.m. Foreign Exchange Services
Sunday: 9.00 a.m.-5.30 p.m. Foreign Exchange Services

Opening hours: June-September: Monday-Friday 9.00 a.m.-6.30 p.m.
Saturday 9.00 a.m.-2.00 p.m. Travel and Foreign Exchange Services
2.00 a.m.-6.30 p.m. Foreign Exchange Services
Sunday: 9.00 a.m.-6.30 p.m. foreign Exchange Services

American Express Office
H-1014 Budapest, Hess András tér 1-3.
Telephone: 214-6446 Foreign Exchange Services
Opening Hours: Monday-Sunday 9.00 a.m.-8 p.m.
Our Card is welcomed in Hungary by 3000 establishments.

*Who dares wins – one of Ágnes Német's outrageous creations at **Manier**. See page 166.*

erature (interesting choices too) and Penguin classics. Very reasonable prices.

Írók Boltja
VI. Andrássy út 45 (322 1645). M1 Oktogon/tram 4, 6.
Open 10am-6pm Mon-Fri. *May-Sept* 10am-1pm Sat.
Credit AmEx, DC, EC, JCB, MC, V. English spoken.
Map D3
The so-called Writers' Bookshop doesn't have a huge selection of English-language books, but fosters a pleasant atmosphere with lots of art books and interesting calendars. There's also a coffee corner.

Litea Bookstore and Cafe
I. Hess András tér 4 (Fortuna Passage) (175 6987).
Várbusz from M2 Moszkva ter/bus 16. **Open** 10am-6pm daily. **Credit** AmEx, EC, MC, V. English spoken. **Map A3**
Doubles as a perfect place for a coffee break while in the Castle District, and offers a multilingual collection of guidebooks, books on art and architecture, prints and a large selection of postcards. Local newspapers and journals in English also available. *See also chapter* **Cafés & Coffeehouses**.

Rhythm 'N' Books
V. Szerb utca 21-23 (266 9833 extension 2226). M3 Kálvin tér/tram 47, 49. **Open** noon-7pm Mon-Fri; 9am-2pm Sat. **No credit cards.** English spoken. **Map D5**
In the same courtyard as the University Theatre, peruse a range of new and secondhand travel books and contemporary literature. Collection of world music on CD and cassettes. Buys and exchanges books and CDs.

Térképkirály
V. Sas utca 1 (117 3130/fax 117 2161). M1, M2, M3 Deák tér. **Open** 9.30am-5.30pm Mon-Fri. **Credit** AmEx, DC, EC, JCB, MC, V. English spoken. **Map C3**
Maps of Budapest and Hungary plus a comprehensive selection of maps from all over the world.

Antiquarian Bookshops

Budapest boasts over 40 antique and used bookshops. A trek starting at Jászai Mari tér (the Pest side of the Margit Bridge), cutting in to Stollár Béla utca, returning to Bajcsy-Zsilinszky út, and then following Károly and Múzeum körút to Kálvin tér, will lead past all the major attractions. The free leaflet *Second-Hand Bookshops in Budapest,* available from many of the shops, includes a map and listings for 25 antiquarian shops.

Font Antikvárium
VI. Andrássy út 56 (332 1646). M1 Oktogon/tram 4, 6.
Open 10am-6pm Mon-Fri; 10am-1pm Sat. **Credit** AmEx.
Some English spoken. **Map D3**
Not much English stuff, but an engaging selection of communist-era books and posters as well as art, architecture, and graphic art books aplenty. Old travel books and maps a plus.

Forgács
V. Stollár Béla utca 12C (111 6874). M3 Nyugati/tram 4, 6. **Open** 10am-noon, 3pm-7pm Mon-Fri; noon-4pm Sat. **Credit** AmEx, DC, EC, JCB, MC, V. English spoken. **Map C2**
Cosy cellar shop crammed with old books. Look out for art and graphics books in an assortment of languages as well as interesting prints and a small collection of books in English. A second location in the Kempinski Hotel has more foreign-language books and rare editions.

Kollin Antikvárium
VI. Bajcsy Zsilinszky út 34 (111 9023). M3 Arány János utca. **Open** 9.30am-5.30pm Mon-Fri. **Credit** AmEx, EC, JCB, MC, V. English spoken. **Map C3**
Skip the shelves full of Hungarian books downstairs and head straight for the second level. First editions in German,

Look for **THE KODAK EXPRESS**
logo wherever **YOU** are,

you WILL *find* TOP **Kodak Quality.**
"1 hour photo development service"

Foto Bázis, 1039 Rákóczi u. 36. • MTI Foto, Krisztina krt. 24. • Kovács Foto, 1026 Szilágyi E. fasor, Budagyöngye • Promt Foto, 1052 Arany J. u.-i Metro • Color Foto Professional, 1065 Nagymező u. 37-39. • Multi Foto, 1182 Üllői u. 201. Europark • Foto Fix, 1123 Alkotás u. 11. • 9 és fél m², 1056 Irányi u. 10. • Rapid Foto, 1031 Római Római tér 2. • Foto Keleti, 1077 Baross téri aluljáró • Gold Foto, 1064 Izabella u. 65. • Pálvölgyi Foto, 1155 Szentmihályi u. 31. • etc.

A Kodak és a Kodak Express védett márkajegyek

English, Hungarian and other European languages, old Baedeckers, tins, toys and other irresistible odds and ends.

Központi Antikvárium

V. Múzeum körút 15 (117 3514/fax 117 3514). M2 Astoria/tram 47, 49. **Open** 10am-6pm Mon-Fri; 10am-2pm Sat. **Credit** AmEx, EC, MC, V. English spoken. **Map D4**
Peruse one of the largest and best selections of secondhand English-language books in the city. Lots of postcards, old posters and prints, along with rare Hungarian books and solid German and Russian sections.

Bibliotéka Antikvárium

VI. Andrássy út 2 (131 5132/331 5132). M1 Bajcsy-Zsilinszky. **Open** 9am-6pm Mon-Fri; 10am-1pm Sat. **Credit** AmEx, DC, EC, JCB, MC, V. Some English spoken. **Map C3**
The corner entrance is for trading and appraising books, walk a few steps up Andrássy út for the main entrance. A large shop, with a huge turnover – people selling books sometimes queue right out the door.

Márffy és Társa Antikvárium és Aukciósház

V. Ferenczy István utca 28 (118 1007/fax 118 1000). M2 Astoria/tram 47, 49. **Open** 10am-12.30pm, 2pm-6pm Mon-Fri; 10am-2pm Sat. **Credit** AmEx, DC, EC, JCB, MC, V. English spoken. **Map D4**
Small, but a treasure trove not only for books, but also for maps, prints, old photo albums and other goodies shelved under the main counter and in racks by the window. Look out for communist-era adverts, postcards, some posters and paintings, stuff in Greek and Latin, and interesting art and graphics books.

Stúdió Antikvárium

VI. Jókai tér 7 (312 6294). M1 Oktogon/tram 4, 6. **Open** 9am-7pm Mon-Fri; 9am-2pm Sat. **No credit cards.** Some English spoken. **Map D3**
Most of the literature is in Hungarian, German and Russian, but there is enough in English to make it worth the trip. Has a small, but rare, Judaica section. Will hold your finds for a week before you part with your forints.

Shop around the clock

With a 24-hour store ten minutes' walk from any point in town except the leafy regions of deepest Buda, Budapest is better equipped than most European cities when it comes to urgent late-night supplies of the three staffs of life: condoms, chocolate and beer.

Non-stop shopping began under communism. Örök Mécses – The Eternal Flame – was the first 24-hour store, so popular that locals still use the name for the faceless Julius Meinl supermarket which currently occupies the Blaha Lujza tér site. The cowboy capitalist early 1990s were the heyday of the non-stops. Clusters of them sprang up around main sites like Nyugati Station, Moszkva tér and the körút, owned by a small, suspicious clique after a fast buck. Many of these remain to this day, much as in 1991, except for a doubling of the prices.

In the next couple of years non-stops were sprouting all over downtown. Customers were pleased not only with the late-night convenience, but also by the range of foreign condoms, beers and chocolate on offer. The shop fronts slowly became embellished by a crowd of local drunks. They'd use the place much like a corner bar – sitting on the doorstep cheerily swigging from bottles and moaning about today's prices. Non-stops began to acquire lives of their own – chubby whores stumbling in for cigarettes, booze hounds in search of the cheapest over-the-counter form of pálinka, and the world and his battered wife stocking up on beer.

Many of the smaller, local non-stops have since closed, or confined their trade to normal business hours. Entrepreneurial dreams foundered on the free-market reality that there simply weren't enough late-night shoppers to support three businesses per street. Meanwhile, in those that remain, the price squeeze has made whores leaner, drunks meaner and in-store security tighter. Theft caused a lot of places to install a small, barred window in the door. Customers must bark their orders through the grate and hope for the best. The standard reply is 'Sajnos nincs', 'Sorry, we're right out'.

In those where you can walk in, expect a low-tech, soft-sell display of basic groceries, alcohol, tobacco and fruit and veg. On particularly humid nights the margarine will be kept nicely chilled in the fridge while stacks of beer bottles boil in the heat. The person responsible for this outrage will be a spotty kid too nervous to start shaving, but stupid enough to hold down his 12-hour-a-night work for a Dickensian pittance. Dozing nearby will be a myopic Alsatian with lice. On the counter will be chocolate, chewing gum and condoms – those Romanian ones that explode on impact and keep tension mounting all month. Behind the counter are spirits and cigarettes.

Certain non-stops stand out. The **Görög Csemege** on József körút offers Mediterranean treats; the **Zöldség-Gyümölcs** stall on Oktogon is packed with pomegranates, pickles and passion fruit; the flower shop on the Pest side of Margaret Bridge is the ideal solution for that late night argument (*see chapter* **Nightlife**).

Scores of stores were killed off by the fierce competition and the fact that MOL, the national oil company, peppered Budapest with nearly as many petrol stations as cars to use them. As Hungarian garages sensibly stock alcohol, the only problem there is being blinded by the strip lighting.

Department Stores

Centrum Áruház Corvin
VIII. Blaha Lujza tér 1-2 (138 4160/138 4330). M2 Blaha Lujza/tram 4, 6. **Open** 10am-6pm Mon-Fri; 10am-1pm Sat. **Credit** AmEx, DC, EC, JCB, MC, V. Some English spoken. **Map E4**
In the process of upgrading from communist-era style, Corvin has reached K-Mart level. Appliances are mostly western, clothes and shoes Hungarian (and priced appropriately). Archaic payment system: take a receipt, go to the *pénztár*, pay, then return to pick up your treasure.

Flavius Center
VII. Rákóczi út 36 (322 1047). M2 Blaha Lujza/tram 4, 6. **Open** 10am-6pm Mon-Thur; 10am-7pm Fri; 10am-2pm Sat. Some English spoken. **Map E4**
With over 40 little shops, this one of the best of the many clothing arcades along Rákóczi út. Full of young Hungarians hunting out the latest look at discount prices.

Fontana Department Store
V. Váci utca 16 (138 2004). M1 Vörösmarty tér. **Open** 10am-6pm Mon-Fri; 10am-1pm Sat. **Credit** AmEx, DC, EC, JCB, MC, V. Some English spoken. **Map C4**
A bit less posh than Luxus, Fontana has clothing, cosmetics, kiddie things, luggage and a nifty rooftop café.

Design & Household Goods

Hephaistos Háza
VI. Zichy Jenő utca 20 (332 6329). M1 Oktogon/tram 4, 6. **Open** 11am-6pm Mon-Fri; 10am-2pm Sat. **Credit** EC, JCB, MC, V. Some English spoken. **Map D3**
Eccentric wrought-iron furniture, fittings and accessories created by owner Eszter Gaál. Own designs can be ordered.

Holló Folkart Gallery
V. Vitkovics Mihály utca 12 (117 8103). M2 Astoria/tram 47, 49. **Open** 10am-6pm Mon-Fri; 10am-1pm Sat. **Credit** AmEx, MC, V. Some English spoken. **Map C4**
László Holló uses traditional Hungarian woodworking techniques and decoration motifs to create furniture in hard woods with soft-coloured, decorative painting.

Opal Art
I. Hess András tér 4 (Fortuna passage) (214 0209) Várbusz from M2 Moszkva tér/bus 16. **Open** 10am-5pm daily. **Credit** AmEx, DC, EC, JCB, MC, V. English spoken. **Map A3**
Zoltán Ács uses the craft of layered glass sculpture, pioneered by Gallé of France, to create beautiful and intricate flowered lamps and delicately landscaped vases.

Household Goods

If you're coming from North America and packing for a longer stay, don't forget that Europe runs on 220v. Include transformers for any appliances or electronics you might bring – they're hard to find in Budapest.

When setting up house, the bits and pieces you might need are found in three types of shops: a *Barkács* for wood and brass fittings, a *Vasedény* for metal things, and a *Műanyag* for plastics.

Bigrav
V. Váci utca 75 (no phone). Tram 47, 49 Fővám tér. **Open** 10am-6pm Mon-Fri; 10am-1pm Sat. **No credit cards.** Some English spoken. **Map C5**

Gadgets galore at **1,000 Apricókk.**

One of the very few places to stock a transformer to convert appliances to European 220 voltage. They'll fill custom orders for larger appliances and computers.

Boszorkánykonyha
V. Petőfi Sándor utca 16 (118 3223). M1, M2, M3 Deák tér/tram 47, 49. **Open** 10am-6pm Mon-Fri; 10am-1pm Sat. Some English spoken. **Map C4**
Country-style housewares – crockery in bold basic colours, green glass vases, and flowery accents. Much of it's too cute and charming, but certainly preferable to the mismatched 'china' likely to be found in a rented Budapest apartment. **Branches:**VI. Teréz körút 58 (312 3089); XV. Pólus Center (419 4096); V. Régiposta utca 13 (266 1331).

Kátay
VI. Teréz körút 28 (111 0116). M1 Oktogon/tram 4, 6. **Open** 9am-6pm Mon-Fri; 9am-7pm Thur; 9am-2pm Sat. **Credit** AmEx, DC, EC, MC, V. Some English spoken. **Map D3**
A centrally located stop for appliances, kitchen utensils, garden tools and miscellaneous DIY supplies.

1,000 Aprócikk
V. Bajcsy-Zsilinszky út 3 (269 6620/322 6420). M1, M2, M3 Deák utca/tram 47, 49. **Open** 9am-6pm Mon-Fri; 10am-1pm Sat. **No credit cards.** No English spoken. **Map C4**
If you melt the rubber gasket in your stovetop espresso maker, this is where to find a replacement, along with 999 other small but useful gadgets.

IKEA Home Furnishing
XIV. Örs vezér tér (252 7675/221 9444/fax 251 9154). M2 Örs vezér tér. **Open** 10am-8pm Mon-Fri; 10am-5pm Sat; 10am-3pm Sun. **No credit cards.** Some English spoken.
No surprises from the Scandinavian chain. Most things are moderately priced (if moderately tasteful) and bigger items can be delivered. The huge out-of-town store has underground parking, cafés, and a supervised playroom for kids.

Keravill

V. Kossuth Lajos utca 2B (118 5008/117 6422).
M3 Ferenciek tere. **Open** 10am-7pm Mon-Fri; 9am-2pm
Sat. **Credit** EC, JCB, MC, V. Some English spoken.
Map C4
Appliances and electronics are generally less expensive in
Budapest than in other major European cities. Keravill has
several outlets in the city, each with its own mix of items.
Branches: VI. Teréz körút 45 (312 2853); VII. Rákóczi út 30
(342 0100); V. Múzeum körút 11 (117 3265).

Fashion

An afternoon of walking around and looking at
what the locals are wearing will give an accurate
impression of what Budapest has to offer. Young
Hungarian women seem to go for the tallest possible platforms with the shortest possible skirts –
even in winter. And that's mostly what you'll find
in shops along the major boulevards. They all
seem to stock the same things – imitations of whatever is coming out of Milan that season. On the
bright side, there are bargains to be had if you
don't mind poking around the sales racks and settling for something that may only last the season.

A more promising trend is the emergence of various young designers. Their experimentation with
fabrics and cuts can produce some brilliant pieces,
though there's often a lack of refinement or a lurking feeling that something's just not right with
many of the garments. The solution is to take matters into your own hands – and this is where the
real fun begins. Most local designers are happy to
modify existing pieces, or incorporate your ideas
to create something new. You'll find that a new
dress or tailored suit made up may cost less than
something off the rack at home.

Accessories & Jewellery

Bijoux

V. Károly körút 3 (117 6450). M2 Astoria/tram 47, 49.
Open 10am-6pm Mon-Wed, Fri; 10am-7pm Thur; 10am-
2pm Sat. **No credit cards.** Some English spoken. **Map D4**
Outrageous and outrageously cheap selection of all that is
fake, fluorescent, flamboyant, fluffy and fun.

Craft Design

VI. Klauzál tér 1 (322 4006/322 7480). M2 Blaha
Lujza/tram 4, 6. **Open** 10am-5pm Mon-Fri. **Credit** JCB,
MC, V. Some English spoken. **Map D4**
Local tanners display their own designs for wallets, hand-
bags, diaries and key-rings. Silk scarves, ceramics, and
accessories are also available.
Branch: Szentendre, Alkotmány út 3 (06 26 313603).

Marácz Kalap

VII. Wesselényi utca 41 (no phone). Tram 4, 6. **Open**
10am-6pm Mon-Fri. **No credit cards.** No English
spoken. **Map D3**
An old fashioned milliner with classic Hungarian fedoras
and women's hats for all occasions.

Ómama Bizsuja

V. Szent István körút 1 (312 6812). Tram 4, 6 Jászai
Mari tér. **Open** 10am-6pm Mon-Fri; 10am-1pm Sat. **No**
credit cards. Some English spoken. **Map C2**

This tiny shop contains a huge collection of antique
Hungarian bijoux (rhinestones, semiprecious costume pieces,
and beads), plus a small selection of women's clothing.

ProMix Manager Shop

V. Szent István tér 3 (117 3569). M3 Arany János utca.
Open 10am-6pm Mon-Fri. **Credit** AmEx, MC, V. Some
English spoken. **Map C3**
A Magyar *menedzer* apparently needs a Parker pen, a digi-
tal travel clock, Samsonite luggage, a classy umbrella, a
leather belt, a silk tie and a selection of imported whiskies.

Sajátos Tárgyak Boltja

VI. Hajós utca 7 (312 0343). M1 Opera. **Open** 10am-
6pm Mon-Fri; 10am-1pm Sat. **No credit cards.** Some
English spoken. **Map D3**
All sorts of accessories, often with an Indian flavour. Picture-
frames, wind-chimes, jewellery, leather bags and incense on
the first floor. Upstairs, a selection of batique and tapestries.

Clothing

Artista

VI. Jókai tér 8 (302 6818). M1 Oktogon. **Open** 11am-
7pm Mon-Fri; 11am-2pm Sat. Closed in summer. **Credit**
AmEx, DC, EC, MC, V. English spoken. **Map D3**
The six designers who make up the Artista collective produce a mixed bag of daring togs. Their prize-winning threads
have starred at shows locally and abroad. Dip into the sales
basket, where some items cost as little as Ft500.

Bon Bon

IX. Baross utca 4 (no phone). M3 Kálvin tér/tram 47, 49.
Open 10am-6pm Mon-Fri; 10am-4pm Thur; 10am-1pm
Sat. **No credit cards.** Some English spoken. **Map D5**
Linen, cotton and woollens made up into sharp but comfy
women's wear. Hats at great prices, along with lots of
Hungarian folk crafts – traditional leather belt bags, candles,
ceramics, wooden jewellery and scarves.

Cox & Hyper

V. Kossuth Lajos utca 20 (267 4511 extension 205). M2
Astoria/tram 47, 49. **Open** 10am-7pm Mon-Fri; 10am-2pm
Sat. **Credit** AmEx, MC, V. English spoken. **Map D4**
Hyper is for girls and Cox, well, you guessed it. Collection of
suits, jackets, shoes and various knick-knacks available for
the males. For women it's disappointing: a Kookai collection,
and more overpriced skimpy garments.

Greti

V. Bárczy István utca 3 (117 8500). M1, M2, M3 Deák
tér/tram 47, 49. **Open** 10am-6pm Mon-Fri; 10am-1pm
Sat. **No credit cards.** English spoken. **Map C4**
The oldest and most respected of Budapest's design houses
creates elegant, conservative looks for women. Work with
Greti herself to make something special, or choose from the
selection of dresses, suits, Italian shoes or sexy under-things.

Rakpart Divattervező Műterem

Bem rakpart 38-39, first floor (214 0940). M2 Batthány
tér/tram 19. **Open** 8am-1.30pm Tue, Thur. **No credit**
cards. Some English spoken. **Map B3**
Six young designers – a leather worker, a weaver, three
seamstresses and a knitter – produce simple frocks, tops and
jackets with a young, but not outrageous feel. Cheap prices.

Home Boy

V. Irányi utca 5 (137 1192/06 30 423 839). M3
Ferenciek tere/bus 7. **Open** 10am-6pm Mon-Fri; 10am-
1pm Sat. **Credit** EC, MC, V. Some English spoken.
Map C5
Baggies for boys with club/skate gear from Stüssy, Fresh
Jive, Dready, Billabong and Adidas, plus a tattoo and pierc-
ing studio in the basement.

V-50 Design – *nifty if impractical headgear.*

Manier

V. Váci utca 48 (118 1812). M3 Ferenciek tere/bus 7.
Open 10am-6pm Mon-Fri; 10am-2pm Sat. **Credit** V.
Some English spoken. **Map C5**
Daring fashion by Ágnes Német. Soft chiffons to knitted
wools, all pieces available to size with alterations. Her stu-
dio across the way has her latest, most outrageous creations.

Orlando

*V. Károly körút 10 (06 30 342 060). M2 Astoria/tram
47, 49.* **Open** 10am-6pm Mon-Fri; 10am-1.30pm Sat.
Credit AmEx, DC, MC, V. Some English spoken.
Map D4
Six designers display their creations in this tiny boutique
filled with almost-sensible suits, dresses and matching hand-
bags. Venture upstairs for gowns, remainders and sale items.
Art'z Modell at the same address is also worth a look.

V-50 Design Art Studio

*V. Váci utca 50 (entrance on Nyáryi Pál utca) (137 5320)
M3 Ferenciek tere/bus 7.* **Open** 1pm-6pm Mon-Fri. **No
credit cards.** Some English spoken. **Map C5**
Valéria Fazekas's big glass case is full of nifty, if sometimes
impractical, headgear. She also procures interesting fabrics
to create subtle dresses and jackets. The Belgrád rakpart
branch features a larger collection.
Branch: V. Belgrád rakpart 16 (137 0327).

Monarchia

V. Szabadsajtó út 6 (118 3146). M3 Ferenciek tere/bus 7.
Open 10am-6.30pm Mon-Wed, Fri; 10am-7pm Thur;
10am-1.30pm Sat. **Credit** AmEx, DC, EC, MC, V. English
spoken. **Map C4**
Five local designers devoted to chic, classically tailored
women's suits and daring evening wear. Awkwardly located on the approach to Erzsébet bridge, but worth a peek at
the window displays which are changed daily.

Persona

*V. Fehérhajó utca 5 (137 9428). M1, M2, M3 Deák
tér/tram 47, 49.* **Open** 10am-7pm Mon-Fri; 10am-2pm
Sat. **Credit** AmEx, DC, EC, JCB, MC, V. English spoken.
Map C4
Similar to Gap, this spacious boutique offers a colour-coor-
dinated range of simple threads and smart accessories. The
shoe collection is worth a peek.

Sixvil Szalon

*V. Kecskeméti utca 8 (117 4834/06 30 422 098). M3
Kálvin tér/tram 47, 49.* **Open** 10am-7pm Mon-Fri; 11am-
4pm Sat. **Credit** AmEx, DC, EC, JCB, MC, V. Some
English spoken. **Map D5**
A new salon for men and women featuring the work of
Vilmos Lostis. Italian fabrics lend a luxurious feel to classi-
cally-cut suits and dresses. Also find a small collection of
Italian shoes plus funky lamps, candleholders, and glass by
another local designer. Stop by in the late afternoon or on a
Saturday to discuss your own creation.

Shoes and Leather Goods

While there's a shoe shop in every courtyard, quantity doesn't always mean quality. Note that your
patent plastic fancies or glam-rock footwear may
only last till the next shoe sensation comes along.

Rácz Mária, Szűcsmester

*V. Bárczi István utca 3 (137 7139/home 185 5985). M1,
M2, M3 Deák tér/tram 47, 49.* **Open** 10am-6pm Mon-Fri;
10am-1pm Sat. **Credit** AmEx, DC, EC, JCB, MC, V. Some
English spoken. **Map C4**
The perfect gift for the politically incorrect is a classic central European fur hat. Mrs Rácz took over her uncle's business, opened in 1946, and still produces classically designed,
and individually tailored stoles, hats and coats. Prices are
reasonable – a ladies hat runs from Ft7,500-Ft15,000.

Kaláka Stúdió

V. Haris köz 2 (118 3313). M3 Ferenciek tere/bus 7.
Open *Oct-Apr* 10am-6pm Mon-Wed, Fri; 10am-7pm
Thur; 10am-2pm Sat; *May-Sept* 10am-7pm Mon-Sat. **No
credit cards.** Some English spoken. **Map C4**
Ágnes Bodor creates affordable and interesting shoes in soft
suedes. Pick a pair to go with something from their small
selection of women's clothing (also by local designers) on the
other side of the shop.

La Boutique

VI. Andrássy út 16 (302 5646). M1 Opera. **Open** 10am-
8pm Mon-Fri; 10am-4pm Sat. **Credit** AmEx, DC, EC, MC,
V. Some English spoken. **Map D3**
Perhaps the largest collection of fine shoes in the city with
prices to match. Owner Irena Dragolevic has a fine eye for
current trends, stocking the best of Italian designers such as
Bruno Magli, Baldan, Genny, Celin, Neri and Fausto Santini.

V.I.P.

V. Károly körút 10 (no phone). M2 Astoria/tram 47, 49.
Open 10am-6pm Mon-Fri; 10am-1pm Sat. **No credit
cards.** No English spoken. **Map D4**
Italian leather boutique with a fine selection of women's
handbags, belts, gloves and wallets. The prices for Versace,
Tacchini and Valentino are a relief after ruinous Váci utca.
No English spoken, but if what you're looking for isn't on
display, they probably don't have it.

Krokodil

*V. Kossuth Lajos utca 15 (137 2619). M3 Ferenciek
tere/bus 7.* **Open** 10am-6pm Mon-Wed, Fri; 10am-7pm
Thur; 9.30am-1.30pm Sat. **No credit cards.** Some
English spoken. **Map C4**

A step up from stodgier competitors Humanic and Salamander, with fashionable shoes at sensible prices. **Branches**: VII. Rákóczi út 38 (342 0954). V. Váci utca 12 (117 6319).

Simetric

V. Múzeum körút 16 (117 5119). M2 Astoria/tram 47, 49. **Open** 10am-7pm Mon-Fri; 9am-1pm Sat. **Credit** AmEx, EC, JCB, MC, V. Some English spoken. **Map D4**
Casual, Italian-made men's shoes and sandals at reasonable prices complement a fine selection of women's footgear. For men, comfortable yet stylish walking shoes, dockers and sandals, with a line of dress shoes that don't necessarily imply a stiff upper lip. Women's shoes walk the edge of fashion without being over the top. Look for bargains in the sale rack.

Shoemakers

The two shops listed make fine quality men's dress shoes. A pair will cost Ft40,000-Ft50,000.

Vass

V. Haris köz 2 (118 2375). M1, M2, M3 Deák tér/tram 47, 49. **Open** 10am-6pm Mon-Fri; 10am-2pm Sat. **Credit** AmEx, DC, EC, JCB, MC, V. Some English spoken. **Map C4**
Men's shoes made to order in about a month, starting from Ft45,000. Discounts are negotiable if you pay cash.
Branch: V. Váci utca 41A (118 0321).

Zabrak Shoes

Kempinski Hotel, V. Erzsébet tér 7-8 (266 8175). M1, M2, M3 Deák tér/tram 47, 49. **Open** 9am-6pm Mon-Fri; 9am-2pm Sat. **Credit** AmEx, DC, EC, JCB, MC, V. English spoken. **Map C4**
Off-the-rack men's shoes reasonably priced. Made-to-order shoes are an extra Ft20,000 and take up to a month.

Tailors

Merino

V. Petőfi Sándor utca 18 (118 7332). M1, M2, M3 Deák tér/tram 47, 49. **Open** 10am-6pm Mon-Fri; 9.30am-1pm Sat. **Credit** AmEx, EC, JCB, MC, V. Some English spoken. **Map C4**
Opened in the 1880s, this is the place to pick out something to be made up by a local designer – or have a suit made by the in-house tailor. Whether looking to buy or not, stop to peek at old wood panelling and shelves piled high with the finest velvets, lace, brocade, silks and woollens. Expert staff are ready to help, but also willing to just let you browse.

Taylor & Scheider Kft.

VI. Nagymező utca 31 (312 0842/06 20 419 721). M1 Opera. **Open** 7am-5pm Mon-Thur; 7am-4pm Fri. **No credit cards.** No English spoken. **Map D3**
Pick from an array of sober fabrics, or bring your own to be made into a suit. Pay Ft35,000-Ft40,000 if you use their fabrics, Ft20,000-Ft30,000 if you bring your own. English or American, single- or double-breasted, they make to order and will even make up something you choose from their current collection of Italian fashion mags (or a picture you bring in) – bring a Hungarian friend for translation, though.

Vintage & Secondhand Clothes

For truly antique clothing (that is to say, anything from before the 1950s), head out to **Ecseri Piac** (*see* **Markets**). For more modern secondhand stuff, *kilós ruha* stores all over the city sell imported secondhand clothing for around Ft1,000 per kilo.

Egyedi Ruha Galéria

IX. Baross utca 4 (118 2056). M3 Kálvin tér/tram 47, 49. **Open** 10am-6pm Mon-Fri. **No credit cards.** Some English spoken. **Map D5**
Unfortunately, the best pieces are kept in the window and not for sale. But there are some treasures to be found on racks stuffed with imported used clothing from western Europe – at prices slightly above *kilós ruha* rates. If you're looking for a Bavarian Dirndl, this is where to find one cheap.

Tweed

VI. Dalszínház utca 10 (332 9294). M1 Opera. **Open** 10am-7pm Mon-Fri; 10am-1pm Sat. **No credit cards.** Some English spoken. **Map D3**
Knitted stripey tops, loud polyester, 1970s vintage platforms and floral dresses.

KaliBoat

I. Batthyány tér (no telephone). M2 Batthyány tér/tram 19. **Open** 10am-7pm Mon-Fri; 10am-3pm Sat. **No credit cards.** Some English spoken. **Map B3**
The most stunning location of any shop in town, the Kali Boat is moored opposite Parliament and filled with a great collection of used clothing. Less refined than Tweed, Kali makes up for it with quantity and the sheer audacity of its location – plus the absurdity of having the thing shift to starboard just as you're trying to slip into a pair of bell bottoms. Cruise the top deck and try on one of a huge collection of leather jackets.

Costume Rental

MAFILM Jelmez és Mértékutáni Ruhaszalon

XIV. Róna utca 174 (251 9778). Bus 7. **Open** 8am-4pm Mon-Thur; 8am-1pm Fri. **No credit cards.** Some English spoken.
Rent out costumes from the MAFILM studio collection for between Ft2,500-Ft5,000. Have your own polar bear outfit specially tailored or get fitted for a sixteenth-century suit and doublet.

flowers
Flowers

If you've forgotten the bouquet on the way to a late-night date, the flower stand on the Pest side of Margit bridge is open 24-hours daily.

Euro Flower Kft.

V. Nádor utca 19 (111 2442/302 5114). M2 Kossuth tér/tram 2. **Open** 10am-6pm Mon-Fri; 10am-1pm Sat. **No credit cards.** Some English spoken. **Map C3**
Lots of house plants, exotic flowers, bouquets made to order and free home delivery for larger items.

Yucca

V. Váci utca 54 (137 3307). M3 Ferenciek tere/bus 7. **Open** 9am-6pm Mon-Fri; 9am-2pm Sat. **No credit cards.** Some English spoken. **Map C4**
The smell of orchids is the first thing you encounter as you walk into this shop filled with unusual fresh and dried flowers available by the stem or gathered into creative custom bouquets.

Flower Delivery

Sasad Virág

V. Haris köz 3 (118 4415). M3 Ferenciek tere. **Open** 9am-6pm Mon-Fri; 9am-2pm Sat. **Credit** AmEx, V. Some English spoken. **Map C4**
Wire flowers through Interflora from this small, central shop.

Folklore

For authentic folk costumes and linens, head to the stalls on the second floor of the Nagy Vásárcsarnok (**Central Market Hall**) on Fővám tér – prices are half what you'd pay on Váci utca. *See also chapter* **Folklore**.

Folkart Centrum

V. Váci utca 14 (118 5840). M1 Vörösmarty tér. **Open** 9.30am-9pm daily. **Credit** AmEx, DC, EC, JCB, MC, V. Some English spoken. **Map C4**
Buzzing with tourists looking for kitsch to take home, the former state-owned folklore shop employs hundreds of craftspeople throughout Hungary to produce machine-tooled woodwork and embroidered linens. The pottery section in the basement has pretty, folksy Korond and dramatic black-on-black pieces from Hódmezővásárhely.

Vali Folklore Souvenir

V. Váci utca 23 (118 6495/137 6301). M3 Ferenciek tere/tram 47, 49. **Open** 10am-7pm Mon-Sat; 10am-1pm Sun. **Credit** AmEx, EC, DC, MC, V. English spoken. **Map C4**
The place to find genuine Hungarian and Transylvanian folk costumes. Beaded and embroidered skirts, blouses and leather vests, pottery and hand-carved wooden things.

Ceramics and Pottery

Haas & Czjek

VI. Bajcsy-Zsilinszky út 23 (111 4094). M3 Arany János utca. **Open** 10am-6pm Mon-Fri; 9am-1pm Sat. **Credit** AmEx, DC, EC, JCB, MC, V. Some English spoken. **Map C3**
Fine selection of Hungarian porcelain and Czech crystal. Rather weak in Herend, look instead to Hollóháza, Alföldi and Zsolnay for reasonably-priced dinner sets and figurines.

Herend Porcelain

V. József Nádor tér 11 (117 2622). M1 Vörösmarty tér. **Open** 10am-6pm Mon-Fri; 10am-1pm Sat. **Credit** AmEx, DC, EC, JCB, MC, V. Some English spoken. **Map C4**
Herend is Hungary's finest porcelain. Queen Victoria picked out their delicate birds and butterfly pattern at the 1896 Paris exhibition to put on her own table.
Branch: V. Kigyó utca 5 (118 3439).

Zsolnay Porcelain

V. Kigyó utca 4 (118 3712). M3 Ferenciek tere/bus 7. **Open** 10am-6pm Mon-Fri; 10am-1pm Sat. **Credit** AmEx, MC, V. English spoken. **Map C4**
Not as refined as Herend, Zsolnay designs are more free-flowing and suited to the Art Deco patterns they commonly use. Most famous for a weather-proof glaze developed in the late nineteenth century which resulted in the beautiful mosaic roof tiles still to be found on the Mátyás templom, the Central Market and the Applied Arts Museum, the firm spent much of the communist era producing insulators for power lines. They've happily returned to fine porcelain, though, and have come out with some bold new patterns in the last few years.

Food & Drink

See also below **Food Delivery**.

Nagy Tamás Sajtüzlete

V. Gerlóczy utca 3 (117 4268/137 7014). M1, M2, M3 Deák tér/tram 47, 49. **Open** 9am-6pm Mon-Fri; 9am-1pm Sat. **No credit cards**. No English spoken. **Map C4**

Some of the better supermarkets have begun to stock a wider variety of cheese, but 'Big Tom' remains the best with around 150 types to choose from. You won't find good brie, parmesan or English cheeses anywhere else.

Coquan's Kávé

IX. Ráday utca 15 (215 2444). M3 Kálvin tér/tram 47, 49. **Open** 8am-6pm Mon-Fri; 9am-5pm Sat; 11am-5pm Sun. **No credit cards**. English spoken. **Map D5**
Hungary's first and only speciality coffee roaster. Pick out a blend from over ten varieties roasted daily, or just stop in for a cappuccino with a delicious carrot cake.
Branch: V. Nádor utca 5 (266 9936).

Kamra

VII. Dohány utca 30A (117 7673). M2 Astoria/tram 47, 49. **Open** 10am-6pm Mon-Fri; 10am-1pm Sat. **No credit cards**. Some English spoken. **Map D4**
Tiny shop selling exquisite organic cheese and wine from Hungary. Sample 'Jew cheese' on a bagel chip – not Kosher, but made from 'an old Jewish recipe' with herbs and garlic.

Kóser Élelmiszer

VII. Nyár utca 1 (322 9276). M2 Blaha Lujza/tram 4, 6. **Open** 7am-6pm Mon-Fri. **No credit cards**. Some English spoken. **Map D4**
Israeli import shop filling the food needs of the Orthodox. Worth a visit for odd things in tins, ramen noodles, sweets and exotic nuts.

Ázsia Bolt

IX. Vámház körút 1 (217 7700). Tram 47, 49. **Open** 10am-5pm Mon; 7am-6pm Tues-Fri; 7am-2pm Sat. **No credit cards**. English spoken. **Map D5**
In the basement of the Vásárcsarnok, Ázsia is expat home cooking central and the prices show they know it. You'll find all the basics for Asian, Indian and Italian cuisine, fancy sauces, black beans, taco shells, frozen squid, barbeque sauce and anything else odd that you might want to cook and eat. Glorious collection of spices.

Húsbolt ABC

V. Belgrád rakpart 23 (118 4836). M3 Ferenciek tere/bus 7. **Open** 8am-10pm Mon-Sat. **No credit cards**. Some English spoken. **Map C5**
The Arabic sign shows you've found the right place. An ordinary ABC on one side, the other is stocked with Middle Eastern goodies – tahini, houmous, fava beans, lentils, Ceylon tea, spices, olive leaves and apricot paste.

Supermarkets

Super Kozért

I. Batthyány tér 5-7 (202 5044). M2 Batthyány tér/tram 19. **Open** 10am-6pm Mon-Fri; 10am-1pm Sat. **No credit cards**. Some English spoken. **Map B3**
Convenient, in a converted market hall but nothing exceptional. Key cutting, shoe repair and other useful services.

Csemege Julius Meinl

VIII. Rákóczi út 59 (133 1061/134 3500). M2 Blaha Lujza tér/tram 4, 6. **Open** 7am-7.30pm Mon-Fri; 7am-2pm Sat. **Credit** AmEx, EC, JCB, MC, V. Some English spoken. **Map E4**
With branches all over town, Meinl is good for culinary basics plus medium-range wines and spirits. This location – known to locals as the 'Eternal Flame' (*see page 163* **Shop around the clock**) keeps later hours than most and accepts credit cards.

Kaiser's Metro

VI. Nyugati tér (332 2531). M3 Nyugati/tram 4, 6. **Open** 7am-8pm Mon-Fri; 7am-3pm Sat. **No credit cards**. Some English spoken. **Map C2**

The package deal

If you are stopped at customs upon entering Hungary (about a 50/50 chance if you're arriving with lots of luggage) make sure to save all of the bits of paper you're given and call a customs expediter. Fines can be outrageous – often more than the value of the article at issue – and the bureacracy staggering. It is not unknown for swarms of customs officials to storm the apartments of those unfortunate enough to have been caught padding their computer monitor with extra socks.

If planning to take home antiques, be aware that, officially, any object over 70 years old requires a special export stamp. Ask your antiques dealer for details.

For more modest parcels, Magyar Posta is an alternative, though one fraught with infernal bureaucratic complexities. Packages up to 2kg with a maximum value of Ft10,000 can be sent surface to any destination for Ft1,245. Bring your own packed box, or purchase one from the *Csomagfelvétel* window (in three sizes and costing between Ft70-Ft150). At the same window, ask for the blue *Vámáru-nyilatkozat* (customs form – conveniently in both Hungarian and French). Itemise the contents of your package and the approximate value of each item and fill in sender/receiver details. Next, seal your box with both the packing tape and the string you have remembered to bring with you, then find the queue at the *Levélfelétel* window for final weighing and processing.

A final warning: post from Hungary is notoriously slow (allow at least a month to the US, and two weeks to the UK), and both incoming and outgoing letters and parcels – and bits of parcels – have an annoying habit of getting lost, especially popular cassettes and articles of clothing. To track a parcel or letter, fill in the small white *Ajánlott* form also to be found at the *Levélfelvétel* window. This gives you a serial number which can be traced from both the sending and receiving end and adds Ft120 to the price of your parcel.

RGW Express

XIV. Hungária körút 67 (tel/fax 252 2190/222 0140). M2 Népstadion. **Open** 8am-5pm Mon-Fri. **No credit cards.** English spoken. **Map F1**
Will pack your things, get them through customs, deliver them to the airport and put them on the plane. Friendly, English-speaking staff and reasonable prices.

Business Umbrella

V. Aranykéz utca 2 (tel/fax 118 4126/118 7244). M1 Vörösmarty tér. **Open** 9am-5pm Mon-Thur; 9am-3pm Fri. **Credit** AmEx, DC, EC, JCB, MC, V. English spoken. **Map C4**
Those planning an extended stay in Hungary might do well to make the acquaintance of the Business Umbrella. In addition to shifting your things around (and getting you through customs), they will expedite your work permit, register your car, and help you set up your own company. *e-mail: busumb@dial.isys.hu*

German chain that stocks just about everything you'd want in a supermarket. Quality fresh meats and a good selection of delicatessen cuts and cheeses. Late hours another bonus. **Branch:** XI. Október 23 utca 6-10 (185 0189).

Rothschild

VII. Károly körút (342 9733). M1, M2, M3 Deák tér/tram 47, 49. **Open** 7am-10pm Mon-Fri; 8am-6pm Sat; 9am-5pm Sun. **Credit** DC, EC, JCB, MC, V. Some English spoken. **Map C4**
Late hours, imported 'western' food and other groceries, free next-day delivery for purchases over Ft2,500, but not cheap.

Vegetarian & Health Food

For basics, head to a larger supermarket like Kaiser where interesting dry soy products, crackers, rolled grains, soy and hot sauces can be found. For spices, herbs, and speciality items, head for one of the shops below. The best places to get good quality vitamins are body-building shops like **Mini-Mix Gyógynövény.**

Bio-ABC

V. Múzeum körút 19 (117 3043). M3 Kálvin tér/tram 47, 49. **Open** 10am-7pm Mon-Fri; 10am-2pm Sat. **No credit cards.** Some English spoken. **Map D5**

Soy sausages, carrot juice, organic produce, whole grains, natural cosmetics, herbal teas, essential oils and dried herbs.

Egészégbolt

XII. Csaba utca 3 (212 2542). M2 Moszkva tér/tram 4, 6, 18. **Open** 8.30am-7pm Mon-Fri; 8.30am-1.30pm Sat. **No credit cards.** Some English spoken.
Convenient location with food basics, vitamins, cosmetics and fresh breads.

Mini-Mix Gyógynövény

VI. Oktogon tér 4 (no phone). M1 Oktogon/tram 4, 6. **Open** 8.30am-6pm Mon-Fri; 8.30am-2pm Sat. **No credit cards.** Some English spoken. **Map D3**
Cosmetics, aromatherapy, basic foods and imported vitamins.

Galgafarm

VII. Eötvös utca 8 (351 2441). M1 Oktogon/tram 4, 6. **Open** 8am-7pm Mon-Sat. **No credit cards.** No English spoken. **Map D3**
Organic produce, wholegrain breads, natural and organic food and cosmetics, plus the only juice bar in town.

Calendula Natura

V. Bárczy István utca 1-3 (06 30 446 161). M1, M2, M3 Deák tér/tram 47, 49. **Open** 10am-6pm Mon-Fri; 10am-1pm Sat. **No credit cards.** Some English spoken. **Map C4**

Tiny but well-stocked with familiar American, English and German brands. Veggie ingredients, naturopathic remedies, fresh teas, vitamins, organic soaps, shampoos and incense. If you're after particular herbs, look up the Latin names before you go, as the literature on hand cross-references in Hungarian, German and Latin.

Wine

Barrique Borszaküzlet
VI. Jókai utca 40 (153 2484/06 20 268 226). M3 Nyugati/tram 4, 6. **Open** 10am-6pm Mon-Fri; 10am-1pm Sat. **Credit** AmEx, EC, MC, V. Some English spoken. **Map C3**
A comprehensive selection of reasonably priced Tokaj wines plus selections from Hungary's other major wine regions.

La Boutique des Vins
V. József Attila utca 12 (117 5909). M1, M2, M3 Deák tér/tram 47, 49. **Open** 10am-6pm Mon-Fri; 10am-3pm Sat. **Credit** AmEx. Some English spoken. **Map C3**
The former sommelier of Gundel (*see chapter* **Restaurants**) presides over an excellent collection of quality Hungarian and select imported wines in the city's oldest private wine shop. Find some of the best reds and rosés from the Villány region under the owner's own Sommelier label.

Food Delivery

Il Treno Pizzeria
Districts V, VI, VII, VIII, IX XII, XIII, XIV: VIII. József körút 60 (269 9223). M3 Ferenc körút.
Districts I, II, X, XII, XIII: XII. Alkotás utca 15 (156 4251). M2 Déli. **Delivery** 11am-midnight daily. **No credit cards.** No English spoken.
Thick crust pizza with occasional token oregano and basil in the sauce – order extra. Otherwise, an acceptable full service Italian restaurant. Free delivery to districts as listed.

Király Pizzeria
VI. Király utca 38 (351 1530). M1, M2, M3 Deák tér/tram 47, 49. **Open** 10am-10pm daily. **No credit cards.** Some English spoken. **Map C4**
Delivery in the area within thirty minutes. No extra charge.

Maharaja
III. Bécsi út 89-91 (250 7544/fax 188 6863). Tram 1. **Open** noon-midnight Tue-Sun. **No credit cards.** English spoken.
Standard Indian eats delivered city-wide during business hours. Deliveries out of business hours only for large orders.

New York Bagel
VI. Bajcsy-Zsilinszky út 21 (111 8441/131 9579/06 60 336 635). M3 Arany János utca. **Open** 10am-8pm daily. **No credit cards.** English spoken. **Map C3**
The bagels aren't much like what you'd get in NYC, but the bagel sandwiches aren't bad. Ridiculously slow service.

Pink Cadillac
IX. Ráday utca 22 (216 1412/218 9382). M3 Kálvin tér/tram 47, 49. **Open** 11am-11pm Mon-Thur; 11am-1am Fri; 1pm-1am Sat; 1pm-11pm Sun. **No credit cards.** Some English spoken. **Map D5**
Excellent salads and pastas. Free home delivery for districts V and VIII and parts of IX, I, II, XI, and XII.

Sushi An
V. Harmincad utca 4 (117 4239). M1 Vörösmarty tér. **Open** 5pm-10pm daily. **No credit cards** for delivery. Some English spoken. **Map C4**
Sushi any day delivered anywhere for no extra charge except for the taxi fare to get it to you.

Hair & Beauty

Most major brand names are on or around Váci utca: Clinique, Estée Lauder and Christian Dior between numbers 8-12; Guerlain on Haris köz 6; and Yves St. Laurent in the Kempinski Hotel.

Azúr
V. Petőfi Sándor utca 11 (118 5394). M3 Ferenciek tere/bus 7. **Open** 8am-8pm Mon-Fri; 9am-2pm Sat. **Credit** AmEx, EC, MC, V. Some English spoken. **Map C4**
For all general health and beauty needs. Look for Hungarian-made, natural cosmetics by Helia-D, Ilcsi, and Dr Juga.

Nature Blue Natural Cosmetics
VII. Károly körút 23 (267 2045). M1, M2, M3 Deák tér/tram 47, 49. **Open** 9am-7pm Mon-Fri; 9am-4pm Sat. **No credit cards.** Some English spoken. **Map C4**
An inadequate substitute for Body Shop, the California-based firm has a line of natural skin and hair products without animal by-products and not tested on animals.

Kállos Illatszer és Fodrászcikk
VII. Nagy Diófa utca 1 (268 0930). M2 Blaha Lujza tér/tram 4, 6. **Open** 10am-6pm Mon-Fri; 9am-1pm Sat. **No credit cards.** No English spoken. **Map D4**
Well-known names such as Nivea, L'Oreal, Anaconda and Freeman at great prices. Huge selection of hair colours.

Beauty Salons

Facials, pedicure, manicure, and massage are dirt cheap by European standards, and quite good too. A great way to take a break from sightseeing and a heavy club schedule.

Exclusiv Szépségszalon
V. Veres Pálné utca 2 (266 7228/266 7229). M3 Ferenciek tere/bus 7. **Open** 8am-8pm Mon-Fri; 8am-2pm Sat. **No credit cards.** Some English spoken. **Map C4**
A huge selection of cosmetic treatments are available at reasonable prices in this bustling salon. Aside from all the usuals there is 'hand and foot care with paraffin', 'body shaping with acupuncture', and a 'Dibi centre' (mechanical face massage).

Picurka Salon
VII. Lövölde tér 2 (341 2339). Tram 4, 6. **Open** 7am-7pm Mon-Fri. **No credit cards.** No English spoken. **Map E3**
Use sign language to negotiate the treatment you want, then sit back and enjoy. Much less expensive than downtown salons and said to have the best facial in town.

Vivien Talpal
II. Fillér utca 10B (213 1445). M2 Moszkva tér/tram 4, 6, 18. **Open** 8am-6pm Mon-Fri; 8am-noon Sat. **No credit cards.** Some English spoken.
Good things for your feet with pedicures, foot massage and computer assisted examinations for custom-fit insoles. These cost Ft1,600 and are ready within a week

Hair Salons

Jacques Dessange
V. Deák Ferenc utca 10 (266 8167/266 1000 ext 885). M1, M2, M3 Deák tér/tram 47, 49. **Open** 9am-8pm Mon-Fri; 9am-4pm Sat. **Credit** AmEx. English spoken. **Map C4**
A full-service salon in the Kempinski Hotel. All receptionists are multilingual as are most of the staff. Fashionable cuts, Dessange hair-care projects, facials, body treatments, manicure and makeovers by 'award-winning' consultants.

On track for all sorts of junk at **Városligeti Bolhapiac**. *See page 172.*

Perino Péter

VI. Izabella utca 45 (352 1404). M1 Vörösmarty utca. **Open** 7am-9pm Mon-Fri; 7am-1pm Sat. **No credit cards.** English spoken. **Map D3**
Be sure to call first for an appointment with Peter or Roland – Hungarians swear by them both. Their spacious studio is stocked with Tigri, Paul Mitchell and other quality hair care products, and a cosmetician is on hand for facials, waxing, and other fun. Most expensive haircut costs Ft1,500.

Zsidró

IV. Andrássy út 17 (342 7366). M1 Opera. **Open** 8am-9pm Mon-Fri; 9am-2pm Sat. **No credit cards.** Some English spoken. **Map D3**
Trendy, promising stylists. They do it all, not just men's and women's hair: cosmetic 'cures', waxing, and massage. By appointment, or chance a walk-in. Join the belles of Budapest for an overpriced coffee and magazines gratis while you wait.

Barbers

Férfi Fodrász

XI. Karinthy Frigyes út (371 0042). Tram 16, 19, 47, 49. **Open** 7am-8pm Mon-Fri; 7.30am-1pm Sat. **No credit cards.** No English spoken. **Map C6**
No English spoken, but this is the place for an inexpensive trim. A real neighbourhood barber complete with classic 1970s light fixtures, a TV older than most of the stylists, and out of date hair-model pictures on the walls. The ladies behind the chair are expert, though, and a wash and trim will cost about Ft1,000. Alcohol scalp massage too.

Fodrász

Rudas Baths, I. Döbrentei tér 9 (212 3687). Tram 18, 19/bus 7. **Open** 9am-6pm Mon-Fri; 10am-1pm Sat. **No credit cards.** No English spoken. **Map C5**

Turn left at the bottom of the stairs to the Rudas changing rooms to enter a distinctly male environment – painted in Ferencváros colours, covered in Ferencváros posters and boasting an impressive stack of Hungarian hardcore porn mags. Józsi will shear your locks for Ft1,000-Ft1,500 and his alcohol scalp massage is very possibly the best in town. Sometimes a long wait, especially on Saturdays.

Laundry & Dry-cleaning

Patyolat is the Hungarian word for laundry. Prices go by the kilo and folding and ironing are usually included. Be wary of signs claiming 'dry-cleaning' services. In some instances this just means a bigger washing machine; in others, a lingering chemical smell and feel as well as creeping greyness.

Irisz-Szalon Textiltisztító

VII. Rákóczi út 8B (269 6840). M2 Astoria/tram 47, 49. **Open** 7am-7pm Mon-Fri; 7am-1pm Sat. **No credit cards.** Some English spoken. **Map D4**
The closest thing to a coin-operated laundry in Budapest – you have to pay someone else to load the machines for you. The price isn't bad, though – up to 7kg is Ft640 and they'll fold everything for you. Ironing on request.

Crystal

V. Arany János utca 34 (131 8307). M3 Arany János utca. **Open** 7am-7pm Mon-Fri; 8am-1pm Sat. **No credit cards.** No English spoken. **Map C3**
Next-day dry-cleaning, as well as leather clothing and winter jackets within a week.

The Home Laundry

II. Radna utca 3 (200 5305). Bus 5. **Open** 8am-7.30pm Mon-Fri; 9am-1pm Sat. **No credit cards.** English spoken.

Now with four locations (unfortunately all in Buda) the Home Laundry is the most trustworthy place to send your dry-cleaning. Regular laundry by the kilo for sheets, underwear and towels (Ft449-Ft699). Other clothing charged by the piece (Ft300-Ft600) with extras like folding, ironing, and hanging and starching for shirts. Pick up and delivery in inner Budapest costs Ft699. Choose from regular or express services with friendly English-speaking staff.

Malls

See also page 173 **Magyar malls**.

Duna Plaza
XIII. Váci út 178 (268 1288). M3 Gyöngyösi út. **Open** 10am-9pm Mon-Fri; 10am-7pm Sat-Sun.
Nothing spectacular about the mall or the shops, but worth a visit for the Virgin Megastore, or to spend an hour in the excellent video arcade or for a few lanes at the bowling alley.

Pólus Center
1152 Szentmihályi út 131 (410 2405/410 8951). Special bus, Nyugati, Keleti. **Open** 10am-8pm Mon-Fri; 10am-7pm Sat-Sun. **Credit cards** vary.
Begin your adventure to deafening pop music in the special buses from Keleti and Nyugati. Disembark in deathly quiet acres of empty parking lot. Cruise down Sunset Boulevard or Rodeo Drive to reach the real destination – Tesco. Everything from home including HP sauce, Branston pickle, Marmite, PG Tips, Patak curry pastes and cheap underwear. Checking out can take upwards of half an hour.

Europark
XIX. Üllői út 201 (282 9266). M3 Határ út. **Open** 10am-6pm Mon-Fri; 10am-1pm Sat.
Converted sports arena in southern Pest that still has a massive discount sporting goods shop. Otherwise, the usual mall shops and restaurants little else to recommend it.

Markets

Ecseri Piac
XIX. Nagykőrösi út 156. Bus 52 from Boráros tér. **Open** 7am-early afternoon Mon-Sat. **Admission** free.
If travelling by bus, get off when everyone else around you starts shuffling and the used car market comes into view on the left. Merchants inflate their prices for westerners, so be prepared for tough haggling. Still the best place for folk costumes and textiles, Communist artefacts and all sorts of interesting junk. Arrive early Saturday for the best pickings. The outside stalls often yield the most unusual finds.

Józsefvárosi Piac
VII. Kőbányai út 21-23. Tram 28, 37. **Open** 6am-6pm daily.
Shoppers are generally Hungarian, Polish and Romanian, stall-holders primarily Chinese, their assistants Gypsy and the money changers Turkish. Don't expect antiques, but be aware that much of the clothing in trendy no-name shops downtown comes from here and avoid the mark-up. It's also good for discount south-east Asian sneakers (made by the same folks who bring you Nike and Adidas). Watch out for pickpockets and enjoy both the wheeler-dealer bustle and the assortment of absurd fake brand names.

Városligeti Bolhapiac
Petőfi Csarnok, XIV. Zichy Mihály út (251 2485). M1 Széchenyi Fürdő. **Open** 7am-2pm Sat-Sun. **Admission** Ft20. **Map F2**
Ecseri's smaller cousin and considerably easier to get to. Thin on Communist relics these days, but look out for toy Trabis, old instruments and lots of other interesting junk.

Music

See also chapters **Folklore** *and* **Music: Rock, Roots & Jazz** *and* **Music: Classical & Opera**.

CD Bar
VIII. Krúdy Gyula utca 6 (138 4281). M3 Kálvin tér/tram 47, 49. **Open** 10am-8pm Mon-Fri; 10am-4pm Sat. **No credit cards**. English spoken. **Map D5**
Take your time choosing from a good selection of contemporary and classical jazz in a relaxed atmosphere. Sip a tea on the house and settle down in the comfy chairs to have a listen to whatever strikes your fancy. Classical, pop, world and folk music also on offer.

Concerto Records
VII. Dob utca 33 (268 9631). M1 Opera. **Open** noon-7pm Mon-Fri; noon-4pm Sat. **Credit** AmEx, DC, EC, MC, V. English spoken. **Map D3**
This crowded but charming shop right beside the Orthodox Synagogue offers a unique and impressive collection of new and secondhand vinyl and CDs. Although there's the occasional rap or funk treasure, the stock is mostly classical and opera, with a little bit of jazz and folk.

Fotex
V. Szervita tér 2 (118 3395). M1 Vörösmarty tér. **Open** 10am-9pm daily. **Credit** AmEx, DC, EC, JCB, MC, V. Some English spoken. **Map C4**
The Magyar megastore – huge amounts of depressingly mainstream pop, but it's central and offers the convenience of shopping for all genres in one store.

Rózsavölgyi Zeneműbolt
V. Szervita tér 5 (118 3500). M1, M2, M3 Deák tér/tram 47, 49. **Open** 10am-7pm Mon-Fri; 10am-5pm Sat-Sun. **Credit** AmEx, DC, EC, JCB, MC, V. Some English spoken. **Map C4**
Don't be put off by muzak wafting out the door or the easy-listening pap at the front. Head straight for the back where you'll find justification for Roszavölgyi's claim to be the biggest classical music store in the region. Large collection of sheet music, too, plus some bizarre vinyl bargains.

Wave/Trance
VI. Révay köz 2 (269 3135). M3 Arany János utca. **Open** 11am-7pm Mon-Fri; 11am-2pm Sat. **No credit cards**. English spoken. **Map C3**
Two adjacent branches. Wave provides a solid choice of alternative guitar-based rock, while Trance focusses on techno, drum & bass, trip hop and house.

Opticians

Ofotért-Optinova Magyar-Amerikai Optikai Kft.
V. Múzeum körút 13 (117 3559/266 2137). M2 Astoria/tram 47, 49. **Open** 10am-6pm Mon-Fri; 10am-1pm Sat. **Credit** AmEx, DC, EC, JCB, MC, V. English spoken. **Map D4**
English-speakers will conduct examinations for glasses or contact lenses. Head here to replenish stocks of contact cleaning supplies. Also find a large selection of international (expensive) and Hungarian (cheaper) frames.

Photocopying and Printing

Copy General
V. Semmelweis utca 4 (266 6564/fax 266 6563). M2 Astoria/tram 47, 49. **Open** 7am-10pm Mon-Fri; 9am-6pm Sat. **No credit cards**. English spoken. **Map D4**

Magyar malls

Duna Plaza – *just don't expect bargains.*

It was like a twisted anthropological experiment. In 1996, chunks of American suburbia were air-dropped into Budapest to create Magyar malls, bizarre groupings of heavily decorated retail outlets, apparently meant to look the way Hungarians think shops in the States should look.

There is something surreal – and not at all American – about the Limousine Juice Bar, built around the body of a 1950s Cadillac, or the Western City food court, with its wooden, corral-fence motif. Like their counterparts in the States, these consumer meccas boast fast food, anchor stores and scores of teenage mall rats in flashy attire. But only in Budapest will you find lard and onion sandwiches for sale in Western City. And you know you're in a unique video arcade when you spot a dozen or so Gypsy women and children in ornate traditional costumes watching the elder men in the family gun down animated attackers. Local shoppers carefully inspect strange mer-chandise that they couldn't possibly need, and almost certainly can't afford. Although 40 years under a command economy have turned Hungarians into eager consumers of trinkets and gadgets, it seems that not enough are consuming them at the malls. Already the **Pólus Center** is experiencing hard times.

But although they're not spending, Hungarians do venture out to the malls. Mr and Ms Magyar apparently love to take their 1.6 children here for ice skating and ice cream, making these great locations for observing the typical Hungarian family in an unnatural habitat. When not people-watching, you can also get some shopping done. Just don't expect bargains. Hard-to-find western items are for sale here, but often at ruinous prices.

Each of Budapest's three main malls has a different atmosphere. **Duna Plaza** is more upscale, with a wide range of fashion shops, more foreigners and a multi-screen cinema. **Europark** is the smallest and cheapest, and the only one where people seem to buy anything. Pólus Center is harder to get to, but rewards the trip with its high surrealism quotient. You can ride bumper cars in the dark, go bowling with people who've never seen the game before, or just gawk at the country folk visiting the big city and the hordes of Austrians in search of bargains.

The losses suffered by shops in the Pólus, and grassroots opposition to the construction of new malls, may put a damper on the growth of these places in Budapest. Fortunately for the city's smaller shops, it seems that the Magyar mall experiment has not been terribly successful.

Nine locations offer efficient and comprehensive photocopy services. Pick up and delivery for a nominal fee (Ft500 each way). The Lónyáy utca branch is open 24 hours and offers desktop publishing and computer rental in addition to its regular services. The self-service centre is next door. **Branches** I. Attila út 12 (202 0906/fax 212 0862). IX. Lónyáy utca 36 (218 5155/fax 218 5156). V. Alkotmány utca 18 (312 7636/fax 332 2563).

Photography

Ofotért
V. Károly körút 14 (117 6313/fax 117 5986). M2 Astoria/tram 47, 49. **Open** 9am-7pm Mon-Fri; 9am-2pm Sat. **Credit** EC, MC. Some English spoken. **Map D4**
Film processing in Hungary isn't any cheaper than at home, and probably not as good unless you go to a professional studio. Nevertheless, Ofotert is considered to maintain higher, more consistent quality than competitor Fotex. Will develop B&W, colour, and slides and carries Kodak supplies.

Fotolux
V. Károly körút 21 (342 1538). M1, M2, M3 Deák tér/tram 47, 49. **Open** 8am-9pm Mon-Fri; 9am-7pm Sat. **No credit cards.** Some English spoken. **Map C4**
Budapest's certified Nikon dealer has camera supplies, colour and slide processing and will help you find camera repair services.

Antique & Secondhand Cameras

Soós Kereskedés
V. József Attila utca 84 (117 2341). M1, M2, M3 Deák tér/tram 47, 49. **Open** 9am-5pm Mon-Fri; 10am-1pm Sat. **No credit cards.** Some English spoken. **Map C3**
Could easily be mistaken for a jumble shop from the outside. All kinds of camera equipment – new and used, western and eastern makes – fight for shelf space with typewriters, glass bottles, antique(ish) porcelain, faux pearls, and stationery supplies. Not to mention a film-processing service, spare wires and cables, used enlargers, and miscellaneous electronics parts. Semi-annual auctions, too.

Bicycle Repair

Túra Mobil Discount Store

VI. Nagymező utca 43 (312 5073). **M1 Opera. Open**
9am-6pm Mon-Fri; 10am-3pm Sat. **No credit cards.** No
English spoken. **Map D3**
Reliable and professional staff repair mountain and touring
bikes. You'll also find accessories, parts for DIY repairs and
a small stock of new bikes.

Computer Repair

Re-Mac Computer Kft.

V. Bajcsy-Zsilinszky út 62 (312 5870/269 1600). M3
Arany János utca. **Open** 9am-6pm Mon-Fri; **No credit
cards.** English spoken. **Map C3**
Authorised service and sales of Apple computers.

Digit Modul Kft

VII. Thököly út 32 (351 7980). **M2 Keleti. Open** 9am-
5pm Mon-Thur; 9am-3pm Fri. **No credit cards.** Some
English spoken. **Map F3**
Sales and repairs of Wintel computers. Will take a look at
your laptop, though their speciality is desktop machines.

Appliance Repairs

Time rather than price is the problem in getting
appliances repaired in Budapest, and much energy can be wasted in trudging from shop to shop
looking for someone that can handle your particular job. Telinformix (269 3333/open 8am-8pm
daily) will direct you to the nearest and most suitable repair shop for your appliance. Have a
Hungarian on hand to explain your predicament –
not many Telinformix staff speak English.

Bigrav

V. Váci utca 75 (137 6226). **M3 Kálvin tér/tram 47, 49.**
Open 10am-5pm Mon-Fri. **No credit cards.** Some
English spoken. **Map C5**
Will repair stereo equipment, convert appliances to 220v cur-
rent, and make transformers for larger appliances.

Luggage Repair

Flekk GMK

VI. Podmaniczky utca 19 (111 0316). **M3 Nyugati/tram**
4, 6. **Open** 9am-6pm Mon-Fri. **No credit
cards.** Some English spoken. **Map D3**
Odd little family-run shop offering zip and luggage repair
within a few days, or shoes heeled and keys cut while you
wait. There's also an eclectic jumble of DIY essentials.

Mountex

IX. Üllői út 7 (217 2426). **M3 Kálvin tér/tram 47, 49.**
Open 9am-6pm Mon-Fri; 10am-1pm Sat. **Credit** AmEx,
DC, EC, JCB, MC, V. Some English spoken. **Map D5**
Mountaineering store with equipment for climbing, caving
and hiking. They also have a repairman on staff for back-
pack blowouts and other equipment repairs.

Shoe Repair

Mister Minit

Skála Metró Áruház, VI. Nyugati tér (153 2222). M3
Nyugati/tram 4, 6. **Open** 9am-6.30pm Mon-Fri; 9am-2pm
Sat. **No credit cards.** Some English spoken. **Map C2**

Cameras are a snap at **Soós Kereskedés.**

The American chain has 20 branches in major shopping centres in Budapest for while-you-wait key copying, knife sharp-
ening and shoe repairs.
Branch: Centrum Áruház Corvin, VIII. Blaha Lujza tér 1-
3 (138 4160 ext 28).

Watch & Jewellery Repairs

Orex Óraszalon

V. Petőfi Sándor utca 6 (137 4915). **M3 Ferenciek**
tere/bus 7. **Open** 10am-6pm Mon-Fri; 10am-1pm Sat.
Credit AmEx, DC, EC, MC, V. English spoken. **Map C4**
Although you can replace a worn-out watch battery in
most jewellery and watch shops, the experienced repair
staff at this location speak English and offer reliable repair
services.

Magic Football Shop

VI. Teréz körút 40 (312 1332). **M1 Oktogon/tram 4, 6.**
Open 10am-6pm Mon-Fri; 10am-1pm Sat. **No credit
cards.** Some English spoken. **Map D3**
Apart from the one at Ferencváros, the only store in town
for Hungarian football souvenirs – all the main Budapest
teams are featured. Plus a good selection of Italian, German
and Spanish gear. Tucked in a courtyard – watch out for the
display of scarves and pennants outside on the körút.

Mallory Sport

VII. Király utca 59 (342 0744). **Tram 4, 6. Open** 10am-
6pm Mon-Wed, Fri; 10am-7pm Thur; 10am-1pm Sat.
Credit EC, MC, V. Some English spoken. **Map D3**
Named after the famous mountaineer, Mallory carries indoor
and outdoor sporting supplies covering everything from aerobics to racquet sports.

Arts & Entertainment

Baths

The history, atmosphere, medicinal waters and sheer sensory delight of Budapest's bathhouses make a long, slow soak the hedonistic highlight of any visit.

The Ottoman mosques, monasteries and schools that once filled the streets of Buda are all long gone, but the Turks did leave one enduring contribution to the life of the town: the bathhouses, several of which, centuries later, continue to offer variations on the theme of an Oriental soaking experience.

Bathing in Buda had been a tradition since Roman times, but it was under the Ottoman empire that the culture of the baths reached its apogee. Buda has around 120 thermal springs and mineral-rich waters have long gushed up from the city's bedrock to fill the pools at sites such as the **Király** and **Rudas** baths.

This natural and abundant supply, combined with the demands of Islam that its followers adhere to a strict set of rules for ablutions before praying five times a day, inspired an aquatic and hedonistic culture that still thrives today. The older Budapest baths are some of the finest remains of the city's Ottoman architecture, complete with domed roofs and arches. Lolling in the warm water while the morning sun cuts through the rising steam, it's easy to imagine yourself as an Ottoman Pasha or *valide sultan* (Sultan's mother) reviewing the new recruits to the harem.

The original Turkish baths have mostly been added to – their original domes and pools now surrounded by more recent structures – and newer thermal facilities have been built in a similar tradition, such as those at the **Gellért Hotel**, or the **Széchenyi** complex in the Városliget.

For an English speaker without much command of Hungarian, entering the baths for the first time can be a baffling experience. Most are still state-run and subsidised to keep prices down. Lengthy menus offer such treats as ultra-sound or a pedicure as well as massage. Instructions in Hungarian, German and Russian explain that customers can stay for an hour and a half, although this rule is not strictly enforced.

The routine is similar in all the Turkish baths, though it varies at the mixed facilities. After buying a ticket you enter a warren of passageways, the entrance to which is guarded by a white-clothed attendant. Hand over your ticket and you will be given a white (well, it was white once) flap of cloth which is to be tied around your waist for

modesty's sake. The ones for women also have an apron-like addition that supposedly covers the breasts, but few women bother to wear them at all. Men tend to keep theirs on, though, sometimes swivelling them round behind to prevent scorched buttocks on the wooden sauna seats.

Once in the changing rooms, either the attendant will show you a cubicle, or else you find one yourself, but each is locked twice and reliably secure. The attendant has one key and you keep the other: tie it to the spare string on your once-white cloth flap thing.

The baths generally have one or two main pools and a series of smaller ones around the perimeter, all of different temperatures, ranging from dauntingly hot to icily cold. The precise drill depends on individual preference, but involves moving between different pools, taking in the dry heat of

Thermal Hotel Margitsziget – *see page 178.*

the sauna and the extreme humidity of the steam rooms, alternating temperatures and finally relaxing in gentle warm water.

An hour or two of this is usually sufficient and extremely relaxing. The waters also ease stiff joints and rheumatic complaints. Afterwards you shower (take soap) and in many places are provided with a towel (so you don't always have to bother taking one of those). All the baths have a rest-room, where customers can take a short nap and recover for a while before changing back into street clothes. On the way out, drop off your used towel and tip the attendant Ft30-Ft50.

Apart from pools, saunas and steam rooms, most sites also offer a variety of medical treatments such as massages. These come in two types: *vízi* (water) massage and *orvosi* (medical) massage. Avoid the former, unless you want to feel as if you have been put through a meat grinder. The medical massage is a gentler experience. Masseurs are professional but inattentive, chatting away to their colleagues as they work. Tip them Ft100 or so.

A full visit to the baths demands a whole morning or afternoon. There's usually somewhere in the foyer to get a cold drink or a coffee, and a stall selling soap and other toiletries. Don't expect to have the energy to do much afterwards except settle down for a long lunch or dinner, or head off home to stretch out for a nap.

Apart from the baths listed here, there are also limited thermal facilities at the **Palatinus** and **Dagály** strands. (*See also chapters* **Sport & Fitness** *and* **Gay & Lesbian**.)

Note that ticket offices shut up shop an hour before listed closing times.

The Baths

Gellért Gyógyfürdő

XI. Kelenhegyi út 4 (166 6166). Trams 18, 19, 47, 49/bus 7 to Gellért tér. **Open** 6am-6pm daily. **Admission** Ft1,200; Ft600 concs. Mixed. Some English spoken. **Map C5**

The most expensive of all the baths, but you do get an Art Nouveau swimming pool chucked in for your money. Probably the best of all the sites, at least in the summer, when your Ft600 also allows access to the several outside pools (the wave machine is popular with children) and sunbathing areas, complete with terrace restaurant. There was a hospital on this site – the waters are suitable for treating invertebral disc and spine problems, arthritis and gout – as early as the thirteenth century, and the Turks also had a spa here. Now the beauty of this Art Nouveau extravaganza, built in the interwar years, is matched only by the surliness of most of its staff, who all seem to be graduates of the Josef Stalin charm school, class of 1950. The separate thermal pools – one for men, and one for women – lead off from the main 33-metre swimming pool, which also has its own small warm water pool. The secessionist theme continues in the maze of steam rooms and saunas which gives the Gellért a different atmosphere to the Turkish Rudas or Király. The clientèle are also quite entertaining, composed mainly of startled tourists and, in the male half, gay men on the prowl or happily reclining in each others' arms. The rest room is sometimes extremely active. Crowded during tourist season. The ther-

Top of the Turks – the **Rudas**, *page 178.*

mal water here contains a lot of carbonic gases and is recommended for people with blood pressure problems and coronary heart diseases.

Király Gyógyfürdő

II. Fő utca 84 (201 4392). M2 Batthyány tér. **Open** *men* 6.30am-7pm Mon, Wed, Fri; *women* 6.30am-7pm Tue, Thur, Sat. **Admission** Ft300. No English spoken. **Map B2**

Along with the Rudas, the Király is one of the city's most significant Ottoman monuments, particularly the sixteenth-century pool. It takes its name from the nineteenth-century owners, the König (King) family, who changed their name to its Hungarian equivalent – Király. Construction began in 1566 and was finished by Pasha Sokoli Mustapha in 1570. The Király follows the traditional pattern of a main pool, surrounded by small ones of a different temperature, together with saunas and steam rooms, but is not as beautiful as the Rudas. The bath's environs are lighter and airier though, and three Turkish-style reliefs mark the entrance corridor. The Király has a reputation for being a gay male pick-up joint.

Lukács Gyógyfürdő és Strandfürdő

II. Frankel Leó út 25-29 (326 1695). Tram 4, 6. **Open** 6am-7pm Mon-Sat; 6am-5pm Sun. **Admission** Ft300. No English spoken. **Map B1**

A complex of two outdoor swimming pools set in attractive grounds and thermal baths, in this case the Turkish-period Császár Baths, although there aren't that many original features left and the layout is quite different from the other Turkish places. The baths are mixed which also gives them a different atmosphere to the Rudas or Király. There's something of an institutional feel to this warrenous facility which some may find off-putting, but the setting is verdant and restful. On the wall outside the entrance to the changing rooms, you'll find a selection of old stone plaques, testaments

Testimonials in stone – Lukács, page 177.

from satisfied customers – the waters are said to be efficacious for orthopaedic diseases. Bring towel and swimming costume.

Rác Gyógyfürdő

I. Hadnagy utca 8-10 (156 1322). Tram 18, 19, 47, 49. **Open** 6am-6pm *women* Mon, Wed, Fri; *men* Tue, Thur, Sat. **Admission** Ft300. No English spoken. **Map B5**
Tucked under Gellért Hill, with a pleasant outdoor café overlooking the Tabán, the Rác baths are named after the Hungarian word for the Serb community that once lived by the river. Though the exterior is nineteenth-century, the octagonal pool and dome inside date back to Turkish times, although they're drabber than those at the Király or Rudas. The Rác offers the same menu of pools, steam and sauna as the other two Turkish-built facilities and has the most active gay scene of the all the baths. Its thermal waters are suitable for treating chronic arthritis, muscle and nerve pain.

Rudas Gyógyfürdő

I. Döbrentei tér 9 (156 1322). Tram 18, 19/bus 7 to Döbrentei tér. **Open** 6am-7pm Mon-Fri; 6am-1pm Sat, Sun. **Closed** Sun during summer (15 June-31 Aug). **Admission** Ft300. No English spoken. **Map C5**
This is the finest and most atmospheric of Budapest's original Turkish baths (men only, although the swimming pool is mixed), especially when rays of sunlight stream through the windows in the domed roof, cutting through the steam. The first baths on this site dated from the late fourteenth century. The new site was constructed by the Pasha of Buda in the sixteenth century and a plaque in his name still stands in the main chamber. The original cupola, vaulted corridor and main octagonal pool all remain, although they have been heavily restored. The Rudas has three saunas and two steam rooms as a well as six pools of differing temperatures. This is the straightest of the baths, although if you visit alone and someone comes to sit next to you he probably wants to be friends.

Széchenyi Gyógyfürdő és Strandfürdő

XIV. Állatkerti körút 11 (121 0310). M1 Széchenyi fürdő. **Open** *strand* 6am-7pm daily. *Mixed thermal baths (Apr-Sept)* 6am-7pm daily; *Oct-Mar* 6am-5pm Mon-Sat; 6am-4pm Sun. **Admission** Ft300. No English spoken. **Map F1**
In the middle of the Városliget, an attractive complex of swimming pools and thermal baths, complete with restaurant, the Széchenyi is one of the largest health spas in Europe. Its waters are used for treating arthritis, gout, chronic gynaecological and respiratory diseases and, if you drink them, gall bladder disease. Outside stands a statue of Zsigmond Vilmos, who discovered the thermal spring that fills the outdoor pool. The Széchenyi is probably the best choice for a day of watery relaxation as it offers outdoor thermal and swimming pools as well as the usual indoor assortment of thermal baths and steam rooms, so customers can exercise and laze about all on one site. Also, unlike

Turkish baths such as the Rudas or the Király, it is open all weekend, when the crowds of customers of all ages give the site an endearing holiday atmosphere. The outside pools are beautifully laid out in a complex of ivy-clad buildings and include a cold water swimming pool as well as a thermal one, open all year round, where guests play chess on floating boards, with steam rising up around them. Drinks and, of course, cigarettes are available.

Spa Hotels

The facilities at all these hotels can also be used by non-residents.

Thermal Hotel Margitsziget

XIII. Margaret Island (311 1000). Bus 26. **Open** 7am-8pm daily. **Admission** *day ticket* Ft1,200. English spoken.
A modern luxury hotel in the middle of Margit island, the Thermal offers a squeaky clean complex of three mixed thermal pools, swimming pool, sauna and steam room. A different experience to one of the Turkish baths, more orientated towards sport and fitness than hedonism. The Thermal Hotel also offers a solarium, a pedicure and two sorts of massage – sport and Swedish – which sounds intriguing. Carlos the Jackal apparently used to stay here, though whether or not he used to take the waters is still open to conjecture.

Thermal Hotel Aquincum

III. Árpád fejedelem útja 94 (250 3360). Tram 1 from M3 Árpád híd. **Open** 7am-9pm daily. **Admission** *weekday tickets purchased before 10am* Ft650; *otherwise* Ft1,200; *weekend day ticket* Ft1,600. English spoken.
A not-quite-luxury hotel named after the ancient Roman town that once stood in this district. The Romans had baths around here and now the Aquincum offers a modern complex of thermal baths, steam room, sauna, whirlpool, swimming pool and gym.

Thermal Hotel Helia

XIII. Karpát utca 62-64 (270 3277). M3 Dózsa György út/trolleybus 79 to Karpát utca. **Open** 7am-10pm daily. **Admission** *weekday morning ticket to 3pm* Ft1,000; *3pm-10pm* Ft1,900; *weekend or full day ticket* Ft2,500. English spoken.
Perched by the river, on the edge of a working-class suburb, this luxury hotel has a modern complex of swimming pool, thermal pools, sauna, steam room and exercise machines. Massages (Ft950) must be booked in advance. Popular with 'businessmen' from the former Soviet Union discussing contracts as they soak. There is also a roof terrace.

Farther-flung Facilities

Dandár utcai Gyógyfürdő

IX. Dandár utca 5-7 (215 7084). Bus 33. **Open** 6am-6pm Mon-Fri; 6am-noon Sat. **Admission** Ft180. No English spoken. **Map E6**
A good way off the tourist trail, in District IX, the Dandár utca mixed thermal baths are small and crowded with locals rather than expats or visitors. Bring a swimming costume and a towel and watch a working-class suburb of Budapest take the thermal waters.

Pestszenterzsébet jódos Sósfürdő

XX. Vízisport utca 2 (283 1097). Bus 23 from Boráros tér. **Open** *men* 7am-3pm Tue, Thur, Sat; *women* 7am-3pm Mon, Wed, Fri. **Admission** Ft180. No English spoken.
Cheapest and most distant of the thermal baths, way out in District XX. This spa offers salty water and the usual assortment of steam room, sauna and thermal pools.

Children

From the mundanely modern to the delightfully dated, Budapest boasts bundles of entertainment for the little ones.

Send in the clowns – the **Circus**, *page 180.*

Budapest still has a lot of appealingly old-fashioned entertainments for children: puppet theatres, folk dance clubs, eccentric conveyances and prehistoric fairground rides. If kids don't find these interesting, then there are all the usual hamburgers, playgrounds and video arcades. Even on a long stay, visitors will find enough child-orientated entertainment to keep everyone amused.

THE HUNGARIAN FAMILY

Hungarians love children. Don't be surprised if people, especially old ladies, stop to stroke and praise your child. Still, the Hungarian family is getting smaller. Young parents usually can't afford more than one or two kids and the housing problem is so serious that young families often live at their grandparents' house.

The Hungarian family is still fairly traditional in its approach to child-rearing. You don't see too many parents with small children in restaurants, or other 'grown-up' places, because children are supposed to stay at home with their mothers until they learn how to behave like little adults.

PRACTICALITIES

Under-12s may not travel in the front seats of cars, but seat belts and baby-seats are not compulsory in the back. Children under six travel free of charge on all public transport vehicles.

If you plan to eat out with your kids, don't take high chairs and child-size meals for granted. On the other hand, disposable nappies, baby food and other essential baby and child equipment are available all over the city.

DIFFICULTIES

Heavy traffic and air pollution mean that long weekday walks along busy downtown streets are not advisable. Instead try the Danube Korzó, the pedestrian streets around Váci utca, or one of the parks and playgrounds listed below.

If travelling with a young baby, you should know that only the narrowest pushchairs can get through the doors of buses and trams. Access can also be a problem when shopping, except in a few new, spacious western-style shops in the downtown area or in the recently built shopping malls in the outskirts.

ENTERTAINMENT

Check the listings in English-language weeklies, *Magyar Narancs* or *Pesti Műsor* or telephone **Tourinform** (117 9800).

Children's Activity Centres

These activity centres offer a variety of programmes for children during the school year and organise day-camps and special events when school is out. Regular activities include craft workshops, language, computer, karate and dance courses as well as playgroups.

The most popular centres are listed below. It is advisable to check current programmes and prices with the venues.

Almássy tér Recreation Centre

Almássy téri Szabadidő Központ
VII. Almássy tér 6 (352 1572). M2 Blaha Lujza tér.
Open 8am-8pm daily (or later depending on events).
Closed in summer. **No credit cards**. English spoken.
Map E3
One of the best kids' castles in town is open every Sunday morning from September to June. Activities include craft workshops, singing, dancing, stories and puppet shows. Special events range from giant hands-on toy exhibits to performances by popular children's entertainers such as Jutka Halász or the Hegedős folk music band. The centre also offers crafts and karate courses for children and has a nice swimming pool.

Marczibányi tér Culture House

Marczibányi téri Művelődési Ház
II. Marczibányi tér 5/a (212 4885). M2 Moszkva tér.
Open 9am-8pm daily (or later depending on events).
Closed in summer. **No credit cards**. Some English spoken. **Map A2**
Craft workshops, a folk dance club, a yoga course for 10-14 year olds and an excellent playground for younger kids. Special events include concerts, puppet shows and pet fairs.

Children's Theatres

Budapest Puppet Theatre

Budapest Bábszínház
VI. Andrássy út 69 (321 5200). M1 Vörösmarty utca.
Shows 3pm Mon-Thur; 10.30am, 4pm, Fri-Sun. Closed in
summer. **Admission** Ft300. **No credit cards. Map D2**
International fairy tales and Hungarian folk stories make up
the repertoire. Language is usually not a problem and the
shows are excellent and highly original. Book at weekends.

Kolibri Theatre

VI. Jókai tér 10 (153 4633). M1 Oktogon. **Shows** 10am
daily; 3pm Fri-Sun. **Open** box office 2pm-6pm daily.
Closed in summer. **Admission** Ft150-Ft350. **No credit
cards. Map D3**
Small theatre that presents fairy tales.

Circus

XIV. Állatkerti körút 7 (343 9630). M1 Széchenyi Fürdő.
Shows 3pm, 7pm Mon-Sat; 10am, 3pm, 7pm Sun.
Admission Ft200-Ft350 Mon-Thur; Ft250-Ft500 Fri-
Sun. **No credit cards. Map F1**
A permanent building with shows year-round, although
inside it looks just like an old-fashioned travelling circus.
International and Hungarian performances with acrobats,
magicians, jugglers, clowns and animals. Book in advance
to avoid sitting next to the deafening orchestra.

Planetarium

People's Park (Népliget), south-west corner (265 0725).
M3 Népliget. **Open** 9.30am-3.30pm Mon-Fri; 9am-4pm
Sat, Sun. Laser shows 7pm. **Admission** Ft250. Laser
shows Ft1,190; Ft790 children. **No credit cards.**
Temporary exhibits as well as educational children's shows.
Popular with older kids.

Eating Out

Although the number of restaurants that carry
high-chairs and have children's menus has been
growing, it's a good idea to call and enquire and
maybe even reserve a high chair. A lot of Hungarian
restaurants aren't very child-friendly, but **Náncsi
Néni, Bagolyvár, Gundel, Tabáni Kakas** and
Fészek are exceptions. You can also be sure of
enjoying a meal with your kids at **Shalimar, Café
Kör, Lou Lou, Gandhi, Via Luna, Pinocchio**
and **Dionysos.** *See chapter* **Restaurants.**

Films & TV

Several cinemas show cartoons and children's
films – most, however, are dubbed. Check film listings in *Pesti Műsor* or *Magyar Narancs* under
Gyerekeknek ajánlott filmek (films recommended
for children) or look in the local English-language
papers. Most hotels and flats for rent have satellite and/or cable TV, including the Cartoon
Network. *See chapter* **Media.**

Folk Dance Clubs

The folk music movement (*see chapter* **Folklore**)
does not leave kids out of the fun. The following
Dance Houses (*táncházak*) are for children.

Muzsikás táncház

Fővárosi Művelődési Ház
XI. Fehérvári út 47 (203 3868). Tram 47. **Open** 5.30pm-
6.30pm Tue. Closed in summer. **Admission** Ft200; Ft100
children. **No credit cards. Map C6**
Muzsikás, the best-known Hungarian folk band, offers a
weekly *táncház* (Dance House) for youngsters: live folk music
and the teaching of traditional dances, including folk tales
and games in a playful atmosphere.

Kalamajka táncház

Belvárosi Művelődési Ház
V. Molnár utca 9 (117 5928). M3 Ferenciek tere. **Open**
5pm-6.30pm Sat. Closed in summer. **Admission** Ft100
children. **No credit cards. Map C5**
This children's *táncház*, which turns into a wild grown-up
táncház at night, is right in the city centre. Songs, dances and
folk tales are taught by talented folk singer Éva Fábián.

Museums

Museum of Transport

Közlekedési Múzeum
*XIV. Városligeti körút 11 (343 0565). Trolleybus 72, 74
or walk across City Park from M1 Széchenyi Fürdő.*
Open 10am-5pm Tue-Sun. **Admission** Ft100; Ft50
students; free for under 6s. **No credit cards. Map F2**
Life-size and model trains, cars and ships. You can climb the
steps of an old train engine and peek into the wagons, you
can also turn a ship's wheel, but that's it for hands-on stuff.

Museum of Aviation

Repüléstörténeti Múzeum
*Petőfi Hall (Petőfi Csarnok), XIV. Zichy Mihály út 16
(343 0009).* **Open** 10am-6pm Tue-Sun. **Admission**
Ft100; Ft50 students, free for under 6s. **No credit cards.**
Map F2
Small and life-size aeroplanes, helicopters and spaceships.

Military History Museum

Hadtörténeti Múzeum
*I. Tóth Árpád sétány 40 (156 9522). M2 Moszkva tér
then Várbusz.* **Open** 10am-5pm Tue-Sat; 10am-6pm Sun.
Admission Ft100; Ft50 children. **No credit cards.**
Map A3
Uniforms and shining suits of armour, the history of war in
photographs and old cannons outside to climb on.

Underground Railway Museum

Földalatti Múzeum
Deák tér metro station. M1, M2, M3 Deák tér. **Open**
10am-6pm Tue-Sun. **Admission** Ft35 or one metro
ticket. **No credit cards. Map C4**
The old-fashioned 'little metro' (M1) can be fun in itself, but
checking out the even older carriages in this small museum
will also be interesting for most children.

Palace of Wonders

Csodák Palotája
XIII. Váci út 19 (201 9483). M3 Lehel tér. **Open** 9am-
5pm Tue-Fri; 10am-6pm Sat-Sun. **Admission** Ft350;
Ft200 children. **No credit cards. Map D2**
An excellent interactive scientific exhibit where school-
children can learn through experiments. There are a hundred hands-on tools and instruments to try out including
giant magnets, spinning wheels, strange mirrors and a 'real'
TV studio.

Telephone Museum

Telefónia Múzeum
I. Úri utca 49 (212 2243). M2 Moszkva tér then Várbusz.
Open 10am-6pm Tue-Sun. **Admission** Ft80; Ft30
children. **No credit cards. Map A3**

A small museum where children can call each other, push buttons, send faxes and try everything out.

Stamp Museum

Bélyeg Múzeum
VII. Hársfa utca 47 (342 3757). Tram 4, 6 to Wesselényi utca. **Open** 10am-6pm Tue-Sun. **Admission** Ft50; Ft30 children. **No credit cards. Map D3**
Over 11 million stamps on 3,000 pull-out glass plates in one big room. A must for philately fanatics.

Outdoor Activities

Zoo

Állatkert
XIV. Városligeti körút 6-12 (343 6075). M1 Széchenyi Fürdő. **Open** *summer* 9am-7pm daily; *winter* 9am-4pm.
Admission Tue-Sun Ft300 adults; Ft250 students; Ft200 children; free for under-2s; Mon Ft200 for all. **No credit cards. Map E1**
The Zoo has begun to change from the sad, old facility it used to be. There are new green areas and more animal-friendly cages and a new playground is promised. Animal names are written in English as well as Hungarian, and an English-language booklet with a handy map is available for Ft200. You need three or four hours to see everything here. As well as the usual lions and monkeys there are also aquaria, nice art-deco buildings, pony-carts, a beautiful exotic bird house, a small domestic animal petting corner and the only public nappy-changing room in town.

Amusement Park

Vidám Park
XIV. Városligeti körút 14-16 (343 0996). M1 Széchenyi Fürdő. **Open** *summer* 9.45am-8pm daily; *winter* 9.45am-sunset daily. **Admission** free; Ft100-Ft500 a ride. **No credit cards. Map F1**
A big tacky old place with a rickety wooden roller coaster, big wheel, ancient merry-go-round and ridiculously unfrightening ghost trains next to newer, scarier rides. Next door is the tiny and somewhat decrepit children's fun fair (Kis Vidám Park) for toddlers and pre-schoolers.

Parks & Playgrounds

There are plenty of parks and playgrounds in Budapest, but with air pollution and poor safety standards it's best to stick to the following places.

Margaret Island

Margitsziget
Tram 4, 6 to Margaret Bridge or bus 26 from Nyugati station. **Map B1**
This Danube island is one huge recreational area with lots of green grass, enormous old trees, swimming pools, playgrounds and a small zoo with domestic animals. You can rent bicycles, four-wheel pedalos and tiny electric cars for children at both ends of the island. Horse-drawn carts and open-topped minibuses leave on round trips of the island every half hour. The best playground is near the Alfréd Hajós swimming pool on the south-west side. The island is also well-sprinkled with kiosks selling snacks, drinks and ice cream in summer. (*See also chapter* **Sightseeing**.)

City Park

Városliget
M1 Hősök tere. **Map E1**
Lots to do here apart from the Zoo, Amusement Park and Circus listed above. **Heroes' Square** (Hősök tere) is teen Budapest's favourite skate-boarding area. Behind it is a boating pond with ducks and swans, some of which turns into

Hand in glove – **Puppet Show** *page 182.*

an ice-skating rink in winter. Beyond the lake is Vajdahunyad Castle, which houses the **Museum of Agriculture** (Mezőgazdasági Múzeum) with lots of stuffed animals and tools. Safety standards are low on the slides and wooden castles in the south corner, although there is a new fenced-around playground for school-children with a tree house, safe slides and monkey-bars. The playground between the zoo and the pond is also in good shape and has a trampoline area where children can bounce up and down for Ft100 for five minutes. There are also ping-pong tables. For ball games you should check out the football fields, basketball and tennis courts behind Petőfi Csarnok on the east side of the park. (*See also chapters* **Sightseeing** *and* **Museums**.)

Óbuda Island

Óbudai/Hajógyári sziget
HÉV to Filatorigát, bus 142 or boat from Vigadó tér.
An island full of green areas and long slides just north of Árpád bridge (Árpád híd).

Károlyi Garden

Károlyi kert
M2 Astoria, M3 Kálvin tér. **Open** 8am-sunset daily.
Admission free. Dogs not allowed. **Map D4**
One of the few clean fenced-around playgrounds downtown. Sand box, slide, ride-on toys, two ball areas and no dogs.

József Nádor tér

M1, M2, M3 Deák tér. **Open** 7am-sunset daily.
Admission free. Dogs not allowed. **Map C4**
A great new playground complete with wooden castles, a ship with slides, swings, ride-on toys, a sandpit and a stream with tiny dams for watery experiments. The main drawback is the heavy traffic in the neighbourhood, particularly on weekdays.

Train & Boat Rides

You can go up to the Buda hills for some fresh air on the cogwheel train that departs across the street from the Budapest Hotel (M2 Moszkva tér then two stops on trams 18 or 56). If you take it all the way up to Széchenyi hill (Széchenyi hegy), which takes about 25 minutes, you can also walk across the park to the Children's Train which is operated by children, except for the engine drivers. This does not run very often, so it's best to check the schedule when you get there and spend waiting time in the neighbouring playground (*see also chapter* **Getting Around**).

Chairlift

Libegő
M2 Moszkva tér then bus 158. **Open** *summer* 9am-5pm, *winter* 9.30am-4pm, daily. **Fare** Ft100; Ft 60 children.
This ski-lift-style ride goes to the top of János hill (Jánoshegy). The view is best on the way down.

Sikló

I. Clark Ádám tér. Tram 19. **Fare** Ft180; Ft100 children. **Map B4**
The renovated funicular (Sikló) goes from Clark Ádám tér up to the Castle District. It's a short ride, but the view is great and the carriages are cool. (*See also chapter* **Sightseeing**.)

Boat Trips

There are several possibilities for boat rides on the Danube. Cheapest is the ferry between the Pest end of Petőfi bridge and Pünkösdfürdő in the north end of the city which picks up and drops off at each of the bridges and at Vigadó tér. This is free for under-4s and about Ft250 for everyone else (*see chapter* **Getting Around**). A sightseeing cruise costs about Ft600-Ft800 (half price under-14s) and offers a bigger boat and a tour guide. Call Ibusz or Tourinform for details (*see chapter* **Essential Information**).

Baby-sitters

Hungarian parents tend to use grandmothers as baby-sitters (always enthusiastic and free!). If you didn't bring granny with you, the agencies listed below offer the most reliable and best qualified child-minding services in town. You may also be able to arrange baby-sitting through your hotel.

Minerva Family Helping Service

Minerva Családsegítő Szolgálat
VIII. Szerdahelyi utca 10 (113 6365). Tram 28, 29. **Open** 24-hour answering machine. **No credit cards.** English spoken. **Map F4**
English-, German-, French- and Spanish-speaking baby sitters and full- or part-time nannies. Rate for sitting is Ft400 an hour.

Ficuka Kid Center

Baby Hotel & Baby-sitter Service
V. Váci utca 11/B, First Floor (138 2836). M1, 2, 3 Deák tér. **Open** 9am-5pm daily. **Prices** average Ft400 per

hour. **No credit cards.** English spoken. **Map C4**
Leave your kids here while you shop on Váci utca or call them for night-time baby-sitting.

Health

In an emergency call 104 or 311 1666 and ask for someone who speaks English. With sick children you can also go to Heim Pál Children's Hospital 24 hours a day.

Heim Pál Gyermekkórház

VIII. Üllői út 86 (314 1262). M3 Nagyvárad tér. **Map F6**

International Schools

Magyar-British International Elementary School
XI. Kamaraerdei út 12-14 (209 1218). Bus 87.
American International School of Budapest
XI. Kakukk utca 1/3 (175 8685). Bus 21.
International Kindergarten & School
XII. Konkoly Thege utca 19B. (175 8258). Bus 21, 90.

Shopping

Budapest has plenty of clothing and toy stores and children's sections in the bigger department stores. Here are some of the best places.

Matti

VII. Erzsébet körút 38 (122 2160) Tram 4, 6 to Wesselényi utca. **Open** 10am-6pm Mon-Fri; 9am-2pm Sat. **Credit** AmEx, DC, JCB, MC, V. Some English spoken. **Map D3**
A wide selection of toys, clothes and other baby and toddler equipment.

Totyi & Tini

V. Bárczy István utca 1-3 (117 9429). M1, M2, M3 Deák tér. **Open** 10am-6pm Mon-Fri; 10am-1pm Sat. **Credit** AmEx, DC, JCB, MC, V. Some English spoken. **Map C4**
Hungarian-designed dress-up and play clothes at reasonable prices.

Gondolkodó Toy Store

VI. Király utca 25 (322 8884). M1 Opera. **Open** 10am-6pm Mon-Fri; 9am-1.30pm Sat. **No credit cards.** Some English spoken. **Map D3**
Toys and games from the best chess software to beautiful wooden puzzles and local hero Rubik's latest brain-teasing inventions.

Burattino

IX. Ráday utca 47 (215 5621). M3 Kálvin tér. **Open** 10am-6pm Mon-Fri; 10am-1pm Sat. **No credit cards.** **Map D5**
A great selection of wooden blocks, trains and puzzles.

Puppet Show

V. Párizsi utca 3 (118 8453). M3 Ferenciek tere. **Open** 10am-6pm Mon-Fri; 10am-1pm Sat. **No credit cards.** **Map C4**
A little shop in a courtyard with lots of cute animal puppets. Friendly staff demonstrate how to make them move.

Fakopáncs Fajátékbolt

VIII. Baross utca 50 (137 8448.) Tram 4, 6 to Baross utca. **Open** 10am-6pm Mon-Fri; 9am-1pm Sat. **No credit cards.** Some English spoken. **Map E5**
Great wooden trains, garden tools and looms.

Film

Magyar movies are making a slow comeback against the wave of Hollywood fare served up in the city's new multiplexes. But one branch of the local industry is booming – Budapest has become the capital of Europorn.

Hungarians love movies. Although the local industry is small, Hungarians have always been interested in international cinema. Budapest has over 30 cinemas and movies from all over the world can be seen in subtitled versions. Along with mainstream US and UK films, European art house movies are extremely popular, but lately more and more Hungarian productions have found their way into the theatres. Many of these have been renovated and two new shopping-mall multiplex cinemas outside the city centre offer the biggest screens, the newest sound systems and the latest Hollywood blockbusters, many dubbed into Hungarian. Budapest cinemas are comfortable and, by western standards, relatively cheap, though for many Hungarians they have now become too expensive.

Although Hungarian cinema has attracted international attention with directors such as Miklós Jancsó, Márta Mészáros and István Szabó (whose *Mephisto* won the Oscar for best foreign-language film in 1982), most of the famous directors and cinematographers became successful after they left Hungary. Notable exiles include Mihály Kertész, aka Michael Curtiz, who went to Hollywood and made *Casablanca*, George Cukor (*The Women, A Star is Born*), Alexander Korda (*The Private Life of Henry VIII*), George Pal (*The Time Machine*), László Kovács, the cinematographer of *Easy Rider*, and Vilmos Zsigmond, who won an Oscar for his camerawork in Spielberg's *Close Encounters of the Third Kind*.

For film-makers who didn't leave the country, things have not been easy in the post-communist world. Inflation, alternative sources of entertainment and reduced leisure spending have hit the Hungarian movie business hard. Many older filmmakers feel blocked in dealing with commercialism and a distribution policy dominated by American product.

Financing a film in Hungary is difficult. There are better investments than film and sponsorships are not tax deductible. Many films are co-produced with other countries, mainly Germany and France (Hungary is also a popular location for international companies, many of which come to shoot here, keeping locals in work).

The curvaceous new **Corvin** *– page 184.*

Despite a few recent Hungarian box-office hits, the Hungarian film industry is still in a state of depression. Many filmmakers look back in nostalgia to the 1960s, when Hungarian films captured attention all over the world. Movies such as *Szegénylegények* (The Round-Up, 1965) by Miklós Jancsó, István Szabó's *Apa* (Father, 1966), Péter Bacsó's *A Tanu* (The Witness, 1968), or Károly Makk's *Szerelem* (Love, 1970) gave Hungary a reputation as one of the most important film centres in Europe. Recently, films like Róbert Koltai's *Sose Halunk Meg* (We Never Die, 1993), nominated for the Academy Awards in 1994, István Bujtor's *A Három Testőr Afrikában* (Three Guards In Africa, 1996), a crime comedy based on Jenő Rejtő's popular adventure novels, and *Csinibaba* (Dollybirds, 1996) by Péter Timár, a quirky musical that takes place in 1962, the first year of the 'goulash consolidation', have all been major successes. But they can't hide the fact that 88 per cent of all films released in Hungary are American products; only 5.6 per cent are Hungarian films.

Still, it seems that audiences are finding their way back to those cinemas which play Hungarian movies, co-productions are being made and several new studios are forming. Out of the 15-20 films which are made each year, more and more are finding distributors and making it to the big screen.

PROGRAMME INFORMATION

The best guide for US and British films are the cinema sections of the English-language weeklies *Budapest Week* and *Budapest Sun*, on sale in hotels and at newsstands. Both specify times and venues, although the *Week*'s is a clearer guide; both can also be unreliable at times. Also useful are the Hungarian magazines *Pesti Műsor* and *Pesti Est* – the latter can be picked up free at many cinemas – which often list features, special screenings and festivals that may not find their way into other programmes. The entries will state if a film is subtitled (*feliratos*) or dubbed (*szinkronizált*). Films in French (*francia*), German (*német*), Russian (*orosz*) and Italian (*olasz*) are also often screened in Budapest. Seats can be reserved ahead of time in most major venues.

Átrium – *best in Buda for Hollywood fare.*

In large theatres, seating is assigned by seat and row number. Note that *szék* is seat; *sor* is row; *bal oldalon* designates the left side, *jobb oldalon* the right side, *közép* the middle; and *erkély* is the balcony. In some Hungarian programmes, E refers to show times: n9 is 8.15pm, f9 is 8.30pm, h9 is 8.45pm. *De* means morning, *Du* is afternoon, *este* is evening and *éjjel* refers to late shows.

Cinemas

Átrium

II. Margit körút 55 (212 5398). Tram 4, 6. **Box office** from 10.30am, **last show** 8.30pm; 10pm Fri-Sat. **Tickets** Ft300-Ft380. **No credit cards.** One screen. Some English spoken. **Map A2**
One of the few large houses on the Buda side of the Danube and a major venue for mainstream Hollywood fare.

Broadway

VII. Károly körút 3 (322 0230). M2 Astória/tram 47, 49. **Box office**, **last show** 8.30pm. **Tickets** Ft350. **No credit cards.** One screen. No English spoken. **Map D4**
Formerly a film museum, this interestingly steep and semicircular 600-seater, built in the 1930s, specialises in French and Italian features and also screens Hollywood fare.

Metró

VI. Teréz körút 62 (153 4266). M3 Nyugati/tram 4, 6. **Box office** from 11am, **last show** 9pm; 10pm Fri-Sat. **Tickets** Ft400. **No credit cards.** Two screens. English spoken. **Map D2**
Budapest's most eclectic cinema, Metro's main screen features popular commercial releases, while its second screen (the *Kamaraterem*) mostly plays Hungarian-made movies and foreign art films. The ceiling of the main room is retractable and is often opened on hot summer nights. The Metro number is also the main Budapest office for cinema information, although this service is Hungarian-only.

Puskin

V. Kossuth Lajos utca 18 (118 6464). M3 Astoria. **Box office** from 11am, **last show** 9pm; 11pm Fri. **Tickets** Ft300-Ft380. **No credit cards.** Two screens. Some English spoken. **Map D4**
This 420-seat house features major Hollywood releases. Its second screen plays previously released movies and art films – both Hungarian and western-made. Constructed at the turn of the century, its upstairs lobby is not as ornate as the nearby **Uránia**'s, but is worth visiting.

Uránia

VIII. Rákóczi út 21 (118 8955). M2 Astória/bus 7, 7A, 78. **Box office** from 11.30am daily, **last show** 8.15pm Mon-Thur, Sun; 10.15pm Fri-Sat. **Tickets** Ft400. **No credit cards.** One screen. Some English spoken. **Map D4**
Built in 1896 as a theatre, the Uránia is one of the grandest cinemas in the country – gold chandeliers and Persian carpets decorate its mezzanine waiting area. Today it is a 684-seat venue for contemporary movies. It gets stifling in the summer.

Multiplexes

Corvin Budapest Filmpalota

VIII. Corvin köz 1 (333 5707). M3 Ferenc körút/tram 4, 6. **Box office** from 10am, **last show** 11pm. **Tickets** Ft300-Ft500. **No credit cards.** Six screens. Some English spoken. **Map E5**

Örökmozgó – 'A szék *on the* jobb oldalon *of the third* sor, *please, for the f9 show this* este.'

Renovated and updated with the newest techniques in projection and sound, this extremely comfortable cinema is also the new venue of the Magyar Filmszemle (Hungarian Film Festival). The building was a headquarters for the resistance during the 1956 revolution (*see* **title of box** page XXX). There is a café and a branch of Odeon Video Rental (*see below*).

Hollywood Multiplex

Duna Plaza, XIII. Váci út 178 (465 1165/66/67/68). M1 Gyöngyösi út. **Box Office** from 10am, **last show** 10.15pm. **Tickets** Ft300-Ft430. **No credit cards.** Nine screens. Some English spoken.

The more central of the two new purpose-built out-of-town multiplexes. It shows mainly mainstream blockbuster movies and has all the charm of the cheese counter in your local supermarket.

Art Cinemas

Most art houses are small venues where seating is not assigned and specialise in non-commercial films. Peter Greenaway, John Cassavetes and Hal Hartley are especially popular in Hungary.

Blue Box

IX. Kinizsi utca 28 (218 0983). M3 Ferenc körút. **Box office** 3pm, **last show** 9pm. **Tickets** Ft200-Ft250. **No credit cards.** One screen, two in summer. Some English spoken. **Map D5**

Former nightclub that now screens everything from Tom & Jerry to Tarkovsky. Seating is removed for occasional events such as jazz concerts and raves. In the summer they also show movies in the garden, convivially equipped with a bar.

Cirko-gejzir

VIII. Lőrinc pap tér 3 (266 1920). M3 Kálvin tér. **Box office** 6pm, **last show** 9pm; 10.30pm Fri-Sat. **Tickets** Ft150-Ft200. **No credit cards.** One screen. Some English spoken. **Map D5**

A tiny cinema with about 30 assorted and mostly uncomfortable chairs and sofas and a programme of obscure independent movies, especially Russian ones. Small bar in the front. Occasional photo exhibitions.

Hunnia

VII. Erzsébet körút 26 (322 3471). M2 Blaha Lujza tér/tram 4, 6. **Box office** from 4.30pm, **last show** 9pm; 10pm Fri-Sat. **Tickets** Ft270. **No credit cards.** One screen. No English spoken. **Map E3**

The Hunnia has only one screen, but presents a varied line-up of Hungarian and foreign films that changes daily. It's owned by the Hunnia film studio (one of Hungary's major movie-makers) and is a main venue for Hunnia releases. The café on the second floor is open from 3pm-midnight and is a popular meeting place no matter what movies are showing.

Művész

VI. Teréz körút 30 (332 6726). M3 Nyugati/tram 4, 6. **Box office** from 4.30pm, **last show** 9pm; 10.30pm Fri-Sat. **Tickets** Ft380. **No credit cards.** Five screens. Some English spoken. **Map D2**

One of the most stylish art cinemas in the city. Its five halls feature previously released classics and contemporary art films. There is a restaurant in the basement, the Federico, after Fellini. This cinema is popular, so get there early.

Örökmozgó Filmmúzeum

VII. Erzsébet körút 39 (342 2167). Tram 4, 6 to Wesselényi utca. **Box office** from 4.30pm, **last show** 8.30pm, daily. **Tickets** Ft250. **No credit cards.** One screen and video gallery. Some English spoken. **Map D3**

Known for its eclectic weekly schedule of everything from silent classics to documentaries. Foreign films in this small house are often played in their original sound with simultaneous Hungarian translation via headsets. There is a coffee shop in the lobby, and an adjoining book store with a few English titles.

Szindbád

XIII. Szent István körút 16 (131 8573). M3 Nyugati/tram 4, 6. **Box office** open 3pm, **last show** 8.30pm. **Tickets**

Hardcore Hungary – A Star is Porn

While most Hungarian movie producers struggle along on a shoestring, one branch of the local film industry is booming. With over 150 sex films a year produced in Hungary, close to 20 per cent of the European total, Budapest has become the capital of Europorn

In the old days, films and magazines had to go under the eye of the communist censor and a glimpse of breast was about as spicy as it got in Hungarian cinemas. Serious porn, brought home by individuals from Austria or Germany, was passed around in samizdat fashion. But after the change of system, a large, greasy photo-journalist by the name of István Kovács spotted a market and began recruiting for his Luxx Video titles.

Kovács' tiny, seedy office on Baross utca, close to Rákóczi tér – the long-time home of Budapest's downmarket whores – is a museum to hardcore Hungary. By his desk are signed photos from his stable of Hungarian porn stars. Downstairs in the shop, films are available featuring Hungarians in action with all manner of humans, animals and domestic appliances.

But like many in the business, Kovács does most of his work as a fixer for the foreign directors who are increasingly choosing Budapest as their location. The reasons are obvious – low cost and attractive venues, cheap film crews and a large pool of attractive, young Hungarians willing to do almost anything for a wad of Deutschmarks.

Film-makers have made the most of the available resources. Porn films have been shot in the famous baths of the Gellért Hotel. American director Patrick Collins was even able to rent the number 18 tram, which wound its way through the Tabán in broad daylight, as a location for his film *Budasex*. The venue which caused the biggest uproar was the Festetics Palace, at Keszthely on the Balaton, a 300-room Baroque pile that is a popular destination for school trips and tourist parties. This was used as the set for Italian director Gianfranco Romagnoli's porn version of the life of spy Mata Hari.

Romagnoli, a caricature of a porn director with his shades and oversized sheepskin coat, is the man behind Hungary's most successful porn export – Anita Rinaldi. She began her working life as a hairdresser in the industrial town Dunaújváros, before starring in a porn version of Snow White which also featured real-life Hungarian dwarfs. But, with the help of her boyfriend Romagnoli, Rinaldi has become a star of higher-class Italian porn and posed for photo spreads in *Penthouse* and *Hustler*. Italians are no strangers to Hungarian porn stars – Cicciolina, who went on to further fame as an Italian Radical Party MP and the muse of American artist Jeff Koons, began life as Ilona Staller of Budapest.

Unlike Cicciolina, Rinaldi has stayed in Hungary where she and Romagnoli run Touch Me Productions – yet another company recruiting fresh talent, setting up shoots for foreign directors, and continuing to ensure that at least in this one segment of the film industry, Hungary stays ahead of the pack.

Ft300. **No credit cards**. Two screens. No English spoken. **Map C2**
Right by the Vígszínház, not as elegant within as it looks from outside, but a decent two-screen art movie house with an interesting programme of independent films. They also have a small video rental outlet. Air-conditioned.

Tabán

I. Krisztina körút 87-89 (156 8162). Tram 18 to Krisztina tér/bus 5, 78, 105 and red 4. **Box office** from 4.30pm-5.30pm, **last show** 8pm, daily. **Tickets** Ft200. **No credit cards**. One screen. Some English spoken. **Map A3**
Nestled in the old Serbian quarter of the city, this tiny theatre usually plays several English-language gems a week. German and French films also feature. Sound and picture quality are never great, but the lobby and café were recently renovated. They also have a video rental library, including a handful of English-language movies.

Toldi Stúdió Mozi

V. Bajcsy-Zsilinszky út 36-38 (111 2809). M3 Arany János. **Box office** from 3.30pm-4.30pm, **last show** 9.30pm, daily. **Tickets** Ft340. **No credit cards**. Two screens. Some English spoken. **Map C3**

Large venue for contemporary art releases (from Hartley to Tarantino) and Hungarian features both old and new. There is a small bar and a gift shop (posters, books, postcards, CDs). In October of every year, György Horváth, the former head of the Filmszemle, organises the Titanic International Filmpresence Festival here, a priceless showing of new arthouse and cult movies.

Video Rental

Budapest has many video rental shops. Most English-language videos are dubbed into Hungarian, but older releases are often available in subtitled form. Video boxes will indicate whether a film is dubbed (*szinkronizált*) or subtitled (*feliratos*) from English (*angol*). Any of the city's video shops will have some titles in English to choose from.

British Council Library

VII. Benczúr utca 26 (321 4039/37/38). M1 Bajza utca. **Open** 11am-6pm Mon-Thur; 11am-5pm Fri; 9.30am-noon Sat. **Map E2**

Step this way for contemporary art releases – the **Toldi Stúdió Mozi** *page 186.*

Membership (Ft1,000 per year) is essential for access to this extensive video library. Superb selection of British TV shows: everything from documentaries to sitcoms.

English Language Video Club and Shop

VI. Zichy Jenö út 44 (302 0291). Tram 4, 6 to Oktogon. **Open** *12pm-8pm Sun-Thur; 12pm-10pm Fri-Sat.* Membership Ft2,000. **Rental** Ft150-Ft500 per video per night. **Map D3**

A wide range of Hollywood blockbusters, independent films and European art house movies. Offering over 1,000 films in English, or with English subtitles, this is definitely the best place to rent movies that were never shown in Hungary or have not yet made it to Hungarian screens. Also a selection of children's movies in English.

Odeon

XIII. Hollán Ernő utca 7 (131 6776). Tram 4, 6 to Jászai Mari ter. **Open** *2pm-9pm daily.* **Rental** Ft150 per tape per day (plus refundable Ft1,500 deposit). Some English spoken. **Map C2**

Original soundtrack videos of US and UK feature films. It's also highly regarded for its large collection of Hungarian classics subtitled into English. Videos can be watched in a viewing room on the premises.
Branch: Corvin Multiplex, *VIII. Corvin köz 1 (333 5707).*

Film Festivals

Magyar Filmszemle

c/o Filmunio Hungary, VI. Városligeti fasor 38 (351 7760/61/fax 351 7766).

This is the major event in the Hungarian film calendar. Each February at the Corvin, the Magyar Filmszemle (Hungarian Film Festival) shows feature films, documentaries and shorts that have been produced in the previous year. There's a competition with one big prize for the best movie, plus several smaller awards. Some movies are also shown outside the competition. Fear not: simultaneous translation by earphone is available.

Invisible Film Festival

contact: Tarek Kaszim at Deiss Kaszim Film, Montázs 2000, V. Október 6, utca 14 (131 5402/fax 131 5402).

This eclectic annual event, where no prizes are awarded, shows a huge variety of films and videos from Hungary and the rest of the world. The worthy intention is to give mostly young film-makers the opportunity to exhibit their works to a wider audience and 'build a new kind of distribution network'.

Mediawave

Festival office H-9028 Győr, Soproni út 45 (449 444/328 888/fax 449 445/415 285).

Otherwise known as the International Festival of Visual Arts in Győr, 125 km west of Budapest, and basically characterised by productions from central and eastern Europe. The festival runs every year for five days at the end of April, shows independent films and videos, and claims to be a festival, where 'artists with different ways of thinking and free thoughts' come together. An international jury awards a main prize. Independent of categories, special prizes are also presented. There are exhibitions, lectures, concerts and an 'à la carte' room, where any works entered in the festival can be viewed on request.

Film Studies

Színház- és Filmművészeti Főiskola

(Academy of Drama and Film)
H-1088, Budapest, Szentkirályi utca 32/a, (138 4855/fax 138 4560). Head of Film faculty: János Zsombolyai.

The Academy of Drama and Film is where directors such as István Szabó and cinematographers such as Vilmos Zsigmond studied the craft of film-making, it offers the only university-level education for dramatic and film arts in Hungary. In 1991 the Academy opened an International class, which, for an annual student fee of $10,000 (entrance exam costs $100), teaches a four-year course in film and TV directing and cinematography.

Gay & Lesbian

Budapest's brilliant baths and steamy saunas are only the most unique feature of a steadily more visible scene.

Knees bend, arms stretch, **Ca-pe-lla***!*

Lesbian and gay life in Budapest is sometimes referred to as a body with only a half-visible face. The visible features are the nightlife, the sex industry, annual film festivals, candlelight march and 'pink picnics'. In these, for even the 'trendy' straight crowd, being *meleg* (the Hungarian word for gay – literally 'warm') is cool. And, of course the most unique feature of Budapest's profile is its fantastic assortment of baths and saunas.

While most of the visible gay and lesbian life in Budapest has emerged since 1989, Hungarians wouldn't say that there is a lesbian, gay or bisexual history in the country, but there is. Now unquestionably claimed as a lesbian is last generation's female sex symbol, Katalin Karády, Hungary's answer to Marlene Dietrich. Her life ended in obscurity in New York, where she died unknown and working as a waitress. People still sometimes leave flowers at the memorial plaque outside her old apartment at V. Nyári Pál utca 9. Other historical individuals said to have had homosexual relations include writers Péter Nádor, Erzsébet Galgóczy and Attila József, and actress Hilda Gobbi.

Yet despite Hungary's self-perception as liberal and tolerant, openly gay individuals are hard to find. In this poor society, most sexual minorities still live in fear of losing their jobs or housing, or of family scandals, and choose to live a double life. Despite relatively liberal laws, discrimination remains active and for the most part unchallenged.

In Hungarian culture sexism is, in any case, fundamental. Men must be masculine and unaffected, and women must be emotional and an object for the pleasure of men. You will rarely see men touch beyond a sportsmanlike handshake and kiss on each cheek, or manly pat on the back. If you try and hug a gay man in public, be prepared to be pushed away, only because it is not socially accepted. Women, on the other hand, are often seen being affectionate with each other.

Still, Hungarian lesbians, gay men and bisexual people have not only come to accept themselves, but are also beginning to develop structures and networks, and prepare for the integration of sexual minorities into the social, political, economic, and overall life of Hungary.

Watch out for situations where westerners are perceived as walking wallets. Use common sense: put your money in a safe place if you go into the darkrooms at the bars, and watch out for people who sit down with you, order a drink, then walk away leaving you to pay. Yet most lesbians and gay men in Budapest come from the heart and are genuinely nice people. Budapesters are used to foreigners, and like them, and most everyone under 30 speaks at least a little English.

For the best information about events, either pick up a copy of **Mások** or **Labrisz**, or call **Háttér** (*see below* **Organisations**), or check out the gay website at *http://ourworld.compuserve.com/homepages/budapest*. This houses listings of current events, clubs, services, and practical information in Budapest (in German, English and Hungarian).

Mások
1461 Budapest, PO Box 388 (266 9959).
Published as a monthly magazine since 1989 and available at newsstands, especially those near the train stations. Contains articles, information on current events, personals, and contact information for resources and services.

Labrisz
1554 Budapest, PO Box 50 (312 5844).
Hungary's first lesbian magazine, published bi-monthly since September of 1996.

Bars

Action Bár
*V. Magyar utca 42 (266 9148). M3 Kálvin tér/tram 47,
49.* **Open** *9pm-4am daily.* **Admission** *Ft500 minimum
charge.* **No credit cards.** **Map D4**
Popular bar with the darkest darkroom in town and lots of
traffic. Condoms sometimes available from the bartender –
it depends if he likes you. The Ft500 'consumption charge'
must be paid on the way out – even if you haven't drunk
Ft500's worth.

Angel Club
*VII. Szövetség utca 33 (no phone). Tram 4, 6/nightbus
6E, 7E.* **Open** *10pm until daybreak Thur-Sun.*
Admission *Ft300 members, Ft500 non-members.*
Annual membership Ft2,000. **No credit cards.** **Map E3**
Since 1989 the Angel Club has been the disco of choice for
most gay people and tourists – this is its fourth incarnation.
Disco, shows and various programmes every Friday and
Sunday. Saturday is men only. Downstairs there's a well-lit
basement bar, overly crowded cave-like disco and dark room
(active on Saturdays). Upstairs there's a restaurant and a
stage for drag shows. Friday is favoured by dykes. Sunday
is generally a mixed crowd with a large straight clientèle
seeking a gay environment.

Bíbor-Club
*VIII. Üllői út 34 (no phone). M3 Ferenc körút/nightbus
6E.* **Open** *9am-7pm, 9pm-4am daily.* **Admission** *Ft500
when there's a show.* **No credit cards.** **Map D5**
Gay-owned, straight-staffed bar with the atmosphere of a
club, private video booths for two, and lots of trade. Mixed
public during the day, men only from 9pm to 4am.

Capella
V. Belgrád rakpart 23 (118 6231). Tram 2. **Open** *7pm-
2am Mon-Tue; 5pm-4am Wed-Sun.* **Admission** *Ft400 at
weekends or when there's a show.* **No credit cards.**
Map C5
Rivalling the Angel club in popularity, a cellar labyrinth
with disco and drag shows. Basement atmosphere with an
eclectic mix of wall art, black light corridors and soft porn
portraits hung indiscriminately around. Located on the
Danube just beyond the cruising strip. Rarely gets going
before midnight. On Wednesdays there's a 1am strip show.

Darling
V. Szép utca 1 (no phone). M3 Astória. **Open** *7pm-5am
daily.* **No cover charge.** **No credit cards.** **Map D4**
A small cosy bar seating a few downstairs. Upstairs are
bench-lined walls for intimate video viewing, with a larger
video room behind the bar. Tapes are changed monthly.

A meleg *welcome at the* **Mystery Bár-Klub**.

Lokál
*VII. Kertész utca 31 (no phone). Tram 4, 6/nightbus 6,
7E.* **Open** *10pm-4am daily; drag shows Fri, Sat,*
Admission *Ft500.* **No credit cards.** **Map D3**
Budapest's oldest gay bar run by transvestite personality
Terry Black and newly redefining itself as a drag club open
to straight clientèle. Lots of hustler traffic.

Mystery Bár-Klub
*V. Nagysándor József utca 3 (312 1436). M3 Arany
János utca.* **Open** *9pm-4am Mon-Sat.* **No cover charge.**
No credit cards. **Map C3**
This was the second gay bar to open in Budapest and offers
a low music, friendly sit-down environment to meet your
friends and chat.

No Limit Club Café
*V. Semmelweis utca 10 (no phone). M3 Astoria/tram 47,
49.* **Open** *10am-5am.* **No cover charge.** **No credit
cards.** **Map D4**
Elegant hustler bar with club rooms for intimate meetings
between friends and rented acquaintances. The merchandise
is the only reason to visit.

Eating Out

Amstel River Café
V. Párisi utca 6 (267 0285). Tram 2. **Open** *9am-11pm
Mon-Fri.* **Average** *Ft1,500.* **No credit cards.** **Map C4**
Cosy pub and restaurant on the Danube *korzó* with a gay
staff and clientèle, beer on tap, plus tourists attracted to the
outside tables. A handy rest stop on the Danube Cruise.

Club 93 Pizza
*VIII. Vas utca 2 (no phone). M2 Blaha Lujza tér/tram 4,
6.* **Open** *11am-midnight.* **Average** *Ft700.* **No credit
cards.** **Map D4**
A popular pizza place that's gay-owned, gay-staffed, and frequented by local lesbians and gay men. A nice place to meet
your friends before going out.

Fenyőgyöngye Vendéglő
*II. Szépvölgyi út 155 (325 5006). Tram 17 to Kolossy
tér/bus 65 to terminal.* **Open** *noon-10.30pm daily.*
Average *Ft800.* **Credit** *AmEx, MC, V.*
A little far out but easily accessible from the centre of the
city at Hármashatár Hill. Everybody is welcome but gay people get a bit more courtesy here.

Saunas

See also chapters **Baths** *and* **Sport & Fitness**.

Gellért Gyógyfürdő
*XI. Kelenhegyi út 4 (166 6166). Trams 18, 19, 47, 49 or
bus 7 to Gellért tér.* **Open** *6am-6pm Mon-Sun.*
Admission *Ft1,200; Ft600 concs. Mixed.* **Map C5**
Proceed to the last door on the right, give in your receipt, collect towel, turn right, go upstairs or downstairs to dressing
cabins. Dry sauna, steam bath, three pools of varying temperatures and massage. Gorgeous Art Nouveau interior.
Clientèle includes tourists, expats and hustlers. Frequented
by straights, too, so discretion should be used.

Király Gyógyfürdő
II. Fő utca 84 (201 4392). M2 Batthyány tér. **Open** *men
6.30am-7pm Mon, Wed, Fri; women 6.30am-7pm Tue,
Thur, Sat.* **Admission** *Ft300.* **Map B2**
This is the second nicest original Turkish bath. Also quite
carnal with the tourists, trade and elderly. Dry sauna, steam
bath, three pools of varying temps and massage. Take swimming gear.

*Girls' night out – **Club 93 Pizzeria** page 189.*

Lukács Gyógyfürdő és Strandfürdő
II. Frankel Leó út 25-29 (326 1695). Tram 4, 6. **Open** 6am-7pm Mon-Sat; 6am-5pm Sun. **Admission** Ft300. **Map B1**
Seek the 'Mud Bath' (*iszapfürdő*). Wild action at dusk. Filthy water. Afterwards, cruise the park between the Lukács and the Danube. Cruising continues in Germanus Gyula Park to the south. Take swimming gear and towel.

Palatinus Strandfürdő
XIII. Margitsziget (340 4505). Bus 26 from Nyugati station. **Open** 8am-7pm daily. **Admission** Ft170.
Nude sunbathing occurs on top of the changing rooms, and is practised almost exclusively by gays.

Rác Gyógyfürdő
I. Hadnagy utca 8-10 (156 1322). Tram 18, 19, 47, 49. **Open** *women* 6am-6pm Mon, Wed, Fri; *men* 6am-6pm Tue, Thur, Sat.* **Admission** Ft300. **Map B5**
Terribly gay, lots of steamy sex among the war veterans, hustlers and tourists. Dry sauna, steam bath and three pools of varying temperatures. Take swimming gear and wait in the hallway for your number to be called.

Cruising areas

The Danube Cruise, running along the Pest embankment between Vigadó tér and the statue of Petőfi near Erzsébet Bridge, is active day and night with locals, foreigners and hustler trafficking. Hustlers are mostly transient youth from neighbouring countries trying to make a buck on their way to the west, or students supplementing their income. Generally those in modest attire are independent novices, while flashier clothing and cellular phones signal the veteran or pimped variety. Rates run about Ft 5,000. Not everyone looking for action will be a hustler, and watch out for police passport checks, looking for illegal transients.

Also known for continuous activity is Vérmező park near Déli station, though in the daytime it's mostly dog-walkers. Less populated with hustlers and better for meeting locals are the Germanus Gyula Park at the north entrance of Margaret Bridge in Buda and the Népliget in the area around the Planetarium. Both are only active at night.

Travel

Cruise Victory Co.
V. Váci utca 9 (267 3805). M1 Vörösmarty tér. **Open** 9am-5pm Mon-Fri. **Credit** AmEx, DC, EC, JCB, MC, V. **Map C4**
Member of the International Lesbian and Gay Travel Association.

Pipacs Minipanzió
V. Kossuth Lajos utca 11-12 (117 7394). M3 Ferenciek tere. **Rates** *double* DM85-DM110. **No credit cards.** **Map C4**
Small comfortable guest house in the heart of the city. Gay owned and operated. Breakfast served.

Homosexual Organisations

Habeas Corpus Jogsegély
1360 Budapest, PO Box 1 (0640 630 036).
Group addressing legal issues of sexuality in Hungary.

Háttér Baráti Társaság a Melegekért
1554 Budapest, PO Box 50 (302 5080).
Gay, lesbian and bisexual telephone hotline, operated daily from 6pm to 11pm. The largest and most active all-volunteer gay, lesbian and bisexual groups in Hungary.

Kesergay
1066 Budapest, Zichy Jenő utca 29 (312 5844).
Hungarian Jewish lesbian and gay social group.

Öt Kenyér
1461 Budapest, PO Box 25 (312 5844).
Lesbian and gay Christian group. Alternates social and prayer meetings every other week.

HIV/AIDS Organisations

Anonim AIDS-segélyszolgálat
XI. Karolina út 35/b (166 9283).
Confidential HIV test site. Some English spoken.

AIDS Telefonsegély
(166 9283) **Staffed** 9am-8pm Mon-Sat.
AIDS information hotline. Some English spoken.

Sex Shops

Intim Center
V. Károly körút 14 (117 0918). M2 Astoria. **Open** 9am-8pm Mon-Fri; 9am-6pm Sat. **No credit cards.** Some English spoken. **Map D4**
Wide selection of toys and magazines. Twenty video cabins, rented by the hour or half-hour. Stocks water-based lubricants.

Apolló Video Shop
VI. Teréz körút 3 (342 1911). M1 Oktogon. **Open** 10am-8pm daily. **No credit cards.** English spoken. **Map D2**
Air-conditioned video screening room and shop with a principally gay clientele. Large video selection.

Intim Lapüzlet és Videotéka
VII. Dob utca 17 (no phone). M1, M2, M3 Deák tér/tram 47, 49. **Open** 10am-6pm Mon-Fri; 10am-2pm Sat. **No credit cards.** **Map D4**
Shop and video-screening rooms with mixed clientèle. Wide variety of selections, and also known to keep water-based lubricants in stock.

Media

Sleaze and self-censorship infect a press only 'partly free'.

For a country with a population of only around ten million, Hungary has an enormous selection of periodicals, with no less than 12 national dailies competing for market share. In broadcast media, by contrast, diversity has been sorely lacking, with only three national broadcasters, all state-run. This, however, may finally be changing with the 1997 privatisation of television frequencies.

But the free press is perhaps one of the biggest disappointments of Hungary's post-communist transition. For all their new-found liberties, the country's news organisations have changed merely in the addition of capitalist greed to their traits of gross political subjectivity and bloated self-importance. The result is an industry still widely distrusted and more corrupt than ever.

The first democratically elected government, a conservative coalition, blocked privatisation and interfered horribly with state-run electronic media. Their meddlings climaxed in a scandalous purge from national radio and television of supposedly Communist elements (liberals who worked there before 1990). The conservatives' successors, the Socialists, simply proved more sophisticated in manipulating the national media.

Blatant interference has disappeared but self-censorship remains rampant among media executives and editors with close personal connections to leading politicians. Equally troubling is the corruption of editors and reporters for financial gain. Scan through Hungarian dailies for an otherwise normal-looking news article bearing a small '[x]' at the bottom. The [x] denotes that the article, likely covering some boring corporate announcement, was paid for. Despite such advertorial being widespread, a recent survey found that fewer than 13 per cent of Hungarian readers know what that little [x] means. What's more, it is an open secret that companies can have the [x] dropped if they merely fork out a bit more. National television and radio are known to follow similar practices.

With these flaws in mind, Freedom House, the international press watch foundation based in New York, graded Hungary's press in 1997 as only 'partly free' for the second year in a row.

The 1997 sale of two national television frequencies and two national radio frequencies is one step in the direction of a media independent from government. At press time, the dust was still settling on this deal, but the next parliamentary elec-

tions (due before September 1998) should provide the first true test of this new status quo. Still, it will probably take a generation for Hungarian media to change, as old personal contacts dating back to before the change of systems are finally eroded by the arrival of younger blood.

The Press

Newspapers

Népszabadság
The most widely read national daily, once the official mouthpiece of the Communists, remains aligned with today's Socialist Party. *Népszabadság* claims a readership of over one million, a dubious figure implying it is read by one-tenth of the population. Dry-looking and the closest thing Hungary has to a paper of record, it resembles the French *Le Monde*.

Magyar Hírlap
Bright and colourful, the *Hírlap* has been one of the largest and most influential dailies since 1968. Closely aligned with the Alliance of Free Democrats (SZDSZ), it has a liberal attitude and a sharp focus on economy and finance. Published by the Swiss Marquard group.

Népszava
In the former regime, 122-year-old *Népszava* was the organ of the trade unions and remained relatively independent. Sustained by a loyal but ageing readership, it is close to the Socialist Party but more critical than *Népszabadság*.

Világgazdaság, Napi Gazdaság
Financial dailies that cover business and money market issues and are often the least biased sources of information on the government's political and economic policies.

Nemzeti Sport
The national sports daily, and Hungary's third most widely read paper, it is heavily weighted toward football coverage with a decided bias in favour of Ferencváros (*see* chapter **Sport & Fitness**).

Mai Nap, Blikk, Kurír
The tabloid triumvirate. *Mai Nap* is the smallest and most serious, *Blikk* the most colourful and wacky and *Kurír* has the most gossip.

Expressz
Daily classifieds paper and the ultimate place to look for everything from flats to pets. Budapesters, aware the paper is available the afternoon before official publication, queue outside the offices to get the first crack at bargains.

Periodicals

Heti Világgazdaság (HVG)
Hungary's version of *The Economist*, covering politics, economics, finance and corporate news. The most influential Hungarian weekly for more than two decades.

All the news you can stand on Váci utca.

Magyar Narancs

Launched by FIDESZ (Federation of Young Democrats) in 1990, *Magyar Narancs* ('Hungarian Orange') is now owned by one of Hungary's largest banks. Fresh language, alternative views, comprehensive listings and an unprecedented tolerance toward minority, gay and drug issues have won it a loyal, young readership. It has continually shrunk in size, however, as it struggles under persistent losses.

Nők Lapja

Women's magazine that is also Hungary's best-selling periodical. It offers a mixture of fashion, recipes and celebrity gossip with the occasional serious article on women's issues.

Listings Magazines

Pesti Műsor

What's-on weekly with comprehensive listings (some in English) of theatre, films, museums, galleries and concerts.

Pesti Est

Pocket-sized, useful and free from cinemas and bars around town. The emphasis is on films, concerts and nightlife.

Foreign Press

International newspapers and magazines are available at hotels, from vendors on Váci utca, in the Castle District and at some kiosks. Apart from the *Guardian International* and *International Herald Tribune*, only yesterday's papers will be available. Foreign dailies run out by early afternoon.

English-language Publications

Budapest Week

The oldest independent English-language paper in the former Soviet Bloc, around since 1991. The *Week* has steadily deteriorated but is still the only place to find off-beat features about life in Hungary, though often these are laughably ill-informed. Contains the best English-language films listings.

Budapest Sun

Once intensely American in its focus, the *Sun* has done an about-face since being acquired by Britain's Associated Newspapers. It now resembles a British regional paper, with heavy emphasis on crime and scandal, a fawning social column, and piss-poor cultural coverage.

Budapest Business Journal

The most professional, and only profitable, of the three English-language papers in Budapest. The *BBJ* is part of a chain that also covers Prague and Warsaw. Its coverage focuses on economic, financial and business issues.

The Hungarian Quarterly

Academic journal in English with essays on Hungarian history, politics, art, literature and current affairs, plus book, theatre and film reviews and the occasional chunk of reportage. Usually contains something interesting. It's available in Budapest bookstores or call 175 6722, fax 118 8297 or e-mail *hungq@hungary.com* for subscription information.

E-mail & Fax Services

Hungary Around the Clock

An English news digest compiled from the Hungarian press and faxed or e-mailed to subscribers by 9am each business day. Subscriptions are available at an introductory rate of $150 for three months, or $450 for a year, by e-mailing *info@kingfish.hu* or by calling 351 7142. To receive this discount, you must mention the codename 'Tom'.

Econews

A daily economic and business news service in English published by the Hungarian state news agency, MTI. Monthly rates are $87.50 for daily delivery by post and $187.50 for delivery by e-mail. To subscribe, call or fax 201 2690.

Hungary Report/HAC News

Free weekly batch of features and columns in English e-mailed to subscribers. Regular topics include politics, history, arts and recipes. For a fee, a weekly digest of political, economic, corporate and other news from Hungary is also available. Subscriptions are $25 for three months, $60 for one year. E-mail *hungary-on@isys.hu*.

Television

The tube options for ordinary Hungarians continue to grow. Two new private stations were about to begin broadcasting as this book went to press. They are owned by Scandinavian Broadcast System and European broadcasting group CLT-Ufa. Already existing channels include:

TV1

The main state-run channel. Besides the daily news programme *Híradó*, TV1 features minority, religious and children's programmes, soap operas, quiz and talk shows, documentaries and dubbed foreign movies in the evening.

TV2

With its terrestrial frequency sold, TV2 was set at press time to become a satellite broadcast channel, continuing its live coverage of Parliament, political debates and sports.

Cable

Each Budapest district has one or two cable companies. The basic menu of unencrypted channels includes CNN, Sky News, NBC Europe, Eurosport and TNT/Cartoon Network in English, plus an assortment of European channels.

Many of Budapest's districts boast a local cable channel, though some are limited to listing what other cable channels are available. Other local cable broadcasts include: **Duna TV**, a public satellite channel beaming news and cultural programming across the country and to ethnic

Forbidden Frequency

'Tilos' means forbidden, which is exactly what Tilos Rádió was when it began broadcasting. Its founders came from the same student groups that spawned the Young Democrats (FIDESZ) and *Magyar Narancs*, and Tilos aimed to be community radio for a young intellectual crowd yearning for something different. It has spurned commercial sponsorship and worked hard to remain in touch with its audience.

Launched in spring 1991, Tilos was too late to be banned by Communist officials. But that didn't stop it getting in trouble. The first democratically elected government restricted the distribution of new radio and television frequencies as it wrangled with the opposition over a media law. The few frequencies it did award were dealt out for political or financial reasons. Exasperated by its inability to get a licence, Tilos took to the air as a pirate station, infuriating officials not only by defying the law, but also with a mix of music and politics that was shocking to the crusty conservatives in power. Thus followed two years of dodging the law. Usually transmitting from a mobile studio set up in someone's apartment, the Tilos crew often had to shut down and escape through a window as police, homing in on their signal, arrived to raid the building.

In August 1993, Tilos stopped broadcasting to seek a legal place on the air after the government announced a limited distribution of new frequencies. Vengeful officials spurned their application. There followed a bitter debate within Tilos over whether to return as a pirate station or continue to pursue a legal frequency.

In the end, those longing to make the station a more stable and professional entity won out – and Tilos finally became a legal radio broadcaster on 1 September 1995.

Tilos can be heard on 98.0 FM nightly from 10pm to 10am, a refreshingly eclectic change from the mainstream rubbish that mostly clogs the Hungarian airwaves. Evenings begin with public service programmes, often topical discussions of current events or cultural, minority or gay issues. Purely music programming kicks in later with theme nights covering anything from Gypsy folk to 'alternative' rock and avant-dance. DJs are mostly Hungarian, though Russian, Serb and American DJs each have weekly programmes.

Keep an eye on listings magazines and street posters for announcements of Tilos Rádió benefit concerts. These are popular, unpredictable and benefit a worthy cause.

Hungarian communities in neighbouring states; **M-Sat**, which, apart from dubbed Benny Hill and Muppets, also shows English Premiership highlights on Monday night; **Szív TV** and **TV3** which show dubbed foreign films and low-budget local programming; and **ZTV**, a 24-hour music video channel backed by Time-Warner.

Radio

Apart from **Tilos Rádió** (*see above* **Forbidden Frequency**), the FM band is mostly crammed with rubbish. Apart from state-run broadcasts filled with endless talk, you'll otherwise find a boring blend of trashy pop, dance mixes and Hungarian rock from stations such as **Sztár Rádió** (92.9 FM), **Danubius Rádió** (103.3 FM), **Juventus Rádió** (89.5 FM). Each has news in Hungarian every hour. **Radio Bridge** (102.1 FM) provides Voice of America's English-language news daily at 8pm and midnight.

The state-run broadcasters are **Kossuth** (66.14-72.98 FM; 540 and 1,116 AM; 6,025 SW) from 4.30am to midnight daily with hourly news in Hungarian and foreign-language programming for ethnic minorities; **Petőfi** (66.02-72.77 FM; 873 and 1,350 AM) with news, pop music, sports and political discussion; and **Bartók** (67.04-72.08 FM) which plays classical music, both canned and live.

BBC World Service

The following are the best frequencies for reception. All times are GMT.
3am-7.30am 1,323 kHz SW
9am-11.30pm 1,323 kHz SW
3am-7.30am 6,180 kHz SW
5pm-10pm 6,180 kHz SW
4am-6.30am 6,195 kHz SW
5pm-10.30pm 6,195 kHz SW
3am-10.30pm 9,410 kHz SW
4am-10.30pm 12,095 kHz SW
6am-7.30am 15,565 kHz SW
6am-9pm 15,575 kHz SW
8am-3pm 17,640 kHz SW

Music: Classical & Opera

Struggling with the transition from state support to corporate sponsorship, a plethora of orchestras and ensembles strive to do justice to Hungary's classical tradition.

Just one of Budapest's 30 orchestras.

In no other country east of Germany will you find a musical identity as potent as that of Hungary. Thanks to the efforts of Béla Bartók and Zoltán Kodály, who in the early part of the twentieth century ventured out into remote regions of Greater Hungary to document the vanishing folk song heritage, Hungarians are raised with an elemental sense of their rich musical heritage. Bartók, assimilating the experiences gained in ethnomusicological research, went on to become one of the giants of twentieth-century music. Kodály, meanwhile, strove to create an all-embracing music education system based on the folk songs they collected. As a result, every Hungarian knows a folk tune or two. Kodály, decidedly the more messianic of the two, shaped musical appreciation in Hungary for generations to come.

During Communist times, the government pumped money into the diverse-if-unambitious musical culture, seeing it as a relatively inexpensive way to keep the masses happy. This posed enormous problems with the change of government in 1990. State subsidies fell dramatically, forcing many of Hungary's best musicians to flee abroad in search of economic security.

Miraculously, although Hungary is still overpopulated with people trained in music, not a single orchestra or ensemble active before 1990 has had to close, though most have been forced to trim their schedules. Even more surprising is that a number of new ensembles and orchestras have sprung up over the last few years. Things are slowly changing from a fully state-supported arts system to one that is heavily supplemented by corporate sponsorship. Both sides – the musicians and the corporations – still have a lot to learn, and musicians' salaries remain far below those of their western counterparts, but the balance has at least assured Hungarian musicians that they are no worse off than any other salaried worker.

You can count on two or three concerts every night of the week during the concert season, which runs from late September to early June. In the summer, the major orchestras pack up and go on either vacation or foreign tours, leaving smaller ensembles and ad-hoc groups to entertain the tourists. Repertoire tends to stick to basic German Romantic fare, though there are a few specialised groups doing contemporary or baroque music.

A free monthly listing of classical concerts, *Koncert Kalandárium* (only in Hungarian), is available at all ticket agencies and some record shops. Listings in English can be found in the *Budapest Week* and *Budapest Sun*.

Principal Orchestras

Budapest has more than 30 orchestras and chamber orchestras, but few are of an international standard. Part of the blame can be laid on a lack of rehearsal and practice time (compounded by a lack of money); the rest of it on an acute shortage of good conductors. The exception is the **Budapest Festival Orchestra**, which started out as an ad-hoc group of Hungary's best musicians and became a full-time orchestra in 1993. With more corporate funding than any other orchestra, the BFO is able not only to offer the highest salaries to its excellent musicians, but is also in a position to invite renowned international soloists and conductors, who are preferred to the band's regular conductor Iván Fischer. Their programming is imaginative and most concerts sell out.

After the BFO, the playing and artistic standards are more inconsistent. **The Hungarian State Orchestra**, though handicapped by the unimaginative programming of their hyperactive and popular conductor Ken-Ichiro Kobayashi, can usually give a solid performance. Their taste in guest conductors, however, is often questionable.

Recently severely threatened with closure, the **Hungarian Radio and Television Orchestra** continues to operate on a truncated schedule. Although their repertoire rarely ventures beyond the established warhorses, performances, led by conductor and pianist Tamás Vásáry, are usually very musically rewarding.

The future is looking up for one orchestra, the **MATÁV Symphony Orchestra**. Formerly the Orchestra of the Hungarian Post Office, the group received in 1996 an unprecedented commitment from the Hungarian telephone company MATÁV, who want to make what was once one of the city's weakest ensembles into one of the best, and have fronted the cash to support this ambition. Former HRTO conductor András Ligeti has been signed up to whip the group into shape. Although it's still to early to see results, MATÁV looks to be in it for the long run.

Venues

Despite the large number of musicians and performing ensembles, there is a severe shortage of appropriate concert venues in Budapest. Only one orchestra (the MATÁV) has its own concert hall, the rest have to fight over the ones listed below. Competition gets fiercer in the summer when the larger venues close, making just about any courtyard or garden a good place for a concert.

Principal Concert Halls

Zeneakadémia
VI. Liszt Ferenc tér 8 (342 0179). M1 Oktogon/tram 4, 6 Király utca. **Open** *box office* 1pm-8pm Mon-Fri; 10am-noon, 4pm-8pm Sat and Sun when there is a concert. **Credit** AmEx, MC, V. Some English spoken. **Map D3**
The Zeneakadémia is really a music school, the legendary Franz Liszt Music Academy, built in 1907. Nearly all of Hungary's musicians learned their craft here from some of the most respected names in music – who did the same a generation earlier. Concerts are held nearly every night in the 1,200-seat Nagyterem (Large Concert Hall), which serves as the country's primary classical music venue as well as a major source of income for the Music Academy. The ornate wood-panelled interior provides the best acoustics this side of the Danube for both chamber recitals and orchestral concerts. There is also a smaller hall, the Kisterem, with less flattering acoustics. The centre is closed in late July and August, but recently amateur groups touring Europe in these months have given them an excuse to light the stage for a night.

Pesti Vigadó
V. Vigadó utca 5 (138 4721). M1 Vörösmarty tér. **Open** *box office* 10am-6pm Mon-Fri; 10am-2pm Sat; 5pm-7pm Sun when there is a concert. **No credit cards**. Little English spoken. **Map C4**
Toilet-bowl acoustics coupled with an interior that might be similarly described make this one of the worst concert halls in town – something definitely went wrong when it was rebuilt after bombing in World War II. Nevertheless, the Vigadó has a colourful guest register, including Brahms, who visited at the end of the nineteenth century. Nicely situated on the bank of the Danube, it's mainly used during festivals and by ensembles who couldn't get into the Zeneakadémia that evening. Closed during July and August.

Other Venues

Budapest Congress Centre
Budapest Kongresszusi Központ
XII. Jagelló út 1-3 (186 9588). M2 Déli/tram 61. **Open** *box office* 2pm-6pm Wed, Fri or on day of concert. **No credit cards**. Some English spoken. **Map A5**
Modern convention centre with poor acoustics, but a larger seating capacity than the Zeneakadémia.

Óbuda Social Circle
Óbudai társaskör
III. Kiskorona utca 7 (250 0288). M3 Árpád híd/tram 1. **Open** *box office* 2pm-6.45pm or one hour before performance. **No credit cards**. No English spoken.
A charming little building in the middle of a Lego-land housing estate, the Óbuda Social Circle hosts recitals and some chamber orchestras. Intimate, and often the site of some of the best concerts around.

Bartók Memorial House
Bartók Emlékház
II. Csalán utca 29 (176 2100). Bus 5, 29. **Open** *no box office; museum* 10am-5pm Tue-Sun; *tickets* on sale one hour before performance and during museum hours. Closed Aug. **No credit cards**. No English spoken.
Bartók's last residence before emigrating to America, now a museum, gives a series of Friday evening chamber concerts by the best of Hungary's musicians. Sometimes also used on other days of the week. Low ceiling promotes claustrophobia, which is perhaps why the chairs are the most luxurious and comfortable of any venue in Budapest.

MATÁV Zeneház
IX. Páva utca 10-12 (215 7901). Tram 4, 6 Boráros tér. **Open** *box office* 9am-3pm Mon-Fri. Closed July. **No credit cards**. No English spoken. **Map E6**
Recently renovated 200-seat home of the MATÁV Symphony Orchestra. What it lacks in seating capacity it makes up for in great acoustics. Likely to be used more and more in the coming years.

Mátyás Templom

I. Szentháromság tér 2 (no phone). M2 Moszkva tér then Várbusz/bus 16. **Tickets** on sale at the venue one hour before performance. **No credit cards.** Some English spoken. **Map A3**

Top venue for organ recitals and sporadic choir concerts, especially in the summer. Despite the typically drowning acoustics, works for choir and orchestra are also sometimes given here, particularly during festivals.

Opera

Although the **Hungarian State Opera** is the only opera company in Budapest, it divides its repertoire of nearly 60 opera and ballet productions a year between two houses, making it seem like there's always something to see on any given night. Most of the higher-profile productions are held in the historic **Opera House** on Andrássy út, a gem of a theatre which has everything an opera house should have except top-notch performers. The other house, a stark monument to Socialism so big it almost seems empty even if it's full, is the **Erkel Színház**. Productions here are usually in need of updating. Recently, however, an attempt has been made to create new productions which suit the dubious qualities of the theatre.

Despite the rich history of the Opera House (Gustav Mahler and Otto Klemperer both had regimes here) the 1990s have proved trying. Threats of bankruptcy hang in the air while old-style mismanagement has successfully squandered most of the company's best talent. The brightest young singers stay around only long enough to be spotted by some international agent, leaving most of the singing duties to well-intentioned veterans. Worse off are the musicians in the pit, who are overstaffed, underpaid and usually under-rehearsed.

But, depending on the director, productions by the State Opera are not always without a sense of invention: what a production lacks in musical or dramatic talent is sometimes balanced by a creative set design and original staging. With at least four opera and three ballet premières a year, the State Opera is trying to cultivate an image of resourceful innovation in the face of impending financial ruin. Often the results are very rewarding. International diva Éva Marton usually performs on the stage that started her career at least once a year, as does up-and-coming divette Andrea Rost. Spring of 1998 sees the completion of its marginally successful Ring Cycle under the baton of

Bach to the Future

One of the first cultural casualties of the change of system in 1990 was the reputable Hungarian classical record label Hungaroton. Once the best-selling east European classical label in the West, Hungaroton hit rock bottom in 1994 when it filed for bankruptcy. A consortium of western investors and the Hungarian government bailed it out, and since then the company has been on a steady rise back to its former glory.

Although many of Hungaroton's staple artists and ensembles have moved on to get contracts with larger western labels, the company has recruited newer ensembles (Cristofori Trio, Affetti Musicali, Forrás Chamber Music Workshop) and younger musical talent (violinist Vilmos Szabadi, pianist Márta Gulyás) to grab back its image as an adventurous label. The last two years' releases have been imaginative and courageous, including repertoire that big western labels wouldn't touch.

Among these are the late Spanish baroque composer Sebastian Albero's *Sonatas for Harpsichord* (Anikó Horváth, HCD 31621), Telemann's *Solo Cantatas* (Affetti Musicali, HCD 31597), C. Ph. E. Bach's *Accompanied Keyboard Sonatas* (Cristofori Trio, HCD 31619) and works by relatively obscure Czech com-

posers such as Jiri Antonin Benda, Leopold Kozeluch and Josef Myslivecek.

The label has also renewed its commitment to contemporary Hungarian music with discs devoted exclusively to some composers not yet well known in the West, such as László Tihanyi, Zoltán Jeney and György Orbán. And, of course, there is always their priceless back catalogue of Bartók's works by great Hungarian interpreters like Antal Doráti, Zoltán Kocsis, the Franz Liszt Chamber Orchestra and Bartók himself. (Such as the 6-CD *Bartók At The Piano: Music by Bartók, Debussy, Kodály, Liszt and D. Scarlatti*, HCD 12326/31)

The main point about Hungaroton is that in Hungary their discs are at least half the price they sell for anywhere else in the world. If you want Magyar artists on a western label, buy those at home and get your Hungaroton CDs in Hungary.

Amadeus CD Shop

V. Szende Pál utca 1 (118 6691). Tram 2 Vigadó tér. **Open** *June-Sept* 9.30am-9.30pm daily; *October-May* 9.30am-7.30pm. **No credit cards.** Some English spoken. **Map C4**

On the busiest stretch of the Danube *korzó*, the widest selection of classical and jazz CDs in the city, including the biggest stock of Hungaroton Classics, and Budapest's lowest prices for non-Hungarian CDs.

Kodály – *decidedly messianic musicologist.*

former Bolshoi conductor Yuri Simonov, while contemporary Hungarian composer János Vajda's much awaited new opera will be premièred in the autumn of 1998.

The State Opera publishes a monthly schedule, available at the Opera House and at some ticket agencies. Opera listings can also be found in the free monthly *Koncert Kalandárium.*

Opera House

Magyar Állami Operaház
VI. Andrássy út 22 (153 0170). M1 Opera. **Open** *box office* 10am-7pm Tue-Sat when there is a performance; 10am-1pm, 4pm-7pm Sun when there is a performance. **Credit** AmEx. Some English spoken. **Map D3** *See also chapter* **Sightseeing**.

Erkel Színház

VIII. Köztársaság tér 30 (333 0540). M2 Blaha Lujza tér. **Open** *box office* 10am-7pm Tue-Sat when there is a performance; 10am-1pm, 4pm-7pm Sun when there is a performance. **Credit** AmEx. No English spoken. **Map E4**

Ticket Agencies

Few classical concerts in Budapest sell out. With the exception of the Festival Orchestra, tickets are usually available and affordable unless a major international artist is involved. Tickets for most concerts are available at **Nemzeti Filharmónia** and **Fortissimo-5**. What isn't available there is best bought at the venue an hour or so before the performance. Tickets for the State Opera and Erkel Színház are only available at the respective box offices and at the State Opera Ticket Office a few doors down Andrássy út. Most places only accept cash, but ticket prices are nowhere near those in the West. For further information, check *Koncert Kalandárium*, which specifically lists where tickets are available for each event.

Nemzeti Filharmónia

V. Vörösmarty tér 1 (118 0281). M1 Vörösmarty tér. **Open** 10am-1.30pm, 2pm-6pm Mon-Fri. Closed July. **No credit cards**. Some English spoken. **Map C4** The state concert agency, this should be your one-stop destination, with tickets for nearly everything and loads of concert schedules and information. Particularly impatient service.

Fortissimo-5

XIII. Hollán Ernô utca 7 (359 5395). Tram 4, 6. **Open** 10am-6pm, Mon-Fri. **No credit cards**. Some English spoken. **Map C2** Private agency inside the Odeon Art-Video store. Tickets for Festival Orchestra concerts and almost everything else are available.

State Opera Ticket Office

VI. Andrássy út 20 (131 2550). M1 Opera. **Open** 10am-5.30pm Mon-Thur; 10am-4.30pm Fri. Closed July-Aug. **Credit** AmEx. No English spoken. **Map D3**

Festivals

After nearly 15 years of the gargantuan Spring Festival, Budapest is now currently without a major international festival. In 1997 the cultural extravaganza, which focused mainly on classical music, was pruned down from 30 days to just 14 and offered mainly local talent, making it not unlike any other fortnight and less of a reason to visit Hungary. It has a new organiser now, but not the financial support and high standard it once garnered. Judging from the 1998 programme, it's certain that the festival will survive, but not that it will ever be the event it once was.

Perhaps as consolation, there are a number of smaller festivals. The Autumn Festival, also more modest of late than in previous years, focuses on contemporary music, as does the 27-year-old Music of Our Time festival, which has gained new life (read: funding) after several years of uncertainty.

Fans of pre-romantic music shouldn't miss the Early Music Festival in late May and early June. This is really the only time one can hear Hungary's few but talented early and Baroque music ensembles perform at home.

Budapest Spring & Autumn Festival

VIII. Rákóczi út 66 4th floor door 66 (210 2795/133 2337/fax 133 2075). M2 Blaha Lujza tér/tram 4, 6. **Open** 10am-6pm. **No credit cards**. **Map E4** *Central Office, Interart Festival Center, V. Vörösmarty tér 1 (117 9838/fax 117 9910/118 9943). M1 Vörösmarty tér.* **Open** 10am-4pm Mon-Fri. **Map C4**

Music: Rock, Roots & Jazz

Budapest's moribund music scene is enlivened by a few laudable exceptions – such as violin virtuoso Félix Lajkó.

The Hungarian music industry isn't working. So much that in the West is taken for granted – a decent range of venues, a healthily critical music press, adventurous radio and television coverage, a competitive and customer-friendly retail side – are either in short supply or simply don't exist.

The constraints of an economy struggling to meet EU membership criteria have hardly helped matters since the arrival of the major labels in 1992-93. Energy prices soar while the forint gets weaker by the day, forcing ticket prices, particularly for western acts, beyond the limited spending power of the average student or job starter. To balance the books and lessen logistical headaches, many Budapest club owners now just shell out for a few DJs and leave live bands to fend for themselves on a circuit of less than a dozen venues.

Nevertheless, there are various acts worth catching. The quirky, danceable sound of Kispál és a Borz, the infectious fun of Publo Hunny, the versatile instrumental jazz-punk of Masfél, or the humourous young rap of Animal Cannibals would grace anyone's CD player. Some Hungarian-language acts from beyond the borders, such as the venomously inventive Tudósok from Novi Sad, or Jutott Neki, Slovakia's answer to The Undertones, are also worth a listen. A major tour by the more popular acts is often made possible with sponsorship from a soft drinks, alcohol or cigarette company.

Yet even the best bands remain trapped with a language they can't export and a sound they haven't the money to improve. Few are prepared to experiment with adding new elements with Hungary's rich folk traditions. One laudable exception is fiddle virtuoso Félix Lajkó (*see page 201* **Fiddler on the Loose**), with leftfield avant-gardists Kampec Dolores a noble second.

For those working in the mainstream, a crash course in conversational German often comes before nurturing any innate musical talent – churning out cut-rate rock and roll standards in provincial Austria is the unhappy lot of many a Hungarian band. Even if one had a finer sense of artistic endeavour, publicity and distribution would be the first of many headaches.

Although there are now two monthly music magazines – the entertainingly idiosyncratic but financially unstable *Wanted* and the pitifully unadventurous *Q* knock-off *Z* – space has to be fought for with competition from the West. It's the same story in the shops. Although the retail situation has picked up with the chain of Fotex stores and a modest Virgin Megastore at the **Duna Plaza** mall (*see chapter* **Shopping**), the majors are more likely to push foreign acts, the importing of whose publicity material is far cheaper and easier than dreaming up whole new campaigns for artists whose catchment area is a city of two million people. Distribution in the provinces remains neanderthal.

For the visitor, the live scene is an affordable curiosity. Apart from the bands already listed, a few veteran outfits from the 1980s Hungarian underground are still treading the boards. Vagtazó Halottkémek – the Galloping Coroners, or VHK – cross fearsomely loud rock 'n' roll with shamanist influences. Balaton, led by Mihály Víg, a romantic loser in the Pete Shelley mould, continue to pour out unbeatably blue pop/rock melodies. And ef Zambó, from the seminal underground outfit Bizottság, still journeys weekly from his artist's studio in Szentendre to play in Budapest with his Happy Dead Band. For an evening of sheer hilarity, you can do worse than catch one of the 1970s supergroups' revival shows. See Hungária, Illés or Omega, and thank someone up there that you weren't brought up in Hungary.

For one week in mid-August, the whole local music scene comes together for the biggest festival east of Vienna. The Sziget ('island') Fesztival consists of some 200 bands playing on ten stages over seven days on a normally deserted island in the Danube (*see chapter* **By Season**). With at least three dance tents, dangerously cheap beer and loss-making ticket prices, the Sziget not only attracts Magyar music fans from across the spectrum; financial input from Pepsi has helped attract acts such as Iggy Pop, David Bowie and The Prodigy – in turn luring MTV and foreign film crews to focus for a while on Hungary and its cash-strapped music scene.

Tickets and information

Concert details and previews can be found in *Budapest Week*, *Budapest Sun* and *Pesti Est*. Concerts rarely sell out but advance tickets can be bought at:

Music Mix-33

V. Váci utca 33 (138 2237). M3 Ferenciek tere/bus 7. **Open** 10am-6pm Mon-Fri; 10am-2pm Sat. Closed on Sat in summer. **No credit cards.** English spoken. **Map C4**

Venues

Large venues include **Népstadion** and **Budapest Sportcsarnok** (*see chapter* **Sport & Fitness**). Central smaller venues in *chapter* **Nightlife** will also feature live music.

Almássy tér Recreation Centre

Almássy téri Szabadidőközpont
VII. Almássy tér 6 (352 1572). M2 Blaha Lujza tér/tram 4, 6. **Open** from 7pm on concert nights. **Admission** Ft300-Ft500. Some English spoken. **Map E3**
Of all the cultural centres in town, the one most willing and most suitable for live music of non-folk genres – though there's plenty of folk here too. With its bars upstairs and down, mid-size concert hall and central location, possibly the best place to catch a quality underground rock combo.

Banán

III. Mátyás király út 13-15 (168 9049). HÉV to Csillaghegy. **Open** *Sept-June* 8pm on concert nights. **Admission** Ft250-Ft350. Some English spoken.
A fair way from the centre of town, but one of the few places left offering affordable non-mainstream music for a friendly circle of young musicians and their aficionados. The stage

is large enough to accommodate occasional theatre performances, the hall's circular shape allowing all a good view of the proceedings. Decent bar away from the numbers. Worth the trek for the right band. Concerts begin 9.30pm-10.30pm.

Barlang

Dunakorzó 11a, Szentendre (06 26 312 657). HÉV to Szentendre. **Open** 6pm-1am Thur-Sat. **Admission** Ft250-Ft400. English spoken.
Officially known as the Dunaparti Művelődési Pomáz, Szentendre's 'The Cave' is the most attractive out-of-town venue for its riverside setting, easy access by public transport and eclectic programming. The large concert hall features jazz, blues, rock and folk acts, but is best known for large, smelly gatherings of punks from nearby Pomaz. At its best in the summer when the courtyard makes for extra bar space. Oasis of unpretention in otherwise snooty Szentendre.

Boogie Thing Blues Kocsma

XII. Krisztina körút 25 (155 7383). Tram 18. **Open** noon-midnight daily. Closed in August. **Admission** Ft100 for live acts. Some English spoken. **Map A4**
Cheap, friendly, old-style family-run pub with modest local acts on at 8.30pm most evenings, mainly in the jazz/blues vein, not too loud to destroy conversation, not too quiet if you fancy dancing. Planned refurbishment should not disturb a cosy ambience engendered by the regulars.

Budai Parkszinpad

XI. Kosztolányi Dezső tér (166 9849). Bus 7. **Open** from 7pm. **Admission** Ft300-Ft1,000. Some English spoken. **Map B6**
The main summer outdoor venue – a few hundred chairs and a huge stage in the park area near Kosztolányi Dezső tér. Concerts are mostly Hungarian pop, although the venue hosts the annual World Music Festival in June (*see chapter* **Budapest By Season**) and various folk dancing events. The stewards can get a bit rough with screaming teenagers.

The Glamour, the Glory, the Giraffes

Grammies for the Yanks, Brits for the Brits. What could possibly be the highest honour awarded to a Hungarian musician? You guessed it. A Giraffe.

The Golden Giraffes (unkindly nicknamed the Golden Baboons) have been dished out by Hungary's music publishers' association, MAHASZ, annually since 1993. They're named after the symbol the association settled on for its holographic anti-piracy stickers. Needing some form of simple movement for the design, MAHASZ rejected even more bizarre suggestions to plump for a docile, nodding giraffe. Hence a row of nine-inch tall, gilded giraffes patiently wait to be picked up by Hungary's loudest and finest at a modest media bash every spring.

The event at the otherwise sedate surroundings of the Stefánia Palace, in the leafy area between Keleti Station and the Városliget, has all the excitement of a village fete. Hungary's music industry moguls switch off their mobiles for the short ceremony, filmed and photographed mainly for local TV and tabloids. The Giraffes are awarded accord-

ing to two sets of criteria: performance in the weekly top 40 album chart, and artistic merit as defined by a middle-aged jury of seven.

There are 12 awards in total, presented and accepted with all the glamour and glory of an infant school sports day. The industry's a bit too young for anyone yet to be receiving awards for lifetime achievement. The one to watch for – mainly because it's not merely based on chart performance – is the Golden Giraffe for Best Newcomers. Kimnowak, Nyers and Animal Cannibals, all past winners, went on to higher and better things with a Giraffe nestling safely on their mantelpiece.

After winners have posed with the obligatory bimbos, everyone floats to an adjacent room to talk shop and munch smoked salmon. Most of those assembled – musicians, producers, A&R people – have a job for life, so local gossip overshadows anything as irrelevant as artist development or next year's potential sales figures. Another day, another giraffe.

Evaluating the latest vinyl shipment at **Underground**. *See page 201.*

E-Klub

X. Népliget 2 (263 1614). M3 Népliget/trolleybus 75.
Open 8pm-5am Fri-Sat. **Admission** Ft400-Ft750. Some
English spoken.
Impersonal venue for rich kids in an otherwise versatile setting (one large concert hall and several smaller rooms) next
to the Planetarium in the Népliget park. Whether a live band
– generally bog standard hard rock – or a plain discotheque,
the flashy clientèle seem immune to the over-amplification
and the strict frisk by the monkeys on the door. Watch out
for the hefty bar prices.

Globe Royal Mulato

*III. Csemete utca 5 (250 3329). Tram 17/bus 6, 29, 60,
65, 65a, 84, 165.* **Open** 7pm-1am daily. Concerts from
10pm. **Admission** Ft500-Ft750. Some English spoken.
Digitally-amplified, sit-back-and-appreciate concert venue
for musos and well-heeled thirty-somethings. Dancing would
be frowned upon even if it were possible in the narrow spaces
between the waited-at tables, and regular unplugged sessions by Hungary's top guitarists hardly encourage aban-
don. Jazz and blues also popular, as are the restaurant and
pool tables upstairs.

Made Inn Music Club

VI. Andrássy út 112 (111 3437). **Open** 8pm-5am daily.
Open 8pm-5am daily. **Admission** Ft300-Ft600. Some
English spoken. **Map E2**
Two crowded, overlit disco floors, an upstairs room for
assorted local bands to perform intimate sets around midnight, and a spacious bar/restaurant terrace attached. Well-
dressed young clientèle.

Petőfi Csarnok

*XIV. Városliget, Zichy Mihály út 14 (343 4327). M1
Széchenyi Fürdő/trolleybus 70.* **Open** from 8pm.
Admission Ft500-Ft2,000. English spoken. **Map F2**
Large events hall in City Park. Indoor arena too large for
most Hungarian bands but most mid-range western acts
passing through Budapest will stop off here. It's also the
venue for the annual Hungarian Jazz Festival. The PeCsa
started life as the Metropolitan Youth Centre in 1984 and still
provides the Depeche Mode Fan Club with a venue for their
monthly events. The main hall is a soulless barn with poor
sound; in summer, the outdoor concert area has a better
atmosphere. Both hold around 2,500 people.

Riff-Röff Rock Club

XI. Fehérvári út 120 (206 1225). Tram 19, 47.
Open 2pm-2am Sun-Tue ; 2pm-4am Wed-Thur; 2pm-5am
Fri-Sat. **Admission** Ft300-Ft500. Some English spoken.
Map C6
Bare rock cellar club down in Buda which attracts the city's
biker community, whatever the live act. The programme
ranges from blues to hard core, but mostly centres on
straight rock. Watch out for MagyaROCK nights on a
Wednesday, which feature a handful of up-and-coming local
acts struggling to distract Buda's grebos from the pool table
in the back. Pleasant terrace section despite the clientèle.

VMH

VIII. Golgota utca 3 (313 8430). Tram 23, 24/bus 99.
Open from 7pm Fri-Sat. **Admission** Ft300-Ft750. Some
English spoken.
Former home of the Black Hole, Budapest's punk venue of
yesteryear, the VMH is the place for scores of misplaced ado-
lescents to waste their pocket money on cheap glue and
lighter fuel. You've got to really, really want to see a thrash
band to come here, having run the gauntlet of change-beg-
gars all the way down the bleak expanses of Golgota utca.
A shame, because it's an excellent space inside, with a rea-
sonably-sized concert room and bar next door.

Wigwam

XII. Csörsz utca 14 (319 9292). Bus 12, 139. **Open** 8pm-
5am Thur-Sat. **Admission** Ft300-Ft400. Some English
spoken. **Map A5**
All bands on the circuit play this spacious former socialist-
realist restaurant in the Buda heights behind the Novotel,
whose vast windows have been covered with teepee-like
skins. The theme is accentuated, if not abused, by a country
and western feel to the wooden furniture. For all that there's
a large stage, decent sound, and two bars, three in summer
when the terrace is open. Clientèle slowly being yuppified.

Jazz venues

Most clubs are too small for top western acts, so
the music on offer is usually home-grown. Tobacco
and spirits companies sponsor regular jazz festivals, so good domestic talent can be nurtured. The

Dresch Quartet deserve your attention, as does saxophonist Mihály Dresch when he is playing solo. Trio Midnight are also worth a look, as are solo shows by their pianist Kálmán Oláh. Aladár Pege is Hungary's king of double bass. Gyula Babos, former leader of seminal group Saturnus and jazz chair at the Liszt Ferenc Music Academy, is the one Hungarian artist who has earned recognition abroad.

Fél 10 Jazz Club

VIII. Baross utca 30 (60 318 467). M3 Kálvin tér/tram 4, 6 Baross utca. **Open** noon-late Mon-Fri; 7pm-late Sat-Sun; concerts from 9.30pm. **Admission** for major acts Ft400-Ft1,500, free otherwise. English spoken. **Map D5**
Not simply a jazz club, but an acoustically perfect if logistically flawed venue to catch local or international blues, funk or various forms of dance music. A lot has been spent on curtains and tiles to enhance the sound emanating from the corner stage downstairs to the people gathered around the main bar/balcony area on the ground floor; little thought has been given to the potential bottlenecks in the doorways below. Ventilation is another problem, and the main bar at stage level is frustratingly tucked away far from the stage. Great on a quiet night, hellish for a name act.

Long Jazz Club

VII. Dohány utca 22-24 (322 0006). M2 Astoria/bus 7, 9/tram 47, 49. **Open** 4pm-2am Mon-Sat. **Admission** free. English spoken. **Map D4**
Budapest's newest jazz club, and a most pleasant one it is too. More L-shaped than Long, it has a small, intimate stage in the corner, visible but not overbearing for those seated at either of the two bar areas. The backdrop is of New York's Chrysler Building, with caricatures of jazz legends on the red walls. A little more money spent on the air conditioning and this could be one of the best live venues in town. Good place to catch up-and-coming local acts. Quick, friendly service.

Jazz Café

V. Balassi Bálint utca 25 (269 5506). Tram 2, 4, 6. **Open** 6pm-3am daily. **Live music** 8pm-10pm Tue-Sat. **Admission** free. English spoken. **Map C2**
The trendiest jazz venue in town with blue lights, draught Kronenbourg, pool in the back room and trendy statues in the main room. Stage area a little cramped for the musicians. Generally decent background music after showtime. Cool atmosphere almost despite its efforts to engender one.

Specialist Shops

See also chapter **Shopping & Services**.

Underground

VI. Király utca 54 (352 7116). Tram 4, 6 Király utca. **Open** 10am-10pm Mon-Fri; 10am-6pm Sat. **No credit cards.** Some English spoken. **Map D3**
Primarily a DJ shop. Current dance stuff from Berlin, London and New York arrives in twice-weekly shipments.

Z Hanglemez

VIII. Rákóczi út 47 (133 0143). M2 Blaha Lujza tér/tram 4, 6. **Open** 1pm-6pm Mon-Fri. **No credit cards.** English spoken. **Map E4**
Tiny courtyard shop devoted to nothing but the works of Frank Zappa: LPs, CDs, cassettes and videos. The friendly proprietor bears more than a passing resemblance to FZ himself and will cheerfully try to track down rarities he doesn't have in stock.

Felix Lajkó – Fiddler on the Loose

Of all the names that crop up regularly on the Budapest gig listings, fiddle-player Félix Lajkó (*left*) is the one to watch out for. Not just in the sense that his concerts are worth seeing – although they most certainly are. But also because, out of the current crop, he's the one Hungarian artist with the talent, passion, vision and manifest potential to transcend his particular context – despite, or perhaps because of, the defiant Hungarianness of his music.

Still in his early 20s and a native of Subotica, Vojvodina – the region of northern Serbia with a large Hungarian-speaking population – Félix Lajkó is a conservatory-trained violinist who successfully fuses jazz, classical and folk influences into something entirely his own. Exuding an other-worldly charisma, he plays the fiddle with all the drama that instrument can afford, mixing restrained classical figures with wild Gypsy melodies in a manner that involves as much improvisation as composition.

He performs with various permutations of traditional Magyar folk instrumentation: cimbalom, zither, double bass, milk-can percussion, drums. A decidedly temperamental artist who plays from mood, his improvisational strategy is risky. When it works, which is most of the time, he's spine-tinglingly good. Occasionally, though, his shows fall flat. Either way, it's never boring.

His 1997 CD, the self-produced *Lajkó Félix és Zenekara* (Félix Lajkó and his Orchestra) (Maszk MZS22), is widely available around Budapest and a highly recommended purchase. Two previous albums, one recorded with respected Hungarian free jazz saxophonist Mihály Dresch, are now unavailable. Another, with double-bass player Attila Lőrinszky, was being recorded as this book went to press.

By all accounts something of an eccentric, Félix Lajkó has so far resisted all overtures from major labels. It's clear he's a talent which needs to go its own way – and also has a long way to go.

Nightlife

Budapest is a fine city for night owls – enough cafés and clubs, strip joints and pubs, to keep you amused until dawn.

Bahnhof – *music, excitement, romance, danger and lots of model trains. See page 203.*

By five in the afternoon, you can almost feel something pulling you out. People in Budapest are getting off work and you've arranged to meet an acquaintance for a drink and then dinner. At the restaurant, your companion runs into an old friend – everyone seems to know everyone in this town. The friend suggests a bar, maybe a party. The pull gets stronger. You stop at a café; someone tells you about some new dance place. The club and the drinks are cheap, and so is the cab that will take you to the door. You're caught up in it now.

There is just something natural about going out in this city. You can stay up until dawn without even thinking about it, or if you do think about it, it seems like a good idea. The pull is all the more subtle because the capital's night spots have a low profile. There's no central neighbourhood for partying, no hub of bright lights like you find in other cities. There are also no spectacular, must-be-seen-in clubs for an exclusive crowd.

What Budapest does have is a growing number of decent clubs and late-night food and drink emporia spread throughout the city. Fortunately,

getting around is easy: the night transport system is pretty useful, regular buses and trains start running by 5am and taxis can be very affordable – as long as you're careful enough to get the right kind (*see chapter* **Getting Around**).

It's a convenient city for night owls. You can talk until dawn in a quiet café, find a rave in an open field, play pool and video games all night or make the rounds of the city's pricey casinos and sex bars. If these activities make you hungry, you can find sustenance at one of several 24-hour restaurants, snack places or grocers.

And it is a relatively safe city, too. There may be pickpockets on some of the busier transit routes, but actual muggings are rare. Perhaps the most dangerous characters you'll meet at night are the bouncers – *see page 206* **The Doormen of Doom**. Do not annoy, speak to, or attempt to feed the goon at the door and you'll be fine.

For the most part, the people you meet in the bars and clubs of Budapest will be friendly, welcoming – and just like you – ready to succumb to the lure of the night.

Clubs

Bahnhof

VI. Váci utca 1 (no phone). M3 Nyugati/tram 4, 6/night bus 6É, 182É. **Open** 6pm-4am Mon-Sat. **Admission** Ft300. **No credit cards**. Some English spoken. **Map C2**
Music, excitement, romance and danger mingle in this spacious hall that used to be part of neighbouring Nyugati Station. On any night but Sunday, the two dance floors (one disco, one house and 'alternative') are packed with blatantly beautiful young Hungarians. The railroad theme of the décor is well executed, and includes a model train that runs under glass for the length of the main bar. Between dances you can cuddle in the booths along the wall and in the back room. The danger is provided by the bouncers, who are notoriously Neanderthal and should be avoided.

Bamboo

VI. Dessewffy utca 44 (312 3619). M1 Oktogon/tram 4. **Open** 3pm-4am Mon-Fri; 7pm-4am Sat, Sun. **Admission** Free to Ft300. **No credit cards**. Some English spoken. **Map D2**
Tropical-style theme bar in a small cellar. Usually packed with a young crowd, especially early in the week, when there's no admission. Funk and 1970s disco classics.

Capella

V. Belgrád Rakpart 23 (118 6231). M2 Ferenciek tere/tram 2. **Open** 7pm-2am Mon-Tue; 5pm-4am Wed-Sun. **Admission** Ft400. **No credit cards**. English spoken. **Map C5**
One of the city's premier gay clubs (*see chapter* **Gay & Lesbian**) deserves a mention here because even heterosexuals can appreciate a good time. Drag show starts around midnight. As soon as that's over, a mixed gay and straight crowd packs the floor for danceable house and disco mixes.

Coctail Disco

III. Szépvölgyi út 15 (no phone). Tram 17/bus 86. **Open** 7pm-2am Sun-Tue; 7pm-4am Wed-Sat. **Admission** Ft500. **No credit cards**. Some English spoken.
This Óbuda meat market is far from the centre of town if all you're looking for is disco hits of the 1970s and 1980s, but most patrons are also here for romance. This is the preferred hang-out of local 'models' and there are certainly plenty of beautiful people to gawk at. Nice and spacious with several bar areas, a decent-sized dancefloor and a terrace serving reasonably priced Italian and Hungarian food. Sometimes house and techno displaces disco in the small hours.

E-Play

VI. Teréz körút 55 (302 2849). M3 Nyugati/tram 4, 6/night bus 6É, 182É. **Open** 6pm-4am Mon-Sat. **Admission** Ft800. **No credit cards**. Some English spoken. **Map D2**
The name doesn't necessarily mean that the young crowd here is chemically altered – though a few of them certainly seem full of energy. Even if you're on nothing stronger than orange juice, you're likely to catch a buzz from the pumping beat of the high-street house music, the lurid neon decor, the deadly serious go-go dancer, the smoke machine and the can't-stop-grinning, can't-stop-moving mob on the mirrored dance floor upstairs. Ascending the illuminated stairs from the downstairs bar area is a trip in itself.

Hully Gully

XII. Apor Vilmos tér 9 (175 9742). Tram 59/bus 105, 112. **Open** 9pm-5am daily. **Admission** Ft700; Ft2,000 for shows. **Credit** AmEx. Some English spoken.
Everything naff about a night out in Budapest conveniently located in one club: scary bouncers, go-go dancers, prostitutes at the bar, a regular clientèle that could work as extras in a budget mafia movie and shady taxi drivers outside, waiting to overcharge you for your ride home.

Kepi Blanc Bistro Musique

XI. Üllői út 45-47 (217 4100). M3 Ferenc körút/tram 4, 6/night bus 6É, 182É. **Open** 9pm-3am Wed-Thur; 9pm-5am Fri-Sat. **Admission** Free most week nights. Ft500 weekends and on special party nights. **No credit cards**. Some English spoken. **Map E5**
Attempts to exude a sophisticated, upmarket feel, with bouncers enforcing an arbitrary dress code – men, don't wear shorts. The club has two dancefloors, smaller one for house music, larger one for dated disco, and draws a good-sized crowd, especially later on weekends. Meet men who want to be yuppies – and the women who want to have their babies. Themed to evoke the French Foreign Legion.

Nincs Pardon

VII. Almássy tér 11 (351 4351). M2 Blaha Lujza tér/tram 4, 6 Wesselényi utca/nightbus 6É, 78É. **Open** 8pm-4am daily. **Admission** Ft200. **No credit cards**. Some English spoken. **Map E3**
A small bar in the front, decorated with interesting Gaudi-like shapes and tile mosaics, and dated disco animating the modest dancefloor in back. Useful spot when in the increasingly lively Almássy tér area. The name means 'no excuse'.

Piaf

VI. Nagymező utca 25 (112 3823). M1 Oktogon/tram 4, 6/night bus 6É. **Open** 10pm-6am daily. **Admission** Ft350. **No credit cards**. Some English spoken. **Map D3**
Don't go before 1am and expect an initial chill from the woman at the door. Use the entry ticket she sells you to get a drink at the bar. Upstairs, in a red-velvet room that resembles a bordello, showbiz types take refuge from 'Budapest's Broadway' outside. The atmosphere is sophisticated and decadent, and the music, whether from a piano player or the stereo, is jazzy. Sometimes a snooty and aggressive barperson will insist you're not allowed upstairs. Step carefully down the nerve-wracking staircase to the L-shaped cellar space below. The postage stamp-sized dancefloor is filled with people dancing to good old disco hits. By the time you resurface, the sun will be up and the buses will be running.

Süss Fel Nap

V. Honvéd utca 40 (374 3329). Tram 4, 6/night bus 6É, 182É. **Open** 3pm-3am daily. **Admission** Ft 250. **No credit cards**. Some English spoken. **Map C3**
Spacious cellar club with lots of cozy corners for a young, cheerful, unpretentious crowd. The DJs are nothing special, but the dancefloor keeps moving. The name means 'let the sun rise'; it's hard to spot it, stencilled near the door. Look for the sign with a picture of the sun, or the yellow sheep painted on the door. Charmingly innocent atmosphere.

Trocadero Presszó

V. Szent István körút 15 (111 4961). M3 Nyugati/tram 4, 6/night bus 6É, 182É. **Open** 9pm-4am Mon-Thur; 9pm-5am Fri-Sat. **Admission** free to Ft400. **No credit cards**. English spoken. **Map C2**
Ignore the tuxedoed thugs outside; they're trying to steer you to the sex club next door. Follow the sign back to Trocadero, the only Latin disco in town. Live salsa and merengue acts show up sporadically and the joint is packed when there's a show (weeknights it can be a thin crowd). It's tough to stay seated for too long, but those who want a rest can get a quiet gallery table and look down at the refreshingly multinational crowd on the floor. The lights are low, the beat is up and homesick New Yorkers may find just what they're missing.

Undergrass

VI. Liszt Ferenc tér 10 (322 0830). M1 Oktogon/tram 4, 6/night bus 6É. **Open** 6pm-5am daily. **Admission** Ft300. **No credit cards**. English spoken. **Map D3**
Under the Café Mediterran (*see chapter* **Pubs & Bars**), in the pedestrian zone that has become a hub of Pest nightlife. Medium-sized cellar space can seem pretty small, but only

Hot to trot at the **Trocadero**. *See page 203.*

because the place is packed with a happy crowd of drinkers and dancers. Dancefloor cut off from the rest of the bar, so you can chat if you like. Music is mostly unimaginative but danceable 1980s disco, though occasionally they have house DJs (*see page 205* **Breakbeats, Raves and DJ Kicks**).

Late-Night Bars

Alagút
I. Alagút utca 4 (212 3754). Bus 2, 16, 86, 105, 116/tram 4. **Open** 24 hours daily. **No credit cards.** Some English spoken. **Map A4**
Classic all-night bar clouded by traffic fumes from the nearby Alagút, or tunnel, patronised by alcoholics from all walks of life and all parts of Buda. Chess and card games popular, breakfast served almost in recognition of making it through another night.

Alkotás Presszó
XII. Alkotás út 47 (212 3745). M2 Déli/tram 61. **Open** 24 hours daily. **No credit cards.** No English spoken. **Map A3**
One of the more atmospheric 24-hour bars in town. Terrace outside and lots of tables inside. The bar is like a long spacious hall, divided by big red velvet curtains to give the place a cosy feel. Ice cream for sale in the front. Piano in the back.

Biliárd Szálon
VI. Dessewffy utca 8-10 (131 6103). M3 Arany János utca/night bus 6É. **Open** 2pm-4am daily. **No credit cards.** Some English spoken. **Map C3**
Billed as a pool and darts club, and renting big Brunswick tables for a few hundred forints an hour, but this place transcends eight ball. Walk down from street level to find old favourites on the juke box, one of the few in town. There are

quiet tables for post-pool patter, pinball machines, an air-hockey table and an atmosphere that convinces you tonight was made for play. It's actually called Noiret, but the name doesn't appear outside.

Dreher Játékterem
XIII. Váci út 6 (153 4765). M3 Nyugati/tram 4, 6/night bus 6É, 182É. **Open** 24 hours daily. **No credit cards.** No English spoken. **Map C2**
Part of the all-night scene around Nyugati. Játékterem means game room, and in the back there are fruit machines and electronic roulette. But most of the space is for drinkers and late-night conversation. Grab a table inside and watch TV, or sit out under the awning and watch Pest go past.

Holsten Söröző Darts Club
IX. Boráros tér underpass (no phone). M3 Ferenc körút/tram 4, 6/night bus 6É. **Open** 24 hours daily. **No credit cards.** No English spoken. **Map D6**
At the centre of a system of walkways beneath the traffic tangle of Boráros tér is a convenient non-stop bar with year-round terrace seating in the half-open underpass. Good spot to post-mortem the evening you haven't quite yet finished.

Museum Cukrászda
VIII. Múzeum körút 12 (266 4526). M2 Astoria/tram 47, 49/night bus 78É, 182É. **Open** 24 hours daily. **No credit cards.** No English spoken. **Map D4**
Though they do offer coffee, sweets and salads around the clock, most of the patrons here after hours seem to want something stronger. Centrally located, impressive selection of affordable imported beers and the outdoor tables in warm weather are a fine place to watch the rush hour begin.

Néró Sörbár
V. Belgrád Rakpart 3-4 (no phone). M2 Ferenciek tere/tram 2. **Open** 24 hours daily. **No credit cards.** No English spoken. **Map C5**
If in the south Váci area and wanting one more, this little waterside hole-in-the-wall awaits. The service is kind of surly but there is light and dark Amstel on tap and sandwiches and rolls are served. Bring your own atmosphere.

Night and Day
VI. Andrássy út 46 (no phone). M1 Oktogon/tram 4, 6/night bus 6É. **Open** 24 hours daily. **No credit cards.** Some English spoken. **Map D3**
There's a small games room in the back, where a forlorn-looking man in a black bow tie stands next to an electronic roulette table and a few idle fruit machines. But most of this spacious, centrally located bar is taken up by two rooms of tables and there's a terrace in warmer weather. Cheerful bar staff serve imported beers from the tap at reasonable prices.

Randevú Junior Sörbár
VI. Nagymező utca 31 (no phone). M1 Oktogon/tram 4, 6/night bus 6É. **Open** 8am-6am daily. **No credit cards.** No English spoken. **Map D3**
The exterior is flashy and naff, and the décor inside isn't much better, but this can be a charming place. Downstairs the bar staff is friendly. In the small gallery upstairs, you can sometimes catch Rudolf Bodrics, the not-quite-king of Casio. His sporadically scheduled 'nostalgia music show' features old chestnuts, and his warm stage presence more than makes up for his mediocre musical talent. Be sure to request Frank Sinatra.

Tulipán Presszó
V. Nádor utca 34 (269 5043). M2 Kossuth tér/tram 2. **Open** 24 hours daily. **No credit cards.** No English spoken. **Map C3**
Friendly 24-hour bar that's a favourite of cab drivers. The 1970s-era posters, card games in the big back room and the feeling that everyone knows each other add to the charm.

Outdoor tables in summer, ideal at night, when this neighbourhood, near Parliament, is relatively traffic-free. If the patio is full, there's usually a place free at the neighbouring Little Irish Coffee Bar, also open 24 hours. Toasted sandwiches available.

Téj Bar

VII. Madách tér 7 (no phone). M1, 2, 3 Déak tér/tram 47, 49/night bus 78É, 182É. **Open** 6am-4am daily. **No credit cards.** No English spoken. **Map C4**
The name translates as milk bar, but that means nothing. A good spot to push your night too far. Funky, run-down place where you may have to wake up the barman to get service, but he doesn't seem to mind. Sometimes he forgets to close up and it becomes a 24-hour joint.

Yes

XIII. Hegedűs Gyula utca 1 (269 3105). M3 Nyugati/tram 4, 6/night bus 6É, 182É. **Open** 8am-4am daily. **No credit cards.** Some English spoken. **Map C2**
Daft late-night haunt of alcoholics and company-seekers. Yes answers all questions: 'Do I really want that one last beer?''Yes.' 'Am I bashing the hell out of the downstairs pinball machine?' 'Yes.' 'Aren't those mafia types in the corner amusing?' 'Oh God, did I really spend Ft5,000?' 'It can't be 4am already?' 'Yes.'

Restaurants & Fast Food

Most of the late-night bars listed above serve snacks and sandwiches, ranging in quality from not bad to awful. The window of the McDonald's near Keleti Station serves until 6am and the McDonald's next to Oktogon is open 24 hours. Here are some alternatives:

Berliner

IX. Ráday utca 5 (217 6757). M3 Kálvin tér/tram 47, 49/night bus 182É. **Open** 9am-3.30am Mon-Sat; 10am-

Breakbeats, Raves and DJ Kicks

Devotees of underground dance will find a small, active but hardly ground-breaking scene in Budapest. Though few of the DJs would last five minutes if transplanted on to a western dancefloor, it is, partly by virtue of having sprung up here later than in most other places, still a fresh and friendly milieu. Drugs are present but not ubiquitous (here the moral panic started before anything was even available) and outdoor raves in summer make for convivial Saturday nights.

A couple of downtown clubs – **Képi Blanc**, **Undergrass** – have house, techno or trip hop nights, but most resident DJs still paddle in the shallows of 1980s disco. Club DJs to look for include Budai (house), Jutasi (house and garage) and Tommyboy (house and acid jazz). Only **E-Play** has a consistent house and techno policy – and that's a bit of a crap shoot, full of slick boys and girls in lime-green hotpants dancing to punchy but uninspiring mainstream techno. Sometimes they have name DJs. Laurent Garnier has played here. But then so has Josh Wink. Once they even had a jungle night. Hardly anyone came.

The best music downtown is probably in **Underground** (*see also chapter* **Pubs & Bars**), where acid jazz and trip hop DJs mix mellow stuff for the drinkers and diners. Occasionally people gyrate in the aisles, but there's no proper dancefloor and the sounds aren't intended to fill one.

The Saturday night hardcore crowd will head out of town to Club Speed in Szigetszentmiklós (Gyári út, tel 06 20 294 404). It's a long trek to this sizeable warehouse space, with one dancefloor, a couple of bars and a crowd that grinds its teeth until dawn – Club Speed is no misnomer. Take your passport; they often get raided.

But don't despair. There's a year-round supply of one-off parties and club nights at places like **Fáklya** (VI. Csengery utca 68), the **Almássy tér Recreational Centre** (*see chapter* **Music: Rock, Roots & Jazz**) and **Vox** in Buda (*see chapter* **Pubs & Bars**). The scene is most entertaining in summer, when raves occur on Buda hills and Danube islands. Look for posters or pick up flyers at **Underground** or **Trance** (*see chapters* **Music: Rock, Roots & Jazz** *and* **Shopping**). Any event involving DJs Titusz, Palotai, Oleg, Virág, Dorka or Naga is likely to draw a crowd.

Titusz drifts between trip hop, acid, house and occasionally dub. Oleg and Virag spin Goa. Dorka plays Detroit, as does Naga, mixing into trip hop and acid. Palotai is the most challenging, the one Budapest DJ deploying a real sense of tension as he veers from Detroit to drum 'n' bass. A lot of Hungarians end up appreciating it from the edge of the dancefloor, though, unable to dance to so many weird rhythms they've never heard before.

midnight Sunday. **Average** Ft1,000. **No credit cards.** No English spoken. **Map D5**

Small bar upstairs. Spacious cellar with big wooden booths for late dining. Hearty helpings of basic Hungarian food and a served until at least 1.30am weekdays.

Grill 99

VII. Dohány utca 52 (no phone). Bus 7/night bus 7É. **Open** 24 hours daily. **Average** Ft500. **No credit cards.** Some English spoken. **Map D4**

Eggs are hard to find in Budapest restaurants but always available at this Magyar-style greasy-spoon diner. The menu includes some Hungarian standards – most deep-fried to help prevent a hangover – as well as eggs served in most styles, with or without ham or sausage. There's a small gallery for those who prefer to dine above it all. Boxing posters pass for décor, patrons include every kind of person of the night.

Hepicentrum

II. 1027 Bem alsó rakpart near Margit Bridge (212 4479). Tram 4, 6/night bus 6É. **Open** 24 hours daily. **Average** Ft450. **No credit cards.** Some English spoken. **Map B1**

Salad bar on the Buda side of Margit Bridge also serves a limited variety of sandwiches.

Montana Pizza

XII. Alkotás utca 2 (no phone). M2 Déli/tram 61. **Open** 24 hours daily. **Average** Ft550. **No credit cards.** Some English spoken. **Map A3**

Brick-oven pizza and friendly service make this the best 24-hour establishment in the strip of shops next to the tracks of the Déli train station. Pleasant interior. Nice terrace too, but the traffic may be a bit much during the day. They also serve pasta, steak and turkey dishes, and have a small salad bar.

Nagymama Palacsintazoja

I. Hattyú utca 16 (201 8605). M2 Moszkva tér/tram 61, 59, 4, 6/night bus 6É/night tram 49É. **Open** 24 hours daily. **No credit cards.** No English spoken. **Map A2**

Small self-service place offering good, cheap pancakes, with a wide range of toppings. Dodgy clientèle late at night.

Szent Jupát

II. Retek utca 16 (212 2923). M2 Moszkva tér/tram 61, 59, 4, 6/night bus 6É/night tram 49É. **Open** 24 hours daily. **Average** Ft700. **No credit cards.** Some English spoken. **Map A2**

The king of Budapest late-night eateries, attracting crowds by offering huge plates of Magyar cuisine. So popular that you may find yourself waiting for a table at almost any time of night or day. But the booths are roomy, and if you don't mind sharing space you should be seated pretty quickly.

Szieszta

XIII. Szent István körút 10 (131 8180). M3 Nyugati/tram 4, 6/night bus 6É, 182É. **Open** 8am-4am daily. **Average** Ft550. **No credit cards.** Some English spoken. **Map C2**

Good pizza, decent pasta and ice cream served late in the upstairs restaurant, usually accompanied by eighties disco classics. Downstairs a spacious bar area attracts a friendly young crowd. Szieszta claims to be open until 4am, but have been known to close the kitchen earlier on slow nights. Still a pretty safe bet for food before 3am.

The Doormen of Doom

The beefy bouncer has become a depressing blot on the Budapest nightscape. Sure, there isn't a city in the world that doesn't have brawny bone-heads working the doors of bars and clubs. But though every nation's doormen look frightening, in most places they only bound into action to break up brawls. And unless you are a Saturday night fighter, the only time they're likely to piss you off is when they refuse you entry.

But the Magyar morons are a different breed. Horror stories abound, such as the British girl who mistakenly entered the men's toilets and was punched in the face, the *Times* correspondent who was floored after protesting when a bouncer called his Hungarian girlfriend a 'whore', and the *Time Out Budapest Guide* contributor who had to have extensive dental work after asking a DJ to play a New Order record.

Those who have complained to club owners get the same story – 'we can't control the doormen'. This is because the clubs don't actually employ the bouncers. A new place opens, along come the heavies and 'explain' to the owners that they will ensure the security of his venue in return for a slice of the cover charge. The 'offer' is rarely refused. At one Budapest disco, the doormen illustrated their power by refusing entry to the owner's wife.

There seem to be four gangs who run the doors racket and only one is headed by a Hungarian – the other three are in the hands of Russian and Ukrainian mafias. But the doors racket is small fry for the mafia groups. Most of the sex clubs and topless bars are in the hands of the mobs. Restaurants and casinos are other favourites as well as the usual guns, drugs and prostitution.

Those who believed that Hungarian tales of mafias were largely fantasy had those illusions crushed in the spring of 1997 when a full-scale war broke out between rival gangs. Over 20 shootings and grenade attacks were reported within the space of two months – the bulk of them taking place at upmarket nightlife venues. It seems that a new head of the Russian mafia had come into town and wasn't satisfied with the territories agreed with rival Hungarian, Ukrainian and Serbian gangs.

The good news is that mafias usually shoot each other and not tourists or local punters, so you are unlikely to return home with a Tarrentinoesque story to tell your friends. But if you don't want to return with a black eye and a busted lip, pay the man, smile and don't get clever sonny.

Young guns at **West End Shopping Centre.**

Underground
VI. Teréz körút 30 (111 1481). M3 Nyugati/tram 4, 6/night bus 6É, 182É. **Open** 3pm-3am daily. **Average** Ft800. **No credit cards**. Some English spoken. **Map D3**
Most of the party crowd here seems more interested in the booze and schmooze opportunities offered in this creatively decorated bar (*see chapter* **Pubs & Bars**). But the food is unique and tasty, and offered until late. The menu, printed in the form of a humourous newspaper, lists unusual starters such as gazpacho, chilli con carne, and tortillas; and hearty main dishes like steak, salmon and fowl. The hamburger is one of the best in Budapest, though that's not saying much.

West End Shopping Centre Ételbár
VI. Nyugati Station (no phone). M3 Nyugati/tram 4, 6/night bus 6É, 182É. **Open** 24 hours daily. **No credit cards**. No English spoken. **Map C2**
Next to the arcade by Nyugati, several booths offering street food for courageous diners. Even if you've had a lot to drink, you probably shouldn't eat anything that you can't identify. The gyros aren't a bad risk, and the hot sandwiches are often quite palatable, but deep-fried could be suicide. Maybe you should go round the corner to the fruit stand.

Arcades

Labirintus
VI. Teréz körút 55 (06 30 403 351). M3 Nyugati/tram 4, 6/night bus 6É, 182É. **Open** 2pm-10.30pm Mon-Tue; 24 hours daily Wed-Sun. **No credit cards**. Some English spoken. **Map D2**
State-of-the-art video excitement.

West End Shopping Centre
VI. Nyugati Station (no phone). M3 Nyugati/tram 4, 6/night bus 6É, 182É. **Open** 24 hours daily. **No credit cards**. No English spoken. **Map C2**
Kill animated attackers, drive a racing car or just shoot pinball until the sun comes up.

Casinos

Budapest has ten casinos – five on the strip between Roosevelt tér and Elizabeth Bridge. The best is the **Várkert**, worth visiting for the build-

ing, a neo-Renaissance former pump-house for the Royal Palace designed by Miklós Ybl. Its chief rival, the Las Vegas, offers glitz rather than glamour. Take your passport and lots of hard cash.

Várkert Casino
I. Ybl Miklós tér 9 (202 4244). Bus 86, 116/tram 19. **Open** 2pm-5am daily. **Admission** free. **Games** American roulette, poker, blackjack, punto banco, dice. **Credit** MC, V. English spoken. **Map B4**

Las Vegas
Atrium Hyatt Hotel, V. Roosevelt tér 2 (117 6022). Tram 2/bus 16, 105. **Open** 2pm-5am daily. **Admission** free. **Games** American roulette, poker, blackjack, punto banco, dice. **Credit** AmEx, DC, JCB, MC, V. English spoken. **Map C4**

Non-Stop Shopping

There are dozens of late-night shops selling cigarettes, basic groceries, and sometimes much more. Below is a list of a few conveniently located non-stop shops. *See also page 163* **Shop Around the Clock.**

Hús Hentesáru
I. Alagut utca 1 (no phone). Bus 2, 16, 86, 105, 116/tram 4. **Open** 24 hours daily. **No credit cards**. No English spoken. **Map A4**
Butcher shop sells sandwiches and basic food items.

Super Sarok
II. Fillér utca 1, next to Retek utca. (no phone). M2 Moszkva tér/tram 61, 59, 4, 6/night bus 6É/night tram 49É. **Open** 24 hours daily. **No credit cards**. No English spoken. **Map A2**
Standard items and an eclectic collection of gourmet treats to please the high-rent crowd of the Rózsadomb.

Dóm Market
V. Bajcsy-Zsilinszky út 24 (no phone). M3 Arany János utca/night bus 182É. **Open** 24 hours daily. **No credit cards**. Some English spoken. **Map C3**

Görög Csemege
VIII. József körut 31b (no phone). Tram 4, 6 Rákóczi tér/ night bus 6É. **Open** 24 hours daily. **No credit cards**. English spoken. **Map E4**
Mediterranean treats in the red-light district.

György Fleur
V. Erzsébet tér. Next to the bus station on the Deák tér side. **Open** 24 hours daily. **No credit cards**. Some English spoken. **Map C4**
Tiny stall next to fruit stand has coffee, cigarettes, snacks, soda and a nice selection of booze.

Nyugati ABC
VI. Nyugati Station (no phone). M3 Nyugati/tram 4, 6/night bus 6É, 182É. **Open** 24 hours daily. **No credit cards**. No English spoken. **Map D2**

Zöldség Gyümölcs
VI. Nagymező utca 50 (no phone). M1 Oktogon/tram 4, 6/night bus 6É. **Open** 24 hours daily. **No credit cards**. No English spoken. **Map D3**

Makulet
VII. Nagy Diófa utca 5 (no phone). Bus 7/night bus 7É. **Open** 24 hours daily. **No credit cards**. No English spoken. **Map D4**

Zugevő Gmk., Non-Stop ABC

IX. Üllői út 119 (215 9655). M3 Ferenc körút/tram 4, 6/night bus 6É, 182É. **Open** 24 hours daily. **No credit cards.** Some English spoken. **Map E5**

AVT ABC

XII. Nagyenyed utca 2 (no phone). M2 Déli/tram 61. **Open** 24 hours daily. **No credit cards.** Some English spoken. **Map A3**

Good selection of essentials and then some in this large grocery story just across from Déli station.

Stalls

Florists

V. Jászai Mari tér (no phone). Tram 4, 6/night bus 6É. **Open** 24 hours daily. Some English spoken. **Map C2**

Two shops, opposite each other on the Pest side of Margaret Bridge, offer flowers, cigarettes and canned drinks.

Greengrocers

Zöldség Gyümölcs

V. Jászai Mari tér (no phone). Tram 4, 6/night bus 6É. **Open** 24 hours daily. **No credit cards.** Some English spoken. **Map C2**

Ínyenc Zöldség Gyümölcs

VI. Oktogon (no phone). M1 Oktogon/tram 4, 6/night bus 6É. **Open** 24 hours daily. **No credit cards.** Some English spoken. **Map D3**

Lots of choices of soft and alcoholic beverages along with a decent selection of fruits and veggies.

Zöldség Gyümölcs

VI. Teréz körút, at Podmaniczky utca. (no phone). M3 Nyugati/tram 4, 6/night bus 6É, 182 É. **Open** 24 hours daily. **No credit cards.** Some English spoken. **Map D2**

Exotic range of fruits and drinks. Always one of the first places in town to get mangoes or avocados in season.

Video Shops

Non-stop video shops insist that you have an ID with a Budapest address. All of them have at least something in English, but remember to check whether the movie's been dubbed or just subtitled.

Fotifon Videoklub

XIII. Pannónia utca 13 (132 5027). Tram 2, 4, 6/night bus 6É. **Open** 24 hours daily. **No credit cards.** Some English spoken. **Map C2**

Six month membership costs Ft500. Video rentals Ft300 per day.

Branch: XIV. Erzsébet királyné útca 41/a (251 9496).

Fókusz Téka

VII. Wesselényi utca 54 (121 6435) Tram 4, 6/night bus 6É. **Open** 24 hours daily. **No credit cards.** Some English spoken. **Map E3**

Ft200 for a 12-hour video rental and a Ft1,000 deposit.

Other Shops & Services

See chapter **Essential Information** for 24-hour medical, dental and veterinary services.

Folkart Centrum

V. Váci utca 14 (118 5840). M1 Vörösmarty tér/M2 Ferenciek tere. **Open** 9am-4am daily. **Credit** JCB. English spoken. **Map C4**

Presumably because of the roulette tables upstairs, this tacky tourist shop is open while the rest of Váci sleeps or hustles. It makes little sense, as their attitude seems to be that if you're up this late, you're probably a shoplifter who must be watched, hawk-like, by a surely uneconomic plethora of surly assistants. There is nothing in here worth nicking anyway: just overpriced strings of dried paprika and nasty folkloric ornaments.

Copy General

IX. Lónyay utca 36 (216 8880/217 6184) Tram 4, 6/night bus 6É. **Open** 24 hours daily. **No credit cards.** English spoken. **Map D5**

Round the clock photocopying and related services.

Ibusz Travel Agency

V. Apáczai Csere János utca 1 (118 5776). M3 Ferenciek tere/night bus 78É. **Open** 24 hours daily. **Credit** AmEx. Some English spoken. **Map C4**

Can arrange accommodation at all hours.

Ibusz Bank

V. Petőfi tér 3 (118 4848) M3 Ferenciek tere/night bus 78É. **Open** 24 hours daily. **Map C4**

Change money at all hours of the day or night.

Sexpensive Bars

Take a walk down Váci utca after dark. Within twenty yards you'll be handed a leaflet about a topless bar. There'll be a map and a promise of 'the companionship of extremely pretty girls'. It'll warn you to ignore the recommendations of taxi drivers or touts from rival establishments. Walk around a while and you can collect dozens of these things, and probably also get approached by a hooker or two.

Sex tourism is big business in Budapest. There are literally hundreds of topless bars and strip joints around town, the busiest making up to $500,000 a year from foreign businessmen and tourists on junket trips. Many, but by no means all, are fronts for prostitution. Even in those that aren't, overcharging is the name of the game, and the 'consume girls' take a large cut of the expensive 'cocktails' you're encouraged to buy them. Many of the women are Ukrainian or Russian and adept at negotiating customers back to the nearest hotel or an apartment hired by the club. Most of the trade is controlled by the Ukrainian mafia.

If a bunch of lads are in town, wedged up and on the hoy, chances are they'll find their way over to The Blue Angel (VIII. Baross utca 5), which stays open from 9pm to 5am daily and charges no entrance fee. If you must try one of these places, that one's as good (or as useless) as any. We're not getting a cut from them. Honest.

Sport & Fitness

Flashy fitness clubs and golf courses for the nouveau riche, a day at the races or a football match for more downmarket delights.

Hungary's outstanding Olympic record is not matched by success in the major spectator sports. There has been plenty of gold in kayak-canoe, fencing, water polo, swimming and modern pentathlon, but in tennis, basketball and football Hungary is at the foot of European rankings.

The biggest event in the sporting calendar is the Hungarian Grand Prix or *Hungaroring*, attracting fans from all over west and central Europe. With the decline of domestic football most fans do their watching in the living room and take in international events on cable TV.

Under Communism, students and workers were actively encouraged to take part in sports and every workplace and college had a sports club. Privatisation has seen most of these clubs fold. In their place, flashy fitness clubs have sprung up all over the city, offering as much aerobics and bodybuilding as the *nouveau riche* can take.

Major Stadia

Népstadion

XIV. Istvánmezei út 1-3 (251 1222). M2 Népstadion.
The national stadium, built by and for the people (*nép*), in 1953. Its capacity is 76,000, only filled when major rock bands come to town. A roof would allow it to host major international sporting events; until one arrives, its biggest attraction are the Stalinist statues outside.

Budapest Sportcsarnok

XIV. Stefánia út 2 (251 9759). M2 Népstadion.
With a 10,000 capacity, the major indoor sports venue.

Spectator Sports

Basketball

Hungarian basketball has been enjoying a mini-revival – with more and more kids shooting hoops rather than goals and with a handful of American NBA rejects playing in the professional league, crowds and interest are booming. Unlike in most countries, the women's game is given as much coverage as the men's and draws similar crowds. The season runs from early September until late May. For fixture details see *Nemzeti Sport* or call the **Hungarian Basketball Federation** (251 0554).

Danone Honvéd

XIV. Dózsa György út 53 (340 8915). M3 Dózsa György út.
The most successful of the men's teams, Honvéd, once the Army team, are now sponsored by dairy company Danone.

Magyar footie fans – Hungary for success.

Ferencváros

VIII. Ferencváros Népligeti Sportcsarnok, Kóbanyai út (260 5859). M3 Népliget.
The most popular women's basketball team, who play their games in a newly-built sports hall. Rowdy supporters.

Football

Hungarian football fans are fed up – fed up with hearing how good Hungary were in the 1950s, when they destroyed England 6-3 at Wembley, tired of being told that there is no money in Magyar football when today's players, incapable of defeating the likes of Iceland and Australia, are earning ten times the average Hungarian salary. For hardcore loyalists, Hungarian football is a painful sufferance. But those nostalgic for the days before all-seater stadiums and franchise catering will find it a welcome escape from commercialisation. If you never stood in the open at Wigan

Athletic in 1982, with a load of beer inside you, surrounded by crumbling terraces, piss-stinking loos and a gang of lads yelling obscenities, then this is your chance to simulate the experience.

Club football attracts average crowds of around 4,000, with admission about Ft300-Ft500. The first division, NB1, has 18 teams, one-third of them from Budapest, and the season runs from mid-July to late November, and then again from March until June. Although hooligan firms and ultra groups do exist, there is little danger, except sometimes at Budapest derbies. The biggest is that between Ferencváros and Újpest – they hate each other badly and there is usually trouble in the metro stations, bottle chucking and plenty of arrests.

Ferencváros

IX. Üllői út 129 (215 3856). M3 Népliget.
The best supported and most successful club in Hungary, though the fans of 'Fradi' have the worst reputation for vandalism, racism and all-round unpleasantness. The club claim that they were independent under communism (though funded by the Ministry of Agriculture) and since the change of system every populist politician has declared loyalty to the green and whites. The tabloids, lapping up the financial scandals and personality clashes at the club, have managed to turn Ferencváros into the nation's number one soap opera.

MTK

X. Salgotárjan út 12-14 (303 0590). Tram 1 to Salgotárjan út.
Traditionally the club of Hungary's Jewish community, MTK have recently experienced a revival since millionaire Gábor Várszegi took control of the club – in 1997 they won the double. Sadly, crowds still only hover around the 3,000 mark. Yet the ground retains a romantic appeal, enhanced by its use as location for cult football film *Escape to Victory*. Yes, Sylvester Stallone and Pelé were together on this field.

Újpest

IV. Megyeri út 13 (390 6181). M3 Újpest Központ, then bus 104, 104a, 96 or red 96 to Megyeri út.
Once the team of the Interior Ministry, today Újpest can boast the most colourful, creative and passionate supporters. The Ultra Viola Bulldogs and friends do their best to create a Latin atmosphere in a badly decaying stadium and sometimes, with the help of flares, drums and huge lilac flags, they manage to pull it off. After struggling in recent years, Újpest have lately enjoyed a revival.

Vasas

XIII. Fáy utca 58 (120 8697). M3 Forgách utca.
Apart from some 1960s success, Vasas have always been one of Budapest's smaller teams. Their spartan stadium is in working-class Angyalföld and the supporters are a friendly bunch of retired trade unionists and drunken engineers. The main attraction is the Santa Fé Étterem behind the goal where you can sit with a cold beer and a grilled chicken sandwich while the boys in red, white and blue stumble around.

Horse Racing

In its socialist 1960s heyday, Hungarian racing offered a rare chance of easy riches, dodgy dealing and cheap thrills. But these days the race courses are a crumbling mess, with a dwindling band of veteran punters struggling to keep up the banter. Hungarian tax authorities ensure that returns are ludicrously low and the gambling is the equivalent of playing cards for matchsticks.

A win is *tét*, a place *hely*. For some chance of paying for the next beer with your winnings go for a box bet: *hármas* is 1,2,3 in order or a *befutó* is the top three in any order. There are rows of windows, where you announce your bet to the grandma by the computer and she gives you a slip. Getting the odds is difficult, especially for boxes, but the odds for wins are shown on the scoreboard, based on a nominal Ft10 bet. The numbers 3-25 would mean that horse 3 winning will give you Ft25 for your Ft10 wagered, or, in British terminology, 5/2. To check out the form, pick up a copy of *Magyar Turf* (Ft100) which has a list of all the runners in the field with details of their last five outings.

Flat Racing

Galopp
Kincsem Park X. *Albertirsai út 2 (263 7858). M2 Pillangó utca.* **Open** *April-Nov* from 2-7pm Sun. **Admission** Ft300. **No credit cards**. No English spoken.

Trotting

Ügető
Ügetőpálya VIII. *Kerepesi út 9-11 (334 2958). Bus 95.* **Open** *all year* from 2pm Sat; from 4pm Wed. **Admission** Ft300. **No credit cards**. No English spoken.

Ice Hockey

Unusually for a former Communist country, Hungary has never produced a top ice hockey team. But interest is growing and with foreign players and coaches working in the sport the quality of the Hungarian game is slowly improving. There are four professional teams in the Extra Liga, including Újpest and Ferencváros from Budapest. Play-offs take place in February at the **Budapest Sportcsarnok**. Fixture details from the **Ice Hockey Federation** (157 0007). Ferencváros play home fixtures at the Kisstadion, next door to Népstadion; Újpest play at the rink beside their football stadium.

Motor Racing

When the Hungarian Grand Prix was reintroduced in 1986 after a 50-year absence, it was the first time Bernie Ecclestone's circus had ventured behind the Iron Curtain. The event often appears to be in jeopardy but is now guaranteed until at least 2000.

Hungaroring

20km east of Budapest off M3 motorway at Mogyoród (06 28 330 040). **Information** *Formula 1 Kft, V. Apáczai Csere János utca 11 (118 7610). M1, M2 or M3 to Deák tér.* **Open** 8am-4pm daily one month before event. **Date** second Sunday in August. **Admission** from Ft4,000 for the cheapest standing ticket on race day to Ft48,000 for a three-day seat. **No credit cards**. English spoken.

Swimming & Water Polo

Hungary continues to produce Olympic and World champions in swimming such as Krisztina Egerszegi and Tamás Darnyi. In water polo, club sides such as Újpest, BVSC, Vasas and Ferencváros regularly feature in the finals of the major European competition and those games guarantee a full house and a noisy atmosphere as the football fans head for the pools.

For details of competitions call the **Hungarian Swimming Association** (326 1584) or the **Budapest Water Polo Federation** (118 0933).

Komjádi Béla Sportuszoda

III. Árpád fejedelem útja 8 (212 2750). Bus 6, 60, 86. **Map B1**
Hungary's national swimming stadium, named after the coach who, in 1932, led Hungary to its first Olympic gold in water polo. Expect a full house for top water polo matches and international swimming galas.

Activities

Cycling

Cycling is illegal on motorways and major roads, and inadvisable during rush hour. Bikes can be taken on certain trains, normally the first or last carriage, but not on trams or the metro. The bike path alongside the road to Szentendre makes for a pleasant afternoon's ride. Margaret Island has two stalls by the roundabout near Margaret Bridge, generally open from 8am-dusk, where you can rent bikes for use in town.

The Friends of City Cycling Group

III. Miklós tér 1 (111 7855). Tram 1/bus 6, 86. Some English spoken.
Produces a *Map for Budapest Cyclists*, showing bike lanes, riding conditions and service shops.

Hungarian Camping & Caravan Club

VIII. Kálvin tér 9, First Floor (218 5259). M3 Kálvin tér. Some English spoken. **Map D5**
Can provide information if required.

Hungarian Cycling Association

XIV. Szabó József utca 3 (252 0879). Bus 7. Some English spoken.
The Millenáris cycle track here is the only one in Hungary.

IBUSZ Leisure Department

V. Ferenciek tere 10, III/5 (118 2967). M3 Ferenciek tere. **Open** 9am-4pm Mon-Thur; 9am-3pm Fri. **Credit** V. Some English spoken. **Map C4**
IBUSZ can arrange cycling trips through the Danube Bend, in the Puszta and across southern Hungary for an average DM1,750. This covers two weeks' half-board for a double room and bike hire.

National Rail Office (MÁV)

VI. Andrássy út 35 (322 8275). M1 Opera. **Open** *Apr-Sept 30* 9am-6pm Mon-Fri; *Oct-Mar* 9am-5pm Mon-Fri. **No credit cards.** Some English spoken.
The National Rail Office (MÁV) can provide a list of cycle-friendly stations and the surcharges per kilometre for cycling tickets (*kerékpárjegy*).

Schwinn-Csepel

VI. Hegedű utca 6 (342 4620). M1 Oktogon. **Open** 10am-6pm Mon-Wed; 10am-7pm Thur; 10am-6pm Fri; 10am-1pm Sat. **No credit cards.** Some English spoken. **Map D3**
A bike shop with a service and repair department.

'*How do I work this thing, anyway?*'

Extreme Sports

Tourists at Heroes' Square often spend more time watching kids doing jumps and turns on skateboards and in-line skates than admiring the statues of the seven Magyar tribal chieftains. Extreme sports are big among Hungarian teens, who with their reversed baseball caps and Nike trainers have adopted the street image of cola commercials.

Rollsport – In-line Skate Center

IX. Kálvin tér 7 (217 4397). M3 Kálvin tér. **Open** 10am-6pm Mon-Fri; 10am-1pm Sat. **No credit cards.** English spoken. **Map D5**
Caters to the skate rat's every need. Wide range of in-line skating equipment including skates, protectors, clothing and helmets – all major brand names. Also a good place to find out the latest on competitions and venues.

Görzenál Skatepark and Freetime Centre

III. Árpád fejedelem útja 125 (250 4800). Szentendrei HÉV to Tímár utca. **Open** 10am-8pm. **Admission** Ft300; Ft200 under-12s. **Rental** Ft300 for three hours. **No credit cards.** English spoken.
A teenage paradise. In one closed-off area there is a roller-skating track, skateboard park, BMX and cycle track and jumps, two basketball courts and several 'freestyle' areas with ramps and jumps for bike, skate or board.

Golf

See page 212 **Fairway to heaven.**

Birdland Golf Country Club

240 km from Budapest. M1 toward Györ, route 85 to Csorna, route 86 to Hegyfalug, route 86 toward Sopron,

through Tompaládony to Bükfürdő. Thermal körút 10 (94 358 060/94 359 000/fax 94 359 000). **Open** daily 8am-dusk. **Fee** Ft6,150 per round Mon-Thur; Ft7,200 per round Fri-Sun. **Club rental** Ft5,260 Mon-Thur; Ft6,000 Fri-Sun. **Credit** AmEx, V, M. English spoken.
Hungary's best course: championship-rated and sited in beautiful hills close to the Austrian border.

Budapest Golfpark & Country Club

40 km north of Budapest. Route 11 past Szentendre to Kisoroszi (26 392 463). **Office** *V. Bécsi utca 5 (117 6025).* **Open** *March 15-Nov* 7am-8pm daily. **Fee** DM43 per round Mon-Fri; DM54 on weekends and holidays. **Club rental** DM12. **Credit** AmEx, DC, EC, JCB, MC, V. Some English spoken.
Closest course to Budapest, but experienced golfers will curse its cow-pasture quality.

Hencse National Golf & Country Club

175km south-west of Budapest at Hencse, Kossuth Lajos utca 3 (82 481 245/fax 82 481 248). **Open** 7am-dusk daily. **Fee** *day card* DM50 Mon-Fri; DM66 Sat, Sun. **Credit** AmEx, DC, EC, JCB, MC, V. English spoken.
Splendidly sited in a National Park. Rooms cost DM100 for a single, DM125 double, with negotiable group fees.

Hotel Wien

XI. Budaörsi út 88-90 (310 2999). Bus 40 from Móricz Zsigmond körtér. **Open** noon-10pm (call to reserve). **Fee** Ft 2,500 per hour. **Credit** AmEx, DC, JCB, MC, V. English spoken.

Indoor simulated golf. Whack the ball at the padded screen showing the fairways and greens of the Pebble Beach Country Club, California, and a computer calculates the distance and direction of your shot.

Pannónia Golf & Country Club

38 km west of Budapest at Máriavölgy. From M1 west of Budapest take Bicske exit, Rt 100 toward Tatabánya, Rt 811 to Alcsútdoboz, turn left, course is 3 km. (22 243 243). **Open** 8am-8pm daily. **Fee** Ft5,000 per round Mon-Fri noon; Fri noon-Sun Ft9,000. **Club rental** Ft2,100. **No credit cards**. English spoken.
On the former family estate of the Habsburg-Lothringens.

The 19th Hole Driving Range

Petneházy Club Hotel, II. Feketefej utca 2-4 (06 30 441 185/06 30 544 017/fax 393 1407). Tram 56 from Moszkva tér then bus 63. **Open** 9am-9pm Mon-Fri; 9am-8pm Sat-Sun. **Fee** Ft500 for a basket of 35 balls and Ft200 per club. **No credit cards**. English spoken.
On a quiet Buda hill, hone your swing from covered stalls.

Health & Fitness

Young Hungary has gone fitness mad. Gyms and solariums have sprung up all over town, though many are unregulated and unprofessional. Better clubs, such as those listed here, meet standard safety regulations. Aerobics is also booming and the

---

Fairway to heaven

Á Tanu (The Witness), a once-banned Magyar film classic, depicts one József Pelikán bumbling through a series of bizarre misadventures that came to symbolise for Hungarians the comedy and terror of life under Soviet communism. Perhaps it is not so strange that when a sequel was made in the 1990s depicting the new comedies and terrors of life under capitalism, Józsi ends up clad in gaudy trousers and hacking his away around Hungary's first golf course.

It didn't take long for this decadent bourgeois pastime to establish a toehold in Hungary. There are four golf courses in the country, ranging from cow-pasture quality to very good. And the sport has taken off among a small slice of Hungarian society – basically businessmen who don't want to be left behind when their foreign colleagues or clients head for the links. Apart from its role as an expensable business activity, golf club membership also ranks up there with a second BMW in terms of status symbols among Hungary's conspicuously consumerist *nouveau riche*. Hungarian golfers even commit the cardinal sin of bringing their mobile phones on to the course.

There are, however, no golf terms in Hungarian. You will not find 'double bogey' in an English-Magyar dictionary. Thus, it is not unusual when standing behind a Hungarian foursome on the first tee to hear something that will sound to the foreign visitor like: 'Blah-blah, blah-blah *send trep*.' Or, 'Blah-blah, *peeching vedge*, blah-blah.' You can then try to guess which of the blah-blahs was an expletive.

Of the four courses to try, the two best are a good haul from Budapest. **Hencse National Golf & Country Club** is near Lake Balaton – a long course and well-maintained with wide, forgiving fairways. The toughest course is the championship-rated **Birdland Golf Country Club** in the resort town of Bükfürdő near the Austrian border. Fairways are tight, surrounded by woods, and the course has more water than you'll be able to stand by the end of the day. There is also a nine-hole par-three course.

Closest course to town (40 km) is **Budapest Golfpark & Country Club**, at the northern extreme of Szentendre Island in Kisoroszi. The setting offers the unique experience of whacking a little white ball around in the shadow of Visegrád Castle, where Vlad the Impaler (inspiration for Dracula) supposedly spent a decade under house arrest. Otherwise it's awful. Greens are slow and bumpy, tees are indistinguishable from fairways – except for the tee markers – and fairways are a mess. Appropriately, this is where Józsi Pelikán went golfing.

national team recently lifted the World Cup. For information contact the **Hungarian Aerobics Federation** *V. Széchenyi utca 8 (312 5699).*

Andi Stúdió

V. Hold utca 29 (111 0740). M2 Kossuth tér, or M3 Arany János utca. **Open** 7am-8pm Mon-Fri, 8am-2pm Sat-Sun. **Rates** Ft500 (aerobics); Ft400 (gym). **No credit cards.** Some English spoken. **Map C3**
Budapest's first western-style fitness club, with an on-site cosmetician and a bar and café.

Eurofit

I. Pálya utca 9 (156 9530). M2 Deli/bus 2, 78, 105. **Open** 7am-11pm Mon-Fri; 9am-9pm Sat-Sun. **Rates** Ft450 (aerobics); Ft1,200 (squash); Ft800 (gym). **Credit** AmEx, DC, EC, JCB, MC, V. English spoken. **Map A4**
Wide range of services including sauna, steam bath, solarium and restaurant. The most upmarket fitness club in town.

Arnold Gym

III. Szépvölgyi út 15 (439 7165). Tram 17. **Open** 7am-11pm. **Rates** Ft800 (includes gym, aerobics and sauna); Ft800 (squash before 4pm); Ft1,500 (squash after 4pm and at weekends). **No credit cards.** Some English spoken.
Young clientèle, fun atmosphere and reasonable rates make this one of the busiest clubs in Budapest. Book in advance.

Marriott World Class Fitness Centre

Apáczai Csere János utca 4 (266 7000). M1 Vörösmarty tér. **Open** 6am-11pm daily. **Rates** Ft1,600 (aerobics and gym); Ft 2,700/hour (squash). **Credit** AmEx, DC, EC, JCB, MC, V. **Map C4**
Personal trainers; rowing, cycling and running machines; sauna, solarium, squash court; Thai and Swedish massage.

Kayak & Canoe

In the 1950s, the Danube was peppered with families canoeing away a Sunday afternoon. While boating has lost its attraction as a pastime, Hungary remains one of the top nations in kayak and canoe and the country is host to a number of international competitions, usually held in Szeged.

Béke üdülőtelep

III. Nánási út 97 (188 9303) Bus 34. **Open** 7am-8pm June-July; 7am-7pm August. **Rates** Ft600-Ft800. **No credit cards.** English spoken.
On the banks of the Danube close to the Hotel Lidó. Kayaks and canoes of various sizes available to rent.

Riding

Horsemanship is popular with Magyars, perhaps dating back to when they rode into Europe from Asia. There is a well-developed tourist industry on the Puszta, especially at Hortobágy.

IBUSZ Leisure Department

V. Ferenciek tere 10, III/5 (118 2967). M3 Ferenciek tere. **Open** 9am-4pm Mon-Thur; 9am-3pm Fri. **Credit** V. Some English spoken. **Map C4**
IBUSZ organises a variety of regular group tours to the Puszta from DM690 for a six-day trip, up to DM2,000 for a nine-day trip. All trips include full board, a professional riding instructor and a multi-lingual guide.

Kayak & Canoe – *a Magyar gets his oar in.*

Petneházy Riding School

II. Feketefej utca 2-4 (176 5937). Tram 56 from Moszkva tér then bus 63. **Open** 9am-noon, 2pm-4pm daily. **Closed** Mon. **No credit cards.** English spoken.
Next door to the Petneházy Club Hotel around 10km from the city centre. For beginners the price is Ft900 per hour, for those with some riding knowledge the price is Ft1,100 – those with experience can take part in short forest tours.

Squash

City Squash Club

II. Marczibányi tér 13 (212 3110). Tram 4, 6. **Open** 7am-midnight daily. **No credit cards.** Some English spoken. **Map A2**
Four courts, Ft1,800 per person per hour (Ft2,400 per hour 5-10pm Mon-Fri). Racquets cost Ft400 per session. Light-coloured soles must be worn.

Eurofit

I. Pálya utca 9 (156 9530). M2 Deli/ bus 2, 78, 105. **Open** 7am-11pm Mon-Fri; 9am-9pm Sat-Sun. **Credit** AmEx, DC, EC, JCB, MC, V. English spoken. **Map A4**
Two courts, on hire for Ft1,200 per hour until 4pm, Ft2,000 from 4-11pm. Racquet hire: Ft200 per session.

Hotel Marriott

V. Apáczai Csere János utca 4 (266 7000). M1 Vörösmarty tér/tram 2. **Open** 7am-10pm Mon-Fri, 10am-8pm Sat-Sun. **Credit** AmEx, DC, EC, JCB, MC, V. English spoken. **Map C4**
One court, costing Ft2,700 per hour. Racquet hire Ft300.

Swimming

Hungary has enjoyed remarkable success in competitive swimming. Alfréd Hajós won gold medals at the first modern Olympics in 1896, then built the pool on Margaret Island where generations of champions trained. In summer, open-air pools are popular. Certain pools and 'strands' (pools with an area for posing and sunbathing) require swimming hats to be worn by both sexes. Day tickets, except at the **Gellért**, cost approximately Ft200 and books of 25 tickets cost around Ft3,000. *See also chapters* **Baths** *and* **Gay & Lesbian.**

Gellért Gyógyfürdő

XI. Kelenhegyi út 4 (166 6166). Trams 18, 19, 47, 49 or bus 7 to Gellért tér. **Open** 6am-6pm daily. **Admission** Ft1,200; Ft600 concs. Mixed. Some English spoken Some English spoken Some English spoken. **Map B5**

Grand, if expensive, setting for knocking out a few lengths. Warm indoor pool, relaxing outdoor pool, wave pool, children's pool, thermal pool and sauna. Gay afternoons in the thermal pool on Wednesdays and Sundays.

Hajós Alfréd Nemzeti Sportuszoda

XIII. Margaret Island (111 4046). Tram 4, 6 then bus 26. **Open** 6am-5pm Mon-Fri; 6am-6pm Sat, Sun. **Rates** Ft200 day ticket, Ft120 under-18s. Some English spoken. **Map B1**
Named after its architect, who won Hungary's first Olympic gold medals for swimming and appeared in the first Hungarian national football team. Public use of the three pools – two outdoor, one indoor – is limited by training or competitions. Sunbathing terrace and restaurant.

Lukács Gyógyfürdő és Strandfürdő

II. Frankel Leó út 25-29 (326 1695). Tram 4, 6. **Open** 6am-7pm Mon-Sat; 6am-5pm Sun. **Admission** Ft300. No English spoken. **Map B1**
Nineteenth-century bath house with two swimming pools, four thermal pools, a spa, a Finnish sauna, a mud bath and physiotherapy. Caters for an older set.

Széchenyi Gyógyfürdő és Strandfürdő

XIV. Állatkerti körút 11 (121 0310). M1 Széchenyi fürdő. **Open** *strand* 6am-7pm daily. *Mixed thermal baths (Apr-Sept)* 6am-7pm daily; *Oct-Mar* 6am-5pm Mon-Sat, 6am-4pm Sun. **Admission** Ft300. No English spoken. **Map F1**
Hottest thermal pools in Budapest. The Széchenyi, in an elegant neo-Baroque building in City Park, comes into its own in winter. Hardy folk trek over the ice from the thermal section to spend an afternoon playing chess in the outdoor pool under clouds of steam. A host of treatments also available.

Hotel Aquincum

III. Árpád fejedelem útja 94 (250 3360). Tram 1 from M3 Árpád híd. **Open** 7am-9pm daily. **Admission**

Palatinus – *what more could a boy want?*

weekday tickets purchased before 10am Ft650; otherwise Ft1,200; weekend day ticket Ft1,600. English spoken.
A boon for guests, a bit expensive otherwise. Three pools, sauna and solarium.

Thermal Hotel Helia

XIII. Karpát utca 62-64 (270 3277). M3 Dózsa György út/trolleybus 79 to Karpát utca. **Open** 7am-10pm daily. **Admission** *weekday morning ticket to 3pm* Ft1,000; *3pm-10pm* Ft 1,900; *weekend or full-day ticket* Ft2,500. English spoken. **Map C1**
Thermal waters transported from Margaret Island by tube. A wide range of thermal treatments on offer. Four pools, two thermal pools, sauna, underwater massage services.

Thermal Hotel Margitsziget

XIII. Margaret Island (311 1000). Bus 26. **Open** 7am-8pm daily. **Admission** *day ticket* Ft1,200. English spoken.
Built on the thermal springs of an old spa, this Margaret Island complex has three thermal pools – at 33, 35 and 39 degrees – two swimming pools, two single-sex saunas, a 28-degree swimming pool and a sunbathing terrace.

Strands

Doing the strand is an essential part of the Budapest summer, posing by the open-air swimming pool and dealing with the occasional beer, swim and *lángos*. There are 12 strands in Budapest. Some visitors stroll topless, while others go naked in certain sections of the Csillaghegyi Strand.

Csillaghegyi Strand

III. Pusztakúti út 3 (250 1533). HÉV Csillaghegy. **Open** *1 May-15 Sept, swimming pool open all year* 7am-7pm daily. **Rates** Ft240 day ticket, after 5pm Ft180. No English spoken.
Four pools in a picturesque setting, with a combined capacity of 3,000. Nude sunbathing on the southern slope.

Dagály

XIII. Népfürdő utca 36 (120 2203). M3 Lehel tér then bus 133. **Open** 6am-8pm daily. **Rates** Ft300 day ticket, Ft200 under-18s. No English spoken.
Twelve pools with a capacity of 12,000. Also a sauna and keep-fit rooms.

Palatinus

XIII. Margaret Island (340 4505). Tram 4, 6 then bus 26. **Open** *1 May-15 Sept* 8am-6pm daily. **Rates** Ft250 day ticket. Some English spoken.
Seven pools include a thermal pool, two children's pools and a teaching pool, plus slides and wave machines. Capacity of 10,000 and on a hot Saturday afternoon in July it can feel like standing-room only.

Római

III. Rozgonyi Piroska utca 2 (188 9740). HÉV Rómaifürdő. **Open** *1 May-15 Sept* 8am-7pm daily. **Rates** Ft240 day ticket. No English spoken.
Three pools and a water chute.

Tennis

There are around 30 tennis clubs in Budapest, most with clay courts, charging between Ft500-Ft1,000 per hour, and some offer coaching lessons. Hotels also rent out courts to non-guests. The following is a selection from different areas of town.

Where to catch the match

Strangely for a city full of theme bars, there is no football pub in Budapest. The new bar owners are all competing for the trade of twentysomethings with plenty of cash and the stereotypical Hungarian football fan is a fortysomething with a beer belly bigger than his disposable income.

If you desperately need to catch the live Sky Sports English Premiership game then **Becketts** (*see chapter* **Pubs & Bars**) is sadly the only option. The sound of Andy Gray in full flow sometimes breaks through the gaggle of business chatter and the loud guffaws of the rugby boys. Watching Manchester United fans in suits celebrate winning the league here has to be one of the most depressing experiences imaginable. If you can make do with the highlights then Hungarian channel M-SAT carries a wrap-up of the weekend's action at 9pm on Monday nights. *Nemzeti Sport,* Ft56, provides the Premiership results.

For European cup games **Kétballábas** (*see chapter* **Restaurants**) has waiters who know what they are talking about and if the owner György Bognár, coach of BVSC and 50 times capped for Hungary, happens to be in with his friends, you can expect plenty of Magyar footballing banter. The walls are decked with flashbacks from his career and no one complains about having the television on.

If you have just witnessed a great Ferencváros victory then the Simon Pince at XIII. Hegedűs Gyula utca 2, owned by tough-tackling Tibor Simon, the Fradi full-back, will be venue for the

Going into extra time at **Becketts.**

post-match celebration. The food is rather dull Hungarian but the pictures on the walls are surprisingly discreet and don't overpower what is a essentially a typical Hungarian cellar söröző.

Most of the hundreds of smelly borozós hidden in the cellars of apartment blocks will have the telly on for Hungarian and international games. To get a feeling of the bitterness and frustration of the average fan these places are perfect. Sadly, the one borozó dedicated to football has no television, but if the idea of a Ft25 spritzer, a lard sandwich and a picture of Puskás turns you on then the 6-3 Borozó at IX. Lónyay utca 62 is a must. It's a scruffy little tribute bar to the side which defeated England at Wembley in 1953. Sadly, like the side itself, it packs up before it should do and closes around 7pm.

Hungarian Tennis Association

XIV. Dózsa György út 1-3 (252 6687). M2 Népstadion. English spoken.
The Association holds a full list of clubs and courts.

BHSE

XIII. Margaret Island (339 8672). Bus 26 from Nyugati Station. **Open** 7am-9pm daily. **Rates** 7am-3pm Ft450 per hour; 3pm-8pm Ft600 per hour; floodlit court Ft1,000 per hour. Eight courts. **No credit cards.** English spoken. **Map B1**

Római Teniszakadémia

III. Királyok útja 105 (160 8616). Bus 34. **Open** 6am-11pm daily. **Rates** 6am-1pm Ft600 per hour; 1-5pm Ft700 per hour; 5pm-10pm Ft800 per hour. Nine courts. **No credit cards.** English spoken.

Szépvölgy Tennis Centre

III. Virág Benedek utca 39-41 (388 1591). Bus 65. **Open** 6am-midnight daily. **Rates** outdoor 6am-3pm Ft800 per hour; 3pm-8pm Ft1,000 per hour; indoor Ft900-Ft2,400. Six courts. **No credit cards.** English spoken.
Three indoor courts, three outdoor. Excellent lighting and ventilation.

Városmajor Tennis Academy

XII. Városmajor utca 63-69 (202 5337). Bus 21, 121. **Open** 7am-10pm Mon-Fri; 7am-7pm Sat; 8am-7pm Sun. **Rates** Ft550-Ft650 (plastic court); Ft650-Ft750 (clay court); Ft750-Ft850 (green set court). Five courts. **No credit cards.** English spoken.
Two clay courts and three green set courts. Also a tennis school with qualified instructors.

Vasas SC

II. Pasaréti utca 11-13 (156 6537). Bus 5. **Open** 6am-8pm daily. **Rates** Ft800 per hour. Six courts. **No credit cards.** No English spoken.

Ten-Pin Bowling

MVA Bowling Centre

Duna Plaza XIII. Váci út (465 1155). M3 Gyöngyösi út. **Open** 10am - 1am daily. **Rates** 10am-3pm Ft1,000 per hour; 3pm-6pm Ft1,500 per hour; 6pm-1am Ft2,000 per hour. **Credit** AmEx, DC, JCB, MC, V. Some English spoken.
In the Duna Plaza mall (*see chapter* **Shopping & Services**), ten alleys for ten-pin bowling plus bar and restaurant.

Theatre & Dance

Budapest strives hard to become a city of theatres once again.

*One of those monolithic institutions – the current **National Theatre**. See page 217.*

There are about three dozen working theatres in Budapest. The mainstream places still pack 'em in with international musicals and the same old Shakespeare and Hungarian classics, but interesting alternative productions are few and far between. Money is short, and while various foundations around the city will support fine art and literary activities, theatre lags way behind with most funds siphoned off into keeping the opera and big city stages alive.

But there is hope. Many of the bright young things who left several decades ago, fleeing cultural stagnation, are returning as mature artists to liven things up. People like Péter Halász, who 20 years ago came up with the idea of 'room theatre' – groups performing in private flats to avoid censorship. Halász went on to New York with his company, Squat Theatre. In one production since his return, the cast bought a newspaper and made a performance out of its contents in just 24 hours. Another emigré, László Hudi, worked with the movement-based József Nadj Theatre in Paris before coming back to found the Moving House Theatre (Mozgóház). The company was acclaimed for its musical *Beckett's Songs* in Berlin in 1997.

Ironically it was a Habsburg Emperor, Joseph II, who first encouraged official Hungarian-language theatre in the late eighteenth century. By doing so he unwittingly set in motion a new art form that would contribute much to the national revival movement throughout the next century. Anglophile and reformer Count Széchenyi made great efforts to secure a National Theatre, seeing it as a crucial institution in the emergence of a new Magyar state. Originally on a site at Astoria, the National Theatre opened its doors in 1837 with a performance of the Magyar classic *Árpád's Awakening* by national poet Mihály Vörösmarty. The building was declared a fire hazard in 1908 and moved to a Neoclassical pile on Blaha Lujza tér. Here it remained until 1964 when the Communists pulled it down in order to build the metro. It then moved to its present hideous premises in the District VII backstreets beyond the Nagykörút. The site of the National Theatre remains a subject of bitter debate and there are plans to move it once again into new premises on Erzsébet tér, where the bus station now stands.

Over the centuries Hungary built up a respectable tradition that looked west for its inspiration. Naturalism was introduced in the early twentieth century when the Reinhardt company came regularly to the city. Foreign work was often staged and, although it took the Hungarians 400 years to translate Shakespeare, they were staging Wilde and Gorky within a few years of their appearance. Stanislavski also made an impact on the Hungarian stage and his realist method continues to hold sway today.

The Soviet takeover in 1948 shifted Hungary out of the European mainstream. Budapest had been a city of theatres. József körút, for example, had a playhouse every third block or so, and the city offered revues, cabarets and farces alongside less populist pieces. The Communists closed many houses, imported dull socialist-realist work, and theatre went into decline. But the Stalinist regime was not unaware of the power of the medium, and in 1951 the State Village Theatre was formed. A horse-drawn ensemble, it toured the villages staging didactic pieces on collectivisation and Stakhanovism.

One of the first projects undertaken by the first post-communist City Council was to renovate the **Vígszínház** (Comedy Theatre) on Szent István körút, an indication of its importance as a symbol. Built a century ago in the Neo-baroque style so beloved of the Austro-Hungarian Monarchy, it became the prototype for theatres all over the country. There are currently plans to build and open new arts centres all around the city. These would replace the communist-inspired Houses of Culture that did little to promote anything except folk dancing and Young Communist meetings. Fired more by enthusiasm and energy than funds, it is hard to predict whether they will come off, but Budapest is certainly keen to become a city of theatres once again.

Curtains usually rise in Hungarian theatres at 7pm or 7.30pm. If not open all day, Budapest box offices begin selling tickets an hour prior to curtain. Wheelchair access and hearing systems generally are unavailable, even in the State Opera House. Often there are no programmes and the coatcheck is usually mandatory, to the point of confrontations with stroppy theatre ushers.

Unless otherwise indicated, credit cards are not accepted at venues and agencies listed.

Ticket Agencies

Some English is usually spoken. If not, ask around. Transactions are invariably in cash, and only in forints.

Central Theatre Booking Office

VI. Andrássy út 18 (312 0000). M1 Opera. **Open** 9am-1pm, 2pm-6pm Mon-Fri. **Map D3**
Tickets for all performance arts can be purchased here. **Branch:** II. Moszkva tér 3 (135 9136).

Music Mix-33 Ticket Service

V. Váci utca 33 (138 2237/117 7736). M3 Ferenciek tere. **Open** 10am-6pm Mon-Fri. Closed in summer. **Map C4**
Tickets for theatre, dance, also rock and classical music concerts and tickets for events abroad.

Dance & Theatre Listings

Pesti Est and *Pesti Műsor* cover just about everything that happens in Hungary. The *Budapest Week* and *Budapest Sun* also run incomplete and often inaccurate listings (*see chapter* Media). The monthly guide *Nézőpont* is available at Ft69 from most ticket bureaus.

Theatres

Establishment Theatres

Katona József Színház

V. Petőfi Sándor utca 6 (118 6599). M3 Ferenciek tere/bus 7. **Open** box office 10am-6pm daily. **Map C4**
Long considered the best Hungarian theatre, this company of players excels in the classics. Their productions of Victor Hugo's *The Laughing Man* directed by András Jeles and Jasmina Reza's *Art* directed by Tamás Ascher (both of whose work is worth watching out for) are outstanding.

Municipal Operetta Theatre

Fővárosi Operett Színház
VI. Nagymező utca 17 (269 3870). M1 Oktogon/tram 4, 6. **Open** box office 10am-6pm daily. **Map D3**
Colourful productions of Hungarian operettas by composers such as Franz Lehár, Imre Kálmán and Pál Ábrahám. Catch the very best Hungarian operetta – Kálmán's *The Csárdás Princess*. A beautiful late Habsburg venue, scheduled for restoration.

National Theatre

Nemzeti Színház
VII. Hevesi Sándor tér 4 (322 2879/342 6175). Tram 4, 6 Wesselényi utca. **Open** box office 1pm-7pm Mon-Fri; 1 hour before curtain Sat, Sun. **Map E3**
For over 200 years – since the 1960s in this ugly socialist-realist building – the National has been producing Hungarian and international dramas and musicals. Founded to promote Hungarian at a time when all other theatres performed in German, nowadays the National has a reputation for conservative programming and mediocre performances.

Pesti Színház

V. Váci utca 9 (266 5245). M1, M2, M3 Deák tér/tram 47, 49. **Open** box office 1pm-7pm Mon-Fri; 1 hour before curtain Sat, public holidays. **Map C4**
The sister theatre of the **Vígszínház** runs classics by Chekhov, Gogol, Miller and Shakespeare.

Vígszínház

Comedy Theatre
XIII. Szent István körút 14 (111 1650). M3 Nyugati/tram 4, 6. **Open** box office 1pm-7pm Mon-Fri; 1 hour before curtain Sat, Sun. **Map C2**
This Habsburg jewel, Budapest's biggest theatre, houses one of central Europe's most dynamic acting companies, particularly suited to big musicals.

Alternative Theatres

Bárka Theatre

VIII. Ludovika tér 1 (303 4713). M3 Nagyvárad tér. **Open** depends on performances. **Map F6**
Formed in 1996 by famous theatre folk and young hopefuls and given a base at the Orczy-Kert park in District VIII. The company concentrates on contemporary works and stages literary, film and musical events. The aim is to appeal as broadly as possible and benefit the local community.

Merlin Theatre

V. Gerlóczy utca 4 (117 9338). M1, M2, M3 Deák tér/tram 47, 49. **Open** 10am-6pm daily, and 1 hour before curtain. **Map C4**
A theatre and restaurant which often stages touring English productions as well as small concerts and cabarets. Visiting writers also come here to give readings and lectures.

Mú Theatre

XI. Kőrösy József utca 17 (166 4627). Tram 4, 47, 49 Fehérvári út. **Open** box office 8am-7pm Mon-Fri; 1 hour before curtain Sat-Sun. **Map C6**

This House of Culture gives space to small alternative companies, musicians and dancers but has no resident company of its own. Certainly worth checking out if you want to see what is new on the Hungarian theatre scene.

Új Színház
VI. Paulay Ede utca 35 (269 6021). M1 Opera. **Open** 1pm-6pm Mon-Fri; 1 hour before curtain Sat. **Map D3** The 'New Theatre', designed by Béla Lajta (*see chapter* **Architecture**) stages small off-beat productions. Cervantes' *Don Juan* and Lorca's *Blood Wedding* are recommended.

Dance

Although dance is very much part of Hungarian folk life, zest for the genre has not really crossed over to the stage. Many productions are either old-fashioned in the extreme, or else stilted and angst-ridden. The Hungarian National Ballet, for example, pride themselves on a *Nutcracker Suite* which hasn't changed for nearly a century.

The modern dance scene has benefited from visits by international companies but remains low on cash and ideas. There are, however, some interesting ensembles. Yvette Bozsik & Company is the current darling of the moderns. This former HNB ballerina has adroitly swung sponsorship her way and presents half a dozen programmes of modern choreography throughout the year. She is based in the Bethlen Cinema on Rózsák tere in District VII. The Artus Táncszínház, another worthwhile modern ensemble, are hoping soon to move operations to a boat on the Danube.

Information

Contemporary Dance Theatre Society
Kortárs Táncszínházi Egyesület *XI. Kőrösy József utca 17 (166 4627). Tram 4, 47, 49 Fehérvári út.* **Open** 4pm-7pm Tue-Thur. Contact Adrienn Szabó. **Map C6** Represents most of the modern Hungarian dance groups in the city and have information about what is new in town.

Szkéné Theatre
Műszaki Egyetem, XI. Műegyetem rakpart 3-9 (463 3741). Tram 18, 19, 47, 49. **Open** 9am-4pm Mon-Thur; 9am-2.30pm Fri; 1 hour before performance Sat, Sun. **Map C6** Venue that also provides information about dance and alternative theatre, and sponsors the **International Meeting of Moving Theatres** (*see below*), at which obscure, talented dance groups gather from all over Europe to expose themselves in this tiny black box.

Táncfórum
I. Corvin tér 8 (201 8779). M2 Batthyány tér/tram 19. **Open** 2pm-6pm Mon-Fri. **Map B3** Can provide information regarding Tranz Danz, Yvette Bozsik, Army and other dance companies. They also arrange the dance section of the Spring and Autumn Festivals.

Venues & Offices

Hungarian National Ballet
Magyar Nemzeti Balett *Magyar Állami Operaház, VI. Andrássy út 22 (153 0170). M1 Opera.* **Open** *box office* 11am-7pm Tue-Sat; 10am-1pm, 4pm-7pm, Sun when there is a performance. **Map D3** *Erkel Színház, VIII. Köztársaság tér (333 0540). M2 Keleti.* **Open** *box office* 11am-7pm Tue-Sat; 10am-1pm, 4-7pm, Sun when there is a performance. **Map E4** The Hungarian National Ballet, performing both in the splendid Opera House and its ugly sister, the Erkel, relies on Russian classical technique. The repertoire is weak on modern pieces although Bartók's *Miraculous Mandarin* is worth seeing.

Hungarian State Folk Ensemble
Magyar Állami Népi Együttes *I. Corvin tér 8 (201 5017). M2 Batthyány tér.* **Open** *box office* 2pm-6pm Mon-Fri. **Map B3** This company (which also tours internationally) specialises in authentic presentations of folk dancing and music from Hungary and the surrounding region. For more on folk dance *see chapter* **Folklore**.

Festivals

Further information can be had from either the Central Theatre Booking Office or the National Philharmonic Ticket Office (*see chapter* **Music: Classical & Opera**).

Csepürágó Festival, in the first week of June, is an all-day fest performed on Castle Hill. After that, from 10-18 June, actors, singers and mimes perform in squares and on street corners. Hungary's most prominent theatre artists, as well as the newest and rawest, all turn out for this.

Budapest Spring & Autumn Festival
VIII. Rákóczi út 66 4th floor door 66 (210 2795/133 2337/fax 133 2075). M2 Blaha Lujza tér/tram 4, 6. **Open** 10am-6pm. **No credit cards. Map E4** Central Office, Interart Festival Center, *V. Vörösmarty tér 1 (117 9838/fax 117 9910/118 9943). M1 Vörösmarty tér.* **Open** 10am-4pm Mon-Fri. **Map C4** Held each March and April, and again in October, these also feature many local and international guest theatres and dance companies. *See also chapters* **Budapest By Season** *and* **Music: Classical & Opera**.

Alternative Theatre Festival
Alternatív Színházi Fesztivál *Contact: Szkéné Színház, XI. Műegyetem rakpart 3 (463 2451/fax 463 2450).* Established in 1994 by ten local performance companies, working without government or corporate sponsorship, this is a 12-day festival of theatre and contemporary dance, held every April.

International Meeting of Moving Theatres
IMMT: Nemzetközi Mozgásszínházi Találkozó *Contact: Szkéné Színház, XI. Műegyetem rakpart 3 (463 2451/fax 463 2450).* Biannual festival since 1978 featuring dance and theatre, a segment of the **Budapest Autumn Weeks** (first week of October – *see chapter* **Budapest By Season**).

Budafest
VIP-Arts Management, VI. Hajós utca 13/15 (332 4816/302 4290). M1 Opera. **Map D3** Presents second-string international ballet dancers. Expensive, but your only chance to see ballet in August. The same organisation also stages a costumed ball at the Opera House every New Year's Eve. *See also chapter* **Budapest By Season**.

Trips Out of Town

Getting Started

Travelling out of Budapest is affordable, amenable and accomplished on an assortment of conveyances.

Budapest contains 20 per cent of Hungary's population. No other town is a tenth of its size. Away from the capital and the major tourist destinations of the Balaton, you'll find a different world: sleepy, backward, friendly. Trips out of town can be like stepping back in time.

Hungary is a small country. By bus, rail or car, two or three hours is the longest it'll take to get just about anywhere. At a more leisurely pace, boats serve destinations along the Danube. Hitching is popular among young Hungarians, especially around the Balaton in summer, but unless you're suddenly stranded or on an absurdly tight budget, it's not worth the bother. Trains and buses are frequent, reliable and very cheap.

Driving on Hungary's single-carriageway road system can be hazardous and hair-raising (*see chapter* **Getting Around**). New motorways are either being planned or under construction.

The better hotels will be able to help you with information and transport bookings. For more information about travel outside Budapest, try:

Ibusz

V. Petőfi tér 3 (118 5707). M3 Ferenciek tere. **Open** 24 hours daily. **Credit** V. **Map C4**
The national tourist agency has branches all over Hungary and can book accommodation, organise tours and train travel and provide information.

Tourinform

V. Sütő utca 2 (117 9800). M1, M2, M3 Deák tér/tram 47, 49. **Open** *2 Mar-14 Nov* 8am-8pm daily; *15 Nov-1 Mar* 8am-3pm Sat, Sun. **Map C4**
The helpful, multilingual staff can dispense lots of information about destinations outside Budapest.

By Bus

Buses are cheap and reasonably comfortable. Prices are per kilometre, with no discount for returns, except for Bratislava and Vienna. All other prices listed below are for one-way tickets, which can be bought in advance or on the coach. There are three main bus terminals:

Erzsébet tér

V. Erzsébet tér (117 2138/117 2966/int 117 2562). M1, M2, M3 Deák tér/tram 47, 49. **Open** 6am-9pm daily.
International destinations, south and west Hungary.

Népstadion

XIV. Népstadion (252 4496). M2 Népstadion. **Open** 6am-8pm daily.
Serves the north and east

Árpád híd

XIII. Árpád híd (117 2318/117 2966). M3 Árpád híd.
Destinations north along the Danube

To **Balatonfüred** (132km): *Erzsébet tér.* Journey time about two hours 30 minutes. Price Ft554. Three buses daily 6.30am-4.40pm. Last return 4.20pm.
To **Eger** (128km): *Népstadion.* Journey time about two hours. Price Ft554. 14 buses daily 6.15am-8.45pm. Last return 6.45pm.
To **Esztergom** (66km): *Árpád híd.* Journey time about one hour 15 minutes. Price Ft196. Frequent buses 6am-10.50pm. Last return 9.25pm.
To **Keszthely** (190km): *Erzsébet tér.* Journey time about three hours 40 minutes. Price Ft799. Two buses daily 6.30am-3.40pm, two extra Sat, Sun. Last return 4.30pm.
To **Pécs** (198km): *Erzsébet tér.* Journey time about four hours. Price Ft849. Five buses daily 6am-4.20pm. Last return 4.30pm.
To **Siófok** (106km): *Erzsébet tér.* Journey time about two hours 15 minutes. Price Ft512. Six buses daily 6.30am-4.40pm. Last return 6.15pm.
To **Sopron** (210km): *Erzsébet tér.* Journey time about four hours. Price Ft813. Four buses daily 6.30am-4pm, two extra Mon-Fri. Last return 2.15pm.
To **Szentendre** (20km): *Árpád híd.* Journey time about 30 minutes. Price Ft84. Frequent buses 7am-10pm. Last return 7.20pm.
To **Visegrád** (43km): *Árpád híd.* Journey time about one hour 10 minutes. Price Ft172. Frequent buses 7.30am-8.30pm. Last return 8.25pm.
To **Bratislava** (Pozsony) (300km): *Erzsébet tér.* Journey time about four hours. Price single Ft1,600, return Ft2,600. One bus daily 7.20am. Last return 4.45pm.
To **Vienna** (Bécs) (265km): *Erzsébet tér.* Journey time about 4 hours 45 minutes. Price single Ft2,450, return Ft3,450. Three buses daily 7am-5pm. Last return 7pm.

By Train

Trains are cheap and relatively reliable. Avoid személy trains, which stop at all stations. Gyors are so-called fast trains. InterCity trains are the speediest and most comfortable, equipped with buffet cars and air-conditioning that sometimes works.

Tickets are priced by the kilometre with no discount for returns. For InterCity trains you have to reserve a seat for Ft160. At rush hours arrive about half an hour before the train is due to leave, as there will be queues at station ticket offices. You can also buy tickets from the conductor on the train, though you may have to fork out a small fine.

No one speaks English at stations. Yellow departure timetables are posted at all of them. At ticket offices it's easiest just to write what you want on a piece of paper: destination, number of tickets, and the time of the train you want.

Oda-vissza means return. An R in the timetable means that you have to reserve a seat. International student cards are not valid but you can get a 33 per cent discount if you are under 26 or look like it (ask for *harminchárom százalék*).

The three main stations are Keleti, Nyugati and Déli, all of which are on underground lines. There is no real logic as to which train goes from which station so always make sure you check.

MÁV Information

VI. Andrássy út 35 (322 7860). M1 Opera. **Open** 9am-6pm. **No credit cards.**
You can buy train tickets here, they have all necessary information, and there's usually someone who speaks English. Phone line manned until 8pm.

To **Balatonfüred**: *Déli.* Journey time about two hours 20 minutes. Price Ft504. Six trains daily 6.25am-5.20pm. Last return 5.20pm.
To **Eger**: *Keleti.* Journey time about two hours. Price Ft504. Four trains daily 7.05am-7.20pm. Last return 8.36pm.
To **Esztergom**: *Nyugati.* Journey time about 90 minutes. Price Ft192. Ten trains daily 6.35am-10.20pm. Last return 6.55pm.
To **Pécs**: *Déli.* Journey time about two hours 30 minutes. Price Ft840 plus Ft160 reservation. Four InterCity trains daily 7.30am-7.30pm. Last InterCity return 6.10pm.
To **Keszthely**: *Déli.* Journey time about three hours 15 minutes. Price Ft720. Five trains daily 7.10am-5.10pm. Last return 6.20pm. Make sure you're sitting in the right carriage as the train sometimes splits.
To **Siófok**: *Déli.* Journey time about 90 minutes. Price Ft432. Six trains daily 7.10am-9.10pm. Last return 8.15pm.

To **Sopron**: *Keleti.* Journey time about three hours. Price Ft780 plus Ft160 reservation. Three InterCity trains daily 7.20am-5.25pm. Last InterCity return 6.36pm.
To **Szentendre**: *HÉV Batthyány tér.* Journey time 40 minutes. Price Ft89. Trains every 10-15 minutes 3.50am-11.40pm. Last return 11.30pm.
To **Bratislava** (Pozsony): *Keleti/Nyugati.* Journey time about three hours. Price one way Ft3,500, return Ft2,500 payable in hard currency or in forints. Ten trains daily 6.25am-9.30pm. Last return 8.43pm.
To **Vienna** (Bécs): *Keleti/Déli.* Journey time about two hours 30 minutes. Price one way Ft4,000 payable in hard currency or in forints. Eight trains daily 6am-9.25pm. Last return 7.05pm.
To **Zagreb** (Zagráb): Keleti/Déli. Journey time about seven hours. Price one way or return Ft5,300 payable in hard currency or in forints. Four trains daily 6.20am-5.30pm. Last return 4.10pm.

By Car

Most roads in Hungary are single carriageway and everybody seems to be in a hurry. You'll see some pretty hair-raising manoeuvres. The 1996 completion of the Budapest-Vienna motorway does, however, mean that you'll miss the delights of the Győr-Hegyeshalom stretch, fondly nicknamed Halál út – Death Road.

Getting out of Budapest is easy and routes are well signposted. From Buda follow M1 signs for Vienna and Sopron, M7 for destinations to the Balaton or then down to Zagreb, and the single carriageway E73 for Pécs. From Pest follow M3/E71 signs for Eger. From Árpád híd take the 10 for Esztergom and the 11 for Szentendre and Visegrád, following the west bank of the Danube.

No air-con but full of character – Hungary's trains are cheap and reliable.

There's more than one way to get out of Budapest – and more than one way to do it.

There are often lengthy queues on the M1 at the Hungarian-Austrian border. At weekends and high season you might have to wait an hour or so.

By Boat

In summer, leisurely boats and nippy jetfoils cruise up the Danube to Szentendre, Visegrád and Esztergom. Jetfoils will also whisk you onwards to Vienna via Bratislava. Although it's interesting to arrive in a new country by river, the jetfoil to Vienna has no real deck area to catch the view, and not much of a view anyway after you've passed the Danube Bend. There's an expensive bar on board, but only the most rudimentary selection of sandwiches and cold cuts if you get hungry on the six-hour journey. Take a picnic and a good book.

All boats to and from Esztergom stop at Visegrád. Most Szentendre boats continue to Visegrád, making a total of five boats to Visegrád every day. It's easy to visit Visegrád plus either Esztergom or Szentendre in a day-trip. Taking in all three by boat on one day is theoretically possible but pushing it. Some Japanese seem to manage it, though.

Boats run daily from 1 April-23 September. Esztergom jetfoils run from 26 May-3 September on Saturdays and holidays, and also on Fridays between 30 June-3 September. Vienna jetfoils run daily from 8 April-29 October and are priced in Austrian schillings, though any hard currency should be acceptable. Get those ones in advance. Tickets for other boats can be bought on board or

in advance at major hotels or the MAHART Tours booking office on Belgrád rakpart.

Boat to **Szentendre** and **Visegrád**: *Vigadó tér terminal (118 1223)*. Journey time to Szentendre about one hour 40 minutes; to Visegrád about three hours 30 minutes. Price to Szentendre Ft260; to Visegrád Ft290. Three boats daily 7.30am-2pm (on the 2pm change at Szentendre for Visegrád). Last return from Szentendre 7.40pm; from Visegrád 6.30pm.

Boat to **Visegrád** and **Esztergom**: *Vigadó tér terminal (118 1223)*. Journey time to Visegrád about three hours 20 minutes; to Esztergom about five hours 20 minutes. Price to Visegrád Ft290; to Esztergom Ft320. Three boats daily 7.45am-2pm. Last return from Visegrád 6.30pm; from Esztergom 5pm.

Jetfoil to **Esztergom**: *Vigadó tér terminal (118 1223)*. Journey time one hour 10 minutes. Price Ft600. One jetfoil at 9.20am Saturdays and holidays, 26 May-3 Sept, and also on Fridays between 30 June-3 Sept. Return 4.30pm.

Jetfoil to **Visegrád**: *Vigadó tér terminal (118 1223)*. Journey time 50 minutes. Price Ft600. One jetfoil at 9am on Saturdays and holidays, 26 May-3 Sept, and also on Fridays between 30 June-3 Sept. Return 4.40pm.

Jetfoil to **Bratislava**: *International terminal, V. Belgrád rakpart (between Elizabeth and Szabadság híd) (118 1743)*. Journey time about four hours 30 minutes. Price AS685 one-way, AS1,100 return. One boat daily at 9am. Return 10.20am. Arrive one hour prior to departure for check-in and passport control.

Jetfoil to **Vienna**: *International terminal, V. Belgrád rakpart (between Elizabeth and Szabadság Bridges) (118 1743)*. Journey time about six hours. Price AS750 one-way, AS1,100 return. Discounts for students; children under 6 free, 6-15 half-fare. One boat daily at 9am April-May, Sept-Oct. Two boats daily at 7.40am and 2pm June-Aug. Return 9am April-May, Sept-Oct, 8am and 2.50pm June-Aug. Arrive one hour prior to departure for check-in and passport control.

The Danube Bend

Slide upstream to see the river's most scenic stretch.

The Danube Bend, 40 kilometres north of Budapest, is spectacular and beautiful: certainly the most scenic stretch on the river's 3,000-km course from the Black Forest to the Black Sea. Here the Danube widens and turns sharply south into a narrow valley between the Börzsöny and Pilis Hills before flowing onwards to Budapest.

The two main settlements on the west bank, Visegrád and Esztergom, were respectively a Hungarian medieval capital and royal seat. Both are easily accessible as day-trips by train, bus or regular summer boats from Budapest (*see chapter* **Getting Started**). Visegrád's hill-top citadel, the ruins of a thirteenth-century palace, is breathtaking. Esztergom, centre of Hungarian Catholicism, is dominated by the nation's largest cathedral.

Although both places can be fitted into one day, most visitors also aim for Szentendre, a quaint former Serbian village and artists' colony. Taking in all three will be stretching a day to its limits, so a couple of hotels in Esztergom, terminus for the Danube Bend ferry service, have been included.

Szentendre

If the visitor to Budapest takes only one day trip, invariably it will be to Szentendre, a settlement of 20,000 people 20 kilometres from the city.

Without a solid grasp of history, however, many will leave disappointed. After the pleasant 40-minute suburban train journey alongside the Danube, Szentendre looks like the classic tourist trap: pony carriages, tacky shops, naff galleries and, most of all, tourists. The trick is to take Szentendre for what it really is, or was before the tourist industry grew up around it: an eighteenth-century Serbian settlement. Treat yourself to a Sunday there. Follow the smell of the incense wafting out from the Serbian churches. It's a rare atmosphere untarnished by tack.

A wave of Serbian refugees moved here after the Turks won the Battle of Kosovo in 1389, building many small wooden churches. The Turks then invaded Hungary. Although Szentendre was liberated in 1686, the Turkish recapture of Belgrade four years later caused a second flood of Serbian refugees. They enjoyed religious freedom under Habsburg rule and traded in leather and wine. Szentendre prospered and the Serbs rebuilt their churches, this time from stone. Although with western Baroque exteriors, the interiors preserve

Orthodox traditions. All places of sanctuary had to face east, irrespective of dimension or streetscape. The resulting disjointed lay-out gives Szentendre its distinct Balkan atmosphere.

The first church the visitor comes to is the Pozarevacka, in Vuk Karadzics tér. For a token admission fee, an old lady will put Slavonic church music on the cranky reel-to-reel. The candlelight and Szentendre's oldest icon screen do the rest. You can still smell the incense in the Balkan Adria café opposite. In the main square, Fő tér, Blagovestenska Church provides a heady mix of deep music, incense and a huge, glorious iconostasis. The most stunning is the Belgrade Cathedral, seat of the Serbian Orthodox Bishop, with its entrance in Pátriáka utca. This is only open for Sunday services, but these offer a moving experience. On the same grounds is a museum of Serbian Church Art, containing bishop's garments and icons, but don't expect any decent documentation.

In 1774 a royal decree demanded the Serbs take an oath of allegiance to Hungary or be otherwise forbidden to trade. This killed Szentendre as a trading centre. A series of floods and epidemics did the rest. Most Serbs moved on.

When a group of artists discovered Szentendre in the 1920s, they were delighted to find a living museum of Serbian houses and churches. Encouraged to stay, they formed an artists' colony. The Barcsay Collection, Dumtsa Jenő utca 10, contains the abstract works of one of the colony's founders. Later generations set up dozens of galleries, with varying degrees of artistic success (*see chapter* **Art Galleries**).

The alternative set who formed the underground music and art group Bizottság still enjoy, check out the weird statues in ef Zámbó's garden, in Bartók Béla utca. Musical activity is otherwise focused on the Dalmát Pince, Malom utca 5, a cellar ideal for regular live jazz gigs, or the Barlang at Dunakorzó 11a, a riverside cultural centre with eclectic musical programming and hordes of punks. See chapter **Music: Rock, Roots & Jazz**.

Bars are either trendy (the Art Café in Fő tér) or rip-off (the Régimódi diagonally opposite). The Montenegro in Kossuth Lajos utca is just right: full of local characters and fake leopardskin furniture.

Tourism took a strange turn in the 1960s, when the government decided to site the huge Open-air Ethnographical Museum a short bus journey from Szentendre. Still being constructed 20 years after its opening, its aim is to show village life over three centuries from ten designated regions of Hungary. So far only three areas are complete. The museum is closed in winter. *See also chapter* **Folklore**.

Tourinform

Dumtsa Jenő utca 22 (26 317 965). **Open** *May-Sept* 8am-5pm Mon-Fri; 10am-2pm Sat, Sun. *Oct-April* 8.30am-4.30pm Mon-Fri.
Helpful and English-speaking.

Visegrád

Despite the spectacular mountain-top Citadel overlooking the most beautiful stretch of the Danube, the village below is small and sleepy with only the ruins of the lower Palace to make it worth a visit.

The Citadel and Palace were built in the thirteenth and fourteenth centuries. The latter was the setting for the Visegrád Congress of 1335, when the kings of Hungary, Czechoslovakia and Poland quaffed 10,000 litres of wine while discussing trade strategy. In a similar but more sober event 656 years later, the Visegrád Group of Hungary, Poland, the Czech Republic and Slovakia planned gradually to remove trade restrictions by 2001.

King Mátyás Corvinus overhauled Visegrád Palace in splendid Renaissance style. All this fell into ruin after the Turkish invasion and mud slides buried the Palace. It wasn't until bits of it were discovered in 1934 excavations that people believed there had ever been anything there in the first place. What you'll see today is mostly ruins. There are modern replicas of the Lion Fountain and the Hercules Fountain, but otherwise your imagination will have to do the rest. Some original pieces uncovered during excavations can be found at the Mátyás Museum, in the Salamon Tower halfway up the hill to the Citadel.

There are three ways up to the Citadel: a strenuous walk up the stony Path of Calvary (25 literally breathtaking minutes); one of the thrice daily buses from the village (ten minutes); or a taxi (call 328 202) or car up Panoráma út. You won't be disappointed. The exhibitions are naff and boring, but the view from the Citadel walls is magnificent, and worth the journey alone.

Once back to earth, we'd recommend a beer in the eighteenth-century Baroque former royal hunting lodge, now a tennis club at Fő utca 41. For lunch, the Fekete Holló, Rév utca 12, with its open fire, can rustle up reasonably priced chicken or trout with all the trimmings.

Probably the best way to see Visegrád is from the bank opposite. Take the hourly ferry across to Nagymaros, and splash around at the only spot on the river where it's possible to swim.

Visegrád Tours

Rév utca 15 (26 398 160). **Open** 9am-6pm daily.
They're a bit sullen here, but it's the only information office in town.

Esztergom

Although Esztergom is Hungary's most sacred city, home of the Archbishop and the nation's biggest church, it has a real-life edge that makes it worth a night's stopover. Not all of its 30,000 inhabitants are pious; there's a huge Suzuki car factory on the outskirts and in town a string of run-down bars full of drunken fishermen.

It is the past that brings visitors here, however. Esztergom was Hungary's first real capital. The nation's first Christian king, Szent István, was crowned here on Christmas Day 1000. He built a royal palace, unearthed in 1934, parts of which can be seen in the Castle Museum south of the Cathedral.

For nearly three centuries Esztergom was the royal seat until the Mongol invasion all but destroyed the city. It suffered more damage under the Turks, but most of what's worth seeing was rebuilt in Baroque style some 250 years ago: the Víziváros Parish Church on Mindszenty tere; the Christian Museum on Berényi Zsigmond utca and the Balassi Bálint Museum in Pázmány Péter utca.

It's the Cathedral that dominates, though. What strikes most is the size of the thing. When the Catholic Church moved its base back to Esztergom in 1820, Archbishop Sándor Rudnay wanted a vast monument on the ruins of a twelfth-century church destroyed by the Turks. It took 40-odd years and three architects and fairly bleak it is too. Main bright spot is the Bakócz Chapel, built in red marble by Florentine craftsmen, dismantled during the Turkish era and reassembled in 1823.

The Treasury holds a collection of golden treasures rescued from the medieval church. The crypt contains the tomb of Cardinal Mindszenty, who was tortured by the Communists in 1948 and then holed up in the American Embassy for 15 years.

In town you'll find a dozen or so reasonable restaurants; the Csülök Csárda, Batthyány utca 9, is as good as any. The dilapidated Hotel Fürdő, Bajcsy-Zsilinszky utca 14 (311 688), can provide a cheapish double room and some old thermal baths. The Hotel Esztergom, Nagy Duna sétány (312 883), is a more expensive modern job with a river terrace and sports centre.

For the best view of Castle Hill and the city, walk up St Thomas Hill to the east. Although all you'll see there now is a modest nineteenth-century chapel – the original was destroyed by the Turks – this was the site of a religious chapter named after Thomas à Becket. It was founded by French princess Margaret Capet whose father-in-law, King Henry II of England, was implicated in Becket's murder – appropriate for a town that is essentially the Magyar Canterbury.

GranTours

Széchenyi tér 25 (33 313 756). **Open** 8am-4pm Mon-Fri; 8am-noon Sat.
Efficient and English-speaking.

Szentendre – *follow the smell of incense and escape from tourist tack. See page 223.*

The Balaton

On the shallowest of inland seas, an excursion into deepest naff.

Hungary is a land-locked country, which perhaps explains why locals get so hyperbolic about the Balaton, largest lake in western and central Europe. Take these words from turn-of-the-century writer Károly Eötvös, often quoted in Hungarian guide books:

'Lake Balaton is fantasy and poetry, history and tradition, a volume of bitter-sweet tales, the age-old home of wild Hungarians; it is both the pride of our past and a brilliant hope for our future.'

But while Hungarians experience the Balaton from the comfort and seclusion of weekend cottages, for the foreign tourist it's a different story: high-rise hotels and concrete beaches, white plastic chairs and advertising umbrellas, a string of over-priced resorts, the breeding-ground of wild mosquitoes.

Though there are some beautiful spots on and around the lake, particularly along the north shore, a trip to the Balaton is first and foremost an excursion into deepest naff – which doesn't mean to say that it can't also be a lot of fun.

Wild Hungarians may still be found in the bars and discos of Balatonfüred or Siófok, but this area was also an age-old home for all sorts of other folk, even before the lake formed around 20-22,000 years ago. Between then and the arrival of the Magyars in the late ninth century, there were Celts, Romans, Huns, Lombards, Avars, Franks and Slavs, whose word for swamp, *blatna*, probably gave the shallow lake its name. The Magyars brought fishing, agriculture, livestock-breeding and built a lot of churches before the Mongols came and trashed the place in 1242. The Turks later occupied the south shore and scuffled with Austrians along the other side throughout the sixteenth and seventeenth centuries. Once they were driven out, the Habsburgs came along and blew up any remaining Hungarian castles.

Most of the interesting sights, therefore, date from the eighteenth century, when agriculture and viticulture began to flourish and Hungarian landowners brought in Slav, German and Croat peasants to work their estates. It was a time of Baroque building and decoration, the best remaining examples of which are the Abbey Church in Tihany and the huge Festetics Mansion in Keszthely. Wine is still produced in large quantities, particularly in the area around Badacsony – full of small cellars where you can taste the wares and buy by the five-litre plastic container.

Although Balatonfüred was declared a spa in 1785, it wasn't until the nineteenth century that bathing and the therapeutic properties of the area's thermal springs began to draw the wealthy in large numbers. In 1836 Baron Miklós Wesselényi, leading reformer of the period, was the first to swim from Tihany to Balatonfüred. Lajos Kossuth suggested steamships, and Count István Széchenyi rustled some up. Passenger boat services still link many major resorts, although the ferry from the southern tip of the Tihany peninsula to Szántód – a ten-minute journey spanning the lake's narrowest point – is the only one that takes cars.

The southern shore – these days one 80-kilometre stretch of tacky resort after tacky resort – was developed after the opening of the railway in 1861, which runs along the lake en route from Budapest to Zagreb. The line along the hillier and marginally more tasteful north shore wasn't completed until 1910. Even so, the Balaton didn't become a playground for anyone but the well-to-do until after World War II, when the Communists reconstructed the area with an eye to mass recreation. You'll still see a category of lodging called an *üdülő*. Once holiday homes for the workers of particular factories or trade unions, many *üdülők* are now privatised.

Before the fall of the Wall, Hungary was one of the few places where East Germans could travel and the Balaton became the place where West Germans would meet up with their poor relations. Tourism is still heavily geared towards the needs of Germans and Austrians – as testified by all the bar bands playing oom-pah music – and a smattering of Deutsch will be more useful than English in these parts. Though a trip to the Balaton is hardly getting away from it all, you'll at least be going somewhere not often frequented by Brits – which also makes for some entertaining English on restaurant menus, such as 'Propositions of the chef: Sailor Dish (for two persons)' or 'In the over preparing paste'.

The lake itself is weird. A 77-kilometre-long rectangle, 14 kilometres at its widest, it covers an area of about 600 square kilometres but is shallow throughout. Lake Geneva contains 20 times as much water. At its deepest (the so-called 'Tihany

*Crass or calming – though it hustles at night, **Siófok** can be relaxing in the daytime.*

Well' off the tip of the peninsula that almost chops the lake in half), the Balaton reaches only 12-13 metres. At Siófok and other south shore resorts you can paddle out 500-1,000 metres before the water gets up to your waist, which does mean it's very safe for children.

But it's not ideal swimming water. It's silty and milkily opaque and feels oily on the skin. The shallowness also means it warms up quickly, and isn't the most refreshing splash on a brain-baking July afternoon. It does, however, freeze well in the winter and is apparently good for ice-skating, but if you visit before May or after October (high season is July and August), you won't find very much open even in the larger towns.

Motor boats are strictly forbidden here but you'll find sailing and windsurfing on the lake. Fishing's popular, too. The Balaton is home to around 40 varieties of fish – including fogas, the Hungarian pike-perch, which is unique to the lake and a suitable accompaniment for one of the many drinkable local wines. The lake is also teeming with eels.

At high season there are also too many mosquitoes. Once the government sprayed both the lake and the Danube to curb the bug population. Now this job has supposedly devolved to local councils, who say they can't afford to deal with it. The result is so many mosquitoes that you often can't go out at night without lathering yourself in repellents.

Another downer is the pegging of prices to the Deutschmark, which means the Balaton is getting expensive for everyone except the Germans. Affordable hotels do exist, but you pay a lot for what you get. Fine dining is hard to find, as is anything cheap and cheerful apart from the occasional pizza. Moderately expensive Hungarian restaurants serving up standard meat and vegetable dishes are the order of the day. Vegetarians will find little.

Nevertheless, the Balaton can make for a fun trip out of town. Most destinations can be reached by train in two or three hours. Siófok and other resorts at the western end of the lake are doable in a day. Perhaps the most agreeable method is to take a long weekend circumnavigating the lake, stopping here and there for a swim or a beer, and driving up into the hills behind the northern shore. Here you've got rolling countryside, quiet villages, the occasional ostrich farm and roadsides decked with wild flowers. From the oddly-shaped volcanic hills above Badacsony (the Kisfaludy Ház restaurant, although somewhat tackily folkloric in theme, has a beautiful terrace), the view across vineyards and the milky green waters of the lake, ploughed by a steamship or two and fading into a distant heat haze, is pretty enough to touch a chord in even the most cynical of travellers.

Balatonfüred

The north shore's major resort is also the Balaton's oldest and has long been famed for the curative properties of its waters. The State Hospital of Cardiology and the Sanitorium dominate the Baroque and these days somewhat dilapidated Gyógy tér at the old town centre. In the middle of the square the Kossuth Well dispenses warm mineral-rich water, which is the closest you'll get to the thermal springs without checking into the hospital.

There also used to be a theatre here, built in the mid-nineteenth century when Balatonfüred was a major hangout for nationalist writers, artists and politicians. 'Patriotism towards our nationality' read the banner outside, and the theatre was intended to encourage Hungarian writing and acting at a time when German was still more widely spoken. Ironic, then, that tourism has reinstated German as the region's lingua franca.

There is a busy harbour with a pier, a shipyard, promenade, six major beaches and an assortment of not terribly inspiring things to see. Popular romantic writer Mór Jókai cranked out many of his 200 novels here, and his summer villa (at the corner of Jókai Mór utca and Honvéd utca) is now a memorial museum. Across the road is the neoclassical Kerék templom (Round Church), built in 1846. The Lóczy Cave (*barlang*), off Öreghegy utca on the northern outskirts of town, is the largest hole in the ground hereabouts.

The Hotel Flamingo at Széchenyi utca 16 (87 340 392) is par for the tacky course, but has a private beach and rooms with balconies more or less overlooking the lake. Modest but comfortable is Hotel Thetis on Vörösmarty utca 7 (87 341 606).

Perhaps because of the many oldsters coming to take the waters, Balatonfüred is a calm and almost genteel place, although there is life after dark. The Fregatt Pub on Blaha Lujza utca is a good spot for an early evening beer and also stays open until the small hours. After dinner at one of the many restaurants all along Tagore sétány and up Jókai Mór utca, the Wagner Club and Galéria offer pop techno, go-go dancers and teenagers on the dance floor moving just as if they were cheerfully kicking pennies, foot to foot. The Déjà Vu music club, above the Pinocchio pizzeria on Széchenyi setány, is a disco popular with locals rather than tourists.

From the end of the pier, with the lights of Siófok in the distance and the Tihany peninsula looming darkly to the west, the lake looks lovely by moonlight.

Balatontourist Balatonfüred

Blaha Lujza utca 5 (87 342 823). **Open** *June-Sept* 8.30am-6.30pm Mon-Sat; 8.30am-noon Sun. *Oct-May* 8.30am-4pm Mon-Fri; 8.30am-noon Sat.

Hot in summer but cool for kids – Lake Balaton is Europe's largest paddling pool.

Tihany

Declared a national park in 1952, the Tihany Peninsula is one of the quietest and most unspoilt places in the Balaton region – though even in this picturesque, historic spot, summer means the blooming of Coke and Lucky Strike umbrellas.

The 12 square kilometres of the peninsula jut 5km into the lake, almost cutting it in half. Tihany village lies by the Inner Lake, separate from the Balaton. On the hill above stands the twin-spired Abbey Church, completed in 1754. This is one of Hungary's most important Baroque monuments, and not just because of its outstanding wood-carvings – though there are certainly plenty of those. King Andrew I's 1055 deed of foundation for the church originally on this site was the first written document to contain any Hungarian – a few score place names in a mainly Latin text. (It now resides at the Pannonhalma Abbey near Győr.)

The Abbey museum in the former monastery next door has exhibits about Lake Balaton and a small collection of Roman statues in an enjoyably cool cellar. If you get tired of the splendid views right across the lake, nearby there are also museums dedicated to folklore, fishing, puppetry and pottery.

There isn't much else to see or do in Tihany, however. The Kakas, in a rambling old house below the Erika hotel, is an agreeable spot for lunch or dinner and, unusually, open all year round. Places to stay are limited, although the Hotel Park by the lake on Fürdőtelepi utca (87 348 611), formerly a Habsburg summer mansion, offers a modicum of elegance and its own private beach. Go for rooms 15, 16 or 17 (the expensive ones with grand balconies), and just say no if they try to stick you in the ugly 1970s annex on the same grounds. Otherwise private rooms in Tihany village can be arranged through Balatontourist.

We'd recommend staying in Balatonfüred, just 11 kilometres distant, and doing Tihany as a side-trip or stopover on the way to the next town.

Balatontourist Tihany

Kossuth utca 20 (87 348 519). **Open** *June-Sept* 8.30am-6.30pm Mon-Sat; 8.30am-noon Sun. *Oct-May* 8.30am-4pm Mon-Fri; 8.30am-noon Sat.

Keszthely

The only town on the Balaton that isn't totally dependent on tourism, Keszthely has a mellow feel quite different from other lakeside resorts. The two busy strands seem to swallow up all the tourists, while the agricultural university means a bit of life off-season as well as some variety at night.

Main tourist attraction is the Festetics Palace, a 100-room Baroque pile in pleasant grounds at the north end of the town centre. The Festetics family owned this whole area and Count György (1755-1819) was the epitome of an enlightened aristocrat. He not only constructed the palace but also built ships, hosted a salon of leading Hungarian literary lights, and founded both the Helikon library – now in the southern part of the mansion and containing more than 80,000 volumes – and the original agricultural college, these days the Georgikon Museum at Bercsényi utca 67.

The Gothic Parish Church on Fő tér has a longer history than most Balaton buildings. Originally built in the 1380s, it was fortified in 1550 in the face of the Ottoman advance. Though the rest of the town was sacked, it managed to hold out against the Turks. In 1747 the church was rebuilt in the Baroque style.

The Hotel Bacchus at Erzsébet királyné utca 18 (83 314 096) is a small and friendly modern hotel, ideally located halfway between the town centre and the strand, with a terrace restaurant that's one of the best in town. If you'd prefer a place by the lake try the Béta Hotel Hullám at Balatonpart 1 (83 315 950), a 1930s joint with airy, high-ceilinged rooms.

There are many bars and restaurants on and around Kossuth Lajos utca, the main street. The Donatello Pizzéria at Balaton utca 1 (83 315 989) is an acceptable Italian restaurant. There's a beautiful garden out the back with fishpond, fountain and rockery, and one feature all too rare in this part of the world: staff who try hard.

Keszthely is an excellent base for venturing up the lake towards Badacsony with its wine cellars and volcanic hills or the cute little village of Szigliget with its fourteenth-century castle ruins. Hévíz, eight kilometres inland, has the largest thermal lake in Europe. Bathing is possible all year round (in winter the lake steams dramatically). The slightly radioactive water is covered in lilies and is recommended for the treatment of locomotive disorders and nervous ailments.

Tourinform

Kossuth Lajos utca 28 (83 314 144). **Open** *June-Sept* 9am-5pm Mon-Fri; 9am-1pm Sat, Sun. *Oct-May* 8am-4pm Mon-Fri; 9am-1pm Sat.

Right across the street there's also a branch of Ibusz and a similar concern called Keszthely Tourist.

Siófok

Siófok is Balaton's sin city: big, loud, brash and packed in high season. Although it's the lake's largest resort – Greater Siófok stretches for 15 kilometres along the shore – there really isn't much in the way of sightseeing. Here hedonism reigns. By day people do the strand. Nights are devoted to drinking, dining, dancing and sex.

The Petőfi sétány strip runs for about two kilometres between the harbour, where the Sió canal meets the lake, and the four big Communist-built hotels – the Pannonia, Balaton, Hungaria and Lido. Ugly concrete blocks, their classy old neon signs nevertheless look great at sunset. In between are bars with oom-pah bands, amusement arcades, western-style steakhouses, topless places, portrait painters, video game arcades, parked cars blasting pop techno, naff T-shirt stalls, a reptile house full of scary snakes and an endless procession of Hungarian, German and Austrian tourists.

The Roxy at Szabadság tér 4 is a decent brasserie where the drinks are well-made. Flört at Sió utca 4 is one of Hungary's best nightclubs: two dance floors (one techno, one tacky), some occasionally excellent DJs, a succession of bars on different levels of the barn-like main room, and a roof terrace overlooking the Sió Canal. In summer young Budapesters sometimes drive down for the night just to come and dance here. Its main rival is The Palace, just out of town. Coca-Cola have sponsored the Beach House on the main strand, offering occasional live concerts, dancing on the beach, and aerobics in the daytime.

There are restaurants everywhere, rather too many of them catering to German tastes. The Pizza Bella at Szabadság tér 1 (84 310 826) serves up average Italian eats. On the strip there are all sorts of food stalls. The Diana Hotel at Szent László utca 41/43 (84 315 296), one of the best in town, also has a restaurant that, if you're going to try it anywhere, is the place to eat fogas. The Janus at Fő utca 93-85 (84 312 546) is another good new hotel, though pricey – but you'll not find very many bargains in this town. On the strip and a little cheaper, the Hotel Napfény by the harbour at Mártirok utca 8 (84 311 408) at least has good big rooms with balconies.

Tourinform

Fő tér 41 (84 310 117). **Open** *June-Sept* 8am-8pm daily. *Oct-May* 9am-4pm Mon-Fri; 9am-1pm Sat.

In summer there's a also a small Tourinform office in the water tower on Szabadság tér. All the other tourist agencies have offices nearby.

Overnighters

Eger and Pécs, Sopron and Szeged – cities to explore at all points of the compass.

Eger

A sweet little town, 128 kilometres east of Budapest at the foot of the Bükk Hills, Eger is famous for three things: its fine Baroque buildings; a siege at which locals repelled the Turkish army; and Bull's Blood, the heavy red wine known in Hungarian as Egri Bikavér.

It's a playful sort of place. Children play Pooh sticks on bridges over the Eger stream. In summer half the population seems to be on in-line skates: gangs of schoolchildren cling to the backs of buses for an illicit tow up Kossuth Lajos utca; whole families skate across pedestrianised Dobó tér.

They take their history seriously, though. The siege of Eger, in which a force of local defenders held the Castle against a much larger Ottoman army, is one of Hungary's few famous victories. The Turks came back and finished the job 44 years later, but the earlier siege of Eger was fixed in the nation's imagination by Géza Gárdonyi's 1901 adventure novel *Egri csillagok* (published in English as *Eclipse of the Crescent Moon*), required reading for every Hungarian schoolkid. Indeed, Gárdonyi's version seems almost to have replaced the actual history. There's a statue of the author within the Castle walls, plus a Panoptikum featuring wax versions of his characters. Copies of the novel are on sale all over town, and on Gárdonyi utca, there's the Gárdonyi Géza Memorial Museum, where his house has been preserved.

The Castle was later dynamited by the Habsburgs in 1702. What remains is big but pretty dull, although a walk along what's left of the battlements affords a fine view over Eger's Baroque and remarkably flatblock-free skyscape. The one remaining Turkish minaret (the corner of Knézich utca and Markó Ferenc utca) also has a great view, although it's a long and claustrophobic climb to get to it.

Eger's Baroque buildings are splendid, most notably the 1771 Minorite church, centrepiece of Dobó tér. There are more listed buildings in this town than anywhere else in Hungary bar Budapest and Sopron. The Bazilika on Eszterházy tér is an imposing neo-classical monolith crowned with crucifix-brandishing statues of Faith, Hope and Charity. There are also many curious buildings along Széchenyi utca and Kossuth Lajos utca.

Eger *Castle – novel setting for a siege.*

Small and with a mostly pedestrianised centre, Eger is ideal for strolling. There are some wonderful old shops, including a beautiful bookbinder's on Szent János utca. One could easily do Eger in a day, but it's a relaxing and rewarding overnighter. The Senátorház hotel at Dobó tér 11 (36 320 466) is comfortable and ideally situated. The Minaret Hotel (right beside the actual Minaret) at Knézich Károly utca 4 (36 410 020) is cheaper.

Local wines are most entertainingly sampled just out of town at Szépasszony-völgy, the Valley of Beautiful Women, a horseshoe-shaped area of dozens of wine cellars, many with tables outside. Wine is cheap enough to allow a level of consumption that would diminish anyone's standards of feminine pulchritude (hence the name), Gypsy fiddlers entertain drinkers, and parties come to eat, dance and make excessively merry. Afternoon is best, as places start closing by early evening. The

Valley bustles most during the two-week harvest festival in September. It's a ten-minute walk or a cab ride. (You'll almost certainly have to walk back.)

For lunch try the Gyros Greek restaurant at Széchenyi utca 10. It's inconsistent but they seem to do their best. For dinner we'd recommend the Talizmán at Kossuth Lajos utca 19, a laid-back and inexpensive cellar restaurant offering everything from Hungarian standards to low-calorie and vegetarian dishes.

After dinner take a stroll by the Eger stream, listen to the croak of the occasional frog, and eye the plaque of Esperanto inventor Zamenhof on Eszperantó sétány.

Tourinform

Dobó tér 2 (36 321 807). **Open** 9am-6pm Mon-Fri; 10am-6pm Sat-Sun.
Friendly and helpful, but not always an English-speaker in evidence.

Eger Tourist

Bajcsy-Zsilinszky utca 9 (36 411 724). **Open** *May-Sept* 8.30am-7.30pm Mon-Fri; 9am-1pm Sat. **No credit cards**. Can help you find accommodation.

Pécs

Spread out on the southern slopes of the Mecsek Hills, down near the ex-Yugoslavian border, Hungary's fourth-largest city has a warm and sheltered climate, enough fig trees and Turkish monuments to lend it a vaguely eastern air, a curious collection of architecture and a clutch of interesting art museums. It's a peaceful place by day, especially in summer, when it acquires a distinctly lazy feel. At night there are plenty of bars, cafés and restaurants – a reflection of both the town's large student population and its lively trade in conferences and festivals. If you're only going to make one foray out of Budapest, Pécs must be the main contender.

Romans settled here and called their town Sopianae – a name that survives as a Hungarian cigarette brand. Assorted tribes asserted squatting rights before the Magyars set up shop at the end of the ninth century. The town prospered on the trade route between Byzantium and Regensburg, King Stephen established the Pécs diocese in 1009, and Hungary's first university was founded here in 1367.

And then came the Turks in 1543, pushing the locals outside the walls that still define the city centre, and flattening the rest of the place. Thus, as in the rest of Hungary, little pre-Turkish stuff survives. But after staying here 143 years, the Turks did leave a couple of mementoes – the most significant Turkish monuments remaining anywhere in the country.

On Széchenyi tér stands the former mosque of Pasha Ghazi Kassim, built from the stones of the gothic church that formerly occupied this site, and later converted back into a church by the Jesuits. These days it's the Belvárosi Plébániatemplom (Inner City Parish Church), but, domed and angled towards Mecca at variance with the square's north-south orientation, still lends an eastern feel to the city's main intersection. The minaret was demolished in 1753.

The mosque of Pasha Hassan Jokovali, complete with minaret, is at Rákóczi utca 2. The most intact Turkish structure in Hungary, this was also converted into a church but later reconstructed as a mosque. The entrance hall houses a small and not terribly interesting exhibit of Ottoman finds.

After the Turks, Pécs was slow to revive. Coalmining spurred prosperity in the nineteenth century. Since World War II there has been uranium-mining and, during the Balkan War, a thriving black market trade with nearby Serbia. Waves of prosperity are clear in the architecture: the forms of the Baroque and Art Nouveau buildings in the old centre are echoed in the 1970s shopping centres and office blocks down the slope.

Pécs is built around two main squares: the aforementioned Széchenyi tér and Dóm tér, at which stands the four-towered, mostly neo-Romanesque Basilica of St Peter. Below this is Szent István tér, with Roman ruins and a small park with cafés and a weekend market.

Káptalan utca runs east off Dóm tér. Pécs teems with art museums and many are to be found up here. Those dedicated to Csontváry, Hungary's answer to Van Gogh (nearby in Janus Pannonius utca 11) and Magyar op-artist Victor Vasarely (Káptalan utca 3) are the most interesting. Zsolnay tile, that coloured stuff you see on top of Budapest's more extravagant Dual Monarchy buildings (and in Pécs on top of new buildings too), is made in this town, but the Zsolnay Ceramics Exhibit just over the street from the Vasarely museum isn't that interesting: it's mostly vases in glass cases.

The Santa Maria, at Klimó György utca 12, with an inexplicably nautical interior built into the old city walls, is a good spot for dinner. Otherwise Király utca, the pedestrian street off Széchenyi tér, bustles at night with bars, cafés and restaurants. You'll probably want to look at the neo-Renaissance Pécs National Theatre, which is just down here. You might also inspect the interior of the István Pince wine cellar at Kazinczy utca 1 – a fine old example of the borozó genre.

Pécs' best hotel, the Art Nouveau and genuinely elegant Palatinus, is down here at Király utca 5 (72 233 022). The friendly Hotel Fönix at Hunyadi út 2 (72 311 680), just north of Széchenyi tér, is much cheaper and just as central.

At weekends, on the outskirts of town, Pécs has one of Hungary's largest flea markets. Catch bus 3 or 50 from the station, or else hail a cab and ask for the Nagyvásár. You'll find acres and acres of junk at the end of the ten-minute ride.

Tourinform

Széchenyi tér 9 (72 212 632). **Open** 9am-5pm Mon-Fri; 10am-3pm Sat. **No credit cards.**
Can provide information and help with accommodation.

Sopron

Sopron is way up in the north-west of Hungary, in a little Magyar nodule that extrudes into Austria. The location has had two effects on this fascinating small, old town. The first is that it escaped devastation by both Mongols and Turks and has managed to retain a medieval feel you won't find anywhere else in Hungary outside Budapest's Castle District. The second is that Austrians flood over the border to go shopping on the cheap.

The Várkerület, which encircles the Old Town, bustles with tiny shops selling bargain booze and cigarettes, budget salamis and household gadgets. Opticians proliferate. There are dentists, hairdressers and beauticians everywhere. Just about every business doubles as a money-changer.

Stepping from all this through one of the entrances into the Old Town is like cracking open a stone to find an extraordinary crystal formation within. Here cobbled, medieval-patterned streets are relaxed and traffic-free. Practically every building is listed: medieval dwellings rub gables with Gothic churches and Baroque monuments. Commerce continues, but quietly, in discreet boutiques and jewellery shops nestling by small museums.

The Firewatch Tower, symbol of Sopron, sums up the town's history and offers a view that takes it all in. It's built on Roman foundations, with a twelfth-century base, a sixteenth-century column and balcony, a seventeenth-century spire, and a 'Fidelity Gate' installed in 1922 to mark the town's decision (they voted on it) to remain part of Hungary after Trianon. From the top you can see the streets and walls of the Old Town, following the lines of the previous Roman settlement, and the vine-covered hills beyond the outskirts.

Though there's plenty to look at it in the daytime – the various old houses and museums around Fő tér and the Medieval Synagogue at Új utca 22 are particularly interesting – it's at night, after the day-trippers have all gone, when Sopron is at its most atmospheric. Wandering the medieval streets, quiet except for the chatter and clatter from restaurants and wine cellars, only a rare parked car intrudes between you and the illusion that you have stepped back several centuries.

For breakfast or coffee try the restored 1920s Várkapu coffeehouse at Hátsókapu utca 3. For lunch the restaurants Gambrinus (inexpensive Hungarian standards) and Corvinus (reasonable pizzas) both have tables outside on Fő tér, centrepiece of the town. The baroque Gangel restaurant at Várkerület 25 is probably the most handsome spot for dinner. Strangely, the John Bull pub at Széchenyi tér 12 isn't bad either – and despite a menu with shepherd's pie and trifle, none of the staff speak English. The Mekong at Deák tér 46 offers some Vietnamese variety.

The Palatinus Hotel at Új utca 23 (99 311 395) is ugly and has small, dark rooms but is right in the middle of the Old Town. The Pannonia at Várkerület 75 (99 312 180) is roomier but more expensive. Cheap rooms can be found at the nameless pension at Damjanich utca 9 behind the bus station.

Although most of the sights are in the Old Town, even the determinedly profit-seeking Várkerület contains some curiosities. Inspect the 1623 pharmacy at number 29, or the ancient Goger opticians opposite.

Locomotiv Tourist

Új utca 1 (99 311 111). **Open** *Sept-April* 9am-5pm Mon-Fri; 9am-1pm Sat. *June-Aug* 9am-5pm Sat.
Sopron station, Állomás utca 2 (99 311 422). **Open** 6am-5pm daily.
Friendly and helpful, with some English speakers on staff. The Új utca branch is above some Roman ruins, now the Forum Museum, which they'll show you around.

Express

Mátyás király út 7 (99 312 024). **Open** 8am-3.30pm Mon-Fri.
Can assist in finding accommodation.

Szeged

The first-time visitor to Szeged is invariably struck by its space and grandeur. One's immediate impressions of Hungary's third largest provincial city are of greenery and plazas, of broad boulevards and proud municipal buildings. Yet they hide a multitude of sin and misfortune, tied to history and geography of this strangely atmospheric southern outpost. Szeged is very much a river city, but its position at the confluence of the Tisza and Maros rivers have not always done it great favour.

Szeged was all but wiped away in the Great Flood of 1879. Thanks to foreign aid, architect Lajos Lechner could produce an adventurous blueprint for a new model city of the late nineteenth century, meticulously planned with a uniform skyline. What remained of the city's era as a Turkish stronghold was washed away; Communism arrived too soon for its architects to affect the lie of the land. Across the river, Újszeged is blighted with tower blocks, but this rarely concerns most visitors. They pour into central Dóm tér in August for the annual open-air music and theatre festival. Out of season, Dóm tér is bold and imposing, with the twin spires of the Votive Church, built as a symbol of the city's post-flood renaissance, its main feature. Széchenyi tér further north is the heart of the city, however – 50,000 square metres of trees, fountains and statues, presided over by the Town Hall.

But it is the Tisza river which is the city's leitmotif. It has both attracted and repelled scores of invaders, it made Szeged an important trading centre in the Middle Ages, and it brought the city to the centre of political debate in the middle of the last century, dividing reformers like Széchenyi who wanted to regulate and engineer against flood, and those whose livelihood had depended on it for generations. It was Count Széchenyi himself who sailed the first steamship down the Tisza to Szeged in 1833, riding through the waves in triumph as if in some Rodgers and Hammerstein musical, while Serbian women watched aghast, crossing themselves in fear.

The Tisza-Maros junction became a convenient backdrop for the redrafting of national borders following the Treaty of Trianon in 1920, which left the city vulnerable to whichever military or economic misfortunes would later befall Serbia and Romania, too often too close for comfort. With the war in Yugoslavia and subsequent economic sanctions, many became involved in the lucrative trade in smuggling petrol down south, and Szeged became synonymous with corruption and gangland killings. Economic migration from Romania is still as visible today as the scores of dodgy shops, bars and businesses opened with fast buck petrodollars.

On the surface, however, the river is a pleasant amenity, convenient for summer disco boats like the Szürke Haja and the Hajó, ideal for the mosquitos that feed off their clientele. Szeged's status as a university town does mean that much of its nightlife is affordable and lively. The JATE Klub, Toldy utca 1, attached to the college, offers a regular selection of name Hungarian bands during term time. The Tisza Gyönge on Közép-kikötő sor across the river is in a similar vein. For something more upmarket, try the Laguna cocktail bar, Hid utca 6, with its unusual decor and large collection of tropical fish.

The local dish is fish soup, halászlé, spiced with paprika, introduced by the Turks and as an important source of revenue to Szeged as mustard to Dijon. The Leső Harcsa Halászcsárda, Roosevelt tér 14, can serve up a mean one and certain tables offer a view of the main bridge, if not of the river itself. The most prestigious joint in town, the Alabárdos, Oskola utca 13 (06-62-312-914), requires reservations.

Although the Royal, Kölcsey utca 1 (06 62 475 275) is Szeged's most famous hotel – Romanian gymnast Nadia Comaneci took refuge here after defecting – it is in urgent need of renovation. Try the cheaper Hotel Tisza, Wesselényi utca 1 (06 62 478 278) or the budget Bornemissza panzió, Szent György tér 5 (06 62 323 330).

Szeged Tourist
Klauzál tér 7 (06 62 321 800). **Open** 9am-5pm Mon-Fri; 10am-2pm Sat. **No credit cards.**
Can also book accommodation in private rooms. For festival tickets and other cultural information, go to the Szabadteri Jegyiroda in the same office.

Szeged's Dom – heading the central square of the same name.

Flood Memorial – **Szeged**'s *position at the Tisza-Maros junction has not always been a boon.*

Vienna

Budapest's bigger, smugger and considerably more expensive sister.

Vienna is still often thought of as Budapest's 'sister city'. A big sister, certainly – and for most of history an extremely bossy sister too (though once it got tired of having its pigtails pulled, Budapest did learn how to fuss and scratch and get its own way sometimes).

Close but competitive in the Dual Monarchy days, the Danubian siblings long ago went their separate ways. You can still see they're related, though. Budapest and Vienna share Habsburg-era similarities but are distinguished by some very stark postwar contrasts – a mix that makes a visit to the Austrian capital a particularly rewarding side-trip. Where Budapest has been run-down by decades of Communism, Vienna has actually benefited from being on the frontline of western capitalism. Where Budapest is poor, self-conscious and shabby, Vienna is prosperous, smug and almost disconcertingly clean.

Budapest is very much a national capital, its whole nineteenth-century shape designed around a monumental celebration of Hungarian identity. Vienna, on the other hand, seems less the capital of Austria than a combination of the dynastic city-state it once was, and the present-day world city that is headquarters for so many international institutions. Long a cosmopolitan melting-pot, today registered foreigners count for more than one in ten of its 1.5 million inhabitants.

In Budapest the Danube dictates the whole feel of the city; in Vienna you'd hardly notice it was there. Arriving by jetfoil (*see chapter* **Getting Started**) you're dumped at a modern ferry terminal on the Danube Relief Channel, with nothing to see but a few cranes, dredgers and United Nations buildings, so far out of town that it can be hard even to find a taxi. Arriving any other way, you might not see the Danube at all, unless from the top of the big wheel in the Prater – a landmark still much the same as it was in Harry Lime's day, except with safer doors.

But prices are the first thing that hit home. A Wiener melange in a famous Viennese coffee house such as Sacher or Demel costs four or five times as much as a similar cup in Budapest's Művész. But at least Vienna can still afford its coffee houses and a couple of dozen old places are still pretty much intact and alive. Sacher is crap, mind you. Demel, on the other hand, at Kohlmarkt 14, is a trip: dauntingly Baroque, with waitresses who speak an absurd formal German no one uses any-

where else, and just about the most chocolatey chocolate cake in the world. At Central, on Herrengasse, where Trotsky once sat sipping coffee and planning the Russian Revolution, sits a dummy of poet Peter Altenberg, who in life more or less lived in the place.

While Budapest's ancient centre is now perched out of the way up on Castle Hill, the medieval heart of Vienna is still the city centre today. You could spend a couple of days exploring without ever having to step beyond the Ringstrasse – the circular avenue which follows the line of the old city walls. From the pedestrianised Stephansplatz, where St Stephen's Cathedral provides Vienna with its centrepiece, history radiates in concentric circles. In the medieval streets around the square and off bustly Kartner Strasse, you'll find backstreet palaces, small churches, atmospheric old squares and alleys, and any number of houses where Mozart once lived.

The area between the Cathedral and the Danube, on and around Rotenturmstrasse, is known as the Bermuda Dreiecke (Bermuda Triangle). This is the main nightlife area, where the visitor can disappear into one of dozens of late-night bars.

The next band of history, over in the south-west corner of the Innere Stadt, is dominated by the 59-acre Hofburg complex: a sprawl of palaces and parks, statues and fountains, Baroque squares and still-functioning imperial stables. This was the seat of the Habsburgs (among all the treasures and monarchical glitz you can still view the spartan iron bed that nightly reinforced Emperor Franz Joseph's sense of imperial duty) and the feeling of power and wealth, concentrated here for centuries, is still quite palpable.

The Ringstrasse (serviced, like Budapest's Nagykörút, by trams) runs in a polygonal horseshoe shape, beginning and ending at the Danube Canal. This was the line of the old city walls. Vienna has always been a border town, and the defences were knocked about and reinforced time and again throughout history (it was here that the Ottoman advance into Europe was halted in 1683) before Franz Joseph began demolishing them for good in 1857. Along the Ring, punctuated by gardens, are all the monumental public buildings of late Imperial Vienna: the ugly Opera House, the Natural History and Art History Museums (on a rainy day, check out the Breughels), the Parliament, City Hall, University and Burg Theater.

The Opera House – just one of late Imperial Vienna's monumental public buildings.

It's all pretty dry stuff, in weighty neo-Gothic and neo-Renaissance styles.

It was in reaction to the pretentiousness of this façade that architect Alfred Loos designed his 'house without eyebrows' – utterly without ornamentation of illusions of past grandeur – which stands cheekily on the Michaeler Platz, opposite the gate into the Hofburg. (Griensteidl, on the ground floor, is a reasonable spot for lunch.)

For more of a taste of turn-of-the-century Vienna, move beyond the Ring to the next concentric circle. At Friedrichstrasse 12 stands the gilt-domed Sezession – home for Gustav Klimt, Otto Wagner and the 17 others who 'seceded' from the Viennese art establishment to found the local version of Art Nouveau. Northwards on the same radius you can visit the Sigmund Freud Museum at Berggasse 19, where the psychoanalyst's working rooms are now a public exhibit.

Beyond this outer ring lie the suburbs and working-class estates, breeding-ground of unrest and revolution in the city that Karl Kraus, on the eve of World War I, dubbed the 'proving-ground for world destruction'. The bureaucratic towers of UNO City, headquarters for the International Atomic Energy Authority, the United Nations Industrial Development Organisation and an assortment of other UN organisations, are the principal monuments to Austria's post-war neutrality.

Contemporary Vienna, removed from the centre-stage of history, is a relaxed and sleepily prosperous place where nothing very much happens any more. You can find just about anything you want in the shops and also eat very well. (After heavy Hungarian food, Neue Wiener Kuche is a light and pleasant shock to the system.) You'll mostly have to pay well for the privilege, though the Naschmarkt (just south-west of the Sezession) offers a centrally-located Saturday morning flea market and daily stalls serving every kind of food you can imagine, from Japanese seafood to (presumably) Hungarian 'Hussar Sausages'. Vienna is full of shops selling pricey executive toys, designer fountain pens and improbable furniture, but second-hand book and music stores are dotted all over too.

Accommodation is expensive. If you want to splash out and get a true taste of *mitteleuropäisch* elegance, try the Bristol at Kärtner Ring 1 (00 43 1 515 160) or the Sacher round the corner at Philharmonikerstrasse 4 (00 43 1 514 56). There's no particularly good area for finding cheap hotels, but the Vienna Tourist Office will be able to help.

It's possible to get to Vienna and back in a day, but scarcely worth the bother. An overnighter makes more sense, but we'd recommend two nights as the ideal short stay. Just expect to spend about as much in 48 hours as you would in a week in Budapest.

Vienna Tourist Office

1025 Augardenstraße 40 (00 43 1 211 140). **Open** 9am-7pm daily.
Helpful and with English-speaking staff. For last-minute room bookings go the office at 1010 Kärtner Straße 38. **Branch**: West Station (00 43 1 892 3392)

Bratislava

The sleepy Slovak capital goes its own sweet way.

Just down the Danube from Vienna, and on road and rail routes between Budapest and Prague, Bratislava is the runt of the Habsburg urban litter. In the days of Czechoslovakia, this city was to Prague what, say, Cardiff is to London. Since 1 January 1993 it's upgraded to bona fide capital of authentically independent Slovakia, but still has something of the puffed-up provincial town.

It's an odd place, Slavic with a Magyar edge, like a cross between Prague and a Hungarian provincial town – with a population of around 450,000 it's less than half the size of the Czech capital, twice as big as any Magyar metropolis bar Budapest. Bratislava wears a muted smile of optimism, youth, the thrill of the new – curious in a city that's existed in some form or another for over 2,000 years. But though settlements and fortifications at this site date back to the Iron Age – it was here that the Amber Road, ancient north-south trade route, forded the Danube – it has only been a Slovak city for an eyeblink of that long history.

Only in 1919, after independent Czechoslovakia was carved from the ruins of the Habsburg Empire, did Slovaks take over the city and name it Bratislava. Once it was the Roman town of Posonium, perched out at the edge of empire. As Breszalauspurc in the ninth century it had been part of the slavonic Great Moravian Empire. For most of the rest of history it was an Austro-Hungarian city known as Pressburg to the Germans, who provided around half its inhabitants until 1945, and as Poszony to the Hungarians, who used it as their capital for several centuries after the Turks occupied Buda in 1541. (There are still around 700,000 ethnic Hungarians in Slovakia, and though official statistics maintain that they comprise only 0.02 per cent of Bratislava's population, you'll often hear Hungarian spoken hereabouts.) Though the Slovakian nationalist movement began to figure in the city from the early nineteenth century, at the turn of the century only a smattering of its then 60,000 inhabitants were Slovaks.

Slovakian Bratislava is thus subtly dislocated from the history which has left it with an Old Town of fine Habsburg baroque, and a Castle that looks like a giant upturned bedstead. The twentieth century has more than made up for this, however. The newer parts of town, now ringed with ugly housing blocks, sliced through by unwelcoming avenues, have the sad, desensitized air of every gutted east bloc metropolis.

There are two sights which can properly be described as unmissable – both in the sense of must-see and of can't-be-avoided. One is the castle, up on its hill, where there's a splendid view of the Danube below and the river plain to the south and east, from which barbarian hordes might have arrived in a cloud of dust at any point in history. The other is the Most SNP – Bridge of the Slovak National Uprising, also known as the Nový most, or New Bridge – a splendid example of spacey communist design. It's a unique single-span suspension affair, sporting a café like a flying saucer, high above the Danube on its one double pylon. From this there are also fine views, both north across the city centre to the vineyard-covered Small Carpathian foothills, and south over Petržalka where a third of Bratislava's population – 150,000 people – inhabit a grim forest of prefabricated communist blocks. (To abet the allure, until 1989 this estate was also ringed with barbed wire and watchtowers, for Austria lies just beyond.) It has the highest suicide rate in Slovakia and is best viewed from the café's toilets.

The Old Town is peaceful, compact and just about big enough to get lost in for a while. This area's had a lick of new paint in the post-communist shake-up, although the effect is often more sterilising than rejuvenating. Here are squares and statues, shops and cafés, baroque monuments and an assortment of Slovak national institutions. Much of Bratislava's nightlife is also in this area, dotted with restaurants, sidewalk cafés and wine cellars. Slovaks display two important differences from their Czech cousins. They are more Catholic – there are nuns and monks scuttling round all over the place. And they drink wine rather than beer. For both quality of tipple and authenticity of Slovakian experience, it's best to follow suit.

A series of broad squares marks the boundary with the rest of town. Kamenné námestie, a gaping intersection on which stands the K-Mart department store, is the real city centre. To the north-west, Námestie SNP centres on a Monument to the Slovak National Uprising – a botched and belated 1944 rebellion against the Nazis, much played up by the Communists to assert some local anti-fascist credentials. Other

Bratislava Castle – dominating the city skyline like a giant, upturned bedstead.

vestiges of Communism include tales of continued government phone-tapping, hotel porters who offer to change money on the sly, and the vast Námestie Slobody featuring a Fountain of Friendship, the world's largest post office, and the extraordinary inverted pyramid which houses Slovak Radio.

Bratislava needs a couple of days to sink in. Hotels are rarely full and often offer discounts at weekends. The Perugia at Zeletná 5 (07 5331 818) looks the best of the posh new Old Town hotels. Fans of tatty Communist modernism will enjoy the skyrise Kyjev at Rajská 2 (07 361 082), just behind K-Mart, with its delightfully dodgy nightclub and excellent views across the city. Most cheaper options tend to be a little out of town. **BIS** can help in finding accommodation.

There are a variety of cafés and restaurants around the Old Town, but don't expect much in the way of fine dining. Café Roland on Hlavné námestie is popular, grand and unmissable, offering surly service amid an assortment of historic buildings. On Venturska just north of Panská is a strip of bars with pavement tables in summer – a lively spot in the evenings until everything begins to close around 11pm.

As midnight approaches, the Old Town quickly becomes deserted. A plethora of police and uniformed security guards at major intersections lends the impression that this is a tacit curfew, but there are late-night options scattered around town. KGB on Obchodná is a teenage hard rock beer cellar. The smoky U Club offers techno until 2am in a World War II air raid shelter beneath the castle – it's beside the entrance to the tram tunnel on Nábrežie gen. Ludvika Svobodu. Charlie's at Špitálska 4, just behind the Kyjev, is a complex featuring a cinema, café and late-opening pub – big, loud, noisy, mixed, friendly and the one place where all the foreigners end up.

There aren't too many foreigners in Bratislava, though, and certainly few English-speaking ones. A smattering of schoolbook German (or, indeed, a little Hungarian) will get you further in most places than any amount of English. A handy pocket-sized guide and street atlas is available in most central bookshops. The dreary local English-language paper, the fortnightly *Slovak Spectator*, is good for listings of venues and events, if sadly for little else.

BIS (Bratislava Information Service)
Klobúčnická 2 (07 533 3715). Open 8am-7pm Mon-Fri, 9am-2pm Sat, Sun.
Can help with accommodation, as well as providing information. Not too much English spoken, though. Small selection of guide books on sale.
Branch: Hlavná stanica (Main Station) (533 4370).

Zagreb

The Croatian capital exudes a weird post-war atmosphere.

'The Upper and the Lower Town, and New Zagreb, the three parts of Zagreb,' waffles the text on a Croatian tourist board map, 'mutually interact to form this typically Zagrebian atmosphere....'

Does this sound like a city grasping for an identity, or what?

'Perhaps you did not know,' gushes the official Zagreb Tourist Association guide, delighted to unearth at least one famous Croat, 'that the first mechanical pencil was invented by Slavoljub Penkala of Zagreb in 1906 and that Zagreb was the European centre for the production of writing equipment between 1914 and 1926.' And sure enough, replicas of Penkala's propelling pencil are on sale (exorbitantly) at the main Ban Jelačić tourist office.

Does this sound like a culture clutching at straws, or not?

Just six hours by train from Budapest – a cheap and interesting if initially often overcrowded ride that runs along the south shore of the Balaton – Zagreb is an attractive city. Sited on the north bank of the river Sava where the last foothills of the Alps shade into the Great Pannonian Plain, the Croatian capital is over 900 years old. In the middle ages it comprised two autonomous towns on neighbouring hills – the Kaptol, seat of the Zagreb bishopric; and what is now the Gornji Grad (Upper Town) – which squabbled and warred for centuries before the Habsburg Donji Grad (Lower Town) began stretching out on to the plain below. The Kaptol's main landmark is the Cathedral. The loftier Gornji Grad, centred on St Mark's Church and reached by a funicular from Tomićeva off Ilica, resembles Budapest's Castle District, only smaller, and without a castle. The rest of Zagreb's centre is leafy, elegant, occasionally baroque and laid out around expansive squares. Smart residential districts dot the hills above; ugly communist housing blocks dominate the skyline south of the main station.

But despite superficial similarities and historical overlaps (most of what is now Croatia was essentially part of Hungary from 1102 up until 1918), Zagreb offers a real contrast to Budapest, making the Hungarian capital seem like a big, vital, cosmopolitan centre.

Especially since the recent war, which has changed Zagreb for ever. Serbs, Slovenes and other non-Croats have mostly moved out. In turn upwards of 100,000 Croats, in a city of only around one million inhabitants, have arrived from Bosnia and elsewhere abroad. More cosmopolitan Croats may be heard muttering that many of these new arrivals – one out of every ten people! – 'just don't fit in', but the fact remains that Zagreb, after all the ethnic displacements of the war, is now culturally and racially an almost absurdly homogenous place.

Thus, despite officialdom's assertion of prodigious age and tradition, this is essentially a young city, capital of a new country. Croatia's only previous period of 'independence' was a few years as a Nazi puppet state during World War II. Available histories gloss over the fascist Ustaše's murder of anything between 350,000 to one million Serbs, Gypsies, Jews and opposition Croats (the exact figure is still being disputed) and, worryingly, Franjo Tudjman's current government seems to be subtly rehabilitating that regime. Croatian army brigades were named after Ustaše war criminals; the new Croat currency is called the kuna, just as in fascist times; and the former Square of Victims of Fascism has been renamed, absurdly, the Square of Croatia's Great Men.

Nationalism is unremitting. Even the city's football team has changed its name from Dinamo to Croatia Zagreb. The national flag flutters everywhere – a horizontal red, white and blue tricolour with a red-and-white checkered coat of arms in the middle. We challenge you to find any spot in the city where you can't spy at least one of them. At markets, next to all the fruit and veg, stalls selling Croatian flags, Croatian keyrings, Croatian candles, ashtrays, baseball caps, shot glasses, t-shirts, footballs, wooden handicrafts, even Croat cruets, do a roaring trade – not to tourists, but to the locals. 'Our flag's getting awfully tatty. What will the neighbours think? Let's replace it with that handsome new drip-dry version.' 'Yes dear, and we could brighten our breakfast table with that lovely Croat cruet set!'

Contemporary Zagreb, still digesting the political and spiritual effects of the war, is a city preoccupied with itself – hard-faced, distracted, not very friendly. Outsiders are mostly ignored, but it can be a relief to sojourn in a city not wholly dedicated to parting you from your hard currency. Not to say that Zagreb is cheap. Hotel prices are every bit as steep as Budapest, with few downmarket options save the Youth Hostel at Petrinjska 77 (434 964), not far from the station. The 'B' category

The funicular terminus on Tomićeva – one way up to Zagreb's Gornji Grad.

Astoria nearby at number 71 (430 444) is reasonably comfortable and serves a decent breakfast. The Dubrovnik is also mid-range and centrally located near Ban Jelačić Square at Gajeva 1 (455 5155). There's a Sheraton (455 3535) and an Inter-Continental (455 3411), but for locally flavoured luxury you'd be better off in the Esplanade near the station at Mihanovićeva 1 (456 6666).

Changing money is easy and there are a few ATM machines dotted around, but Croatia's economy, like its nationalistic culture, is swimming against the homogenous European tide. From the visitor's point of view, this adds up to a lot of curious local products where normally one might expect multinational names, such as cigarette brands called Benston, Ronhill, Triumph Lights and (of course) Croatia and Zagreb. From Kraš confectionary shops you can buy chocolate Croatian passports. From the rival Kandit chain you can get Vukovar chocolate bars, complete with a bombed-out townscape on the wrapper.

There isn't usually much going on. A monthly guide, *Zagreb Events and Performances*, available free from tourist offices, lists a desultory selection of sports events, classical concerts and exhibitions. There's also a booklet called *Zagreb Gastro*, listing 90 or so restaurants with little clue as to which might actually be any good. Don't expect much. Korčula at Nikole Tesle 17 (422 658) serves more than acceptable fish. Pizzeria Nocturno, handily located off Tkalčićeva at Skalinska 4 (276 428), can

rustle up a decent pizza. Klub Maksimir, out near the football stadium at Oboj 1 (241 189), offers finer dining in the former pavilion of a small sports field. For fast food try the Pingvin sandwich booth at Nikole Tesle 7 or the Tosteria Sunce round the corner at Bogovićeva 3.

At night, most of the action begins on and around Tkalčićeva, a narrow street full of bars that runs off Ban Jelačić Square and weaves up the gulley between Kaptol and the Gornji Grad. After chucking-out time (around 1am) Gjuro II (Medveščak 2) will serve for some dated disco dancing. The Jabuka, a cab-ride up into the hills (Jabukovac 28), is about as rockily alternative as it gets. The occasionally riotous bar in the middle of Ribnjak park, just behind Kaptol, has both a 'classic rock' disco and tables outside and stays open until around 4am.

Zagreb is an easy city to get around in. Though taxis are ruinous, the tram network, centred on Ban Jelačić Square and running from 5am to midnight, is cheap and simple to figure out. Tickets can be purchased at newsstands. Most distances are in any case walkable, and going out for a stroll is certainly the best way to soak in Zagreb's weird post-war atmosphere.

Tourist Information

Trg bana Jelačića 11 (00 38 51 481 4051). **Open** 8.30am-8pm Mon-Fri; 10am-6pm Sat; 10am-2pm Sun.
On the main city square. English spoken, lots of useful free leaflets and maps, plus Penkala's mechanical pencil on sale. **Branch**: Trg Nikole Šubića Zrinjskog 14 (455 2867).

Further Abroad

One step beyond Budapest, the Wild East awaits.

Budapest is an excellent staging post for an assortment of uncommon destinations. UK citizens require visas for Romania, Serbia and the Ukraine, but not for Slovakia or Slovenia. Citizens of other countries should check with their embassies.

Romania

In Transylvanian Romania, you still see horses and carts sharing roadspace with oil tankers, and in parts some folk customs have remained largely unchanged for centuries.

In the cities, hotel prices are pegged five times higher for foreigners than for locals. Food and service are appalling and outside hotel bars and discos there is a lack of anything resembling nightlife. The people, though poor, are friendly enough. A visit to Romania, even nine years after Ceauşescu, is still a shock to the system. Visiting some rural areas is like travelling back in time to fourteenth-century Switzerland. Don't expect modern creature comforts, and if intending to stay in the country, remember to pack some flea powder.

Most Romanian cities are easily accessible from Budapest by rail, but expect some uncomfortable train journeys.

Serbia

It's difficult to get a visa without a letter of invitation, but if you know someone who knows someone, that should do the trick. Belgrade is seven hours by train from Budapest, including a tedious one-hour wait at the border.

Serbia is very much a nation in transition – still suffering from the effects of wartime sanctions and groping after a new national identity. Expect lots of impassioned political discussion, hordes of Bosnian Serb refugees, rampant poverty and black-market trading, gold-chained gangsters zooming around in fast cars, bumped-up hotel prices for foreigners, and distinctly mediocre food. The Kalemegdan fortress overlooking Belgrade is the capital's only real tourist attraction and most of the rest of the city is composed of crumbling Communist blocks. But Serbs like to party and the city comes alive at night with a few trendy designer bars and a handful of clubs playing excellent house and techno.

Slovenia's Lake Bled – popular destination.

Slovakia

Beyond Bratislava, the Tatras, up on the border with Poland, are like a mini-Alps with possibly the cheapest skiing in Europe. Tatranska Lomnica is the most distinguished resort. Košice in East Slovakia is the country's second-largest city – a rough and ready place with big Gypsy and Hungarian populations (it was for many centuries the Magyar city Kassa).

Slovenia

This small former Yugoslav state, with Alps and a short Adriatic coastline within 40 minutes of each other, is like a budget version of Austria. Lake Bled, surrounded by woodland and mountains, is a popular destination, but the capital, Ljubljana, is the main attraction (seven hours from Budapest by rail). A long-established radical art scene – this is the home of NSK (Neue Slowenische Kunst) a multi-headed arts organisation centred on the group Laibach – is reflected in some interesting nightlife options.

Ukraine

Poor and in places irradiated, with highwaymen who rob buses (and even give you a receipt you can show the next band of highwaymen to prove you've already been ripped off), a trip to the Ukraine really is a journey into the Wild East. Visas are issued only to people who have a letter of invitation from an official organisation. Kiev is beautiful, though.

Directory

Essential Information

Crime

Although crime – particularly organised crime – has risen considerably in the 1990s, Budapest remains a relatively safe city. But as anywhere, a little common sense goes a long way. Watch out for pickpockets and purse-snatchers around Váci utca, the Castle District, Heroes' Square and at stations. Don't exchange money on the street. Be careful on trams 2, 4 and 6 where gangs sometimes operate. The prostitutes on Rákóczi tér are also reportedly adept at lifting items from pockets. Be careful if walking alone at night around outlying areas of town or District VIII around Rákóczi tér.

If you are black, Asian or Middle Eastern in appearance, be wary of the growing number of racist, skinhead gangs. They hang around in outlying areas and metro stations, so consider taking a taxi if alone or in a dodgy-looking neighbourhood. The police tend not to be of much assistance.

You are obliged by law to carry identification on you at all times and the police can make spot checks. In practice you are unlikely to be checked.

See **Police** *page 249, and* **Criminal Capers** *page 242.*

Customs

Coming into Hungary, any items of clothing or objects which could be deemed to be for personal use are exempt from duties. Individuals over 16 years old are also allowed to bring in 200 cigarettes, 20 cigars or 100 grams of tobacco, also five litres of wine, one litre of spirits and five litres of beer. Merchandise up to a value of Ft24,000 is allowed duty-free after which a 15 per cent duty and 2 per cent customs tax are payable in addition to 25 per cent ÁFA (VAT). In practice, foreigners are rarely checked. There is no limit to the amount of foreign currency that you can bring in.

It is forbidden to bring in drugs or arms.

On exit the following limits apply:

- wine – 2 litres;
- spirits – 1 litre;
- 200 cigarettes or 20 cigars or 100g of tobacco;
- Ft245,000 of gifts.

It is also forbidden to take more than Ft100,000 out of the country.

Dentists

See **Health**.

Disabled Travellers

Despite being home to the world famous Pető Institute, which treats children with cerebral palsy, Budapest does not have much access for the disabled. Public transport is basically inaccessible, apart from the M1 metro line. There are, however, some possibilities. The airport minibus is accessible. There is a special BKV bus, use of which can be arranged through MEOSZ, who also have their own minibus and can provide a helper. The **Museum of Fine Arts**, **Museum of Applied Arts** and **Foundry Museum** (*see chapter* **Museums**) are now accessible, as is the **National Foreign Language Library** (*see below* **Libraries**).

Wherever new stretches of street are built, there are ramps in kerbs to facilitate access for wheelchairs, and all new buildings, such as Budapest's three shopping malls (*see chapter* **Shopping & Services**) or the numerous new office blocks, are now designed with the disabled in mind. There are also a limited number of trips available such as Balaton by train once a week. For more details phone:

Hungarian Disabled Association
MEOSZ
III. San Marco utca 76 (368 1758). Tram 1. **Open** 8am-4pm Mon-Fri. English spoken.

Doctors

See **Health**.

Driving in Budapest

Budapest has all the traffic problems of most modern European cities with a few extra ones thrown in. Hungarian driving is not good. Hungarians have constant urges to overtake in the most impossible places, they lack concentration and jump traffic lights. There are a lot of accidents, mostly cars going into the backs of other cars. Many vehicles are of poor quality. Roads are even worse. Cobbled streets abound, designed to tax even the sturdiest suspension. There has been a huge influx of western cars in recent years, increasing traffic levels and daytime

Criminal capers

Among their regular advertisers, popular Budapest radio stations have a new and unusual genre of clients: victims of car theft. The ads come nearly hourly, and go something like 'Please call the following number if you have information about a blue Mercedes, registration number....' But the advertisers aren't appealing to the average listener who might have seen the car. It's more a not-so-subtle code that allows the thieves to contact the owner, who can then reclaim their underinsured car (policies for luxury cars are ridiculously high) for a sizeable ransom. The exchange usually takes place in some lonely city outskirt in scenes reminiscent of a spy thriller, complete with paper bags full of cash left at public phone booths in the dark of night. Such is the new Budapest.

Since the political changes, crime has spiralled in Hungary. In addition to car theft, burglaries, muggings and spectacular armed robberies have become a regular part of the evening news. The rise of organised crime has caused the most worry, however. According to local journalists and businessmen, gangs organised by and connected to larger groups in Russia, Ukraine and China now do business here alongside homegrown syndicates. Typically these gangs engage in smuggling, racketeering and extortion – which is most often cloaked under the guise of 'security'.

Until recently, these mafia groups had managed to coexist. But an apparent turf war erupted in late 1996 marked by over two dozen late-night bombings and shootings. Though most of the attacks seemed aimed at simply damaging nightclubs or restaurants as a warning or retribution, three people died along the way. Additional casualties were Hungary's two top cops, who both lost their jobs after police failed to make swift arrests in connection to the attacks.

But Budapest's crime rate only seems remarkable compared to the sleepy days of goulash communism. Next to nearly any large western European or American city, Budapest remains a fairly safe sort of place.

parking problems. Practically all central streets are jammed from 7am-7pm on weekdays due to roadworks and detours. This is just the beginning of the long process of replacing cobblestones and old tram tracks, and making pavements inaccessible for parking cars. Talk of restricting traffic in certain areas has not yet amounted to much.

There was a time when a western car would almost certainly get stolen and taken somewhere in the former Soviet Union. This trade has diminished but it is wise to take precautions. Keep cars locked and fitted with an alarm if possible. Take the radio out and do not leave anything visible inside. If you cannot find your car where you left it, it does not necessarily mean it has been stolen. It may have been towed for illegal parking. If so, go to the nearest police station. In the centre this is at V. Szalay utca 11-13 near the Parliament.

• Seatbelts must be worn at all times.

• Always carry your passport, driving licence (not necessarily an international one – UK and US ones are generally accepted), vehicle registration document, evidence of motor insurance (green card insurance is not compulsory for those insured in the UK), and *zöldkártya* (exhaust emissions certificate) for cars registered in Hungary.

• Do not leave anything of value in the car, especially car documents.

• Headlights are compulsory by day when driving outside town, although not on motorways.

• Priority is from the right unless you are on a priority road, signified by a yellow diamond on a white background. Whatever the case, drive with caution on one-way roads.

• Watch out for other drivers. They may not be watching out for you.

• Watch out for trams, particularly in places where the passengers alight in the middle of the road – this can take some getting used to for people who come from non-tram towns.

• Watch out for drunks, people walking on country roads at night and bicycles without lights or markings.

• The speed limit on motorways is 120 kph, on highways (signified by a white car on a blue background) 90 kph, on all other roads 80 kph unless otherwise indicated, and 50 kph in built-up areas. Speed traps abound, with spot fines that vary greatly, especially for foreigners. These are sometimes negotiable, however.

• The alcohol limit for driving is basically zero (0.08 per cent) and there are many spot checks, especially at night, with severe penalties for the guilty. Take a taxi if drinking (*see chapter* **Getting Around**.)

Breakdowns

A 24-hour breakdown service is provided by the Magyar Autóklub. They have reciprocal agreements with many European associations, so check before you come. English and German are usually spoken, but if not they will ask you for the model (*típus*), colour (*szín*) and the number plate (*rendszám*) of the vehicle and also the location. Assistance is usually fairly rapid.

Magyar Autóklub

(212 3952). **Open** 24 hours daily. **No credit cards** but will accept a credit letter from affiliated organisations. English spoken.

There are also these private breakdown services:

Túra Team Club Breakdown Service

(262 0189). **Open** 24 hours daily. **Credit** AmEx, EC, MC, V. English spoken.

Budasegély

(269 7062/269 7218). **Open** 8am-7pm daily. **No credit cards.** No English spoken.

Start

(276 8302). **Open** 24 hours daily. **No credit cards.** Some English spoken.

Parking

Parking is not easy any more and towing and wheel clamping are in force. Most town parking is on the pavements – just copy everybody else. Certain areas have parking meters which, during working hours, cost Ft120 an hour in the centre for a maximum of two hours, and Ft50-Ft80 in other districts. Certain central areas are controlled by parking attendants – V. Március 15 tér,

or under the Nyugati Station flyover, for example, where prices are Ft60-Ft80 an hour. There is a multi-storey car park on V. Bárczy István utca 2 just off Petőfi Sándor utca, and another at V. Türr István utca 5, both cost Ft180 an hour or Ft2,160 per day.

Petrol

Most filling stations are open 24 hours and sell all types of fuel. Unleaded is *ólommentes*. Stay away from any fuel marked with a K as this is for lawnmowers and Trabants.

Most stations are self-service but some still have attendants, to whom people generally give a modest tip. Nearly all petrol stations accept credit cards and sell tobacco and basic groceries.

Car Service Agents

BMW

XIII. Kassák Lajos utca 75 (140 7640). M3 Árpád híd. **Open** 9am-5pm Mon-Fri. Closed in August. **No credit cards.** Some English spoken. **Map D1**

Citroen

IX. Könyves Kálmán körút 26/b (216 7100). M3 Nagyvárad tér. **Open** 8am-5pm Mon-Fri. **No credit cards.** Some English spoken.

Fiat

VIII. Kálvária utca 9 (134 4531). **Open** 8am-5pm Mon-Thur; 8am-3pm Fri. **No credit cards.** Some English spoken. **Map F5**

Ford

XIII. Váci út 84 (270 3433). M3 Dózsa György út. **Open** 7am-4.30pm Mon-Fri. **Credit** AmEx, DC, JCB, MC, V. English spoken.

Honda

XIII. Frangepán utca 36 (149 5763). M3 Nyugati. **Open** 7am-4pm Mon-Thur; 7am-1pm Fri. **Credit** EC, MC, V. Some English spoken.

Mercedes Benz

XIII. Kárpát utca 21 (129 9990). Trolleybus 79. **Open** 7am-8pm Mon-Fri. **Credit** AmEx, DC, EC, JCB, MC, V. English spoken.

Opel

XIV. Mexikói út 15/19 (251 8555). M2 Népstadion. **Open** 6am-6pm Mon-Fri. **No credit cards.** No English spoken.

Peugeot

XI. Szurdok utca 4 (246 4270). **Open** 7.30am-6pm Mon-Fri. **No credit cards.** Some English spoken.

Renault

XI. Budaörsi út 121 (246 3900). Bus 40. **Open** 7am-5pm Mon-Fri. **No credit cards.** Some English spoken. **Map A6**

VW/Audi

III. Mozaik utca 1/3 (250 0222/250 0247).
HÉV Filatorigát. **Open** 5.30am-9.30pm Mon-Fri.
Credit EC, MC, V. Some English spoken.

Drugs

Drugs are illegal in Hungary and the police regularly raid certain discos and bars in Budapest to make sure everybody remembers this. According to excitable police estimates there are 220 nightclubs and discos in the country where 'people use large amounts of drugs'. (Quite where all these places is a mystery to us.) While in 1990 the police caught people with a total of 3.9 kg of heroin and 2.4 kg of hash, by 1996 these figures rocketed to 319 kg and 816 kg respectively.

If you are caught with a small amount of drugs, you will be required to attend six months of weekly group therapy sessions 'to prevent addiction'. A small amount means less than 10 joints, 20 tabs of LSD, 50 tabs of ecstasy, 2 grams of cocaine or 0.6 grams of heroin. If you have more than this, you will be arrested and taken to court. However, the definition of 'a small amount of drugs' is likely to change in the near future and even smaller amounts will be tolerated.

Drog Stop Hotline *(267 3344).* 24 hours daily
Drog Ambulancia *(270 4221).* 10am-4pm Mon-Fri.

Education

See also chapter **Children**.

Directory

Universities

Central European University (CEU)

V. Nádor utca 9 (327 5000/fax 111 6073). M2 Kossuth Lajos tér. **Open** 9am-5pm Mon-Thur; 9am-3pm Fri. **Map C3**

Founded in 1991 by George Soros, CEU offers postgraduate courses for students from central and eastern Europe and the former USSR. Departments include History, Legal Studies, Gender Studies and Political and Environmental Sciences.

Eötvös Loránd University

Eötvös Loránd Tudományos Egyetem (ELTE)
International Secretariat – V. Pesti Barnabás utca 1 (postal address 1364 Budapest, Pf 107) (267 0966 ext 171/fax 266 3521). M3 Ferenciek tere. **Open** 10am-2pm Mon-Thur; 10am-noon Fri. **Map C4**

The largest and oldest Hungarian university, it was founded in 1635 in Nagyszombat (now Trnava, Slovakia), moved to Buda in 1777, and to Pest in 1784. Today there are 12,000 students at the Faculty of Humanities, Sciences, Law and the Institute of Sociology.

Budapest University of Economic Sciences

Budapesti Közgazdaságtudományi Egyetem (BKE)
International Studies Centre – IX. Fővám tér 8 (217 0608). Tram 2, 47, 49. **Open** 8am-4.30pm Mon-Thur; 8am-2pm Fri. **Map D5**

An independent institution since 1948, the BKE (known as the Közgáz – 'public gas' – a pun on the Hungarian for economics: *gazdaság*) has 4,000 students, and issues diplomas in Business Administration, International Economics and Business, and Social and Political Studies.

Budapest Technical University

Budapesti Műszaki Egyetem (BME)
International Student Centre – XI. Műegyetem rakpart 3 (463 1408/fax 463 2520). Bus 86. **Open** 9am-4pm Mon-Thur; 9am-2pm Fri. **Map C6**

Established in 1782, the BME has over 9,000 students studying at seven faculties that include Architecture and Chemical, Electrical and Civil Engineering. The education is highly practical, and BME is among the few Hungarian institutions whose diplomas are accepted throughout the world.

Semmelweis University of Medicine

Semmelweis Orvostudományi Egyetem (SOTE)

English Secretariat – VIII. Üllői út 26 (266 0452). M3 Klinikák. **Open** 9am-3pm Mon-Thur; 9am-1pm Fri.

Over 200 years old, but only in its current form since 1955, when the faculties of Pharmacy and Dentistry were incorporated. Ignác Semmelweis, who discovered the cause of puerperal fever, was a professor here last century.

Learning Hungarian

Arany János Nyelviskola

VI. Csengery utca 68 (111 8870). M1 Oktogon/tram 4, 6. **Open** 10am-5.30pm Mon-Thur; 10am-3.30pm Fri. **Map D2**

One of the largest language schools, offering courses in most European tongues. 60-lesson courses are available at Ft25,200 and you can take five, ten or fifteen weeks to attend this many lessons. International student ID nets a 10 per cent discount.

Eötvös Loránd University, Faculty of Humanities

V. Pesti Barnabás utca 1 (267 0966/extension 5107). M3 Ferenciek tere. **Open** 9am-4pm Mon-Thur; 9am-2pm Fri. **Map C4**

ELTE organises a summer university for foreigners with Hungarian-language classes. During the academic year, a two-term Hungarian course is available. Participants are registered as regular students, and, if they study at a college in their home country, may use the credits they receive here. ELTE also offers 20-week intensive Hungarian courses. Survival evening courses cost around Ft600 for 45 minutes.

Hungarian Language School

VI. Eötvös utca 25A (312 5899). M1 Oktogon/tram 4, 6. **Open** 9am-4pm Mon, Tue, Thur, Fri; 9am-7pm Wed. **Map D3**

Two-, three-, and four-week courses throughout the year at different levels. A four-week survival course costs $100, a three-week intensive summer course with cultural programmes is around $210.

Kodolányi János Institute

XI. Zsombolyai utca. 3 (185 2646). Bus 7. **Open** *office* 8am-4pm Mon-Fri. **Map B6**

Intensive Hungarian courses for $1,300- $2,000 per semester depending on whether you take 14, 20 or 28 lessons a week.

Katedra Nyelviskola

V. Fővám tér 2 (118 2051). M3 Kálvin tér. **Open** *office* 8am-4pm Mon-Fri. **Map C5**

Intensive and not-so-intensive Hungarian courses at different levels. For between Ft10,000 and Ft20,000 for five or 10 weeks.

Electricity

The current used in Hungary is 220v which works fine with British 240v appliances. If you have US 110v gadgets you will need a current transformer. These are available in Budapest only from **Bigrav** on Váci utca (*see chapter* **Shopping & Services**). Plugs have two round pins so bring an adaptor for any other plug.

Embassies & Consulates

For a full list of embassies look in the phone book or yellow pages under *Külképviseletek*.

American Embassy

V. Szabadság tér 12 (267 4400/after hours 153 0566). M3 Arany János utca. **Open** 8.30am-11am Mon-Fri. **Map C3**

Australian Embassy

XII. Királyhágó tér 8/9 (214 2091). M2 Déli. **Open** 9am-noon Mon-Fri.

Austrian Embassy

VI. Benczúr utca 16 (269 6700). M1 Bajza utca. **Open** 9am-11am Mon-Fri. **Map E2**

Belgian Embassy

I. Toldy Ferenc utca 13 (201 1571). M2 Batthyány tér. **Open** 9am-noon Mon-Fri. **Map B3**

British Embassy

V. Harmincad utca 6 (266 2888). M1, M2, M3 Deák tér. **Open** 9.30am-noon, 2.30pm-4pm, Mon-Fri. **Map C4**

Canadian Embassy

XII Budakeszi út 32 (275 1200). Bus 22. **Open** 9am-11am Mon-Fri.

Danish Embassy

XII. Határőr út 37 (155 7320). Bus 39. **Open** 10am-1pm Mon-Fri.

Dutch Embassy

II. Füge utca 5/7 (326 5301). Bus 11. **Open** 10am-noon Mon-Fri. **Map A1**

Finnish Embassy

XI. Kelenhegyi út 16/a (185 0700). Bus 7. **Open** 9am-noon Mon-Fri. **Map B5**

French Embassy
*VI. Lendvay utca 27 (332 4980). M1
Hősök tere.* **Open** 9am-noon Mon-Fri.
Map E2

German Embassy
*XIV. Stefánia út 101/103 (467
3500). Bus 7.* **Open** 9am-noon Mon-
Fri.

Indian Embassy
*II. Búzavirág utca 14 (325 7742).
Bus 11, 91.* **Open** 10am-noon Mon-
Thur.

Irish Embassy
*V. Szabadság tér 7/9 (302 9600). M2
Kossuth tér.* **Open** 9.30am-12.30pm,
2.30pm-4.30pm, Mon-Fri. **Map C3**

Israeli Embassy
*II. Fullánk utca 8 (200 0781). Bus
11.* **Open** 9am-noon Mon-Fri.

Italian Embassy
*XIV.Stefánia út 95 (343 6065). Bus
7.* **Open** 9am-noon Mon, Wed, Fri.

Japanese Embassy
XII. Zalai út 7 (275 1275). Bus 156.
Open 8.45am-12.15pm, 2pm-3.30pm
Mon-Thur; 8.45am-12.15pm Fri.

New Zealand Consulate
I. Attila út 125 (131 4908). M2 Déli.
Open 9am-noon Mon, Wed; 1pm-
4pm Tue, Thur. **Map A3**

Norwegian Embassy
*XII. Határőr út 35 (155 1811). Bus
39.* **Open** 10am-1pm Mon-Fri.

South African Embassy
*VIII. Rákóczi út 1/3 (267 4566). M2
Astoria.* **Open** 9am-12.30pm Mon-
Fri. **Map D4**

Spanish Embassy
*VI. Eötvös utca 13 (342 9993). M2
Oktogon.* **Open** 9.30am-12.30pm
Mon-Fri. **Map D3**

Swedish Embassy
*XIV. Ajtósi Dürer sor 27/a (268
0804). Bus 7/trolley bus 72, 74, 75.*
Open 10am-noon Mon-Fri. **Map F2**

Swiss Embassy
*XIV. Stefánia út 107 (343 9491).
Bus 7.* **Open** 10am-noon Mon-Fri.

Health

Despite severe cutbacks and
restrictions, the Hungarian
health service is still considered
one of the best in eastern
Europe. The service provided is
adequate, although a lot of
queuing is involved. Most
doctors speak English.

Emergency care
is provided free to citizens of
the UK, Finland, Norway,
Sweden and former Socialist
countries, although it is
probably wise to have medical
insurance. Those living here
should get a TB (social
security) card through their
company, to obtain free state
health treatment, and register
with a local GP. Private clinics
now offer the opportunity to
avoid the queues and discuss
problems in English.

Emergencies/Hospitals

In an emergency the best thing
to do is to go to the casualty
department of any hospital.
Take along a Hungarian
speaker and always carry some
form of identification.

Ambulances

The normal emergency number
is 104. Or call 311 1666 where
they speak both English and
German.

Private Clinics

IMS
*XIII. Váci út 202 (129 8423/149
9349). M3 Újpest Városkapu.* **Open**
8am-8pm Mon-Fri. **Credit** AmEx,
MC.
A 24-hour emergency service is
available on 250 3829, but this service
does not accept credit cards.

Professional Orvosi Kft
*V. Múzeum körút 35, Third Floor,
no 6 (117 0631). M2 Kálvin tér.*
Open 4pm-8pm Mon; 8am-noon Tue,
Thur; 8am-noon, 4pm-8pm, Wed. **No
credit cards. Map D4**

SOS Emergency Medical Service
*VIII. Kerepesi út 15 (118 8288/24-
hour 118 8212). M2 Keleti.* **Open** 24
hours daily. **Credit** AmEx, MC. **Map
F3**

R Klinika
*II. Felsőzöldmáli út 13 (325 9999).
Bus 29.* **Open** 8am-6pm daily, 24
hours in emergencies. **Credit** AmEx,
JCB, MC, V.

Pharmacies

Pharmacies (*patika* or
gyógyszertár) are marked

by a green cross outside.
Opening hours are generally
8am-6pm or 8am-8pm Mon-Fri,
with some also open on
Saturday mornings. Some
English will be spoken in all of
these pharmacies. The
following pharmacies are open
24 hours:
*II. Frankel Leó utca 22 (212 4406).
VI. Teréz körút 41 (342 1189).
VII. Rákóczi út 39 (314 3695).
IX. Üllői út 121 (215 3800).
XII. Alkotás út 29 (155 6482).*

Dentists

Although there is state dental
care, most people go private if
they can. Prices are reasonable
compared to the West, as
evidenced by the number of
Austrians flocking over the
border to have their molars
scrutinised. German and/or
English are spoken in the
clinics listed below.

Dental Co-op
*XII. Zugligeti út 58/60 (176 3049).
Bus 158.* **Open** 9am-6pm Mon-Fri;
1pm-6pm Thur. **Credit** AmEx, MC,
V.

Super Dent
*XIII. Dózsa György út 65 (129 0200
ext 180). M3 Dózsa György.* **Open**
8am-2pm Mon, Wed, Fri; 8am-7pm
Tue, Thur. **Credit** AmEx.

SOS Dental Clinic
*VI. Király utca 14 (267 9602/269
6010). M1, M2, M3 Deák tér/tram
47, 49.* **Open** 24 hours daily.
Credit AmEx, DC, JCB, MC, V.
Map C4

Chiropractor

Dr Jack Conway
*XI. Györök utca 2 (185 2515). Tram
19, 49.* **Open** 8am-noon, 1.30pm-
4pm, Mon, Thur; 8am-noon Tue,
Wed, Fri. **No credit cards.** English
spoken.

Poison Control Centres

Erzsébet Kórház
*VII. Alsó erdősor utca 7 (322 3450).
M2 Blaha Lujza tér.* Some English
spoken. **Map E3**

Heim Pál Kórház
*XI. Üllői út 86 (210 0720/269 9398).
M3
Nagyvárad tér.* Some English spoken.
Map F6
For children only.

Directory

AIDS & Sexually Transmitted Diseases

AIDS remains at a relatively low level in Hungary, although this may increase with the influx of foreigners and high promiscuity.

AIDS hotline
(138 2419) 6am-4pm. Some English spoken.

Skin & Genital Clinic
Bőr és Nemikórtani Klinika
VIII. Mária utca 41 (210 0310). M3 Ferenc körút. **Open** 8am-4pm Mon-Fri. Some English spoken. **Map D5**
This is the place to go if you have STD problems. An AIDS test here costs Ft4,000.

Anonymous AIDS Advisory Service
Anonim AIDS Tanácsadó Szolgálat
XI. Karolina út 35B (166 9283). Tram 61. **Open** *hotline* 9am-8pm Mon-Sat; *in person* 5pm-8pm Mon, Wed, Thur; 9am-12.30pm Tue, Fri. English spoken. **Map A6**
Free anonymous AIDS tests available.

Alcoholics Anonymous
VII. Kertész utca 28, First Floor (267 9348). M2 Blaha Lujza tér. **Map E4**
Meetings in English on Tuesdays at 5.30pm and Fridays at 6.30pm. Call László at the above number for details.

Domestic Violence

NaNE – Women United Against Violence
Nők a Nőkért Együtt az Erőszak Ellen
IX. Vámház körút 7 (216 5900/6pm-10pm daily 216 1670). M3 Kálvin tér. **Open** 9am-6pm Mon-Fri. English spoken. **Map D5**
Offers support and information to battered and raped women and children.

Veterinarians

Budapest Állatkórház
XIII. Lehel út 43/47 (270 0361/270 1166). M3 Árpád híd/tram 1. **Open** 24 hours daily. Some English spoken.

Contraception & Abortion

Condoms are available at chemists, Azúr shops and many supermarkets.

Abortion is legal and widely used, although not as widely as

under Communism, when contraception was not easily available. For abortions you should refer to a local doctor or gynaecologist.

Alternative Medicine

Alternative medicine is very much in its infancy in Hungary, with much talk of wonder cures but as yet little organisation or substance.

There are now several Chinese doctors with acupuncture and massage therapies. Pick up a copy of the magazine *Harmadik Szem* for listings of homeopaths and Oriental practitioners. Or try:

Dr Funian Yu
Józsefvárosi Klub, VIII. Somogyi Béla utca 13/15 (118 7930). M2 Blaha Lujza tér. **Open** 1pm-6pm Mon-Fri (by appointment). English spoken. **Map E4**

Magyar Homeopathic Doctors' Association and Homeocentrum Pharmacy
XI. Ratkóz köz 4 (246 2132). Bus 139. **Open** 2pm-7pm Mon, Wed, Fri; 9am-1pm Tue, Thur. Some English spoken.

Britain, Norway, Finland, Sweden and the former Warsaw Pact countries have reciprocal agreements guaranteeing free emergency treatment to their citizens. Non-emergency treatment is not covered though, and it is probably best to take out travel insurance if only to avoid the long queues at the state hospitals. This will also cover you for lost or stolen valuables.

Internet

The best places for internet access are the cyber cafés in the recently built shopping malls (*see chapter* **Shopping & Services**). You can also try c3 (Center for Culture and Communication) (*see chapter* **Art Galleries**).

The local dial-in number for Compuserve is 291 9999. The number for America Online and Prodigy is 457 8888. Microsoft Network is on 267 4636.

Plaza Internet Club and Cyber Café
Duna Plaza Shopping Center, XIII. Váci út 178 (465 1126). **Open** 10am-10pm daily. **Price** Ft600/hour. English spoken.

MATÁV Telefónia üzlet
Europark Shopping Center, XIX. Üllői út 201 (281 1857). **Open** 9am-8pm daily. **Price** Ft500/hour. Some English spoken.

Language Schools
See **Education**.

Left Luggage

Twenty-four-hour left-luggage facilities are available at Nyugati and Keleti stations: Ft120 or Ft240 for large items. Prices run from midnight to midnight. Lockers do exist at all three main stations but are rarely available. These cost Ft150. There are also facilities at Erzsébet tér bus terminal, open 6am-7pm Mon-Thur; 6am-9pm Fri; 6am-6pm Sat, Sun. Price Ft150 per item.

Legal Help

If in need of legal assistance contact your embassy who will provide you with a list of English-speaking lawyers. (*See also chapter* **Business**.)

Libraries

The American Library
V. Szabadság tér 7 (302 6200). M2 Kossuth tér. **Open** 11am-5pm Tue, Thur. **Map C3**
Membership free to anyone over 16.

The British Council Library
VI. Benczúr utca 26 (321 4039). M1 Bajza utca. **Open** 11am-6pm Mon-Thur; 11am-5pm Fri. **Map E2**
Excellent magazine and periodicals section and English-teaching section, also a huge video library.

Directory

Magyars do it doggie style

A recent poll of European countries returned the results that Hungarians are far and away the most avid dog owners in Europe, if not the world. Budapest, city of dreams and love, is also a city of dogs, as well as their attendant and loving owners, and a virtual mountain of dog shit.

Hungarians love dogs. Every fourth folk song is about a loyal sheepdog, and poodles seem to be issued to every elderly citizen at retirement. A sheepdog is essential equipment to Hungarian manhood, while women tend towards cute little furball breeds. Old women sit in the park accompanied by herds of precious little dogs, shampooed and bedecked with ribbons, while the young set would never be seen without some kind of 'statement dog'. Dobermans are popular with the black leather crowd, pit bulls with skinheads, German shepherds with families.

And of course there are the noble Hungarian breeds. Vizslas, a sort of sleek Habsburg *Uber-hound*, nuzzle their loving masters with wet tan noses, while hoping to flush quail from beneath parked cars. Mystically dreadlocked pulis, the world's greatest sheepdogs, look like canine Rastafarians barking insanely at each and every crossing light. Their ropey, dreadlocked hair was originally a trait that protected them against attack by wolves, but now seems little more than a fashion statement. And of course, many of the most beloved pets are simply smelly mutts.

Even in Budapest, dogs are not without their detractors. A recent fad for attack dogs has led the government to move for legislation against fighting breeds like pit bulls and rottweilers. And a walk though any residential area or park will show that in fact, most of these dogs are not really 'walking' at all. One can think of them as millions of beings who do little but roam the streets of Budapest buck naked, wheedling on the sidewalk and taking dumps on every kerb. If these beings were two-legged, nobody would stand for it. Yet they are not only tolerated but given nice homes, fed well, cuddled, and cooed over.

If anyone needs proof, take a tour of District VII. Marek József utca has probably the highest concentration of dogs in the city. And they all have to 'go' somewhere. A few blocks north is the leafy Városligeti fasor and the beginnings of the embassy district. Here the tree-lined streets are wonderful for an evening walk – just watch where you step, and don't wear shoes with cleated soles.

Membership open to anyone over 16 for a one-off fee of Ft500.

The National Foreign Language Library

V. Molnár utca 11 (118 3188/118 3688). M3
Ferenciek tere. **Open** 9am-8pm Mon, Tue, Thur, Fri; noon-8pm Wed. English spoken. **Map C5**
Only foreigners with residence permits and a passport may check out books here. Good periodicals section; helpful staff.

National Széchényi Library

I. Buda Palace Wing F (175 7533).
Várbusz from M2 Moszkva tér.
Open 9am-9pm Tue-Sat during academic year. English spoken. **Map B4**
The biggest national public library in Hungary with a large collection of foreign-language books, periodicals, microfilms and inter-library services. Useful for research but you can't check books out.

Lost Property

If you lose something, you can enquire at the police station in the area where you thought you lost it, but don't hold out much hope. Take along a Hungarian speaker, especially if you need a statement for insurance purposes. Hungarian police are not renowned for their language skills.

At Ferihegy Airport 1 phone 296 7690 and at Ferihegy 2 call 296 8108. For anything left on trains, go to the station you arrived at and be persistent but pleasant; it has been known to get results. For taxis, phone the company you rode with. Fõtaxi claims to hold on to items left in their vehicles for five years.

BKV Lost Property Office

Talált Tárgyak Osztálya
VII. Akácfa utca 18 (322 6613). M2 Blaha Lujza tér. **Open** 7.30am-3pm Mon-Thur; 7.30am-7pm Wed; 7.30am-2pm Fri. No English spoken. **Map E4**

Maps

There is a wide selection of new Budapest maps available, but the old one is still the best: Cartographia's *Budapest Atlas* at Ft2,000. In handy book form, it contains all public transport lines, house numbers, a full street index and is sturdy enough to stand some battering about. For lovers of origami there is also a wide range of fold-out maps. Free maps of central Budapest can be picked up at **Tourinform** (*see above*) and should be enough to see you through a short stay.

Maps are available at most bookshops and travel agents, at Tourinform and at some newsstands. A good specialist map shop is **Térképkirály** (*see chapter* **Shopping & Services**).

Money

The Hungarian unit of currency is the forint, usually abbreviated as HUF or Ft – the convention we have used in this guide. Forint coins come in denominations of Ft1, Ft2, Ft5, Ft10, Ft20, Ft50, Ft100 and Ft200.

Notes come in denominations of Ft100, Ft500, Ft1,000, Ft5,000 and Ft10,000. The Ft50 note is brown. The dark red Ft100 has a picture of Lajos Kossuth, the nineteenth-century revolutionary. The blue Ft500 features poet Endre Ady. Béla Bartók's profile graces the green Ft1,000, and the orange Ft5,000 depicts István Széchenyi, the nineteenth-century moderniser of Hungary. The new and fancy-looking Ft10,000 features Szent István and has Braille writing on it together with a metal strip and some other anti-forgery devices.

Banks

Banks give better rates than change kiosks, but it is worth shopping around as rates do vary. Traveller's cheques are exchangeable at both banks and change kiosks, although sometimes at a worse rate than cash.

Black market exchange is no longer worth it and don't be tempted to change on the street with various dubious characters. They are usually part of some organised mafia and will try to leave you with useless Yugoslav dinars or lighten your wallet by some similar con.

Forints can be changed back into hard currency at any bank and at the bureaux de change in the airport. When changing back large amounts, some places may still demand exchange receipts with your passport number stamped on them.

The usual **opening times** for banks are: 8.15am-6pm Mon; 8.15am-4pm Tue-Thur; 8.15am-1pm Fri. Apart from cash and traveller's cheques, most banks will also advance money on a credit card, but Postabank and Ibusz accept only Visa.

Bureaux de Change

These are now all over the main tourist areas and usually open from 9am-10pm daily. English is spoken in all of the places listed below. Rates are often poor but try:

Exklusiv

V. Váci utca 12 (117 2596). M1, M2, M3 Deák tér/tram 47, 49. **Open** 9am-6pm daily. **No credit cards**. **Map C4**

IBB/Intergold

VI. Teréz körút 62 (131 8361). M3 Nyugati/tram 4, 6. **Open** 10am-5pm daily. **No credit cards. Map D2**

24-hour Exchange Facilities

There are cash machines all over town and you should find one on any busy shopping street. Apart from machines connected to the Cirrus and Plus systems, allowing you to draw on a foreign bank account or credit card, there are also exchange machines. You slip in a foreign banknote, they spew forth forints. American Express has a 24-hour machine and both Nyugati and Keleti stations have round-the-clock exchange facilities.

Ibusz Bank

V. Petőfi tér 3 (118 5707). M3 Ferenciek tere. **Open** 24 hours daily. **Map C4**
Will change cash and traveller's

cheques or else advance money on Visa, Diner's and JCB cards.

American Express

V. Deák Ferenc utca 10 (credit card 267 2313/traveller's cheques 266 8679). M1, M2, M3 Deák tér/tram 47, 49. **Open** 9am-6.30pm Mon-Fri; 9am-2pm Sat. **Map C4**
Currency exchange, moneygrams, mail and fax delivery for card and traveller's cheque holders, hotel reservations, airline tickets and cash advances in hard currencies, all for various fees.

Credit Cards

Credit cards are becoming more widely accepted and American Express, Visa and Mastercard are accepted in several thousand outlets. This usually indicates that these establishments are tourist-orientated and therefore more expensive than the norm. For cash advances see previous section.

Newspapers

There are three English-language weekly newspapers: *Budapest Week*, *Budapest Sun* (both with listings and entertainment guides) and *Budapest Business Journal*. Most newspaper kiosks and hotel lobbies will have foreign newspapers either same day (the *Guardian International* or *International Herald Tribune*) or one day old (any other newspaper). **Bestsellers** bookshop carries many newspapers and magazines as well as a large stock of books in English. (*See also chapters* **Media** *and* **Shopping & Services**.)

Opening Times

Hours vary according to the type of shop. Most shops open from 9am-5pm Monday-Friday, and 9am-1pm on Saturdays. Department stores usually open from 10am. Supermarkets, greengrocers and bakeries usually open at 6.30am or 7am and close around 8pm Monday-Friday, switching to 1pm-3pm on Saturdays. There are many non-stops, small 24-hour corner shops, where you can buy basic groceries, tobacco and booze. Most restaurants close by 11pm or midnight.

Passports

You're required by law to carry your passport with you at all times, although in practice you will rarely be checked.

If you lose your passport, report it immediately to the local police station and then also to your consulate who will issue you with an emergency passport. You will not be allowed to leave the country without it. *See also* **Visas**.

Pharmacies

See **Health**.

Police

The stupidity of Budapest police is the subject of many Hungarian jokes. You will have little contact with them unless you have something stolen or commit a crime. The police can stop anyone and ask for identification but this is unlikely unless they think you look like an illegal immigrant. If robbed or you lose something, report it to the police station in the district where the incident took place. Take a Hungarian speaker with you and count on filling in forms for the rest of the day without much chance of ever retrieving your stolen property. It's not really worth it unless it was something really very valuable, or unless you need the forms for your insurance company.

Post

The Hungarian postal service is reasonably efficient despite employing some of the stroppiest staff in the business. Letters from the UK generally

take about four days to arrive. Post boxes are square red things sporting post horn and envelope symbols. These are relatively rare, though, and it's more usual to take your letters to the post office where the person behind the desk will put the stamp on and post it for you. Expect to queue a bit, especially at Christmas. Most post offices are open from 8am-7pm on weekdays. There are no late-night post offices, but the ones at Keleti and Nyugati are open 7am-9pm daily.

Postal Rates & Post Boxes

Letters weighing up to 30g cost Ft20 within Budapest and Ft27 to the rest of Hungary. A letter up to 20g to neighbouring countries (those literally bordering on Hungary) costs Ft27. A letter to anywhere else in the world costs Ft90 up to 20g, Ft180 up to 100g. To send them airmail (*légiposta*) is an extra Ft24. Postcards to neighbouring countries are Ft20 and Ft60 elsewhere in Europe and Ft72 overseas.

To send something registered (*ajánlott*) is an extra Ft120 and express an extra Ft150.

PO boxes are obtainable at most post offices for a fee of Ft1,500 for three months. Poste Restante letters will go to the office at Nyugati Station.

For courier services and express mail *see chapters* **Business** *and* **Shopping & Services**.

American Express

Card-holders or clients with American Express traveller's cheques can use their mail service. Letters should be addressed to: American Express Travel Service, Client Mail, Deák Ferenc utca 10, 1052 Budapest (266 8680). M1, M2, M3 Deák tér.

Sending Packages

The Hungarian postal system has an insanely complicated system for sending packages depending on what it is and on when and how you are sending it. Try to keep the package small, under 2kg. This will ensure the cheapest rate: Ft480 up to 500g, Ft1,200 up to 2kg. Packages should also be done up with string and you will also need a blue customs declaration form (*vámáru-nyilatkozat*) from the post office.

Also try to keep the value to a minimum, as sending anything worth over Ft10,000 is so complicated it's hardly worth the bother. Special boxes can be purchased at the post office. Most post offices can also supply a booklet in English detailing postal charges. (*See also chapter* **Shopping & Services**.)

Public Holidays

New Year's Day (*Új Év*); 15 March, National Holiday; Easter Monday; 1 May, Labour Day; Whit Monday; 20 August, St Stephen's Day; 23 October, Remembrance Day; 25, 26 December.

There is usually something open on most holidays apart from the evening of 24 December when Budapest becomes a ghost town and even the non-stops shut. New Year's Eve is very lively, as is St Stephen's Day on 20 August, with fireworks launched from Gellért Hill. *See also chapter* **Budapest By Season**.

Public Toilets

There are public toilets at various locations for which you will have to pay a small fee to an attendant. It's easier to pop into a bar or café, although here too you often pay. Ft20-Ft50 is normal.

Religious Services

International Church of Budapest

III. Kiskorona utca 7 (176 4518). M3 Árpád híd.
Multi-denominational worship in English and children's ministry on Sundays at 10.30am.

International Baptist Church

Móricz Zsigmond Gimnázium, II. Törökvész út 48-54 (Pastor Bob Zbinden 250 3932). Bus 11.
Services on Sundays from 10.30am.

Jézus Szíve Templom

VIII. Mária utca 25 (118 3479). M3 Ferenc körút.
Catholic mass in English on Saturdays at 5pm.

Anglican Services

St Columbia Church of Scotland, Presbyterian and St Margaret's Anglican/Episcopal Chaplaincy

VI. Vörösmarty utca 51 (no phone). M1 Vörösmarty utca. **Map D2**
Anglican eucharist on first and third Sundays at 11am. Anglican Holy Communion second, fourth and fifth Sundays of the month at 9am. Presbyterian services second and fourth Sundays at 11am. Joint Presbyterian/Anglican service fifth Sundays at 11am. Sunday school at 11am Sept-May.

Jewish Services

Central Synagogue

VII. Dohány utca 2 (no phone). M2 Astoria/tram 47, 49. **Map D4**
Services take place at 9am Saturday; 6pm Sunday-Friday.

Jewish Community Centre

VII. Síp utca 12 (342 1335). M2 Astoria/tram 47, 49. **Open** 8am-noon Mon-Fri. English spoken. **Map D4**
Summer services in Hebrew.

Renting Accommodation

The most reliable way of finding a place to rent is through word of mouth. If someone knows of someone whose aunt has a flat to rent, take it. Otherwise you are likely to be overcharged

because you are a foreigner (and so must have tons of money). Hungarians consult the national classifieds daily, *Expressz*. Other apartments are advertised among the classifieds in the *Budapest Week* or *Budapest Sun*, where you will usually also find ads for accommodation and real estate agencies. (*see chapter* **Media**).

Repairs

See also chapter **Shopping & Services**.

Exoterm

XI. Bogdánfy utca 8/a (209 2494). **Open** 8am-5pm Mon-Fri. Some English spoken.
Plumbing, gas and heating repairs

Evitex

VI. Színyei Merse utca 7 (312 4835). **Open** 7am-4pm Mon-Fri. English spoken. **Map D2**
Electricity repairs. Send a fax after 4pm and they will call you back.

Zárcentrum

II. Margit körút 54 (201 3928). **Open** 9am-6pm Mon-Fri, 9am-1pm Sat. Some English spoken. **Map A2**
Key copying and lock repairs, great selection of the latest locks for sale. **Branch**: XI Fehérvári út 24 (166 5654).

Residency

See **Work Permits**.

Seasons

Although Budapest can get very cold in winter and infernally hot in summer, the climate is basically agreeable. However, the weather has proved unpredictable in recent years. *See also chapter* **Budapest By Season**.

Spring

Average temperatures 2-10 degrees C in March; 11-22 degrees C in May.
May is probably the most pleasant month. Winter attire gets discarded though rain can sometimes dampen spirits.

Summer

Average temperatures 16-32 degrees C.
Most Hungarians leave Budapest whenever possible for the Balaton or the weekend house. It can get very hot, especially in July, but is otherwise fairly pleasant, especially when there's a breeze coming down the Danube. When there isn't, expect a pall of pollution.

Autumn

Average temperatures 7-23 degrees C.
The weather is lovely in September but does start to get cold in October when everything moves inside and the heating gets turned on.

Winter

Average temperatures minus 4-4 degrees C.
Winters are cold and quite long but not unbearably so: the air is very dry and the central heating is good. Snow usually falls a few times a year giving Budapest a completely different light. Smog can descend if there is no breeze to blow away the fumes from the coal used for heating.

Smoking

Smoking is banned on public transport, in theatres and in cinemas but allowed everywhere else. Hungarians are among the heaviest smokers in Europe. It is quite normal for people to ask strangers for a cigarette or a light on the street and cigarettes are still often sold singly at kiosks and non-stops.

Street Names

Hungarian varieties of street can be confusing. The most common is utca, often abbreviated as 'u.', meaning simply 'street'. This should not be mixed up with an út (útja in

Directory

the genetive), which is (usually) a big, wide, straight street or avenue – unless it's a körút, which means a ring road.

A tér (tere in the genetive) is a square, a körtér is a circle or circus. Other varieties of Hungarian thoroughfare include: köz (lane), fasor (alley), sétány (parade), udvar (passage, arcade or courtyard) and rakpart (embankment).

Temperatures

See **Seasons**.

Telephones

The old phone system has largely been modernised and phoning home rarely presents a problem, although remember there are no cheap hours for international calls. Don't be surprised if you get cut off in the middle of a conversation and remember that an engaged tone doesn't always mean what it seems. If at first you don't succeed, dial, dial and dial again.

Public Phones

Most of these have been modernised. Some take Ft10, Ft20 and Ft50 coins. Others are card phones. Cards cost Ft750 for 50 units or Ft1,600 for 120 and can be bought at post offices, newsagents, small tobacco shops and from the men at stations with trays like cinema ice-cream sellers (though be careful, especially at Nyugati, as some of these guys are selling used ones for collectors). Cards will also be on sale at most metro stops.

Making Calls

To make an international call dial 00, wait for the second purring dial tone, then dial the country code and number. Australia 61, Austria 43, Canada 1, France 33, Germany 49, Ireland 353, New Zealand 64, UK 44, USA 1.

Useful numbers

Inland operator: 191
Inland directory enquiries (in Budapest): 198
(outside Budapest): 198
International operator (English spoken): 190
International directory enquiries (English spoken): 199
Police: 107
Fire/emergency: 105
Ambulance 104 or (in English): 311 1666
Sending telegrams (charged to your phone bill/English spoken): 192
Wake-up service: 193
Exact time: 080

To call other places in Hungary from Budapest or to call Budapest from the rest of the country you have to dial 06 first, wait for the second tone, and then follow with code and number. You also have to dial 06 before calling mobile phones, which are common in Hungary.

To call Hungary from abroad dial 36 and then 1 for Budapest. International rates are the same at any time of the day or night. There are no cheap hours.

Faxes

Some post offices have a fax service but this involves a lot of waiting around. Major hotels also have fax services. Otherwise try the phone, fax and telex centre at:

MATÁV
V. Petőfi Sándor utca 17 (117 5500).
M3 Ferenciek tere. **Open** 8am-8pm Mon-Fri; 9am-3pm Sat. **No credit cards**. Some English spoken. **Map C4**

Mobile Phones & Pagers

If you need a phone but your apartment doesn't have one, mobile phones or pagers are the best bet. The digital GSM system is fully established here and reliable, although costly: a phone and connection card will set you back around Ft150,000.

To buy the connection card you either need a resident's permit (*see* **Work Permits**) or must get it through the company you work for. For more details, try the two GSM companies which operate in Hungary. English is spoken in all of the places below.

Westel
V. Petőfi Sándor utca 12 (266 5723).
M3 Ferenciek tere. **Open** 9am-8pm Mon-Fri; 9am-5pm Sat, Sun. **Credit** AmEx, JCB, MC, V. **Map C4**

Pannon GSM
XIII. Váci út 37 (270 4130). M3 Dózsa György út. **Open** 9am-7pm Mon-Fri; 9am-2pm Sat. **No credit cards**.

There are two pager companies, both of which have English services. A pager will cost in the region of Ft50,000.

Eurohívó
XIII. Váci út 37 (270 4160). M3 Dózsa György út.
Open 8am-6.30pm Mon-Fri; 8.30am-1.30pm Sat. **No credit cards**.

Operator Hungária
XIV. Dózsa György út 84-86 (267 9911). M1 Hősök tere/trolleybus 75, 79. **Open** 9am-3.30pm Mon-Fri. **No credit cards. Map E1**

Time

Hungary is on Central European Time, which means it is one hour ahead of British time except for two brief periods at the beginning and at the end of summer.

Tipping

There are no fixed rules about tipping in Hungary but it is customary to round up the bill or leave about ten per cent for waiters in restaurants or bars (this is often their only wage).

As you pay, tell the waiter how much change you would like. Saying *köszönöm* (thank you) as you hand over a note means you want them to keep the change. The same applies to taxis. You usually have to pay toilet attendants Ft20.

It's also customary to tip hairdressers, cloakroom attendants, repairmen, changing room attendants at baths and swimming pools, even doctors and dentists.

Tourist Information

The best place is **Tourinform**. The other national tourist agencies can also help you, though not necessarily with a smile – the attitude seems to be that they are doing you a favour just by being there. Services are often duplicated. **Ibusz** is the best agency for accommodation. **Express** is essentially (though not exclusively) a student travel agency. Some sort of English will be spoken in most of these places.

The easiest way to find out what's going on in Budapest are the weekly English-language newspapers *Budapest Week* and *Budapest Sun*. The more linguistically adventurous could try the free weekly listings publication *Pesti Est* (with film listings in English) or *Pesti Műsor* from newsagents for Ft49. *See chapter* **Media**.

Tourinform
V. Sütő utca 2 (117 9800). M1, M2, M3 Deák tér/tram 47, 49. **Open**
9am-7pm Mon-Fri, 9am-4pm Sat, Sun. **Map C4**
Staff are friendly, helpful, multilingual and have all the information you'll need for travel, sightseeing and entertainment.

Ibusz
V. Petőfi tér 3 (118 5707). M3 *Ferenciek tere.* **Open** 24 hours daily. **Credit** V, EC, JCB, MC. **Map C4**
The national tourist agency has branches all over Hungary and can book accommodation, organise tours and provide information as well as all the other normal travel agency services (flights, trains, holidays). The Petőfi tér branch
will change money at all hours. There are branches at all main railway stations.

Budapest Tourist
VIII. Baross tér 3 (333 6587). **Open** 9am-5pm Mon-Fri. **No credit cards. Map F3**
Nyugati Station (332 6565). **Open** 9am-5.30pm Mon-Fri; 9am-12.30pm Sat. **No credit cards. Map D2**
Déli Station (155 7167). **Open** 9am-5pm Mon-Fri. **No credit cards. Map A3**
Money exchange, information, tours, holidays, flights.

Cooptourist
Nyugati Station (312 3621). **Open** 9am-4.30pm Mon-Fri. **No credit cards. Map D2**
Money exchange, information, tours, holidays, flights.

Express
V. Zoltán utca 10 (111 9898). M2 *Kossuth tér.* **Open** 8am-4pm Mon-Fri. **Credit** AmEx. **Map C3**
Friendly staff, currency exchange, some information, flights, student cards, youth hostel cards.

Universities

See **Education**.

Visas

Citizens of the United States, Canada and all European countries apart from Turkey and Albania can stay in Hungary for up to 90 days without a visa; only a passport is required. South Africans can stay up to 30 days. Citizens of Australia and New Zealand still need visas, which are valid for up to 30 days. Visas can be obtained from Hungarian

consulates, on the border if arriving by car, although not by train, and at the airport.

The simplest way to get a new stamp in your passport or renew a visa is to take a day trip to Vienna (*see chapter* **Trips Out of Town**) or take the train to Komárom (from Keleti or Déli) and walk over the bridge to Komarno in Slovakia. (To meet Slovakian currency requirements, you'll need to have a credit card or the hard currency equivalent of \$15 in your pocket.) Do this too often, though, and you might get trouble from border officials. Visas can also be renewed in Budapest at your local police station if you can produce exchange receipts to prove you have been keeping yourself. In theory, all foreigners are required to show that they have access to the equivalent of Ft1,000 per day. In practice, such proof is rarely requested. If you do get asked, the production of a credit card will usually suffice. *See also* **Work Permits**.

Water

The water is clean and safe to drink. In some old houses there are still lead pipes so run the tap for a few minutes before drinking.

Weights & Measurements

Hungary has its own unique system for measuring out solids and liquids. A *deka* is ten grams; a *deci* is ten centilitres. In a bar, for example, you might be asked whether you want *két deci* or *három deci* (0.2 or 0.3 litres) of whatever liquid it was you just ordered. Wine in bars (but not in restaurants) is usually priced by the *deci*. At a fruit stall, if you want 300 grams of apples, you would ask for 30 *dekas – harminc deka alma.*

Budapest by numbers

(Data are for 1995 unless otherwise indicated)

Population of Budapest **2.1 million**
Area of Budapest in square km **525**
Population of Hungary **10.3 million**
Area of Hungary in square km **93,030**

Ethnic divisions: Hungarian **94.5%**
Gypsy **4.5%**
German **0.4%**
Croatian **0.2%**
Romanian **0.1%**
Slovak **0.1%**

Religions: Roman Catholic **65%**
Protestant **25%**
Eastern Orthodox **4%**
Jewish **3%**

Number of English-speaking expats with resident permits: **2,769**
Number of English-speaking expats according to media: ca. **20,000**

Natural growth of population: **-3.3 per one thousand inhabitants**
Life expectancy: men **65.3 years**; women **74.5 years**

Global ranking of Hungary for:
heart diseases **1**
tobacco consumption **2**
suicide **2**
alcohol consumption **3**
Olympic medals **9**

State budget revenues: **Ft 3,501 billion**
State budget expenditures: **Ft 3,581 billion**
Budget deficit: **Ft80 billion**
GDP: **$4,273 per capita**
Growth rate: **1.5%**
Expected growth rate in 1997: **2.5%**
Estimated ratio of the black economy: **30%**
Inflation in 1991: **35%**
Inflation in 1997: **18.6%**
Ratio of the private sector in the economy in 1997: **70%**
Number of enterprises with foreign direct investment and capital: **24,950**
Ranking of Hungary in region for foreign investment: **1**

Claimant unemployment in Hungary in August 1997: **10.4%**
Claimant unemployment in Budapest in August 1997: **4.7%**
Average net monthly earnings of full-time employees (first half of 1997): **Ft35,000**
Price of a modest two-room flat in the outskirts of Budapest (1997): **Ft3,500,000**

Number of national daily newspapers published in Budapest: **12**
Number of political parties sitting in Hungarian Parliament: **7**
Total number of political parties: **52**
Number of legal suits filed by MPs against MPs for slander in 1996: **6**

Number of telephone lines in Hungary in 1980: **617,243**
Number of telephone lines in Hungary in 1996: **2,661,600**
Number of mobile phones in 1996: **473,100**

Number of American-style shopping malls built in Budapest in 1996-97: **3**
Number of American fast food joints in Budapest: **over 100**
Total number of cars in 1997: **2,265,000**
Number of working Trabants in 1997: **302,148**

Litres of wine consumed a year by a Hungarian: **30**
Estimated percentage of wine sold in Hungary that is not made of grapes: **68%**

Annual expenditures of households (Ft/capita) on:
tobacco **3,683**
alcoholic beverages **2,937**
books **513**
fresh vegetables **447**
theatre and cinema **166**. ????

Estimated number of dogs in Budapest: **160,000**
Amount of dog turd on the streets every day: **40 tons**

Number of revealed criminal cases in 1996: **466,050**
Proportion of crimes cleared up: **50.2%**

Information essential

When in doubt, do it backwards – that's the rule of thumb in these parts. Hungarians put their family names first and their first names last. Addresses begin with the postcode, are followed by the city, then the street name and finally the house, floor and flat numbers.

All the stuff that would go in the top right hand corner of a British or American letter (address, date etc) in Hungary, of course, is placed in the bottom left hand corner. And don't forget that dates are written year/month/day.

Perhaps this follows from the Magyar tongue, which sort of works backwards as well. It's what linguists call an agglutinative language, in which all the defining bits of a word – the work that in English is done by prepositions and prefixes – get stacked up at the end of it. This is so different from English that it makes the process of learning Hungarian a little like having to rewire your brain. (*See chapter* **Language**.)

Also, remember that when going into a restaurant or bar, Hungarian men always enter before women. The final, surreal, touch is that Hungarians say 'Szia!' (pronounced 'seeya') where we would say 'hello' and say 'helló' where we might say 'see you'.

Helló!

Women

Although men and women are equal by law in Hungary, there are countless problems from the wage differentials to sexual harassment at work, and from an unfair division of labour to domestic violence. Several women's organisations (see the list below) have been set up since 1989 to help solve these problems, but the word feminist is still an ugly word in Hungary. Feminists are seen as a bunch of militant, man-hating, masculine women who fight for something that most Hungarian women think they already have: equality.

The 'new' values imposed upon the traditional division of labour by the Communist regime meant that women kept their traditional roles, but were suddenly expected also to work eight hours a day outside the home. Thus were the problems of 'emancipation' solved in Hungary in the 1950s. Meanwhile, women were made to believe that driving tractors meant that they had achieved equality with the stronger sex. By 1967, when it had become obvious that women were exhausted by the double shift, the three-year child-care allowance system was introduced. Since fathers were not expected, and until 1982 not allowed, to stay at home with their children as primary carers, women, who often spent three to ten years at home with the kids, fell hopelessly behind in their professions. Another by-product of this arrangement was that since the mother was at home, she performed all the housework, socialising the children in the good old traditional gender roles.

Thanks to the women's movement this picture has started to change. Abortion is legal and easily accessible, women's wages are rising, sexual harassment at work and wife battering get more and more often reported and punished by law, and an increasing number of men are ready to mop the floor or cook dinner. Still, if you are from the West, expect to experience traditional values that may surface as sexist remarks in the street, gentlemanly courtesy towards women among friends or family, funny looks if you enter a restaurant or bar alone, and condescending macho attitudes in any social setting.

Ariadne Gaia Foundation

Ariadne Gaia Alapítvány
V. Szép utca 3 III/1 (117 4779). M3 Ferenciek tere. Contact Magda Roháńszky or Ágota Ruzsa. English spoken. **Map C4**
Offers courses on women's assertiveness, counselling training, group therapy and counselling, in English if required.

Feminist Network

A Feminista Hálózat
Budapest 1399, PO Box 701, 1092. Contact Judit Acsády. English spoken.
The first real grass-roots campaign group for women, the Network organises meetings, training and campaigning sessions and publishes a quarterly magazine, *Nőszemély (The Female Person)*, – which includes essays and articles on women's social and political situation in Hungary today.

NaNE – Women United Against Violence

NaNE – Nők a Nőkért Együtt az Erőszak Ellen
IX. Vámház körút 7. Postal address: Pf 660, 1462 Budapest (216 5900/helpline 216 1670). M3 Kálvin tér/tram 47, 49. **Open** *office* 9am-5pm, *helpline* 6pm-10pm, daily. Contact Ildikó Szineg. English spoken. **Map D5**
Rape and domestic violence are low-profile issues in Hungary. There is no law against marital rape and little sympathy for rape victims. This telephone helpline was set up in 1993 to give support and information to

Directory

battered and raped women and children, to campaign for changes in law and policy, and to challenge social attitudes to violence.

Association of Hungarian Women

Magyar Nők Szövetsége
VI. Andrássy út 124 (131 9734/fax 112 5071). M1 Hősök tere. **Open** 10am-3pm Mon-Fri. President Judit Thorma. Some English spoken. **Map E2**
Now independent, the original communist-era women's association has survived to fight another day. Understandably, they're not particularly radical – they have seen it all before. It has 40 member organisations, 500 individual members and aims 'to work for the equal opportunity of women and participation in social and political life'.

Union of Women Entrepreneurs

Vállalkozó Nők Egyesülete
VI. Andrássy út 124 (131 9734/fax 112 5071). M1 Hősök tere. **Open** 10am-3pm Mon-Fri. Contact Katain Köves. English spoken. **Map E2**
Set up with a gift of money from an American women's group, this sounds more impressive than it actually is, and gives legal and professional advice to around 300 members.

MONA Hungarian Women's Foundation

Magyarországi Női Alapítvány
XIII. Tátra utca 30B (270 1311/fax 120 1115). Tram 4, 6. **Open** 9am-5pm Mon-Fri. Contact Mária Neményi or Gabi Szilárd. English spoken. **Map C2**
Since 1992 MONA has been doing its best to draw together women from various campaign organisations and interest groups. They launched themselves with a round table on why there is no strong women's movement in Hungary and since then have held meetings for women mayors, women journalists and women in business. If you want to get a perspective on the women's movement in Hungary, then MONA is the place to start.

Ombudswoman

Ombudsnő
VIII. Múzeum körút 4C (266 9833 ext 2308). M2 Astoria/tram 47, 49. **Open** 2pm-6pm Thur. English spoken. **Map D4**
The Ombudswoman programme provides a Women's Information and Resource Centre which puts women in touch with psychiatrists, lawyers and social workers. There's also an information hotline and a recently established media group. A ground-breaking interdisciplinary Gender

Studies Centre, including a library, is now in its nascent stages.

Work Permits

Non-Hungarian citizens who wish to live in Hungary have to apply for a residence permit. But before you do that, you have to have a work permit, a steady job and a permanent address. The process of obtaining all the necessary documents should be started before your visa expires and three months before you actually start working for a company.

First you have to sign a contract with your future employer, and take this contract to the **Fővárosi Munkaügyi Központ** (Capital City Labour Centre) where they will assess whether there is really no Hungarian to fill your future position. This will take them 30 to 60 days.

During this time you can have your diplomas and certificates officially translated, obtain a compulsory medical certificate and fill in a great number of forms. Once you have submitted your application for a work permit with all the attachments, you will have to wait for another month to receive an answer from the Labour Centre. If you are lucky, your company will offer to do some of these unpleasant duties on your behalf.

Once your work permit is in your hands, you can apply for a residence permit, which means several more weeks, if not months, of standing in line at **KEOKH** and **ÁNTSZ** (see below) among other places. Requirements for a residence permit include a work permit, an $40 visa obtained at a Hungarian embassy abroad (if you didn't get one before you left home, you'll have to go to Vienna), a legal permanent

residence, an AIDS test at Ft12,000, a chest X-ray, numerous value stamps that you buy at post offices (ca. Ft5,000), countless application forms and passport photos, your passport, and official translations (ca. Ft3,000 per page) of every foreign-language document with stamps on them. The whole process is bound to be long and annoying even if you speak Hungarian. And if you end up getting a residence permit, you can only take a couple months break from the bureaucratic hell, because you will have to renew all your papers within a year – unless you decide to marry a Hungarian, in which case the process will be different and probably easier. But then again, getting a divorce is also no piece of cake. According to official statistics, 2,769 US and UK citizens had residence permits in 1996. According to unofficial estimates, there are over 20,000 native speakers of English living here.

Fővárosi Munkaügyi Központ

Capital City Labour Centre
VIII. Kisfaludy utca 11 (303 0720) Tram 4, 6. **Open** 8.30am-3pm Mon-Thur, 8.30am-1pm Fri. Some English spoken. **Map E5**

Orvosi Rendelő

XI. Budafoki út 111-113 (203 0091). Bus 3, 10, 10A, 83, 110. **Open** 8am-noon Mon-Fri. No English spoken. **Map E6**

KEOKH

VI. Városligeti fasor 46/48 (118 0800). M1 Hősök tere. **Open** 8.30am-6pm Tue; 8.30am-1pm Wed; 10am-6pm Thur; 8.30am-noon Fri. Some English spoken. **Map E2**

Állami Népegészségügyi és Tiszti Orvosi Szolgálat

XIII. Váci út 174 (129 0490). M3 Újpest Városkapu. **Open** 8am-noon Mon-Fri; 1pm-3pm Mon-Thur. No English spoken.

US Chamber of Commerce

V. Deák Ferenc utca 10 (266 9880/fax 266 9888). M1, M2, M3 Deák Ferenc tér. **Open** 9am-5pm Mon-Fri. **Map C4**
Consultations by appointment only.

Országos Fordító Iroda
VI. Bajza utca 52 (269 5730). M1
Bajza utca. **Open** 9am-6pm Mon-
Thur; 8.30am-12.30pm Fri. English
spoken. **Map E2**

Settlers Hungary
XII. Sashegyi út 18 (165 1990).
Tram 59. **Open** 8am-5pm Mon-Fri.

No credit cards. English spoken.
This agency will help you sort out
your work permit for Ft25,000 and
organise your resident's permit for
Ft40,000.

Business Umbrella (*see
chapter* **Business**) will help

you get your work permits and
residence permits, so you don't
have to stand in line for months
and deal with lots of red tape.
(Work permits for Ft18,000
plus VAT, residence permits
for 30,000 plus VAT).

Getting Around

Budapest is easy to explore on
foot. Most of the places you
might want to go to fall within
a relatively small central area,
the rest of the urban sprawl
consisting mostly of
uninspiring tower blocks. If
your feet get tired, use the
comprehensive metro, tram,
bus and trolleybus network.
This is efficient and cheap and
will get you within a couple of
hundred yards of any
destination. Taxis are cheap if
you stick to recommended
companies.

Budapest is constructed
around a series of concentric
ring roads, with other main
roads radiating from the
centre. Traffic has increased in
recent years. Although
congestion has not yet reached
western levels, lack of parking
means it's best not to use a car
during daytime.

Arrival in Budapest
By Air

Ferihegy airport (296 9696) is
20km (15 miles) to the south-
east of Budapest on the E60
road. There are two terminals,
5km apart.

Ferihegy 2
*(arrivals 296 8000/departures 296
7000).* English spoken.
A modern terminal that deals with all
Malév, Lufthansa, Alitalia and Air
France flights.

Ferihegy 1
(296 7155). English spoken.
Closer by 5km. Older than Ferihegy 2,
it handles other flights.

Airport Minibus Shuttle
(296 8555). **Open** 5am-10pm or until
the last flight. English spoken.

The best way into town: for Ft1,200
they will take you to any Budapest
address. Buy a ticket at the counter in
the arrival hall, tell them where you're
going, then wait for a driver to call
your destination when they know
how many others are going your way.
This can take anything from five minutes to, on a bad day, half an hour. It
also works the other way round: call
them to be picked up from anywhere
in the city and taken back to either
terminal. Accessible to wheelchair
users.

Public transport
A Mercedes minibus with Centrum-
Airport on the side runs from outside
the terminal to Erzsébet tér bus
station. Tickets, Ft600 (free for under-
6s), are bought on the bus, which
leaves every half-hour from 6am-
10pm. You can also take the 93 bus to
Kőbánya-Kispest metro station and
the blue M3 metro from there for the
cost of one public transport (BKV)
ticket for each (Ft35 from the airport
newsagent). Last buses are at
10.40pm from Ferihegy 2 and
11.34pm from Ferihegy 1. Last metro
leaves at 11.10pm, or there's the 182É
night bus from the station.

Taxis from the airport
The taxis outside both terminal
buildings are controlled by a mafia
who fix prices at several times the
norm. A taxi from the centre with a
reputable company should cost
Ft2,000-Ft2,500.

Car hire
All the major car hire firms have
stands at the airport (*see below* **Car
Hire**).

Airlines
Air France
*V. Kristóf tér 6 (118 0411/airport
294 4201). M1, M2, M3 Deák tér.*
Open 8am-4.30pm Mon-Fri. **Credit**
AmEx, DC, MC, V.

Austrian Airlines
*V. Régiposta utca 5 (327
9080/airport 292 1970). M1, M2,
M3 Deák tér.* **Open** 8.30am-12.30pm,
1.30-4.30pm, Mon-Fri. **Credit** AmEx,

DC, MC, V.

British Airways
*VIII. Rákóczi út 1/3 (266
6696/airport 296 6970). M2 Astoria.*
Open 8am-5pm Mon-Fri. **Credit**
AmEx, DC, MC, V.

Delta Air Lines
*V. Apáczai Csere János utca 4 (266
1400/266 6420/airport 296 8860).
M1, M2, M3 Deák tér.* **Open**
8.30am-5pm Mon-Fri. **Credit** AmEx,
DC, MC, V.

KLM
*VIII. Rákóczi út 1/3 (373
7737/airport 292 4070). M2 Astoria.*
Open 8.30am-4.30pm Mon-Fri.
Credit AmEx, DC, MC, V.

Lufthansa
*V. Váci utca 19/21 (266
4511/airport 292 1970). M1, M2,
M3 Deák tér/tram 47, 49.* **Open**
8.30am-5pm Mon-Fri. **Credit** AmEx,
DC, MC, V.

Malév
*V. Dorottya utca 2 (266 5616). M1
Vörösmarty tér.*
*V. Ferenciek tere 2 (266 5913) M3
Ferenciek tere.*
Both: **Open** 9am-5.30pm. **Credit**
AmEx, DC, MC, V.
Malév's 24-hour information service
for both terminals is on 157 9123. In
addition, they have an office at each
terminal: Ferihegy 1 (157 7554);
Ferihegy 2 (157 7179).

Swissair
*V. Kristóf tér 7/8 (267
2500/airport 157 4370). M1, M2,
M3 Deák tér/tram 47, 49.* **Open**
8.30am-5pm Mon-Fri. **Credit**
AmEx, DC, MC, V.

By Bus

If arriving by bus you will be
dropped at the bus terminal on
Erzsébet tér (117 2562, 6am-
6pm Mon-Fri; 6.30am-4pm Sat,
Sun. No English spoken). There
are exchange and **left luggage**
facilities here (*see chapter*
Essential Information).

Directory

Piracy on the high streets

Taxis in Budapest are in theory an extremely reasonable form of transport. In practice taxi drivers are a bunch of unscrupulous pirates who scour the streets for suckers, wind up fares to the limit, take kickbacks from hotels and dodgy nightclubs, and generally exploit the fact that few non-Hungarians speak a word of the local lingo.

Hail a random taxi on the street – there are hundreds; supply far outstrips demand – and you're liable to get fleeced in one or more of several tried and tested methods. Drivers leave the meter off (claiming it is 'kaput' if you point this out) and double the number they first thought of at the end of the journey. Or they doctor the meter so the digits whizz by like that thing they used to have in Times Square showing the growth of the US Budget Deficit. Or they whisk you off on an unsolicited sightseeing tour of the city before returning to a destination about two blocks from wherever it was you started. Any dissent concerning the proposed fare structure is met with either threats of physical violence or the old 'I only speak Magyar' routine.

The solution is to do as the Hungarians do: hail a Főtaxi. Recognisable by their oval 'taxi' light and red-and-white checkered livery, Főtaxis (the name means 'main taxi') are one of the few companies that is both efficient and honest. There are others (Tele 5, Volán Taxi and City Taxi are all mostly reliable, and often have better cars) but the welcoming gleam of the oval Főtaxi light can be spotted from a distance at night.

Free marketeers take note: this paragon of integrity and affordable urban travel is a state-run company (due to be privatised, alas). It's the individual entrepreneurs who cause all the trouble. Some of the pirates have even taken to impersonating Főtaxis by adding a red-and-white stripe. Watch out and don't be fooled.

There is currently talk of regulating uniform taxi prices and cutting the total number that cruise the streets. In the meantime, if you are lucky enough to find an honest driver, be sure to give the good fellow a handsome tip.

By Train

Budapest has three main stations: Déli (south), Keleti (east) and Nyugati (west), all of which have metro stops of the same name. The Hungarian for station is *pályaudvar*, often abbreviated (in writing but not in speech) to *pu*. There is no real rhyme or reason as to which station serves which destination. Keleti is the main station serving most trains to Vienna, Bucharest, Warsaw, Bulgaria, Turkey and north-western Hungary. Déli also serves Vienna and Austria as well as Croatia, Slovenia and south-eastern Hungary. The magnificent Nyugati is the main point of departure for Transylvania and Bratislava. Always check the station, though, as services get moved around.

On arrival you will be bombarded with offers of taxis and accommodation. The latter can be worth checking out, although the barrage of hostel hustlers at Keleti (sometimes they board the train an hour out of Budapest) can make for an extremely off-putting arrival. Avoid taxi touts and stick to the recommended companies in the ranks outside stations. All three stations have exchange facilities and tourist information but only Keleti and Nyugati have 24-hour left-luggage facilities.

MÁV Information

VI. Andrássy út 35 (322 8275/national enquiries 322 7860/international enquiries 342 9150). M1 Opera. **Open** *Apr-Sept* 9am-6pm Mon-Fri; *Oct-Mar* 9am-5pm Mon-Fri. **No credit cards.** Some English spoken.
Often the easiest place to buy tickets in advance. Phone lines are manned until 8pm. After that, call one of the stations listed below.

Keleti station

VIII. Baross tér (613 6835). M2 Keleti/tram 44, 67, 23, 24, 36. **Lines open** 8pm-6am. Some English spoken.

Nyugati station

VI. Nyugati tér (149 0115). M3 Nyugati/tram 4, 6. **Lines open** 8pm-6am. Some English spoken.

Déli station

I. Alkotás út (175 6293). M2 Déli/tram 18, 59, 61. **Lines open** 8pm-6am. No English spoken.

Public Transport

The Budapest transport company (BKV) is cheap, efficient, and gets you to within about a hundred yards of any destination. Walking is not fashionable here. The network consists of three metro lines, trams, buses, trolleybuses and local trains. In summer there are also BKV Danube ferries. Maps of the system can be bought at main metro stations for Ft190. Street atlases (Cartographia's at Ft650 is the handiest) also mark the routes.

Public transport starts around 4.30am and finishes around 11pm although there is

Directory

Stalin isn't stalling

They've tried to remove his name and his image all over Hungary, but the ghost of Josef Stalin still shambles maniacally through downtown Budapest, shooting out sparks and throwing commuters off balance. The city's trolley buses, painted in festive, communist red with grey trim, serve as (literally) moving memorials to the former Soviet dictator who created, terrorised and systematically depopulated the East Bloc.

The trolley bus system provides convenient connections throughout the inner city. It was inaugurated in 1949, the year in which Stalin was 70 years old. The Communist leadership of the time thought it would therefore be appropriate to call the first trolley bus the No. 70. Other lines were added to the system and each was numbered according to how old Stalin was that year. Even though Stalin died in 1953, the last line in the trolley bus system was the No. 83, a sort of posthumous birthday present inaugurated in 1961, when Stalin would have been 83.

Half bus and half tram, these clunky vehicles make for lively travel. At times it seems that their electric motors only have two speeds: dead stop and too fast. Even though there are straps to hang on to, you should grab a seat if you can: the ridiculous speed and angles at which the drivers take corners can throw anyone off balance. It doesn't help that the trolley buses go through some of the more run-down parts of District VII and VIII where the streets are heavily cobblestoned. Thrill-seekers who enjoy a bumpy ride can try the seat over the back wheel.

The trolley buses' power source is overhead lines. Two poles stretch up from the roof of the vehicle to contact the lines. The contact points often spew sparks, a phenomenon which is especially visible after dark and lends mystery to the badly lit inner-city. The power poles occasionally bounce so badly that their contact with the overhead wires is broken. Then traffic comes to a halt while the driver reestablishes contact with a special yellow stick, carried just for this purpose.

Shortly after the Communist party lost power in 1989, statues and place names that commemorate Stalin, Lenin and other Communist heroes were eradicated all over the country. But for now, the trolleys still lurch through Budapest, like some last final vengeance of the mad dictator.

a limited night bus network along major routes. Tickets can be purchased at all metro stations, also at some tram stops and newsstands. A ticket is valid for one journey on one piece of transport (except the ferries, which have a separate system), so if you change from metro to tram, or even from metro line to metro line, you have to punch a new ticket.

On trams, buses and trolleybuses the contraption for validating your ticket is not intuitively designed. Punch your ticket by sliding the business end (the bit with the circled numbers) into the black slot at the top of the red box, then pull the slot-thing towards you hard until it clicks. Maybe it's best first to observe how locals do it.

Day, three-day, weekly, fortnightly and monthly tickets are also available from metro stations although you will need a photograph to obtain anything but a one-day or three-day pass. Take your photo to Deák tér metro to be issued with a photopass. For a ticket longer than one day you have to ask for: *egy napi bérlet* (one day), *egy heti bérlet* (one week), *két heti bérlet* (two weeks) or *egy havi bérlet* (one month). All these tickets run from the day of purchase apart from the monthly which is valid per calendar month. It is possible to ride without a ticket, but plain-clothes inspectors (who put on a red armband before demanding your ticket) are common and can levy somewhat arbitrary on-the-spot fines, usually around Ft600. Playing the dumb foreigner doesn't usually work.

Prices
Single – Ft60
Metro ticket for up to 3 stops – Ft40
Metro ticket for up to 5 stops – Ft65
Metro transfer ticket – Ft100
10 tickets – Ft540
20 tickets – Ft1,000
Day – Ft500
3-day – Ft1,000
Week – Ft1,300, Ft1,230 (not buses)
Passes (with photo) Week – Ft1,230
2-week – Ft1,640
Month – Ft2,460

BKV Information
(117 5518/342 2335).

Metro

The Budapest metro is safe, clean, regular and simple. There are three lines: yellow M1, red M2 and blue M3.

These connect the main stations and intersect at Deák tér. The recently renovated M1 line, originally constructed for the 1896 exhibition, was the first underground railway in continental Europe. The other lines, constructed post-war with Soviet assistance, still have Russian trains.

Trains run every two to three minutes (length of time since the last train is shown on a clock on the platform). Single tickets, three-stop, five-stop and metro transfer tickets can be purchased from either the ticket machines or ticket office in the stations. Validate tickets in the machines at the top of the escalators and in Deák tér passageways when changing lines.The first trains run from 4.30am and the last ones leave around 11pm.

Buses & Trolleybuses

There is a comprehensive bus and trolleybus network, the main lines being the 1 from Kelenföld train station to the centre and then following the M1 metro line, and the 7 connecting Bosnyák tér, Keleti station, Blaha Lujza tér, Astoria, Ferenciek tér, Móricz Zsigmond körtér and Kelenföld station. The castle bus (*Várbusz*), goes from Moszkva tér round the castle area and back. Buses with red numbers are expresses that miss out certain stops. Most stops and buses have times and stops listed. *See also page 258* **Stalin isn't stalling**.

Trams

Like many central European cities, Budapest has retained and expanded its tram network. The most important routes are the 4 and 6 which follow the Nagykörút from Moszkva tér to Fehérvári út and Móricz Zsigmond körtér respectively, the 2 which runs up the Pest side of the Danube, and the 47

and 49 which run from Deák tér to Móricz Zsigmond körtér and beyond into wildest Buda.

Local Trains (HÉV)

There are four HÉV lines. You will probably only need the one to Szentendre from Batthyány tér, price Ft128 although a normal BKV ticket is valid as far as Békásmegyer. After that it's an extra Ft60. First and last trains from Batthyány tér are at 3.50am and 11.40pm, and from Szentendre 3.30am and 10.30pm. Other lines run between Örs vezér tere and Gödöllő, Vágóhíd and Ráckeve, and Boráros tér and Csepel.

Night Buses & Trams

A reduced but reliable service works at night following the main routes and is usually full of drunks on week nights and teenagers at the weekends. Handiest are the 6É following the Nagykörút, the 182É following the blue M3 metro line, and the 78É from Döbrentei tér on the Buda side of Erzsébet bridge to Örs Vezér tere following, from Astoria, more or less the M2 route. On these routes buses run every 15 minutes.

Danube Ferries

Undoubtedly the most civilised method of travelling within Budapest, the BKV Danube ferries also offer a river ride which is exceedingly cheap when compared with the various organised tours. The local service runs from May to the end of September between Pünkösdfürdő north of the city and Boráros tér at the Pest foot of Petőfi bridge, stopping at most of the bridges, Vigadó tér and either end of Margaret Island. Fares vary between Ft50-Ft200. Boats, however, only run once every couple of hours, with extra services at weekends.

Timetables are posted at all stops. Boats to Szentendre, Visegrád and Esztergom on the Danube bend leave from Vigadó tér. (*See also chapters* **Trips Out of Town** *and* **Getting Started**.)

Ferry Information
Jászai Mari tér terminal (Margaret Bridge Pest side) (129 5844). Or try BKV information as listed above.

Eccentric Conveyances

Budapest has an assortment of one-off public transports.

The cog-wheel railway, for the price of a normal BKV ticket, takes you up Széchenyi-hegy. It runs from opposite the Budapest Hotel, two stops from Moszkva tér on tram 56 or 18. Last train down is at 11.30pm.

Across the park from the cog-wheel railway is the terminal of the narrow-gauge Children's Railway (*gyermekvasút*) which wends through the wooded Buda hills to Hűvösvölgy. Formerly the Pioneer Railway, then run by the Communist youth organisation, many of the jobs are done by children. Trains leave hourly between 9am-5pm and tickets cost Ft200 (depending on distance).

Another way up into the hills is the chair-lift (*libegő*) up to Jánoshegy – at 520 metres the highest point of Budapest. Take the 158 bus from Moszkva tér to the terminus at Zugligeti út. It costs Ft180 (Ft100 children) and runs between 9am-5pm from May-September, 9.30am-4pm October-April. There are cafés and bars at the top, and you can walk to Erszébet lookout tower or the Jánoshegy stop on the children's railway.

Tamer but more central, the funicular (*sikló*) takes a minute to run up from Clark Ádám tér to the Castle District. It's a short, vertiginous ride but the view is good. This runs from 7.30am-10pm and a one-way ticket costs Ft180 adults, Ft100 children.

Taxis

Rates in Budapest vary from the cheap to the outrageous. Stick to cabs displaying the logo of one of the companies mentioned below. Others often have tampered meters or will take you by the scenic route. Avoid expensive western-model cars hanging around outside hotels and tourist spots. They are usually crooks. Not that drivers of small cars are necessarily above ripping you off too. The cheap and reliable **Fötaxi** have red-and-white checkered patterns on their doors and can be spotted from a distance by their oval-shaped lights. Watch out for impostors, though. If you're calling for a cab, the people at **City Taxi** speak English. If you're always calling from the same address, City Taxi have a databank which records your address the first time, meaning you merely have to give your telephone number on subsequent calls.

A receipt should be available on request. Say: *számlát kérek*. A small tip is usual but not compulsory. All legitimate taxis should have yellow number plates, but having yellow plates doesn't guarantee that they won't try to fleece you. *See also* **Piracy on the high streets** page 257.

The most reliable companies are the following:

City Taxi *(211 1111)*.
Fötaxi *(222 2222)*.
Tele5 *(155 5555)*.
Volán Taxi *(166 6666)*.

Car Hire

Cars and rates vary from Ladas to limousines. A credit card is usually necessary for the deposit. Check that the price includes ÁFA (VAT). There's an insurance charge and varying rates of mileage from free, a fixed amount free and a per kilometre charge. Longer-term rates are available. The main companies have desks at both airport terminals.

Americana Rent-a-car *Pannónia Hotel Volga, XIII. Dózsa György út 65 (120 8287). M3 Dózsa György út* . **Open** 8am-7pm Mon-Fri; 8am-3pm Sat; 8am-1pm Sun. **Credit** AmEx, DC, MC, V. English spoken.

Avis *V. Szervita tér 8 (118 4685). M1, M2, M3 Deák tér*. **Open** 8am-6pm Mon-Sat; 8am-noon Sun. **Credit** AmEx, DC, MC, V. English spoken.

Budget *I. Krisztina körút 41-43 (156 6333). M2 Déli pu.* **Open** 8am-8pm Mon-Sat; 8am-6pm Sun. **Credit** AmEx, DC, MC, V. English spoken.

Europcar *VIII. Üllői út 62 (313 1492/Ferihegy One 296 6680/Ferihegy Two 296 6610). M3 Ferenc körút.* **Open** 8am-7pm Mon-Fri; 8am-noon Sun. **Credit** AmEx, DC, MC, V. English spoken.

Fötaxi *VII. Kertész utca 24-28 (210 1374). M2 Blaha Lujza tér.* **Open** 7am-5.30pm Mon-Thur; 7am-2pm Fri. **Credit** AmEx, DC, MC, V. No English spoken.

Bicycles

Budapest is not bicycle-friendly. Pollution is high and drivers are not used to cyclists. Bike use is on the increase, though, and the city has installed a few bicycle lanes. Bikes and tandems can be hired on Margaret Island opposite the bus stops at both ends.

Maps

City centre maps and metro maps are included at the back of this guide. Free maps are also available from Tourinform. All metro stations have detailed street and transport maps placed near the entrance.

Tourinform
V. Sütő utca 2 (117 9800). M1, M2, M3 Deák tér/tram 47, 49. **Open** *2 Mar-14 Nov 8am-8pm daily; 15 Nov-1 Mar 8am-3pm Sat, Sun.*

Business

Two years ago Hungary's economy was described as the hare that had become a tortoise. Once the shining star of the new market economies in eastern Europe, it was hobbled by a lack of reform. Belt-tightening began in 1997 and austerity has been painful. While the country's fiscal and trade deficits have been impressively cut, average earnings plummeted by 12 per cent in 1995-96 to about $200 per month, and this just as social services were deeply cut.

Yet the economy has started to respond, with 1997 showing significant growth and generating confidence for the final years of the decade. Unemployment has fallen, particularly in Budapest. The reforms have been especially helpful in reassuring foreign investors, who have continued to pump billions into the country. Since 1989, Hungary has garnered $16 billion – more than half of the total foreign investment in the former Soviet satellite countries of eastern Europe.

Privatisation and corporate restructuring have also continued at breakneck pace, transforming some state-owned dinosaurs into formidable competitors. For example, drug company Richter Gedeon and truck-maker Raba have emerged from the post-Communist mess to become international players. Some of the first private start-ups allowed by the Communists in the late 1980s, particularly high-tech firms such as Graphisoft (architectural software) and Semilab (makers of machines that test silicon wafers) have also gone international.

Hungary is now on track to join the European Union by about 2002, with economic reforms in place and most major regulatory legislation already passed. In addition, the

Directory

Hungarian forint has become fully convertible for businesses, with only a few restrictions remaining for individuals. The central bank has also been largely protected from sudden fluctuation by fixing it to a set schedule of monthly devaluations, due to be phased out sometime in 1998.

Hungarian business culture, however, is still characterised by some highly dodgy practices. Excessive taxes make for rampant evasion and a black economy that thrives despite every effort to crack down. Even many legally established businesses routinely evade taxes, ignore creditors and breach contracts. While some western businessmen may break the law to gain an advantage and hope they won't get caught, an enormous percentage of their Hungarian counterparts do it in order to keep up and simply know they won't get caught.

A parallel phenomenon is deep Hungarian distrust for legal transactions and the public institutions that manage them. This came through in spades on 28 February 1997 when a rumour spread that one of the country's largest banks, Postabank, was on the brink of declaring insolvency. Despite a PR offensive by the bank (who called the public stupid) and reassurances from the government, thousands queued at branches across the country to withdraw their savings – Ft24 billion's worth (and perhaps public distrust was not so misplaced – the government later had to stump up Ft12 billion to guarantee Postabank's bad loans).

The bottom line is that Hungarian business culture will take at least a generation to adapt fully to western ways. Meanwhile, business travellers might appreciate some out-of-date Hungarian habits. While they have taken obsessively to cellular phones, Hungarians

still prefer face-to-face meetings for even minor conferences. Strong business relationships are also much more dependent on well developed personal relationships. And bring plenty of business cards. Hungarians scatter them about at any opportunity.

Note: Rt – similar to PLC; Kft – limited company.

Stock Exchange

In the Habsburg days Budapest was the financial capital of the Austro-Hungarian empire and the Budapest Stock Exchange (BSE) was Europe's second most active. After a 40-year interlude, the BSE re-opened in June 1990, the first *bourse* to recommence in the former Communist countries. With only 45 companies listed, the BSE is not representative of the Hungarian economy as a whole, but has managed to attract serious interest. In 1996 it was the second fastest growing bourse in the world (after Moscow's) and a 1 January 1996 investment of £10,000 on the BSE index would currently be worth an astounding £24,000. Government securities still account for the overwhelming majority of transactions, while foreign institutional investors account for well over half the equity turnover.

Budapest Stock Exchange
Budapesti Ártéktőzsde
V. Deák Ferenc utca 5 (117 5226/fax 118 1737). M1 Vörösmarty tér/tram 2, 2A. **Open** 10.15am-1.15pm Mon-Fri. English spoken. **Map C4**
Visitors can watch trading through the glass walls. To organise a tour ring Sándor Lévai (266 9566/fax266 6203).

Budapest Commodity Exchange
Budapesti Árútőzsde
XIII. Róbert Károly körút 61-65 (269 8571/fax 269 8575). Tram 1, 12, 14. **Open** 9.30am-noon Mon-Fri. English spoken.
Visitors are welcome to see the Exchange in action. Officials recommend 10.30-10.45 as the best time. Contact Péter Jánoska.

Banks

In 1988, the National Bank of Hungary (NBH) was split up into three large commercial banks – Magyar Hitel Bank, Budapest Bank and K&H Bank – which all had bad loans to large state enterprises. Each have since been restructured and two have been privatised.

New joint venture banks and subsidiaries of foreign banks have increased their presence in recent years, intensifying competition and spurring the consolidation of smaller banks with larger players. The result has been improved services for customers, including slightly speedier service (using a Hungarian bank can still be a painfully slow process when it involves anything but the simplest transactions) and the advent of electronic banking. Credit and debit cards connected to any of several international clearance systems can be used to receive forints at more than 1,000 ATMs in Hungary – most in Budapest. Wire transfers are now quick and easily arranged (with a one-day delay). Cheques, however, are practically non-existent and cannot be cashed in less than three weeks, and then only at grievous expense.

The following are the head offices for the major banks in Budapest.

ABN Amro
XII. Nagy Jenő 12 (202 2722/fax 201 3685). Tram 61 Csörsz utca. **Open** 9am-2pm Mon-Thur; 9am-noon Fri. English spoken.

Budapest Bank
V. Alkotmány utca 3 (269 2333/fax 269 2400). M2 Kossuth Lajos tér/tram 2, 2a. **Open** 8am-5pm Mon, Thur; 8am-1pm Tue, Wed, Fri. Some English spoken. **Map C2**

Central-European International Bank (CIB)
Közép-Európai Nemzetközi Bank
V. Váci utca 16 (212 1330/fax 212 4200). M1 Vörösmarty tér, M3 Ferenciek tere. **Open** 9am-noon, 1pm-2.30pm Mon-Thur; 9am-noon Fri. English spoken. **Map C4**

Citibank Budapest
*V. Váci utca 19-21 (374 5000). M1
Vörösmarty tér, M3 Ferenciek tere.*
Open 9am-5pm Mon-Thur; 9am-4pm
Fri. English spoken. **Map C4**

Creditanstalt
*V. Akadémia utca 17 (269 0812/fax
153 4959). M2 Kossuth Lajos
tér/tram 2, 2a.* **Open** 9am-3pm Mon-
Thur; 9am-1pm Fri. Some English
spoken. **Map C3**

Hungarian Foreign Trade Bank
Magyar Külkereskedelmi Bank Rt
*V. Szent István tér 11 (269
0922/fax 268 8245). M1 Bajcsy-
Zsilinszky, M3 Arany János utca.*
Open 8am-2pm Mon-Thur; 8am-
1pm Fri. Some English spoken.
Map C3

Hungarian Credit Bank
Magyar Hitel Bank
*XIII. Pozsonyi út 77 (270 2944).
Trolley bus 76, 79.* **Open** 8am-1pm
Mon-Fri. Some English spoken. **Map
C1**

Internationale Nederlanden Bank
*VI. Andrássy út 9 (268 0140/fax
268 0159). M1 Bajcsy-Zsilinszky.*
Open 9am-3.30pm Mon-Fri. English
spoken. **Map C3**

Commercial and Credit Bank
Kereskedelmi & Hitel Bank (K&H)
*V. Vigadó tér 1 (267 5000/fax 266
9696). M1 Vörösmarty tér.* **Open**
9am-5pm Mon; 9am-4.30pm Tues-
Thur; 9am-noon Fri. English spoken.
Map C4

OTP Bank
*V. Nádor utca 16 (153 1444/fax
312 6858). Bus 15, 105.* **Open**
8am-4pm Mon-Wed; 8am-3pm Thur;
8am-1pm Fri. Some English spoken.
Map C3

Postabank
*V. József Nádor tér 1 (118 0855/fax
117 1369). M1 Vörösmarty tér.*
Open 8am-6pm Mon, Thur; 8am-
1.30pm Tue, Wed, Fri. No English
spoken. **Map C4**

Government Organisations

Hungarian Investment and Trade Development Agency
Magyar Befektetés és Kereskedelem
Fejlesztési Rt
*V. Dorottya utca 4 (266 7034/fax
118 6064). M1 Vörösmarty tér/tram
2, 2a.* **Open** 8am-4.30pm Mon-Fri.
English spoken. **Map C4**

ITD is a good first point of contact for
businessmen. They have a useful
library and can provide plenty of
information.

Hungarian National Bank
Magyar Nemzeti Bank
*V. Szabadság tér 8-9 (269 4760/fax
332 3913). M2 Kossuth Lajos tér/bus
15.* **Open** 8am-1pm Mon-Fri. Some
English spoken. **Map C3**

Ministry of Industry, Trade & Tourism
Ipari, Kereskedelmi és Turisztikai
Minisztérium
*V. Honvéd utca 13-15 (311 1448/fax
302 2394). M2 Kossuth Lajos
tér/bus 15.* **Open** 8am-4.30pm Mon-
Thur; 8am-2pm Fri. English spoken.
Map C3
The information department is very
helpful and staff speak good English.

State Privatisation and Holding Company
Állami Privatizációs És
Vagyonkezelő Rt
*XIII. Pozsonyi út 56 (269 8600/fax
149 5745). Trolleybus 76, 79.* **Open**
8am-4pm Mon-Thur; 8am-3pm Fri.
Some English spoken. **Map C1**
The organisation responsible for
selling state-owned assets.

Embassies & Agencies

American Embassy (Commercial Department)
*V. Bank Center Building, Szabadság
tér 7 (302 6100/fax 302 0089). M2
Kossuth tér.* **Open** 8.30am-4.30pm
Mon-Fri. **Map C3**
Hosts new electronic business library
(11am-5pm Tues and Thur) including
extensive business databases.

American Chamber of Commerce
*V. Deák Ferenc utca 10 (266
9880/fax 266 9888). M1, M2, M3
Deák Ferenc tér.* **Open** 9am-5pm
Mon-Fri. **Map C4**
Consultations by appointment only.

British Embassy (Commercial Section)
*II. Hűvösvölgyi út 54 (202 2526/fax
202 2526). Bus 56.* **Open** 8.30am-
5pm Mon-Fri.

British Chamber of Commerce
*I. Iskola utca 37, First Floor, Flat 4
(201 9142/fax 115 5496). M2
Batthyány tér.* **Open** 9am-noon, 2pm-
5pm, Mon-Fri. **Map B3**
Consultations by appointment only.

Business Services

Accountants & Consultants
All the 'Big Six' are in Budapest
and have been for a number of
years. Office hours given are
official ones, but you can often
reach someone much later.

Arthur Andersen/Andersen Consulting
*VIII. East-West Centre, Rákóczi út 1-
3 (327 7100/266 7707/fax 327
7199/266 7709). M2 Astoria/bus 1,
7, 7A, 9, 78/tram 47, 49.* **Open**
8.30am-5.30pm Mon-Fri. **Map D4**

Coopers and Lybrand
*II. Lövőház utca 30 (345 1100/fax
345 1104). M2 Moszkva tér/tram 4,
6.* **Open** 8.30am-5.30pm Mon-Fri.
Map A2

Deloitte and Touche
*V. Vármegye utca 3-5 (267 2062/fax
267 4182). M3 Ferenciek tere/bus
15, 15A.* **Open** 8.30am-5.30pm Mon-
Fri. **Map C4**

Ernst and Young
*XIV. Hermina út 17 (252 8333/fax
251 8778). Trolleybus 72, 74.* **Open**
8.30am-5.30pm Mon-Fri. **Map F1**

KPMG Reviconsult
*XIII. Váci út 99 (270 7100/fax 270
7101). M3 Forgách utca.* **Open**
8.15am-5pm Mon-Fri.

Price Waterhouse
*VII. Rumbach Sebestyén utca 21
(269 6910/fax 269 6936). M1, M2,
M3 Deák Ferenc tér.* **Open** 8.30am-
5.30pm Mon-Fri. **Map D4**

Conference Facilities
As well as the places below,
most of the major hotels also
host conferences.

Budapest Convention Centre
Budapest Kongresszusi Központ
*XI. Jagelló út 1-3 (166 9625/fax 185
2127). Tram 61/bus 8, 8a, 12, 112,
139.* **Open** 8am-7pm Mon-Fri.
English spoken. **Map A5**

European Serviced Offices (ESO)
*VI. Révay utca 10 (269 1100/fax 269
1030). M1 Bajcsy-Zsilinszky út.*
Open 24 hours daily. English
spoken. **Map C3**
As well as conference facilities, ESO
lets out office suites on short-term
leases and offers multilingual
secretarial services.

Directory

Regus Business Centre

VII. Emke Building, Rákóczi út 42 (267 9111/fax 267 9100). M2 Blaha Lujza tér/tram 4, 6. **Open** 8am-6pm Mon-Fri. English spoken. **Map E4**
Offices can also be leased on short-term contracts with multilingual secretarial services.

Couriers

These companies will pick up packages. Sending a document to the UK or US costs Ft3,500-Ft6,500.

DHL Hungary

VIII. Rákóczi út 1-3 (266 5555). M2 Astoria/tram 47, 49. **Open** 8am-6pm Mon-Fri; 8am-noon Sat. **Credit** AmEx, MC, V. **Map D4**

Royal Express

IX. Nádasdy utca 2-4 (216 3606/216 3707/fax 218 3808) **Open** 8am-6pm Mon-Fri; 9am-1pm Sat. **Credit** AmEx, V.
Federal Express affiliate.

TNT Express Hungary

X. Fertő utca 5 (431 3000/fax 431 3096). **Open** 8am-4pm Mon-Fri. **No credit cards.**

UPS

X. Kozma utca 4 (262 0000/fax 262 1111). **Open** 8am-5pm Mon-Fri. **Credit** AmEx.

Commercial Estate Agencies

Office space has increased dramatically since 1990 with the construction of a number of western quality office blocks. In mid-1997, top quality office space cost DM35-DM45 per square metre per month. Rents are stated in Deutschmarks as a hedge against inflation, though it is illegal to charge rent in foreign currency.

British firms dominate the commercial property scene so all the offices listed have English-speaking staff.

Colliers International

II. Horvát utca 14-24 (214 0601/fax 201 3041). M2 Batthyány tér. **Open** 8am-6pm Mon-Fri. **Map B2**

DTZ Hungary

VII. Rumbach Sebestyén utca 21 (269 6999/fax 269 6987). M1, M2, M3 Deák Ferenc tér/tram 47, 49. **Open** 8.30am-5pm Mon-Fri. **Map D4**

Healey and Baker

VII. Emke Building, Rákóczi út 42 (268 1288/fax 268 1289). M2 Blaha Lujza tér/tram 4, 6. **Open** 8.30am-5.30pm Mon-Fri. **Map E4**

Jones Lang Wootton

VIII. East-West Centre, Rákóczi út 1-3 (266 4981/fax 266 0142). M2 Astoria/tram 47, 49. **Open** 9am-6pm Mon-Fri. **Map D4**

Lawyers

The following firms have English-speaking lawyers.

Allen & Overy/Déry & Co.

Madách Trade Centre, VII. Madách Imre út 13-14, Floor 4 (268 1511/fax 268 1515). M1, M2, M3 Deák Ferenc tér/tram 47, 49. **Open** 9am-6pm Mon-Fri. **Map C4**

Baker & McKenzie

VI. Andrássy út 125 (352 8800/fax 342 0513). M1 Hősök tere. **Open** 8am-8pm Mon-Fri. **Map E2**

Clifford Chance/Köves és Társai

Madách Trade Centre, VII. Madách Imre út 13-14 (268 1600/fax 268 1610). M1, M2, M3 Deák Ferenc tér/tram 47, 49. **Open** 8am-8pm Mon-Fri. **Map C4**

McKenna and Co/Verőci, Örmai és Társa

V. Bank Center building, Szabadság tér 7 (302 9302/ fax 302 9300). M3

Arany János tér, bus 15. **Open** 8.30am-8pm Mon-Fri. **Map C3**

Relocation Services

The following companies help deal with residence and work permits.

Business Umbrella

V. Aranykéz utca 2 (118 4126/ fax and phone). M1 Vörösmarty tér. **Open** 9am-5pm Mon-Thur; 9am-3pm Fri. **Map C4**
Also arranges translation, interpreting and customs clearance.

Settlers Hungary

XII. Szánkó utca 3 (319 1500/fax 319 1759). Bus 8/8A **Open** 8.30am-4.30pm Mon-Thur; 8.30am-4pm Fri.
Also helps with finding schools, registering cars and customs clearance.
e-mail:
100263.1233@compuserve.com

Staff Hire Agencies

Inflation can cause rates to vary wildly.

Adecco

VI. Bajcsy-Zsilinszky út 27 (269 1164/fax 269 3774). M1 Bajcsy-Zsilinszky út. **Open** 10am-3pm Mon-Fri. **Map C3**

Select

XIII. Szent István körút 4, first floor, No. 2 (269 3944/fax 269 3945). M3 Nyugati/tram 4, 6. **Open** 9am-5pm Mon-Fri. **Map C2**
A multilingual secretary charges Ft800-Ft1,200 per hour.

Online Services

The local Budapest dial-in number for Compuserve is 291 9999. The number for America Online and Prodigy is 457 8888. Microsoft Network can be accessed on 267 4636.

Further Reading

Books from Corvina, City Hall and other Hungarian publishers are unlikely to be readily available in the UK or US. In Budapest you'll find them in good general Hungarian bookshops as well as in those

specialising in English publications. At Bestsellers bookshop and its academic branch at the CEU, you should be able to locate most anything on Hungary in print. *See chapter* **Shopping & Services.**

History

Bender, Thomas & Schorske, Carl *Budapest & New York: Studies in Metropolitan Transformation 1870-1930*
Patchy compilation of academic essays comparing the two capitals.

Buza, Péter *Bridges of the Danube* (City Hall)
Everything you ever wanted to know about Budapest's famous bridges, with occasional absurd asides.

Crankshaw, Edward *The Fall of the House of Habsburg* (Papermac)
Solid, and solidly anti-Hungarian, account of the end of the Habsburg dynasty.

Garton Ash, Timothy *We the People: The Revolution of 1989 Witnessed in Warsaw, Budapest, Berlin and Prague* (Granta, 1990)
Instant history by on-the-spot Oxford academic.

Gerő, András *The Hungarian Parliament (1867-1918): A Mirage of Power* (Columbia University Press)
Academic analysis of Parliamentary representation during the Dual Monarchy period.

Gerő, András (ed.) *Modern Hungarian Society in the Making* (CEU Press)
Collection of essays on the last 150 years of Hungarian political, social and cultural history. Includes a particularly interesting piece on Széchenyi.

Hoensch, Jörg K. *A History of Modern Hungary 1867-1994* (Longman)
Updated from an original 1986 edition, a thorough account of Magyar mishaps from the beginnings of the Dual Monarchy to the present.

Kovács, Mária M. *Liberal Professions and Illiberal Politics: Hungary from the Habsburgs to the Holocaust* (Woodrow Wilson Center Press/Oxford University Press)
Detailed account of the struggle between liberal and anti-semitic politics during the Horthy years.

Lázár, István *Hungary: A Brief History* (Corvina)
This 'colourful essay presenting the story of the Hungarians as one person sees it' is mostly a load of bollocks – unfortunately the only single-volume history of Hungary available in English.

Litván, György (ed.) *The Hungarian Revolution of 1956: Reform, Revolt and Repression 1953-1963* (Longman)
Five Hungarian members of the Institute for the History of the Hungarian Revolution offer a blow-by-blow account of the uprising.

Lukács, John *Budapest 1900* (Weidenfeld)
Extremely readable and erudite literary and historical snapshot of Budapest at its height. Probably the best book about the city's history and culture currently in print.

Swain, Nigel *Hungary: The Rise and Fall of Feasible Socialism* (Verso)
Authoritative explanation of the demise of goulash socialism.

Taylor, AJP *The Habsburg Monarchy 1809-1918* (Penguin)
Terse history of the twilight of the Habsburg era.

Biography, Memoir & Travel

Brook, Stephen *The Double Eagle: Vienna, Budapest & Prague* (Hamish Hamilton)
Fussy but entertainingly detailed travelogue of the Habsburg capitals in the early 1980s.

Fermor, Patrick Leigh *Between the Woods and the Water/A Time of Gifts* (Penguin)
In the 1930s Fermor took a bike from Holland to Istanbul, stopping off in Budapest along the way. These picaresque and evocative memoirs were the result.

Magris, Claudio *Danube*
Excellent literary travelogue following the course of central Europe's main waterway. The chapter on Budapest is short, but gets the point.

Márai, Sándor *Memoir of Hungary 1944-1948* (Corvina)
Detailed and insightful memoir by exiled Magyar author.

Pressburger, Giorgio & Nicola *Homage to the Eighth District* (Readers International)
Authentic and touching street-level recollections of the now-vanished Budapest Jewish society before and during World War II.

Rimmer, Dave *Once Upon a Time in the East* (4th Estate)
Communism seen stoned and from ground level – eccentric travelogue of lamentable behaviour in Berlin, Budapest, Romania and assorted east European revolutions. Both comic and touching.

Szep, Ernő *The Smell of Humans*
One survivor's short, stark memoir of the Hungarian Holocaust.

Literature & Fiction

Ady, Endre *Neighbours of the Night: Selected Short Stories* (Corvina)
Prose pieces from the poet featured on the Ft500 note. Somewhat stiffly rendered in English, but at least they translate, unlike his gloomy but stirring poetry.

Alexander, Lynne *Safe Houses* (Penguin)
Brilliant, disturbing novel of Hungarian emigrés in New York.

Esterházy, Péter *A Little Hungarian Pornography* (Corvina/Quartet)/*Helping Verbs of the Heart* (Corvina)/*The Glance of Countess Hahn-Hahn* (Weidenfeld & Nicholson)/ *She Loves Me* (Corvina)
One of Hungary's most popular

contemporary writers, Esterházy's postmodern style renders a radical break with Hungarian literary tradition.

Fischer, Tibor *Under the Frog* (Penguin)
Seriously funny and impeccably researched Booker-nominated romp through Hungarian basketball, Stalinism and the 1956 revolution.

Göncz, Árpád *Homecoming & Other Stories* (Corvina)
Dry short stories from Hungary's popular President, playwright and translator of Hemingway.

Konrád, George *The Case Worker/The Loser* (Penguin)
Dark, depressing stuff by Communist Hungary's most prominent dissident.

Kosztolányi, Dezső *Skylark* (Chatto)/*Anna Édes* (Corvina)/ *Darker Muses, The Poet Nero* (Corvina)
Kosztolányi, who wrote these novels in the 1920s, was probably the best Magyar prose writer this century. Hungarians claim his translations of Winnie-the-Pooh are even better than the original. But they would.

Lengyel, Peter *Cobblestone* (Readers International)
Big philosophical detective novel set in turn-of-the-century Budapest, rendered more-or-less unreadable by the exceedingly irritating translation of all place names: 'Elizabeth Ring' for Erzsébet körút, 'New Pest' for Újpest etc. Leave it on the shelf.

Örkény, István *One Minute Stories* (Corvina)
Vignettes of contemporary Budapest: absurd, ironic, often hilarious and all extremely short.

Anthologies

Hungarian Plays (Nick Hern Books)
Four modern Magyar playwrights in English translation: Péter Kárpáti, András Nagy, Ákos Németh and Andor Szilágyi.

In Quest of the Miracle Stag: An Anthology of Hungarian Poetry from the 13th Century to the Present (Atlantis-Centaur/Corvina/M. Szivárvány)
Huge and dauntingly comprehensive survey of Hungarian poetry in English translation.

The Kiss: Twentieth-century Hungarian Short Stories (Corvina)
From Ady to Eszterházy: 31 short stories add up to a good sampler of modern Magyar lit.

Children

Dent, Bob *Budapest for Children* (City Hall)
Slim volume full of suggestions for how to keep the little blighters entertained.

Directory

What's in a name day?

Hungarians pounce upon any excuse for a party, which is perhaps why they created name days – turning the old tradition of honouring saints into a new tradition of getting pissed up at the workplace every other day.

Everyone with a Hungarian name can celebrate at least one name day every year; some more popular names have two days assigned to them. While birthdays remain a more important celebration, on those days you must buy the drinks. On name days everyone buys the drinks for you. And of course, there's no escape from the party because everyone knows when it's your name day. Most Hungarian calendars list the names that are associated with each day of the year. There's also a web page where you can where you can find out whose name day it is, or look up the day for a specific name: *www.isys.hu/nevnap*.

Foreigners are encouraged to celebrate their own name days – yet another excuse for a party. Most common names have a Hungarian counterpart – Lászlo is Leslie, for example, and Ferenc is Frank. If your name doesn't translate, ask a Hungarian friend. They're usually happy to pick a name for you, either because it sounds like your name, or just because they think it suits you.

The custom of celebrating name days originated in the Catholic tradition of commemorating saints' feast days. As the tradition changed from being strictly Catholic to something more Hungarian, other non-Christian Magyar names have been added to the name-day calendar. This ensures that even people with pagan names such as Árpád, Attila or Emese each have their day.

For instance, Saint Stephen, the king-saint credited with killing his brother and uniting several Magyar tribes to form the Hungarian nation, has his feast on 20 August. The entire nation pays homage to their founder with fireworks in all the bigger towns. But the same day is also the name day for anyone called Vajk – the original pagan moniker for Stephen before he converted himself and his country to Roman Catholicism.

When name days roll around, you can celebrate with small gifts, a card, flowers, a party, or a round of pálinkas. In many cases, just saying 'boldog névnapot', or 'happy name day', is enough to show you care and impress the locals with your knowledge of their culture. Especially when you then get the drinks in.

Directory

Gárdonyi, Géza *Eclipse of the Crescent Moon* (Corvina)
Boy's-own adventure about the 1552 Turkish siege of Eger – one battle the Hungarians actually won.
Molnar, Ferenc *The Paul Street Boys* (Corvina)
Turn-of-the-century juvenile classic of boys' gang warfare over a derelict District VIII building site.

Art & Achitecture

Gerle, János *The Turn of the Century* (City Hall)
Walking tours round Budapest's most interesting architecture.
A Golden Age: Art & Society in Hungary 1896-1914 (Corvina)
Colourful coffee table compendium of turn-of-the-century art and architecture includes examples of work by all the Hungarian greats. Drab essays, though.
Art and Society in the Age of Stalin (Corvina)
Interesting collection of essays on socialist realism.

Budapest Architectural Guide (6 BT)
Building by building guide to Budapest's twentieth-century architecture. A useful handbook, though the commentary (in both Hungarian and English) isn't terribly illuminating.

Language

Payne, Jerry *Colloquial Hungarian* (Routledge)
Much more entertaining than most language books, drawing on interesting and potentially romantic situations for its dialogues.
Hungarian-English English-Hungarian Tourist's Dictionary (Akadémiai Kiadó)
Cheap, serviceable and pocket-sized.

Miscellaneous

Bodor, Ferenc *Coffee Houses* (City Hall)
Utterly brilliant vignettes of Budapest coffee culture.

Ernyey, Gyula *Made in Hungary: The Best of 150 Years in Industrial Design* (Rubik Innovation Foundation)
Entertaining coffee table compendium of Hungarian innovation, including the Biro, Unicum bottle, Rubik's Cube and various kinds of bus.
Gundel, Károly *Gundel's Hungarian Cookbook* (Corvina)
The best of Hungarian recipe books, by the man who more or less invented Hungarian cuisine.
Kocsis, Irma *A Tour of our Locals* (City Hall)
Idiosyncratic and personal crawl around dozens of old Budapest bars. Not as good as Bodor's similar Coffee Houses (*above*) but still interesting.
Lang, George *The Cuisine of Hungary* (Bonanza)
Detailed study of the development of Magyar cuisine.
Restaurant of Days Gone By (Tegnap és Ma Alapitvány)
Available at the Museum of Commerce & Catering: absorbing and beautiful collection of photos and memorabilia from the golden age of Magyar gastronomy.

Advertisers' Index

Please refer to the relevant sections for
addresses/telephone numbers

Index

S

Maps

Budapest

Districts - Kerületek

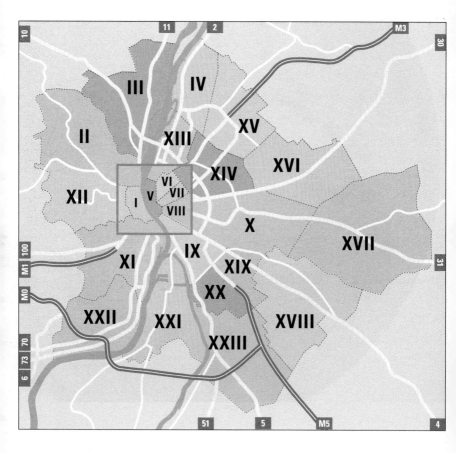

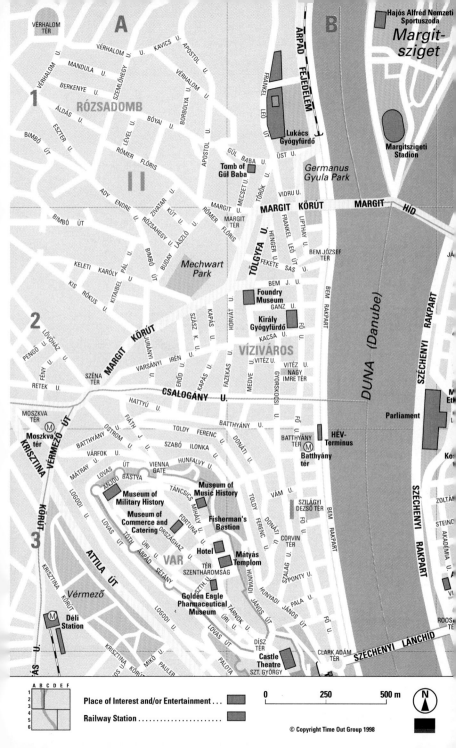

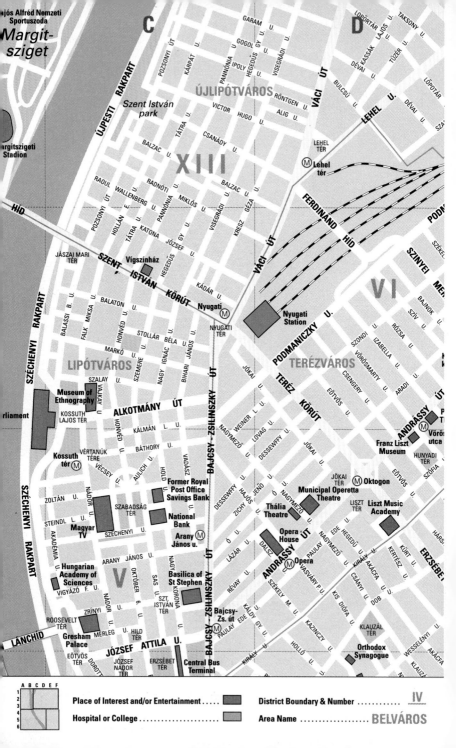

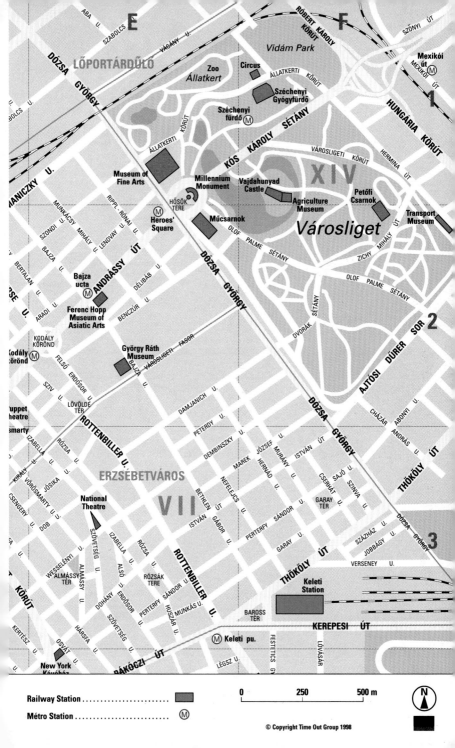

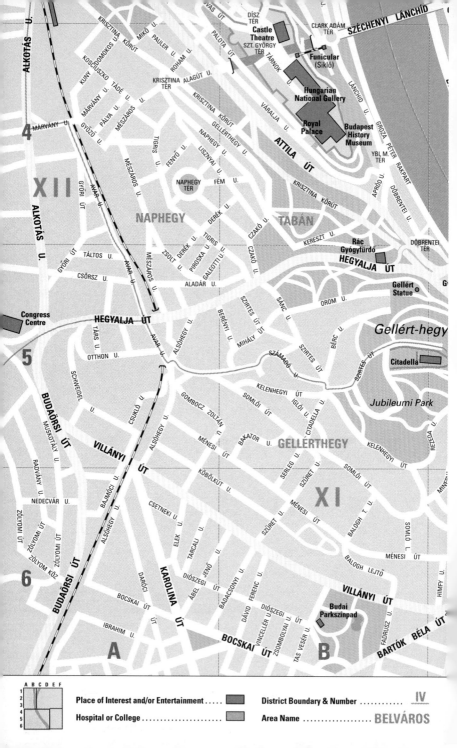

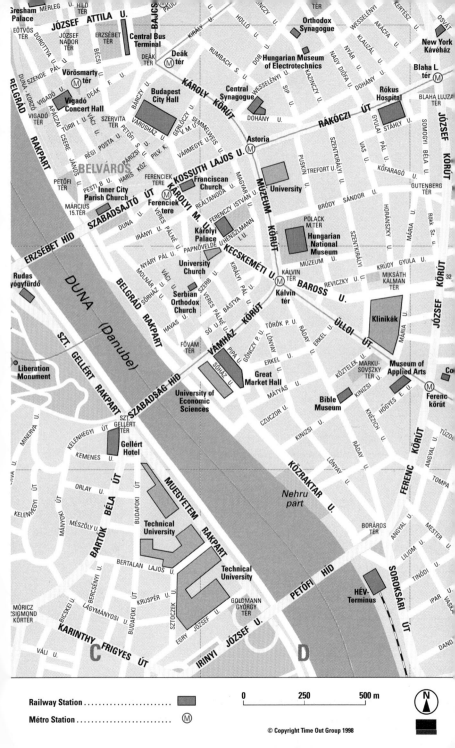

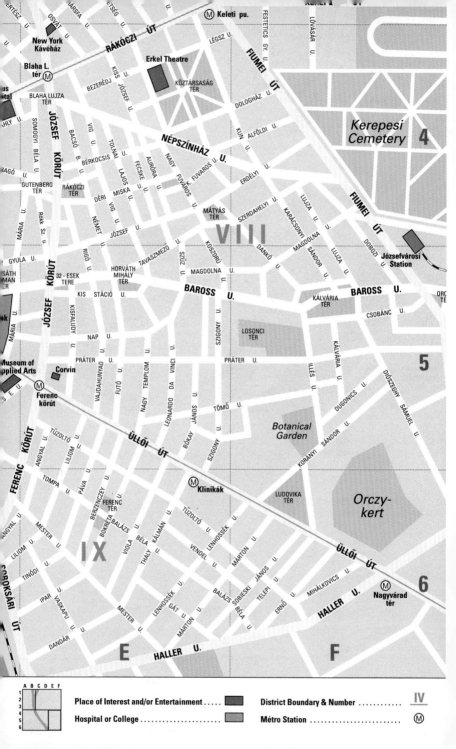

Street Index

Without it, you're nowhere.

The AT&T Global Calling Card. It'll save you.

If you want to get somewhere fast, it pays to travel with the AT&T Global Calling Card. It costs nothing to get, and has all the calling conveniences of the AT&T Calling Card. Plus, it offers competitive prices and a 10% discount on calls you make to and from any one country you choose—all on one simple bill to your credit card. You can save on every card call you make around the world. But you need the AT&T Global Calling Card to enjoy the savings. To get an application or information about our services call our local office at 267-1980 Ext. 2156.
And if you wish to access **AT&T Direct**[SM] Service to place a call with your AT&T Calling Card or to call collect, from Hungary dial 00-800-01111*. You just won't find benefits like these with any other card.

*Public phones require coin or card deposit.

©1997 AT&T

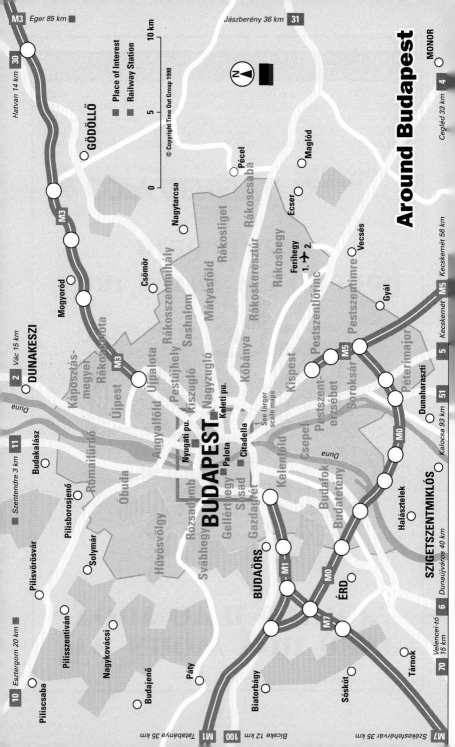

Around Budapest

We know you have your own copier.

That's why we opened nine stores.

COPY GENERAL
Full Service Copy Centers

We use
Kodak COPIERS

1093 Bp., Lónyay u. 13., Tel.: 217-1592 • 1054 Bp., Alkotmány u. 18., Tel.: 332-2563
1111 Bp., Bercsényi u. 4., Tel.: 166-7205 • 1052 Bp., Semmelweis u. 4., Tel.: 266-6564 • EMKE Center, 1072 Bp., Rákóczi út 42., Tel.: 268-1326 • 1016 Bp., Krisztina krt. 83-85., Tel.: 212-0862 • 1087 Bp., Fiumei út 3-5., Tel.: 133-4059 • 6720 Szeged, Jókai u. 1., Tel.: (62) 323-773 • 8000 Székesfehérvár, Fő u. 15., Tel.: (22) 348-111

CZECH REPUBLIC • POLAND • HUNGARY
WASHINGTON DC • RUSSIA • CHINA

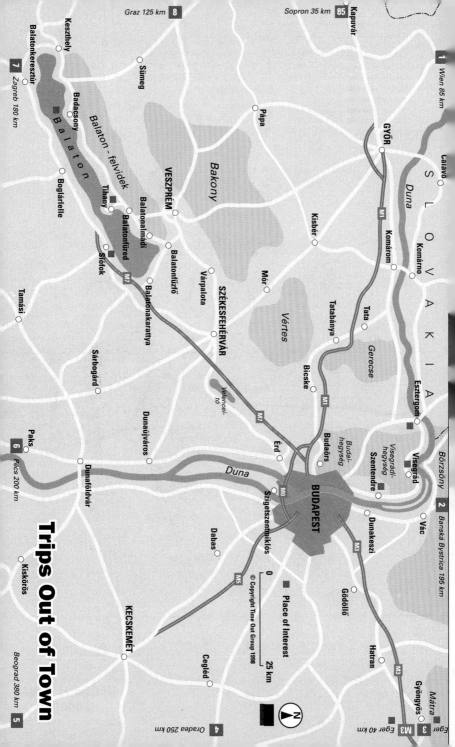

Trips Out of Town

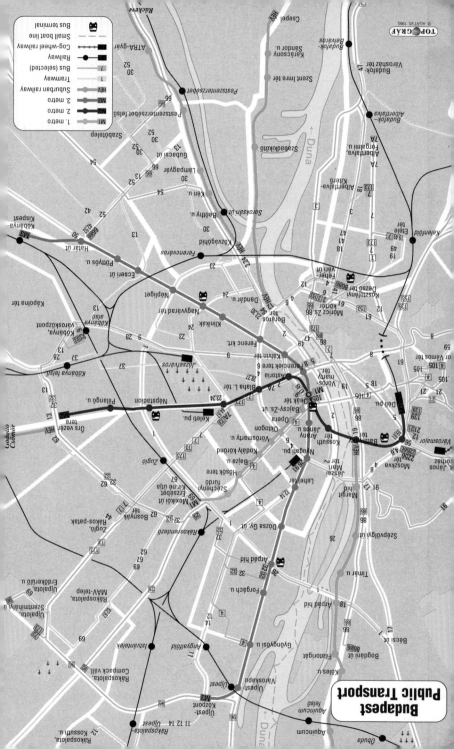

Budapest Public Transport